INTANGIBLE EVIDENCE

BERNARD GITTELSON

LAURA TORBET

A FIRESIDE BOOK · PUBLISHED BY SIMON & SCHUSTER, INC.
NEW YORK · LONDON · TORONTO · SYDNEY · TOKYO

SIMON AND SCHUSTER/FIRESIDE BOOKS
PUBLISHED BY SIMON & SCHUSTER, INC.
SIMON & SCHUSTER BUILDING
ROCKEFELLER CENTER
1230 AVENUE OF THE AMERICAS
NEW YORK, NY 10020
SIMON AND SCHUSTER AND FIRESIDE AND COLOPHONS
ARE REGISTERED TRADEMARKS
OF SIMON & SCHUSTER, INC.

DESIGNED BY BONNI LEON

MANUFACTURED IN THE UNITED STATES OF AMERICA

1   3   5   7   9   10   8   6   4   2

LIBRARY OF CONGRESS CATALOGING IN PUBLICATION DATA

GITTELSON, BERNARD.
INTANGIBLE EVIDENCE.

"A FIRESIDE BOOK."
BIBLIOGRAPHY: P.
INCLUDES INDEX.
1. PSYCHICAL RESEARCH.   2. OCCULT SCIENCES.
I. TORBET, LAURA.   II. TITLE.
BF1031.G47   1987   133.8   87-15046

ISBN 0-671-64800-4
0-671-62541-1 PBK

Acknowledgment and thanks are made to the following for permission to quote from previously copyrighted materials:
Arthur C. Clarke's World of Strange Powers, by John Fairley and Simon Welfare. Copyright © 1984. Reprinted by permission of William Collins Sons and Co., Ltd., London.
Journeys Out of the Body, by Robert Monroe. Copyright © 1971. Reprinted by permission of Doubleday and Company, Garden City, NY.
Life After Life, by Raymond A. Moody, Jr. Copyright © 1976. Reprinted by permission of Stackpole Books, Harrisburg, PA.
The Magical Child, by Joseph Chilton Pearce. Copyright © 1977. Reprinted by permission of E. P. Dutton, New York.

(continued at back of book)

ACKNOWLEDGMENTS

Jack Maguire and Mardee Regan made substantial contributions to the research and preparation of this book. I am also grateful for the contributions of Annette Brody, Fides Guanlao, Debby Roth, Hap Hatton, and Jean McGovern.

Several professionals in the field were especially generous with their time and guidance. Dr. Keith Harary, Dr. Marcello Truzzi, Dr. Nikolai Kholkhov, Martin Ebon, and Dr. Stanley Krippner. Dr. Krippner and Jerry Solfvin graciously gave us permission to use research for their Sand Éditions book *Parapsychologie: science ou illusion?* Librarian Wayne Norman at the Parapsychology Research Foundation and Laura Nipe at the American Society for Psychical Research also deserve special mention.

Finally—and I hope I have not omitted any names—I would like to thank those who so kindly provided me with research materials and/or spent generous time in interviews, in person or on the telephone: Luis Valle Antuna, Julien Armistead, Doug Baker, Tim Ballingham, Pat Barnes, Alex Bavelas, Dr. John Beloff, Clarisa Bernhardt, Dr. Elizabeth Brandt, Dr. Julie Bresciani, Gene Brog, Gerardo Cabezudt, Lenore Cantor, Nadya Olyanova Carruthers, Phillip Cassadore, John Copland, Tony Cordero, Dr. Phillip Costin, Maria Crummere, Fredrick Davies, Dr. Douglas Dean, Linda Delgado, Ellin Dodge, Ed Dunn, Orlando Duran, Rebecca Eisenberg, Arthur Ellison, Dr. Hans Eysenck, Bill Feighan, Diane Frattini, Dr. Vivian Garrison, Luiz Gasparetto, Françoise Gauquelin, Dr. Michel Gauquelin, Uri Geller, Dr. Allan Goldstein, Howard Goodman, Dr. Stephen Jay Gould, Barbara Harding, Elsa Hart, Dr. John Hasted, Gilbert Holloway, Susan Holmes, Charles Honorton, Dr. Steven Howard, Irene Hughes, Valerie Hunt, Dr. Jay Hyman, Brian Inglis, Scott Jones, Anke Junge, David Kneightley, John Krysko, Trudy Laprade, Felix Lehman, Dr. Lawrence LeShan, Rachel Levy, Tony Y. J. Lin, John Mareschella, Zoltan Mason, Dr. Ed May, Faith McInerny, Trudy Mellon, Ruth Montgomery, Dr. Robert Morris, Thelma Moss, Maria Napoli, Rolla Nordic, Bob O'Dell, Eleanor O'Keefe, Sydney Omarr, Brendan O'Regan, Dr. Karl Osis, Marion Palmer, Morning Pastorok, Dr. K. Ramakrishna Rao, Beatrice Rich, Dr. John Roberts, D. Scott Rogo, Dr. Bernard Rosenblum, Dr. Elizabeth Rauscher, Caroline Rob, Sister Sarita, Ron Schapel, Stephan Schwartz, George Serban, Dr. Susan Shargal, Stan Sherman, Pam

Silber, Judy Silver, Alan Simon, Prince Hirindira Singh, Bob Slatzer, Joe Sugarman, Ingo Swann, Russell Targ, Ian Turnbull, Mark Vito, Larissa Vilenskaya, John Von Mieres, Donald West, Ruth West, Anthony White, Ellie Willat, John Williamson, Carroll Righter, Dr. Robert Wuthnow.

To Rosalind, Louise, and Steven, who patiently endured my traveling all over the world and spending endless days away from home to complete my research, I am grateful with all my love.

CONTENTS

CONTENTS

PREFACE

"I knew who was calling before I picked up the phone."

"As we drove through the town, I knew what we would find around every corner, though I'd never been there before."

"I had a dream that you would call me and tell me that you bought a piano."

"Something told me to stop; the next thing I knew, a car spun out of control into the intersection."

"A tarot-card reader at a party foretold that I'd lose my job within a month. It was completely unexpected, but she was right."

"I woke up with an urge to call my brother, to whom I had not spoken in months; I called and learned he'd had a serious heart attack in his sleep."

"Before he spoke, I knew what he would say."

"Suddenly I saw the lost bracelet in my mind's eye, and sure enough, it was there in the glove compartment."

If you have ever—even once—had an experience like those above, and you would like to learn more about it, and about how you might enhance your ability to have and use such experiences, this book is for you.

It is not for people who have convinced themselves that their own experiences were mere coincidence. Nor is it for those who believe the study of such phenomena should be confined to the lab, or who think that we can learn about psychic functioning from card-guessing experiments, but not from a psychic reader or a healer.

This book is about a serious subject that has profound implications for man's self-understanding and for his future. It's time to bring it out of the closet.

INTRODUCTION

I trace the beginning of my journey into the world of the paranormal, and therefore the genesis of *Intangible Evidence*, to an incident that took place in the ballroom of London's Mayfair Hotel in 1962. At the time, I was president of a large, bustling public relations firm that represented such clients as the European Common Market, the West German Government, and many large corporations here and in Europe. One night, Katina Theodossiou, a prominent English astrologer whom I'd hired to entertain at a press conference, told me in all seriousness that the second part of my business life would put me in the forefront of astrology and other psychic studies. Though many things she told me that prophetic night about my past and my character were chillingly accurate, I laughed off her prediction for my future as nonsense. Me, involved in astrology, or any other psychic razzle-dazzle? It would require an all-but-unthinkable turnaround in the life (and personality) of a pragmatic, hard-driving businessman like me.

Yet her prediction has come true. Now, I didn't suddenly have some mystic conversion or vision. In the late 1960s, I was looking for a change from the constant travel my work involved. I've never had trouble coming up with new business ideas, and it wasn't long before I'd solved my problem, simply by putting two and two together. Noting that just about every newspaper and magazine I read ran an astrology column (it was, after all, the dawning of the Age of Aquarius), and taking advantage of the public's new interest in computers (those room-size IBM behemoths), I computerized astrology—working with a top astrologer and a brilliant computer programmer. The whole astrological ephemeris went into the computer, to provide different birth-time calculations—and interpretations—for every five minutes, for every latitude and longitude, over a hundred-year period. The phenomenal success of these computer-generated mail-order horoscopes made headlines all over the world. For the first time, the output of a computer was a *product*—a new industry was born.

Then I happened to catch a radio interview with a man talking about something I'd never heard of—biorhythm—and I was off and running again. I computerized biorhythm and wrote a book on the subject, working with mathematicians to create a simple do-it-yourself formula for the complicated calculations that normally required access to a big IBM 360 computer, or a complex math formula and the plotting of three sine curves on a graph. I expected to sell perhaps five thousand copies to researchers who didn't have their own computers (this was 1970). To my surprise, the book has sold millions of copies worldwide; it has helped make biorhythm a household word, and my computerized biorhythms continue to be popular. Computerized numerology, tarot, and the I Ching followed. This work has been written up in cover stories in *Time, Life, Reader's Digest,* and *The New York Times Magazine,* and has been featured in hundreds of news and magazine stories. Having met and worked with many of the leading adepts in these fields, I can certainly say that I am "in the forefront of astrology and other psychic studies"—at least as an entrepreneur.

During the first years of my life in this new field, it was interesting to me only because it was business. When people asked me if I believed in what I was doing, I'd tell them I believed it all the way to the bank. But as I got more involved, I met extraordinary people—people whose ability to see beyond the present seemed obvious and genuine. It became impossible to keep my disbeliever's credentials in order.

Here were perfect strangers who told me incredible things about myself. One clairvoyant assured me that a deal I was certain of closing would fall apart, but would work out three weeks later with another investment group. It did. Working from photographs, a psychic told me that my son would end up in the hospital during the coming month for his back, but that he would be fine; I was quite shaken when he called two weeks later to tell me that he had had to be hospitalized for three days while he got a cortisone shot to ease his back pain. I was told that my assistant would meet a man from Connecticut through a classified ad. Soon after, she met her new friend through a classified ad for a co-op apartment; the man was selling because he had just bought a house you-know-where. Always healthy, I paid no attention when an astrologer told me in November 1984 that I would have problems with my heart in "one year and ten months." When I had a mild heart attack in 1986, I remembered his prediction and went back to my files to check the timing: one year, ten months, *and two weeks* from the time I interviewed him.

It became harder for me to explain the unexplainable according to the rigid rules of logic that were so dear to me. It became impossible to dismiss the stories I heard from the rational, accomplished, intelligent people who consult these practitioners. In the end, it was impossible to maintain my detachment.

I went through the stage called "there must be something to this." Still the doubter, still looking for the rational explanation, or the quackery, I tried to find out more. As I found myself delving deeper and deeper into psychic phenomena, I discovered a whole new world which extended well beyond the scope of the psychic arts. I found that serious people at respected institutions and corporations are turning their attention to the study and use of psychic ability. In the past couple of years, I've talked to scientists at universities, research laboratories, think tanks, and even in the U.S. Government who are working in this fascinating field, and who under carefully controlled laboratory conditions are turning up evidence for everything from clairvoyance to psychokinesis and out-of-body travel. I've talked to critics who feel that all this stuff is hogwash, or at the very least brainwash. I've interviewed dozens of adepts in the psychic arts, seeking to learn more about how they view their role and their powers, seeking insight into the nature of their abilities, their successes and failures. Too, I wanted to know more about their clientele: who came to them, and why; how did they serve their clients? As I traveled across the country, and to Canada, England, Scotland, France, Germany, Japan, Mexico, China, Korea, and Hong Kong, ordinary people told me their own astounding stories. Perhaps because of my unique position as a businessman in this 'other' world, many people I met, sensing in me a sane and sympathetic ear, recounted experiences they had been reluctant to divulge even to family and friends.

I'm not arguing for the validity of psychic phenomena as much as I am arguing against closed-mindedness. Even if 98 percent of reported psychic phenomena are nonsense, the other 2 percent are important, and must be examined and understood. The field of parapsychology and the psychic arts deserve a fair, open forum, which I hope to provide with *Intangible Evidence*. My goal is to demythologize, to destigmatize, and to legitimize the exploration of expanded psychic horizons. I want to encourage people to make their own inquiries, to be their own researchers, and to become aware of their own abilities beyond the limits of the five senses.

A BRIEF LOOK AT *INTANGIBLE EVIDENCE*

Book One of *Intangible Evidence*, which surveys the broad field of psychic phenomena, is presented in three sections. Part I is meant as a broad overview of the subject: a history of psychic phenomena and the paranormal around the world, especially the modern era of psychical research, with a look at current public attitudes and interests. In Chapter 3 the fur flies—there is hardly a more controversial subject than the issue of whether there is such a thing as psi, and about what constitutes reliable evidence. There are, of course, many fanatics on both ends of the psi spectrum: hard-core believers who are pushovers for everything from extraterrestrials in their backyard to aroma therapy, and rabid disbelievers who deny the mere possibility that a premonition could exist in this most rational of all worlds. Sometimes they're cute when they're mad.

Having failed—of course—to settle the question of psi's legitimacy, we move on anyway to Part II, where we look at the many ways in which psychic abilities manifest themselves, in chapters on ESP and psychokinesis. Here we see the parapsychologists at work, trying to capture, to explain, to measure psychic functioning. It's no easy task, for psi is a slippery quarry, and parapsychologists work under intense scrutiny from scientists in other disciplines. One chapter focuses on the psychics themselves: What are they like, and what is it like to have psychic ability? The final chapter in Part II tackles the tough questions: What is psi? Where does it come from? And how does it work?

Part III surveys the most promising applications for psi—everything from business (where they're careful to refer to hunches rather than premonitions), to oil exploration, stock-market forecasting, personnel evaluation, healing, finding missing persons, solving crimes, archaeological exploration, earthquake prediction, warnings of danger, and psychiatry. (I should mention here that black magic, spiritualism, and many other "fringe" areas of psi, especially where serious research has been limited, are merely touched on.) The last chapter in Part II discusses the age-old question posed by mystic, parapsychologist and physicist alike: Does consciousness survive the death of the body? In addition, dozens of fascinating stories that were told to me, or that I read, during the course of writing this book are recounted in sections called "Interludes," one each in Parts I, II, and III.

Book Two is the place where you can investigate and test psi for yourself. There are chapters on everything from developing your own extrasensory abilities to calculating your biorhythm, learning how to analyze handwriting, or learning how to cast the I Ching. These disciplines are the tools, the means of access to the kinds of information and functioning detailed in Book One. This material is not meant to enable you to master these complex skills; the intent is to get you interested and give you enough information so that you can get a feel for where your own abilities lie and what interests you enough for you to follow it up with further study or consultation with a professional.

TWO NOTES: One, all the anecdotes in this book either are recorded in the parapsychological literature or were told to me firsthand, and have been checked where possible. Unfortunately, some of the anecdotal material is unattributed. Many people are still afraid to publicly own up to their interests or experiences with psychic phenomena. A good example is a New York psychiatrist who has been very successful at getting background information on his clients from charts cast by an astrologer he works with. "I am able to cover material and elicit information that would normally take me six months or more in the normal course of analysis. I check it all out with the patient, of course. It's tremendously efficient, and often astoundingly accurate. But you can't use my name just yet. I'm writing a book about psychotherapy, and it won't have any credibility if it's known that I'm a believer in astrology." Another shy believer is an Oscar-winning actor who tells some fascinating stories about his experiences using numerology and the tarot. "But my agent says that if I use my name, it will cost me roles. Besides, when I go on promotional tours, all the audience will want to hear about is this stuff. They won't even remember the name of my film."

Two, there is what, for lack of a better term, I'll call a "communal 'I' " used in the writing of this book (you've heard of the "royal 'We' "?). Many of the anecdotes and several of the interviews were collected by my coauthor, Laura Torbet, but we retained the first person singular throughout for the sake of consistency.

Intangible Evidence will illuminate the paranormal landscape, too long shrouded in hocus-pocus, fear, and ignorance. As I have been the catalyst for so many people to open up and tell me their stories, so might this book be the catalyst for a broader public to come out of the psi closet. Most of all, I hope that readers of *Intangible Evidence* will get caught up in the same sense of wonder and adventure that continues with me on my journey through the land of psi.

Bernard Gittelson
New York, 1987

BOOK ONE

GETTING TO
KNOW THE
UNKNOWN

PART · ONE

OUT OF OUR SENSES?

CHAPTER · ONE
A WALK ON THE PSI SIDE

"There are more things in heaven and earth, Horatio,
Than are dreamt of in your philosophy."
—*William Shakespeare*, Hamlet

Intangible Evidence is about the unexplained bits and pieces that get swept under the rug of twentieth-century rationalism. Scientists refer to them as anomalies, by which they mean anything that's out of whack somehow, anything not understood within the boundaries of established knowledge. While not all anomalies fall within the category of psychic phenomena, most psychic phenomena are anomalous.

We're flush with terminology for these mysteries. The term "paranormal"—beyond (or parallel to) the normal—is used, as is "parapsychological"—beyond the mind, or psyche. We use the label "psychic phenomena" for anything that appears to overstep the confines of known physical laws. "Psi" (pronounced SIGH) is a useful contemporary term, implying as it does the overlapping psychic, psychological, and even physical nature of the unexplainable. In short, psi encompasses all information processing unaided by known sensory perception or analytic input. All the above terms encompass extrasensory perception, or ESP—experiencing information not available through the five senses—and psychokinesis, or PK—the seeming ability of the mind to influence matter. ESP in turn includes telepathy, the ability to communicate paranormally, without words or other sensory means; clairvoyance, knowledge acquired paranormally; and precognition, knowledge of the future that there is no way of deducing from available sensory information. That provocative collector of anomalies, Charles Fort, skipped over all the fancy terminology and got right to the point when he referred to all that puzzling and problematic stuff under the rug as the "damned facts."

The "damned facts" are many and varied, and it is surprising to find some of them keeping company. They turn up unexpected (and unwelcome) in the laboratory of the Dean of Engineering at Princeton University, where students are able to skew what should be the random "landing pattern" of steel balls dropped through a chute. They turn up, more predictably, in the den of a gypsy tea-leaf reader in a storefront on New York's Fifth Avenue who reels off the initials of the two people I've just been with. A dowser, using a forked twig from a willow tree specially flown in from North Carolina, finds water in Africa for General Patton. A manufacturing executive I meet at a black-tie dinner at the Waldorf-Astoria recounts, not without embarrassment, his visit to a Filipino healer who cured the water on his lungs, "punching his fingers into my chest," just days before he was to undergo major surgery to correct the problem. The results of thousands of card-guessing trials performed over more than twenty years by Duke University's pioneer researcher J. B. Rhine, when analyzed, good and bad thrown together, show a probability above chance expectation of *millions* to one! Two skilled psychics, monitored and recorded in a laboratory, "fly" to Mercury and report strikingly similar visions; but the real clincher comes two weeks later when *Mariner 10* sends its reports back and confirms their findings, right down to the (most unexpected) rarefied atmosphere, the auroral glows, and the magnetic rings "pushed out into space" on the dark side of the planet. At Newark College of Engineering, scientists Douglas Dean and John Mihalasky test more than five thousand executives for ESP abilities, and find that the more successful an executive is, the more likely it is that he will score high in predicting the hundred-digit numbers a computer will generate at random. Perfectly sane and reputable people have reported UFO sightings, have remembered "past lives" under hypnosis, or have recalled out-of-body experiences that took place when they nearly died during surgery. Others claim they see an aura or light around people, or swear they've changed their luck by changing their name, or regularly consult their astrologer about their stock portfolio. And perfectly sane and reputable scientists are proving, to the satisfaction of all but the most adamant disbelievers, the reasonable likelihood of everything from telepathy to the fact that *it is possible to see the future*: you just have to know how to tune in to it. Moreover, if you can tune in, you have the power to modify that future. Six hundred people, after but a four-hour training session, walk across a bed of hot coals in a supermarket parking lot in Boulder, Colorado. (Soon after, horrified scientists perform the equally remarkable feat of jumping through verbal hoops trying to show that there's a perfectly logical explanation for it.)

Evidence of seemingly paranormal goings-on come in from all over —from many different fields, from many different belief systems, from all corners of the earth. It seems to come from space in the form of UFO sightings and "astral travel." It comes from beneath the earth, where dowsers find gold and psychics pinpoint archaeological treasure hundreds of feet underwater on the ocean floor, or beneath the sands of the Sahara. It fraternizes with physicists breathing the rarefied air of relativity theory, astrologists charting the stars, and mediums claiming to carry messages from beyond the grave. It includes the forbidding-sounding "mind control" and "psychic warfare" hinted at from behind the iron curtain. Yogis who reputedly can control their breathing and materialize objects from thin air come into the picture somehow, as do a carefully investigated (though still suspect) group of Chinese children who seem to be able to "read" with their fingers, and any number of "psychic" surgeons who seem to operate with rusty knives and without anesthesia. Engineers with their random-number generators, and even quantum physicists, cannot escape the clutches of psi.

It is hard to make sense of psi, so elusive and varied and dazzling and puzzling are its many facets. Is it an issue of mind, or one of matter, or one of mind over matter? Of brain, or body, or the connection between them? Is psi a little-understood aspect of nature, or is it something from "outside"? And how shall we make sense of it? Should we stand back, and look at the whole; or is any one particle, as in a hologram, a microcosm of the whole, able to tell us about all the others? Are we talking about many things, or are they all manifestations of a single phenomenon with a unifying explanation?

Psi is a subject that engages the attention of philosophers and psychologists, mediums and mystics, theologians and scientists. Are they like the proverbial blind men examining the elephant, each seeing what will turn out to be the same thing, but each from a different perspective? Most important, will they remove their blindfolds and see the elephant for what it is?

Though explanation eludes us, and heaven knows we try ridiculously hard sometimes to find "rational" explanations, the things reported in *Intangible Evidence* exist—if only in the minds of those who experience them. I say "if only" with tongue in cheek, because it may turn out to be the wildest conceit to say that something which happens in the mind is not real, while something that reduces to matter is. Perhaps, as some suggest, we've got it backward, and matter itself is a creation of the mind that enables us to function in the "real" world. Psychology professor Nikolai Khokhlov of the University of California at San Bernardino put it this way: "Matter is the vehicle in which we ride."

The happenings reported in *Intangible Evidence* are not rare exotica; they are but a small sampling of things that happen all the time, to millions of people in thousands of forms. We may live in a scientific age; we may worship facts and deride fiction; but that hasn't stopped people from having prophetic dreams, from having the feeling they've "been here before," from acting on a hunch, or from walking unharmed on beds of hot coals. To quote the nineteenth-century investigator Charles Richet on his experiences with the paranormal: "I will not say that it is possible; I only say that it is true."

Paradoxically, it is our increasingly powerful computers, our ever-more-sophisticated methods of statistical analysis, and the troubling holes that today's physicists are punching into the once-inviolable monument called scientific objectivity that are forcing us to seriously confront the unexplainable—and perhaps on terms that make those very scientists squirm. The rug of rationalism is getting lumpy; it is becoming harder to walk across it without some embarrassing anomaly oozing out. Besides, I suspect that there are priceless treasures under that rug, for you and me and for our planet. *Intangible Evidence* is going to take a good, hard look at what's under there.

LOOKING AT PSI FROM ALL SIDES

I am afraid that *Intangible Evidence* is going to be upsetting to many of the researchers I spoke to, and for whom I have the utmost respect. Psi researchers are understandably sensitive about speaking openly to inquisitive laymen like me. They have plenty of experience with being misquoted, and are afraid of unguardedly saying something that would make them seem the flaky, foolish, blind believers and charlatans they're so often said to be. "I would not want to say that psi exists," they say; "I'm just investigating the possibility." "Don't lump me in with the aura readers and the Kirlian photographers." "You can't believe stories that people tell you; all that counts is what can be reliably replicated in the laboratory."

I've taken their cautions and admonitions very much to heart, agreeing with them wholeheartedly that it is of the utmost importance to make distinctions between, for example, a telepathic experiment that has been repeated dozens of times in dozens of labs, the accumulation of beyond-the-laboratory-walls evidence of telepathy collected by serious researchers, and the story told to me by my next-door neighbor about the telepathic message she received from her husband while driving to the airport.

On the other hand, I consider all these sources of information about psychic phenomena valid on some level. The hard-core lab research is generally accepted by all but the most adamant critics. While no one has been able to "prove" reincarnation, Ian Stevenson's *Twenty Cases Suggestive of Reincarnation* is an investigation worthy of consideration by serious inquirers. Stories told to me of out-of-body experiences, healings, and precognitive dreams (all checked out where possible) by reputable, levelheaded, in some cases well-known people, who have no reason to lie and who are themselves often baffled by their experiences, cannot be dismissed out of hand. It must be said, too, that most such experiences are far more powerful and vivid than the limited glimmerings usually elicited under the dampening influence of laboratory testing.

The question of whether psi is amenable to verification in a laboratory, and to what degree, is a valid one. The psi findings that emerge from the lab are often pale shadows of the paranormal experiences people report in everyday life. A psi subject wired for sound in a steel-encased room so that a researcher can "prove" that a psi experience is taking place is bound to be under some constraint; he is much more likely to have a psi "hit" while relaxing on Sunday morning, or when there is a real reason to do so—a friend has had an accident, or he's trying to pick a winning horse at the track. The outspoken and gifted psychic Ingo Swann's abilities have been tested under laboratory conditions with significant success on everything from describing geographical sites all over the globe, with only map coordinates to guide him, to "disturbing" the electromagnetic field of a supposedly impenetrable detector hidden in a chamber under several feet of concrete. In his autobiographical *To Kiss Earth Goodbye,* he says that while he sympathizes with the need of the scientific mind to understand and analyze psi, the heavy-handed methods of scientific investigators are "grinding the diamond into a dust pile while trying to capture the sparkle." The manifestations of psi in the laboratory, while they are often statistically impressive and go a long way toward building the case for psi, will probably always be somewhat limited. Will it ever be possible to pull off a reincarnation in a lab? Will enough research subjects ever be fortuitously hooked up to measuring devices when word "comes through" that their mother is ill? As many people who take psi in stride have said in one way or another: "I don't need proof that psi exists. I know it does, because I use it."

Book Two will be especially exasperating to the scientists (I can see them tearing out their hair now), for it covers everything from astrology to tarot and biorhythm. But I have studied and written on biorhythm extensively, I've had too many convincing experiences with gifted tarot-card readers and psychics, and I've heard too often from people I respect about their similar experiences to write them off without further exploration. However shaky their premise may seem to the doubter, I have come to believe that in many cases the mantic arts—for all their elaborately developed technique—serve to a great extent as *devices or tools for accessing a common source of psychic information.* If Book One is about the many forms of psychic processes, Book Two is about how to learn to tune in to them, or to make use of people who can help you to do so. These skills, and those who practice them, are available to the general reader to check out for himself. Certainly, Chapter Twelve, on improving your own ESP abilities, is a valuable entree to experiencing paranormal phenomena for yourself.

The field of psychic research needs very much to have its conservatism and complacency jolted, to have its progress prodded along a bit. For while the scientists are busy measuring psi phenomena in precious, rigidly controlled experiments, the psychic "action" is swirling all around them. Time is a-wasting. I have made every attempt to separate the scientific and verifiable from the anecdotal. But I believe they are all pieces of the same issue, and I feel that they complement each other, side by side between the covers of this book.

A SKEPTICAL BELIEVER

By now, you can see where I stand on the subject of psi: I'm a believer. Now, I don't believe everything—some of this stuff sounds pretty farfetched to me, the product of overfertile imaginations, or perhaps of profit-minded quacks. In the quest for an understanding of psi, an open mind should be balanced by a healthy skepticism, so that the "gee-whiz" aspects can be separated from the hard science. But I find credible Charles Honorton's (of the Psychophysical Research Laboratory in Princeton) reports that the long-term rate of psi "hits" in his highly controlled *Ganzfeld* telepathy experiments is a whopping 38 to 45 percent (25 percent would be expected by chance). I believe that the plants from barley seeds nurtured on water held by healers in Doug Dean's (and others') repeated experiments grew substantially higher than untreated plants. And I also, I confess, believe in the abilities of the psychic who correctly told me my son would be in the hospital the following month, and the astrologer who described events and the tenor of my childhood with uncanny accuracy. Some things I investigated just didn't pass muster—Scotland's legendary Findhorn, for example, where giant vegetables were reported to grow in barren soil: To me it just seemed like a pleasant commune, and I saw no 10-pound rutabagas. Kirlian photography didn't convince me, though I was impressed with some of its supporters. I'm not so sure about the medium who passed along the message from my deceased mother, and I'm not ready to pass judgment on UFOs. Pyramid power? Crystal healing? As they say in Missouri—show me.

Perhaps you bought this book because you're curious about the unknown, or you have had personal experiences you can't explain. But you may also be embarrassed—and afraid. It's not surprising. What we are learning about paranormal phenomena flies in the face of everything we have been taught about the nature of reality. It upsets our carefully constructed view of the world, a world in which we already have enough in the way of change and upheaval and newness to cope with anyway. If psychic functioning is real, it demands that we rethink many of our ideas and beliefs, and it opens up a whole world shrouded in mystery, and a good deal of mumbo jumbo. It means that we must consider seriously things we've brushed aside—with a laugh, or with a rationalization. A top researcher at prestigious SRI International, formerly the Stanford Research Institute, has had plenty of experience with people's resistance to evidence of the paranormal, by both the general public and the scientific community. He calls it the "scared shitless" factor.

I can only encourage you to leave your fears and prejudices behind as you read *Intangible Evidence*. I assure you that nothing dangerous or scary has happened to me in my pursuit of psi—just many fascinating and exciting and life-enhancing things. Everything I have learned points to the fact that psi is inherent in us, an aspect of nature itself; it is not separate or "different." It is a rich but latent side of our human nature, a set of abilities and sensibilities neglected by most of us and thus atrophied in obeisance to science and fear. What we are now learning about psi challenges us to rise to the occasion, to allow ouselves to perceive things in a new way, to stop equating the paranormal with the strange, to embrace this neglected aspect of ourselves. We must resist the temptation to hold on fearfully to the picture of reality we feel so safe with; it imposes harsh limits.

Of course, there are people who go too far, who fall into the dark crevices of the occult and must be rescued. But there are also those who become enmeshed in bizarre religions, who play golf as long as there is daylight, who become addicted to alcohol or drugs, who live vicariously through TV soap operas, who become obsessed with their computers, or Dungeons and Dragons, or "survival" games. It's a matter of temperament, not content. You're an adult, you're not overly gullible, you make your own decisions. You chose your doctor and your accountant; you can certainly make up your mind about whether to see a psychic or a healer. If you consult a psychic about a stock buy, it only adds to the information your broker gives you, and you can decide how much weight to give to his advice. It is unlikely that you would forgo your doctor's help because you were also consulting a healer.

Many people I've met have learned to make psi work for them, and have learned to integrate it into their everyday lives. They don't go into a trance; they haven't changed their way of living. They don't think of psychic ability as a cure-all for life's problems, and they know it works at unpredictable times. But they've come to realize that some of their dreams and daydreams and hunches have their origin in a place that they don't fully understand, but which they're learning to tune in to and to trust. For them, it is not the strangeness but the "everydayness" of psi that is most striking.

Even many conservative researchers feel the evidence points to the fact that most of us have some psychic ability—whatever it is. In *The Mind Race*, Keith Harary and Russell Targ cite the "enjoyment of having an additional perceptual ability with which to experience all aspects of your life and environment. We should develop these skills because it is possible to do so, and because doing so will enrich our lives."

Go slowly. Read carefully. Test for yourself whether psi has any value for you. Find your own way, your own level of interest, your own sense of how psi fits into your life. Doubt where doubt seems appropriate, but don't be afraid to believe and to use psi. Most of all, don't miss out because of fear or embarrassment. Life's too short, and too fantastic. You'll be sorry if you miss this one.

INTERLUDE · ONE
TALES OF THE
PARANORMAL

In my psi journey, I've never ceased to be amazed at the stories I've heard—and at the unexpected people who told them. It was the rare occasion, once I mentioned the topic of this book, that at least one captivating tale was not forthcoming. Some were told to me in hush-hush whispers over a business lunch. Others regaled rapt audiences at dinner parties. Some came in the form of idle conversation during a plane flight or even as I waited in line at a movie. Stories came in on fancy letterheads from the desks of prominent executives who had heard of my project. Friends I'd known for years suddenly confided their strange tales.

Some of these stories, along with tales from psi researchers and some classic anecdotes from the annals of psi, are recounted here, and in subsequent Interludes in Parts Two and Three. I'm sure that you will find them as fascinating as I do, and that they will pique your interest in all the many mysterious manifestations of the paranormal. Most of all, I hope they will demonstrate to you that unexplainable experiences are not rare, but common, and that they happen to sane and levelheaded people—like you and me.

"I almost always 'know' the person I am speaking to over a telephone without ever meeting that person," says Jane Gosselin, a professional astrologer who acknowledges the psychic component of her craft. "I am very cautious and responsible. People who come to an astrologer often need therapy, and for this reason, it is the burden of ethical astrologers to guide the client positively where he or she can get the most help.

"Four years ago, a woman in her fifties came to me for a reading. The person she was concerned about was her daughter. I requested a picture, and as she went through her wallet, my eyes became drawn to a different picture—of a little boy about three years old. I could not let it go, and I could not concentrate on the picture of her daughter until I could see the other picture. As I result, when holding his picture I saw him in pajamas, getting up from his bed, passing through rooms, going to the bathroom. As he got just outside the door, there was the sound of a scuffle in the living room. I saw a bike, a Christmas tree, and a man attacking a woman on the living-room sofa, and I felt fear in me, as though I were the small boy. I related this to the woman.

"It turned out that the little boy was her grandson—the son of the daughter for whom she desired this reading. It seems the daughter was separated from her husband at the time (which was a year or two prior to this reading—the boy now being about age five), and at Christmas time, her ex-husband was visiting and raped her on the couch—exactly as I saw it from the little boy's eyes. Also, no one, neither the mother of the boy nor the grandmother, knew that the boy had witnessed this. He had eventually developed a stuttering problem, this woman told me, and he had intermittent emotional trouble. No one knew why or even thought about why. They took it for granted that it was a part of his emotional makeup or that he was having difficulty adjusting to his parents' separation.

"In effect, this reading helped one small boy and helped a family. A psychologist might never have discovered this incident, since most likely it would have been buried in the subconscious mind of a little boy at age three."

Psychic John Krysko, whose area of expertise is economic and market forecasts, tells the following tale: "A doctor in Queens came to me for help on the advice of a friend. He'd been attacked by masked men who took money and some drugs, and he was afraid they'd come back. I was able to do a reasonable drawing of the three men, and told him that the police would find them in the Bronx, driving— I remember exactly—a brown '68 Electra, and gave the license-plate number. I told him that if they weren't caught, at three weeks from that date a robbery would take place in Brooklyn in a hardware store near an elevated train. Somebody would be shot, I added, and the car would go over the Verazzano Bridge. When the police got this information, they asked the doctor about it, and he told them he had gotten it from a psychic. Of course they totally ignored it; it was a dead issue. I had even provided a tape, which I generally do as a backup. Well, it was sad, because the robbery took place in Brooklyn on the appointed day—at an auto-parts shop, near the elevated train. A cop who knew about my information recognized the car double-parked nearby. As the police approached, three guys came running out of the shop, and one of the policemen was shot and killed. I was one digit off on the license plate, and the men strongly resembled the pictures I had drawn."

British Professor of Experimental Physics John Hasted recounted for me a classic story about Australia's famous Melbourne Cup horse race. "The owner of one of the horses had a dream in which he saw his horse winning the Melbourne Cup two weeks later. But there was something curious in the dream: His jockey was wearing a black armband. He repeated the dream to several people, so it was well documented. Well, the dream did not, in a sense, come true, because although the jockey did win the Melbourne Cup on his horse and was wearing a black armband, the owner did not see him—because he had died in the intervening two weeks. The armband was for *his* death."

This next story was told to me by a very close friend of the woman to whom it happened. I have verified it through the doctor in the story, and through medical records. "This is the story to end all stories. It happened to my friend Colette, a very sensible, down-to-earth Frenchwoman, who returned to France last summer as part of her duties as governess to two children of an American couple. Colette lost her husband, Freddy, about five years ago, very suddenly; he died in an auto accident. Now, one strange thing about this was that he had had an accident exactly one year earlier, in which the car had been completely destroyed, but from which he escaped unscathed. But everything changed after that: He had a fear of getting back into the car, his business went down the drain, he went bankrupt, he was constantly depressed. Then, the very first time he got into a car, a week short of a year later, he was instantly killed in an accident. This time the car was unscathed, but he struck his head and died.

"Five summers later in France, my friend woke up one night with internal bleeding. She called around, was directed to the hospital, got into a cab, and went to the emergency room. It was deserted at two in the morning, so she walked around until she found the woman she had talked to on the phone earlier, and introduced herself. The woman turned out to be a doctor. She said to Colette, 'You sit here, and you come with me.' Colette looked around and didn't see anybody and thought that maybe she had heard wrong. So she went inside, went through the whole examination, and asked the doctor what was wrong. The doctor said to her, 'Would you like to have your husband with you while we discuss this?' And Colette laughed and said, 'Oh, I'd love to have my husband with me, but my husband died five years ago.' The doctor said, 'Well, who's that gentleman you walked in with?' So Colette said, 'I didn't come in with anyone.' 'Madame, of course you did,' countered the doctor. 'The gentleman is waiting for you in the lobby.' Colette said, 'No man came in with me,' and then she said, 'Describe the man.' This doctor described her dead husband to a T—his height, the thinning hair, everything. At which point Colette sat down and said to her, 'Where did you see him?' The doctor replied, 'When you came in through the open door the man was holding your arm, and he came in with you, and I asked him to sit down in the chair while you came with me to the examining room.' The two women then went back outside, and of course he wasn't there anymore. So Colette said to the doctor that she must be imagining things, and the doctor got very upset, and went on about how she was head of emergency services and had been there for many years. . . ."

There are many reported cases in which people famous for their creativity reveal that their inspiration came to them in a dream. Friedrich Kekule, a nineteenth-century organic chemist, was searching for the correct model of the molecular structure of benzene. The best current hypothesis suggested a chainlike linear structure, but such a design did not fit all the experimental data. One night in a dream, Kekule was struck by the vivid image of six snakes in a ring, each swallowing the tail of the next. Remembering the dream in the morning, he realized that if benzene was structured in the same hexagonal arrangement, then all the experimental data would be explained.

On November 17, 1986, Captain Kenju Tenuki was piloting a Japan Air Lines cargo jet from Reykjavik to Anchorage when he spotted "two columns of light" ahead and to his left. He thought it might be a military aircraft, for Anchorage flight control had no other aircraft listed. Then the lights approached to within 500 or so feet of his craft —"two dark cylinders with row after row of spinning amber lights" that were incredibly bright, yet cast no shadows. The cylinders flew in formation with him, and Tenuki realized that the craft was under careful control, so he was not afraid of collision. When the strange craft suddenly sped away, he saw two fluorescent white lights about eight miles distant; he was able to get a radar blip of the craft on his screen. When he caught up with it over Fairbanks, he saw a giant ball the size of "two aircraft carriers" with protruding lights. He called for a reading from U.S. Air Force military control center; the controller reported a blip, but it disappeared a minute later. As Tenuki changed course to avoid the unidentified craft, the craft followed him, again in careful formation. While investigation was unable to confirm the strange sighting, no one accuses Tenuki, a veteran pilot with an unblemished record, of hallucination, intoxication, or falsifying his report.

Writer and columnist Leonore Fleischer relates this incident which occurred as a friend was driving her to her house in the country. "We got to talking about the tragedy of my old lover Douglas' suicide. It had always been a mystery to me, but as we talked I mentioned that with all his early promise, Doug had felt distraught when his novel wasn't successful; that he had felt trapped in Miami, where he had been living, and by the circumstances of his life. But I still didn't really understand it. Suddenly a car pulled in front of us so sharply that we had to put on the brakes. I looked up and the car had a New Hampshire license plate, with its motto, 'Live Free or Die.' The license plate read: DOUG. I think it was a message from Doug trying to explain to me why he chose to commit suicide."

Attorney Peter Morrison, a client of psychic Beatrice Rich, tells the following story: "My wife happened to see Beatrice shortly after we found a house that we had made an offer to buy, and asked her about it. Beatrice described the house in some detail, even pointing out that the entire roof would have to be replaced; this was later confirmed in the engineer's report. But she also remarked to her that some unpleasant things had gone on in the house . . . 'nothing demonic or anything, just not nice, not right, bad practices.' We pretty much forgot about this until about a month later, when I saw Beatrice. Beatrice did not connect me with my wife—we use different names, and Beatrice never remembers what she tells her clients anyway. The first thing she said to me was that I seemed to be very much involved in a real estate transaction, that I was buying something, it looked like a place where I was going to live, not an investment, and it looked as if it were happening right now. Well, we had just signed the contract *that afternoon*. Later in the reading, I asked Beatrice to tell me about the house. 'Well, I don't know what this has to do with your house, but I see a very large cat.' In fact, there was a very large cat that seemed to reside at the house, even though no one was living there—it would jump on us whenever we arrived to look at the property. Then she said that there were some unsavory people who used to live there, that there was something not right about whatever went on in the basement. This, combined with what she had told my wife, Laura, made me decide to check up on the owner, because we were getting a bit suspicious anyway: We were negotiating through a lawyer, the owner was nowhere to be seen, and the house was being left to total neglect. Beatrice saved the day. When I tracked this guy down, it turned out that he was a fugitive from a drug indictment in California, and that the basement had been used to stash drugs. The house was tied up in the indictment, and if we'd gone through with it, it would have been an illegal transaction; we could have lost the house."

Arthur Osborn, the author of *The Future Is Now*, relates this story: "The report is by Mademoiselle Dulay, of the Comédie Française. It concerns the tragic end of the young actress Mademoiselle Irène Muza. Mlle. Muza was in a hypnotic trance when she was asked if she could see what awaited her personally in the future. She wrote the following:

'My career will be short: I dare not say what my end will be: it will be terrible.'

"Naturally, the experimenters, who were greatly impressed by the prediction, erased what had been written before awakening Mlle. Muza from the trance. She therefore had no conscious knowledge of what she had predicted for herself. But even if she had known, it would not have caused the type of death she suffered.

"It was some months later that the prediction 'My career will be short' was fulfilled. And indeed, her end was 'terrible.' Her hairdresser had allowed some drops of an antiseptic lotion made of mineral essence to fall on a lighted stove. Mlle. Muza was instantly enveloped in flames, her hair and clothing were set afire and she suffered burns so severe that she died in a hospital a few hours later."

Washington-based scientist Allan Goldstein, whose recent research has focused on multiple personality, admits, a bit reluctantly, that he sometimes senses an aura around certain people, or at unpredictable times can read others' thoughts. "For example, when my wife, Linda, and I first moved to Washington, we were having a drink after a play at the Kennedy Center. Sitting next to us were two strangers, two women who had gone to the show. Now, I don't ordinarily start talking to strangers, but I started talking to one of the women. I felt as if I had a line of communication, a sense of recognition of things, and of some of the events that had to do with her. During the conversation she told me about a friend of hers who was a neurosurgeon. That very morning the man, a very well-known surgeon, had been in my office. I didn't quite understand why I was attracted to this woman, why I was inclined to talk with her, but I think it was that recent connection."

Susan White tells the following romantic story: "When I was thirteen, I lived in Southern California and had a boyfriend, Larry, who lived next door. During the days we'd play at the beach, and at night I'd dream of growing up and marrying him. Then disaster struck! My dad was going to be transferred back East, and we had to move by the time school started again in September. In one month we were gone. I was devastated.

"Needless to say, I did survive the trauma. I made new friends and went to college in Massachusetts. Years later, at the age of twenty-nine, I went to a convention in San Francisco. The day it ended, I experienced a very strange sensation: I *had* to go back to Santa Monica (four hundred miles away). I rented a car and drove south through Big Sur.

"I reached the Santa Monica beach in the afternoon. It was summer, and the beach was full. After an hour, I began to feel that something was wrong. I loved being at the beach, but something was telling me I wasn't supposed to be there. I started to leave, feeling very perplexed.

"I got in the car, started the engine, and pulled away from the curb. I didn't know where I was going, but by this time I began to realize that some subconscious force had taken control of my direction. I trusted this force. Then it became clear to me: I was heading toward my old block to visit my old house! When I pulled up, the house wasn't there. Instead, there was a four-story condominium building. A nice-looking man came out from behind the building. He saw me wiping tears from my face and asked if I was okay. I nodded and mumbled, 'I used to live here.' He looked directly into my eyes and said, 'Stick?' It was Larry—calling me by an old nickname! He had become a beautiful man.

"Larry, a writer living in San Diego, had also felt drawn to return to Santa Monica at the very same time I had. Although I am a firm believer in the psychic sciences, I couldn't believe this was actually happening. It wasn't until we had shared our lives over a cup of coffee and realized our many parallel experiences that it was clear how natural our meeting really was.

"That was one month ago. I am now back home in Boston. Oh, yes—Larry is coming to visit me in a few weeks."

"Numerology never made any sense to me," reports a business associate, "but last year I met a numerologist at dinner at a friend's house, and he told me, on the basis of the numbers of my name and birth date, that I would have tremendous difficulties in my marriage in the year ahead; he even went into some detail. I was taken aback, because in fact those difficulties were already showing themselves, and they got worse in the ensuing months. Yet I wrote his predictions off to coincidence and quickly forgot about them. Almost a year later I ran into him again. This time he told me that I was right on the point of making a major decision—a crucial life change, which would involve a major relationship in my life. That morning I had found an apartment, and five days later I separated from my wife."

CHAPTER · TWO
WHAT'S GOING
ON HERE?

"Astrology is stupid and you are a typical Gemini."
—Scientist, speaking to Bernard Gittelson

Confucius said: "May you live in interesting times." If this cryptic remark was meant as a blessing, we are surely fortunate. We find ourselves living in an era in which a near worship of science and technology coexists with an expanding interest in the paranormal, the occult, and the nature of human consciousness, where psychics and physicists cross paths on the road to enlightenment.

Paranormal phenomena, by whatever name—occultism, supernaturalism, metaphysics, anomalistics—have always encompassed whatever it was that man did not understand at any given time in his development. And man's attempts to understand these phenomena have always been framed in terms of the historical, religious, intellectual, scientific, and social ideas of his culture. In the course of time the terminology, the frame of reference, the interpretation, and the level of acceptance of the seemingly extraordinary have changed in keeping with cultural attitudes, and with man's wherewithal to understand them. But the nature of paranormal events themselves has shown a remarkable consistency: Precognitive dreams, clairvoyance, telepathic communication, apparitions, miraculous healings, divination, and messages from beyond the grave have always been the stuff of which the paranormal is made. It is only because people have had such experiences—in all cultures, in all eras—that we have any basis for psychical research.

Though the primary concern of *Intangible Evidence* is the vibrant modern era of parapsychology research and the public's keen interest in psi, a brief "whirlwind tour" through the history of paranormal phenomena and parapsychology will help put the present era in perspective.

IN THE BEGINNING

The earliest myths and legends were created to explain the forces and patterns of nature that so ruled the life of primitive man—the moon and tides, the rains, the day and night, the seasons, and the creation of the world in which he found himself. As knowledge was acquired, the myths changed to accommodate it, though myth and the "facts" were often inextricably intertwined. As man's knowledge increased, and explanations became clear for what had seemed impenetrably mysterious, the distinction between the mystical and the material was more carefully delineated. There also arose a distinction between the occult, or unexplainable, and the so-called magical—phenomena ostensibly created by those who claimed especial "powers," the shamans and sorcerers.

Though the shaman's role varies from culture to culture, the tradition of shamanism in one form or another is pervasive in all cultures. The shaman is often chosen by the tribe because he or she is seen, often at an early age, to possess attributes which qualify him to act as spiritual guide and advisor: As a child the budding shaman may be clairvoyant, may hallucinate or have visions, may choose to spend long periods in isolation and meditation, may easily enter a trance state, or even a state of apparent possession, from which he emerges with predictions or advice thought to be vital to the community.

In *The Occult*, Colin Wilson recounts the experience of Sir Arthur Grimble, once British land commissioner for the Gilbert and Ellis Islands in the South Pacific, who witnessed the "calling of the porpoises" by the native shaman. The shaman retired to his hut to enter into a dream in which he invited the "porpoise-folk" to a dance and feasting in his village. Hours passed, with the villagers silent and waiting. At last, the porpoise-caller rushed from his hut and fell on his face, clawing at the air and whining in a queer, high note. He then bade the villagers arise and follow him into the water. The porpoises came, Grimble reports, "moving toward us in extended order with spaces of two or three yards between them, as far as my eye could reach. So slowly they came, they seemed to be hung in a trance . . . the villagers were welcoming their guests ashore with crooning words. . . . It was as if their single wish was to get to the beach." The porpoises were then killed for the feast.

In February of 1986, *The New York Times* devoted half of page 2 to an account of a shaman of Brazil's Txucarramae tribe who had saved a prominent and beloved naturalist from certain death from the bite of a poisonous toad. The president of Brazil called in the shaman when all standard medical help had failed, and the country watched and listened as the shaman's three days of incantations, hallucinogenic "cigars," and herbal baths were carried out in full public view. The picture accompanying the article shows the feathered and beaded shaman, Raoni, with his protruding lip plate, standing next to the recovered Augusto Ruschi, in pith helmet and jungle khakis. Four months later, the *Times* reported Ruschi's death. Critics felt this proved the uselessness of the shaman's intervention; believers feel the shaman gave the scientist months of productive life, at a time when death seemed imminent.

Shamanism turns up again, in contemporary Haiti, in Harvard ethnobotanist Wade Davis' *The Serpent and the Rainbow*, a fascinating account of his journey through the labyrinth of the voodoo culture to track down the true nature of zombiism.

Divinatory practices were common in such early cradles of civilization as Mesopotamia, Egypt, India, and China. The patterns discerned in the heavenly bodies under which all men lived were the basis for astrological forecasts in virtually all early civilizations. In Mesopotamia, astrological records date from 8000 B.C.; omens were given special status, for every omen was believed to have a personal meaning to the observer. The Egyptians, whose pyramids are thought to have been aligned for astrological sightings, focused on life after death, the survival of the spirit or soul—as did the culture of India. Indian tradition has so carefully spelled out many facets of human nature and consciousness that they have survived and crossed cultural lines to find acceptance in Western man's quest for understanding: Terms like asana, chakra, mantra, kundalini, nirvana, mandala, siddhi, and yoga would be found in any contemporary dictionary. The idea of meditation as a means of gaining conscious control over inner states comes to us from India, though we may as soon pursue it these days in the more acceptable name of biofeedback, or guided imagery, as in yoga. From China comes another system of philosophy and divination, the I Ching, which has found favor in the West, as has acupuncture, a technique for freeing up the vital life force called "qi," or breath of life, so that it flows freely through the twelve meridians of the body. *Qigong*, a form of training used to manipulate these vital-energy centers, has lately found favor on our shores. Masters of *qigong* have such powerful "qi" that they purportedly can heal those with diminished qi. Yet another Oriental discipline which has sneaked in is *feng shui*, which stresses the proper placement and alignment of buildings, furniture, and the like according to ancient laws of nature worship and yin/yang relationships. When Raymond Hung, the president of a leading electronics company, planned to locate his new plant in Secaucus, New Jersey, he sent both his astrologer and his *feng shui* advisors to plan the placement of the furniture.

It was the Greeks who first actively sought to understand how the world worked and how man fitted into that world. They called their quest philosophy: the love of wisdom. Sophisticated mathematical sytems, astronomical advances, the science of numbers (the foundation for numerology), a theory of atomic energy—that is to say, rational, empirical ideas of form and substance—emerged, albeit hand in hand with highly developed ideas about the spiritual nature of man and the human condition. What Dr. Jeffrey Mishlove refers to as the first parapsychology experiment was carried out by King Croesus of Lydia in 550 B.C. (and reported by the historian Herodotus) to determine which of the oracles he should consult about his proposed campaign against the Persians. He sent a messenger to each of the seven oracles of highest reputation; on the hundredth day after their departure, they were to ask the oracle what Croesus was doing at that moment. Even before she was told of her assignment, the oracle at Delphi, in a trance, made her pronouncement to the holy men of the temple. The oracle's message translated as follows:

> I can count the sand, and I can measure the ocean;
> I have ears for the silent, and know what the dumb man nameth;
> Lo! On my sense there striketh the smell of a shell-covered tortoise,
> Boiling now on the fire, with the flesh of a lamb, in a caldron—
> Brass is the vessel below, and brass is the cover above it.

When all the messengers returned to Lydia, King Croesus read the predictions of all the oracles, and immediately declared the oracle at Delphi to be the only true oracle, for she had divined what he was doing at the prescribed moment—a task he had chosen because he felt it would be impossible to guess. He had taken a tortoise and a lamb, torn them apart with his own hands, and boiled them together in a brass caldron with a brass lid. In appreciation of the oracle's gifts, Croesus made an enormous sacrifice of several hundred animals, then sent a gift of gold to Delphi worth, by today's standards, more than $150 million! The ironic postscript to this story is that when he consulted the oracle at Delphi to find out if an empire would fall in his campaign against the Persians, the oracle replied in the affirmative. What the clever woman didn't tell him, perhaps fearing for her life, was that the empire to fall would be his!

Portents also figure prominently in Roman history—in its Shakespearean version. Many of us will remember from our school days that Caesar's wife dreamed on the eve of the Ides of March of his blood being spilled, and that a comet was believed to portend his death. Plutarch felt that man had a natural capacity for divination, if used under the right conditions. Socrates acknowledged the prophetic voice of his dreams, trances, and visions. While Pliny the Elder dismissed magicians as impostors, he felt that some magical techniques had been proved. And Ptolemy's books on astronomy, though misguidedly earth-centered, are considered the basis of modern astrology.

The Bible is riddled with accounts of supernatural phenomena: dream visions, apparitions of God, prophecies, healings, speaking in tongues. The Jewish tradition is filled with references to prayers as a way of achieving altered states of consciousness. Central to the Kabbalah, the Jewish mystical tradition, is a hierarchy of mystical and enlightenment stages through which man might pass to achieve union with God. These stages are often depicted as a tree of life. The elaborate symbology of the ten spheres of the tree of life, and other Kabbalistic imagery, are primary influences in numerology, as well as in the Major Arcana of the tarot, and their connection to astrology.

In Christianity we find the miracles of Jesus, whose austerities became the basis of the monastic tradition: flagellation, fasting, celibacy. Later on, of course, many unpleasant apparent psychic phenomena were said by the Catholic Church to be the work of the devil, and were dealt with through the ritual of exorcism. One voice of reason during this period was an eighteenth-century church official by the name of Prospero Lambertini. Assigned to probe claims of miracles and paranormal phenomena, he concluded that psychic experiences were not the sole province of the religious, but could occur to anyone (even to animals), more often in dreams than while awake, and often in symbolic rather than literal form—and that they were *innate human capabilities* rather than some demonic or spiritistic manifestation.

Church—and sometimes state—persecution of those who pursued the occult, and of those who felt that such phenomena need not have a religious explanation, drove the study of occult phenomena underground, into secret societies that preserved ancient knowledge while they sought further to expand their grasp of the human condition and consciousness. The Kabbalah was studied in secret, as was alchemy. Alchemy, incidentally, has turned up separately in many cultures. Understood to literally mean the art of changing lead into gold, it was more accurately a metaphor for the transformation of one's consciousness. Some believers held that the alchemist could transmute lead into gold when he had elevated his own consciousness onto a higher plane whereon he could achieve the transformation of any matter by reducing all (including himself) to one primordial substance, and then re-creating another—in this case gold. For this, he had to be in possession of the symbolic "philosopher's stone," the attainment of a full understanding of the powers of the mind through such means as meditation, dreams, and visions. (Some current theories of psi propose a collective consciousness in which all people and things are connected; it is through concentration and discipline that we can recognize and tune in to that connection.) Various cults sprang up, such as the Hermetic Order, which again turned for its imagery to the tree of life. The order's main thesis can be deduced from its motto, "As Above, So Below," meaning that man, himself a microcosm of the universe, can find its secrets within himself.

Giant leaps were made, beginning in the sixteenth century, with Copernicus' pronouncement that the earth moves around the sun. This heretical concept was soon expanded and elaborated by Johannes Kepler, Galileo, and Sir Isaac Newton (1642–1727). Newton's revolutionary laws of mechanics, calculations of the movements of the heavenly bodies, and gravitational theories overshadow in the modern mind the fact that he was an *alchemist* with a profound interest in the occult and esoteric. Cartesian logic—"I think, therefore I am"—added another piece to the developing scientific method of reasoning and understanding, though it is interesting to note that Descartes, no friend of the occult, attributed his ideas to images that came to him in dreams or in the in-between stage just before awakening. Sir Francis Bacon in the seventeenth century, promoter of the inductive method of reasoning—from observation to hypothesis to confirmation through experiment—first proposed that psychic phenomena could be studied scientifically through the "guessing of cards" and the "throwing of dice."

This was an era when rationalism reigned, and man walked the fence between science and the "otherworldly," not acknowledging that the two might not be mutually exclusive, and that both might be part and parcel of "human nature." Science writer Martin Ebon postulates that the history of parapsychology is really the history of a series of individuals, whose "fascinations and achievements," rather than the "force of History," shaped its course. If that is so, Dr. Emmanuel Swedenborg (1688–1772) was a pivotal figure, the epitome of the man who combined intellectual and scientific sophistication with an intense interest in the paranormal. Linguist, inventor, engineer, craftsman, scientist, he pursued interests ranging from anatomy, economics, physiology, and crystallography (a science he founded) to bookbinding, marquetry, watchmaking, and the development of everything from a submarine to an ear trumpet and a glider. Having mastered the outer world, he turned to the inner world, seeking, through intense immersion in study and meditation, to understand it as he had come to grips with natural phenomena. From 1744 until the end of his life at age fifty-six, he professed to have access to the other, spirit world as easily as to that reality in which we normally exist. He claimed that his prolific writings on the nature of the soul, the spirit world, and life after death, written in his usual careful, scientific tone, were possible because of his guiding angels. Many of his colleagues thought he'd gone off the deep end. But a clairvoyant vision of a fire going on in a town 300 miles away, attested to by witnesses, seems to have solidified the credibility of his later writings. The philosopher Kant, the poet Yeats, the visionary artist Blake, and the poet and dramatist Goethe were all profoundly influenced by Swedenborg. Swedenborg's lasting impact may owe not so much to the content of his writings as to his approach and attitude, which constitute the ideal approach to things paranormal: an acceptance of them as latent human capabilities, central to man's full potential, a side of our nature that runs parallel to the sensory world we know.

The mid-eighteenth to the mid-nineteenth century—a period covering the Age of Reason or the Age of Enlightenment—was a time of intense scientific advancement. A worship of science was characterized, predictably, by vehement skepticism toward all things "paranormal," as man became able to explain more and more of his world in physical terms. Rationality overwhelmed popular "superstition" and religious dogma; this attitude was most prominently embodied in the writings of the eighteenth-century Scots philosopher Hume. As Brian Inglis notes in *The Paranormal,* only Catholicism still allowed for the occasional miracle; essentially this attitude has continued to this day.

Parapsychologists Stanley Krippner and Jerry Solfvin point out in

Parapsychologie: science ou illusion? that "The dialectic process typically produces an 'anti-thesis' in response to the thesis. In response to the 'thesis' of science arose the romantic 'anti-thesis.' " Science, the classical stance, was understood to be descriptive and value-free: It gloried in the physical, the sensible, the natural, the regular; while the romantic stance glorified the unique, the spontaneous, the irregular, and the richness of diversity. It emphasized intuition, creativity, and imagination, and insisted that understanding depends on the context of a phenomenon and on such nonsensory and nonquantifiable aspects of experience as spirituality and beauty. The philosopher Jean-Jacques Rousseau best personifies the romantic battling the narrow-minded materialistic approach of "pure science." As happens in such cases, the debate eventually led to the search for a solid position in the middle ground. Franz Mesmer's theory of energy flow in humans as a form of magnetism seemed to appeal to the need for a "rational" explanation of the unexplainable. Mesmerism, the bizarre technique in which patients were submerged in baths full of iron filings to induce trance states as a means of bringing about healing, was probably as tremendously popular as it was because it seemed to put a scientific foundation under ideas and states of consciousness once derisively lumped in with the "occult." Not that the occult had completely disappeared. There was widespread interest in the tarot, and many new tarot decks were designed and became popular during this period. Even more popular was the "science" of handwriting, which was receiving tremendous attention both in the salons and in the universities of Europe. In the nineteenth century, Goethe and the philosopher Schelling were the catalysts for so-called natural philosophy, offered as a synthesis of physical and spiritual phenomena. Goethe foreshadowed Jung with his belief that the archetypal influences in his poetry were universal. By the late nineteenth century, the rationalists had again fought back against naturalism, in the form of the German experimentalists and what was called "logical positivism." It was this atmosphere of controversy and conflicting viewpoints which set the stage, in the 1880s, for the founding of the societies for psychical research in England and America.

Krippner and Solfvin argue that "the psychical research societies represented an aspect of revision that had an eloquent voice in the writings of the French mathematician Henri Poincaré and the German theoretical physicist Albert Einstein. Neither scientist was an advocate of psychical research nor much interested in the topic. Yet both acknowledged the creative and intuitive values of scientists in forming scientific knowledge. Both dealt in objectivity, yet understood the critical role played by value-laden assumptions in generating the theoretical structures of science." Einstein wrote of his work in special relativity: "I despaired of the possibility of discovering the true laws by means of constructive efforts based on known fact—the longer and more despairingly I tried, the more I came to the conclusion that only the discovery of a universal formal principle could lead us to assured results."

The particular focus for the founding of the psychical research societies was the investigation of spiritualism, which was cutting a broad swath through society on both sides of the Atlantic. Spiritualism was first heard from in Hydesville, New York, in 1847, when the Fox family, in particular sisters Margaretta and Catherine, claimed they were visited in their old farmhouse by a series of strange rappings and noises. After initial fright, they found them to be "spirit communicators" who would respond to their questions with a code of rapping sounds that signified "yes," "no," and individual letters of the alphabet. The rapping spirits soon spread from the Fox household into the community and, as people discovered they could produce the rappings and associated phenomena in their own seance groups, across the country. Soon tables were turning, and spirits paying visits, from coast to coast. In some cases, the claimed effects were even more spectacular: objects wandering erratically through the air, a piece of chalk incribing words on a slate, musical instruments playing themselves, small items materializing in thin air.

The Fox family made a career of their spirit communications, traveling around the country in a swirl of controversy. They were often challenged and tested by skeptical researchers, both here and abroad. In England the esteemed physicist Sir William Crookes thoroughly investigated the Foxes, and was convinced that no trickery was involved. Others came up with plausible explanations of their trickery. In 1888, Margaretta Fox suddenly asserted that their results were obtained by fraudulent means—though some say she wrote her confessional book to get money from those interested in debunking spiritualism, in order to support her alcoholism. But it was too late to save the world's sanity: By the time Margaretta 'fessed up, there were well over a hundred mediums practicing in New York City alone. It should be said that at no time in their career were the Foxes ever caught in a fraudulent act.

Madame Helena Petrovna Blavatsky, who founded the Theosophical Society in 1875, also caused quite a stir, claiming that her psychic powers came from her membership in a Tibetan spiritual brotherhood. It was one of the brotherhood, a *mahatma* in Hindu garb, who "appeared" at the first official meeting of the Theosophists, leaving a package containing the constitution and rules of the organization. Such luminaries as Gladstone, Alfred Lord Tennyson, Arthur Conan Doyle, and Thomas Edison sat in on the wondrous goings-on at the Theosophical Society before Madame moved to India to continue working her wonders, which included apparitions and mysterious letters. Though many were convinced of the authenticity of her miracles and Theosophy bloomed, in 1884 the inevitable scandal—provoked by an investigation of Blavatsky by the fledgling Society for Psychical Research, eager to prove its members' seriousness and lack of gullibility—finished it off. The authenticity of Madame Blavatsky has remained controversial, and that controversy surfaced again in 1986 when a critique by forgery expert Dr. Vernon Harrison challenged the evidence—mostly handwritten letters—that had been used to discredit Blavatsky. His carefully documented presentation shows that those letters were themselves forgeries, and the case mounted against her was so weak, partisan, and confused that "it might just as easily have been shown that Blavatsky wrote *Huck Finn*." He blames the society for publishing the report and for wasting the opportunity to investigate an important occultist properly. However, even though it has taken a hundred years to exonerate Madame Blavatsky, the Theosophical Society has managed to survive, and Theosophical teachings have made their mark on our culture.

The Society for Psychical Research (SPR) was founded in 1882 in London by a coalition of scholars and spiritualists at Cambridge University for the purpose of "making an organized and systematic attempt to investigate the larger group of phenomena designated by such terms as mesmeric, psychical, and spiritualistic." The preeminent medium David Douglas Home, who never took money for his seances and openly deplored fraudulence in the field, was also repeatedly tested by Crookes. (Despite Home's apparently impeccable reputation, he was denounced by Robert Browning, who frowned on his wife's interest and belief in him, in a poem called "Mr. Sludge, the Medium.") Home, who numbered among his patrons Napoleon III of France, Tsar Alexander of Russia, and numerous scientists and literati on both sides of the Atlantic, was what is called a physical medium; reportedly able to actually materialize spirits, he included among his feats levitation and the ability to hold hot coals.

The success of the SPR, guided by Cambridge University professor of philosophy Dr. Henry Sidgewick, led to the founding, in Boston in 1885, of the American Society for Psychical Research by a group of academicians that included the renowned English-born philosopher/psychologist Dr. William James (whose influence, until recently, was undermined by his close association with spiritualism). In ensuing years, many mediums were studied and tested by the society. But spiritualism proved a tricky subject for scientific investigation—too weird, and too vulnerable to accusations of fraud and trickery. The goals of the societies evolved into a broader mission of attempting to understand the nature of the human personality and the mind/body problem, of which spiritist phenomena (automatic writing, levitation, disembodied voices, and so on) were but one manifestation. There unavoidably came a breach between the scholars and the spiritualists, the upshot being that the latter lost ground and eventually left the research societies to the scholars and researchers, with their drier, more scientific approach. Always challenged and ridiculed, they nevertheless, as Alan Gauld states in *The Founders of Psychical Research*, "amassed in favor of paranormal phenomena evidence which would in the case of almost any other kind of natural event have been unhesitatingly and almost universally accepted."

While research on the European continent was sparse, a few pockets of activity are worth mentioning. One is the extensive researches of the Nobel Prize–winning Parisian physicist Dr. Charles Richet. Most notable among them were his card-guessing experiments, to which he applied probability theory with great success. He was also involved in the extensive investigations of the physical medium Eusapia Palladino, a Neopolitan peasant whose repertoire included levitation, ectoplasmic excretions, voices, bizarre odors, and strange taps and touches—even when her hands and feet were held by Richet and other investigators, to prevent cheating. For Eusapia did cheat. From time to time, the experimenters would give her the opportunity by releasing her hands and arms or conducting seances in semidarkness. Surprisingly, her efforts at fraud were often quite clumsy and easy to detect. Palladino herself never denied that she was capable of cheating, claiming that she was always in a trance, and therefore unaware of what she was doing. She maintained that it was the investigators' responsibility to keep her from cheating. Usually they did; but reluctant as most people are to give credence to the unbelievable, her record remains tarnished and suspect despite numerous testimonies in her favor submitted by eminent eye-witnesses over a twenty-year period. From working with Palladino,

Richet conjectured that so-called paranormal powers were really "un-recognized latent powers in the human organism."

A medium by the name of Lenore Piper became William James' Fox sisters. Extensively tested by James, and subsequently by Dr. Richard Hodgson and Dr. James S. Hyslop, she eventually convinced them all of her gifts. William James said of Mrs. Piper: "For me the the thunderbolt [of fact] *has* fallen, and the orthodox belief has not only had its presumption weakened, but the truth itself of the belief is decisively overthrown."

Most mediums during the era of spiritualism were so vulnerable to charges of fraud that parapsychologists developed theories to explain the problem: Does the overwhelming pressure to perform and to convince skeptics force psi-gifted individuals to cheat when their abilities aren't "on"? Do they do so against their wills? Is it instead a matter of natural temperament or personality: Are mediums some-how disposed to play tricks, like amoral poltergeists? Does the expla-nation lie in the supernatural world: Does psi power protect its mystery by compelling demonstrators to confuse the issue with "staged" effects? Is it possible that psi-gifted people are simply the victims of prejudicial scrutiny, when in fact their behavior has the same ratio of honesty to dishonesty as the average person's behavior?

Whatever the explanation, no quantity of tests and testimonials could convince the skeptics who had not witnessed spirit mediums firsthand. By the mid-1930s public interest in mediumship and psychical research had died down, and the field was decimated by unceasing attack and skepticism, from without and within. There occurred a shift in the societies, in both America and England, from mediumship and physical manifestations to the mental capabilities implied by telepathy and clairvoyance, both of which met the impor-tant criterion of being more amenable to laboratory study, using more sophisticated statistical models and techniques. Several events seemed to bring into focus this new era—the modern era of psychical research. Among them were the 1920 arrival of Dr. William Mc-Dougall at Harvard University, where he reintroduced hypnotism to American psychology, and the pursuit of other psychical experi-ments under the auspices of Dr. Gardner Murphy, whom many con-sider the single most important figure in the reemergence of psychical research. Another was the 1930 publication of *Mental Radio* by Upton Sinclair, an accounting of years of dramatic telepathic ex-periments carried out with his wife, Mary, in which she was consis-tently able to reproduce drawings made by others, usually from an adjacent room, but on occasion over distances measured in miles; the book's introduction was written by no less a figure than Albert Einstein. René Warcollier's *Mind to Mind* was also influential.

But the true arrival of the modern era of psychical research was heralded by William McDougall's move in 1927 to Duke University in North Carolina as head of the psychology department, with Dr. J. B. Rhine and his wife, Louisa, hot on his heels. The Rhines, believers in psychic functioning but discouraged by the difficulty of establishing "proof" through their investigations of spiritualism, hoped to put psychical research on a sounder footing. The Duke University Parapsychology Laboratory was formally established in 1934—the same year in which Rhine published *Extra-Sensory Perception*, a study of research at Duke with students. Here for the first time was academic evidence that paranormal powers were the province not just of the medium and the mystic, but of all of us. So began the modern era of psychic research.

MODERN PSI

The importance of the Parapsychology Laboratory at Duke and J. B. Rhine's impact on the field are hard to overstate. While nothing in Rhine's approach was revolutionary (certainly nothing since has matched the sensationalism of spirit phenomena), he brought respectability, responsibility, and in some measure *acceptance* to this controversial arena. This he did mainly by refining the methodology of parapsychological research, seeking to close loopholes and standardize methods of investigation. Believing that psychic functioning manifests itself *infrequently*, *unpredictably*, and *in small doses*, Rhine concentrated on simple, easily controlled, standardized, repeatable experiments, in large samples that could be subjected to rigorous statistical analysis. This he did with the simple, if tedious, expedient of card-guessing—and later dice-throwing—experiments. Rhine's statistics overwhelmed by the sheer quantity of trials on which they were based. While individual tests might show only small deviations from chance, the accumulation of many thousands of such tests was astonishing, with odds against chance reaching into the millions. Another innovative element of Rhine's work was his use of "ordinary" test subjects—college students—instead of "gifted" psychics or mediums. This paid off in two ways: It reduced possible suspicion of cheating by accomplished tricksters, and it reinforced the hypothesis that *just about everyone has some measurable psi ability*.

Rhine's early experiments, and most other investigations during this period, focused on evaluations of ESP in the lab—specifically, of telepathy. But a serious problem soon became apparent: How do you tell telepathy (paranormal communication) from simple clairvoyance? In other words, in the card-guessing experiments central to Rhine's and others' research, could the "receiver" not detect the hidden card directly (clairvoyantly) rather than via the sender's telepathic message?

So the emphasis shifted to testing clairvoyance, and experiments were "purified" to rule out telepathy, so that the experimenter would have no knowledge of the target being guessed at. Very simply, while Rhine's early work involved a subject guessing cards that were being looked at by the sender, the refined later work involved guessing the order of a deck of specially marked cards that had been shuffled by machine, with "hits" or "misses" recorded by machine or by an independent party who had never seen the shuffled deck.

Rhine then turned to experiments in an area that had been largely ignored since the demise of mediumistic interest, now considered so bizarre: physical rather than mental phenomena, or as he labeled it, psychokinesis (PK). The protocol that emerged involved the subject's *willing* the fall of dice thrown by a machine to land on a certain number. Variations of card-guessing and dice-calling were the meat and potatoes of psychical research for more than twenty years, between 1930 and the 1950s.

With what many researchers saw as the tremendous success of these new procedures (at last it seemed that psychic functioning could be repeatably produced and measured under controlled conditions acceptable to many in the scientific community), attention turned to trying to understand the process of psychic functioning, and the conditions for its success. Researchers wanted to know what personality factors were implicated in successful psychic functioning, what laboratory conditions facilitated it, what kinds of experiments brought in high scores, what internal laws governed psi functioning. They sought to understand the importance of time and distance, of subjects' attitudes toward ESP, and the set of variables needed for psi's optimum manifestation.

Not surprisingly, Rhine's work and that of others raised a hue and cry among skeptics. The objections usually took one of two forms: criticism of laboratory protocols or statistical methods, or allegations of outright fraud. Some critics suggested that experimenters could give involuntary signals to research subjects (sensory leakage), that cards were insufficiently shuffled, that there were errors in the recording of data, that the dice were imperfectly made and thus favored certain faces. Other critics didn't bother with specifics; they just said that since such phenomena didn't seem to be explainable according to physical laws, they were by definition impossible.

By 1938, as Krippner and Solfvin report, parapsychology had attracted so much attention that the American Psychological Association sponsored a symposium in which papers written by three parapsychologists (Rhine among them) and three critics were presented. J. L. Kennedy, chairman of the symposium, had been quoted that year in *Time* magazine as saying that he was "working on a coffin for ESP." However, the critics apparently did not present a decisive case. Later that year, the first mail survey of psychologists was published. Of the 58 percent of those sampled by the American Psychological Association who responded to the questionnaire, 59 percent reported that they considered the investigation of psychic phenomena "a legitimate scientific undertaking."

During 1941 and 1942, the American Society for Psychical Research, crippled by earlier scandal over a questionable medium known as Margery, by lack of public interest, and by the intervention of war, was re-formed under Gardner Murphy, and a program of rigorous experimental research was implemented. Its journal, along with the *Journal of Parapsychology* and the British *Journal of the Society for Psychical Research*, became a highly reliable source of information about psi research; standards adhered very closely to those in "orthodox" science. Critical responses to published papers were often featured.

In 1955, the prestigious journal *Science* published a critical article by Dr. G. R. Price which opened by stating that "believers in psychic phenomena . . . appear to have won a decisive victory. . . . This victory is the result of an impressive amount of careful experimentation and intelligent argumentation." Flummoxed by the evidence, Price went on to argue that no amount of evidence is sufficient to prove what is essentially a miracle according to the laws of nature, unless it would be even more miraculous if the testimony were a lie. Fighting words: the implication was that fraud is the only plausible explanation if the experiments cannot be rejected on other grounds. This argument, as Krippner and Solfvin note, was predicted in 1882 by Dr. Henry Sidgewick: "We must drive the objector into a position of being forced either to admit the phenomena as inexplicable, at least by him, or to accuse the investigators of lying, or cheating, or of a blindness incompatible with any intellectual condition except absolute idiocy."

One of the harshest criticisms of parapsychology came from nuclear physicist and past president of the American Association for the Advancement of Science E. U. Condon in 1969: "There used to be spiritualism, there continue to be extra-sensory perception, psychokinesis and a host of others. . . . Where corruption of children's minds is at stake, I do not believe in freedom of the press or freedom of speech." He went on to say that those who publish or teach the "pseudosciences" should be horsewhipped and "forever banned from further activity in these usually honorable professions."

Later the same year, the Parapsychological Association was, after three previously rejected applications, granted affiliate membership in the American Association for Advancement of Science. During the membership hearing, it was reported that scientists in the audience leaped up to make outraged speeches about the impossibility of psychic phenomena. Finally the anthropologist Dr. Margaret Mead made an impassioned plea:

"The whole history of scientific advance is full of scientists investigating phenomena that the establishment did not believe were there. The PA uses standard scientific devices such as statistics, double-blinds, and placebos. I submit that we vote in favor of this association's work."

The Council voted 165 to 30 in favor of the PA's admission. Psi was finally deemed scientific—in its methods if not its beliefs—by the esteemed body.

This momentous milestone did not end the debate, of course; it continues to this day. Now that lab procedures have become more stringent, critics usually concentrate on experimenter fraud or delusion. Because parapsychologists themselves are good at policing their own house, outright fraud is rare, and when uncovered, it is usually uncovered from within. Thus nowadays, when critics speak of fraud, it is usually by way of pointing out that it *could* have occurred. Today the psi-bashing crusade has been taken up by the self-appointed Committee for the Scientific Investigation of Claims of the Paranormal (CSICOP). These would-be psi cops have plenty of anti-psi fervor, and they spread it around liberally. CSICOP and its members are discussed in Chapter 3. Suffice it for now to say that they are ever-vigilant, that their tactics are not always even-handed—and that they have not been free of controversy themselves.

Along with psi's increasing respectability has come a gradual, if sometimes grudging, encroachment of psi into universities and private research foundations, often (again, as Ebon points out) because of the reputation and tenacity of individual researchers. William McDougall's work had been funded at Harvard by some long-buried psychical research funds, though normally it had been the custom of those few academicians in the field to do their research "on the side." It was the brother of one of the founders of Stanford University who endowed the pioneering psychic research done there. Stanford had no choice but to accept the funding, but it is interesting to note that much of the research done at Stanford approached psi from a negative viewpoint; little of it has proved significant. Though still regarded with embarrassment in some circles, research is carried on at a handful of universities—prominent among them Syracuse, the University of Virginia, Princeton, the University of California at Davis, and the City College of New York, as well as a handful of universities in Canada and overseas. There are currently several chairs in Parapsychology: One is held by reincarnation specialist Ian Stevenson at the University of Virginia; another is held by Dr. William Roll at West Georgia College. The newly endowed Koestler Chair of Parapsychology at Edinburgh is held by Dr. Robert Morris. Rumor has it that Cambridge may soon follow. Dr. Ramakrishna Rao, formerly of Duke University, holds the first chair in parapsychology at a university in India. Dr. Martin Johnson holds the chair of parapsychology at the University of Utrecht in the Netherlands. Dr. Hans Bender has a chair at the University of Freiberg, Germany. John F. Kennedy University at Orinda, California, offers a master's degree in parapsychology; for a doctorate, the usual procedure is to take the degree in psychology with a thesis on a parapsychology topic.

Because experimental goings-on in the psi field from about 1960 to the present are the subject matter of Part II, I will only summarize them briefly here in order to round out our whirlwind psi history.

There has been a resurgence of interest in using gifted psychics as research subjects. It was the much-tested medium Eileen Garrett who, determined to learn more about her strange and troubling gifts, started the Parapsychology Foundation in New York, and whose patronage and publishing ventures have been influential in the dissemination of serious information on psi research. Stanford Research Institute (now SRI International) was the birthplace of remote-viewing experiments, in which the subject is asked to describe—in words and pictures—a site visited by a third person (or "beacon") which has been chosen at random by computer from a target pool. Such experiments are a mainstay of current research. Variations with a goal of archaeological exploration have been conducted by Stephan

Schwartz at the Möbius Group. Remote viewing, considered one of the most promising areas of psi research, has proved successful with nongifted subjects as well.

Under Dr. Montague Ullman, Dr. Stanley Krippner, and others at the Maimonides Hospital Dream Laboratory, "senders" in sealed chambers were able to influence the dreams of sleeping subjects by concentrating on slides or pictures. Dr. William Braud and Charles Honorton have worked extensively with the *Ganzfeld*, or "whole field," technique, in which the testing process is carried out in a relaxed state of minimal sensory distraction. Dr. Helmut Schmidt's work with random-number generators (RNGs), which imitate the unpredictable atomic decomposition of radioactive materials such as strontium 90, has made target-guessing procedures truly random, and thus removed the possibility of fraud in target selection. RNGs have added immeasurably to the strengthening of experiment protocols. Dr. Robert Jahn, of Princeton's Engineering School, "found" himself in the field of parapsychology after he discovered, to his consternation, that student volunteers could affect the theoretically impervious output of random-number generators. Dr. Charles Tart, professor of psychology at the University of California at Davis, using as target "visiting sites" holograms selected by computer and projected in steel-encased rooms, has made major contributions to the laboratory investigation of out-of-body experiences, and is known for his work on psychic functioning in altered states of consciousness.

Spontaneous, or anecdotal, psi has been successfully pursued in the area of poltergeists by several researchers; Ian Stevenson has laboriously tracked down dozens of reported cases of reincarnation.

Healing, a major focus of recent psi research, has come a long way since the days when Edgar Cayce was subjected to the pokings and proddings of both critics and researchers. Dr. Dolores Krieger at New York University Hospital has trained and tested thousands of nurses in the "laying on of hands" with enough success that *The New York Times* featured her work on page one of its Science Times in the fall of 1985. The first federal grant in the area of healing was awarded to Dr. Janet Quinn in 1986. Lawrence LeShan, who extensively tested psychic Eileen Garrett, taught himself, and subsequently many others, to heal, in order to show that psi could be harnessed and used by just about anyone.

Others—prominent among them Dr. Gertrude Schmeidler (now retired from City University of New York), Dr. Charles Tart, Charles

Honorton, and Dr. Rex Stanford at St. John's University—are interested in questions of the psychic personality and conditions suitable to psi functioning. Robert Morris has investigated the occurrence of psi in animals, and has made significant contributions to the vital study of "experimenter effect"—how the researcher's prejudices affect the outcome of his experiments, whether because of clues or attitudes imparted to subjects, or hidden bias in his hypothesis, choice of subjects, or any number of factors, including his own psychic ability!

More in Parts Two and Three. But before looking at "popular psi," there's one more topic to address. What about "psychic warfare" and the "mind race" between our government and the Soviet Union? This is a tough question. The extent of government-sponsored psi research, both here and in the Soviet Union, is a mystery nearly as impenetrable as the nature of psi itself.

PSI WARS?

Ironically, the first indication that psychic functioning was being studied for possible military use cannot be confirmed. In 1959, a French newspaper reported that the U.S. atomic submarine *Nautilus* was being used to conduct ship-to-shore telepathic experiments (radio communication is impossible underwater). This report was denied by the government, which accused the Russians of planting the story. *This* explanation was seen by others as a cover-up. No one really ever got to the bottom of it; but it had the effect of galvanizing public attention, and, some say, of creating support for psychic research both here and in the U.S.S.R. Submarine research on psi has since been conducted on both sides of the Iron Curtain.

Interest was further fueled by *Psychic Discoveries Behind the Iron Curtain*, a 1970 book by Sheila Ostrander and Lynne Schroeder based on their interviews and travels in Soviet-bloc countries. The gist of their findings was that there is extensive Soviet Government–funded psychic research activity, that there are at least a couple of dozen research centers, that Soviet research is highly secret, that it is directed toward military applications, and that it is taken quite seriously. Since this time, a few other books have updated their report: *The New Soviet Discoveries* by Henry Gris and William Dick; Martin Ebon's *Psychic Warfare: Threat or Illusion?*; *Mind Wars*, by Ron McCrae, former assistant to investigative columnist Jack Anderson; and Targ and Harary's *The Mind Race*, with its epilogue on the status of psi in the Soviet Union by parapsychologist Larissa Vilenskaya, a defector who publishes a quarterly journal of international psi research, particularly in the Eastern Hemisphere.

Ideologically and philosophically, psi is a tricky subject for the Soviets, because it could easily be seen to be in conflict with Marxist materialistic doctrine; precognition is particularly hard to reconcile with Marxist philosophy. Soviet terminology reflects this: For example, the Soviets refer to "bioenergy" when speaking of healing, not wanting to imply any potential spiritual component. Almost all psychic research is carried out under government auspices; private investigation is discouraged. Dr. Nikolai Khokhlov, professor of psychology at California State University at San Bernardino, feels that the Soviets are far ahead of us, for a couple of reasons. "They have all the money they want in their hands. They want a thousand scientists: They can either lure them or arrest them, and they can put them in a place where they can produce or else. . . . People have to fight for simple things, like your tape recorder, or even a cup of tea. So they have incentive, partially by intimidation, partially by material promises. It's very easy." But certain factors keep the Soviets back. They have a serious computer lag. Perhaps more crucial, as Vilenskaya notes, is that "[most] people who possess these abilities are very much against negative applications. I don't feel that they will find too many sensitives to go along." She recounts the story of a healer, a colleague who was asked to "influence some foreign leaders who are speaking on the radio . . . to change their minds. . . . I refused. I said that I will never do their dirty work."

The United States, on the other hand, is hampered by other problems, according to Khokhlov. Mysticism, dreaming, belief in healing —"never-never land"—are very much alive in the Russian soul, spurred by the dreary everyday reality of the system. Here, on the other hand, despite our talk of mind and soul and religion, we are servants of pragmatism and science. While the Soviets assume the existence of psi, and focus their research on how to use it, we spend most of our time trying to prove to the powers that be that psi exists, so that we can get more funding to do more research to prove that psi exists—and perhaps *eventually* to learn how to use it.

The Soviets are definitely learning how to use psi, and if we can believe the reports, much of their research seems to be focused on rather malevolent, potentially warlike applications. "Action at a distance"—essentially mind control or influence of another, often unsuspecting, person—has turned up in several guises. This might take the form of putting people to sleep, or waking them up, at a distance.

It might involve the transmission of pain from sender to receiver. In one experiment, biophysicist (that's one Soviet euphemism for parapsychologist) Yuri Kamensky imagined he was strangling his partner, Karl Nikolaev: Nikolaev's EEG patterns showed such drastic changes that the researchers were afraid he was suffocating, and thought of stopping the test. When Kamensky imagined beating Nikolaev, Nikolaev felt severe pain and almost fell out of his chair. Incidentally, Kamensky was in Moscow and Nikolaev in Leningrad during these tests.

Nina Kulagina (page 140) is best known for her reported ability to psychokinetically move objects. Widely publicized photographs show her "suspending" a ball in the air, though she has also been caught at fraud. But she really grabbed everyone's attention when she was able to stop a frog's heart from beating by concentrating on it from a distance of about 4 feet. She demonstrated her skills for Vilenskaya, by psychokinetically creating a burn on Vilenskaya's skin which remained visible for five days. She proceeded to cause a burn on her own skin, and then to heal it within ten minutes, as Vilenskaya looked on. Kulagina has been able to cause such a burn even through a lead shield. And she has been able to lower the vital functions of mice so that they appeared near death. Vilenskaya's question is: why are they interested in these devastating applications? Kamensky explained to her that negative feelings are transmitted more strongly than positive ones. Vilenskaya feels that the success of such experiments depends a good deal upon the belief system of the experimenters, and Soviet psi is after negative uses.

You can see how such reports of Soviet experiments could put a scare into the American military establishment. If "action at a distance" really works on demand, it would theoretically be possible to scramble the brains of our military personnel and government leaders (or stop their hearts!), intercept secret communications, and ferret out the exact locations of our missiles and warships.

So, are we worried, and if so, what are we doing about it? The consensus of most people in the field is that we are not doing much, though no one seems to know why we're so complacent. Nikolai Khokhlov, in contrast, states that "the truth is that for years we have super-duper top-secret laboratories that are working twenty-four hours a day on this. . . ."

Mind Wars cites several examples of government involvement, though McCrae, a disbeliever himself, tends to look at most of the research as laughable, and purposely offers examples to make the reader laugh along with him. He alleges that an operative of the Office of Naval Intelligence each month paid a Washington psychic named Madame Zodiac $400 to look at charts and photographs, tell him the location of Soviet missile submarines, and forecast their maneuvers. He reports that a psychic named Charles Whitehouse has a receipt for a "multispectral image analyzer station" which the Navy bought from him, also to be used to locate submarines. This Rube Goldberg contraption purportedly amplified psychic energies: You merely inserted a picture of the sub, and—voilà!—the machine would tell you where it was. There was also supposedly a plan to have psychically directed sea gulls defecate on the periscopes of Russian subs. There's more: a plan to take advantage of findings, pioneered by Cleve Backster, that plants respond to human emotions. As McCrae archly remarks: "You can see the effect this would have: Smuggle a psychic rhododendron into the Kremlin's secret chambers, and their darkest secrets would be ours."

McCrae's condescending report should be viewed in the light of a telling comment he makes in connection with remote viewing: "I did, and still do, find remote viewing as accurate as that claimed for [the gifted psychics] Swann and Price so fantastic as to be ridiculous. I may be wrong, but to quote one eminent physicist who read the report from SRI, the research center where the remote-viewing experiments took place: 'This is something I won't believe even if it turns out to be true.' I might never personally accept the reality of remote viewing, even if it turned out to be true." How's that for open-minded investigation? Too, both Marcello Truzzi, publisher of The Zetetic Scholar, and Keith Harary, Director of Research at the Institute for Advanced Psychology, cautioned me that McCrae's reports might be questionable.

In contrast to McCrae's evaluation, Congressman Charles Rose, chairman of the House Subcommittee on Intelligence Evaluation and Oversight, said of SRI's remote viewing: "What these persons 'saw' was confirmed by aerial photography. There's no way it could have been faked. . . . Some of the intelligence people I've talked to know that remote viewing works, although they still block further research on it, since they claim it is not yet as good as satellite photography. But it seems to me that it would be a hell of a cheap radar system. And if the Russians have it and we don't, we are in serious trouble."

So goes the controversy. Because the subject is so sensitive, and because they are so protective of their skimpy funding, I had a hard time getting straight answers to the question of our government's psi activities from otherwise open researchers. Sometimes they themselves don't know. SRI seems to be primarily funded by government money, though whether it is CIA or Pentagon money is anyone's guess. Ingo Swann spent most of 1978–80 at SRI, probably at the government's expense. Jack Anderson's column of October 24, 1985, seems to confirm stories of SRI funding for remote viewing of Soviet military installations, first with the CIA's "Project Scanate," later reincarnated as the Defense Intelligence Agency's "Project Grill Flame." An SRI spokesman I talked to skittishly claimed that while it does have government projects under way, much of its current work is being done under the auspices of private corporations.

The real story is elusive. It does seem that the Soviets far outspend us, perhaps by a reported ratio of 100:1. The best estimates are that, whatever it is our government is up to so surreptitiously, it probably doesn't involve more than $5 million–$10 million a year.

Can we really harness the ability to blow each other up "psychically"? Most researchers find this idea very farfetched, at least given the present state of the art of harnessable psychic functioning. We can only hope that rumors of malevolent government intentions—and capabilities—are exaggerated, or that good sense, and goodwill, will prevail. Failing that, let's hope that the skeptics are right for a change, and that psychic functioning really is impossible.

POPULAR PSI

While the extent of government-sponsored psi research may be a mystery, and while serious parapsychology research is still but a drop in the bucket of scientific inquiry, public interest in things psychic seems to be coming out of the closet at last. As if thumbing its nose at the waffling wimps of science, the public has embraced the psychic, the occult, the "alternative" in many forms and in many forums. This barely contained groundswell of public interest, still kept somewhat in check by fear of censure and ridicule, seems about to burst the seams of seemliness once and for all.

The signs are everywhere. The fact is that hundreds of millions of people, in this country and all over the world, from all social classes and walks of life, are involved in some sort of psychic or metaphysical discipline. Even in our high-tech society, belief is unexpectedly strong. The editors of *Psychology Today* were astounded when a 1984 poll of its upscale readers revealed that a whopping 85 percent of women and 78 percent of men believe in ESP. A poll taken by *The Times of London* the same year turned up belief above 80 percent. There's much more going on out there than meets the eye.

Tales of astrological forecasts and psychic predictions used to be confined to movie-star confessions in the *National Enquirer* and screen magazines. Today you find them on the front page of *The Wall Street Journal* and in the business section of *The New York Times*, told by stockbrokers and CEOs. *The Wall Street Journal* has run many front-page stories on the paranormal: a report on a convention of psychic surgeons in the Philippines; the story of remote viewing being used to forecast silver futures; a story on brokers who work with astrologers; one on astrologers who work with people buying real estate; a droll treatment of the Fortean Society, which collects anomalies such as toad showers and psychic tooth fillings. *The New York Times* carried the story of a Florida woman who won a $1-million lawsuit (since reversed) after a CAT scan caused her to lose her psychic powers, and another on a psychic excused from jury duty because she claimed to know the verdict of the upcoming trial. Other *Times* stories covered "white-collar psychics" and growing mainstream interest in spiritual concepts. *Dallas* and *New York* magazines have run special sections of sources for psychic practitioners. ABC's July 4, 1985, *20/20* broadcast included a segment on precognition in which Hugh Downs relates a childhood experience in which he "knew" the exact contents of a letter from his grandparents. A police officer goes on to talk about his work with psychic Dorothy Allison on the Atlanta child murders, and a Federal Aviation Authority air controller talks about the calls he received from Cincinnati resident David Booth, who had several prophetic dreams about the 1979 crash of an American Airlines DC-10 out of O'Hare airport. Psychic Alan Vaughan tells of his documented dreams about the murder of Robert F. Kennedy—which led to the founding of Robert Nelson's Central Premonitions Registry as a clearinghouse for predictions.

The emerging connection between business and the psychic arts is fascinating—and makes eminent sense. As Chester Rothman, a vice president with Shearson Lehman Brothers, said in a full-page article on parapsychology in the business section of *The New York Times* in 1985, "If a psychic can better grasp the rationalities of the world than a market analyst, he might well give better business advice." Ron Schapell, former president of the Lear Corporation, periodically consults psychic Clarisa Bernhardt since she correctly told him (at a chance meeting) that a test plane he was about to fly would crash unless he fixed part of the communications system on the exterior of the plane. I recently met a commodities broker who relies heavily on the I Ching, in addition to traditional market indicators, and an oil-company president whose psychic tells him where to drill his wells.

Roy Rowan, in *The Intuitive Manager: Profiting from the Eureka Factor*, reports that H. L. Hunt's son Herbert revealed that when his father consulted a psychic before a series of explorations, she steered him away from the Santa Barbara channel, where there was subsequently a major oil spill. I was told, with strict orders not to reveal names, that the editor of a prominent home-design magazine consults a psychic about the competence and compatibility of anyone she is thinking of hiring. The strong ESP abilities of sucessful executives is amply documented in *Executive ESP* by Douglas Dean and John Mihalasky.

Remember Uri Geller, who seemingly bent keys and forks, and stopped the clocks of TV viewers all over the country? A catalyst for renewed public interest in the paranormal, and consequently the central figure in the raging controversy over claims to paranormal powers, he has given up trying to please the skeptics and concentrates on finding gold and precious resources for large corporations who aren't afraid of being laughed at (all the way to the bank). Geller is now living in a splendid manor house on the banks of the Thames north of London, and claims to have made more than £50 million ($80 million) this way.

Ex-Congressman Bill Feighan of Ohio told me story after story about his conversion from adamant skeptic to believer. He has gotten advice from a number of psychic practitioners—astrologers, tarot readers, clairvoyants—on everything from money matters to choosing business partners, buying land on which to build a house, and campaign strategy. When his mother was terminally ill and various family members were taking turns spending time with her, a psychic told him the time she would die, so that they could all be with her when it happened. Joe Sugarman, president of the JS&A mail-order firm, has been so bowled over by things that have happened to him through psychics that he's finally given up trying to rationalize psi and is just going to "let it take me wherever it leads." He has recently been successful in marketing products which work as a tool for improving psychic abilities. This open-minded, yet skeptical, attitude seems to be characteristic of the many successful business people who are using psi for personal and profitable gain.

Not everyone is so open in acknowledging interest or involvement in things paranormal. Many people have told me stories I would love to share—of precognitive dreams, of a psychic's market predictions, of matchmakings and dealmakings—in strictest privacy. And I have lost count of the times I've stepped out of important business conferences, only to have some sheepish executive surreptitiously slip me his birth time on a crumpled piece of paper, mumbling that I should send him his astrological forecast or biorhythm printout "in an unmarked envelope."

Their caution is not really surprising, for in the halls of power, hard-nosed disbelief still reigns, and fear of reprisal—loss of job or being passed over for promotion—is a very real consideration. When I get frustrated about this head-in-the-sand attitude, I look back at recent history and realize that things are bound to change, for resistance to new and strange ideas seems to be intrinsic in human nature. Space travel, heart transplants, television, and computers have all been deemed impossible by one worthy pundit or another. In response to the premiere of Rossini's *Stabat Mater*, Richard Wagner wrote a satirical review, declaring that the piece was "jotted down by Rossini in a moment of repentance for all the money he had cheated out of a gullible public." Stravinsky's *Firebird Suite*, Martha Graham's "scandalous" modern dancing, and James Joyce's "filthy" *Ulysses* were all greeted with horror and catcalls. *The Experts Speak*, a tongue-in-cheek compendium assembled by Christopher Cerf and Victor Navasky, is a 390-page treasure trove of authoritative statements—all of which proved false. It should be the required antidote for attacks of narrow-mindedness. After all, who would have listened thirty years ago if you'd told people to jog, give up smoking, and eat yoghurt?

Thirty years ago people who consulted psychiatrists kept their dark, dirty secret to themselves; today people make small talk about their psychotherapy over lunch, and corporations have psychologists on staff. Hypnotism used to be a conjurer's act; today it is used by lawyers and police for recall, and by doctors to treat everything from smoking to phobias. Biofeedback is a prime treatment at pain and stress clinics these days; it is really just a more technically refined version of meditation, the now acceptable relaxation technique once practiced only by gurus and their hippie followers. Psychics help police find missing bodies, and advise lawyers on jury selection. Ten years ago acupuncture was on the very fringes of medicine, but today, helped along by the respectability of James Reston of *The New York Times*, who underwent an emergency appendectomy in China with acupuncture as an anesthetic, and reported on his experience, it is used in many hospitals, to treat a wide variety of ailments. Healing itself, once on the very fringes of the occult, has become a central focus of public interest. In England, the General Medical Council permits healers to work with patients, even within the hospital setting, as long as the patient remains under the primary supervision of a doctor. The United States is not at that stage yet. And don't be too eager to tell your doctor that you're seeing a healer; it is often a sure way to damage the relationship, according to a report in *Psychology Today*, August 1985. Most patients have learned to keep their visits to a healer secret from their doctor, even though they are often educated people who keep a perspective on the role of the healer, and even though only 1 percent of healers sampled were hostile to traditional medical treatment. One doctor told his patient, when she told him that a healer had cleared up her skin rash, to go back to the healer next time she was in a car accident.

The article also debunked the myth that only the religious, the uneducated, and the rural succumb to the appeal of the healer. This I have seen for myself. In a church on Central Park West in New York City, healing services regularly draw a crowd of upwards of five hundred people that seems to cut across every social and cultural line this big city has to offer. In a friendly and informal atmosphere, mothers with children, couples, men in three-piece suits, and punk rockers stand in line to wait to consult with one of a dozen healers for their physical or emotional ills, or to "stand in" as the healee for an absent friend or family member.

Paranormal beliefs and practices show up all over the world, for psychic experiences—and man's desire to understand them—are universal. In India, a horoscope is cast at birth for virtually every baby born—of every religion, of every caste. Reincarnation is accepted as fact, and the many stages for the attainment of spiritual life, amply documented in the Hindu tradition, influence the conduct of everyday life. In Japan, a working knowledge of astrology is considered as useful as a working knowledge of electronics. Biorhythm has also been taken up enthusiastically by the Japanese. Some Japanese corporations monitor the daily biorhythms of employees in order to assign tasks more efficiently and cut down on accidents. Workers wear armbands which indicate physically, emotionally, or intellectually critical days, so that coworkers will be aware of their situation. The Japanese Government in 1986 appointed an eight-member committee (*Omni* magazine called it a "Ministry of Telepathy") to study the possibility of telepathy and gravity waves as a means of communication.

In both France and Germany, it is common for companies to have an astrologer and a graphologist on staff, to be consulted in matters of hiring, firing, and promotions. I learned this firsthand many years ago when the president of the giant German corporation Triumph went to a great deal of trouble in a roundabout way to find out my birth time before hiring me as a consultant. My suspicion was confirmed by an executive at Volkswagen, for whom I also consulted: "Of course they checked out your chart, and your handwriting, too, I bet. We always have our astrologer and graphologer evaluate our personnel."

The Chinese throw the I Ching for guidance about everything from business to marriage; this ancient book of wisdom is as fundamental to them as the Bible is to Christian cultures. During the Philippine elections in 1986, the numerologist Edouardo C. Baluno consulted both his Kabbalah and Fatima tables, and pronounced Corazon Aquino a sure winner. In England, there are more than five thousand licensed healers, most of whom belong to the National Association for Spiritual Healing; the stigma still attached to healing in the United States has largely disappeared in the United Kingdom. More than a third of the population of Brazil are Spiritists, members of a quasi-religious cult which combines the influences of European, American Indian, and African culture. The voodoo culture of Haiti is similar, in that it reaches into all areas of Haitian life—personal, social, religious, and spiritual. Within these traditions, trances, spirit possession, and even the ability to walk over hot coals are accepted as normal practices for those who achieve a higher state of knowledge or spirituality. In the United States, fire-walking has been enthusiastically taken up by followers of Anthony Robbins' Neurolinguistic Programming—strikingly parallel to the practices of voodoo culture, but with a modern scientific veneer to make it more palatable to our rational minds. The scientific community has written this entire phenomenon off by ascribing it to the Leidenfrost effect—the tenet of physics that purports to explain away the phenomenon by claiming that anyone can walk over hot beds of coals if his feet are sweaty. I'm more inclined to listen to Wade Davis: "There may, in fact, be an explanation for these extraordinary abilities, but if so it lies in regions of consciousness and mind/body interactions that Western psychiatry and medicine have scarcely begun to fathom. In the absence of a scientific explanation, and in the face of our own certain ignorance, it seems foolish to disregard the opinions of those who know possession best."

In Spanish-speaking communities across the United States, *espiri-*

tistas—combination counselors and spiritual guides—are an integral part of the society, consulted by lawyers and doctors as well as laborers and housewives. Dr. Virginia Garrison, a Columbia University professor who has intimately studied this phenomenon, is extremely impressed with the astute and effective counsel given by the *espiritistas.* Having lived in their community and in their homes, having studied with them and talked to their clients, she has reached the conclusion that the *espiritistas,* with their mix of commonsense advice, charms, and incantations, account for the low incidence of mental-health problems in the community. In the American Southwest, American Indian "sweat lodges" have moved beyond tribal boundaries. These gatherings, a kind of cathartic confessional presided over by tribal medicine men, are intended to induce a higher consciousness through group meditation held in tents heated to high temperatures. Popular on college campuses, they have also sprung up in the prison system, where they are purported to be performing a valuable and effective psychotherapeutic service.

Numerous practices adopted and adapted from other cultures have found their niche in the Western quest for enlightenment. Many forms of yoga and meditation are widely practiced, as are several types of massage therapy, and "bodywork" of every description. Hindu chanting, Buddhist asceticism, and Sufi dancing are all seen as drug-free ways to bring about altered consciousness and thus easier access to the inner, and perhaps "other," self. Carlos Castaneda's immensely popular books about the sorcerer don Juan (which are now generally believed to be works of fiction) have familiarized the public with the Yaqui Indian path to inner knowledge through personal discipline and courage. Interest in life after death has been sparked by the near-death studies of such respected researchers as Dr. Elisabeth Kübler-Ross and Dr. Raymond Moody. This in turn has led to a renewal of interest in reincarnation, hypnotism, and the highly controversial past-lives therapy, in which subjects reportedly regress to the point where they can revisit former lives, and become aware of problems that have carried over into the present one.

THE PSYCHIC SMORGASBORD

The cornucopia of paranormal goodies offered today is awesome, and everyone has a different idea about what is worthwhile: One man's path to enlightenment is another man's balderdash. Astrology makes sense, but UFOs are too farfetched. Meditation is the path to enlightenment, but the I Ching is pure gobbledygook.

Much of what's going on today falls under the heading of "New Age," the more sober and credible heading for what used to be labeled "hippie" or "counterculture." Signs of increased mainstream acceptance of "alternative lifestyles" are everywhere. Look at the popularity of Shirley MacLaine's books about her spiritual travels; the openness with which Tina Turner discusses her long involvement with Zen Buddhism; Sting's combined interest in the occult, psychology, and "a kind of layman's view of nuclear physics." Look around you on the streets of New York, where psychic readers and advisors are turning up in storefronts at very fashionable addresses, along with New Age paraphernalia emporiums with names like "Star Magic" and "Cosmic Light."

One of the best ways to get an idea of just how far-reaching—and sometimes farfetched—this movement is, is to pick up a selection of the free publications, with names like *Whole Life Times* and *Free Spirit*, that are given away at health-food stores and such New Age gathering places as New York's Open Center, Boston's Interface, or Big Sur's Esalen Institute (still going strong). You'll find ads for crystal balls and brain-wave synthesizers, for lenses that purport to enable you to see the human aura, for pendulums and healing crystals.

For firsthand experience (and an enjoyable afternoon), visit one of the psychic fairs that bring together all manner and form of psi-stuff. Some, such as the semiannual Whole Life Expo, are sizable conventions that draw thousands to sample the New Age grab bag. The standard version, much more modest, takes place on a weekend day in a church or hotel suite, where vendors of myriad wares and services set up their card tables, and for $10 or $15 you can have a tarot reading, your handwriting analyzed, your palm read, or your aura checked. There will be books on everything from hypnotism and salt power (yes, salt power) to love trances and wishing dolls. You can buy a biorhythm computer, a numerological forecast, a magnetic healing bracelet, aromatic oils, a moon-phase wristwatch, a cassette tape for testing your psychic powers, or a subscription to *Fate* magazine. There will be lectures on the I Ching, reincarnation, the Kabbalah, witchcraft, trance channeling, and UFOs.

This is just the sort of thing that gives the debunkers and scientific researchers apoplexy, for there's rarely any attempt at quality control, any attempt to separate the effective from the useless, the gifted from the quacks. Some of these people and practices are the very offenders that give the paranormal a bad name; however, since very little of it has ever been subjected to scrutiny by those qualified to pass judgment, who can separate the wheat from the chaff? In the old flat-earth days, mapmakers would write "Here Be Dragons" at the edges of the map, to indicate their belief that beyond the known lay evil and danger. Before we jump to the same conclusion about the flakier fringes of the unknown, we might do well to remember that those areas once marked "Here Be Dragons" are thoroughly accounted for on modern maps. While aroma therapy, pyramid power, Atlantis and the Bermuda Triangle, yeti and bigfoot, runes and cartouches, vampires and ghosts are beyond the scope of this book, and beneath the consideration of all right-thinking rationalists, they are the occultism of choice for many.

Is it quackery or overzealousness that we're dealing with here? At the level of the psychic fair and *Fate* magazine ads, it's probably a combination of the two. Keep in mind that most of it is harmless, that some of it is fun, and that the majority of people have the sense to take it with a grain of salt. On a more poignant level, it is probably an indication that many people are trying to make some sense, and perhaps some use, of psychic abilities—and getting little help elsewhere.

Many psychic practitioners I have met would shun the psychic fair. But they, and their serious counterparts on the side of science, are rarely separated from the silly in most people's minds. For this we can thank the media—for whom psi is both an easy target and a sure attention-getter. In *The Mind Race*, Keith Harary and Russell Targ devote thirty-five pages to a tour of psi in the media; it's quite an eye-opener. They point out the distortion of psi in film and fiction, and by ratings-watching news reporters. They make a damning case against the psychic stereotypes fostered by books and movies—the beautiful, immortal witch of *Bell, Book, and Candle*, the ostracized loner in *Carrie*. Any number of films—*Poltergeist, The Exorcist, The Amityville Horror*—associate psychic functioning with the supernatural, and imply that messing about with psi can be dangerous.

Incidentally, *The Amityville Horror*, which professed to be a true story, turned out, after careful investigation by psi researchers and psychologists, to be a case in which severe mental disturbance on the part of the family involved (intensified by media-fueled hype) was at the heart of the matter: It was a hoax that had nothing whatsoever to do with psychic functioning. According to Harary, it is a classic example of how psychic occurrences in the media are usually made out to be scary and unsettling; too, they are associated with people who are unbalanced. No wonder the general public is scared of psi. The effect is to make people afraid of their own psychic experiences, and feel that they must be crazy. Or they think psychic experiences so strange and powerful that they dismiss their own premonitions or telepathic communications as "less" than psychic.

This state of affairs is unfortunate, for many people are eager for serious information about psi, and for insight into their own psychic experiences. Popular opinion and media distortion obscure the fact that psychic abilities seem to be latent in all of us, that they are "normal," freely available, and can be pursued independently, without a need to turn over one's trust, one's money, or one's intellectual and emotional independence to some spiritual idea or leader. But serious, unsensationalized information is hard to come by, so many people settle for the specious brew offered at psychic fairs, and at extremes are drawn into cults or become enamored of controlling gurus who claim to have the answers. Jim Jones, who led the members of his People's Temple to their deaths in Guyana—inducing hundreds to drink poison in a mass suicide as the authorities closed in on him—was a master at manipulating the media.

Charlatans like Jones, Harary remarks, take advantage of public misconceptions about psi to bind their followers to them. After the People's Temple disaster, stories came to light of Jones' faked psychic performances, cleverly pulled off with the help of his sidekicks. The power of the cult—religious, psychic, or otherwise—can be devastating. Harary was deeply involved in counseling those left confused and anxious in the wake of Jim Jones' devastation; a group called Fundamentalists Anonymous was founded in 1986 to provide support for those disillusioned by their immersion in fundamentalist religious groups. As card reader Bethany Birkett comments, "If someone says there are evil spirits around you, they are trying to soak you for money."

For all the publicity given to corrupt gurus and gypsy tea-leaf readers who con old ladies out of their life savings, it is my feeling that the con and the quack—and the incompetent—are no more common in this field than in many other areas of modern life. There are thousands of unlicensed doctors practicing medicine, and many licensed doctors who are lazy or uncaring or who don't keep up with what's going on in their field; others just don't have the "touch" of a gifted physician. The same parallel can be drawn for teachers, lawyers, accountants, clergymen. Stock frauds, pyramid schemes, insurance scams, corporate bribery, crooked judges, sexually abusive teachers:

defrauding and bilking the public is by no means the exclusive province of gurus and vendors of love potions.

It's not surprising that many people view any form of psychic phenomena as so much flapdoodle served up to a gullible public for monetary gain. Yet my personal experience contradicts this impression almost entirely. The adepts I've met have been serious, intelligent professionals of high integrity. Many have truly outstanding abilities, and many feel they have a "calling" to use their unusual abilities to help people. They don't sit in darkened rooms, gazing into crystal balls; they don't wear bandanas or clanking gold jewelry. Of course, I am talking about respected practitioners with established reputations, not the run-of-the-mill reader at the psychic fair or the shady storefront. I have met very few psychic advisors who I felt were incompetents or charlatans (though I know there are thousands of fraudulent practitioners); and I have met very few people who felt that their visit to one of these practitioners (other than a fairground tea-leaf reader) was useless or fraudulent.

Parapsychology writer Hans Holzer says, "There are about 10 percent truly brilliant professionals. There are 5 percent quacks—those who say that every morning they talk to Marilyn Monroe's spirit. And there's a middle ground of honest people who are just not very good." Even if the advisors' gifts are modest, they give well-intentioned advice, using their specialized skills and training, to people seeking help with the problems of life in a complicated and confusing world: They are "someone to talk to." An article about the popularity of psychic phenomena in the April 1985 issue of *Psychology Today* says that "whether their know-how is sheer coincidence or cogent science, psychics seem to be healing wounds inflicted by massive shifts in social roles since the 1960s." Clinical psychologist Dr. Marilyn Ruman is quoted: "In a time of flux, astrologers, psychics, and fortune tellers are offering what nobody else is—answers, reassurance, and hope."

Sometimes I think the scientific community could learn something from the open-minded attitude of the general public in the search for knowledge about psi and how it could be used to enhance our lives. I doubt that pyramid power—however loony—has done as much harm as those so-called scientists who reject paranormal phenomena because they're impossible, according to the rules of *their* game. Lest we forget: *Newton was an alchemist.*

CHAPTER
THREE

THE
CONTROVERSY:
IS PSI LEGIT?

*" . . . the man who holds miracles to be ceased
puts it out of his own power ever to witness one."*
—William Blake

By now, it seems to me, there is irrefutable evidence that psi is a bona fide phenomenon. To quote Dr. Hans Eysenck, Professor Emeritus of Psychology at the University of London, "To deny the facts would be unscientific."

Yet psi's legitimacy is still hotly debated. Its most extreme opponents are those who insist that there is no such thing as psi, that it is a mass delusion, a creation of the mind for coping with life's mysteries, a solace to those who need to find deeper meaning in the unfolding of life's events. Others act as though the whole field of psi were just one big bunko operation, a fraud perpetrated by everyone from magicians and con men to parapsychologists. Dr. David Marks, writing in the March 1986 issue of the prestigious journal *Nature*, claims that "parascience has so far failed to produce a single repeatable finding and, until it does, will continue to be viewed as an incoherent collection of belief systems steeped in fantasy, illusion, and error." Even the respected critic Dr. C. E. M. Hansel began his investigation of ESP with the assumption that "in view of the *a priori* arguments against it, we know in advance that telepathy, etc., cannot occur." Is this a sound basis for open-minded inquiry? Then there are those who feel that even if psi exists, what good is it? Isn't it just a mixed bag of parlor tricks, a forum for pseudo-gurus, another amusement for the bored citizenry of the Aquarian Age? In this chapter we'll address these provocative questions.

WHAT GOOD IS PSI?

1. *We may use psi in many ways, often unconsciously, to enrich our everyday lives.* These practical applications of psi cover a broad spectrum, from the sublime to the most mundane. When I asked Ingo Swann how psi added to his life, he said it all in a nutshell—and only half in jest: "Well, it's saved me from death a couple of times [via precognitions of danger], and it cuts down on my long-distance phone bills. Those people who are sensitive enough, I can think about them and they'll call me instead of me calling them."

We may use our psychic abilities to find lost keys. It may be ESP that warns us of danger, or plants the suspicion that something is wrong with our child at camp. Psi may enable us to heal ourselves when we're sick, or to wake up with the solution to a problem that's been bugging us. It is one explanation for the lucky streak of the gambler, the peak, almost superhuman performances of athletes— not so different in nature from the seemingly paranormal feats of yogis. More prosaically, it may explain why one cabdriver seems to have a sixth sense for the best way of getting you across town at rush hour, avoiding all the lights, the crowded streets, the unseen traffic accident, the impractical routes, while another has you foundering in traffic, stuck behind a double-parked truck. Psychic sensitivity may explain unusually keen business skills, absolute pitch, the ability to pick a stock that will do well, an intuitive sense about the right person to hire for a job, the ability to detect a phony story. Psi's greatest benefits may be in the area of enhancing our everyday activities.

We don't always acknowledge that we are using psi; we call it a hunch, or intuition, or coincidence—if we recognize it at all. We suddenly have a flash of insight that leads us to something we've been searching for for weeks. We feel we "know" what other people are going to say or do, and this helps us in our dealings with them. Dr. John Roberts remembers the time that a new patient walked into his office, and as they talked he suddenly said to himself, "This woman has bone cancer"—an unfortunately correct diagnosis for which the presenting evidence gave no clue. Dr. Allan Goldstein, a professor of biochemistry at George Washington University who is co-inventor of the artificial hormone thymosin, tells of a very intense discussion among a small group of scientists at a conference in Galveston, Texas. "I remember physically leaving my body, where I was literally looking down at the table and I knew what the person across from me was going to say before he presented it. I was so sharp at that meeting—it felt wonderful. Because I knew what he was going to say, I could really present my argument, and I really won the day. But I can't do it anytime I want—I guess I repress it most of the time. It's actually a little frightening because you think you're going crazy, but it was a wonderful sensation in terms of the ability to prepare myself for that discussion."

Now, most of us don't leave our bodies, but many of us have had the feeling that we knew what someone was about to say, or had the feeling that we should take something along with us when we left the house that turned out to be useful, or had a problem-solving idea come to us in a dream. We've "known" that we should take a different route home from work because there would be traffic, or that we should call a friend whom we hadn't thought of in weeks.

It is not uncommon to feel we have a telepathic link to someone we're close to—a parent, a child, a good friend. Dr. Goldstein went on to say that he often "knows" when to call his mother. "I was in a meeting here in New York, and in the midst of a very important discussion the thought suddenly came to my head that I should call my mother. I stepped out of the meeting and called. She had just hung up the phone after trying to reach me in Washington, to tell me that my father had just been taken to the hospital."

Sometimes we do things, or make decisions, that we seem to have no real basis for, and which we don't ourselves understand. Stories such as this one from Joel Eisenberg are common in the psychical literature: "I woke up in the middle of the night, on a beautiful night, the air fragrant and warm. It was a wonderful night, but I felt like I'd been having a bad dream, or that something was wrong, or that someone was in the house, and I was real nervous inside.

"So I checked the baby—the twins weren't born yet—and went in Jason's room, and the window was wide open and it smelled like the neighbor was burning coal. I went out on the balcony and there was no smell outside, yet I kept smelling this smoke. I bent down to kiss Jason, and his blanket was on fire over on the side of the bed against the wall. I couldn't see or smell the fire until I had bent down close to Jason, though it had probably been smoldering since I woke up. His blanket had fallen down next to the night-light and had just started sparking, and was just about to set fire to his hair. He still won't part with that blanket; it's got the burn hole in it, the edges frayed by the ashes. . . . "

Studies suggest that many of us unconsciously use psi when we need it, without recognizing it as such, to cope with our daily lives.

Rex Stanford calls this unconscious "scanning" of our environment, especially in time of need, Psi Mediated Instrumental Response (PMIR). Researcher William Cox gathered statistics on train accidents on a particular route in Chicago over a period of several years, and found that significantly fewer people took the trains on accident days than took *the same trains* on days when there were no accidents. There's just no telling how many of your daily decisions and actions, life-sustaining or just efficient and practical, are influenced by some measure of psychic information that you're not even aware of being in touch with. Just think of how empowering it would be if you could actively harness even a little bit of your psychic potential, and call on it for everything from deciding if it was safe to take a plane flight to how to deal with your boss.

2. *Psi is a tool to increase self-understanding, to develop our creativity and awareness, and to broaden our horizons.* Renowned psi writer and historian Colin Wilson has said that "art has the power of inducing a degree of Faculty X [his term for psi]. That is why human beings invented it." Only a very small number of people possess extraordinary psychic gifts, but it looks as if most of us have some psychic ability, which can be improved with discipline and practice. This is the attraction, for many, of disciplines ranging from meditation and t'ai ch'i to astrology and the reading of tarot cards: They provide a means of access to normally hidden information.

The psychic ability of children seems to exceed that of adults, indicating that whatever psychic abilities we are born with are mostly drummed out of us by the social and educational programming of our culture. Some few manage to escape this repressive, psi-destructive socialization, or they work to counteract it. Stories abound of writers, artists, composers, and inventors whose creative output was abetted by their dreams, daydreams, and intuition. Composers often report "hearing" a piece of music in its entirety during the process of creation; artists "see" the completed painting. One theory holds that genius itself is a manifestation of powerful psychic functioning, of access to information hidden from us ordinary mortals. Mere precociousness cannot explain the musical sophistication of the young Mozart, the all-seeing eye of a seven-year-old chess prodigy, the man who can calculate *pi* in his head to two hundred decimal places. As mathematician Ronald Graham inquires, in a 1987 article in *The New York Times Magazine* titled "Science on the Track of God," "Was Beethoven discovering the *'Waldstein'* Sonata or did he create it?"

Interviewed by *Publishers Weekly*, writer Paul West declared: "A lot of my stuff comes out of dreaming, not quite trancelike states, but certainly a very inward fingering of potentials. . . . I've always had this enormous amount of stuff floating through my head; it isn't stuff I invented. You can call it collective unconscious or racial memory—I don't know where it comes from . . . I think it's always going on, and there are just times you listen to it more. . . . It's always zooming around or maneuvering or hovering, and when you feel clear-headed or have more mental energy than usual, then you begin to intercept bigger pieces of it. . . . My head's always full of available jazz that I can tune into and exploit . . . a kind of continuum that I can pillage whenever I feel like it."

Novelist Taylor Caldwell believed that she re-created characters from lives she had led in the past. Einstein felt that it was flashes of inspiration, whose source he could not name, which provided him with his revolutionary theories. James Watt had a "vision" while walking through a park in Glasgow of the steam engine in complete detail. One night when Elias Howe was struggling with the technical problems of the sewing machine, he fell asleep ruminating on his predicament, and dreamed that has was captured by savages whose leader gave him an ultimatum: Produce a working sewing machine in twenty-four hours, or die! Terrified, he tried and failed to solve the problem. The savages came after him, brandishing their spears over him. Oddly, the spears had holes in their points. Waking, he realized that his frightening dream had given him the solution to this problem: The thread should go through the *point* of the needle.

3. *Psi intimates the existence of our consciousness beyond the confines of the material world.* Now, this is exactly the sort of spiritual/religious mumbo jumbo that makes the pragmatists and the skeptics throw up their hands in despair. Critic Dr. Paul Kurtz, professor of philosophy at the State University of New York at Buffalo, dismissively calls this "the transcendental temptation," as though a desire to surpass the accepted limits of the everyday world were only for the jelly-brained. The assumption is that the quest for an understanding of the world beyond the senses, or for a larger meaning to our lives, has no validity, or can be assumed to be a delusion.

Yet the field of psi has its roots in the study of mediumship, as a quest for answers to the nature of man, his consciousness and his soul. But psi got sidetracked from these questions by the derision of its critics, by the need to appear scientific and to provide proof of a kind acceptable to the powers that be. There are many who feel that psi has forsaken its proper arena of inquiry and has yet to recover its proper mission. But the universal quest for meaning beyond everyday reality cannot be written off so easily, nor can millions of personal experiences of paranormal functioning be so easily dismissed. It could be argued that the reason people are so attracted to psychics, aura readers, and quasi-religious cults is that the established order, social and scientific, offers little but criticism in response to this genuine need. Nikolai Khokhlov points out that the Soviet Union has been unsuccessful in stamping out religion. "Why? Because religion is one of the avenues of interaction between one individual's biofield and the collective biofield, not only of the now but of forever, the past and the future. . . . Christianity was one attempt to create a huge, collective field of thought. There is still that challenge of fusion in a bigger collective consciousness until someday—hopefully—we have a universal field of collective consciousness."

Novelist Robert Stone, author of *Dog Soldiers* and *A Flag for Sunrise*, in speaking of the transforming aspects of his experience with drugs, told *Publishers Weekly*: "I became less ashamed of confronting religious impulses. . . . One of the reasons for the prevalence of drugs in our society is the aspiration to something transcendent, something above the daily life, something more meaningful than ourselves. . . . All of my characters are looking for transcendence, whether they know it or not." Ingo Swann reminds us of a remark by Van Gogh when he says, "If the physical is considered the be-all, end-all, the universe is truly a horrible, horrible, utterly horrible cage."

Some say that the study of psi leads inevitably to a worldview that transcends the limits of the earthbound world. Stephan Schwartz, codirector of the Möbius Society, states: "This work forces you into a spiritual awareness. There just isn't any way you can continue to do parapsychology and not develop a spiritual sense. I am not a church person. . . . I believe in God . . . more than believe in it. God is real."

In the most profound sense, psi is the full breadth of the nature of man. Serious research has confirmed the potential for communication and action at a distance, and even for highly provocative ideas such as reincarnation. The only logical explanation for our inability to function comfortably in the paranormal arena is that we unconsciously limit our awareness of and access to psychic information. But as Swann says, "It is possible to exist in an awareness beyond things physical, beyond the 'earth' in all things." When we learn to accept, understand, and harness this aspect of our humanness, when we stop treating it as something exotic and forbidding, we may find out what it fully means to be human.

4. *The understanding and application of psychic functioning on a broad scale would have benefits for all of society and for the universe.* In fact, it may be crucial to solving some of the larger problems of our planet.

J. B. Rhine once stated that there is a universal connection between psi and a "good, honorable life." It's a sentiment echoed by others who work in the field. Their point is not that all parapsychologists are swell people, but that learning about psi leads to a belief in the interrelatedness of all things, and that when you recognize this inter-connectedness, you feel less isolated, and less defensive. You realize that everything you do affects everyone else also, and the world in which you live. If you cause harm, you are also harming yourself. As the prophets of the New Age have been trying to tell us, the idea that we are isolated egos, whose individualism is of paramount importance, is hogwash in the cosmic scheme of things. We are all, as the mystics (and now the physicists) have been saying, One, in the most pragmatic and concrete sense. Our oneness is as real as our individuality.

There are many hard-core scientists who believe (and fervently hope) that by getting in touch with the psychic side of ourselves, we will finally understand the folly of killing one another and poisoning the planet: We are fouling our own nest. Lawrence LeShan comments: "Psi's potential benefits I think are absolutely essential and crucial to the fate of the earth. The study of psi is the study of how people can't be separated from each other. In a very real sense, we are not each other's brothers, not our brother's keeper, but we *are* each other. At a time when every other method has failed to help us stop killing each other, stop poisoning our only planet, stop damaging ourselves, stop feeling lonely and alienated, this may be the last answer—the study of how people are together and can't be separated, no matter how they *are* separated. That's why I was in the field for all those years, seeing that potential value."

Nikolai Khokhlov speaks of the ecology of the collective mental field, and what he feels is the ultimate message of all psychic research —that "we are living in an energy field not only of our own thoughts and emotions, but of everyone else's as well. That makes us a world community of thinking, feeling, radiating and receiving beings. If we understand that, many notions will change." Khokhlov feels that if we understand the critical importance of this thesis, we will find it "imperative not to go on polluting our collective consciousness with thoughts of war and violence . . . Unless we nurture that collective field, which subtly, unconsciously influences us, then we will destroy ourselves." He warns of the danger of self-fulfilling prophecies: "If we collectively convince ourselves that there is no way to avoid war, that our enemies are out to destroy us, we will make those constant, collective, reinforced thoughts come to pass." He feels that the most devastating consequences are for future generations. Unless we change our thinking, "we must be concerned that the [psychic] well to which our children will have access may be contaminated. If that well is poisoned, they are lost. They cannot live. We must be concerned about the evolution of this, that the collective field is contaminated." To illustrate what he means, he gives the example of the 15 million people who in just one hour may watch a brutal murder on television, who in turn feed the thoughts and emotions they have during that experience into the collective unconscious. What good, benevolent thought and feeling will counterbalance this kind of powerful, repeated negative input, this continuous broadcast?

Stephan Schwartz stresses the importance of learning to gain access to the collective consciousness: "We are now in a new epoch. We started out in the epoch of fighting; that's two guys hitting each other on the head with sticks. Then we moved to the epoch of war. That's a group of people in a coordinated way hitting each other on the head with sticks or bigger things. We are now in the epoch of gene-pool annihilation. We are at the place where we have the power to destroy the gene pool and hence our species, in fact the whole planet's ability to propagate. Clearly, the answer to resolving that dilemma does not lie entirely in the intellect. If it did, we would have come up with answers. We must begin to look at the other rooms in our consciousness. If we don't I don't think we're going to make it."

FEAR AND LOATHING OF PSI

Evidence indicates that psi may be a neglected aspect of our birthright. If so, why are we not actively seeking to use our psychic potential? Why are we resisting, avoiding, and ignoring it?

There are several contributing factors. One is simply our misunderstanding of the nature of psi, a misunderstanding fostered by sensationalism at both extremes of the psi spectrum. Psi is menaced by true believers who demand full-reality-status papers for bigfoot and the Bermuda Triangle. At the other extreme, it is attacked by the true disbelievers, those who dignify themselves by calling themselves skeptics, but who fervently believe that no one has ever had a premonition or communicated telepathically, crusaders who feel that they are saving the world from the evils of spiritual healers and tarot-card readers. We are brainwashed by movies with titles like *Witches in Space* and *Out-of-Body Rapist*. The public rarely gets good, reliable information about serious research in psychic functioning. This is regrettable, but in a way understandable. Much of the current work in parapsychology is complicated, statistical, and dry. It doesn't exactly grab headlines—not that serious publications are eager to provide the space anyway. Journalist Curtis D. MacDougal, in *Superstition and the Press*, provides a devastating picture of the paranormal in the press; the book is a fat compendium of mostly superficial, uncritical articles on everything from exorcism and sea serpents to doomsday predictions. While MacDougal's mission seems to be to show that the public is being duped by the unselective, sensationalizing reporting of the press, he unwittingly underlines the fact that serious research and theories are largely ignored. Too, he gives his own anti-psi stance away by listing the reading he did in connection with his book—almost all of it critical, debunking literature.

Psi also seems to conflict with our rational, pragmatic Western belief system, and is publicly perceived as an unnatural aspect of human functioning: It doesn't fit. It can't be explained according to the rules we use to explain the world—and the rules are sacrosanct. Though we often pride ourselves on our individualism, bucking the tide comes hard to many of us. The stigma attached to admitting belief (or participation) in anything paranormal is a powerful turnoff. No one wants to be labeled fluff-brained and irrational in an age which respects reason and intellect. As Anthony White, a former partner at Delphi Associates, says: "It's a new closet." Psi gets a blanket condemnation in the public mind; little distinction is made between blind faith in the daily horoscope column and your premonition that a friend is ill, or your belief that meditation is good for your health and well-being and helps you gain access to your inner self. Few of us trust our psychic experiences: We write them off as coincidence, an aberration. We rationalize them, forget about them. We certainly don't mention our involvement in the paranormal to anyone who might misunderstand or abuse the information; thus, we get little reinforcement outside ourselves. It was once thought that people tended to exaggerate their reports of psychic experiences. But studies show that in reality we don't embellish such experiences, we minimize them; and as time goes by, they are diluted and diminished in our memory.

Which brings us to what is probably the core issue when it comes to the legitimacy of psi and the reason for the fervor of its critics: it is *fear*, pure and simple. This is no small consideration. There is a good deal of evidence to indicate that fear of psi is much deeper and more widely held than one might suspect. It hampers our personal pursuit of psi abilities and the strides made by science in trying to understand psi.

An informal experiment conducted by Charles Tart vividly illustrates our unspoken fears of the paranormal. At a reception after a lecture he had given to a group of leading parapsychologists, Tart asked a group of his colleagues to "believe that I have developed a drug, 'telepathine,' which would enable those who took it to telepathically receive all thought and feeling of everyone within a 100-yard range." He went on to say that there was no antidote to the drug. Then he asked them if they wanted the drug. No one responded; instead, a discussion ensued about the implications of such a drug. They were avoiding the issue, so he again asked, "Who wants the drug?" There was more discussion, and still no response, so he shouted "WHO WANTS THE DRUG?" There was silence, and finally his colleagues realized that when they had to acknowledge that telepathy might be a power they would have to own, they were afraid of it. As Tart points out, "This experiment was done with people who were exceptionally interested in psi, willing to sacrifice career success to work in this controversial field. If parapsychologists have fears, what about ordinary people?"

Another example: a parapsychologist at SRI told me that the institute was once turned down for a government research grant because "psi is the work of the devil."

If you think about it for a minute, such fear is not surprising. Do we really want to know what others are thinking; even more, do we want others to know what we are thinking, to have access to the deep, dark secrets and shames that we think are ours alone? Are we not terrified to give up the nice, reasonable cause-and-effect picture we have of the world and how it works, in exchange for one that is strange, forbidding, and seemingly without limits? Who can promise that it is safe to be psychic? Would our psychic abilities not set us apart from others, and make us feel different and left out? Many well-known psychics were tormented during their childhood by the knowledge that what they "saw" and "did" was unacceptable to their family and peers. Some suppressed their abilities in order to live happily in the world. Would having psychic abilities make us feel unsure of who we are, cause us to question the image of ourselves so carefully built up, so grounded in the here and now; would it not cause terrible discomfort? And are psychic powers not evidence of mental instability? Are they not the work of the devil?

In my travels, I met a sociology professor who told me that as a teenager she was going out with a guy named Charlie, but he wasn't calling her. So she sat quietly in a corner and said, "Charlie, call me," repeating the message a few times. And within five minutes Charlie called her. This she was able to do on several occasions. An ardent Catholic, she told this to her priest—who promptly told her that the devil was in her. For many years afterward she was frightened that she had the devil inside her—until she realized that this type of telepathic functioning was not uncommon, and certainly not evil.

We have been conditioned to think of paranormal functioning as so alien to what we think of as our normal mode of operation that our fear is understandable. Mind control, the kind of thing we associate with the psychic-warfare rumors about the CIA and Russia's KGB, is frightening stuff to those who get their psi information from the papers. Yet from what we know of psi, there is little reason for fear. Psi is a weak, subtle signal over which even the best psychics have limited control; it certainly does not always work "on demand." Certainly it seems that you cannot psychically get (or give) information that is private—no one ever psychically turned up a subject's deep, dark secret. As LeShan says, "I think ESP is limited. For example, I don't think it's possible to telepathically pick up information from somebody who doesn't want to give it to you." LeShan was also concerned about potential harm when he was learning to heal, but found that in all the healing he did, and all the healers he worked with, he never ran across an instance in which harm came to anyone. "If that had happened, I would have stopped immediately."

We have made of psi something so strange that we don't know what to do with it. But psi belongs to us. It is an inherent part of our nature that is wasted because it doesn't get nurtured: Our psychic skills should be trained along with our math and language skills. Ingo Swann, who gets a bit frustrated with the "obdurate incapabilities" of us ordinary mortals, refers to our resistance to psi as our "dreary psychological plagues." All indications are that the fear of psi is far scarier than psi itself. Our psi abilities should be empowering, not debilitating. And as LeShan says, "You must act as if you were not afraid."

IS PSI FOR REAL?

The controversy over whether psi exists, and what constitutes legitimate proof of psi, is almost as fascinating as psi itself. The psychologist William Maslin has noted the "tension between the need to know and the fear of knowing." The rabidity and tenaciousness of the critics seem to me more a commentary on man's fear of facing up to the mysterious aspects of reality than an open-minded quest for truth. This resistance is articulated in a remark made by Dr. Warren Weaver, a former president of the American Association for the Advancement of Science, in speaking of Rhine's work: "I find this a subject that is so intellectually uncomfortable as to be almost painful." Intellectual discomfort goes with the territory of psi; if it's safety and orthodoxy you desire, this is a field to steer clear of. Most parapsychologists, and the true skeptics, live with a certain discomfort level in the pursuit of knowledge. Others, who cannot bear the discomfort (or honestly admit to it, as Weaver did), attack psi irrationally at whatever cost, ethical or intellectual. This is my gripe with many of the critics: I feel they don't fight in a straightforward, or even rational, manner.

This book, and the literature of parapsychology and the occult, are filled with instances of apparent paranormal occurrences, many of which have taken place in the laboratory, and which have been subjected to scrutiny that would be considered sufficiently rigorous in any other field. Yet the dissenters are legion, and loud—for psi is no ordinary field. The rules are different for psi; as sociologist Marcello Truzzi has stated, "Extraordinary phenomena demand extraordinary proof." This makes a certain kind of sense, and parapsychologists are used to going the extra mile to prove their case, but it also creates a bizarre double standard. Thus we have the rather ridiculous situation in which the possibility of telepathy or healing is examined far more critically than, say, nuclear-reactor safety or heart-transplant procedures. Psi's critics are adamant about repeatability in psi experiments. Yet, as psychologist Dr. Theodore X. Barker points out, a survey of introductory *psychology* textbooks turned up the word "repeatability" in only 10 percent of the indexes. Another problem is that the skeptics never make clear just what it is that would constitute acceptable proof. Every time parapsychologists feel that they've finally met the challenge, the skeptics will demand they go another step further, and perform just one more miracle, before they give their stamp of approval.

Fear of psi leads to some rather aberrant behavior on the part of otherwise rational people, and their resistance to it takes a number of forms.

The most intractable disbelievers are those who insist that there's no such thing as psi *because it's impossible*. This is the "I won't believe it even if I see it" contingent. Now, it takes a sweeping mind to categorize all the thoughts and research in this broad field as mush-brained drivel, or as outright lies, but that's what this stance amounts to. Here's a colleague of Dr. Carl Sargent, commenting on some ESP research: "The results you presented would convince me of anything else but this: I just cannot believe it, and I don't know why." The pioneering German physicist Hermann L. F. von Helmholtz said that "neither the testimony of all the Fellows of the Royal Society, nor even the evidence of my own senses, would lead me to believe in the transmission of thought from one person to another independent of the recognized channels of sense."

The rabid disbelievers really bend over backward to exclude psi. When I interviewed George Serban, author of *The Tyranny of Magical Thinking*, he explained away one thing after another—psychic crime detection, astrology, tarot, telepathy, well-documented anecdotes. My question: "Is there any time you have found any validity at all to psychic phenomena?" "Simply coincidence—really" was his explanation. Prediction, he explained, "serves a very powerful need." He went on to talk about the "very vague language" of psychics, the phenomena of mass hysteria, of hysterical pregnancies, irrationality, insecurity, religion, and offered lots more talk about coincidence. Not one little opening for consideration of the possibility of psi. My favorite ostrich remark is from a psychiatrist who questioned LeShan's work: "Chance coincidences happen more often than the laws of chance would lead one to believe." Now, there's food for thought.

One prominent critic of parapsychology, C. E. M. Hansel, started with a premise which harks back to pioneer skeptic David Hume, declaring that "any defect such that their result may be due to a cause other than ESP cannot provide conclusive proof of ESP." Thus his conclusions rested on the thesis that, in a careful examination of many research experiments, not one could be found in which the *possibility* of fraud could be completely ruled out (a situation common to, and tolerated in, research procedures in other branches of science). This is the old "a lie is more likely than a miracle" school of debunking. Hansel focused his investigations on the famed Pearce-Pratt experiments. This was a series of card-guessing trials, carried out over eighteen months under ever more stringent conditions, using the gifted subject Hubert Pearce, under the guidance of Gaither Pratt, Rhine's chief assistant at Duke. The odds against chance for Pearce's performance over the entire series were calculated as 1 in 10,000,000,000,000,000,000,000. Now, Hansel did not find fraud, and provided no evidence that fraud had occurred; he just concluded that this was the only possible explanation—far more likely than the possibility that ESP might actually have taken place. You can see that parapsychologists might find this attitude pretty exasperating—and all but impossible to fight. Puthoff and Targ put it this way in *Mind Reach:* "No matter how miraculous the result of an ESP demonstration, an observer tries to discount it as a lucky day."

Dr. Jeffrey Mishlove (who has the distinction of holding the first Ph.D. in parapsychology granted by an accredited American institution, the University of California at Berkeley) accuses some skeptics of deliberately sabotaging open-minded paranormal research. In *The Roots of Consciousness,* he gives as an example a report funded (at over half a million dollars) by the U.S. Air Force and conducted by the University of Colorado. The report concluded that UFOs were unworthy of further investigation, even though not all the sightings were explainable. However, the report is suspect in light of this memo written by the project coordinator to the university:

"Our study would be conducted almost exclusively by nonbelievers who, although they couldn't possibly *prove* a negative result, could and probably would add an impressive body of evidence that there is no reality to the observations. The trick would be, I think, to describe the project so that, to the public, it would appear a totally objective study but, to the scientific community, would present the image of a group of nonbelievers trying their best to be objective, but having an almost zero expectation of finding a saucer."

As Mishlove says, "Why anyone would suggest that science would turn its back on neglected and unexplained phenomena is a mystery." However, it's a mystery that surfaces again and again in the annals of anti-psi activity.

Controversy over the legitimacy of UFOs—and reports of UFO coverups—flared up again in 1987 in the wake of several popular books on "documented" UFO contacts. The debate centered around the "Rosewell Incident" in 1947, the purported crash of a flying saucer in Roswell, New Mexico, after which the remains of four extraterrestrial crew members were found in the wreckage. UFO enthusiasts have long tried to probe what they contend is a complex government cover-up that included the debriefing of witnesses and reporters, and the issuing of false press releases claiming that a weather research balloon had crashed. The reopening of this controversy was sparked by the appearance of a top-secret document relating to the incident: the record of a secret briefing made to incoming President Dwight Eisenhower by the first director of the CIA, Rear Admiral Roscoe Hillenkoeter. The paper describes the operations of Majestic-12, a team established by President Truman in September 1947 to investigate the incident. It describes the dismantling of the alien craft and the conclusion that the biological and evolutionary processes of the humanlike bodies were "quite different from those observed or postulated in homo sapiens." (This incident is detailed in a book published in England, *Above Top Secret: The Worldwide U.F.O. Coverup*, by British UFO researcher Timothy Good.)

Not surprisingly, the debate over the legitimacy of the document polarized opinions, with the skeptics wanting to dismiss it out of hand, or to explain it as the mental aberrations of a culture in which people feel helpless or feel a need to explain earthly problems. "Nonsense . . . an outright hoax," says Philip J. Klass, a noted UFO debunker. Paul Kurtz of CSICOP (see below) says it's "part of a bizarre trend in which there is no sense of standards of evidence." (Science fiction writer Ben Bova compared belief in UFOs to religious fervor, saying that while we used to have gods, we now welcome the idea of extraterrestrials because we "want to feel we're not alone . . . ")

Other scientists, including Navy physicist Dr. Bruce Maccabee, seem more willing to consider the problem, to entertain the possibility, however outrageous or frightening, that UFOs exist. He feels that people who have been trying to ignore the UFO question may be in for a shock. "Some sort of things have been flying around for decades, and they aren't ours . . . the simple fact is that there are unexplained sightings. Over the past 40 years, there have been 100,000 sightings, with 10 to 20 percent that are hard to explain." The logical approach—and the open-minded, scientific one—would seem to be for serious scientists to assiduously investigate the latest surge of reported UFO/extraterrestrial encounters. The reluctance to do so is, in a way, the most impenetrable mystery of all.

The most visible battalion of the anti-psi squad is CSICOP, the Committee for the Scientific Investigation of Claims of the Paranormal. Professing to be a body of neutral skeptics whose mission is to provide the public with the truth about psychic phenomena, it has turned out to be less than even handed in its reporting and evaluation of paranormal phenomena. Though the committee was founded out of a genuine concern about the public's uncritical acceptance of many so-called paranormal phenomena, its mission appears to be merely to stamp out the paranormal. CSICOP's journal is the controversial *The Skeptical Inquirer*. Leslie Shepard points out in *The Encyclopedia of Occultism and Parapsychology* that although the journal's scope of inquiry is wide, and a number of dubious or fraudulent claims are efficiently debunked, "it is difficult to combine an attitude of impartial inquiry with a stance of scientific authority when there is an implicit initial assumption that all claims of the paranormal are erroneous or fraudulent. One searches the pages of *The Skeptical Inquirer* in vain for any instance of paranormal phenomena or parapsychological findings being validated or even tentatively accepted, and opposing voices or protests are quoted only in order to be relentlessly put down without extended discussion. The tone of many articles is sarcastic and hostile rather than impartial, and the frequent appeals to 'scientific evidence' as an alternative to 'false beliefs and delusions' often sound authoritarian."

Since CSICOP is not primarily a research organization, they have the luxury of being able to devote most of their funds and energy to attacking the expensive and time-consuming research of others. Since they have little of their own evidence to present, they have adopted a few tried-and-true tactics. One is merely to act as censors: They have been known to put pressure on newspapers and other publications to cancel their astrology or biorhythm columns. This I know firsthand, as they tried to persuade the publishers of a Buffalo, New York, newspaper to discontinue my biorhythm column.

CSICOP's watchdogs are all over the place. In 1986, Oregon psychic Noreen Renier won a $25,000 defamation-of-character suit against John Merrell, a cofounder of one of the CSICOP sub-groups, the Northwest Skeptics. Merrell got hot under the collar about Renier's claims to have helped the police solve cases and—in a barrage of letters to the media and police—was overzealous in his attempt to undermine her character and abilities.

CSICOP is also fond of attacks on the personal integrity, credentials or misguided softheadedness of individual parapsychologists. When I attended their annual convention in Boulder, Colorado, in 1986, I had to laugh at the way they pointedly referred to Charles Honorton as *"Mister"* Honorton, as though his lack of a Ph.D. was the most damning thing they could think of to say about him. (The story changes, though, when the shoe is on the other foot. In his introduction to the book *Flim-Flam!*, by debunker James Randi [see p. 87], Isaac Asimov extols Randi as the ideal person to do this vital debunking job: "He has no academic credentials, and therefore no academic restrictions. He can call things as he sees them, and is not held back by professional politeness in discussing those scientists who not only fall for the paranormal, but promote it in their ignorance.") At the convention, I noticed that they spent little time trying to debunk serious, replicable research such as Honorton's. Most of the panels and seminars were devoted to easy targets to which *no serious researcher* gives much credibility, such as newspaper astrology columns and such topics as "Past Tongues Remembered?", "Confessions of a Past-Life Therapist," "Creationism and Pseudoscience," "The Giant Pterodactyl Project," and "Winning Through Pseudoscience."

CSICOP gets a lot of attention from the media, but its reputation in the scientific community is considerably blemished. British parapsychology historian and writer Brian Inglis told me that CSICOP often takes a head-in-the-sand approach to serious, replicable research, and that when they choose to look, they do so selectively.

Another classic debunking tactic is to "disprove" psychic functioning by demonstrating that psychic feats can be performed by magicians or mentalists, and are therefore not paranormal at all—merely magic tricks that dupe a gullible public, or gullible researchers. Cornell psychologist and magician Dr. Daryl Bem makes a sideline of giving demonstrations of apparent clairvoyance, telepathy, and precognition—and then informing the audience that it was only conjuring and sleight-of-hand. This looks good on public display, but there are several flaws to this method of debunking. First of all, there is a real distinction between what a mentalist or sleight-of-hand artist can do on a stage and with preparation, and what can be done spontaneously. Yes, a good magician can fake the bending of a spoon; a good mentalist can appear to be picking up "psychic" information from a gullible member of a studio audience, when in fact he is an expert at deciphering body language and other subtle clues, and perhaps has the help of an assistant in the audience. But this is not in any way scientific proof, and it does not rule out the possibility that these things can *also* be done psychically. An analogy could be made to the many healthy young men who, with a combination of over-the-counter drugs, lack of food and sleep, and personal wiles, have been able to convince a draft board that they were unfit for military service. It has long been recommended within the field of parapsychology that magicians or mentalists be on hand during experimental procedures to ensure that no trickery was going on.

When I asked Marcello Truzzi how he accounts for some of the incredible feats of the top mentalists—Eugen de Rubini, Frederick

Marion—he said that their abilities are not fully understood. In other words, while these mentalists *insist* that there is nothing paranormal about what they do, Truzzi isn't so sure; he feels that some of the things they do have not been fully explained by ordinary means. The popular mentalist Kreskin makes a big point of underlining the fact that his abilities are in no way paranormal: It's extra-*sensitive* perception, he says, not extrasensory. Yet he goes on to recount stories of apparent telepathic experiences he's had with people in elevators, or the time he stopped his performance cold because he suddenly "knew" that a woman in the audience was planning to commit suicide that night. It seems to me that some of these critics protest too much. They are so afraid of psi that they rationalize it away even when it is staring them in the face, and when they themselves use it. There is more than one way to skin a cat: It is possible to accomplish the same apparent effect both psychically *and* through trickery.

One of the most colorful of CSICOP's watchdogs is the magician/debunker known as The Amazing Randi. Randi deserves much credit for performing a valuable public service. He has made the public aware of fraud and quackery in the field, and has uncovered many cases of outright trickery, sending scores of phony evangelists, healers, and spoon-benders packing. Randi has made a personal crusade —and a personal reputation—of stamping out the paranormal wherever it surfaces. Randi makes a big public fuss over his annual debunking awards. He calls his trophy a "Uri" (after every debunker's favorite target, Uri Geller); it takes the form of a bent spoon in a Lucite base. For many years now, he has offered $10,000 to anyone who can show him irrefutable proof of paranormal functioning, and keeps himself busy checking out claims, but has yet to pay off.

Randi in 1986 received a much-publicized and much-coveted MacArthur Foundation grant to further his crusade. In a speech entitled "James Randi and Objective Research," published in the September 1986 edition of the Schneider-Gauquelin Research Journal, Hans Eysenck expressed his dismay. On the basis of Randi's post-award television appearances, he states, "Randi was overoptimistic in thinking that a grant's prestige would instantly transform him from a showman into a serious advocate of the establishment." He feels that Randi "has no right to be heard in a scientific debate." The MacArthur Foundation, in Eysenck's opinion, has not added to its prestige by funding Randi's "research," which he believes "has no scientific standing, and which it would be sheer impudence to compare with . . . the Gauquelins'."

Randi's award is a perfect example of the status given to debunking of psi by the media and the establishment, in their zeal to distance themselves from the taint of fuzzy-minded thinking. But it seems a shame that the award couldn't have gone—if not to a serious, struggling psychic researcher—to one of the many dedicated, research-oriented critics of psi whose work is making a constructive contribution to the field.

The blustering of the psi cops discredits them, though the public hasn't the evidence to see the less than forthcoming way in which they sometimes operate. As Harary points out, "They are not the scientific community . . . but they present themselves as judge and jury as though they represent the scientific community. . . . They are a cult of believers in the absence of psychic functioning." People who make their whole career out of hacking at the research and beliefs of others are, he continues, "pathologically very interesting." Anthony White says, "We don't pay attention to people like them anymore, because we're not trying to prove anything to them. We know it works and if they want to sit back there with the Flat Earth Society and say, 'It can't exist because it threatens my world view,' that's fine. We don't burn the Flat Earth people at the stake either. They're just lost in another paradigm that's woefully out of date. We don't waste our time debating with them, because their rules of evidence are different and their preassumptions preclude our existence. . . . "

An argument can be made that CSICOP and other members of the anti-psi contingent perform a valuable service in keeping the public's gullibility in check. And certainly there has been constructive criticism of psi research, which has led to better research protocols and more leakage control. But the unbridled critics are also in a position to do great harm. Aside from the fact that they hamper the progress of new research, they do untold damage by convincing people that their own psychic experiences have no validity. CSICOP's stance could well lead people to believe that their premonitions and dreams are signs of mental instability. In the end, such fervid debunking really boils down to fear: Its members are scared silly of psi, and they hope to convey their fear to you, so that maybe it will all go away.

"ANOMALIES ARE WHAT SCIENCE IS ALL ABOUT"

CSICOP and other debunkers may sometimes act like meddlesome bullies, but mainstream science hasn't exactly welcomed psi with open arms either. Many universities are embarrassed by their resident parapsychologists—if they've been unlucky enough to have such a creature turn up in the first place. Often subtle pressure is brought to bear on the professor with a psychical bent—he may be underfunded, denied tenure, and generally held in mild contempt by his peers. In some cases, it is only the impeccable reputation of the parapsychologist or private funding to the university that keeps him from being run off campus. Douglas Dean told me that the Newark College of Engineering was never happy with the parapsychology research he and John Mihalasky were doing there; as soon as Mihalasky left, the college destroyed the records of their years of research. Parapsychologists don't get no respect! In such a climate, it's not surprising that psi researchers give up trying to swim against the tide. They go back to their original fields (psychology, laser physics), where they can stop having to defend themselves at every turn —and where they don't have to fight for status and money. In the last couple of years Lawrence LeShan, Anthony White, and Russell Targ, among others, have done just that.

In the public mind, scientists are the pioneers of the unknown. We entrust them with the mission to explore new territory, come back and show us their findings in terms we can understand, and make their findings applicable to our lives. But psi gets second-class treatment here too, for science has an especially hard time fitting psi into its worldview and an even harder time expanding and revising that worldview to embrace psi. Dr. K. C. Cole, in an article in *Discover* magazine, September 1985, titled "Is There Such a Thing as Scientific Objectivity?" makes a couple of interesting points. "Facts come clothed in history, colored by context. Science is less a statement of truth than a running argument. As it turns out, the scientific method isn't so scientific after all." Cole continues, "Like the rest of us, scientists tend to see what they expect to see."

At any given time, science is defined by a set of theories, which are tested and challenged, and which slowly evolve to accommodate new knowledge. Quantum functions exhibited no lawful properties, had no explainable basis, until the laws were changed to make them fit into a coherent model. There are many unanswered questions which science manages to work around: Where does thought originate; how does the mind communicate with the body; how does atomic energy work? But science has not been so accommodating to psi, and psi has not had the blessing of a Planck or an Einstein to light the way.

In other areas it is axiomatic that if you are not able to get results with existing procedures, or if the existing theories cannot encompass reported phenomena, your approach needs revamping. You are barking up the wrong tree, asking the wrong questions. Just recently, science has been willing to open its eyes to such ideas as a fifth force of physics—the "hyperforce"—and to a theory that "superstrings" will prove to be the uniting force of nature. Yet many scientists seem determined to force psi into the present paradigm, to demand that it play by the old rules.

Fortunately, some parapsychologists are willing to stick their necks out a bit and have stopped trying so hard to please the establishment. Harary spoke to me of "the slavish belief in scientific facts." Arthur Ellison decried the "naive realism of scientists." Marcello Truzzi compared parapsychology's status to that of psychology fifty or a hundred years ago, when it was the pariah of science. Orthodoxy and discovery have always clashed, a *New York Times* editorial noted on October 17, 1985, pointing out that in 1922, geologists vigorously dismissed the idea that the earth's continents had moved in the geological past; it was not until the 1950s that surveys of the ocean floor compelled them to accept the idea. It was suggested in 1904 that the U.S. Patent Office close because there was little left to be invented. This is a good place to note, too, that Ernest Rutherford, the physicist credited with splitting the atom, was advised by his tutor not to study physics—because science had such a complete picture of physical phenomena that very little remained to be discovered.

It's just possible that our culture's fervent belief in "scientific objectivity" is tripping us up, limiting us in needless ways. As Michael Crichton points out in *Electronic Life*, there are situations in which "scientific bias becomes dangerous. Science is an awfully powerful method for exploring reality, but it is only one method. Whole realms of human experience lie beyond its grasp. In fact, consciousness itself is beyond science . . .

"The failure to recognize this leads to patent absurdities. A team of scientists measuring the heartbeat and rectal temperature of a yogi in a trance is a profound joke. . . . They are in the same position as social scientists who study garbage to determine how people lead their lives; such studies tell you something, but not much. . . . We have a strong tendency to exclude or deny phenomena that don't fit our preexisting schemes." Laurent Beauregard, in the premier issue of *The Zetetic Scholar*, asks, "Might not a sufficiently strong commitment to the existing body of scientific knowledge at a given time contribute to a stagnation of the growth of knowledge?"

Hidebound scientists could learn about open-minded inquiry from the Society for Scientific Exploration. One of the aims of the organization is to encourage and sanction exploration of anomalous phenomena thought to be beyond the pale of serious-minded science. UFOs, extant dinosaurs, placebo healing, automatic writing—all are considered fair game by this cross section of scientists, which includes Robert Morris, Robert Jahn, Keith Harary, Bart J. Bok, Persi Diaconis, James Trefil, Stephan Schwartz, Marcello Truzzi, Hal Puthoff, and president and founder Peter Sturrock. Yet many stay away, wary of censure by their colleagues and the institutions that support them. Something is wrong with this picture. As MIT's Ralph Markson observed at the society's 1983 symposium: "What has happened to science? Why aren't there more scientists here? Anomalies are what science is all about."

FIGHTING BACK

So what do the parapsychologists do to defend themselves? Very little, some say—and therein lies the problem. Much current psi research is done as much to satisfy the skeptics as to expand knowledge of psi. Charles Honorton estimates that "we spend probably one-third to one-half of our time being overtly defensive, because we have to. We've got to survive; we've got to maintain funding to keep the work going." Honorton gave me one of his articles to read; the text of his presentation was seven pages long—followed by close to twenty pages of rebuttals and counterrebuttals. Take a gander at this title from *The Zetetic Scholar*: "Evan Harris Walker replies to Edward W. Karnes's reply (ZS #7) to Evan Harris Walker's Comments on Edward W. Karnes, *et al.*, re: Remote Viewing (ZS #6)." Did I hear you groan? However, many parapsychologists defend this defensiveness. A prominent SRI executive insisted that parapsychology "must make itself acceptable for scientific investigation," and Hans Eysenck cautions against stepping outside the accepted scientific boundaries: "You may throw away some nuggets of gold, but it's safer not to mix the thing."

Ingo Swann has no use for this pussyfooting attitude, and has found his own way to deal with it. He continues to be involved in scientific psi exploration, but has gone underground, and is mum about his current work. "There was a time," he says, "when we were open and as a result spent 98 percent of our man-hours and dollars answering challenges from critics. Any time it looks as if ESP is going to receive legitimacy, the antipsychic critics do a trip to make sure the legitimization of it doesn't come about. It's not their intention to look at serious research. I stepped out from that just to get some work done. It's just purely a defensive step, and it proved a very healthy one. The critics in America are so terribly destructive; they don't hesitate about character assassination or anything. Parapsychology lacks many things, and one thing it lacks on the whole is an aggressive stance. The fault lies with parapsychology. Parapsychology is filled with these introverted types who can't get their act together enough to go out and do the equivalent of kicking somebody in the nuts."

One reason the field of psi is in such a state of paralysis is that in knuckling under to the demands of implacable critics, investigators have not only immobilized themselves, but have abandoned areas of research that are the very bedrock of the paranormal. By this I mean the rich lode of anecdotal experience, investigation of occult phenomena, and *personal* experience of psychic functioning.

Fortunately, this tide seems to be turning, and many parapsychologists are outspokenly encouraging the broadening of psi's reach beyond the stifling confines of the lab. Rhea White, the preeminent archivist and bibliographer of psi, makes a plea for personal involvement: "The most appropriate methodology for understanding what psi is and how it works is for researchers to learn to use psi themselves." Rex Stanford has said that parapsychologists should try personally to experience as many psi phenomena as they can and should "study the practices and beliefs of magic, religion, and mysticism of diverse cultures and times as they relate to possible psi phenomena." Wouldn't it be helpful if psychic researchers could overcome their distaste for the psychic arts, and seriously address the validity of such practices as tarot or numerology? Why not examine how it might be that planets have an influence on our lives, the underlying dynamic of the throw of I Ching coins. How can the numeric value of one's name mirror one's personality? What reasoning might explain the seeming story revealed in the lines of the palm? We might learn something about the nature of psychic functioning—and gain a more rational attitude about the psychic arts—through open-minded investigation.

Keith Harary feels that we must push to make psi more "marketable," more relevant. "It is not enough for us merely to inform the public about current research while we take care not to overstep the limitations and boundaries that cowards and critics have laid out for us."

LeShan concurs: "The field is in a shambles, partly because they've gotten involved with a small group of scientists trying to follow the track of physics and chemistry, where it doesn't belong. They define scientific as the science around 1890, maybe 1882. Reforms will have to come from the outside. . . . If we're lucky, there'll be some guy working in a patent office, like Einstein, to formulate it in some dramatic way."

LeShan brings up a fascinating issue when he talks about how psi has lost its way. "Parapsychology started out as a theory, that there is an afterlife, there is a soul, there is survival. Over the years, the scientistic viewpoint took over, which means everything has to be like physics, and so you got into the laboratory with an immense number of little facts, but no theory, and that's where it is today. It's completely reversed. Nobody talks about the search for a soul, or the search for survival. . . . Your modern scientist is as afraid to find that he has a soul as the medieval monk would have been to find that he didn't." LeShan goes on to say that when he began to assess the level of self-sabotage in the field, he found it to be extraordinarily high. "Just at the time, in the 1930s, when we were learning how to work with mediums under strict conditions, and to quantify the results, we stopped working with mediums." He tells the story of the Maimonides Dream Lab's work with the gifted psychic Eileen Garrett, its first subject. The first target given her was the horse race in *Ben-Hur*. She was awakened and said, "I had a dream where there were four black horses pulling chariots against four white horses; it reminded me of the scene in *Ben-Hur*, except I was holding the black horses with whips." The lab never used her as a subject again.

This sounds implausible, but his explanation is that parapsychologists are interested in getting results, "but not too good results. Too good results are much too frightening to parapsychologists." LeShan worked with Eileen Garrett for five years at the Parapsychology Foundation, which she founded—that is to say, she kept him on staff full-time as a paid psychologist to make sure the experiments were foolproof. The only problem was that no one asked her to take part in experiments. "There's a difference between knowing and believing," LeShan says. Parapsychologists know these phenomena exist, but are terrified of really finding out. "I realized if I wanted to triple the amount of basic data in the field, I could do it in one stroke: by setting up a special committee to pick up lost manuscripts out of Waterloo Station in London." Lost and unpublished research is a psi phenomenon in itself. British parapsychologist Dr. D. J. West said in his retirement speech: "As I look back, I realize I spent all my time looking for significant results, and none of my time in following up significant results that I had."

There are other psi-stifling factors. One major one is the tendency, noted by Gertrude Schmeidler, for researchers to couch their extraordinary findings in such a cloud of guarded language and obfuscating statistics that they get lost. And then there are the researchers who unconsciously, unintentionally, suppress psychic functioning, so that their findings come out very marginal, or at chance levels. John Beloff is, self-admittedly, such a psi-suppressor. As LeShan says, "Beloff can suppress a psi experiment at a thousand yards. He's the perfect example of a dedicated man, a scientific man, a brilliant man, whom I really like and admire, with his life on the line in this field, but he unconsciously suppresses the results. It's the only way to account for what happens. Other people are getting good results with the same protocols."

Sometimes it seems that parapsychologists are their own worst enemies. Their defensive stance makes for some rather lukewarm conversation—at least when they think they might be quoted. There's a lot of mumbling, and almost a physical effort to distance themselves from the lunatic fringe of the paranormal. They hem and haw, and utter bland phrases like "Well, I don't want to say that I believe, but you can say that there are a lot of data." In fact, my experience is that many of them lead a bizarre "double life." Publicly cautious, in private they tell me of their precognitive dreams, or their belief that in the end we'll discover that it's all "one mind." I was astonished that even someone as open and pioneering as LeShan still resists psi. When I asked him about metal-bending, he pulled out of a drawer a spoon that he had "psychically" bent himself. Yet despite his personal experience, he still needed more "scientific" proof. "The thing that convinced me most strongly, by the way, because of the turn of my mind, is George Owens' [metallurgical] analysis of the break in the spoons." Keith Harary, both a pioneering researcher and an accomplished research subject, squirmed like crazy when I tried to question him about poltergeist phenomena, metal-bending, and other psychokinetic phenomena, saying he doubted the veracity or authenticity of almost all of the claims. "Controlled experiments haven't shown convincing results, and aren't always possible to carry out in these reported cases."

Psi is nothing if not elusive. Couple the psi-blocking (and psi-doubting) machinations of the parapsychologists with their fear of being misunderstood; add to that the freaky mishaps, unexplainable equipment breakdowns, and specimen disappearances that are frequently reported when parapsychologists try to record extraordinary phenomena, and you have a rather uncanny set of circumstances. The provocative Jeffrey Mishlove even theorizes that the heated maelstrom created by "muddled viewpoints of emotional believers and hard-nosed skeptics" is itself the thermodynamic consequence of psychic events.

If the field of psi is going to extricate itself from the doldrums, and command the public's respect, it is going to have to adopt a more aggressive stance, and even change the basic rules about how the world works. Stephan Schwartz points out that "science is fighting ESP because it doesn't fit the worldview. It's going to require a change in the metaparadigm." Targ and Harary challenge us all when they ask: "Where will you be standing when the paradigm shifts?"

PART · TWO

SIGNS OF THE

PARANORMAL

CHAPTER
FOUR

PSI AND MIND

"Remote viewing is like playing charades with yourself."
—Keith Harary

"It's like déjà vu all over again."
—Yogi Berra, on the re-rehiring of Billy Martin to coach
the New York Yankees

Parapsychology, notes a prominent researcher, is "a collection of facts in search of a theory." History tells us that one day the pool of informed guesses about psi will achieve a type of critical mass, and a theory will emerge that not only accounts for the facts about psi but also inspires widespread acceptance of those facts. Meanwhile, we are forced to define psi in terms of its effects rather than its causes, and the effects alone are often, well, unbelievable.

Some paranormal effects manifest themselves in the material universe. Friends sit around a table with their hands laid lightly on the top and the table begins to buck. Two teenagers have an argument in a kitchen and dishes stacked in a nearby drainer suddenly shatter. A stockbroker walks barefoot across white-hot coals without suffering any burns or discomfort. In each situation, an unexplained force gives physical evidence of its presence and its power, even though the beast itself eludes detection.

Most often, however, psi is a private affair: Its effects occur within the minds of individuals. A man alone in his study hears the voice of a close friend urging him to hurry over to his house; he does, only to discover that the man has inadvertently locked himself into a windowless cellar room. Working solely with a photograph of a missing person, a woman correctly describes his whereabouts. A tarot-card reader tells a man she's never seen before that his son is having trouble at school. A grade-school pupil dreams one night about a strange orange plane making an emergency landing in a nearby parking lot, and it actually happens two days later. In such cases, there is no concrete evidence of a psychic force at work, only a firsthand report that may or may not be verifiable. To everyone but the psi-struck individual, the event itself—and what caused it—remains hidden, unknown, unknowable.

THE TERMINOLOGY TRAP

In this chapter, we'll look into the mystery of mysteries: the psi events that are private and subjective by nature because they happen only within the mind. Most scientists divide these effects into three broad categories: telepathy, clairvoyance, and precognition. Before focusing on each of these categories individually, let's examine the terms themselves: How effective are they in creating meaningful distinctions? How well do they describe the phenomena they are meant to describe?

TELEPATHY (literally, "distant feeling"): Usually defined as access to another person's thoughts by means not involving the known senses or logical inference, telepathy can assume many different forms.

Very often a person having a telepathic experience acquires a message as a more or less direct communication from another person, such as the case of the man who "hears" his friend calling from the locked cellar room. Other times, the telepathic impression seems to be the result of accidental eavesdropping: A woman has a dream about being chased through a department store by a chimpanzee while her husband in the next room is reading the same incident in a story.

Occasionally the telepathic impression will be nonverbal—a physical or emotional reaction on the part of the receiver that doesn't fit the receiver's situation but does fit the situation of another party. J. B. Rhine recounts an experience of this type in his book *Extra-Sensory Perception*. One day while driving on a New Jersey highway, a friend of his was overwhelmed by a sensation of pressure on his chest. The pain became so great that he thought he was going to die. He struggled to pull the car off the road and sat unable to move for several moments. All at once, the sensation went away and there seemed to be nothing wrong with him. He drove home and discussed the episode with his wife later that evening. They were considering whether or not he should get a medical examination when he received a phone call from Colorado, telling him that his son had been killed that afternoon in a head-on car collision—his chest crushed against the steering wheel.

CLAIRVOYANCE (literally, "clear seeing"): Clairvoyance is defined as the acquisition of information about an object, location, or event by means not involving the known senses or logical inference. In contrast to telepathy, clairvoyance refers to an awareness of physical realities (things) rather than mental realities (thoughts, emotions, and sensations).

Typically, the clairvoyant "sees" something, although the character and clarity of this vision, like the imaging that occurs in a dream, may not correspond to the character and clarity of normal, everyday vision. As such, the vision is "nonlinguistic"—that is, it must be "translated" into decipherable, linguistic terms which describe here-and-now reality. For example, a psychic in San Diego, asked by a client to help locate a lost piece of jewelry, received an impression of "dark and light bars, movement, brightness." Eventually, the client connected the clairvoyant vision to the back seat of her car, which was draped with a fake zebra skin to protect the upholstery from light streaming through an overhead sun roof. The jewelry was discovered beneath the back seat.

In some cases, however, the clairvoyant signal is more analogous to hearing something (technically "clairaudience") or smelling, tasting, or touching something (technically "clairsentience"). For example, a woman on an Oregon farm was jolted awake one morning at 3:40 by the sound of people screaming. The sound quickly vanished, but she felt a smoky, unpleasant taste in her mouth. She woke her husband, and together they scoured the farm but found nothing irregular. That evening on a television newscast, they heard about a plant explosion 90 miles away that started a huge chemical fire which killed six people. The explosion had occured at 3:40 A.M.

PRECOGNITION (literally, "knowing ahead"): Precognition is defined as the acquisition of information about an object, location, or event *in the future* by means not involving logical inference. For example, a man walking down a Detroit street in 1951 was suddenly struck by the thought that the substantial building in front of him would not be there in years to come. Instead, there would be a hill of adobe huts and a waterfall. He dismissed the thought as pure nonsense until twenty years later, when he returned to Detroit after a long absence and discovered a new shopping mall where the building had been: a complex of abobe huts piled alongside and on top of one another with an artificial waterfall as a central feature!

The Austrian philosopher Ludwig Wittgenstein claimed that "philosophy is a struggle against the bedevilment of language." This is particularly true in the case of parapsychology. One major difficulty in arriving at a coherent theory about the nature of psi is that the words we use to talk about it get in the way.

"Telepathy" is a term derived from the world of electromagnetism. It was coined by Frederick Myers in 1882, during an era that saw the newly invented telegraph and telephone as near-miraculous, "invisible" modes of communication. Unfortunately, the unavoidable implication is that telepathic transmission works somewhat like telegraphic or telephonic transmission—that is, through a wave of energy that crosses space from one fixed location (the brain or mind of the sender) to another fixed location (the brain of the receiver). The problem was compounded with the invention of the radio, which led researchers down many false trails in their attempt to relate telepathy to broadcast waves of current. In fact, as we will see, even though the anecdotal and experimental evidence indicates that these electromagnetic analogies are not accurate, they continue to shape the way science investigates telepathy and the way the public regards it.

The term "clairvoyance," with its romantic sound and emphasis on vision, is simply burdened by negative connotations. It suggests a hallucinatory experience—a type of exotic mirage that is engendered by the viewer and magically winds up matching something in the outside world. We can't help thinking of carnival acts, mad prophets, or gypsies in storefront fortune-telling parlors.

The term "precognition" implies *knowing* something as opposed to somehow just *sensing* something—a subtle distinction, but then, the phenomenon itself is subtle. Is the precognitive experience really characterized by intellectual perception or wisdom at some subliminal or intuitive level, as the word would have us believe? The term also reinforces a linear concept of time and bids us look in only one direction along that line. Post-Einsteinian physics, on the other hand, seriously questions the notion that the future has no existence until after the present. As for the demonstrated capacity of people to access information from an unknown past (technically known as "retrocognition"), it gets much less attention, although it's potentially a sign of the reverse kind of psychic activity and an equally valid field of study.

Even the term "parapsychology" itself is probably a misnomer. It suggests a bizarre, "nonnormal" experience. On the contrary, theoretical developments are increasingly pointing toward psychic functioning's being a "normal" part of nature.

Aside from the problem that the terminology is misleading, there's the problem that the categories created by the terminology frequently overlap when it comes to specific cases. If a man I've never met correctly describes the contents of my concealed wallet, is he using clairvoyance to pick up patterns and images from the wallet itself, is he using telepathy to pick up my thoughts and memories regarding what's in the wallet, or is he getting precognitive feedback on his own future knowledge?

Suppose I am suddenly visited with the image of a strange woman by a lake; then, a week later, I see a picture of that same woman next to a newspaper article reporting that she drowned herself the previous night following months of depression. Was the appearance of the image a precognitive experience, or was it an indication that I was telepathically in contact with the stranger while she was contemplating suicide? Most parapsychologists would label the image precognitive, since its key point of interest is its relationship to an incident that occurred later in time. Whether the target of the precognitive episode was the event itself or the newspaper photo is yet another complicated issue! And to muddy the waters still more, Freud would ask the compelling question "Why did you 'tune in' to *that* woman and *that* event?"

Ingo Swann is quite blunt in his opposition to the present terminology. When I asked him why he thought psychic phenomena eluded our understanding, he insisted, "Our concepts of what we're looking at make it difficult. I don't believe there's any such thing as telepathy or clairvoyance. These are buzzwords that caught on some-place in the history of the research and they stuck. There is no evi-dence at all, for example, that what we're calling telepathy does anything remotely like what the definition says it must be doing."

Swann prefers to think of all psychic effects as happenings within a collective universe—happenings which two, three, five or five hundred individuals may be experiencing simultaneously, as each tunes in to the collective field via what Swann calls the individual's "ESP core" (which, incidentally, may help to account for what Jung defines as "synchronicity." This is the purported dynamic that takes place in the shuffle of tarot cards, the fall of the I Ching coins, or the distribution of tea leaves. Some connection is made between the unconscious and the outcome of what should be a random event.) Stephan Schwartz comments: "I don't think telepathy, clairvoyance, and precognition are distinct phenomena. I believe," Schwartz told me, "there's really only one phenomenon, and that's access by con-sciousness into the collective."

Unlike those who are unusually sensitive to the psi component of their own consciousness, and those who have spent their profes-sional lives studying psi, most of us are still pretty much outsiders looking in. We're only dimly aware—on a conscious level—of some of the effects of psi, and we have little or no subjective appreciation for how and why it works. As imprecise as the terms "telepathy," "clairvoyance," and "precognition" may be, they serve an undeni-ably important function: They provide us with an official language for identifying, examining, and discussing psi experience.

At the very least, the terms direct our attention to the special sig-nificance of the effects they attempt to describe. Without them, we are left with such vague substitutes as "intuition," "inspiration," and "hunch." Human nature being what it is, such vagueness is danger-ously attractive. It keeps us from having to acknowledge that we possess capabilities that we don't understand or that go against con-vention (the so-called ownership resistance syndrome). If I went be-fore a board of directors and said that I had a gut feeling that real estate would suddenly boom in Fargo, North Dakota, they might accept my recommendations. But if I went before that same board and said that a numerologist told me that the time was right to buy property in North Dakota, or that I'd had a dream in which I saw tall buildings rising out of the plains of North Dakota and people carry-ing suitcases full of money, they'd throw me out on my pants!

While we need to recognize that "telepathy," "clairvoyance," and "precognition" are interim labels—terms of convenience that function as bridges between past perceptions of these phenomena and what they actually represent—we also need to remind ourselves that most parapsychologists during the past century have used these terms and have managed to advance our knowledge about psi effects considerably. It's impossible to refute Ingo Swann when he says, "We need to work on redefining and renaming these concepts, so that we can approach them with a different mind map and without prejudice." For the present, however, these terms still command the field. At some level, they continue to establish fruitful discriminations, as we'll see when we look at each category separately.

TELEPATHY

Of all psi effects, telepathy is the most commonly reported and receives the most scrutiny by scientists. This may or may not indicate a prevalence of telepathy over other psi phenomena in day-to-day human experience. The more likely explanation is that the concept of telepathy in itself has a unique and powerful appeal to the human imagination. Throughout history, the possibility of direct mind-to-mind communication has held the promise of drawing people closer together and adding to their individual security, comfort, and power. This promise may well load the scales in favor of people's recognizing, remembering, valuing, sharing—and verifying—their moments of telepathy more easily than they do their moments of clairvoyance or precognition.

In most accounts of spontaneous telepathy, an affinity already exists between the two individuals involved (admittedly, it's difficult to verify psi taking place between people who don't know each other). In these accounts, what often seems to trigger the psi experience is one party's pressing need to be in contact with the other. Mrs. Joicey Acker Hurth of Cedarsburg, Wisconsin, vividly recalls an instance of "crisis telepathy" in her own life that occurred in 1955, when her daughter, "little" Joicey, was five years old. Little Joicey had just left home to meet her father and brother at the Rivoli Cinema several blocks away.

"I went on back to the kitchen and I was standing in front of my sink washing a dish or two. All of a sudden I froze and dropped the plate I was holding. I raised my eyes to heaven and said, 'Oh God, don't let her get killed.' I just knew something was wrong. I immediately went to the phone to telephone the theater, and a young girl answered. I said, 'My daughter has had an accident. Is she badly hurt?' and the girl stammered and almost dropped the phone and said, 'J-j-just a minute, it just happened, how did you know?' Then the manager came to the phone, and he said, 'Mrs. Hurth, your daughter was hit by a car. She got up and ran to the side of the road, and your husband is with her now. He's going to take her immediately to the doctor. She doesn't seem to be seriously hurt.' "

Later, little Joicey revealed that immediately after the accident she sat on the curb "crying and saying, 'Mama, Mama, Mama,' " though her screams were inaudible to her mother. The scene of the accident was too far from the Hurth home for Mrs. Hurth to have heard any noise.

The link between two people who share a moment of telepathy doesn't have to be as apparently close as that between mother and child, husband and wife, two lovers, or twins. So far, no data have accumulated to suggest that one kind of close relationship breeds more telepathic incidents than another kind of close relationship. Often the special need of the moment determines just how close a particular relationship is. This is especially true when it comes to incidents of "deathbed" telepathy, which occupy a large proportion of the anecdotal material relating to telepathy. You may be disturbed in the middle of the night by a desperate cry from a long-ago acquaintance you haven't thought about for years. It may be impossible to prove, but perhaps that person had a private reason for desiring your presence before dying or for making sure you carried an indelible memory of that moment. A friend's mother told me this story:

"I was living in London during the war [World War II] while my husband was away in the service. One night I woke up in the middle of the night, restless and tense, thinking of a man named Dan, whom I had dated for several years before I met Albert, and of whom I'd always been fond, though we hadn't had contact for years. But I couldn't sleep, and tossed restlessly, all the time thinking of Dan. Half in and half out of sleep, all of a sudden I was on the floor, and felt like I'd been thrown there. It was a bizarre sensation, and I'd bruised my hip. In the morning, I couldn't remember much about it. But a couple of weeks later I learned that Dan had been blown up by a land mine on the night I had that 'dream.' "

Theoretically, the "information" about Dan's being blown up by a land mine was available in the "collective field" for anyone to dream about, but it came through to my friend's mother because of her relationship to Dan—her "need to know"—and because she recognized it as such. Others may have picked up that same "information": perhaps his mother or a close friend. Strangers may have had the same dream, but could connect it to nothing in their lives. For them, it was just a dream, or a feeling, *not* a telepathic (or clairvoyant) experience.

As I indicated before, the closer the relationship between the two people involved, the easier it is to verify that telepathy has occurred. They're apt to talk together more (and therefore identify telepathic moments that would otherwise be overlooked), plus they're apt to understand each other more deeply (and therefore be able to distinguish exaggeration, emotionalism, and falsehood from the truth). Telepathy could be happening all the time between strangers as well as friends and relatives—but is it truly telepathy unless it is discovered? Keith Harary calls this the "Holiday Inn Effect": If a man staying in a hotel had a heart attack and another man staying elsewhere in the hotel had a dream about someone having a heart attack, but checked out of the hotel the next day without knowing about the man upstairs, he isn't aware of having had a telepathic experience. And there's no way of knowing how often this type of thing happens. If it cannot properly be called "telepathy," certainly it is some sort of psychic phenomenon—in other words, an experience that cannot be explained by any orthodox scientific theory.

All the evidence says that the need to communicate, undeniably an element in a great number of recorded cases of telepathy, is capable of overcoming any physical and temporal barriers that may stand in its way. Scientific experiments by J. B. Rhine and others, for example, have shown that instantaneous telepathic communication can happen between two people situated far away from each other in shielded rooms that are impermeable by any sort of electromagnetic current (a fact which discourages "physical" theories that attempt to explain psi as an electromagnetic transmission). This doesn't mean, however, that the probability of your creating a telepathic bond with someone else increases in direct proportion to the magnitude of your need, the fixity of your intention, or the special "sympathy" you already have with the target recipient. There are clearly other elements involved; including your belief that it can be done.

As we've relied more and more on institutional and mechanical modes of communication—couriers, the written word, electronic transmission—we may have distanced ourselves from a capacity we once had to tap this psi-ability more easily. Anthropologists in the twentieth century have observed members of so-called primitive cultures communicating over long distances in a manner that could be explained only as telepathic. Medical psychologist Thelma Moss, formerly at U.C.L.A., who has studied Australian aborigines, reports that they use telepathy the way we use a telephone (and, as she remarks, "The telephone is as much a mystery to them as their telepathy is to us"). When hunters are about to return home to their village—sometimes a journey of several days—they telepathically communicate to the villagers so that preparations for cooking, feasting, and tanning can be made in advance.

Even today's Native American culture remains what scientists refer to as "psi-conducive" in settings where some of the ancient traditions still hold sway. What science calls "psi," Native Americans call "the outer world," and they claim an ability to shift to that world for numerous purposes. Individuals use it to put forth invitations to social events (in the vernacular, this is known as "using the moccasin telegraph"). Leaders use it for periods of group decision-making, during which all members remain silent and motionless. Shamans use it to help disciples—near or far—who are undergoing vision quests, by entering their visions at critical moments and acting as guides. Spain's Basque culture fosters the active teaching of psychic skills to children.

It could be that even the most mainstream, technologically oriented citizen of the world depends on telepathy continually in his or her daily life and is simply not aware of it. This is the basis of Rex Stanford's fascinating theory, which he labels Psi-Mediated Instrumental Response (PMIR), suggesting that what appear to be lucky coincidences in our daily lives may actually be moments we have engineered by the involuntary exercise of subconscious psi abilities. One of the real-life examples he cites to describe how this nonintentional psi may function when we need it is a story about an army colonel who inadvertently got off at the wrong subway stop in New York and ran into the very people he was intending to visit.

Stanford has conducted several impressive experiments that appear to confirm the presence of PMIR. Since these experiments technically involve clairvoyance rather than telepathy, we'll review them later on. A series of analogous experiments that relate more directly to telepathy was conducted by Douglas Dean and Carroll Nash at the Newark College of Engineering. In one room, a subject relaxed while a plethysmograph measured the moment-to-moment blood volume in his or her finger. In another room, far away from the subject, a "sender" concentrated, one at a time, in random order, on fifteen different names: five from a phone book, five from the sender's own circle of friends, and five from those people known to be important to the subject. Invariably, the subject's blood volume rose whenever the "sender" concentrated on the name of someone important to the subject.

In a minority of the reported cases of telepathy, neither overt nor subliminal need seems to be involved. Somehow, an individual has simply "fallen" into telepathic communion with someone else, and the content of the moment has been relatively trivial. On a summer day in 1984, Bob Everson of Columbus, Ohio, was relaxing by his backyard pool with his family when all at once he was overcome with a feeling of joyful surprise, accompanied by the thought that someone dear to him had come "all the way from India" to see him. Bob was puzzled, since he didn't know anyone in India and the feeling had been so undeniably strong and immediate. He described the odd sensation to his sister-in-law, Beth Everson. The next day at work, Beth overheard one of the secretaries on her floor talking about the shock she had received when her best friend from college, a teacher in New Delhi, had appeared unexpectedly on her doorstep the previous day. Flabbergasted, Beth established that the meeting had occurred at the same time Bob had been subjected to his "odd sensation." The secretary was a stranger to Bob and only a nodding acquaintance to his sister-in-law; and since her house was across the city from Bob Everson's house, there is no way he could have overheard the reunion.

Dr. Jule Eisenbud, a professor of psychiatry at the University of Colorado Medical School, calls this type of telepathy "flaw-determined," as distinct from the more common and more instrinsically meaningful "need-determined" variety. In "flaw-determined" telepathy, there appears to be a temporary breakdown in whatever mental system represses our receptivity to psi information. Given the erratic and inconsequential nature of this kind of telepathy, most of us would never be able to identify its operation in our personal experience, unless, like Bob Everson, an incident were particularly vivid and we were able by some fluke of fate to confirm it. Who knows how common this type of psi-functioning is? Again, can we say that telepathy has actually occurred if the two "participants" remain unaware of its occurrence?

Another perplexing issue is whether or not the subject in any kind of psi test is safe from the possibility of being unintentionally "psychically" influenced by the people who organize and facilitate the test —an influence that may contaminate the result, even though, ironically, it may in itself be a sign of psi in operation. Known as the "experimenter effect," it's one of the more fascinating paradoxes involved in the struggle to analyze psi ability according to orthodox scientific methodologies.

A major concern relating to the experimenter effect is that a subject's performance may be considerably altered by the mere expectations of the person conducting the experiment. It has long been observed that some researchers consistently get better results than others, with identical experiment protocols. Dr. Robert Morris, who holds the Koestler Chair of Parapsychology at the University of Edinburgh, admitted to me:

"There are some people who have argued that all of parapsychology's results are the results of a relatively few gifted and talented experimenters. *They* are actually doing it—manifesting the psi power —and the subject is simply sitting there, coming along for the ride. I don't especially buy that, but it is a possibility."

The experimenter effect can take place in any of the life sciences. In a laboratory test that has become a classic illustration of this curious phenomenon, rats chosen for their similar abilities in maze-running were randomly grouped into two separate cages, one marked "clever" and the other marked "stupid." Each rat was then tested in a series of maze-runs by several different research assistants. The rats taken from the cage marked "clever" invariably produced the better scores, even though the population of each cage was secretly and randomly changed after each run. Could the subjects in a telepathy experiment—or any other experiment for psi ability—be susceptible to a similar performance catalyst? Perhaps wishing *does* make it so.

In another experiment, ostensibly testing the cancer-causing effect of a particular substance on rats, it was shown that the experimenters unconsciously chose the rats previously identified as more prone to cancer for the group to receive the carcinogen. In this case, the latent psychic capabilities of the experimenters were proving themselves in the very act of ruining a carefully controlled experiment. What this implies about the accuracy of any scientific experimentation is frightening!

Outside the strict confines of the laboratory, psychiatrists are well aware of the potential for an analogous kind of "experimenter effect" in their own practices, being frequently surprised by the apparent telepathic links between them and their clients. In what is now a famous and classic case, psychiatrist Montague Ullman provides an intriguing example of the confusion that may result when elements of a therapist's real-life experience somehow get projected into the dream-life experience of his or her patient:

"In his dream, the patient offered a chromium soap dish to a man who blushed when the patient said, 'Well, you're building a house.' The patient could not report any associations to the soap dish. However, the therapist remembered that a year and a half earlier, a chromium soap dish had, by mistake, been shipped to the new house into which he had just moved. In a belligerent spirit, responding to the mounting building costs, he never bothered to return it; but a week before the patient's dream, several architects had come over to inspect the house; and one had spied the soap dish lying unused in the cellar, and had embarrassed the therapist by calling attention to it."

Ullman himself conducted a series of famous dream-telepathy experiments with Stanley Krippner at the Maimonides Medical Center in Brooklyn during the 1960s. Taking as their cue Freud's observation about "the apparently intimate connection between telepathy and dreams" and "the incontestable fact that sleep creates favorable conditions for telepathy," they designed an experiment to test whether actual dream content could be telepathically induced by an outside agent. Electrodes were attached to the head of a volunteer subject, who then slept overnight at the laboratory. As soon as monitors detected the sleeper's rapid eye movements (REMs—a signal of dream activity), an agent in another room would try to transmit a target picture. After a few minutes, the subject would be awakened and asked to recount his or her dream.

In one 1966 experiment, an agent concentrated on projecting the content of a painting selected at random: Hiroshige's *Downpour at Shono.* William Erwin was asleep in another room and reported dreaming about "an Oriental man, a fountain, water spray, walking down the street when it was raining." The center witnessed many other successful episodes of dream telepathy, including a dramatically accurate "hit" obtained by having two thousand people at a Grateful Dead rock concert concentrate on transmitting a color slide projected on stage to a sleeper in the Brooklyn laboratory, which was 45 miles away.

One aspect of telepathy that lurks in the background of all experimentation and darkens telepathy's promise to humankind is the specter of thought control. As I mentioned before (see Chapter 2), the Soviet Union has frequently been accused by observers and former citizens—including Larissa Vilenskaya and Nikolai Khokhlov— of conducting extensive research into the use of "distant influence" for political purposes. For this reason, some Westerners are increasingly worried about the possibility of Soviet sabotage at every encounter between the two cultures. At the 1978 World Chess Championship in the Philippines between the Soviet citizen Anatoly Karpov and the exile Victor Korchnoi, Korchnoi claimed that a member of Karpov's retinue was employing telepathy to disturb his game-planning. Can telepathy be used to manipulate our emotions, our willpower, our attitudes, our ideas, even our actions? What is science able to tell us about this?

Keith Harary compares this controversy to the controversy surrounding hypnosis: Is it possible for someone to experience images from another person's mind and not know that this is happening? Can a person be influenced to do something he or she is not leaning toward doing already? When we discussed this matter, he acknowledged that using telepathy to influence behavior may be within the range of human abilities, but that much more study is needed to determine if and how it works: "Before we go off the deep end about it, we need to consider the relationship between perception and behavior. You perceive something, and how do you respond to it?" Russell Targ adds: "Suppose I show you a picture of bodies half-buried in a mud slide south of the border. If you're a photographer, you might find that a remarkable, incredibly composed photograph. If you're from that area, you might really hurt inside seeing your countrymen buried. If you're an average citizen in the United States, you might say to yourself, 'God, I'm glad I wasn't there!' or 'Holy cow, can you believe that?' So just the fact that you perceive information does not in any sense of the word determine what your response is going to be to that perception. To influence a person by telepathy, you would have to determine a great deal about that person and be very certain that at a given moment he or she would be receptive to your signal."

As for the flip side of the issue—whether someone could use telepathy to see into another person's mind against that person's will— many scientists are in agreement with LeShan, who told me, "I don't think it's possible to pick up information telepathically from somebody who doesn't want to give it to you." Also, from what we know of psi in general, it is a weak, unpredictable signal. Even the best psychics cannot communicate all the time, certainly not powerfully: They can't just command a friend to call, and what information they are able to receive telepathically is often fragmentary and sporadic.

CLAIRVOYANCE

One day in 1956, an amateur pilot taking a flying lesson was about to attempt for the first time a difficult roll in her Piper Cub. Deep in concentration, she was suddenly overwhelmed by a feeling that there was trouble below her. With effort, she put the feeling out of her mind and performed the maneuver. But the sensation that something was wrong kept returning. Finally, she gave up practicing and, guided solely by her instincts, flew 70 miles off her course, where she saw that a car had run off a highway. Landing, she ran to the car; inside, a woman was slumped over the wheel. She pulled her out; moments later the car exploded in flames. The car's passenger was her mother.

At first glance, the young pilot's story seems to illustrate telepathy: Someone very important to her has an urgent need for help, and she is instantly aware of this need, though she is physically distant from that person and preoccupied with her own activity. What makes the story distinctive, however, is not her sensitivity in itself, which, after all, was not focused on a particular person and did not take the form of a coherent thought, feeling, or emotion. The remarkable part is her ability to go directly to the scene of the need, despite the fact that she had no rational way of determining where it was. Parapsychologists attribute this kind of ability to "clairvoyance"—the extrasensory perception of an object, location, or event.

The story I have just recounted offers an excellent example of how psi classifications tend to overlap. It also suggests why parapsychology continues to employ these classifications. For all their imprecision, they do manage to highlight special aspects and applications of psi power. In the case of clairvoyance, what is significant to consider is the possibility for people to extend their witnessing capacities beyond the apparent barriers of space, knowledge, and memory.

There is a theory in the psi world that human beings have gradually all but lost their psychic sensitivity as civilization has become more complex. Many experts interpret present-day clairvoyant experiences as irrepressible signals from an ongoing mental perceiving mechanism each of us possesses as a member of the human species. Once potent enough to enable prehistoric men and women to survive in a savagely inhospitable world, this internal mechanism is now much weaker—neglected in favor of external technologies. As Stanley Krippner said to me, "We've come to rely on instruments rather than our senses. We're like the modern airplane pilot who studies the computer screen rather than the sky itself."

If we accept the existence of a neglected psychic scanning mechanism in human beings, the young pilot's story is analogous to the many documented stories of animals that exhibit uncanny investigative and navigational abilities: cats that stalk other cats separated from them by concrete walls two feet thick; dogs that travel hundreds of miles on their own to be reunited with their owners; turtles that spend months drifting in ocean currents, only to return for spawning to the exact spot on land where they were born.

At the very least, all these stories imply that *need engenders ability*. We see startling examples of this idea, though the underlying mechanism is not necessarily psi, during specific emergencies, such as when a 110-pound woman of average strength lifts a 1,000-pound beam that has just collapsed on her child. This idea may also explain the riddle of how certain feats have been accomplished within cultures that lacked the manufactured devices we require to accomplish the same feats. Wade Davis, in *The Serpent and the Rainbow*, speculates on his inability to see the planet Venus in the sky during the day: "Astronomers know the amount of light reflected by the planet, and we should be able to see it, even in broad daylight. Some Indians can. And but a few hundred years ago, sailors from our own civilization navigated by it, following its path as easily by day as they did by night. It is simply a skill that we have lost, and I have often wondered why."

Comparing clairvoyance to the homing instinct of animals and the hypersensitivity frequently displayed by less scientifically oriented cultures is a possible starting point for understanding the phenomenon, but it doesn't cover the complexity of many experiences parapsychologists have labeled "clairvoyant." With no personal need at stake and no affinity to the target, people have willed or attuned themselves to exercise their clairvoyant talents for an amazing range of purposes: to track down criminals; to locate the most appropriate spots for oil wells, mineral mines, and archaeological digs; to diagnose baffling medical conditions; and to warn private individuals as well as public agencies about tangible present dangers (see Chapter 8). In most such cases, the psychic ability is trained and disciplined; the user learns to pay attention to the psi component of his consciousness.

When we turn to examine spontaneous clairvoyant experiences—many of which feature no need, no affinity and, by definition, no will on the agent's part—the mystery of "how" and "why" deepens. Because they can't be identified on any level as another person's thoughts, feelings, or emotions, spontaneous clairvoyant experiences are usually more difficult to recognize and decipher. Most anecdotes speak of "vague inklings," or "confusing patterns of images," or "a bundle of sense impressions." These are somewhat like the pseudo-sensations we get when we idly daydream; except that in the clairvoyant incident, those pseudosensations seem more insistent, more serious, more invested with a real life of their own. It's as if the signal were an alert, saying, "Something is here that interests you," or "Something is going on that you should know about."

In rare cases, a spontaneous clairvoyant experience will be as clear and as engaging as a concrete, "real-life" experience and, therefore, easier to communicate and to validate. Like so many telepathic incidents, such strong clairvoyant moments are often associated with a crisis situation. Beverley Nichols recounts an incident from his own life in his book *The Powers That Be*. Nichols, a reporter for the Canadian Broadcasting Corporation, was in London one November day to do a broadcast on British royalty. He was in the midst of describing a procession of Queen Elizabeth in her golden coach, attended by the Horse Guards: "Then, without any warning I had a sharp feeling of discomfort, almost of nausea, accompanied by an acute headache. The picture of the Queen and her cavalcade vanished as swiftly as if it had been blacked out in a theatrical performance, to be replaced by an equally vivid picture of President Kennedy driving in an open car, flanked by his escort of motorcyclists with their snarling exhausts. And as though it were being dictated to me, I began to describe the scene."

In his broadcast, he was able to tie in the Kennedy description by comparing the elaborate security measures adopted for the U.S. president with the relatively simple measures adopted for the British monarch. The broadcast over, he was leaving for a drink when a stranger rushed up to him and said, "President Kennedy has been assassinated. Six minutes ago."

Nichols' experience of seeing Kennedy had been so singularly impressive that he was unable to dismiss it as coincidence; and when he played back the tape, he noticed that the whole tempo of his voice was different while he was narrating the Kennedy vision. Perhaps Nichols' clairvoyant episode was empowered by his "need to know" as a reporter. Perhaps it happened in spite of any logical reason, just as the literal occurrence of the clairvoyant moment defied the logic of distance.

It's uncommon for a clairvoyant experience to feel so real and forceful that it completely replaces normal sensory experience. In most cases, it appears to enter the agent's conscious awareness peripherally, as a fleeting glimpse, sound, smell, taste, or touch. This doesn't mean, however, that clairvoyance is strictly an episode in consciousness. Clairvoyance, like telepathy, may operate subconsciously for extended periods of time, influencing our state of mind and guiding our behavior.

To test Stanford's PMIR hypothesis (see page 106) in regard to clairvoyance, parapsychologists Martin Johnson, William Braud, Ramakrishna Rao, and Ephraim Schechter independently performed variations of the same ingenious experiment. Students were asked to take an academic examination. Attached to each student's answer sheet was a sealed envelope. The students were not told what was in this envelope. In some experiments, about half of the envelopes contained correct answers to the examination. In other experiments, each envelope contained correct answers for a selection of questions. The object of all the experiments was to determine whether the students performed noticeably better on the questions for which answers were given in the sealed envelopes. In every experiment of this type, the students did score significantly higher on these questions. They unconsciously used their psychic ability.

By far the most intriguing and convincing scientific research relating to clairvoyance began in 1973 at the Stanford Research Institute (SRI) in Menlo Park, California, under the direction of Harold Puthoff and Russell Targ. Working with Ingo Swann, who came to him with an impressive reputation for psychic sensitivity, they first had Swann clairvoyantly "view" objects that were in another room. But Swann soon became bored with this activity and wanted to try something more interesting and useful. With Swann's input, Puthoff devised a protocol he thought would be especially challenging. Ultimately called Project Scanate (*scan*ning by coordin*ate*), it consisted of giving Swann latitude and longitude indications and asking him to describe immediately what he perceived. To make sure that Swann couldn't be operating from logical inference or eidetic memory (the ability to close one's eyes and reproduce exact images of what one has previously seen), he required descriptive details that he thought would not be available on maps and that would be virtually impossible for

Swann to have seen in his past. As an added precaution, the experimenters working directly with Swann remained ignorant of the target site until after Swann's description. The results were astounding. Swann was able to provide successful descriptions in a surprisingly large percentage of experiments.

In one experiment, for example, a target site was submitted by an East Coast scientist who was skeptical of the undertaking. Here is Swann's response from the laboratory transcript:

"This seems to be some sort of mounds or rolling hills. There is a city to the north; I can see taller buildings and some smog. This seems to be a strange place, somewhat like the lawns one would find around a military base, but I get the impression that either there are some old bunkers around or maybe this is a covered reservoir. There must be a flagpole, some highways to the west, possibly a river over to the far east, to the south more city. . . . There is something strange about this area, but since I don't know what to look for within the scope of the cloudy ability, it is extremely difficult to make decisions on what is there and what is not. Imagination seems to get in the way. For example, I get the impression of something underground, but I'm not sure."

As part of the exercise, Swann drew a picture of what he had seen. The transcript and picture were mailed to the East Coast scientist, who phoned back the results: The target was, in fact, a missile site. Swann's description was accurate in every detail. Even the relative dimensions and distances on his drawing were to scale! The results were definitive. There was no possibility of collusion between Swann and the challenger, and the target site was small and subject to controlled access.

DRAWING BY SWANN OF EAST COAST TARGET SITE

Seeking a neutral term to characterize this ability, Puthoff came up with "remote viewing." He also refined the experimental procedure to placate incredulous members of the scientific community. The use of geodetic coordinates was abandoned. The revised protocol required the subject to describe to an experimenter a site being visited by a third person, called a "beacon." The site would be chosen at random by computer, to ensure that the subject had no basis for guessing details and to eliminate the possibility of deliberate or subliminal cueing by the experimenter. The experiment would be timed so that the subject would wait thirty minutes before beginning his or her description, which often included sketches or drawings. By then, the beacon would be present at the target site. While the subject communicated his or her impressions, the experimenter would employ interview techniques to elicit relevant details, overcome impasses, and steer the subject away from rational comparisons or guesswork.

Following the experiment, the subject would always be given feedback. In many cases, this would involve taking the subject to the actual target site, which accomplished several purposes: The subject could verify his or her psychic experience (again, addressing the issue of whether psi has occurred if there's no feedback); the subject could identify which specific images and impressions were "correct"; and the experiment could be concluded in the subject's mind, leaving him or her fresh for succeeding rounds. Independent judges would compare a transcript of the subject's description with the total pool of random target sites and choose the site they felt matched the description. If the target site matched the target selected by the judges, it was considered a "hit."

Using this revised protocol—first on people known to be psychically gifted, and later on ordinary volunteers—Puthoff, Russell Targ, and, later, Keith Harary have achieved an outstanding 70-percent success rate in dozens of trials (a success rate which has been sustained in dozens of other trials conducted by other researchers). "We still don't understand where the information is coming from," Harary admits, "but we do understand a lot about how people process psychic information, to the extent that we're able to take ordinary people and show them how to recognize psychic impressions and separate them from other, nonpsychic impressions, which we term 'mental noise.' He gave me a brief overview of the particular skills involved in remote viewing:

"Some people feel that they aren't very facile with mental images or that they don't have mental-imaging skills. They have to learn to develop these skills. Some people are very good at describing their own internal experience. There are people who have to learn how to verbalize that. In general, the remote-viewing process is similar to the creative process. It is like learning to take somewhat undifferentiated feelings and sense an impression and express that to yourself and to other people without turning it into something else. And that's like creating a poem, creating a painting. You might say that remote viewing is like playing charades with yourself."

It's important to remember that clairvoyance in general is not always visually oriented. Parapsychologist Stephan Schwartz insists, "I like the phrase 'remote viewing' as a substitute for 'clairvoyance,' but it really should be called 'remote *sensing*.' " Princeton's Dr. Robert Jahn uses the phrase "remote perception." A single clairvoyant experience may engage all the senses. It may also be dominated by a single category of sensations: sounds, smells, tastes, or tactile impressions. Since the major mode of perception for most individuals is visual, however, vague impressions such as those which occur most often during a clairvoyant incident are liable to be translated instantly to what Ingo Swann calls "pictographic language." In the so-called remote-viewing experiments, many of the subjects are more comfortable using drawings than using words to describe what they are experiencing. Unlike verbal language, which articulates names and facts on the basis of rational judgments, pictographic language is mainly concerned with colors, shapes, sizes, and proportions— "universal" qualities that have meaning on the nonfactual level of reality within which psychic information is received.

In some demonstrations of clairvoyance, parts of the human anatomy other than the eyes appear to be capable of "seeing" things. (This, of course, is exactly what many psychic practitioners claim to be able to do.) In the 1960s, Soviet parapsychologists discovered and tested a girl, Rosa Kulesheva, who, while blindfolded, could read ordinary print with her fingers and tell the color of an object simply by touching it. The Soviets called this inexplicable ability "bio-introscopy." In the West, it's now known as "para-optic vision" or "fingertip vision." Reports have lately begun reaching the outside world from China about children who can "see" with their ears, their backs, and their feet. Collectively, the evidence does point to the possible existence of a "field" of sensitivity surrounding the human form that has the potential to function as a type of psychic sensor. It might explain, for instance, how sleepwalkers are able to move about without accident and perform relatively intricate tasks even though their eyes are closed.

One final dimension of clairvoyance worth mentioning is "psychometry," defined as the extrasensory ability to determine information relating to an inanimate object merely by contemplating or handling that object. It's often used in police work with psychics: The psychic will be given an object closely associated with a missing person, like a piece of clothing, and the psychic will use this object as a touchstone for sensing where that missing person can be found.

Lawrence LeShan conducted an especially interesting psychometric experiment with the gifted psychic Eileen Garrett. First he showed her three identical boxes and told her what was inside each of them: One contained a lock of hair from his daughter Wendy, one contained a tuft from the tail of his neighbor's dog, and one contained a rosebud. Then he took the boxes behind a screen setup which allowed Garrett to hold the boxes through sleeves without actually seeing them. In an order determined by random-number tables, he slid each box beneath her fingers. She was always able to identify correctly the contents of the box and to deliver commentary that astonished LeShan. Here is a partial transcript of her comments, interspersed with his comments (to the reader only; no replies were made to Garrett's remarks during the session), when she touched the box containing a lock of his daughter's hair:

G: Oh, that's your daughter. I think I'll call her "Hilary." She'd like that.

L: When my daughter was four years old [eight years previous to this date], she had a "crush" on a girl of six named Hilary. For a year she begged us to change her name to Hilary. Nothing like this had ever happened before or since. It was a private joke for several years thereafter that had never been—to the recollection of my wife or myself—mentioned outside the immediate family. It had certainly *not* been mentioned in at least four years by any of us. . . .

G: She has been very interested in American history these past few weeks, hasn't she?

L: Three weeks before, my daughter had been given an English assignment to do a book review of Howard Fast's book on the American Revolution, *April Morning*. For the first time in her life she became interested enough in a subject to go to the school library and ask for more books about it. . . . To the strong belief of my wife and myself, this was not mentioned outside the house, although her teachers and school friends may have known of it.

G: The Peace Corps? She wants to join the Peace Corps this summer. That doesn't seem right.

L: We had recently decided to send Wendy to a work camp the following summer. She had heartily disliked the idea. The night before, Wendy, my wife and I were discussing the matter. My wife said, "It's sort of a junior Peace Corps." Wendy immediately grasped this concept, became quite excited at the idea, and began to look forward to going to the work camp. The discussion had not been mentioned to anyone else by my wife, my daughter, or myself.

Garrett's prowess notwithstanding, most scientists disparage the notion of treating "psychometry"—or "object reading"—as a distinct clairvoyant phenomenon, fearing that such a move might draw misleading attention to the nature of the inanimate object itself. They prefer to think of psychometry as a ritual means of assisting someone to tap and focus his or her general clairvoyant powers. Some psychics, however, disagree: To them the object is a "telephone number" separating its owner—a stranger—from all others in the universe.

PRECOGNITION

It's one thing to transcend barriers of space. It's quite another thing to transcend barriers of time. Throughout history, no other paranormal experience has aroused so much awe and so much skepticism as precognition.

Famous stories abound. In 1865, Abraham Lincoln told several people about a dream he had had in which he traced strange sounds of mourning to the East Room of the White House: "Before me was a catafalque on which rested a corpse wrapped in funeral vestments. Around it were stationed soldiers who were acting as guards, and there was a throng of people, some gazing mournfully upon the corpse." Since the face was covered, Lincoln asked a guard who it was. "The president," the guard said. The dream continued to haunt Lincoln until a week later, when he was assassinated.

The sinking of the luxury liner *Titanic* in April 1912 sparked a multitude of premonitions. The most incredible story in this regard concerns a book written fourteen years earlier by Morgan Robertson, which describes a liner named the *Titan* that is almost identical in size and features to the *Titanic*, and that sinks after striking an iceberg in the North Atlantic during the month of April.

Like telepathy and clairvoyance, precognition is most often associated with crises. Typically, a spontaneous precognitive experience will function as a type of early warning signal about some danger or misfortune—frequently involving death—that lurks in the future.

What is striking about many such warnings is that they seem to apply more to a community of people, or to a famous person known to a community of people, than to the single person who receives them. This characteristic lends support to the theory that psi phenomena are a manifestation of a link between individual human beings and a collective consciousness (which may generate greater psi-provoking energy around certain people or events and could occasion what C. G. Jung identifies as "synchronicity" in the lives of numerous, otherwise unrelated individuals). In modern times, it has inspired the establishment of two organizations committed to tracking and validating premonitions: the London-based British Premonitions Bureau and the New York–based Central Premonitions Registry.

The British Premonitions Bureau was founded shortly after a tragic disaster at Aberfan, Wales, on October 21, 1966, when tons of coal waste piled into a slag heap fell on top of the Pantglas Junior School, killing 116 children and 28 adults. Reporters from the *London Evening Standard* verified twenty-two different premonitions of the event from people all over Britain, and the newspaper responded by setting up the bureau and inviting readers to contribute accounts of precognitive episodes. Robert Nelson, a former executive at *The New York Times* who also worked at the Maimonides Dream Laboratory, opened the Central Premonitions Registry in 1968. In this case, the motivating incident was a letter from the psychic Alan Vaughan, dated May 28, 1968, to Stanley Krippner, researcher at the Dream Laboratory. Vaughan recounts the contents of that letter in his book *The Edge of Tomorrow*:

"On the morning of May 25 I rose at 5:00 A.M. to record some vividly remembered dreams. In the first dream an American Indian fired a rifle through a grating to murder a person. In the second dream Robert Kennedy became me, walking through a hallway; dirt fell from an overhead grating, which I associated with a kitchen hallway in my boyhood home. I commented in my dream diary, 'A single rifle shot from a grating might be connected with the dirt sifting down from the grating in the second dream. It may be precognitive, but in a very distorted form. The dirt coming down seems ominous.' I took the American Indian to be symbolic that 'the assailant will not be a member of a group thought of as anti-Kennedy.' "

Unable to ignore the vividness of his dream, Vaughan appealed to Krippner: "If you can think of any way of drawing his [Kennedy's] attention to such a threat . . . I would be appreciative. If it happened I think I should have it on my conscience; if it doesn't then I only need feel a bit foolish."

On June 5, before Kennedy could be warned, he was assassinated in a kitchen hallway of the Ambassador Hotel in Los Angeles by a person in hiding who was not a member of a group perceived to be unfriendly to Kennedy. Within the month, Nelson began publicizing the Central Premonitions Registry, hoping that if he received several independent warnings of the same disaster, he might be able to alert those at risk. So far, even though the bureau has received many convincing premonitions of disasters facing prominent individuals or large groups of people, it has proved very difficult to check out the claims, and to separate serious reports from wild rantings. The biggest problem, predictably, is that authorities in charge of safety or security have paid little attention to the bureau's work.

Precognitions indicating crises that are of local, national, and even international concern attract the lion's share of attention, but the major proportion of anecdotal material consists of precognitions relating to one's personal fate. Most of these experiences are not very vivid; in fact, they're not visual at all, merely generalized "feelings." Still, the emphasis is on calamity. In Lady Churchill's autobiography, she tells about a time during World War II when her husband, Winston Churchill, was preparing to return to Downing Street after an inspection tour of London. He was just about to get in on the street side of his staff car, as he always did, when "for no apparent reason he stopped, turned, opened the door on the other side of the car himself, got in, and sat there instead"—something she had never seen him do. On the way back, a bomb fell near the car and would have hurled it over, if Churchill had sat in his usual place. "Only Winston's extra weight," Lady Churchill insists, "had prevented disaster." When she asked her husband about the incident, he could say only that "something" had made him stop, in a way that told him to sit on the other side. Later, Churchill told a miners' group, "I sometimes have a feeling—in fact, I have had it very strongly—a feeling of interference. I want to stress it. I have a feeling sometimes that some guiding hand has interfered."

On October 1, 1985, a last-minute change of plans by PLO chief Yasser Arafat kept him from being blown up when Israeli planes raided his operational base in Tunisia. "Only my sixth sense saved me," a shaken Arafat told reporters outside the ruins of his command post. "I was on my way to headquarters, but at the last moment I decided to meet my people at a villa elsewhere."

There is a happier side to precognition. Often instead of a warning, precognitive experiences seem to be delivering reassurance in the form of an image from the future that implies good news, progress, or hopes fulfilled. Barbara Greene, a friend of mine who is a knowledgeable collector of nineteenth-century furniture, recalls one such incident:

"For many years, Ted and I have dealt with Jack Winston, an antiques and furniture dealer whom we respect very much. At one point we fell in love with a beautiful nineteenth-century French commode, but at that time it was very expensive and out of our price range. But Ted loved that commode, and every once in a while he would go over to the gallery and sigh over the commode. It came to be known to us as 'Ted's piece.' One Monday, he came home crestfallen because he had seen the commode again, but it had been sold. Without knowing why, I said to him, 'That commode will be sitting right in this spot on Thursday,' and I pointed to a place in our library. I immediately felt a little foolish, and Ted thought I was a little nutty, but I forgot about it. On Wednesday morning, we got a call from Jack Winston. 'Mrs. X is driving me crazy. She is buying a group of pieces, and we had negotiated a price on Monday. But this morning she calls me up and she wants to renegotiate. She's done this before, and I've had enough. I know you love that commode. You can have it at my cost—but you have to get it out of here by tomorrow morning, before she comes.' So there it was on Thursday morning, sitting in our library, where it is to this day—still one of our favorite pieces."

One facet of precognition that excites everyone's curiosity is the chance of receiving "inside information"—a tip on the winning lottery number, or a rising stock, or a roll of the roulette wheel. Of course, you have to deal with the fact that precognitive imagery is not always easy to interpret. The following affadavit was made by Mr. M. B. Campbell in Surrey, England, in 1947:

"I certify that during the morning of 10th November 1947, Mr. A. S. Jarman called at this office and told me of a dream that he had had the previous night relating to a horse winning a race, and the figures 2020. We looked together through the morning paper to see if these figures could be relevant to the statistical figures of a horse running that day, but could find nothing apt. The following morning Mr. Jarman showed me a morning paper which reported that a horse named Twenty Twenty had won the 3.45 race at Leicester the previous day. We had not considered the names of the runners when trying to allocate the figures 2020 the previous day."

The above examples are all vivid, live anecdotes. However, most scientific experimentation with precognition has been organized around the same dry, statistical card tests and picture tests used for telepathy and clairvoyance.

Helmut Schmidt of the Mind Science Foundation in San Antonio, Texas, a German-born physicist working for the Boeing Research Laboratories in Seattle, believed that this type of experimentation was open to a great deal of criticism: The subject and experimenter could cheat, a truly "random" selection was difficult to guarantee, and the subject might consciously or unconsciously exert some other psi power to achieve results (such as psychokinesis to force the card shuffle, or telepathy to dictate a particular design to the person ultimately chosen to draw). He developed a machine for precognition testing that features a series of lights operated by electrons emitted in response to the random radioactive decay of the isotope strontium 90. This emission represents a truly unpredictable process that the subject can be asked to anticipate, with minimal possibility for fraud (due to computer compilation of results) and minimal vulnerability to fraudulent tampering. So far, experiments with the Schmidt machine have helped both to verify the existence of precognition and to facilitate the examination of a large number of subjects under the same tightly controlled conditions. The machine has also been used in experiments testing for psychokinesis (see Chapter 5).

A less structured, and more dramatic, precognition experiment was the "chair test" devised by the famous Dutch psychic Gerard Croiset, which perplexed scientists and laypersons all over the world. A chair would be chosen randomly from the seating plan for an upcoming concert or a public meeting in a large hall. The seat would not be a reserved seat, and the hall could be in any city—the location was never revealed to Croiset. Sometimes the seat would be chosen by lot, sometimes by free decision, sometimes by a machine similar to the Schmidt machine. Once the seat had been chosen, Croiset was capable of describing, anywhere from one hour to twenty-six days in advance, the person who would be sitting in that chair during the concert or public meeting. His impressions were always detailed—focusing on facial features, dress, and even incidents from the person's background—and almost always accurate!

For example, two days prior to a 1953 meeting in Hilversum, The Netherlands, a chair was chosen by lot and Croiset predicted, "The person who will sit in that chair was away for a few weeks in another country. I see him walking in a large city. His shoelaces are loose. He leans forward to tie them. As he does so, I see a gentleman walking behind him who bumps into him." At the meeting, the person sitting in the chair said that the incident had occurred on a busy London street corner.

In the face of much skepticism from members of the scientific community, who argued that the experiment's protocol was not free from contamination and that the results were ambiguous and questionable, Croiset and Dr. W. H. C. Tenhaeff, his associate in many of the chair experiments, went so far as to devise their own statistical format for proving the worth of the experiments. It was so convoluted that it only damaged their cause. Commenting on this situation in 1973, Dr. Jule Eisenbud said, "The problem in working with a brilliant sensitive is not that he cannot measure up to the rigorous constraints imposed by statistical analysts, but rather that statistical processes may be unequal to the task of interpreting to best advantage the data he does manage to provide." In the April 1986 *Journal of the Society for Psychical Research*, Eisenbud added, "At the present time I am more than ever convinced, at any rate, that it is the height of folly to try to put psychics such as Croiset into statistical straitjackets."

Malcolm Bessant, the famous English psychic, participated in a cycle of very dramatic precognition experiments conducted by Stanley Krippner at the Maimonides Dream Laboratory. On sixteen occasions, Bessant was told to dream about an event that would be set up for him to experience on the following morning. During the night, he was awakened whenever his brain waves indicated that he was dreaming, and a researcher would record his recital of his dream. In the morning, another researcher—having no contact with the rest of the team—would randomly open a book of dream symbols and devise a "happening" for Bessant to experience when he arose. There was almost always a striking correlation between Bessant's dream content and the content of the next morning's skit. For example, one morning Bessant was surprised by having ice cubes dropped down his back. In one of his dreams the previous night, he had envisioned ice cubes and had felt cold.

Patrick H. Price, a former police commissioner and vice-mayor of Burbank, California, became a full-fledged "psi star" during his run of remote-viewing experiments at SRI during the mid 1970s. One of his most striking demonstrations apparently involved precognition. Originally, the experiment was supposed to follow standard remote-viewing protocol: Price would wait for a target team to reach a location that it had determined by using a random-number generator and target cards, and then he would describe the site the team was occupying. Instead, the team independently decided to follow a "random" drive, in which each turn would be determined by arbitrary factors in the flow of traffic. This way, the team members had no idea where they would be at the time Price was supposed to "psych out" their location.

Twenty-five minutes before the time set for their arrival, while they were still driving around "randomly," Price said to the experimenters at the lab, "We don't have to wait till then. I can tell you right now where they will be." He went on to give the following description:

"What I'm looking at is a little boat jetty or a little boat dock along the bay. In a direction about like that from here [he pointed in the correct direction]. Yeah, I see the little boats, some motor launches, some little sailing ships, sails all furled, some with their masts stepped, others are up. Little jetty or little dock there. . . . Funny thing—this just flashed in—kinda looks like a Chinese or Japanese pagoda effect. It's a delicate feeling of Oriental architecture that seems to be fairly adjacent to where they are."

Price also described decomposed granite slabs leading down to the water. After he finished, the team was still twenty minutes away from its unknown destination. When it returned later in the afternoon, Price and the experimenters with him learned that the team had eventually visited the Redwood City Marina. Price's description matched the area perfectly!

REDWOOD CITY MARINA

While it may be fun to marvel at wondrous precognitive feats, our logical minds are inclined, deep inside, to balk: Precognition can be very fearful to contemplate. Accepting the existence of precognition means accepting that our current concept of time needs radical adjustment. The most difficult problem for most people is entertaining the notion that our lives are predestined, that the individual possesses no free will. Stephan Schwartz refutes this notion by pointing out that there may be innumerable possible futures, instead of just one. "It's possible to get a report back from the future," Schwartz theorizes, "but not a future that happens." Seen from this point of view, the future is malleable—full of what Ingo Swann calls "crystallizing possibilities" that may be influenced by a human being's individual will and conduct.

A famous example of a "future that didn't happen" involved Air Marshal Sir Victor Goddard of the Royal New Zealand Air Force in January 1946, when he was stationed in Shanghai. On the night before he was due to fly home, he attended a party hosted by the British consul and overheard someone behind him saying, "Too bad about Goddard. Terrible crash." The speaker turned out to be a friend of his, Gerald Gladstone (later Admiral Sir Gerald Gladstone). Suddenly face to face with Goddard, Gladstone stuttered, "I'm terribly sorry . . . I mean, I'm terribly glad." He then begged Goddard not to fly that night, claiming that he'd had a strong image of Goddard in a Dakota plane going through a snowstorm, over mountains, and then crashing to his death on a "rocky, shingly shore." He had also envisioned two civilian Englishmen and a woman on board as well as the crew: all killed.

At first, Goddard dismissed the warning; although he was scheduled to fly on a Dakota plane, he was not taking any passengers—only the crew. Within minutes, however, he was advised by radio to take an Englishman named Ogden with him. Later, a male English reporter was also assigned on board; and at the last minute, a female secretary was recruited to accompany Ogden. The group took off the next morning aboard the Dakota plane, named *Sister Ann*. Hours into the flight, the radio broke down, and it began to snow heavily. Eventually mountains were sighted—an indication that they were off course. Their fuel was running out, and they decided to make an emergency landing. Through the now raging snowstorm, they could make out only a "rocky, shingly shore" near a fishing village. After two failed attempts, the *Sister Ann* hit the ground and skidded across the stone shore, tearing its undercarriage. Villagers ran down and rescued everyone. The precognitive vision had been accurate except in one, all-important respect: Goddard was not aboard.

• • •

Many parapsychologists theorize that since no event has a 100-percent probability of occurring until all the conditions of its occurrence have been met, an indefinite number of "alternative futures" may exist that are qualitatively similar. Assuming this is true, then the distinguishing aspect of each "alternative future" would be the magnitude of the probability of its occurrence. In other words, psychic perception of a future event might depend on its probability, rather than its actual occurrence.

Researcher Elisabeth Targ devised a remote-viewing experiment to address this theory, in which showing a viewer a given object in a pool constituted the "actual future." Six objects were chosen to compose a pool of "possible futures." Before each session, one of these objects was randomly assigned a 50-percent probability, while each of the remaining objects was assigned a 10-percent probability. This meant that in a pool of ten objects, five were the same, and there was one each of the five other objects. The viewer, in a distant location, was asked to describe the item he or she would be shown at the conclusion of the experiment. As soon as the viewer finished describing that item, a target object was chosen from the pool by a computer which took into account the probability figures previously determined. In some cases, the computer chose the high-probability object; in other cases, one of the low-probability objects. The probability of the outcome did not sway the subjects, however. The viewers quite consistently described the actual object subsequently chosen by the computer, regardless of the odds for their choice.

A look into the future is much more thrilling to the human imagination than a look into the past, and so the psi phenomenon known as "retrocognition" receives much less consideration than "precognition," though both illustrate possible psychic transcendence of the barrier of time. As distinct from "déjà vu"—the experience we have when we encounter something for the first time and yet feel that we've encountered it before, retrocognition is a direct, fresh perception of a past event. A friend told me about a retrocognitive sensation she had in the summer of 1985, while she was in the hospital recovering from minor surgery:

"I was in a very blah mood, just staring at cracks in the wall of my room, when suddenly a filmy sort of scene unfolded in front of me. There were four women hovering around my bed. Each one wore a voluminous, old-fashioned dress. Three of the dresses were black and one was a lilac color. One of the women in black said to another woman in black, 'Irene, hush, you must not say such silly things.' I could see details on their faces and I could smell a faint odor—a flower I couldn't place. I described the scene to my mother when she visited later that same day. At first, it didn't mean anything to her. Then she thought of something—a distant relative of my father's had been named Irene. She checked with my father and my father checked with his father and, lo and behold, he remembered a distant cousin named Irene who had lived in Ireland in the latter part of the nineteenth century. She had three sisters and eventually had to be confined in a home for the feebleminded. All of this was information I'd never heard before—nor had my mother or father."

Often retrocognition takes the form of what Jung calls "psychic localization": A specific place seems to harbor experiences that can be clairvoyantly perceived by a sensitive visitor. You stay overnight in a country inn and, knowing nothing of its past, dream of a crime that happened there thirty years before. You visit a Civil War battlefield and suddenly hear cannons booming and horses neighing, even though the battlefield is empty. The famous historian Arnold Toynbee cites no fewer than six retrocognitive episodes of this type in *A Study of History*. Among the incidents he psychically witnessed were the suicide of a proscribed Roman rebel in 80 B.C., the Spaniards' first sight of the Aztec capital Tenochtitlán, and a Greek soldier describing how he'd tried to save a girl from rape. But one particular incident provided an overwhelming perspective on a kind of timeless universal consciousness. He reports that he found himself "in communion, not just with this or that episode in History, but with all that had been, and was, and was to come. In that instant I was directly aware of the passage of History gently flowing through me in a mighty current, and of my own life welling like a wave in the flow of this vast tide."

PSI AND ALTERED STATES OF CONSCIOUSNESS

An interesting sidelight of the Grateful Dead concert experiment mentioned earlier is that many of the human transmitters may have been in altered states of consciousness, due to the music itself and the use of psychedelic drugs. Whether altered states of consciousness in general encourage or intensify psi capability—including telepathic communion—has still not been scientifically demonstrated, although the anecdotal information suggests that they sometimes might. When I spoke with Charles Honorton, who assisted in the Maimonides experiments, he said, "Our normal senses are more filters than they are windows to the world. An estimated 50 to 60 percent of spontaneous psychic experiences happen during dreams, probably because dreams are separated from the filter of the senses." By extension, his theory might be applicable to states of mind under meditation, light trance, hypnosis, and even drug influence, a point worth examining.

The most carefully controlled and most oft-repeated experiments of psi in altered states of consciousness use the *Ganzfeld* technique, which was developed in Germany and first applied to psi by Dr. William Braud. In the 1970s, Honorton began accumulating data on the *Ganzfeld*; his research continues to the present. The *Ganzfeld*, or "whole field," technique involves placing the subject in a mildly altered state of consciousness known as "sense habituation." The purpose of the technique is to maintain a subject's sensory inputs at a constant level, so that outside distractions are eliminated and mental attention is redirected to internal events, hopefully including psi experience.

In a typical *Ganzfeld* experiment, the subject (or "receiver") rests comfortably in a chair or on a mattress in a peaceful room. The ears are encased in padded headphones playing white noise or rhythmic sea sounds. The eyes are completely covered with halved table-tennis balls rimmed around the edges with cotton, over which a diffused light (usually red) is cast. Meanwhile, a "sender" sits alone in a soundproof room some distance away. A computer randomly selects a single video clip among 160 possible choices—ranging from Bugs Bunny cartoons to footage of a spider spinning a web—and the sender watches the clip, attempting to transmit its images to the receiver. While this is being done, the receiver "talks out" all the images, sounds, thoughts, and feelings he or she experiences. The receiver's running commentary is monitored by an experimenter who does not know what the sender is viewing. After twenty to forty-five minutes, the receiver watches four different video clips and judges which clip he or she thinks the sender was transmitting. If the receiver matches the clip with the one seen by the sender, the experiment is considered a "hit." So far, after thousands of trials, the incidents of a match have been 38 to 45 percent—which greatly exceeds the chance expectation of 25 percent and strongly suggests the occurrence of telepathy.

Though controversial, *Ganzfeld* is attracting a lot of converts among post–Rhine-era parapsychologists. Many of them are eager to shift psi research away from the behavioral approach of the lab to the more subjective approach that mind/consciousness studies in general have taken since the cultural sea change of the 1960s. William Braud has made systematic comparisons between the scoring of *Ganzfeld* and non-*Ganzfeld* groups, both to judge the effectiveness of *Ganzfeld* and to develop refinements in the *Ganzfeld* protocol. These comparisons imply that a *Ganzfeld* group may yield higher performance scores.

Despite the widespread enthusiasm, *Ganzfeld* is not without its critics. Keith Harary, for example, said to me: "*Ganzfeld* cuts down on environmental noise, but not on mental noise, which may actually be amplified. Psi is available in many normal states of consciousness —including a normal waking state. We need to study the ways in which psi is expressed in these different states, instead of assuming that one state is more psi-conducive just because it's the one we've been studying lately. *Ganzfeld* is artificial. While it may help some people in the beginning to attain a state of attention, it's no good in everyday life. You can't use psi to find a parking space with Ping-Pong balls over your eyes." This image also bothers Russell Targ: "*Ganzfeld* conveys a picture in which psi functioning looks weird, is weird, and requires an altered state of consciousness."

Commenting on *Ganzfeld*, Rex Stanford told me, "Techniques to reduce distractions reduce external 'noise.' As time goes by, they also increasingly produce random functioning in the brain—unusual, bizarre, and unrestrained responses. I believe this definitely offers more opportunities for ESP activity." While the data accumulated so far support the idea that the *Ganzfeld* technique does enhance psi receptivity, there are still many more studies to perform before a definite link is proved.

We've already seen that dreams often include psi information, but what about other altered states of consciousness (ASCs), such as those achieved via meditation, hypnosis, drug-intoxication, or sensory deprivation (for example, by fasting or by submersion in an isolation tank)? All these conditions weaken or remove the rational filters of our ordinary, waking existence. Do they stimulate our psi powers? Are we more likely to experience telepathy, clairvoyance, or precognition while under their influence?

Many scientists believe that ASCs are *possibly* more psi-conducive than the normal state of consciousness; but so far, experimenters haven't been able to confirm this belief with any certainty. One major impediment is the absence of any standard for measuring the degree to which a subject is experiencing an ASC. In the case of hypnosis, there is no physiological indication whatsoever to verify that a subject is actually in some sort of trance. As for meditation and drug-intoxication, which do produce physiological symptoms, the quality and meaning of any change vary greatly from individual to individual, depending on his or her physical, mental, and emotional makeup.

This lack of a standard makes it difficult to draw any cause/effect conclusions regarding ASCs and psi-activation. Some evidence indicates that a relaxed state of mind favors high scores among subjects being tested for psi, but determining where the relaxation factor ends and other state-of-consciousness factors begin is impossible without a more precise measurement than is currently available. We can't even tell if there *is* any factor beyond relaxation, which may in itself be the most significant psi-impacting feature of a given individual's particular ASC experience.

When it comes to judging the effects of meditation, research is complicated by the fact that there are so many different varieties of meditative experience to examine. Working with practitioners of Transcendental Meditation, Honorton was surprised to find that they scored either well above chance or well below chance. According to parapsychologist John Palmer, this may indicate that meditation (and possibly any ASC) affects only the *magnitude* of psi's impact on consciousness. The *direction* of that impact, by contrast, depends on other, unaccountable, and no doubt highly subjective factors. In other words, your performance in an ASC is likely to be very poor or very good rather than simply normal. This accords well with the opinion of many experts, including Keith Harary and Ingo Swann, who contend that because ASCs increase the randomness of a person's thoughts and perceptions, they are just as likely to keep people from being sensitive to psi signals as they are to put people in touch with psi signals.

Studies of ESP experiments performed while the subject was drug-intoxicated or undergoing sensory deprivation (both states highly conducive to hallucination) are similarly inconclusive: There have been single tests demonstrating unusually high results and single tests demonstrating very poor results. The only significant research into the connection between sensory deprivation and psi-receptivity has centered around use of the *Ganzfeld* technique.

Most of the psi experiments involving drugs have shown themselves to be methodologically flawed: They didn't establish the subject's attitudes toward either drugs or psi—attitudes that would very likely affect the subject's performance during testing. After numerous investigations on the subject of drugs and ASCs, Charles Tart had to admit that despite the mass of apparently scientific research, the influence of any type of ASC on psi activity was in many respects "a prescientific area."

CHAPTER · FIVE
PSI AND MATTER:
PSYCHOKINESIS

"PK is consciousness walking around the room."
—*Gertrude Schmeidler*

The word *psychokinesis* has been around only since 1943, but the phenomenon is as ancient and mysterious as Stonehenge or the Pyramids. Egyptian papyri thousands of years old contain stories of households tormented by evil spirits who threw objects against walls and shattered furniture. The Old Testament describes Moses parting the Red Sea; in the New Testament, Jesus dispenses with the formalities and just walks on the water. It was recorded by the Catholic Church during the Middle Ages that Saint Teresa of Avila and Saint Joseph of Copertino were capable of floating in the air before crowds of witnesses. Even Sir Francis Bacon, that skeptical observer of the secular world, wrote in the early seventeenth century about a force within the human mind that could be tested ". . . upon things that have the lightest and easiest motions . . . as upon the sudden fading or coming up of herbs; or upon their bending one way or the other . . . or upon the casting of dice."

All these references suggest that the mind may have a direct and palpable effect on the physical universe, without the intervention of muscular activity or any other motor process. In common speech, the phenomenon is known as "mind over matter." J. B. Rhine, after nine years of observing this capability in the laboratory, labeled it "psychokinesis"—abbreviated as PK—to distinguish it from "extrasensory perception," or ESP. Like ESP, PK is a paranormal mental power that is theoretically unaffected by distance or barriers and appears to contradict established laws of physics. Unlike ESP, PK acts upon matter, producing results that are perceptible to the ordinary senses of an outside observer.

Strictly speaking, PK refers to *movement* or *change* in physical matter caused by mental activity: A glass on a table suddenly spins, or slides around, or rises two feet into the air, or explodes. Most experts, however, use the term in conjunction with any event featuring a paranormal physical manifestation. In addition to the disturbance of objects, this category includes acoustical, electrical, and thermodynamic aberrations, materializations, "supernatural" feats such as fire-walking, metal-bending and levitating, and revelations of psi "energy" such as auras and "psychic" photographs. It possibly includes such phenomena as out-of-body experiences and trance channeling. In this chapter, I'll pursue this broader definition of PK. Some parapsychologists even apply the term to "psychic healing"—the influence of consciousness on biological systems—but since this is a relatively large and distinct subject, I will discuss it separately in Chapter 9.

Spontaneous cases of PK are fairly difficult to recognize and verify. However odd a physical event may be, it isn't likely to have much meaning in itself to make it more memorable. Suppose a teakettle pops off your stove and seems to hover in the air before crashing to the floor. You may be momentarily stunned, but chances are the incident will soon be forgotten, since it's only "something strange" that happened once. If you do continue thinking about it, you'll probably distort your original perception of the event by insisting on a "natural" explanation for it. "Perhaps there was a small seismic disturbance," you might speculate. "Perhaps the teakettle didn't actually hang suspended as long as I thought it did." Or you might say to yourself, "I didn't sleep well last night. I must have imagined it."

It's no wonder, then, that so many anecdotes regarding apparent spontaneous PK revolve around an instant in time that is unforgettable in its own right: the moment when someone dies. The classic example of such a PK effect is a clock-stopping. Louisa Rhine recounts a typical example in her book *ESP in Life and Lab*, reported to her by a man who owned a gold pocket watch given to him by his brother:

"I took leave from my job and sat up nights to help my sister-in-law during the last two days of my brother's terminal illness. He breathed his last at six-twenty-five in the morning. I called the family immediately and we phoned for the doctor and the undertakers. At about seven-thirty we were sitting around a rush breakfast—my two brothers, the widow and the nurse. Arrangements had previously been made to be at the undertaking parlors at nine-thirty. . . . Some one asked me how much time we had, and I took out the pocket watch mentioned above, when, lo and behold, it had stopped at the exact minute of his death. I called the attention of those gathered around the table to the phenomenon and in order to show that it was no common occurrence, asked my brother to wind the watch to make sure it had not run down. It was three-quarters wound."

Spontaneous PK has also been frequently identified with moments of trauma among the living. One of the most famous and bizarre reported incidents occurred during a heated argument between Carl Jung and Sigmund Freud shortly before they severed their professional and personal ties. Curiously, the subject they were debating was the very existence of psychic events. As Jung recalls in his book *Memories, Dreams, Reflections*, he was greatly upset while listening as Freud attacked the possibility of having a psychic experience. All at once, Jung felt his diaphragm become a "glowing vault," and a loud banging noise issued from a bookcase in the room, causing both of them to jump to their feet. "There!" Jung exclaimed. "That is an example of a so-called catalytic exteriorization phenomenon." Freud refused to believe him. "You are mistaken, Herr Professor," Jung insisted, "and to prove my point, I now predict that there will be another loud report." Instantly, a second banging noise came from the direction of the bookcase.

In each of these examples of spontaneous PK, the effect itself is obvious and meaningful; the nature of the effect, however, remains ambiguous. Although we can deduce a plausible reason for *why* the effect was produced, we can't say with any certainty *how* the effect was produced.

The sudden stopping of a watch appropriately symbolizes the end of a person's life, and we're irresistibly compelled to draw a causal relationship here. But how was the watch stopped: by the transformed consciousness of the dying brother or by the shocked mind of the brother who owned the watch? A skeptic might say that the watch-owner accidentally slammed his watch against the wall in his shock at the moment of death, but later forgot about it. In other stopped-clock situations, the two parties were separated by thousands of miles, and the surviving clock-owner was not consciously aware of the death when it happened. Still, the same questions apply: Was it the "spirit" of the dying man or the telepathically informed mind of the survivor that stopped the clock? It seems logical to say that the tension between Jung and Freud resulted in the strange detonation from the bookcase, but how, exactly, was it produced? Was it by Jung's mind, roiling in irritation? Was it by Freud's mind, either indignant toward Jung or subconsciously at odds with his own professed denial of psi? Or was it by some other agent altogether, like a playful ghost who had been eavesdropping?

POLTERGEISTS

Speaking of playful ghosts, the most impressive and baffling incidents of spontaneous PK are those which feature strong effects exhibited intermittently over an extended period of time. Officially, they're classified as episodes of Recurrent Spontaneous Psychokinesis (RSPK). Popularly, they're known as episodes of "poltergeist," a German word that means "noisy and boisterous spirit." Modern movie directors and screenwriters have been enormously attracted to this image of a demonic, otherwordly jokester and have propagated a misleadingly fanciful image of just what is involved in a poltergeist situation. Admittedly, in many RSPK cases, the capricious intervention of a playful ghost seemed the only likely explanation of "why" and "how"—at least for a while.

During the first week of August 1948, unexplained fires began erupting in the Macomb, Illinois, home of the Willey family. Brown spots appeared on the wallpaper and gradually got hotter and hotter until they burst into flames. Everyone in the household—Willey, his wife, his brother-in-law, his nine-year-old niece, and his eight-year-old nephew—kept on the alert to put the fires out before they spread. By the fourteenth of August, the house was so badly damaged it had to be abandoned. The local fire chief, after many fruitless days of leading a search for the cause of the fires, was forced to admit to the press, "The whole thing is so screwy and fantastic that I'm almost ashamed to talk about it."

Throughout the winter of 1967, weird happenings plagued an attorney's office in Rosenheim, West Germany. Initially, the telephone system started misbehaving. All the phones in the office would ring simultaneously and no one would be on any of the lines. A meter registered vast numbers of outgoing calls that could not have been made by the staff. Engineers, electricians, and physicists from the Max Planck Institute were summoned to investigate; and while they were there, light bulbs twisted in their sockets and exploded, file drawers shot out of their cabinets, pictures swung on their hooks, and developing fluid spurted out of a photocopier. In time, one of the psychologists—Dr. Hans Bender—noticed that trouble occurred only in the presence of a nineteen-year-old secretary. The trouble ceased altogether after she quit her job.

In this example—and in many recorded poltergeist incidents—the reported motion of the objects was remarkably different from normal motion, featuring slow, strange trajectories and midair pauses. Even more interesting is that often a child or adolescent was nearby when the effects manifested themselves. On closer examination, the effects actually appeared to center around that young person, who was often found to be singularly unhappy or upset during the time span of their occurrence. This has led many parapsychologists to interpret RSPK as a paranormal outlet for pent-up stress or, in numerous cases, severe mental disturbance: what Stanley Krippner calls the "release-of-effort" hypothesis, and what other authorities identify as "externalized PK." Children and adolescents are typically liable to develop strong frustrations and to suppress them out of fear, shame, or guilt. The RSPK manifestations themselves tend to be in character with the tantrum behaviors of an immature person, who might hurl and destroy household objects, abuse machinery, and even set fires. The trigger for this kind of RSPK episode, however, is usually assumed to be a genuinely neurotic or psychotic condition—not merely a circumstantial fit of anger or a brief period of moodiness.

Unfortunately, children and adolescents are also prone to mischief. Suspicion has been cast over many possibly authentic examples of RSPK because the youthful, insecure "focus" of PK activity, anxious to remain a center of attention, has faked effects when they've ceased to occur on their own.

PK IN THE LAB

Investigations of poltergeist phenomena, like those of spiritualism and mediums, are highly difficult to control, and highly criticized for their vulnerability to fraud. Studies of PK in the lab, while not so exciting, have provided valuable statistical data. Dr. J. B. Rhine's investigations of PK began with a simple dice-rolling experiment. The subject would attempt to will each outcome in a series of dice rolls. If he or she consistently "hit" a targeted number at a level above chance expectation, it was safe to assume that the subject had exercised psychokinetic control over the dice. As the decade progressed, Rhine refined his experiment to make it more methodologically sound: first by having the dice tossed from a cup and then by having the dice tossed by a mechanical device. The faces on each die were also changed from time to time to prevent any physical bias in a roll.

Most of the experiments used students—subjects with no reputation for psychic ability—but the results were singularly persuasive. A sizable number of tests did point to the operation of PK. An especially convincing development was the discovery of "quarter distribution declines" in the scoring. After dividing each of their completed score sheets into four quarters, Rhine and his associates noticed a tendency for subjects to score higher in the first quarter than in the last quarter. This consistent decline effect helped to support the argument that above-chance results in the experiment were due to paranormal influence: There could be no other explanation for such a score-sheet pattern. The decline effect also implied that PK ability might wane over time, at least in the context of dull, repetitive task performance.

Given the modest level of PK that could be elicited under strict laboratory procedures and the mundane nature of the procedures themselves, researchers during the 1950s gradually lost their enthusiasm for this type of testing. The 1960s, however, redirected their attention to PK-related phenomena in a variety of different ways.

At the beginning of the decade, Dr. Bernard Grad of McGill University in Montreal conducted a highly original series of experiments that seemed to establish a scientific foundation for the existence of psychic healing. The first set of experiments used three randomly created groups of laboratory mice whose backs had all been similarly wounded by removal of a small area of skin. The first group was placed in a box that was held by a former officer in the Hungarian cavalry, Colonel Oscar Estebany, who had a reputation for healing army horses. The second group was similarly handled by medical students who had no such reputation. The third group received no handling at all. The individuals monitoring the experiment and caring for the mice were kept ignorant of how the groups were divided, to offset any possible "experimenter effect." The experiment showed significantly faster healing rates among the mice treated by Estebany.

The second set of Grad's experiments centered around barley seeds. Estebany was asked to hold a sealed bottle of saline solution for thirty minutes. Half of the seeds were treated with water from this bottle and the other half were treated with water from a control bottle. The seeds were then planted in separate pots. The pots that received seeds treated with water from Estebany's bottle had more plants growing in them, and the individual plants were considerably taller.

We'll look further into psychic healing in another chapter. As far as general PK goes, the Grad experiments helped to start scientists thinking not only about the practical applications of PK ability, but also about different ways to accumulate evidence of PK's existence, besides the relatively tedious and purposeless dice-rolling approach. Another stimulus to scientific curiosity about PK at this time was a flood of provocative snapshots issuing from behind the Iron Curtain.

PARANORMAL PHOTOS?

In 1964, authorities in the Soviet Union finally gave Semyon Kirlian and his wife their own laboratory and a generous research budget, so that they could verify and extend their twenty-five-year-old photographic experiments. The high-quality pictures they were now able to produce clearly depicted otherwise invisible flares of light surrounding the forms of living organisms. Photographs of human fingers illustrated ray patterns that changed according to the mood and health of the individual. A picture of a leaf that had just had its top third removed showed a sparkling outline of the complete original leaf.

The Kirlian photographs received immediate worldwide circulation and raised a host of questions among scientists and laypersons. In the case of human beings, could these photographs be physical evidence of a psychic force field, known through the ages as an "aura" and to specialized occult groups as an "astral" or "etheric" body? When nineteenth-century mediums spoke of being "sensitive to vibrations" and of seeing "energy clouds" surrounding their clients, were they referring to the glowing corona that encircles the human figure in these photographs?

Parapsychologists and physical scientists continue to debate precisely what this glowing outline represents. When I asked Thelma Moss about it, she dodged the question, saying only that "the Kirlian photo effect is not the aura. By classic definition, the aura extends several feet beyond the body. Kirlian rays extend only about a quarter of an inch beyond the body." Judging by what I learned from all my interviews, I too am skeptical regarding any link between Kirlian rays and the aura; and I'm not convinced that the "effect" produced by Kirlian photographs has anything to do with the paranormal. It seems to be an effect perhaps of moisture; the undeniable presence of the rays does support the conclusion that our physical sphere of influence does not end at the surface of our skin. Thus it is of more interest to those concerned with its potential diagnostic applications.

LOW-LEVEL PK

By the 1970s, interest in PK was undergoing a strong, threefold revival: in the lab, in the field, and among the general population.

Helmut Schmidt's random-number generator, in which a process such as the flashing of different lights is triggered by the totally random radioactive decay of strontium 90, introduced a random-process factor into scientifically formal PK testing that was far more authentic and impressive than the random-process factor in dice-rolling. Now subjects can try numerous different routines to test for "flaw-determined" or "low-level" PK: for example, willing one light to switch on more than another, or willing a special pattern of light ignition, such as a clockwise circular order. Other experiments involve subjects' trying to "psychically" skew a random distribution process—such as the fall of steel balls through a pinball-like machine. The results are mechanically tabulated (and therefore more trustworthy), and experiments in different locations can be more uniform in their protocols and quality control. Very large data bases show rather conclusively that subjects—with no special abilities, training, or induction techniques—can in fact consistently psychically interact with physical systems or processes to a statistically measurable degree.

Dr. Robert Jahn, of the School of Engineering/Applied Science at Princeton University, has been conducting experiments and collecting data on low-level PK for more than a decade. In 1986, he and his colleagues R. D. Nelson and B. J. Dunne published the results of a major survey of six years of experimental data in both "low-level" PK and remote viewing. The report concluded with a new theoretical model for correlation of the experimental data. These findings were reported in the April 1986 edition of the *Journal of the Society for Psychical Research*. While couched in dry, technical language, they are rather extraordinary. Pointing out that existing models cannot accommodate the experimental data, the authors call for a "fundamental reexamination of the assumptions underlying our definition and description of reality, and in particular the role of human consciousness in establishing that reality."

According to their new model, there is no such thing as "reality," or "experience," except as the interaction of consciousness with its environment. Thus, any theories about physical reality are "no more than useful organizing strategies adopted by the consciousness to order the information it processes." (See Chapter 7 for further discussion of this and other theories of psi.) The authors find concepts of quantum mechanics useful as *metaphors* for the interaction of consciousness with physical systems and processes, in a form that encompasses both "normal" and "anomalous" behavior.

Nelson, Jahn, and Dunne go on to talk about applications and implications of their findings in a world in which consciousness indeed seems to be capable of interacting with matter. If, in fact "reality" is what we *think* it is, and our *thoughts* can affect the physical world, then we must look at the possible effects of our consciousness on our environment, in particular on the machines with which we interact. As Jahn, Nelson, and Dunne continue: ". . . the low-level psychokinesis effects . . . suggest obvious ramifications in the military and intelligence sectors, in law enforcement, industrial practice, and in general information management technologies. Specifically, the results with the random event generators raise the generic possibility of anomalous effects arising from conscious or unconscious interactions between human operators and any sensitive microelectronic information processing devices or systems . . . given the array of anecdotal data relating anomalies to extraordinary psychological or neurological states, any microprocessors or functional computers performing critical exercises in proximity to operators subjected to high levels of excitement, stress, or responsibility, may be particularly suspect. Cockpit controls in aircraft or spacecraft, and aircraft and missile guidance and tracking systems would be two evident class examples, but a much broader range of potentially vulnerable man/machine situations can be readily envisaged." They go on to look at more positive applications for this new knowledge, such as the extraordinary possibility that we might learn to willfully control "certain microelectronic functions for utilitarian purposes." Next time you feel too lazy to get up, you might *think* about turning the lights off. And be careful not to get too stressed out around your home computer.

THE GIFTED PSI SUBJECT

For some parapsychologists during the past twenty years a far more revolutionary development than machine-oriented testing has been the return to seeking out psychically gifted people and studying them as thoroughly and imaginatively as possible, both in the field and in more controlled lab environments. Three intriguing subjects have been Nina Kulagina from the Soviet Union, Uri Geller from Israel, and Sri Sathya Sai Baba, an Indian guru whose devoted followers number in the millions.

Nina Kulagina claims that she first noticed her strange powers while she was recuperating from injuries she received fighting in the

Soviet Army during World War II. "I was very angry and upset one day," she remembers. "I was walking toward a cupboard when suddenly a pitcher moved to the edge of the shelf, fell, and smashed to bits." Somehow she knew that she was responsible for this "accident"; and as time went on, she developed the ability to control her PK energy. Among the first to examine her was Edward Naumov, who watched as she successfully moved groups of matches around a table and a single prechosen cigarette inside a sealed jar of cigarettes. The famous Soviet writer Vadim Marin recalls a bizarre event that happened at about this time while he and Kulagina were dining out together:

"A piece of bread lay on the table some distance from her. Mikhailova [Kulagina's maiden name], concentrating, looked at it attentively. A minute passed, then another . . . and the piece of bread began to move. It moved by jerks. Toward the edge of the table, it moved more smoothly and rapidly. Mikhailova bent her head down, opened her mouth, and just as in the fairy tale, the bread itself (excuse me but I have no other words for it) jumped into her mouth!"

In this case, Kulagina apparently willed the movement of the bread; but in many similarly informal moments, bizarre things occurred that were evidently not intended as demonstrations. Out of nowhere, loud noises would interrupt conversations in quiet studies; ashtrays would suddenly crack; books would inexplicably open themselves and pages would begin flapping in perfectly calm air. Kulagina was not exceptional in this regard. Strange things just seem to happen around psychics. When American journalist Dotson Rader was dining with Uri Geller, a saltshaker began crossing the table, even though the two of them were deeply involved in conversation. Said Rader, "It was like watching a tiny bishop wearing a silver mitre shuffle across a snowy field."

The most startling series of controlled experiments featuring Kulagina as a subject were set up by Genday Sergeyev, a neurophysicist at the Utomskii Institute in Leningrad. An egg was broken into a saline solution in an aquarium and Kulagina was challenged to separate the white of the egg from the yolk—a feat that couldn't possibly be attributed to fraud. With cameras recording every minute, Kulagina struggled hard and was able to move the white and the yolk apart from each other. The machines to which Kulagina was attached documented just how hard she had struggled: An electroencephalogram registered great disturbances in the reticular formation, which coordinates and filters information in the brain; a cardiogram showed a pulse rate of 240 beats a minute, four times the normal level; also noted was a sudden rise in blood sugar characteristic of a stress reaction. The test took thirty minutes, and Kulagina lost more than two pounds in body weight. By the end of the day she was reportedly very weak and temporarily blind.

When the Western scientist Benson Herbert, director of the Paraphysical Laboratory in Wiltshire, England, visited Kulagina in July 1972, she declined to offer a formal exhibition of her powers, explaining that she wasn't physically up to it. Nevertheless, she surprised Herbert with an impromptu PK demonstration outside his Leningrad hotel. He recounts the experience in a 1972 issue of *Parapsychology Review*:

"Kulagina gripped my left arm about two inches above the wrist . . . and I waited, not quite knowing what to expect. If anything, I thought I may feel some beneficial or soothing influence, but for two minutes, I felt nothing whatever, save only a natural increase of warmth under her hands. Then, quite abruptly, I experienced a new sensation, which I described at the time as a kind of 'heat' but which now, after much reflection, I believe to be more akin to a mild electric shock. It was however enough to be quite unpleasant; my arm writhed and my face grimaced to the amusement of the onlookers. After perhaps two minutes, I came to the conclusion that I could not endure the sensation a moment longer, and disengaged my arm from Kulagina's formidable handclasp. One interesting feature was that throughout these two minutes, the sensation as far as I could judge remained quite constant; and it began suddenly as if with the turning on of a switch. There was no gradual build-up of sensation and discomfort such as might have been expected through someone gripping one's arm too tightly."

Kulagina, like the great mediums of the nineteenth century, frequently found herself unable—or indisposed—to exercise her startling talents under controlled conditions. To many scientists, this only showed that psi is not a predictable, always available power (a fact which makes the notion of psi-based mind control ridiculous). In other scientists, however, this failure provoked skepticism. If Kulagina truly possessed and controlled such strong PK capabilities, why couldn't she demonstrate them more consistently and impressively in front of scientists? If she could tease observers with all sorts of strange effects outside the laboratory, why did she fail to perform more carefully structured experiments? The on-again, off-again abilities of so many paranormal "performers" is more evidence of quackery to the skeptics.

This issue is even more nettlesome in the case of Uri Geller. Born in Tel Aviv in 1946, Geller first became aware of his PK powers very early. When his mother gave him a watch on his seventh birthday, he realized that he could move the hands ten or fifteen minutes forward or backward just by staring at the dial. Shortly after completing his military obligations, he decided to capitalize on his unusual talent. He became the star of his own conjuring show, with a varied repertoire that included guessing names written on a concealed blackboard, psychokinetically repairing watches, and—the biggest crowd-pleaser of all—bending metal simply by touching it lightly.

Curious about reports of Geller's capabilities that were starting to filter through the international scientific community, Russell Targ and Harold Puthoff invited him to SRI for a series of tests in 1972. Targ and Puthoff were more interested in verifying Geller's ESP powers than his PK powers, and they did this by placing Geller in a sealed chamber and having him describe drawings that were placed on the wall in a remote room. They subjected Geller to a few PK experiments, such as asking him to alter the readings on a magnetometer and offset a one-gram weight placed on an electric scale, but the results of these tests were disappointing. Informally, however, Geller was able to entertain them with a number of spontaneous effects—breaking rings in a living room, interrupting television signals in the lab, and bending spoons in a cafeteria. This baffling inconsistency, coupled with Geller's own flamboyant personality, made Targ and Puthoff very cautious about their claims. Targ, for example, who is interested in magic and therefore especially sensitive to the fine line between fact and illusion, offers this comment in the book *Mind Reach*, which he coauthored with Puthoff:

"To summarize our work with Uri, in the total time that we spent working with him, we must have seen dozens of objects move, bend, and break. It often looked as though they were bent by paranormal means. However, our job was to separate the wheat from the chaff, and we summarily rejected any data obtained under circumstances which might *in principle* permit a nonparanormal hypothesis, even in those cases in which there was no evidence for the proposed alternative. Critics of our work often overlook the fact that as physicists we are the ones who have the greatest motivation to insure that we do not waste the next ten years of our lives writing equations for possibly nonexistent phenomena. Thus we consider only those data we observed under controlled conditions where there was no known possibility for error.

"The experiments conducted under rigid conditions left no doubt as to Uri's paranormal perceptual ability. We are not saying that he doesn't have psychokinetic ability also; we simply were not able to establish it to our satisfaction. The response to our reported results is about evenly divided between those who are upset with us for finding Uri has any paranormal ability and those who are upset with us for not finding more."

On November 23, 1973, Uri Geller appeared on television in Britain and allegedly used his mental powers to bend keys and cutlery and to restart watches that were said to be broken. Much more significant, however, was the fact that scores of viewers wrote in claiming that PK effects occurred in their homes while they were watching the broadcast: Spoons and forks curled up in drawers, small objects flew about in the air, and clocks that had long before ceased to function suddenly started up again! It was immediately dubbed "the mini-Geller effect" and Uri Geller instantly became a worldwide celebrity.

Unhappily for science, this sudden fame and the controversy surrounding it eventually removed Geller from the world of controlled experiments and public performance and sent him into the world of practical business. When I asked Geller about his life since then, he confided:

"I decided to start working mainly for very large companies. For some I've found oil; for some, gold; for some, copper. The very large companies that I've worked for are the ones that dare because they are not afraid of the word 'ridicule.' Still, they instructed me not to talk much about it, because they were afraid of controversy with stockholders. So I've been laughing all the way to the bank while the parapsychologists are jumping all over, saying, 'Does he use sleight-of-hand? Does he have laser beams in his belt buckle?' " (See Chapter 6 for more on Uri Geller.)

The reported PK feats of Sri Sathya Sai Baba are even stranger than the reported PK feats of Kulagina and Geller. In the course of Sai Baba's forty-year career as a religious leader in southern India, thousands of his followers have claimed to witness materializations, levitations, out-of-body experiences, and psychic healings. Parapsychologists Erlendur Haraldsson and Karlis Osis visited him several times between 1972 and 1976 and became personally convinced that he genuinely possesses PK ability, although they had to be content with informal demonstrations. In their report to the

American Society for Psychical Research, they explain Sai Baba's reluctance to be a laboratory subject:

"He tends to belittle the significance of his own psychic phenomena, calling them 'small items,' and he repeatedly stresses the importance of spiritual and ethical issues. Our bid for formal experiments was rejected with the comment that he would only use his paranormal powers for religious purposes such as helping his devotees when they are in dire need or for invoking faith in hitherto agnostic persons, but never for purely demonstrative purposes."

Sai Baba did treat Haraldsson and Osis to numerous spur-of-the-moment apparent displays of PK. He "materialized" holy ash and holy oil (substances that would be difficult to conceal without leaving traces), a gold ring, and even a 29-inch necklace of bulky stones. In each materialization, he would close his fist without having touched anything, then open it and reveal the object lying on his palm. Frequently he permitted Haraldsson and Osis to examine his clothing ahead of time, so they could try to eliminate the possibility that he might have concealed the object on his person. Interviews were never prearranged and always occurred outdoors or in a completely bare concrete room (which they very carefully inspected) where he holds daily public audience.

One of his most inexplicable acts was to make an enamel picture disappear from a ring (which he originally "materialized") that Osis was wearing. The picture was oval, about 1 inch by ¾ inch, and secured to the ring itself by a circular rim on both sides and four evenly spaced protruding notches on the top. Here is their description of what happened:

"In an interview during our second visit when we tried to persuade Sai Baba to participate in some controlled experiments, he seemed to become impatient and said to K.O., 'Look at your ring.' The picture had disappeared from it. We looked for it on the floor, but no trace of it could be found. The frame and the notches that should have held the picture were undamaged; we examined them afterwards with a magnifying glass. For the picture to have fallen out of the frame, it would have been necessary to bend at least one of the notches and probably also to bend the frame at some point, but neither had been done. . . . When Sai Baba made us aware of the picture's absence we were sitting on the floor about five or six feet away from him. We had not shaken hands when we entered the room and he did not reach out to us or touch us. As we sat cross-legged on the floor, K.O. had his hands on his thighs and E.H. had noticed the picture in the ring during the interview and before this incident occurred. E.H.'s first reaction was that the picture had suddenly become transparent. . . . When the picture could not be found, Sai Baba somewhat teasingly remarked, 'This was my experiment.' "

OBEs AND TRANCE CHANNELING AS MANIFESTATIONS OF PK

Two other categories of mediumship deserve mention in the context of psychokinesis: the out-of-body experience (OBE) and trance channeling—the apparent transmission of the spoken word, music, artistry, or writing from disincarnate spirits. These topics will be covered in more detail in Chapter Ten, but let's look at a few examples here.

Ruth Montgomery was a syndicated political columnist and former president of the Women's National Press Club, and she was a skeptic when she began investigating psychic phenomena twenty-five years ago. Under the posthumous spiritual tutelage of famous medium Arthur Ford, however, she gradually developed an extraordinary talent for automatic writing. She admits that she felt foolish when she began experimenting by holding a pencil lightly poised above a sheet of paper:

"Nothing happened. Simply nothing. And after giving it a few minutes each morning I would throw down the pencil and dash off to the Capitol or the White House to earn an honest living. At last, on the tenth morning, some otherworldly force of Herculean strength seemed to grab my hand, and although my eyes were closed, it propelled the pencil into circles and figure eights with such pressure that I thought the lead point would break. I could not have dropped it if I'd tried."

Ultimately more inspiring messages were delivered by a succession of "guides," and Montgomery has since published these messages in a series of best-selling books.

Self-styled "trance painters" and "automatic writers" have demonstrated remarkable feats in the presence of scientists and laypersons alike, but whether or not the limbs of these demonstrators were psychically driven to produce the images or words of dead people remains a matter of personal belief. Skeptics believe such feats are likely to be psychological in nature. What lends credence in some cases to the explanation of psychic channeling is one (or both) of two conditions: Either the products are executed in a manner that the medium is seemingly incapable of reproducing in his or her normal state, or the products bear an unusually close affinity to the works (or possible works) of a person who is no longer alive.

Luiz Antonio Gasparetto is a Brazilian psychologist who has performed hundreds of public trance-painting sessions during the past twenty years. In an astonishingly short period of time (averaging from five minutes to a half an hour), he is able to create a "new" masterpiece by an old master. Not only is his range impressive (he has successfully executed the styles of Leonardo, Rembrandt, Van Gogh, Renoir, Lautrec, Matisse, Modigliani, and Picasso, among others), but he uses no brushes. He paints with his feet as well as his hands, and occasionally channels one artist through his left arm, another through his right arm, and a third through his feet at the same time!

Gasparetto is convinced that the disincarnate masters paint through him for the sole purpose of revealing that life continues after death. His description of what happens to him during a typical trance-painting episode indicates that some sort of psychokinetic force may be at work:

"At the onset I feel a telepathic invitation to work. This is followed by my sensing the fluidic presence of other artist-spirits. Immediately a force overpowers my arms, moving them automatically. I am not guiding them by my intention. I feel the muscles of my arms in response to the spirit's wishes. It is clear to me that my will is free and that I can stop if I want to. However, I am inclined to abandon my own wishes and give myself to whatever happens with this work."

Whatever accounts for Gasparetto's capabilities, the public demonstrations easily persuade observers that some powerful form of inspiration is occurring. Writer Darlene Moore gave me this report of a session held at Fort Mason in San Francisco on the evening of August 11, 1986:

"Keith [Harary, Moore's husband] and I arrived at 7:25, and the demonstration began ten to fifteen minutes after that. It took place in a large, dark room (even with the lights "up," before the demonstration, it was dark). The room was very warm. A woman gave Luiz a brief introduction, saying he has had these experiences since he was a child (I think thirteen years old), that he prefers to work in the dark, and that the most important thing was that the audience be quiet and still through the demonstration. Luiz then walked in and

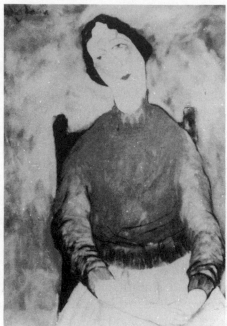

"MODIGLIANI" CHANNELED
THROUGH LUIZ GASPARETTO

"TOULOUSE LAUTREC"
CHANNELED THROUGH LUIZ
GASPARETTO

"VAN GOGH" CHANNELED
THROUGH LUIZ GASPARETTO

spoke for a short time. He said he didn't know what would happen, but he knew that the 'spirits' were there—that he'd made the arrangements with them earlier so no one would be disappointed.

"The lights were turned down and Luiz put on a tape. It was an assortment of classical music that alternated between very tranquil and very stirring selections. The combination of the music, the lighting, Luiz' movements, and the heat seemed to have an almost hypnotic effect on the audience. The demonstration lasted approximately forty minutes. During that time Luiz did at least five drawings and three acrylic paintings.

"I have no idea what was happening during the demonstration, but it appeared to be a mixture of fantasy and inspiration. It was quite an experience. Eight pieces in forty minutes doesn't allow much time for a piece—several of them very interesting. (As someone later pointed out, what kind of work could any great artist do in a few minutes?) Luiz' hands move incredibly fast, and his body moves and gyrates while he works. Through the demonstration, a man steadied the paper or canvas for him. When I noticed, he seemed to work in time with the music. Most of the time, but not always, he looked away from a piece while he worked on it. The first drawing, a 'Rembrandt' in one color, was drawn upside down. The two faces in another were drawn simultaneously, using both hands.

"When the demonstration was over, Luiz thanked God and the spirits for the opportunity to serve them. The lights were turned on and the woman who introduced Luiz wrote on the back of each piece the time it took to complete it. She said the works were for sale and that all proceeds, less expenses for supplies, go to charity."

The out-of-body experience (OBE) is an event during which a person has the sensation of his or her consciousness becoming independent of the body. Throughout the ages, OBEs have been reported by mystics, dreamers, and people who have come close to dying (the so-called near-death experience, or NDE, discussed in Chapter 10). An experiment conducted at the Psychical Research Foundation in Durham, North Carolina, was designed to examine whether out-of-body experiences have any objective reality—in other words, if the sensation felt by the subject of the OBE is associated with any objectively verifiable effects.

The experiment involved both Keith Harary, who is able to self-induce OBEs, and Harary's pet kitten. The kitten was placed in a large container while Harary lay down in a distant room to engage in a series of OBEs. The experimenters, Harary included, wanted to see whether the kitten could detect the presence of Harary's "second body" when it visited the container. Harary was able to signal his fellow experimenters when he was entering an OBE state and when that state was over, and records of these times were later compared with records kept by other experimenters watching the kitten. During non-OBE periods, the kitten was noisy (recording thirty-seven meows during the sessions), active, and anxious to get out of the container. During the times when Harary was experiencing an OBE and focused on the container, the kitten became noticeably quiet and calm. The same behavior emerged throughout four experimental sessions!

GROUP DYNAMICS AND PK

The shift away from the laboratory to the field in the world of PK research is perhaps best exemplified by the growing popularity of grass-roots experimentation. Three widespread social phenomena in particular are receiving more and more attention from the mass media: sitters' groups, PK parties (featuring metal-bending and seed-sprouting), and fire-walking seminars.

PK SITTERS' GROUPS

Sitters' groups hark back to the nineteenth-century days of seances and table-rapping parties. Usually, the same procedure is involved: Individuals gather around a table in a semi-darkened room and attempt to summon a disincarnate spirit or psychokinetic force. In some cases, they practice group concentration, meditation, or visualization; in other cases, they enter some sort of trance state.

In at least one memorable instance, however, the traditional protocol was modified with noteworthy results. During the early seventies, several members of the Society for Psychical Research in Toronto decided to meet regularly in an effort to conjure an apparition that they themselves would create. They invented "Philip," a seventeenth-century English nobleman who committed suicide in remorse over the death of his gypsy mistress, Margo. One of the group members even drew a sketch of Philip in his full aristocratic regalia. The group met every week for a year and attempted to invoke Philip through meditation. Nothing happened. Finally, in the summer of 1973, they tried a new approach, suggested by the writings of K. J. Batcheldor, the leader of several British sitters' groups. Instead of maintaining an atmosphere of quiet attentiveness, the members started directing jokes, songs, and playful exhortations at "Philip." The shift in strategy quickly paid off. According to Iris Owen, leader of the "Philip group":

"One evening, during the third or fourth new session, the group felt a vibrating within the table top, somewhat like a knock or rap. It is correct to say 'felt' rather than 'heard,' because the group was making a degree of noise at the moment so that the unexpected action within the table took them completely by surprise. They were not expecting anything of that nature, so nobody could say for sure whether they *heard* the vibration as a noise, although everybody *felt* the vibration."

Establishing a code of one rap for "yes" and two raps for "no," the group members actually began talking with "Philip," who confirmed almost every aspect of the biography they had created! He did make some changes, however. In keeping with his image as a cavalier under King Charles, he claimed that he was not in love with Margo, insisting that it was only a case of sexual infatuation.

When I spoke with Lawrence LeShan, who analyzed tapes of several Philip-group sessions as well as the actual table they used in their gatherings, he said:

"An oscilloscope pattern of a tap on a sheet of paper or a hard surface is typically high up or high down, and then it tapers off. The Philip taps, on the other hand, are high up or high down or a straight line. There is no tapering off, which is very strange. I spent an hour with that table, trying to produce something like that oscilloscope pattern. I hit it with everything from a paper clip to my toes, till I nearly bit the damned thing. I could not reproduce that pattern."

PK PARTIES: METAL-BENDING AND SEED-SPROUTING

Uri Geller's television appearances in 1973 inspired many people to try out their own PK powers on household silverware. Even without the benefit of a standard procedure to follow, many of their attempts were successful. Self-help workshop leaders were quick to see the potential of metal-bending as a programmatic exercise: It seemed to offer immediate, tangible proof that you can do wonders if you set your mind to it. Since then, metal-bending parties, hosted by all sorts of people who are successful at motivating people and intrigued by mind-over-matter phenomena, have proliferated throughout the United States and Great Britain.

Diana Gazes, a television interviewer and producer who conducts workshops in the New York City area, calls the metal-bending facility "warm-forming" (as do many other metal-benders) and claims that everyone possesses this capability. At her workshops, guests bring their own silverware and run through a variety of techniques for focusing their warm-forming energies, such as doing yogic breath exercises, following guided visualizations, and watching videotapes of people bending forks and spoons. Eventually, the party guests are asked to concentrate on bending the particular spoon or fork they are holding. Usually, the majority of people are able to do this. One such person, a friend of mine who is a prominent attorney, offered the following account of the Diana Gazes session he attended during the summer of 1986:

"There were about fifteen people there, ranging in age from midtwenties to mid-sixties, I would say. There was a teacher, a young paramedic who was entering medical school, an airline hostess, people who had seen Gazes' television show, and people who had heard about metal-bending and wanted to explore their psychic potential in the latest fashion. I was one of two people who told Diana, in answer to her question, that I didn't believe I would bend metal that night. I was somewhat put off by her long spiel and some of the 'New Age' rap that seemed to be part of the evening's package.

"Diana led us through a couple of relaxation exercises, which included breathing and guided imagery, and you could actually feel an increase in some kind of energy in the room. She described the metal-bending process in detail and had us watch films of other groups— some of them TV audiences—bending metal. That was pretty convincing. I didn't know what to expect when she took us through the guided imagery, which was to lead to the actual bending: 'Picture a white light coming down through your head, into your shoulders, etc. . . .' But sure enough, when we all chanted, 'bend, bend, bend,' one woman immediately was able to bend her fork as if it were so much putty. She was astonished and thrilled and began picking up one spoon or fork after another, bending them every which way, exclaiming gleefully with each bend, as we all looked on. Then another person bent, then another. Sometimes, the time during which one could bend lasted for just a second or two; for others, it lasted for twenty or thirty seconds, then the metal would return to normal consistency—rigid, unbendable without a great deal of strength.

"We repeated the imagery process, and this time more people joined those who were able to bend the metal—myself included. A pile of mangled forks and spoons accumulated. In the next round, those who had easily bent metal stood behind those who were still trying to do it, lending their 'energy' to the effort. At one point, one woman was holding a fork by the handle; as we all looked on, the tines of the fork slowly bent and twisted as though they were the petals of a flower in a soft breeze. I can't explain how it felt to bend the metal—it was as though it melted in my hand. It had nothing to do with strength—once the moment passed, it was as hard as ever. But there's no question that I did it, and that I, and everyone who applies himself, have the ability to do this, or any other 'impossible' task."

"When you focus your mental energy on a metal spoon or fork," Gazes claims, "a 'window in time' opens up, and for about two to thirty seconds, the metal becomes warm and soft enough to bend." A more scientific explanation has not been forthcoming, although electron-microscope photographs of PK-bent metal compared with strength-bent metal show significant differences. Lab investigation seems to show that PK-bent metal becomes magnetic at the point of bending, while strength-bent metal does not.

Jack Houck, an advanced-systems technologist at the McDonnell Douglas Corporation, claims to have organized the first PK parties in 1981 and has held more than fifty since then (including a recent party in Vancouver, British Columbia, with four hundred attendees). Usually, Houck's parties focus exclusively on metal-bending, but from time to time he has tried seed-sprouting. Soybean seeds are placed in water at the beginning of a party. Near the end of the party, a few of the beans are placed in the open hands of each guest. According to Houck, at every party, much to the guests' amazement, the beans held in about half of the hands quickly pop open and a few actually grow a small sprout.

"There are not enough data or controlled experimentation at this time to postulate what might be happening in or around the seeds," Houck admits. In searching for an explanation for what is physically happening during metal-bending, Houck speculates:

"Most of the time, the person doing the warm-forming reports feeling the silverware or other object become warm as if heat were coming from inside the object. It is postulated that, somehow, the mind is creating the conditions for energy, of unknown form, to be deposited along the grain boundaries of the metal. The dislocations may somehow act as transducers to receive this energy, possibly from some other dimension. Whatever the form of the energy as it is transduced into the metal grain boundaries, it is then partially converted to heat. This is the same conversion that occurs with a microwave oven, in that the electromagnetic energy is converted to heat when it is attenuated by the meat. In the metal, the grain boundaries become very hot, possibly even molten. When a large portion of the metal has soft grain boundaries, the grains are free to slip or float and the metal temporarily loses its rigidity."

The skeptics, of course, consider all of this highly suspect, and feel that the workshop leaders are putting the participants into a hypnotic state in which they "see" the metal being bent. If so, they are fooling a lot of the people a lot of the time.

FIRE-WALKING

Unlike metal-bending or seed-sprouting, fire-walking has an extensive history as a means of demonstrating the power of the mind over the physical universe. It has appeared indigenously as a spiritual exercise in cultures all over the world: in Greece and Sri Lanka, Fiji and Siberia, Japan and Brazil. The format is virtually the same in each case: A person walks barefoot across a bed of glowing coals—either wood or mineral—and is then examined to see if he or she escaped being burned. As a modern workshop phenomenon, it came of age side by side with metal-bending.

One of the most popular fire-walking workshops is Anthony Robbins' "Fear into Power: The Firewalk Experience." Its sessions consist of chanting and "psych-ups" that empower a person to walk with fire immunity across an 8-foot bed of red-hot coals after about a couple of hours of indoctrination. A part of Robbins' prewalk pep talk is asking participants to go back in their minds to a time when they were "entirely loved and comfortable, creative, confident, curious—like a child."

Robbins credits his powers as an indoctrinator, as well as a firewalker, to "Neurolinguistic Programming," or NLP, which he describes as a "technology for creating transformational experiences and for understanding and influencing others." NLP was developed by a group of therapists and linguists who drew on the techniques of such famous psychologists as Milton Erickson, Virginia Satir, Gregory Bateson, and Fritz Perls. Unlike more traditional psychotherapies, NLP attaches less importance to discovering the "content" of a problem and more importance to attacking its "structure," through a combination of self-suggestion and experimentation in "reality shifts."

Larissa Vilenskaya who "fire-walked" under the guidance of Tolly Burkan, shared these reflections with me:

"The result is not only that there's no burn and no pain—it's a state of 'high': at first, the deep satisfaction that you accomplished something, then the feeling that you are able to do anything. I was skeptical of all this 'positive thinking' talk when I went to Burkan. But then, among all those people there, I had a kind of flash revelation: I have the same skin, the same flesh as these people who have just walked. They are standing there smiling—nothing happened to them; why can't you be calm and do it? And I just did it."

Not surprisingly, fire-walking as a PK demonstration has met with a great deal of skepticism. Some scientists insist that fire immunity in such situations is due to the Leidenfrost effect, whereby a liquid exposed to intense heat—such as a drop of water hitting a hot skillet —will immediately create an insulating layer of steam. Their argument is that the feet of the fire-walker perspire and trigger this protective Leidenfrost effect. Other scientists dismiss this argument as nonsense, especially given the fact that people not "psyched up" to fire-walk are easily burned when their feet step on a hot coal. Whatever one's point of view, however, the fact remains that fire-walking as such is not amenable to rigid scientific examination. Bernard Leikind, a physicist at UCLA who has his doubts about both fire-walking as a PK effect and the relevance of the Leidenfrost effect, points out, "It's not a controlled experiment. People have different feet, different ways of walking, and they take different paths over the coals. It's not that you *cannot* get burned; it's just that it's not nearly as likely as it looks."

INTERLUDE · TWO
MORE TALES
OF THE
PARANORMAL

A psychoanalyst tells me this curious tale about one of his patients: "She has fond memories of visiting her great-aunt as a little girl, and having her aunt read to her from A. A. Milne. Many years later, while in Paris on her honeymoon, she was browsing in one of those bookstalls along the Seine, and spotted a copy of her beloved Milne. She picked it up—to find that it was inscribed to her from her great-aunt: It was the same copy that had been read to her."

Dr. Jerry Goldfisher, chief of medicine at Englewood (New Jersey) Hospital, had this to say to me: "I don't believe in any of the work you're doing, but I must tell you two stories that have baffled me for years.

"One night when I was in medical school, six other students and I were fooling around with a Ouija board for the first time (this was November 1941), and we asked when the invasion would take place that would stop Hitler's Reich. The board said, 'June 6.' When the Normandy invasion actually took place on that date in 1944, we called each other, remembering the Ouija prediction. I truly can't explain this incident.

"The other story concerns a patient who came to me saying that he knew he was going to die on a particular date five years away. After examining him, I could find nothing wrong, physically or mentally. Yet he insisted he would die. In the interim, he invented and marketed 'Paint-by-Numbers' and made a good deal of money for his family.

"He applied for life insurance, and the company contacted me. I reported the man's strange premonition, but also told them I could find nothing wrong. They sent him for a psychiatric evaluation, which he passed, so they insured him.

"A week before he'd claimed he would die he checked into the hospital. All the tests we took were negative. When I visited him on the day he'd named, he was shaving, combing his hair, preparing himself. He died in my arms later that day. An autopsy showed no pathological cause. Could he have willed it? I don't know."

From a professor at a small Eastern college I received this story: "I was walking quickly across campus, late for my class, when I ran across a colleague going the other way. I nodded to him, told him I was in a hurry to catch my bus; he nodded in acknowledgment. When I got to class, the students were buzzing about something; I had a hard time calling them to order. When I asked them what all the tizzy was about, they told me that the professor that I had just run into had died almost two hours earlier."

Theodore Dreiser, the famous American writer, claimed that he was once visited by the spirit of a living friend, John Cowper Powys.

Powys had come to dinner at Dreiser's Manhattan home one evening; and as he was about to leave for his place in the country, he said to Dreiser, "I'll appear before you, right here, later this evening. You'll see me."

"Are you going to turn yourself into a ghost or have you a key to the door?" Dreiser laughed.

"I don't know," said Powys. "I may return as a spirit or in some other astral form."

Dreiser gave no further thought that evening to Powys' promise; but two hours later, as he sat reading all alone, he looked up and saw Powys standing in the doorway between the entrance hall and the living room. The "apparition" had Powys' features, his tall stature, loose tweed garments, and general appearance, but a pale white glow shone from the figure. Dreiser rose at once and strode toward the ghost, or whatever it was, saying, "Well, you've kept your word, John. You're here. Come in and tell me how you did it." The apparition did not reply, and it vanished when Dreiser was three feet from it.

As soon as he had recovered somewhat from this astonishment, Dreiser picked up the telephone and called Powys' house in the country. Powys came to the phone. After he had heard the story of the apparition, Powys said, "I told you I'd be there, and you oughtn't to be surprised." Dreiser was never able to get any explanation from Powys, who refused to discuss the matter.

An especially strange tale was reported in *Newsweek*, January 20, 1986. It involves fifteen-year-old Felipe Garza, who had a crush on a high school classmate, fourteen-year-old Donna Ashlock. Donna suddenly began gasping for breath at the fast-food stand where she worked after school, and where Felipe hung around trying to get her attention. She was diagnosed as having cardiomyopathy—a weakening of the heart muscle—and was given six to eight weeks to live unless a heart for transplant was found.

"I'm going to die so I can give my heart to my girlfriend," Felipe told his mother. Since his parents were not aware that he had recently experienced blackouts and headaches, they paid little attention. Less than two weeks later, a blood vessel burst in Felipe's head, and he was declared brain-dead by the time he reached the hospital. His donated heart saved Donna's life.

In the small upstate community of Canandaigua, New York, on July 25, 1984, two brothers, Michael and Christopher Stott, collapsed and died in separate incidents ninety-two minutes apart, without warning, and for no apparent reason. Michael had been with his girlfriend and another couple at his friend's house watching TV, after having gone bowling, when he suddenly couldn't catch his breath. His friends tried to administer CPR (cardiopulmonary resuscitation, an emergency lifesaving technique) while they called an ambulance and his mother. He died at the hospital an hour later. The mother returned home, where her sister had been called in to watch Michael's young brother, Christopher. When the son heard the news, he had a near-identical attack, was rushed to the same emergency room, and died. The boys' hearts have been microscopically examined at the National Institutes of Health and no irregularities were found. The case has been gone over thoroughly by many medical researchers; many theories have been pursued and abandoned, although one promising one led to a dead end when the cooperation of the boys' (estranged) father could not be enlisted.

There are a couple of interesting sidelights. Two weeks before the deaths, the boys were riding home from the Fourth of July fireworks with their mother when Christopher demanded, screaming, that she pull the car over. He leaped from the car when it stopped and ran around it screaming, "I'm going to die! I'm going to die!" When he calmed down, he refused to explain himself. On the day he died, he didn't want to let his mother out of his sight. Michael's girlfriend, Tracy Baglio, claims that Michael has appeared to her several times since his death: "There was nothing weird about him. He was dressed like he was always dressed. . . . He sat down next to me and told me that he had come to give me a message. He wanted me to tell his mother that he and Christopher were fine and that she shouldn't worry."

Montanan Sally Vargo was walking through a department store with her daughter when suddenly she saw a vision of a fire. As the vision became clearer, she saw a house on fire. She heard the screams of children in an upstairs bedroom, and then a woman trying to get into the house. "She couldn't get past the flames. And I recognized her—she was my next-door neighbor!" Mrs. Vargo snapped out of her trance, grabbed her little girl's hand and ran screaming for a phone. The manager of the store stopped her, and she told him that her neighbor's house was on fire and she had to call the fire department. "Fortunately, he didn't ask how I knew that, and he dialed the phone and handed it to me." Her vision was truly precognitive, because when the fire department arrived, the house was not yet engulfed in flames; the electrical fire in the basement had recently started and was put out before any real damage occurred. But the firemen confirmed that the house would have been completely engulfed in but a few minutes.

George Flours was working on street repairs 10 feet underground with his partner, James Gray, when he had a sudden premonition that an explosion was going to occur. When his partner didn't believe him, he grabbed him by the collar and pulled him out of the hole and ordered everyone to duck. But nothing happened. "The guys started swearing at me, and after a few seconds everyone started to get up; then—*wham!*—an explosion lifted everyone about a foot off the ground." There were two minor injuries, but it could have been worse, because the underground hole was completely filled with rubble.

German parapsychology researcher Hans Bender has among his case histories the following tale of precognition: A man had a dream in which the driver of a hearse said to him, "Come with us." Weeks later, while visiting Paris, he was about to get into a newly installed rapid elevator in a department store when he recognized the elevator operator as the hearse driver from his dream. Startled, he didn't get on the elevator. Moments later, the cable of the elevator snapped, plunging the elevator into the basement, killing and injuring many of those aboard.

On October 10, 1984, parapsychologist Russell Targ, along with six Soviet scientists, went to the home of Moscow psychic Djuna Davitashvili for a long-distance remote-viewing test. They had with them photographs of six San Francisco landmarks, each in a sealed, numbered envelope. Davitashvili's task was to describe the location where Targ's partner, researcher Keith Harary, would be standing *four hours later*. She described a round structure with a cupola, in the center of a small plaza. Inside the round structure, she saw a profile of an animal's eye; the animal, she continued, had pointy ears. Four hours later, Harary randomly chose one of the six possible sites to visit. It turned out to be number 4, a merry-go-round on a pier in the center of a small plaza; the animals on board were horses with pointy ears.

• • •

On May 18, 1974, Dorothy Pritchett, a reporter for *The New Washington Sun*, went to a meeting conducted by psychic Tony Cordero. With her were her friend Virginia Anderson; Virginia's husband; their two sons, Jimmy and Jack; and Jack's fiancée. "As the evening progressed, Tony made many predictions to people in the audience, including myself, and related events that had occurred in the past. Tony then turned to Jack Henderson, my girlfriend's son, and Jack posed this question: 'Am I going to have a long life?' 'We all have to die sometime,' Tony answered. He warned Jack several times to be cautious, because he was going to be involved in a serious auto accident if he was not. Tony asked Jack if he had a new car, or if he planned to purchase a car, or if he had any friend with a car that was new or looked new. To all the questions Jack replied in the negative, though he was annoyed, because the conversation seemed to be leading nowhere. Tony again warned him to be careful if he happened to be riding in a friend's new car, because he visualized an accident involving Jack, a friend, and a speeding new car within the next three weeks. Jack was still expressing doubts after the meeting.

"Unfortunately, Tony's prediction came true with chilling accuracy. On Saturday, June 8, Jack was struck by a speeding car which looked shiny and new, a 1973 Chrysler, as a friend was walking with him. He died the next morning."

In his skeptic's guide to psychics in Dallas, Mark Donald relates a story about psychic Fan Benno. "Once during a reading, she got a strong sense that her client's name was Mary or Margaret; the client claimed her name was Janet. The information came in very strong, and Benno was troubled by the discrepancy. Janet had no knowledge of any Mary or Margaret; she had certainly never used those names herself. Several weeks later Benno heard from Janet. When she confronted her parents about the results of the reading, they admitted to her that she was adopted. The name on her original birth certificate was Margaret."

"I am not a believer in psychic phenomena," says Pam, the president of a marketing firm; "I can't accept these abilities." Yet she has had several "bouts" of apparently psychic experiences in her life. "They come in bunches, and when they happen the information coming through has a quality of absolute certainty. It started innocently enough, with a few incidents right together when I was about twenty-five. I was with my husband at the Hollywood Bowl when complete scenes from the movie *King Solomon's Mines* flashed before me, and I knew my husband was thinking about the movie. Without realizing what I was saying, I turned to my husband and said, 'I saw *King Solomon's Mines* too.' He was shocked. 'How did you know I was thinking about that?' Just a couple of days later I was on the phone with my mother and I had a vision of her going to the refrigerator and getting an apple. 'I'd like an apple too,' I said. The next incident happened a week or so later. My husband and I were watching a morning game show on television—*Jeopardy*. I was in a smart-alecky mood and I said to him, 'I'm going to answer every question.' And I did—every single one, sometimes before the question was complete. Then *To Tell the Truth* came on, and I said to Hal, 'See that guy? He's going to say that he has a collapsible boat in his closet, and he's the one telling the truth.' Of course that's just what happened. It freaked me out; I think I was so scared by it that I didn't have any more experiences for years.

"Then a few years ago, I had another spurt. Like I said, I still don't believe in this stuff. This time, every incident was a premonition of danger, and it would be preceded by a horrible feeling of grayness and dread, a feeling of stifling; it's hard to explain, but it wasn't pleasant. One afternoon I was hanging a picture, trying to straighten it on the wall, when I suddenly heard a sound like a million voices making a deep humming noise inside my head. It was awful, and I put down the picture. It stopped, so I picked up the picture and started in again. But the voices started up, and the room seemed to go gray. I dropped the picture. About twenty seconds later there was an earthquake.

"A few days later I was out with a guy I was dating, and I got that gray, dread feeling again. I couldn't ignore it and had to sort out the feeling, so I asked him what was happening with him. He told me that the next day he was catering a job on a yacht. 'Don't go on the yacht,' I told him; I didn't know why, but it connected with the bad feeling, and I warned him again. But I hadn't been able to give a reason, and he went. Well, he survived, but it was terrible. A freak storm came up; they didn't have their catered meal at all. Fighting the storm, the captain's arm got tangled in the ropes, and he severed an artery; no one could put on a tourniquet, and no one else aboard knew much about sailing. They were tossed about for more than three hours; one person went overboard (and was pulled back), and they almost capsized.

"The next time I got the feeling, I tried to go through the people and things in my life, and the feeling settled on my son, who wasn't home. I knew there was something wrong, and just waited with great anxiety. A couple of hours later he came home. 'Okay, what happened?' I said. His eyes got like saucers. 'How did you know? I wasn't going to say anything about it. I was driving with Bert and the car went out of control. We spun around and went through a red light, and came within an inch of ending up under a truck.'

"The last time it happened was about a week after that. I was in a friend's car driving on the freeway, in the rain, in heavy traffic. I turned to my friend and said, 'The car in front of the car in front of you is going to spin out. Be careful.' Ten or fifteen seconds later, the car two cars ahead went out of control, and several cars piled up. This really spooked me again. I am very uncomfortable with these things, and I haven't had any in a long time."

"You know I'm not a flake," said a friend of mine, "but your readers aren't going to know that. I have very clear memories of when I was a baby, of thinking and trying to communicate with my parents, but not being able to talk. This sounds crazy, but I can remember even before that. I told this to my therapist, but I waited until he knew me pretty well, so he wouldn't think I was a nut case. I remember when I was born. There had been very bright light, then suddenly I was born and it was dark and hard to see, and I thought, 'Oh, my God, what am I doing here?' and a voice—a voice I've heard a few other times in my life—said to me, 'You chose this. This is your mother, this is your father, this is what you wanted, you should make the best of it.' Then it was gone, and I forgot it. The next time I heard that voice, I was in a supermarket, and I was looking at a man behind me in a line, and the voice said, 'This is the man you are going to marry.' And, of course, it was."

By far the most fascinating and convincing accounts of reincarnation have been those researched by Ian Stevenson. Here is a typical example: Shanti Devi, born in Delhi, India, in 1926, was seven when she announced to her parents that she had been born before, in a town called Muttra. She described her previous life in great detail: She had been married and had died giving birth to her third child. Her parents paid little attention to her babblings until one day several years later, when Shanti claimed a businessman who had come to their house for the first time was her "husband's" cousin.

The businessman acknowledged that he was from Muttra and that he had a cousin who had lost his wife in childbirth ten years previously. Later, the "husband" was brought to the house; and Shanti, not told about the visitor, instantly seemed to recognize him and threw herself into his arms! When he then took her to Muttra, she correctly pointed out various people and places from her supposed previous life, and actually initiated conversations with former relatives in the local dialect, despite the fact that she had never encountered it as Shanti. A scientific commission investigating the case found that she was able to direct a carriage through Muttra even while blindfolded. The only person from her former life she was not able to recognize was her third child—whom she had never seen.

CHAPTER · SIX

WHAT IS IT LIKE TO BE PSYCHIC, AND WHAT ARE PSYCHICS LIKE?

"All mystics speak the same language and come from the same country."
—*The visionary Louis Claude de Saint-Martin*

One of the great pleasures of writing *Intangible Evidence* has been meeting some of the world's top psychics. What are these gifted individuals like, and what is it like to be psychic? It is very difficult to generalize, for while the cream-of-the-crop psychics share, in abundance, an ability that most of us have but a bit of, you would never be able to pick them out of a roomful of people at a cocktail party. In fact, you'd never expect to find some of them at a cocktail party to begin with—least of all at the *same* cocktail party.

Let me try to make a few broad generalizations. Most of them demonstrated their abilities very early, though there are exceptions —the controversial Peter Hurkos had the frightening experience of becoming instantly clairvoyant when he came out of a coma after a fall. It took him years to learn to cope with his abilities. Many psychics grew up with at least one family member who was understanding and supportive. Ingo Swann had his psychic grandmother Anna. Alex Tanous' mother herself had psychic abilities, and saved her son from danger several times; his father's friend Kahlil Gibran had predicted before he was born that he would be psychic. Uri Geller's mother played psychic guessing games with him. Not many were as lucky as Beatrice Rich, who was fortunate to have a mother who consulted a psychic to find out how to handle her precocious daughter's abilities.

Having psychic abilities may seem fascinating and romantic, but they have often been a trial and a burden for many; coping with such ill-understood powers calls for enormous inner strength. Supportive family notwithstanding, most psychics had terrible childhood difficulties because of their psychic abilities—they were ostracized and feared by their peers, discredited by neighbors or teachers who refused to believe them. Many had a difficult time assimilating and understanding their own gifts. Several actually repressed their abilities out of fear, or in order to be accepted. Ingo Swann made a conscious decision at the age of eleven to stop traveling among the stars, so that he could be like others, and be a part of "normal" life. Eileen Garrett spent her adult life trying to understand the psychic powers that had caused her so much anguish, and to bring about a more widespread acceptance and understanding of psychic abilities.

Alex Tanous had a horrible experience which made him withdraw and deny his psychic abilities for years: Soon after he told a playmate who taunted him that he hoped he would die, the boy became ill and died; Tanous was terrified that he had caused it, though the child died in an unrelated accident. Years later, Tanous wrote *Is Your Child Psychic?* with the express purpose of helping parents to recognize and encourage their children's psychic abilities, to avoid the youthful traumas he experienced.

There have been reports of psychics who were diagnosed as crazy before they recognized or came to terms with their unusual gifts. Who knows how many psychics have been destroyed by their abilities, or have languished in mental institutions, victims of ignorance and lack of support? Probably because of the difficulties they have had to face in coming to grips with their abilities and in coping with the derision and doubt of others, the people I interviewed, as a group, struck me as strong, sound, well-integrated, highly individualistic personalities.

There, though, the similarities end. As Beatrice Rich notes, "I've seen these abilities in all kinds of people, in odd shapes and places. I don't think education or intelligence has anything to do with it." I agree with her. The temperaments, the personalities, the lifestyles of the great psychics have little in common. Some use their powers for money, some for the greater glory of God, many to help mankind. They all have different ways of operating, and different areas in which they function best—usually because of their particular temperaments and interests. Swann, scientific and inquisitive, is as much the researcher as the researched; he's probably never done a private psychic reading in his life. During his "travels," Ingo sits in a chair smoking a cigar, with his eyes wide open; he "flies" to Jupiter to get a look at the planet before *Pioneer 10* gets there. Beatrice Rich does private readings and works mostly within a framework of six months in either direction. Garrett had her spirit guides who spoke to her while she was in a trance. Ruth Montgomery's guides speak to her through automatic writing. Edgar Cayce made his uncanny medical diagnoses while in a sleep-like state. Peter Hurkos found bodies; Clarisa Bernhardt predicts earthquakes.

Spending time with highly gifted psychic practitioners is something I recommend to all skeptics—though, predictably, the most avid skeptics are usually the most resistant to meeting someone with such abilities. On dozens of occasions now, I have "treated" my skeptical friends to a reading with a top psychic or astrologer or tarot-card reader. They go in saying, "I'm not going to tell them anything," or "They'll just rattle off generalizations and expect me to read into it what I want"—the usual skeptic's rap. I don't try to argue. "Let me know how it goes," I request. I don't usually have to wait long. "That was the most incredible experience I've ever had," they may begin, and then keep me on the phone for half an hour with all the things the psychic told them about their spouse or kids or co-worker. Or they come back with their tails between their legs, their arguments totally deflated, babbling semi-incoherently. "I don't understand it, you must have told him about me . . . " It becomes very hard to hold on to one's cherished worldview in the presence of the genuine article. It goes far beyond "cold reading"—the kind of magician's art based on body language and inadvertent clues. It's far more specific, almost impossible to write off as generalities. In his introduction to his biography of Alex Tanous, *Beyond Coincidence*, Harvey Ardman speaks of doing a "180-degree" flip-flop from his long-held views about science and rationality, of abandoning the beliefs of a lifetime. "I still feel shaken," he confesses.

In the interest of a better understanding of psychic abilities, many researchers—prominent among them Gertrude Schmeidler, Charles Honorton, John Palmer, and Charles Tart—have devoted a great deal of energy to an attempt to define the psychic temperament. Except for a few broad generalizations, however, their efforts have mostly proved fruitless, for the psychic temperament doesn't always fit a carefully prescribed niche. To sum up a great deal of research very glibly: Generally well-adjusted people who believe in psychic phenomena do best in tests of psychic ability. It was Gertrude Schmeidler who first made the distinction, identifying "sheep," those who believed in psi and who performed better on tests than the skeptical "goats." Charles Honorton has accumulated a great deal of data which correlate success in his *Ganzfeld* remote-viewing and low-level PK experiments with a personality profile classified as ENFP—Extroverted (rather than introverted), Intuitive (rather than sensing), Feeling (rather than thinking), Perceiving (rather than judging)—as determined by scores in the Myers-Briggs Personality Type Indicator test.

But these distinctions apply mostly to psychic ability in the general population, not to your top-of-the-line psychic. Talking to the psychics themselves is the best way to see the scope of their abilities, the various ways they work, their varying motives and temperaments. A visit with a sampling of psychics—based predominantly on my personal interviews with them—will give you a feel for what it's like to operate in their rarefied world and how their lives are different from ours—and the same as well.

CLARISA BERNHARDT

Clarisa Bernhardt has her psychic finger in many pies, but she is best known to the public as "The Earthquake Lady." One day in 1974, Clarisa predicted over station KIEV in her hometown of San Jose, California, that an earthquake would hit a particular area of central California on Thanksgiving Day at about 3 P.M. The earthquake hit at 3:01, and Clarisa's life hasn't quieted down since. By now Clarisa has predicted hundreds of earthquakes, duly registering her predictions with the U.S. Geological Survey. Roger N. Hunter, project leader of the government's conservative and rigorous Prediction Monitoring and Evaluation Program, has said of Clarisa, "She has the best track record of two hundred scientists, astrologers, psychics, and dreamers. . . . She's doing better than anyone else, and if she can keep this up, we're willing to listen." All predictions are fed into a computer, which later reveals not only how much correct information was contained in the prediction but also how likely it had been by chance alone—and the results show, Hunter reports, that Clarisa does "ninety-nine percent better than chance."

How does she do it? Clarisa likes the term "Complete Sensory Perception," and says that her information comes to her in many ways. With the earthquake predictions, "I see a calendar with the date circled in red, and the word EARTHQUAKE stamped across it. Then I'll hear the magnitude and I'll hear the location . . . though sometimes I see a map . . . I've seen earthquakes years in advance, and just a day ahead." Sometimes Clarisa gets information in dreams, but most of the time her visions come in the waking state.

In 1979 Clarisa predicted that Phoenix's Route I-10 Salt River Bridge was going to collapse. How did she know? She was visiting Phoenix for a lecture series. Friends drove her from the airport to her first meeting, and she took advantage of the time to try to catch a nap in the back seat. Nearly asleep, she suddenly sat up, having felt what she describes as a "bump in the energy" as they crossed the bridge. She didn't make much of it at the time, but on the way back to the airport the experience repeated itself as she crossed the bridge —except that this time a voice told her that a section of the bridge would collapse in about three weeks.

In 1975, as Clarisa was walking across the grounds of California's capitol in Sacramento, she had a vision of a woman in a red cape (she was reminded of Little Red Riding Hood) pointing a gun at President Ford. When Clarisa contacted the FBI, the local office was unaware of any planned presidential visit, and asked her for a date; she saw September 5. That day, Lynette Fromme, wearing a red cape, was foiled by a bystander in her attempt to kill Ford.

You would think that with a track record like Clarisa's, the police and the FBI would be knocking down her door to get her help. But mostly they ignore her predictions (as they do those of most psychics). Sometimes they keep their involvement very hush-hush—as was the case when the FBI met with Clarisa in a car in an out-of-the-way location after she reported on TV that she had a vision of Patty Hearst with her hair cut short. "It was like something out of a spy movie," she laughs. One suspects, too, that they sometimes follow up on her leads without acknowledging her help.

For example: Clarisa showed me a copy of a March 1983 Mailgram she sent to the Vatican to warn of her vividly detailed vision of an attempt on the Pope's life during an upcoming visit to Poland. As usual, half the letter was devoted to an attempt to list her credentials so that she would be taken seriously. She never heard from the Vatican, nor did she hear of any assassination attempt on the Pope in Poland. That is, until she noticed a January 1985 story in the *Los Angeles Times*: POLES TOLD OF FOILED '83 PLOT TO KILL POPE. While few details were given, the story came out during the trial of a secret-police general. Warsaw denied the story. But the general, Zenon Platek, is quoted: "This information is being disclosed for the first time today. There was a real chance of an assassination attempt on the Pope. We took special steps and arrested several people in possession of explosives and automatic weapons."

In spite of all this, Clarisa says, "the scientists don't seem to be that interested. Some of them just ignore the successes; they are like ostriches. It probably is unsettling to them—geologists, for example, have spent years learning their trade, and they have all their multi-million-dollar equipment, and along comes someone untrained like myself, and I outguess them."

People come to Clarisa for all manner of things, not only, I suspect, because of her wide-ranging abilities, but because Clarisa is a person who truly wants to help, and to use her abilities to be of service. She is an animated, comfortable woman with a wide smile and vivid blond hair cut in bangs; her inquiring eyes peer at you through long black false eyelashes. Words like "integrity," "spirituality," and "ethics" are sprinkled through her wide-ranging conversation on everything from stock market predictions to UFOs—with which Clarisa reports a long-standing communication.

Clarisa remembers being able to see auras when she was three or four, and for a long time thought them normal; and her family accused her of peeking into her Christmas presents. But she dates her real psychic powers from the age of thirteen, when a fall from a horse left her nearly blind. "Three days after the accident, my room seemed to fill with light. Then a beautiful lady walked toward me and told me not to worry. The vision faded, and my sight returned. From then on, I developed psychic abilities."

When Clarisa does private readings, she works with her client's aura—which she believes to be a powerful psychic channel for her ("my equivalent of a 'computer code,' " as she describes it). But she is careful not to pry where she's not wanted. "I don't go around peeking into people's auras," she says, speaking of her ability to turn her skills on and off. Sometimes this is for her own protection. "I like people," she says, "but I don't go out too much, or go to too many parties, because it's hard for me not to be affected by what's going on around me. For one thing, when people drink, their auras open up. If we go to a restaurant, we try always to sit so that I'm the farthest from other diners. Funny things happen sometimes. One day I was at a lunch counter, and suddenly I got this terrific headache. I turned to the person next to me, and confirmed that he had a violent hangover. It gets tricky too with Rick, my husband. I try hard not to tune in on him, but sometimes I just know what's going to happen next. The worst part of what I do is that it can be very isolating. Sometimes I'm aware that people are afraid of people like me. They feel threatened. They assume that since I'm psychic I know everything about them. They think they have something to hide, and they'll say to me immediately, 'I know you probably know this already about me; please don't tell my boss.' It's not true, of course, but it can be difficult for me."

Clarisa told me one story that gave her a lesson about the tremendous responsibility of having abilities like hers. She has many times worked with the police in finding missing people, or bodies, and frequently teaches the "psychic" portion of the search-and-rescue courses taught to law-enforcement personnel and volunteers in several California communities. One time she was called in to help trace a woman named Candy Deavers who was missing in Los Gatos. The woman's husband came to Clarisa with photographs and several of his wife's possessions. Working from a map, she helped locate the missing woman. A picture from the local paper shows Clarisa meeting with the reunited husband and wife. "I was thrilled that I was able to resolve it," she recalls. "But two weeks later I got a call from Mrs. Deavers. She says, 'I'm getting ready to get lost again; don't find me.' I was shattered because I thought I'd done something wonderful, but I realized that I was interfering with her free will. Every adult has the right to get lost if they wish. So there are cosmic or universal or ethical issues to be taken into consideration."

There are many situations in which Clarisa uses her ability to see auras. "A company hired me because they had some money missing from petty cash and the employees' purses. It was getting serious and people were getting paranoid, so they had me come and interview everyone—about ten people. They all knew why I was interviewing. No one likes that kind of accusation, it makes them nervous, so I had to take into account that their auras would be a little darker than normal. After ten interviews I could find nothing more serious than the occasional pilfering of paper clips. But when I questioned one woman, she answered very truthfully that she knew nothing about it—but a truck showed up in her aura, a delivery-type truck. So when I made my recommendations to the manager, I said, 'Do you have a truck that looks like this?' and I described it. And he realized that on Tuesdays when the truck made the deliveries, that's when the money was missing. Well, he couldn't accuse, but he could recommend. He requested a new driver, and that was the end of the problem."

Clarisa does her public-service work without charge—earthquake prediction, search-and-rescue teaching, work with police. For private readings, based on one's aura, she charges a fee. She explained a bit of how this works as she prepared to read for me. "Everyone has an aura; it is something you carry around with you twenty-four hours a day. When you are sleeping it is your hot line to the universe. Most people think of auras as halos, but I have met only two or three people with real halos. I meet some very nice people, but they don't have halos, so I say to myself, What is the difference? I noticed that children have halos until they are three or four or five, but once they start associating with other children, the aura starts going down around the body. And I realized that the three adults with halos were a nun, a nurse, and a prospector—a hermit. All very innocent, protected from the kind of life experiences we all have to go through. Some we don't choose, but we grow from them, so I call the aura that goes all around the person the twentieth-century aura, and I think it is the preferred one to have.

"Now, when I do the reading, I concentrate a few minutes to get in tune with your energy, and then I tell you what I see in your aura —not only the colors and what they mean to me, but I see things, and things happening. At first I lose sight of you. All I see is the colors." Clarisa went on to read my aura: "First of all, I'm very pleased to see that you have a band of lavender on the left side, right in front of you. This is your intuition and also related to your perception, and it shows me that if you haven't been having a lot of dreams lately and remembering them, you will soon have them. . . ." She went on to tell me in great detail about personality traits, about past and upcoming events, all tied in with clues provided by the ever-changing colors in my aura, and seemingly "information" that came to her in connection with seeing the colors.

What happens if she sees negative things? Again, it is a question of ethics. "People who come to me put a lot of trust in me, so I have to be very careful. I can't avoid sensitive issues, but I don't want to scare or mislead people. If I see someone with a really ill aura, for example, I'll say, 'Well, I think your energy is going to be a lot better, but it would be a good idea to get a checkup from your doctor.' Or if I see a physical danger, I might suggest that they change their route to work, change their path, for a few weeks. But I don't want to plant unconscious thoughts that would lead to worry and other problems. It's a fine line."

And where does her information come from? "I just call it the universal consciousness or the universal broadcasting system. All knowledge is there for everyone to know." Clarisa told me that she feels that a higher force or intelligence is at work here, but that she doesn't try to label it. "Religious people often challenge me: 'Do you believe in Jesus Christ?' and so forth. I say this is not a church issue. I'm not challenging religion; this sixth sense doesn't conflict with religion, or with belief in 'science' or 'reality,' for that matter."

Like most psychics, Clarisa feels that all people have, or could develop, psychic abilities. "You just have to tune in to the station and eliminate the static. I have an interest in earthquakes, an interest in the well-being of our country; I'm interested in a lot of things. So that's what I tune in to. I think the universe has all sorts of information if we just learn to tune in."

Clarisa also does an increasing amount of business consulting— finding oil and minerals, picking stocks—and in this area she charges a percentage. Like many psychics, Clarisa keeps a file of testimonial letters, news clippings, prediction documentation, and the like to prove her credibility when called on. In her files too are dozens of letters from business and professional people she's advised, and she gave me many names of people to call to verify her work with them.

I called racehorse trainer Orlando Duran at her suggestion, to get his story of Clarisa's recommendation that he change some equipment to improve the horses' performance. "She was out with me while I was feeding the horses, and she asked me if I was using an iron bit, and I said of course, it was standard. 'Well, it's funny,' she says. 'The horse is telling me he wants something different.' And I ran through some possibilities with her—rubber, leather—and we decided on a bit that was part leather. Then she told me exactly how the horse—Astro Bravo—was going to run in the race the following day: He'd run back for a long time, and then it would become a contest with two other horses, and he'd win. She was right."

Here's what Ron Schapell, former president of the Lear Corporation, told me about how Clarisa detected problems in a plane Lear was about to test. "A friend and I happened to catch Clarisa on a radio show, explaining her earthquake predictions. My friend called her after the show and spoke to her, then asked if there was something I wanted to talk to her about, so I asked her if there would be any problem with the plane we'd be testing in a couple of weeks, the Learjet—I did the original design while I was working for Bill Lear. She asked if it was a type of plane that had a propeller on the tail, and of course she couldn't have known that, but I verified it. She said something about the nose on the plane having a structural problem, so I asked her about the instrumentation box that we would be mounting on the front for the tests. This is a very important stage in testing, where you mount instrumentation forward of the nose, to get accurate readings free of airflow disturbance, and then correlate them with the actual instruments in the plane. She said that would be a problem; there was something wrong with it. I called the office the next morning, and told them to remove the instrumentation and fly the plane without it while they checked the instrument booth for a structural problem. Well, this all panned out over a period of six months, but the analysis showed that it would have failed in flight. The instrumentation booth would have gone through the propeller that was tail-mounted, and it would have caused a very bad incident. Since then I've had her look at other planes that we've designed before they fly."

There are more stories. Former Congressman Bill Feighan told me that Clarisa has counseled him in several business deals, in one case advising him against an investment that turned out to be a major disaster for friends of his who wouldn't listen to her warning. Clarisa showed me a letter—along with a check for $1,300—that she had just received from the Hasbro Corporation's Tony Parkinson, as a 10-percent commission on his profits from the Cities Service stock on which she had advised him.

One of the most fascinating stories came from Bob Slatzer, whom Clarisa had earlier warned not to take a plane that later crashed (page 218). Do you remember the brouhaha in late 1985 when ABC suddenly canceled a planned 20/20 episode that was supposed to·examine a reported cover-up of Marilyn Monroe's death? The story was that Roone Arledge, president of ABC News, canceled the show at the last minute, ostensibly because of his friendship with the Kennedy family: Robert Kennedy (following in the footsteps of his brother John) is said to have been involved in an affair with Marilyn, and to have seen her the night of her death. Years before Marilyn was a big star, Bob Slatzer was married to her for just a few days; their marriage was annulled under pressure from her studio, but they remained close friends. Early on—years before her death—a psychic had told Slatzer that Marilyn would be murdered. Anyway, in 1982, when Slatzer first pressed Los Angeles County to reopen its investigation, Clarisa had told him, "I hate to tell you this, but there is just going to be another massive cover-up. But it's not over yet. Something else will come up in the next couple of years." Time passed and they discussed this matter from time to time, and then, he says, "There I was working with 20/20 on their Marilyn Monroe special, and I'm talking to Clarisa, and she says, 'Do you think they will really air it? I have a funny feeling about that.' Well, you know the story—it was all over, and Arledge was actually accused of censoring the news. Then she told me it might be a blessing in disguise, and that it would serve to get the Board of Supervisors to reopen the investigation. Well, the vote to convene the grand jury has just passed. I talk to Clarisa from time to time, and she advises me on whatever's going on in my life at the moment." (This was October 6, 1985. The evidence was subsequently ruled insufficient and the investigation was again canceled, but Clarisa still feels that there will be an investigation, owing to new evidence that has yet to come to light.)

Earthquakes finally got to Clarisa. She feels that her abilities make her too sensitive to earthquakes, to the anxiety and fear and emotional uncertainty they cause—and she feels that everyone in earthquake areas is affected, even though people may not recognize it. "I don't see California falling into the ocean, as so many have predicted, but it takes its toll in nervousness and negative energies; it affects people's behavior." Clarisa has moved to Canada. Maybe she'll be predicting avalanches next.

TONY CORDERO

Like Clarisa, Cuban-born Tony Cordero showed his stuff when he was very young. "I started foreseeing events when I was about four

—to me it was as normal as breathing. I would tell relatives, play-mates of things I felt were going to happen, and of course, they did. My parents took me to psychologists to see if there was something wrong with my brain. I didn't think about these things—I would feel the vibration, I would feel sensation. I would be playing with toys and I would look at one of my relatives and I would say, 'Be careful about that,' and then I would go on playing. They would ask why I was saying that, and then whatever it was would just close off to me. The psychologists told my family that I was just extremely perceptive and there was nothing wrong. In 1956 I told my family that I saw red flags all over Cuba and they were going to have to leave the country and that a lot of members of the family were going to be shot. This I saw in my mind like a movie. I actually saw people running, I ac-tually saw relatives being shot. I could hear and smell—I could smell smoke and hear the sound of gunfire. I feel like I'm in the situation. I can hear people talking but they cannot hear or see me. It's like traveling into time or something."

Tony also had the experience of receiving information from people who, his parents later realized, were relatives who had died. This was just one more thing that set him apart from others; but a child-hood trauma convinced him that he should dedicate himself to mak-ing people be aware of, and cultivate, their "sixth sense"—for themselves and for the benefit of humanity.

"When I was seven years old, I had spinal meningitis. In the hos-pital I started having convulsions; the doctor later said I'd had a heart attack, and I was pronounced dead. I recall leaving my body. I could actually see a cloud as though my energy was leaving my body; I could look down and sense, see, and smell everything. I could see bright lights and hear strong echoes, and then this energy radiated to me the message that I had to go back inside my body and I was going to be cured in twenty-one days. Then when I started to talk again—I was still paralyzed from the neck down—I told the doctor what I had felt and seen. He said it was part of my delusions from the high fever. That's when I decided, and it stayed with me. I felt that here is all this suffering around me that can be avoided."

When Tony came to the U.S. from Cuba in 1961, his family begged him not to talk about his odd abilities for fear that the family would be misunderstood or even deported; they were in a strange place and feared people would not understand. So he told his family that he would try to be like everyone else, but tragic circumstances soon singled him out. "It was November 1963. All the Cuban kids in school had been gathered around a television set to watch Kennedy at the Orange Bowl, welcoming the prisoners of war from Cuba. It was a small black-and-white TV, and I'll never forget, I could see blood coming out of the president's head, and the blood was in color. I closed my eyes and then opened them and I could see it again—the blood was all over his face. I started hyperventilating; I was really shook up. They took me to Mr. Datson, the principal, and then to the children's hospital in Coral Gables. From there they contacted the FBI in Miami and told them that I was saying that President Kennedy was a good man, and they should stop him from going to Dallas—he was going to be killed. . . . I knew it could be stopped, because all but the blood was in black and white. If the whole thing had been in color, it would have meant that the event was too close to be averted. My mother was worried because she was afraid the FBI was going to harm me, but they told her no, they were just going to take notes. Then it was very upsetting when it happened. I just wanted people to know that if there is something coming, they can prevent it from happening if they know in advance."

The question of whether the future can be altered is a crucial one for psychics, especially because they have a hard time not feeling responsible for things that they see and that go unheeded. This problem is especially difficult for the person who is not in touch with the psychic component of his consciousness, who inadvertently dreams of a disaster—an air crash, a flood—that comes to pass, leaving death and devastation in its wake. In some cases, they are troubled for a long time afterward, suffering from feelings of guilt in the knowledge that they were unable to help.

Tony feels that the future is like a hurricane that is beginning to form, that gathers momentum, becoming more concrete and unavoidable as it approaches. "If someone is on the lookout, on the alert, even if the accident takes place, you can do the right things and decrease the danger," he advises. Tony himself was scheduled to be on the Air Florida plane that crashed into the Potomac in 1984 when the plane's wings iced up. "I got a vibration that I shouldn't be on that plane. I talked to someone at the counter and asked if everything was okay; they looked at me funny and called the security guard because I was asking strange questions. They told me that plane had no trouble with ice. It was a terrible feeling while I was standing there to feel that there would be something wrong—and of course, I have no certainty, no proof. Sometimes this gift is useless: If I try to tell them what's wrong, they think I'm some nut or somebody who wants to sabotage the plane."

Since Tony spends a great deal of time doing radio and television shows, most of his predictions are well documented. His prediction of the Watergate scandal certainly made people take notice. On October 28, 1971, he was on WRC radio's *Speak Out Washington* with Stephanie Coulter. "When she asked me what I felt about President Nixon, I immediately felt connected to a computer of information, and at the same time it was like looking at a slide projector. And I felt the vibration that he was going to have to resign, and she asked, 'Is there a reason?' and I said, 'I feel that he is going to be involved with a scandal that is connected with the Watergate building.' At that time Watergate hadn't been heard of. She said, 'Tony, I hope you're wrong, but you have said other things that have materialized.' And I told her I would write President Nixon a letter and warn him of this scandal."

Tony wrote his letter and received a form-letter reply from Nixon staff assistant David N. Parker, followed by a visit from Philip K. Johnson of the Office of Cuban Affairs, wanting to know why he was saying these things about the president. Tony explained that he was just trying to help avoid a crisis. Then Tony gave the story to Louise Lague at the Washington *Evening Star* and Deane McCollum, who wrote a gossip column called "The Ear." But their paper didn't take the information seriously, and "lost" the story; *The Washington Post* got it first. Meanwhile, Tony was able to tell Lague that her paper was going to have to sell or go out of business.

Cordero, a youthful, energetic man with dark brown eyes and close-cropped hair, claims that he has since been working with the Justice Department and the FBI on a very low-key level, though he is sworn to confidence about the details. "The government is very careful about these things. They don't want the publicity and they don't want the exposure. They know I am in the public eye. They keep asking me what I want, what I want for me. . . . My thing is that I need to get this thing across and I tell them, 'If you're not going to help me, fine, I understand. But don't try to close doors for me, because I will open them one way or another!'"

Tony claims to have done work for both the Israeli and the Peruvian governments. The Israelis, he says, were very open. "They said, 'Look, we don't want to know how you do it, we just want to know what you have to say.' I was able to tell them that Sadat would go to Israel; they looked at me and said it was impossible—and I told them I saw his death three years later, in front of a military parade. All they were interested in was the security of Israel—that's it. I told them that they would purchase radar equipment from West Germany, that it was in Israel's interest, and other things I cannot make public. They asked me why I concerned myself with Israel, and I said, 'On Israel depends the balance of the whole world.' "

Other of Tony's documented predictions include his forecast in 1971 that Red China would be admitted to the United Nations, the death of the Pope in 1978 and the election of a non-Italian Pope (no one believed *that*), Indira Gandhi's death, the earthquake in Mexico City and the volcanic eruption in Colombia in 1985, and the 1986 explosion of the space shuttle *Challenger*.

Tony's mail and news clippings give a picture of the range and accuracy of his abilities, and of the help and comfort he's given to those who consult him. There are testimonials to his integrity and responsibility, as well as to his great talents. There are dozens of letters from radio and TV executives and reporters saying how many people called in after his show, how accurate his predictions were— and, incidentally, how uncannily he had seen their own lives and problems. "I was astounded that you predicted the interference during President Carter's fireside chat only minutes before the broadcast." "On NBC-TV in Phoenix on October 11, 1975, Mr. Cordero predicted that an explosion would take place in southern Arizona, but it would remain a mystery because the Air Force was heavily involved. That evening an explosion did indeed occur south of Tucson. The blast ripped a hole in the ground 300 feet in diameter, and had traffic backed up on Interstate 10 for five miles. . . . Three people lost their lives and a fourth was critically injured. . . . It is now five months later and not a word of explanation of the disaster." "He described my home in detail, including the change made by putting in two new windows. He told me a neighbor's baby would become ill, and two days later he did." "While in Cleveland, one of his predictions about a fire in the Pentagon came true." "This is to verify that at my first meeting with Tony Cordero he was able to inform me in detail of many facts related to the death of my father." "Cordero came across as a total realist, a person totally aware of his 'sixth sense' and how to use it to the best advantage of humanity." "Without ever meeting my mother, Tony told me her name, that she was a twin, and that the delivery was a difficult one for my grandmother. The first two facts I know are correct. The latter I do not know."

What really drives Tony Cordero? It seems to be helping people to recognize their own latent psychic abilities, and to use them responsibly. Tony feels that his classes in ESP and psychic awareness, for adults and children, are the most important part of his work. He showed me letters from people who feel that his classes have helped them cope better with their lives, their careers, their troubled kids, their relationships. He says he has been successful in turning addicts and alcoholics around, in giving hope to the suicidal, comfort to the ill or to the dying. "We have to make ourselves better by learning and understanding, not closing off. It's not a religion; it doesn't conflict with religion. But people are limiting themselves. My crusade—whether it's on radio or TV or in my courses, whether it involves a bit of showmanship and teasing in the audience or it's private counseling—is to make people aware, to expand their horizons, to make their lives better."

BEATRICE RICH

"It seems normal to me. It's what I do." I was asking Beatrice if she felt her abilities set her apart from others, or were a burden to her. "I feel like I've been given a job to do, a service I must perform. I have to do it. It was never a burden to me, but a kind of compelling and fascinating thing. There was a drive to do it when I first started. It seemed like some kind of rarefied, special thing that I had been given, and I had better be careful with it and nurture it and not abuse it or transgress against it in any way; it was not to be used for material gain, or I'd pay a heavy price for it. John [Beatrice's longtime friend who books her appointments for her] is always trying to get me to handicap the horses. He pesters me to death: 'C'mon, give me a number. Who's going to win in the fifth at Aqueduct?' But it doesn't feel right to me. Or he tries to get me to increase my hours. I prefer to work at night and see a limited number of people; it's exhausting to do this, and I feel responsible to be at my best. You know, I sleep late every day, I eat a big lunch, I meditate—it's like being in training. I sort of prepare myself. Outside of hours, I don't do this, I don't 'work'; it's the last thing in the world I want to do."

On the surface, Beatrice seems to fit the classic image of the psychic. She pretty much confines herself to giving private readings —the usual fare about family and career and love and success. No radio and TV predictions, no testing in parapsychology laboratories ("They wanted to hook me up with wires and monitors at Maimonides Hospital. I don't want people watching me when I sleep. No, thank you."), very occasionally a bit of work with the police. But that's where the similarity ends.

For one thing, Beatrice just doesn't look the part, aside from her large, ethereal, almost unblinking blue eyes. Slim, pale, blond, and almost fragile-looking, Beatrice conveys more the impression of a very pretty, fashionably dressed schoolteacher. And the fragility is a bit deceptive. Tactful and kind in her handling of her clients, nevertheless Beatrice, in her shy and soft-spoken way, is candid, outspoken, and very confident of her considerable gifts. When I asked her if everyone to some extent had psychic abilities, she was quick to disabuse me of that notion: "Well, I know that this is heretical, but I really don't think so. Maybe some people have it in a minimal way, where it's not going to change their lives or make a bit of difference, any more than I'm going to become a brain surgeon."

At the outset of a reading, Beatrice asks to hold a personal object that you've brought and waits while you set up your tape recorder, carefully explaining how the reading works—you choose the topics you want to cover; the reading generally spans a period of the past and the upcoming six months; she sometimes confuses past and future (as she sometimes confuses people's children with their pets); she wants you to concentrate on your question while you shuffle the cards. Then she folds her graceful hands on the table in front of her, looks steadily into your eyes, and describes your life to you as though she had seen the whole movie—which is not so far from her description of how she works. It's a jolting experience, all the more so because it's often the mundane, everyday details of your life that unfold in Beatrice's reading. You have the disquieting feeling she's been living your life, watching you let the laundry pile up, seeing you sing along with MTV or read bedtime stories to the kids, feeling your tension headaches or your poison ivy. "You really eat a lot of ice cream," she might say, or "Your wife is getting pretty exasperated with your temper tantrums."

And what does she feel she gives to her clients? Different things to different people at different times, she says. "I help clarify things for them—their lives, their relationships, problems at work. I'm sometimes able to link the past and the future, to tell them about the direction their lives will take. Sometimes they think their lives are going one way, but I see something quite different, and I feel it helps to know, to be prepared. I try to refrain from telling people what to do, unless the situation is so horrendous that if I don't tell them I'm being negligent." Somehow, though, Beatrice often manages to convey, in her tactful way, what she *thinks* you should do.

It all began for Beatrice one day while she was a graduate art student in New York. On a whim, when the movie they had planned to see was sold out, she and a girlfriend dropped in at the Gypsy Tea Kettle on Fifth Avenue to have their fortunes read. "The woman had a deck of cards and read my teacup; she told me a long story about the man I would marry. He rode a motorcycle, came from a large family, was a big sports fan, et cetera. I thought, 'Oh, that's nice,' and forgot about it. A couple of weeks later I was walking down the street and it hit me that this information was for a friend of mine in Florida. So I wrote to her and told her I hadn't taken leave of my senses, but I thought she'd meet someone like this—I described him —and she'd marry him. She wrote back and said she'd already met him—well, it's a longer story, but of course they got married, and I thought, Well, I can do this. Now, this was twenty-plus years ago; there were no classes, few books—it just wasn't popular—but I just sort of thought I could do it. Now, I don't like tea, I like coffee, but she just used a regular deck of cards, so I did the same. The individual cards don't mean anything to me, like the queen of spades means this, or diamonds mean that; at this point they're just a way of focusing, a way of concentrating, a beginning. I just started by reading for friends, and the information just poured through me; it's like a light passes through me, and then it's gone. The cards are catalysts; with four or five cards I get one story, then with the next four or five cards I get another. I ask my client to shuffle the cards and think about the question they want to ask, so I feel that the cards function also to transfer the client's energy."

Beatrice also uses psychometry—picking up information from inanimate objects—and asks clients to bring a personal object for her to hold, something dear to them that isn't used by, or hasn't belonged to, anyone else. This she also taught herself, trying her skills on objects friends sent from people she didn't know. Holding the object, she would sit quietly in a chair, with pad and pencil, making notes of any information that came to her. "I always asked that people send only objects of little value—a comb, a key—but in one envelope nevertheless came a ring set with diamonds, emeralds, and pearls. When I put the ring on, my hand changed. It became tan, with long platinum nails, and along with the hand came a whole story—a divorce, that she was laying big blocks of stone on her patio, an illness. [I have always been fascinated by the odd bits and pieces that psychics pick up—and by the things that get overlooked, or aren't "seen."] Even though I was new to this, it wasn't scary at all to me. A few weeks later, I was at a party. There were about thirty people there, and there was the woman with tan hands and platinum fingernails. I went up to her and said, 'I have your ring.'. . ."

After graduate school, Beatrice left New York to teach art at a junior college in Florida, sometimes tagging along with a friend to lectures on psychic abilities. "Frequently they were on such a low level that I just couldn't sit through them. But something had caught my attention, so I'd go to the next one. At one lecture, I was called up to the front and asked if I could get any information about a man in the group. I looked at him and saw silver spoons, vases, forks moving around his head and shoulders like a rainbow—I just reeled off the items in front of everyone. They were shocked; it even startled me. The man turned out to be an importer of these things. Another time during that period I was working with an object, I don't remember what . . . I saw a blond woman, seated, middle-aged, with a blue dress, but I could only see her from the hips up. I could see her knitting, could see the color of the hangers in her closet, of all things, see a car accident as a child. The image wouldn't fade, but the woman didn't show up in full; I couldn't see her below the waist. Well, it turned out this woman was in a wheelchair and couldn't walk. Sometimes the information comes through and you don't know how to interpret it."

What about Beatrice's childhood? Well, it seems that Beatrice had psychic abilities, but no one made much of them. She has memories of periodically hearing a beautiful voice calling her name; many years later she found out that her brother heard the same voice. And things would occasionally move around on their own—a plate of cheese, glasses. "It didn't scare us, ever. We would laugh; these things happen so fast they don't give you time to be afraid. We'd try to find some rational explanation for it; we'd see if the table was wet—sometimes there is an explanation." Beatrice also has memories of moving along above the ground. "I mentioned this to my mother about a year ago and I almost collapsed when she said, 'Yes, I used to see you do that. I didn't know what to do. I'd try not to scare you; I'd just say, "Put your feet down on the floor, dear," and you'd say, "The floor is cold." ' Mother said she didn't know what to do about that. My mother, who I feel has tremendous psychic abilities and never did anything with them, went to someone who was psychic and asked him what to do about me. He told her not to worry about it, that I'd probably grow up to be psychic, to let me alone and I'd be fine. So, you see, I wasn't traumatized by all this."

I spent a good part of my interview with Beatrice trying to get answers—or at least clues—to the hardest questions of all: What is it? How do you do it? Where does it come from? As Beatrice (like many other adepts I've asked about this) says, "There is no language to describe this." However, Beatrice did make a stab at the answers, often by using stories to illuminate certain issues.

"I'm sure I'm not in this alone, in the sense that I do go into something—it's like a 'shift,' kind of a mild trance, another level or dimension. I don't remember things I tell people—I only keep my eyes open so I won't look too peculiar. People are forever coming to me and telling me things I told them and what happened, and of course I don't even remember their faces, much less what I told them, unless I've met them in a social situation. Much of the information comes to me visually, probably because I'm an artist when I'm not doing this. I think it comes from a similar source; the painting too flows out of me. But with the art and the psychic stuff, there's a tremendous amount of practice and discipline. I'm so comfortable with this that it seems normal. It's like doing a drawing and some-body is watching and they're still asking me, 'How do you draw? How do you get the nose to look like that?' During a reading, I see kind of a transparent movie going on around your head. But there's information that comes with it that's instantly there. I was sitting with a girl and I saw these hats piled up behind her head. I told her her grandfather was Russian, a haberdasher, in the hat business, because the information was attached to the hats.

"Another time I was doing a career reading for a woman who worked on Wall Street, and I kept seeing a little figure behind her head, twirling on the ice in a little skating costume; it wouldn't go away. So I finally said, 'This is too distracting: I keep seeing you in this skating costume,' and she said, 'Well, I'm a part-time skating instructor,' so that was part of her career.

"Another time I was with a woman who asked me about her hus-band, and I saw that he was sick, and I was saying to myself, 'sick, sick,' and it was like you were standing next to me poking an elbow in my ribs and said to me, 'It's a heart attack.' It was as if 'they' were exasperated, like 'C'mon, can't you see that? Let's get on with it.'

"Sometimes this happens: I was with someone and they were ask-ing about a restaurant they wanted to open. And without planning to, a part of me just went there, and I was in this restaurant, looking down at it, describing it. It felt perfectly safe—what the researchers call bi-location.

"Occasionally I see past lives, fragments. An advertising man—he was thirty-one or thirty-two—came to see me, and I looked down at my arms and they were getting huge, muscular; I'm a thickset, squat, terribly muscular man; I can't see my face. Off to the side I see sort of a fort, a beautiful day, with horses, tapestry blankets, probably medieval England, and he is a soldier, an archer—he's practicing. I mention this to him and he tells me that archery is his hobby. A young adman in New York City. Not tennis, not jogging—archery."

Beatrice seems to be particularly good at seeing illness and physical distress. "Why are your hands so numb?" she asked a friend. "There's nothing wrong with your circulation." The woman explained that it was a leftover side effect of a serious nerve disease she'd had a few years before.

The problem with being so attuned to physical problems is that the pain frequently translates itself into her own body. "If their shoulder hurts, if they have a headache, or their stomach is bad, or their feet are swollen, I get that pain, just for a minute. Sometimes it's intense. Once I was with a woman and my hand felt like it was on fire, burning hot, but her hand looked normal—no burns, no blisters, no bandage. Well, it turned out she had completely burned the flesh off her hand in a freak accident three years earlier. Yet I picked it up.

"Another time a friend called and asked me about his sister, who was having a gynecological problem. I wrote down her name, sat down with the paper in my hand to concentrate on her—and I collapsed on the table. My head smashed the table, I couldn't breathe, I was choking. It lasted for about a minute, and it was pretty awful. I called him back and told him I didn't know about the gynecological problem, but that she had blood clots in her lungs. Sure enough, she was brought back after being pronounced dead on the operating table, her lungs filled up with blood."

Sometimes her clients have a reason for keeping their problems secret. Beatrice told me about the time two women dragged a nationally known football player to see her. "He was embarrassed, and he certainly didn't think I could tell him anything. He wouldn't even look directly at me. It took me a while to figure out what he did; all I could see was a tremendous amount of running—it was exhausting —and violence. I asked him about his knee, and he said, 'Sure, everyone who reads the papers knows about my knee.' Of course, I didn't even know who he was. Then I said to him, 'Your other knee hurts too; why haven't you taken care of it?' Well, I thought he would go through the roof! He looked around as if he were being followed. It turned out that his other knee was bothering him, but he hadn't told anyone, because he didn't want to jeopardize his contract negotiations."

Beatrice always asks her clients before a reading if they want to hear bad news, but she doesn't talk about death—"because death is irrevocable; you can't change the course of events." But she often has to deal with what she calls "things I'd rather not know about." In the case of illness, she will offer her diagnosis, but encourages the client to see his or her doctor right away.

This ability can work in a positive way. "Sometimes people think they're ill, and I don't feel it. For example, I've had women come to me who thought they had breast cancer and they didn't—though I always tell them to check it out. After all, I'm not always right.

"One couple came to me who wanted to know about their young son's health, and I said it looked fine, and they said, 'But what about his eyes?' I said there seemed to be no problem with his eyesight. Well, they were very disappointed; they said, 'You're wrong; he's got this terrible eye disease and he's going to lose his vision.' I told them I was sorry, but I didn't get it. About a week later they called saying it was a misdiagnosis, the doctor had made a mistake, the child was fine."

Bad news is always hard to handle, and Beatrice always tries to do it as tactfully and helpfully as possible. "A man came to me whose sister was missing. So I told him that a friend of his sister's had been discovered or would soon be discovered (I often don't know if something has just happened or is about to happen) in a swamp under a bunch of leaves, a black girl, in the Everglades in Florida. What I felt was that his sister was farther into the swamp and dead, and I didn't tell him that. I didn't know what to do.

"It can be horrible. Sometimes I feel that people have got to hear what I say. I saw a woman who was with a man who I knew was violent and eventually was going to beat her up. I just see it happening and he's done it before to somebody else. It's just a matter of time before it's going to happen to her if she doesn't step away from that relationship. I mean, I have to tell people."

I pointed out to Beatrice that she couldn't be seeing what she sees in actual elapsed time, because she seemed to be able to grasp and analyze years of information, to see the whole unfolding of a relationship or a job, to see things about people that might take others years to figure out. As one friend remarked, "You feel like she's seen you in therapy for four years. She described my wife—the bursitis in her shoulder, her frustration with her work, the whole way we behave with each other."

"I wish I could really explain it," Beatrice says. "It's like it's laid out; all the information is there. I see the dynamics of the relationship, I see the quality, I see if it's going to work out. Sometimes I see the relationship before it happens and how it will turn out. A woman came who had her boyfriend waiting downstairs, and I told her he was in the CIA and described his assignment. She didn't believe me, but it was true. I got them married. It's hard to tell people what to do, and I try not to give advice unless I feel it would be negligent if I didn't. Sometimes you see mistreatment and violence, and you just have to speak up.

"This kind of functioning breaks away any kind of barrier to information, including time. If I were to meet you socially, I wouldn't pick up these things. I'd just have my own natural sensitivity or reaction, as anyone does, to people. Goodness, I don't walk around the streets like this. The information is immediately available; it's like reading a little, compressed, short novel. It's all there and I just have to tell the story."

"What you do seems so exotic," I told Beatrice. "It doesn't feel that way to me" was her reply. "I'm very much of this world, and I love all the pleasures of this world—all its delights. Good food and beautiful clothes and movies and the ballet and whatever—though I could use a few less of its problems. I'm like everyone else; I go on living my mundane little life, and I have to pay the rent like everyone else. It doesn't help that much personally on a day-to-day basis. If I see something I don't like, I'm not going to be thrilled about it; it's more difficult to do for myself.

"But this work definitely makes you more spiritual, and I don't mean that in a religious sense. You just lean toward a more spiritual, universal awareness of things. You have a different responsibility from someone who, say, plays music. I think the whole point of being aware of these things is to make you a better person, more loving, kinder; you have more humility, more compassion. I like to feel that I'm helping people, helping this field, giving it some aura of dignity and respect."

INGO SWANN

Just blocks away from the Greenwich Village address where Beatrice Rich plies her trade lives a very different sort of psychic. Ingo Swann is *sui generis*: In pursuit of *Intangible Evidence*, I met no one else quite like him. In fact, I almost didn't meet him at all. Ingo doesn't give interviews anymore, and I had to pass muster before he'd consent to see me. Even then, I felt his attention was a bit perfunctory until I was able to win his respect. Ingo has had enough of misrepresentation by the press and by rabid critics of psi. As he put it, "I've been through the misquoting and holding-up-to-ridicule mill several times now." When I first saw Ingo, he had just had the pleasure of turning down *60 Minutes.*

If you've read *Intangible Evidence* this far, you've already had an earful of Ingo Swann's outspoken views, and read of his spectacular psychic feats; you probably have formed some idea of what kind of man he is: smart, analytical, iconoclastic, opinionated, gifted, involved. But that doesn't tell the whole story, for once you spend a little time with Ingo, he is affable, charming, witty, and forthcoming. Most obvious, when you visit him in his studio in lower Manhattan, is that he is a talented and prolific artist. Lining the walls of his studio are giant canvases of "other worlds," in which magical creatures inhabit cosmically surreal landscapes—places where you and I have never been, but with which Ingo seems to be intimate. You can almost feel his effort to make the earthbound pigments express the otherworldly color and luminosity. The second time I saw Ingo, he was in the throes of writing a major essay on New Age art—another aspect of his effort to explicate and communicate the essence of the related psi/aesthetics/New Age issues. Swann views his art as a synthesis of his whole experience, including his work in ESP. "My work in ESP is precisioned downward to the ESP task and what goes into performing it. That is science, I believe, and the painting is aesthetics. But I feel they are twin issues, and we'll get further if we view ESP as an aesthetic thing rather than as a detached scientific phenomenon. Right now, we use ESP to gather information or convey information, but that's probably a rather infantile or limited form of the greater potential. Because you could use ESP to create information, too."

Ingo went on to say that he feels he creates information in his painting, but not yet in his ESP work. As he says, "There are none of us yet who are total products of the new order. The intention of the New Age artist is totally different from that of the artist born and formed during the modern-art epoch. New Age art speaks to the possibilities of the universal order of consciousness. And modern art spoke to the possibilities of the individual ego. The goal of the New Age artist is to transcend the ego and meld his consciousness into the natural order of consciousness that has been assiduously avoided by science . . . I think the fact of a universal consciousness has been pretty much established in terms of Jung's collective unconscious."

I asked Ingo what he believes influences and creates the collective unconscious. He talked about the shared Jungian archetypes of the collective unconscious, commenting that while Jung felt they were continually added to genetically, there are those who feel they are constantly being added to by every thought and deed. "At some level of consciousness, you're plugged into everything that has happened in the past, with preferences that collect around certain archetypal concepts. But according to occultists, this shared consciousness isn't fixed in present time, but has non-space/time connection, which gives us access to the past and future, to the extent that the future has been formed or crystallized in the collective unconscious."

Aha! Here we are again at that idea of a dynamic, continually forming future. "Does that help explain precognition?" I asked. "Precognition is one of those stupid, stupid words. How can you precognize something? It's more like the person tunes in to these crystallizing postulates of the future, and when he gets enough of the elements, it gets shoved up into consciousness. *Then* it becomes a cognition.

"The disciplines that deal with consciousness have always said the future can change by changing the elements of the present time that are going into forming that future. This is what is behind what I call the New Age Imperative, the idea that if you continue to think in the terms you're thinking in now, you'll get the future that's predicated on those terms. Because the future is building onto it, on these old-age ideas of war and that defensive posture, all of the things that have led to impasse. It's like a self-fulfilling prophecy. The New Age imperative, of course, is just to stop thinking in those terms, and to think of positiveness and hopefulness and calm and peace and beauty. The struggle of the New Age artist is, whether it's expressed as a consciously held conviction or just unconscious feeling, you just abandon the old way of thinking and opt for a self-fulfilling future built on positive ideas; the ego is a very limiting thing, and it drops away. That's why you see this reflected in New Age painting, and that's why unconsciously the public is responding to it. That's why New Age artists have such an enormous consumption in terms of posters and postcards and things like that on the public level. [Ingo has written a book on the subject, *Cosmic Art*.] One main thrust of the New Age thinking goes that those big universal trends and needs and desires and things like that are there in the collective, and that in order to perceive them and work with them, you have to let go of the ego."

While it is obvious that art and the paranormal are closely intercon-

nected for Ingo and deal with the same issues, I wasn't very successful in getting Ingo to talk about his current involvements in
parapsychology. He is determined to hang on to his hard-won privacy, and will only drop tantalizing clues as to what he is up to these
days in the field. As he has already made perfectly clear in Chapter
3, except for some people he highly respects, he hasn't much use for
most of the parapsychology establishment: "If they can't confront the
brave new world, they have no business being brave new scientists."
In his autobiographical *To Kiss the Earth Goodbye*, he makes a priceless
comment about what he thinks of the way the parapsychologists
handle gifted subjects like himself: "The tactic heretofore has been to
capture a subject exhibiting some paranormal potential and grind
that subject through the research mill governed by fashionable, but
by no means conclusive, strategic ideas of human possibility. The
paranormal potential in the subject—if indeed it was there in the first
place—usually was extinguished promptly and the subject himself
fed out the back door in some sort of pulp form."

Ingo feels strongly that working out of the public eye is much
better, that his energy isn't being drained answering challengers and
doubters. He has no doubt that the paradigm, or mix of paradigms,
parapsychology has been using is wrong, and that it is necessary to
go back to the basic ideas governing the paradigm. "If you find the
right way to handle a given phenomenon, it develops right in front
of you. It's like finding a very narrow band on the radio. You can
pass over it unless you have a fine tuner. And the thing that you
make into a finer and finer tuner is the anticipation of the knowledge
of your consciousness about what it is that it's supposed to be looking
for and dealing with. Once consciousness can be reprogrammed and
the mind maps can be redesigned to incorporate these things, then
the channel can be seen more clearly. It's really a rather simple
change. Everyone looked for this complex explanation in parapsychology, and when nothing worked, they made it more and more
complex. But the thing to do was work your way through all the
complex things and reject them and reject them. Finally you found
yourself with some very simple changes and the lights turned on. It
was incredible." Incredible, but frustrating. While Ingo implied that
he was working hard, and closely, with some top parapsychologists,
I couldn't pry any details out of him. We'll just have to wait and see.

If you don't have the right paradigm, Ingo went on, dropping hints
along the way, the experimentation doesn't pan out. "If I've succeeded at all it's simply because I have located a problem for which I

could find adequate information and source material, and I could also relate it to work going on in brain research and neuropsychology or even art. I found one of my greatest clues to ESP in a book on art." Ingo went on to illustrate for me the parallels between children's drawings and the drawings that psychics make for remote viewings or OBEs, the drawings made by brain-damaged patients, and the premises of Betty Edwards' book *Drawing on the Artist Within*—all clues to the pictographic-meaning theory mentioned in Chapter 7.

"There seems to be a genetically existing factor which has capabilities of transcending time and space and does so on a very random basis." That was about as much as Ingo was prepared to say about the nature of psi. But even though he feels that he has made inroads into an understanding of the psi mechanism, Ingo says that because psi happens within the total biological organism, until that organism is better understood, ESP and psi won't be understood. "ESP is a self-evoking phenomenon, and some people can learn to evoke it in themselves; it can operate as a function of the will or the desire for it. Then consciousness has to begin to change its reality to conform with this new familiarity with the unknown part of ourselves." To this end, Ingo has written *Natural ESP*, in which he shows the reader the methodology he's evolved for accessing what he calls the "ESP core," in order to learn to evoke it, to understand it, discipline it, and use it. "Marilyn Ferguson, who is publishing a book called *The Visionary Factor*, teaches seminars in how to bring about a shamanistic change in people's lives. And contacting your ESP potential, I think, does about the same thing at this stage.

"Once you have contacted some semblance of your own ESP processes, they become real, and your whole system adjusts toward accepting them. But you need a reality shift and not a philosophical shift. You have to bring yourself to the point of having an experience that forces you to readjust. In the absence of a personal experience it all stays intellectual and analytical."

It was at this point that I brought up the resistance of most scientists to the fire-walking phenomenon, and their contention that it could all be explained according to the Leidenfrost effect. "They love that," he retorted, "because it reinforces their world against this other, inexplicable world. But it's still a crock of shit." I countered that a couple of scientists have walked on coals in order to debunk the phenomenon. Ingo's interpretation: "If you say there was a scientist who did that and said he believed it was the Leidenfrost effect, he's simply not allowing the reality to shift his mind-set."

To Kiss Earth Goodbye gives a good account of Ingo's childhood, his ideas about psi and its researchers and practitioners, and his multi-faceted involvement in the field. Ingo, with his scientific educational background and inquiring mind, has done a little bit of everything, often as an active participant in developing theoretical premises, as well as the experiments to test them. He introduced himself to plant-psi researcher Cleve Backster and worked with him. With Gertrude Schmeidler, he developed the idea of testing his ability to change the temperature of thermistors sealed in thermos bottles. At the ASPR, he helped develop and performed a series of OBE experiments. He wrote to Hal Puthoff (after seeing a letter from Puthoff on Cleve Backster's desk) and got involved at the ground-floor level with the remote-viewing protocols. He had the idea of choosing remote-viewing sites at random using only map coordinates—longitude and latitude—to guide him. When NASA space probes were due to fly past Mercury and Jupiter, Swann and fellow psychic Harold Sherman "went" there first, describing wonders of space that hadn't yet been seen—specifically revealing that Mercury, unexpectedly, had both an atmosphere and a magnetic field.

Not surprisingly, Ingo's abilities showed up early, and like those of so many other psychics, were probably to some extent inherited. Anna, his German grandmother, was thought by many in the Scandinavian community in which he grew up in the Rockies to be "if not a witch, a possessor of the evil eye." It was naturally to Anna that Ingo, with his unusual and extraordinary awareness, gravitated. He tells a story of how first Anna's and then his own premonitions saved them from being buried by back-to-back avalanches.

Ingo's childhood history, his supportive grandmother notwith-standing, is the usual one of extraordinary perceptions that couldn't be subdued by disciplinary measures or social pressure. Nevertheless they caused such anxiety that he made the decision actively to sup-press these abilities for many years—an effort so successful that he also suppressed his knowledge that he had them. Even from his vantage as an adult, Ingo seems to despair of convincing most people of his childhood experiences. "It is useless to insist in the face of incredulity that what happened to me as a child was a real experi-ence," he writes. "No effort is being made, therefore, to lay it out as fact, and so it can conveniently be told in the third person." He recalls the time he saw Britain's King Edward VIII sitting alone "in a room with big chairs in it, all alone, and he was crying"—agonizing over whether to marry Wallis Simpson—though Ingo was too young to know their names, or to grasp the situation. He tells the story of how he was duped into being anesthetized for the removal of his tonsils, of "leaving" his body to view the operation, seeing the doctor's scalpel slip, hearing the doctor say a "dirty" word that wasn't allowed at home. He saw the doctor drop his tonsils into a jar. When he awoke, he asked for his tonsils and was told that they had been discarded. Another lie!—and one that all the adults seemed to collude in. He saw the war—"people flying in big birds, throwing things at the ground and then great big explosions . . . people across the ocean with huge waves; they have their cars filled with suitcases, and some have horses and carts. There are screams." Though he was loved and spoiled, Anna was the only one he could tell about these things; it was their secret. He saw tornadoes, horse races, earth-quakes—"mountain winds sweeping through forests of pine . . . rainbows forming after the magnificent storms that swept the plains . . . surf pounding on beaches he knew not where . . . glittering phosphorous plankton trailing in eddies from the passing ships at sea during the night." He knew what people were going to say before they said it.

And then he realized that not everyone did what he did, and he felt strange. His growing sense of right and wrong brought terror and depthless compassion at the horrors he would sometimes witness. He withdrew, and tried to confine his "travels" to the beauties of nature. His sensitivities started to diminish. Though he somewhat enjoyed his ability to irk or scare adults, he felt set apart from other children. On the Fourth of July, 1941, he made a conscious decision that he didn't want to be different from others—a choice that he didn't realize was a bad one until many years later. That night, he took one last magnificent trip through space—the swirl of glittering stars and incandescent colors, the sounds of roiling planets. He noticed that the earth was not truly round, but oblate. Then he rushed back, eager to join in the flow of humanity, to check out the possibilities for friendship and interaction, not strained by the burden of his extraordinary abilities. It was not until 1969, when he realized that he had established some kind of telepathic communication with his pet chinchilla, that it all started coming back to him.

URI GELLER

"Where is it written that a psychic cannot make money? I don't think that in history there was a very wealthy psychic. For some reason they always kept to mediumship and spiritualism, reading tarot cards, and some of them were very divine and money was not to be touched, but I am a very contemporary person. All my life I wanted to be wealthy. Maybe it's because I have a Jewish head for business. . . . I remember when I was a kid I always said that if I don't make it, then I'll become a gigolo and marry some rich woman. I mean, you know, I'm not a Getty, but I certainly am in the £50-million [$80-million] bracket. Fifteen years ago, all my possessions were a scooter."

Does Uri Geller need an introduction? Is there anyone who doesn't remember him on the television talk-show circuit, focusing his intent gaze to bend keys and spoons with his psychic powers, telepathically reproducing the drawings of his hosts and audience members, stopping the clocks and appliances of viewers all over the country? All amid a swirl of controversy, which the tall, dark, movie-star–handsome young Geller seemed to relish thoroughly. Geller became a catalyst for the controversy over the legitimacy of psi. Skeptics pointed to Geller as the quintessential magician/showman, capable of fooling not only a gullible public, but gullible parapsychologists. Parapsychologists put him through every imaginable hoop (though some parapsychologists say that Geller often avoided laboratory situations), testing and poking, and some declared that Geller had rather extraordinary powers—though he wasn't above resorting to trickery when his abilities failed him. Everyone I've talked to—on both sides of the fence—has had strong sentiments about Uri Geller, and many have amazing stories of their encounters with the amazing Uri.

You've probably guessed that Geller didn't make that £50 million bending spoons. Tired of being challenged and accused of fraud, Geller dropped out to live quietly in Europe with his family, practically a hermit. Today he claims he is using his psychic powers to locate minerals and precious resources for large corporations—corporations that are interested in results and are not afraid of ridicule. "I've found for some companies oil, for some gold, for some companies copper. I work on a percentage, a very small percentage, but with something like oil or gold, that can be a big amount of money."

It all started about ten years ago when Val Duncan, the director of a bank and president of Britain's Rio Tinto Zinc Corporation, saw Geller on television and wondered if he could learn to dowse for precious minerals. Duncan reportedly took Geller to his property on Mallorca, where he had buried caches of oil and various minerals, and tested him out. Then Duncan showed Geller how to work from maps. Uri has since worked with such companies as South Africa's Anglo-Transvaal mining company and Australia's Zanex. He has a plan to find Lasseter's Reef—a legendary golden mountain that is to Australia what Atlantis is to the rest of the world.

I asked Geller what else lay ahead for him. "Well, there is nothing you can do with so much money. You know if you have five houses around the world, all you do is end up flying between them. And you know once you are in show business, it's hard to totally leave it. So in these last years I kept doing maybe one or two T.V shows that reach millions of people. I do only very prestigious lectures, like the Young Presidents Organization, with people like Kissinger and Gerald Ford. I keep writing books [he has a new one out, *The Geller Effect*], and I basically spend most of the time with my family—my wife and two children. [My son] Daniel has already shown his powers. The critics—the Randis and the like—are still out to get me. I must say, I still enjoy the controversy, and nothing can touch me now."

I told Uri I would love to see him really confound the critics with some unassailable display of his powers. "Yes, well, it will come. I go every eight years to something very big. Eight years I did the shows and all the testing. Now eight years I've done the mining. Very soon I will do something major psychically, whether it's opening the antenna of a satellite that didn't open, or bringing back something that was left on the moon—something so major that it can't be ignored. But I must tell you that even if I do something like that, there will be those who say, 'Well, there were nylon strings attached,' or 'It's coincidence.' " LeShan once joked to Geller that he should be careful if he tries such a trick; he might get confused and bring back the moon itself!

What's Uri Geller's story? He was born in Israel in 1946, and first noticed his powers because of the telepathy between him and his mother; they would play psychic guessing games. (This is an aspect of psi, by the way, that many researchers feel merits further exploration: The mother/child connection is perhaps the original psychic bond.) When he was four, a spoon he was eating with curled in his hand. He grew up in Cyprus, returned to Israel to serve as a paratrooper in the army, and was wounded during the Six Day War in 1967. In the early seventies, having made himself a household name all over Israel for his phenomenal abilities, he traveled to Europe and then to the United States, leaving a trail of astonishment and controversy wherever he went. In Germany he claims to have stopped a cable car in midair, and followed up by halting an elevator in a department store. In England and in the United States, his metal-bending feats were widely reported in the media. He was endlessly challenged to perform new feats under controlled conditions. In England, the metal he bent was found to fracture differently from normally stress-bent metal. He caused a Geiger counter to register five hundred times its normal count, and was able to psychically deform a crystal of molybdenum. At the Stanford Research Institute he caused measurable weight "loss" and "gain" in a one-gram weight. He correctly called eight out of ten dice throws. He repeatedly was able to duplicate drawings made by experimenters while he was sealed in a communicationproof room. At a U.S. Naval research center, Geller caused the recently invented alloy nitinol to become deformed in an uncharacteristic way. In Tokyo in 1984, after two days of trying, brandishing his fist and shouting commands, he was able to stop and erase the image on a Hewlett-Packard computer-graphics system. Later that year he garbled a floppy disk in an Israeli computer system.

But the most fascinating of Uri's feats take place away from the television cameras and recording instruments of the lab. One reason for this may be that such things as cameras and recording instruments seem to go haywire in Uri's presence. By now I've heard countless stories from researchers about the equipment Uri screwed up. As Puthoff and Targ report in *Mind Reach*, "An almost limitless list of equipment failures was associated with our attempts to observe Uri's paranormal ability." In one instance, they had set up an experiment in which Uri was to try to displace a laser beam. They pointed out to Uri that if he was successful, the result would show up via a deflection of the pen on the recording instrument. Uri bypassed the laser beam. He just turned and raised his fist to the recorder and said, "Move!" The pen moved all the way across the paper and never moved again. Uri had burned out both channels of the recorder.

Because of happenings like this, and because many of the most spectacular things that happen with Uri happen outside the lab, many researchers have had to be very restrained about the claims they made for Geller's abilities. As Targ and Puthoff say, "The line we are drawing is one that gives us no pleasure, and it provides a lot of discomfort. It is our impression that Uri possibly did perform a number of genuine psychokinetic feats in the laboratory [Geller was unable to bend metal under experimental conditions at SRI], but in the world of science, no one at all cares what we think possibly may have happened."

Some of Geller's spontaneous feats are quite something, to hear witnesses tell it. The first time Targ and Puthoff met Geller, after an evening in which Geller had eagerly shown off several of his effects, they found that the metal post supporting a STOP sign at the foot of the driveway where they met was twisted into three complete loops. Andrija Puharich, the American physician who worked for years with Geller, claims that at one point his Mercedes-Benz disappeared from in front of his house and reappeared at the edge of a lake 100 yards away.

At Uri's urging, I called Bob Williamson, who owns a hotel company in Los Angeles. "I'll tell you about the part that changed my life for me. I met Uri in about '73 and he bent a key for me. As soon as he did it, funny feelings went through me and I realized it was like a thousand doors were opening up. I'm a little slow, but I figured that if one person can bend one key one time, just once, then despite all the things I was taught and conditioned to believe, there was more to the world than I realized.

"Anyway, at the point I met Uri, I had just lost about forty or fifty pounds, but I was a very heavy drinker on my way to becoming an alcoholic. We were at my apartment, talking, playing some music. I had a little flask, a half-pint silver flask. Uri was after me just fierce, and he gets very fierce: 'You must stop drinking.' (Geller himself leads a rather ascetic life; he is a vegetarian who neither drinks nor smokes, and who exercises regularly.) Later we were walking to the car—it was a clear evening—when off to the side, materializing in the middle of the air, came this flask; and instead of tumbling or falling down, it just came much slower than regular speed and hit the grass and plopped down beside us. We were very shocked, even Uri; even though he had seen this many times, he is still shocked when something like this happens. I had seen two or three other versions of this with him, so I knew what was taking place. But I did realize the symbolic importance of it. A short time after that I just said a prayer to lose the desire for alcohol, and I stopped drinking— that was eleven or twelve years ago. The message was pretty strong. Uri doesn't claim that he caused the flask to come out of the sky, but these things happen around Uri."

One of the most amazing encounters with Geller is recounted by journalist Dotson Rader in an article for *Esquire* magazine in the mid- 1970s, during Uri's first visit to the United States. Rader set out to find out what this brash, charming, extraordinary young Israeli was like and got more than he bargained for. They met at a restaurant for dinner and Geller, in his usual irrepressible, boyish way, wanted to show off. He bent spoons. He described the personal history of a watch and a bracelet Rader was wearing; he reproduced drawings that Rader drew on table napkins; he caused Rader to guess correctly a number he (Uri) had written down. A voluble Geller expounded his belief in the unknown entities around him, and in the extraterrestrials with whom he says he has extensive communication.

It was after dinner, when they retired to a small apartment Geller kept, that things got very strange. Geller was in an excitable, agitated mood, and talked volubly: He wanted very much to know where his powers were coming from, voicing his concern that you could go crazy from having to deal with these things. He said he felt that there were people in madhouses because they couldn't understand or cope with their powers: They were trying to cope with too much data; they were living with one foot in the unknown. Rader felt the room getting warmer, actually oppressive. As Geller rambled on, and Rader became more uncomfortable, they started hearing strange knocking sounds. Meanwhile, Geller was expounding on his theory of extraterrestrial intelligence as the controller of psychic powers, stopping at one point to accurately read Rader's mind. ("Why are you thinking about a fish?" Geller demanded. Rader was thinking of a fish-shaped wine bottle.) Suddenly a heavy, hand-shaped wooden sculpture that was sitting on a table flew across the room, struck the far wall, and fell to the floor. Rader was terrified, but Geller was only annoyed. "It happens all the time. Don't get upset." As the atmosphere got even hotter, a spoon flew into the room; when Geller picked it up, Rader reports, it melted in his hand. Geller was upset that Rader was frightened. In fact, he was terrified. Rader didn't want Geller to come near him. Geller tried to apologize. "Things fly around the room all the time. My secretaries always see it; they are used to it. I do not make them fly. I don't want them to damn fly." Then a rock seemed to fall from the ceiling. "He didn't like having me, his guest, upset," Rader writes, "and I was really upset. 'Now what?' Geller was finally fed up. He sounded like a frazzled housewife whose kids are constantly breaking things every time her back is turned." There was more of this, and then suddenly the atmosphere returned to normal and things quieted down.

The finale came a couple of days later, when Rader returned to the apartment during the day to meet Geller for a drink. When he arrived, Geller was dressing. While he was waiting for Uri, Rader took the hand sculpture and put it under his seat cushion so that it wouldn't misbehave. He and Geller left and walked to the elevator.

There was the hand standing in front of the elevator. The terror had gone, Rader reports; it seemed like the most natural thing in the world.

A few observations should be made here. One is that Geller seems to have around him some of the same kind of energy associated with poltergeist phenomena. Another is that Geller has since been more circumspect about sharing with the public his far-out ideas about extraterrestrial intelligences and unseen entities, and gives very little clue that anything strange is going on behind the scenes. Also, Rader's article was evidently weird enough that *Esquire* included a commentary from a doctor, in a little box that ran within the article, giving possible psychomedical explanations for the Geller effects, or Rader's state of mind.

Geller's clipping file is filled with quotations from several prominent scientists attesting to his abilities. Wernher von Braun: "Geller has bent my ring in the palm of my hand without ever touching it." John Hasted: "The Geller method of breaking steel is unlike anything described in the [metallurgical] literature." Dr. Friedbert Karger of the Max Planck Institute of Plasma Physics: "Based on preliminary investigations of Uri Geller, I cannot establish fraud. The powers of the man are a phenomenon which theoretical physics cannot yet explain." Then there are the stories written by reporters who had their skepticism and their minds blown (as one of them put it) when they met Geller. And indeed, though Uri's powers aren't always "on" when he wants them to be, and he is not above using sleight-of-hand when he has to perform on command, he has done enough right-before-your-eyes demonstrations to boggle the eyes of all but the blind. My own meeting with Geller was pretty amazing. Brian Inglis had called Geller on my behalf and arranged our meeting. I found him living in a veritable castle on the Thames outside London. Though calmer and more mature than I remembered him from TV a decade earlier, he was still boyishly eager to show me his stuff. I think Uri still feels the bite of his critics, though he says, "I know that I have these powers; no one can come and tell me I don't.

"Show me one person that didn't once in his life have a déjà vu or a telepathic experience. I'm not saying there are not coincidences. Wait, I will show you telepathy. First of all, I cannot guarantee that whatever I'm going to show you will work." In fact, everything seemed to work, rather marvelously. "Draw something and cover it —turn around, don't show it to me. Okay, visualize it in your mind, draw the line in your mind, concentrate. I get a triangle . . . now I

get an upside-down triangle . . . a Star of David. You
see? Now, a magician would not be able to duplicate
this, only if he comes with a prepared pack and he
uses your same drawing pad. . . . I don't think I'm
unique to do this. There are are dozens of children in England who
can bend metal, whom Hasted has worked with. There are other
people who can locate minerals, who can do remote viewing much
better than I can, who are great healers." Then Uri wanted to show
me his metal-bending prowess. "You brought a spoon with you, no?
Did Brian [Inglis] tell you to bring a spoon? [I had picked up a spoon
in a restaurant en route.] Good. Come on over here where there's
more metal; that helps." Geller led me over near the television set.
"You see, I stroke it very gently. Can you see it?—I don't want to do
it too much. There's no trickery, no chemicals. See, it's still bending,
by itself; the molecular structure is
changing. I don't know myself
how I do it; the mind is very powerful.

"Unfortunately, the hard scientific community of the world mostly
thinks that psychic phenomena are basically fraudulent. There are a
few who understand—Hasted, Targ, Inglis, Puthoff but even Honorton and Morris, in my opinion, are closed-minded. The Russians
get the upper hand because just one big boss has to decide and they
put $100 million into it: They send headhunters into tiny villages to
find the people with the psychic powers, peasants; find them nice
little apartments and a nice little salary; and they're happy. But I
don't think they—or I—can use psychic powers to do damage. They
try to use it for evil purposes, but it just doesn't work. But I don't
know. Maybe in Russia if there's a guy like me and they train him
for twenty years, maybe he can stop someone's heart or bring down
a missile or trigger an atomic warhead. Could I go to Heathrow and
detect bombs? Well, to train people to detect bombs—not the bombs,
but the people who have them—is a process of many years, sharp-
ening your powers to do that, and still you couldn't do it all the time.
It took me many years to polish my telepathy so that I could reproduce it in drawings. You have to use these things. The aborigines
can do these things because they're part of their life; they are always
practicing and polishing. But as we become older, we become more
skeptical, more mechanized and computerized; we tend to let our
psychic abilities fade out. If we didn't, we wouldn't need tele-
phones."

I left convinced of Uri's talent, notwithstanding his penchant for showmanship in a pinch. His failures at critical times are unfortunate and seem to mirror what happens with many psychics under pressure to perform. Maybe now that the pressure is off, he'll pull off that extraordinary, unmistakable psychic feat that will force people to take notice of psi's full potential.

CHAPTER SEVEN

IS THE UNKNOWN UNKNOWABLE? THE WHY OF PSI

"Discovery consists of seeing what everybody has seen and thinking what nobody has thought."
—Albert Szent-Gyorgyi

"Time and space are modes by which we think, not conditions in which we live."
—Albert Einstein

"The more we come to understand the universe, the less it looks like a great machine, and the more it looks like a great thought."
—Sir James Jeans

Understanding psi's true nature has proved a formidable task. It may be, as Lawrence LeShan muses, that psi is a wildflower that grows only spontaneously, and fares poorly under cultivation. Findhorn's Ian Turnbull referred to it as "the shyest creature." There are some who even insist that psi doesn't want to be discovered, and throws up all sorts of smoke screens and false clues to avoid detection. Given the fact that psi's core essence manages to elude the most dogged searchers using state-of-the-art machinery and sophisticated statistical protocols, this seems almost plausible. But then the inimitable Ingo Swann puts his two cents in: "I think that's garbage. They're projecting their own inadequacies onto the problem and blaming the problem."

The problem is a formidable one nonetheless, and one that is crucial to parapsychology's—and man's—progress. What is psi? Where does it come from? What is its function? Such questions continue to baffle not only the researchers, but the psychics themselves. Even the most gifted and articulate of them cannot solve the central riddles of psi.

The work of parapsychology is greatly inhibited by the lack of a coherent theory which everyone agrees fits the observed data—not that the observed data, in this case, are a matter of agreement to begin with. Yet theory is the building block of research; it classifies, organizes, explains, predicts. It is the foundation against which new ideas and progress are measured. Theory enables us to formulate the right questions, to approach psi in a way likely to bear fruit. As physicist W. F. Barrett put it, "Without a theory, facts are a mob, not an army."

What psi has at the moment is many facts—mountains of anecdotal and experimental data—and many theories and bits of theories. Some of them dovetail nicely; some clash violently. What it adds up to is many tantalizing glimpses into the innards of psi. In this brief chapter, let's look at some of the more promising clues, and see if we come any closer to revealing psi's secret heart.

DOES PSI PHYSICALLY FIT?

The all-too-human temptation to find an explanation for psi in the everyday world is powerful. The conventional physics theories claim that the data of psi are faulty, or that they can be explained by conventional means. It would certainly be comforting to feel that our ideas about the world require no wrenching change to make room for psi, that there is no need to change the paradigm of how the world works. A great deal of attention has been devoted to such physically manifested effects as those of Kirlian photography, and the effects of the electromagnetic field on psychic behavior. But most such ideas are not holding up well to close scrutiny.

"Kirlian photography," says Nikolai Khokhlov, "is a lemon that was dumped on us by the Soviets, and we picked it up because we didn't know better. It is about 85 to 90 percent high-voltage corona, creating some visible light, radiated electroenergy." Electromagnetic theories began with the discovery by German physicist Hans Berger in 1940 that rhythmic electric currents emanate from the brain; he invented the electroencephalograph (EEG) to monitor them. The theory is that physical changes in the brain are transformed into mental energies which travel in a wavelike manner through space, affecting the brain of another. But "transmission" theories ignore the fact that time and distance don't seem to be factors in psi. (The "long-distance" psi experiment most familiar to the public was astronaut Edgar Mitchell's communication from space with a colleague back on Earth.) It was probably the apparent similarity to radio communication that seduced scientists into thinking that similar forces were at work. But while a radio signal gets fainter the farther you get from its source, this has not proved true of psychic "transmissions." And how do we account for psychic information from the past—or the future? (Einstein remarked that the distinction between past, present, and future is an illusion, albeit a stubborn one.) Eysenck and Sargent in *Explaining the Unexplained* refer to the "fruitless pursuit of electromagnetism."

Several recent studies purport to show a connection between periods of extremely low-frequency (ELF) electromagnetic activity (on a global scale) and increased psychic activity. These studies too are highly disputed. It has been pointed out that individuals are influenced far more by localized electromagnetic energy—in the form of televison, home appliances, passing subway trains—than they are by the global ELF field. Some researchers feel that electromagnetic-field theories are suspect because of the difficulties of getting true measurements of global ELF activity in which localized activity is properly shielded. Keith Harary calls the interest in ELF theories, and the implied desperation to find an explanation for psi in the everyday physical world, "almost like superstition."

Then there are the physical "field" theories, a field being defined as an arena of mutually interdependent coexisting phenomena. Field theories solve the transmission problem by stating that everything within a given field is influenced by other elements in the field. The Soviets, led by biophysicist Victor Inyushin, use the term "bio-plasma" to refer to a "particle soup consisting of free protons, free electrons, and free ions," which exist around and within living organisms, creating individual, but interconnected, "biofields." Other theories postulate different but overlapping "matter fields," "behavior fields," and "psi fields."

British biologist Rupert Sheldrake has been a center of controversy for his theory of "morphogenic fields," which refers to the theoretical sphere of influence that a group of organisms exerts over others of the same species. These morphogenic fields play a role in the development and maintenance of the group, the cumulative fields of all past systems influencing all subsequent systems across time and space. In concrete terms, the theory goes, once some members of a group of organisms learn a new pattern of behavior, subsequent members of the species can learn that behavior without being directly taught. For example, once a number of rats in a London laboratory learn to navigate a particular maze, similar rats in New Zealand are able to learn the same maze more quickly; this behavior, if reinforced, remains a part of the morphogenic field of that species. To some people, this sounds suspiciously like psi with a more acceptable new name: the ability to tune in and acquire useful information stored in a universal consciousness.

The analogy of a hologram is often advanced to explain how field theories work. A hologram is a record, a 360-degree image, of an object, constructed by the interfering waves of laser beams. If the record is then illuminated by similar laser waves, the image becomes visible. The information captured by the beams is so evenly distributed that any fragment of the original can reproduce the whole record. The microcosm reflects the macrocosm, and is reflected by it. As Krippner and Solfvin remark, "There's no need to explain how information travels from one point to another if it's already present at the second point. If the brain is a hologram interpreting a holographic universe, psi is a necessary component of that universe; holographic theorists would have had to hypothesize psi had not parapsychologists already done so."

Physicist David Bohm does not accept the seeming contradiction between physics and psychical data, between the internal mechanism of psi and the external world of observed experience. The relationship of mind and matter is one of participation, rather than interaction; information activity is perceived as meaning. Bohm's theories do not separate mind from body, observer from observed, subject from object; rather, he sees universal consciousness as the basic makeup of both the implicate and explicate orders.

THE PHYSICS CONNECTION

Many theories coming out of advanced physics in recent years, specifically quantum physics, have bolstered arguments for psi. A world in which one object can be in two places at the same time, in which (according to relativity theory) time slows down as an object approaches the speed of light, where an electron can change from one orbit to another around the nucleus of an atom without traversing the space between the two orbits, is certainly as bizarre as a world in which two people can communicate psychically. Why is it, then, that the wild and woolly world of physics is accepted, even revered, by the establishment, while psi is still considered beyond the pale of rationality? As Elizabeth Rauscher, a theoretical physicist and parapsychologist with a list of credentials as long as your arm, says of psi, "If you can believe modern physics, you can believe this stuff."

One implication of physics is that we live in what Max Planck labeled a "multitracked universe," in which there are several discrete levels of functioning. On each level the rules for the behavior of time, space, and matter are different. One set of laws operates in our everyday sensory world, quite another on the level of Einstein's relativity theory, and yet a third on the submicroscopic level of quantum particles. But in each case such behavior is considered normal within the framework of the rules understood to govern that "track" of the universe. Charles Fort referred to these sets of rules as "nothing more than the right costume to wear." Lawrence LeShan makes the point that the level on which psi functions is different from our sensory reality, and that while we are in what he calls the "clairvoyant reality" it seems normal. Many psychics I talked to spoke of the "shift" they make into the mode they use to function psychically: They organize reality in such a way that it seems normal at that level.

There are several striking parallels between quantum physics and psychic phenomena. For one thing, as with psi, the events of quantum physics are nonlocal. Distance is not a factor, and an event in one location can affect an event at another location, with nothing going on in between. Time and space are treated identically in quantum physics; as with psi, time does not appear to be a barrier. Correlated or synchronous events, rather than the transmission of energy, is involved—an idea we'll come back to later.

Another parallel to psi is the unpredictability of matter at the quantum level, akin to the randomness of psi. At the quantum level, it is possible to predict only the probability, or the statistical chance, that something will happen, not the specific event. (This is the premise behind experiments using Helmut Schmidt's random-number generators.)

In the world of quantum physics, a particular event, until it is observed, exists only as a set of parameters, called the "state vector," a term that describes the infinite range of simultaneous positions and velocities that a particle might take—its probabilities. But we cannot observe all the probabilities, only the one that occurs when we observe it. A case in point: an electron within an atom has a known probability of being in one or another of its possible orbits. But until it is observed, it is not in any one of those orbits, but in its state vector. Only when the observation occurs does the state vector "collapse" into one of the probable states, the one that was seen and measured. Its true orbit is determined; one event is selected from many possible states. This is the conundrum described by the Heisenberg Uncertainty Principle, which states that you can measure the position *or* the velocity of an electron, but not both. Put another way, all measurements affect the system being measured in such a way that we cannot see it as it would be if we did not look: that is to say, you don't see something as it is, you see it as *you* see it. As with psychic events, any observer, anytime, anywhere, may affect these processes by the simple act of observation. It is thus conceivable that all the other possibilities encompassed by the state vector are observed by someone, somewhere.

With the act of measurement, we know that one specific result has occurred: The state vector has collapsed. In other words, a part of reality that was previously in a superposition, a kind of limbo state, goes into a firm position at the time of measurement. Marcello Truzzi points out that some psi proponents, like Dr. Robert Jahn, argue that consciousness of a thing is a measurement of something and therefore effects the collapse of a wave function so as to "create" a reality (that is, get it out of a state of superposition).

There arose the concept that *consciousness creates psi events* by influencing the collapsing of the state vector; it affects the physical system. Without the observation, there is no "event." As physicist Eugene Wigner states it: "Consciousness itself is the true variable in physics."

Just as observation is a necessary criterion for events in quantum physics, there is no way of knowing that a psychic event has taken place unless there is evidence that it happened—either in the form of the results of a lab experiment, or in the confirmation of a premonition or a hunch. A dream, a passing thought, is not seen as being precognitive unless we recognize it as such; otherwise, it apparently never happened: It is as though psi had not occurred. In the case of psi, the effect of consciousness in collapsing the state vector should be measurable, the measuring scale being the statistical results of the psi subject's observations.

Certainly psi is not inconsistent with the findings of physics; but physics deals with matter, and psi information has no known physical properties. While there are many who feel that psi will eventually be explained within the ever-expanding framework of twentieth-century physics (again that longing for a comforting alliance with matter), it seems a more promising approach to think of quantum physics as a useful and illuminating analogy to (and a useful language for talking about) the phenomena observed in the world of psi. Elizabeth Rauscher remarks that there appear to be clues to the nature of consciousness in the structure of physical theory; that in fact, the so-called internal journey (of yoga, meditation, psychotherapy) and the external validation system of science may be leading us along the same path of knowing.

In *The Medium, the Mystic, and the Physicist*, Lawrence LeShan illuminates this particular clue with a clever and eye-opening exercise. After pointing out the similarities of mystical knowledge in different times and cultures (and referring to mystics as "the most thoroughgoing empiricists of all"), LeShan challenges the reader to determine, from a list of about sixty-five quotations, which were made by mystics and which by physicists. He even provides a list of the mystics and physicists quoted. Separating the statements of those on the inner path from those following the outer way is not so easy. Try it yourself. Here are six examples, two from mystics and four from physicists:

"Nature gets credit which in truth should be reserved to ourselves; the rose for its scent, the nightingale for its song and the sun for its radiance. The poets are entirely mistaken. They should address their lyrics to themselves and should turn them into odes of self-congratulation on the excellency of the human mind. Nature is a dull affair, soundless, scentless, colorless, merely the hurrying of material, endlessly, meaninglessly."

"It is the mind which gives to things their quality, their foundation, and their being."

"When we thought we were studying the external world, our data were still our observations; the world was our inference from them."

". . . the reason why our sentient, percipient and thinking ego is met nowhere in our world picture can easily be indicated in seven words: because it is ITSELF that world picture. It is identical with the whole and therefore cannot be contained in it as part of it."

". . . all phenomena and their development are simply manifestations of mind; all causes and effects, from great universes to the fine dust only seen in the sunlight, come into apparent existence only by means of the discriminating mind. Even open space is not nothingness."

"Pure logical thinking cannot yield us any knowledge of the empirical world; all knowledge of reality starts from experience and ends in it. Propositions arrived at by purely logical means are completely empty of reality."

Even before you find out who said what, you can concede the similarities in thinking. And the answers are: Alfred North Whitehead (P), The Dhammapada (M), H. Dingle (P), P. Schroedinger (P), The Suringama Sutra (M), and Albert Einstein (P).

PSI AS CONSCIOUSNESS

A theoretical model for psi advanced by Robert Jahn and his colleagues at Princeton holds that "reality, or experience, is constituted only in the interaction of consciousness with its environment, via the exchange of information, and thus . . . any physical theory, or any other scheme of conceptual organization, can only properly address the interaction, and not the environment or the consciousness, per se. . . . the common concepts and formalisms of physical theories [are] no more than useful organizing strategies adopted by the consciousness to order the information it processes." Elizabeth Rauscher has similar sentiments: "The more you do physics, the more it looks like psychology."

Which brings us to what seems to me to be the most promising vantage point from which to view psi: as a manifestation of, as caused by, or as mediated by consciousness itself. If we look at it this way, a great deal falls into place. We have already seen the inseparability of consciousness from events in quantum physics, and there are further clues and theories which implicate consciousness—the universal consciousness that, as Keith Harary puts it, "permeates nature," and the consciousness implied by our individual personalities, our needs, and our interaction with our environment.

William James spoke of a subliminal cosmic consciousness that occasionally broke through into normal awareness: "We with our lives are like islands in the sea, like trees in the forest. The maple and pine may whisper to each other with their leaves. . . . But the trees also commingle their roots in the darkest underground, and the islands also hang together through the ocean's bottom. Just so there is a continuum of cosmic consciousness, against which our individuality builds but accidental fences. . . . Our normal consciousness is circumscribed for adaptation to our external earthly environment, but the fence is weak in spots, and fitful influences from beyond leak in, showing the otherwise unverifiable common connection."

H. H. Price, who was head of the Society for Psychical Research from 1939 to 1941, and taught in the United States at Princeton and UCLA, first suggested that the human mind of necessity developed a mechanism to repress the continuous flow of information from the collective unconscious, to prevent being flooded with the thoughts and emotions of others. During dreams and relaxation, this repressive mechanism is off guard, and psychic functioning surfaces. Henri Bergson—in what became known as the "Bergsonian filter" theory —felt that because the mind was capable of perceiving everything, it was necessary to screen out a great deal.

The view of psi as consciousness is related to psychoanalyst Carl Jung's conception of "archetypes"—universally understood and agreed-upon symbolic concepts of man. Nikolai Khokhlov views archetypes as products of the collective unconscious. According to him, archetypal images have power because they are a coalescence of like thoughts and experiences shared by many people over time. Thus those thoughts which are frequent and repeated in human experience reach a critical mass that gives them added power in the collective; infrequently held thoughts or transient ideas get lost in the vast field. The archetypes evolve as human thought evolves, to reflect the common perception of the world.

Khokhlov gives an example of how the collective consciousness may be molded. "If an old man is sitting in Central Park and says to himself, 'I really would like to butcher that squirrel,' it is a sick but logical thought for some of mankind; yet that sort of thought will fly out and go away because it is rare. On the other hand, if he thinks, 'It is nice to have your family around when you're old; they all enjoy being with their grandfather,' he is feeding the archetype of the wise old man. . . . The archetype of the wise old man, which we share, will be strengthened. Other families will also share and use it. Other generations will continue to support it. Then it will persist; it will continue to exist. It will be a permanent pattern of thought in the collective unconscious. . . . But it can change. Today the wise old man, the grandfather, is often looked upon as a fool. If that thought becomes common, the image of the wise old man will change, a new archetype will form, and new generations will perceive that old man differently. . . . Archetypes must be maintained and nourished. They can be lost. We have archetypes of loyalty, for example, but they are losing their strength. It is possible that over time, the archetype will become weak and lose coherence; loyalty might be disregarded and cease to exist as a concept."

The idea of a universal consciousness implies that all of man's (and perhaps other organisms', earthbound and elsewhere) thought and experience is available to everyone, anytime, anywhere. In this view, psi effects may be explained as two or more people tuning in simultaneously to common experiences in the collective unconscious, what Jung called "synchronicity," what we usually call coincidence—and what many psychic practitioners feel they are tapping into with their cards, their numbers, or their star charts. Ingo Swann feels that "the collective unconscious is really a very fertile ground for research. . . . The best hypothesis right now has to do with synchronicity, and the fact that at various times, things happen together even though they happen to two people apart . . . for reasons that aren't well understood, identical frameworks collapse and become real within the mind of two different people. For all we know it can be five or six or two thousand people. But it is a collective phenomenon of some kind."

Some researchers—Gardner Murphy, William Roll—have conceptualized the psi situation as one in which overlapping "psi fields" make contact. Murphy saw psi as a matrix of information, constantly added to, from which psi impressions proceed. Roll felt that memory is part of the psi field; he suggested that—as with memory—recency, frequency, and vividness of experience govern the reception and transmission of ESP.

More possible evidence for the connection of psi and consciousness is evidence which suggests that our personal experiences and temperaments may determine what links in the collective are likely to break through to our awareness. Thus two people with experiences and goals in common—mother and child, therapist and patient, longtime friends, coworkers, subject and target in a psi experiment —appear likely to tune in synchronistically to the common pool of consciousness and bring back similar experiences. They are predisposed to share psychically available information by their common needs and experiences. Rex Stanford calls this apparently psi-dis-

posed system "conformance behavior." Psychoanalyst Jan Ehren-
wald even conjectured that psi might be the most important
connection in the mother/child symbiosis. I have asked psychics to
explain how it is that they are able to get information about people
their clients ask about, isolating that individual from everyone else
in the world, just from a name, an initial, or a picture. The answer
seems to be that the connection is already there; all that is needed is
the "address," some small byte of information that separates that
person from all others. One psychic remarked to me that we are all
connected by telephone, but you have to know the number of the
person you want to call; even then the meaningfulness of the conversation is up to the participants: At the very least, they should have a
language in common.

William Roll felt that the need or desire for a certain event to
happen increases the probability of its occurrence; thus he explained
cases of precognition in which the events foreseen were prevented
from happening by the action taken because of knowledge gained
through the act of precognition. Another aspect of the possible effect
of need or desire on psychic functioning is the often-observed group
dynamic. When many people have the need for certain information,
or desire a certain effect to be produced, it seems more likely to
happen. Thus, premonitions about famous people (whom many people care about) or about groups of people who are in danger (from
an air crash, or an earthquake) are common in psychical annals. (It is
argued, however, that there may be just as many precognitions about
individuals or unknown people that we never hear about, or never
recognize.) Groups of like-minded people seem to be an important
factor in such psychokinetic effects as metal-bending and PK "sitter
groups," or seances. Certainly the experience of the "Philip" group
(page 150), who "created" in detail the "spirit" who communicated
with them, lends credibility to this theory.

Many indicators point to the fact that psychic information must be
meaningful to us to break through to consciousness. This is why
some researchers feel that we got off the track with experiments
involving card-calling and dice-rolling: We didn't need to know the
answers, beyond our desire to do well in the test. When J. B. Rhine
wanted to test psychic Gerard Croiset using the Zener card deck,
Croiset declined, saying, "I respect your work very much, Dr. Rhine,
but I do not like just to guess cards. I have to be emotionally involved, in a case like that of a missing child or somebody in trouble."
Croiset's remark illustrates why we seem more likely to have—or to

recognize—psychic experiences only in "emergencies," when some-one is in danger or dying. The idea of a universal consciousness implies that the psychic information that your child is in danger is available to everyone, but it comes through *noticeably* only to you, or your mate, because your need to know overcomes the barriers you have built against recognizing such information. Some stranger may have picked up that same information in a dream, or a random thought, but he is unlikely to recognize its meaning, or to know that it is "psychic" information. For him, the information about the dan-ger your child is in was not a conscious psychic experience unless he somehow learns what happened to your child.

The way in which we receive and process psi information may also be affected by personality factors. Someone who is well adjusted and not defensive may be more open to receiving psychic information and to sharing psychic space with others. Such a person is less apt to distort that information, and more likely to recognize it for what it is.

The selectivity in what psychic practitioners seem to pick up during a reading—the information they discern and that which they don't—is fascinating. One sees your house in great detail—the color scheme, the lace-edged pillowcases, the unfinished fireplace—but misses the four cars in your driveway. Another goes on at length about your kids, your mate, your friends, all the relationships in your life, but has little physical sense of your home or office. For some reason, a piece of jewelry on your dresser, a stack of books in the basement, your penchant for raiding the refrigerator in the wee hours, a dream you had about Paris comes through to them. This seems to be another clue about the importance of meaning in psychic receptivity: The interests and experiences of the psychic seem to influence what he or she is likely to tune in to about you, and what he is likely to overlook. Gerard Croiset had a strong emotional iden-tification with those who consulted him; there would often be an "associative relationship" between something in his own life and what he would see in the life of the client who consulted him. In one instance, when he went to visit a doctor and his wife, the doctor teased Croiset, asking him if he could see anything in his wife's past. Croiset looked at the woman and said, "I see you as a little girl of about twelve years with some girlfriends. You are sitting on a fence with them. One of the girls pushes you in fun on the back and you fall awkwardly—a bad fall. One of the spikes from the fence pierces the lower part of your abdomen." Croiset was right. But what is interesting is that what he picked up about the doctor's wife connected to a similar incident in his own childhood, when a playmate accidentally pushed him off the narrow railing of a bridge in his native Amsterdam.

I think this same phenomenon may have been operating in an incident concerning Eileen Garrett reported by Lawrence LeShan. He had prepared a group of small objects, each sealed in a box, for Garrett to examine using psychometry. During the preparations, a secretary had come into his office and picked up one of the objects, a small clay tablet, chatted for a few minutes, and left. When Garrett "read" the objects, she came to the clay tablet. Passing over any information connected to its ancient Babylonian history, Garrett talked only about "a woman associated with this," describing in detail the secretary who had held the tablet: her unique hairstyle, two scars, her special relationship with her daughter. My guess is that she was more psychologically connected to—or more interested in—the woman than she was in ancient Babylonia. As LeShan observes, "What we perceive is at least as much our invention as our discovery."

Most information in the theoretic collective unconscious is not particularly important, certainly not vital enough to divert our attention from the hustle-bustle of our everyday world. As Nikolai Khokhlov points out, there are billions of bits of information out there that are not critical; yet all of them combine to determine, to bring about, the future. As long as we do not influence them—because they are of no particular consequence, or because we are unaware of them—the future is determined. However, if we get hold of a bit of information about the future, we are sometimes able to change it—to avoid a personal disaster, for example. To that extent, we alter the course of events, on a minute, personal level; the future has a certain malleability. But, Khokhlov asks provocatively, "Does the future include only the likelihoods generated by human beings? If you limit it to that, it gives us the smug feeling that we are masters of the universe. I am convinced that there are parts of the universe where higher intelligence exists; if we are open-minded we have to grant the scientific possibility of that. So is the future only dependent on us? In an everyday way, yes, but beyond that . . ."

The concept of a free-access pool of universal consciousness gains credibility from findings coming out of the study of information theory, and the workings of the computer. As Robert Morris observes of computer theft, "You can steal something that is still there." So too is information in the collective consciousness available to everyone, always. As Willam James put it decades ago, "The space of my imagination in no way interferes with yours. We can all have the same dream."

So what is it that we see or apprehend when we get psychic information? Laboratory experiments have been unable to find any physical correlation between a particular target and success at identifying it. A target on microfilm appears to be just as guessable as a target the size of an ocean liner. The order of twenty-five cards in a stack may be psychically seen as clearly as twenty-five cards separately laid out face down on a table. Gertrude Schmeidler and others speculate that the target, the thing we "see" in psychic functioning, is not the object, or the experience, itself, but an information pattern—the *meaning* of the object or experience. More evidence for this thesis is available when you read transcripts of remote-viewing or OBE experiments. The reports usually focus on shapes and colors, fleeting images and smells, spatial relationships and feelings. The viewer is rarely able to name an object or a site; in fact, "facts" are usually misleading. If a subject says he sees a big stadium "like the Hollywood Bowl," you can be pretty sure he's not seeing the Hollywood Bowl, and that he is allowing his rational mind to interfere with his psychic functioning. When someone has a premonition of danger, she often doesn't see the details of that danger: She wakes up with a feeling of dread connected to someone or some place; perhaps she smells fire, or hears a crash, or has a sinking feeling when entering a particular room. The meaning is conveyed, rather than the analytical details.

Looking at the sketches that psi subjects make is another clue to how psi works, says Ingo Swann. "No matter how good an artist a psi subject is, the drawings look like these," Ingo says, showing me a book of drawings by children. "These are not aesthetically correct, but they carry the meaning they have for the child. Psychic drawings are the same; they carry the meaning of the thing rather than the visual perspective of it. I made huge, huge inroads into understanding psi because of this book. Then I found a book on neuropsychology, with drawings by brain-damaged people. And they were drawing meaning again. Betty Edwards in her book [*Drawing on the Artist Within*] doesn't make the ESP connection, but it's there to be made."

To make sense of psychic information, we have to translate it into terms we can understand, for the ESP core deals with information in an unfamiliar way that is different from our everyday mental processes. We have to, as Keith Harary says, "play charades" with the information. We have to take ideographic information, information that is universal beneath all language—colors, textures, shapes, forms—and deduce what it is in the real world that is being referred to. The processing of these pictographic information packets must be done with as little interference as possible from our emotional and rational minds; the danger is that the information gets so analyzed and overprocessed and overlaid with "mental noise" that by the time it is articulated in our awareness, it is a but a pale shadow of our psychic perception of it.

NATURAL PSI

Sigmund Freud—who, incidentally, said that if he had it to do over again, he would devote his life to psychical research—believed that a telepathic message received in a dream would be treated like any other stimulus. This led Jule Eisenbud to view psi as a constant influence on our behavior, whether or not we are aware of it. This is very much like Rex Stanford's premise that we use psi constantly, unaware, to scan our environment for information we need to make our lives run more smoothly.

Eisenbud conceived of psi as an integral part of nature which functions to bring order to an otherwise chaotic universe. Though he saw psi as goal-oriented, he felt that its goals were "not those of the individual at all but of an ascending hierarchy of interrelated systems in which the individual is merely a messenger."

Keith Harary takes psi one step further and proposes that psi permeates nature as a basic, underlying lawful structure of perceived events. In this view, psi is seen as an information-organizing principle in nature which permeates everything, but which we tap into only intermittently, randomly, imperfectly. According to the "psi as nature" model, we are not able to see psi for what it is because we exist *in* it; it is not separable from our perception of it. This phenomenon is apparent when six people are asked what they saw at the scene of an accident; each of the six will have seen it differently. The environment cannot be distinguished from our perception of it; so-called objective reality doesn't exist independent of the observer.

According to Harary, "Psi might be defined as certain aspects of nature's normal functioning that observers do not usually notice." In these terms, we are swimming in an information universe. He uses the analogy of a swimming pool. "It all looks like water, but I know it is filled with microorganisms. I can put a dye in the pool that will turn the microorganisms red. I still can't see the microorganisms, but I can see the red; and that red pattern may give me information. I can use it and attach other information to it." Harary, like so many others, sees cultural conditioning as one reason why we perpetuate such a limited view of reality, and why some cultures seem to be more attuned to psychic information than others. In Tibet, where there is no word for *paranormal*, what are to us paranormal occurrences are common to the local culture—from the believed-in reincarnations of the Dalai Lama to a rinpoche's holding off a storm cloud so that a festival can take place. By this thesis, nonhuman life—plants, animals—might be more directly responsive to psi because of the lack of cultural repression.

Psi tantalizes us; it occasionally embraces us. "Certainly," Harary comments, "psi research is uncovering as much about the limits of human awareness as it is about psi itself. As long as we view psi as abnormal, different, or odd, we will subconsciously view nature as somehow disorganized or chaotic." And as Colin Wilson says, the idea that nature is chaotic is "like asking us to believe that a pile of rusty cars in a scrap yard might be blown together into a Rolls-Royce." As long as we indulge ourselves with this view of nature, we will continue to think of psychic functioning as an aberration, a random subversion of nature's disorder, something "supernatural." Such a view permits us to abdicate responsibility for any control we might have over our psychic functioning. If consciousness is the dominant factor in our perception of psi—and indications are that this is so—then psi is as much a philosophical and psychological issue as it is scientific.

We have to change the way we think about psi. Our ability to access psychic information seems random because of our limited knowledge of how it works. Learning to function psychically may simply (!) be a matter of searching for hidden evidence of underlying order in what appear to us to be random processes. It would involve measuring and paying attention to information that is in and around us, and exerting a purposeful influence over it. It may also require belief: After all, if consciousness determines psychic experience, maybe you *cannot* experience what you do not believe.

If psi is consciousness, what you look for is what you will find, whether it is a subatomic particle or a vision of the future. As Ingo Swann says, "Psi is easy if you find the right way to look at it."

PART · THREE

PUTTING

PSI TO

WORK

CHAPTER
EIGHT

APPLYING PSI

"Where oil is first found, in the final analysis, is in the minds of men."
—Thomas Gold

Through the ages, human beings have been tantalized by the prospect of harnessing psi power and putting it to beneficial personal and social uses. Today, when we're on the threshold of so many discoveries about consciousness and the mind/brain connection, it is important to consider how psi might be employed to make our lives more secure, enriched, and productive. By considering the evidence at hand, and forming our own ideas and objectives, we prepare ourselves for handling our psychic capabilities effectively and responsibly.

At first, it may seem premature to talk about the practical applications of psychic abilities. If we don't know what psi is, or the manner in which it works, how can we put it to constructive use? We need to remind ourselves that we know very little about the basic nature of many of the power systems we utilize, such as electricity, atomic energy, or human intelligence. The record shows that psi can provide valuable information about real-world people, places, objects, and events. However mysterious psi may be, it's a capability that can help individuals and groups to achieve their goals; and the means of employing it are seemingly available to everyone.

The advice most experts offer for tapping our psi abilities sounds deceptively simple. We have only to believe in the existence of psi, without necessarily understanding it, and then to maintain a responsiveness to its subtle signals, whether we choose to call those signals "gut feelings," "intuitions," or "hunches." In a society that places a high value on activity and precision, it's difficult for many people to have faith in this kind of passive alertness, and even more, the patience to practice it. In specific incidents, a psychic signal may be so strong that it is unmistakable; but to develop an ongoing psychic sensitivity, most of us need to go through the relatively slow process of learning to distinguish psychic signals from impressions that originate in the memory, the imagination, the emotions, or the immediate environment—all forms of "mental noise." According to the reports of those who persevere, the rewards of the process far exceed the difficulties. In the short term, one enhances one's general powers of awareness. In the long term, one learns to exercise his or her personal capabilities to avert dangers, uncover opportunities, solve baffling problems, and make inspired decisions.

Some people who wish to avail themselves of psi capability prefer to rely on the guidance of gifted psychics or practitioners of psychic disciplines, many of whom have evolved their own specialized procedures for invoking psychic signals. In this capacity, modern psychics are reclaiming the social function of psychics in ages past, before scientific methodology eclipsed other modes of information-gathering. They are helping private individuals, business people, and government officials accomplish specific projects with a swiftness and a degree of success that in many cases would have been unattainable through standard operating procedures.

In this chapter we'll consider the wide range of potential practical uses for psi, as reflected in real-life accounts. Some of the examples involve people who found themselves responding to their psychic insights almost against their will—as if they were psychically driven to behave in a certain way that was in their interest. Other examples feature people who consciously sought psychic insight—either from themselves or from those with psychic abilities, were they healers, astrologers, or dowsers—and acted accordingly. In either category, the evidence supporting psychic ability as a useful tool is overwhelmingly convincing.

PERSONAL USES

Here is a story told to me by a woman who is a cinematographer: "I was flying back from Los Angeles on the 'Red Eye,' and slept most of the way back. I woke up in a sweat, having dreamed that a man dressed in black had broken into my apartment and was standing at the foot of my bed—it was frightening, and a strange dream. I went home, took a nap, ran some errands, and was supposed to be getting ready go to a meeting uptown at three o'clock. Two-thirty came and I was still sitting at my dining-room table and reading magazines. I kept telling myself that I had to stop, I had to get going to the meeting, but I couldn't seem to get myself moving. At three I'm still sitting there, when I hear a crash in the garden; I thought it was the superintendent being his usual clumsy self. A minute later, I looked up and there was a man dressed completely in black with his face pressed against the window. Well, you know me. I started screaming at him and ran to the door shouting, 'You better get out of here, you creep, or I'll bash your face in.' The guy turned and ran out the way he came—up a hose that he'd lowered into the garden. If I hadn't been there, he could easily have cleaned me out—all my equipment and everything; it would have been a disaster."

Accounts in which a person experiences some sort of paranormal warning are common in psychical literature. Crisis-oriented telepathy, clairvoyance, or (as in this case) precognition often occurs while the recipient is dreaming or in a relaxed state of awareness: Distractions in the physical environment are minimal, and an extrasensory alerting mechanism automatically kicks in. As this case shows, the warning itself is frequently accompanied by a *passive* tendency to act in such a way that the misfortune will be prevented. In situations where the danger is more urgent, or the recipient is more sensitive, the signal may be strong enough to break through any sensory noise and credible enough to provoke drastic activity. This is particularly evident in the context of a parent/child relationship. Russell Targ offers an illustration from his own life:

"We were at a dinner party at the home of my colleague Hal Put-hoff and his wife, Adrienne. We were all very happy to be joined by a mutual friend who lived out of town. In the middle of this cheery get-together, [my wife] Joan stood up from the table and said we had to go home immediately! Everyone wanted to know why. But Joan could not think of a reason. . . . In fact, when we arrived home a few minutes later, we opened the front door and faintly heard someone coughing. We went into the bedroom of our ten-year-old son, Sandy, and found him quietly choking to death. He had already turned blue from lack of oxygen. Joan, a registered nurse, knew what to do. She dragged him into the bathroom, turned on the hot shower full blast, and turned the room into a large croup tent. Within a few minutes the room was filled with steam. Sandy resumed breathing and went back to sleep."

Commenting on this kind of nonspecific psychic warning, Targ theorizes that "most people have such experiences, but do not pay much attention to them." Presumably they aren't able to differentiate a psychic signal from a random thought or emotion or dream image. Even people who are markedly predisposed to respect psychic messages may have trouble doing this, and so they listen carefully to gifted psychics. Bob Slatzer, a friend of psychic Clarisa Bernhardt, was talking to her one day and mentioned that he was going to Chicago to be on the *Phil Donahue* show:

" 'Don't take any flights that add up to the number eleven,' she warned me. I took out my ticket and sure enough, my flight to Chicago added up to something like a six or seven, but the flight back tallied eleven. Well, I didn't change my plans right away, but I kept it in mind. I did my show, but then several plans that I had made seemed to fall through or get switched around, and, to make a long story short, I got to thinking about what Clarissa had said, and I decided to fly home the night before my scheduled flight. Well, it wasn't as easy as I thought, because most flights were all booked up for the booksellers' convention out in Los Angeles; but the ticketing agent got me on a flight that meant packing and leaving the hotel within ten minutes—she told me to take my baggage right onto the plane—and they literally had to phone down to the gate to hold the plane. On the plane next to me were Ben Gazzara and Peter Bog-danovich, with whom I had cancelled party plans earlier. 'Things didn't work out,' one of them said, 'so we decided to go back early too.' Well, you know the end of the story. The next day I had slept late, got up, and was shaving when the bulletin came over the radio that the flight on my original ticket, Delta flight 191, had crashed on takeoff after its stopover in Dallas, killing almost everyone aboard, including many publishing people on their way to the convention. I had to get on the phone and call my brother right away, because I had taken out one of those flight-insurance policies, naming him as beneficiary. I had mailed it to him, enclosing a Xerox of the ticket. Fortunately, he didn't receive it until later that day."

In many cases, the psychic warning signal is quite clear and direct: so much so, in fact, that it compels the recipient to pay attention to it without any conscious decision-making. A woman I met playing tennis told me that she had recently had this psychic dream experience:

"In the dream, I was driving along, when a big truck went out of control and came over to my lane and headed straight at my car. It was a scary dream, but I shook it off. The next day I was driving to pick up my son at school. Stopped at a traffic light, I noticed a large tractor-trailer coming up to the light from the other direction. Suddenly I realized it was the scene from my dream, and I knew that the truck would not be able to stop. Without thinking, I put my car in reverse and backed quickly off to the side of the road. The truck plowed right through the light and into the place where I had been waiting for the light."

A friend of mine who is a film sound recordist had this to say:

"As far back as I can remember I've felt that I had what I call a guardian angel watching over me, protecting me—not that I could see the angel; it was more like a presence—and several times in scary situations, or an emotional crisis, I've had the sensation of a hand on my shoulder, pulling me back, saving me from danger, or keeping me from making a bad decision.

"In one of the earliest incidents I can remember, I was with my sister, Monica, standing on the back porch of my friend Mary Louise's house, across the street. They had bought an old house and were renovating it. Suddenly I heard a voice that said, 'Move!' and felt that hand on my shoulder. I jumped to one side and pushed Monica out of the way—just as a huge beam came crashing down right at the spot where we'd been standing."

Often, people have psychic revelations about events that are going to happen to other people they know. Alec Guinness, in his 1986 autobiography, mentions one that struck him quite vividly. When he met James Dean, Dean showed off to him a Porsche he had just bought. Guinness immediately had a flash in which he saw Dean in an accident in the car. The impression was so startling that he told

Dean not to drive the car, or he'd be dead within the week. And that is exactly what happened.

Psi ability can have a much broader and happier role in daily life than warning people of danger: It can actually allow people to "tune in to" distant friends and loved ones. Keith Harary conducted an impromptu "remote-viewing" experiment in June of 1983 to see how Russell Targ was faring while on a trip to Europe. Unaware of Targ's itinerary, Harary concentrated on "seeing" Targ at ten o'clock one morning:

"During the viewing, I . . . recorded strong feelings of Russ' being 'hot but happy, almost at peace, sending very positive thoughts.' I went on to describe 'something very beautiful here . . . blue stone . . . crystal blue water . . . steps . . . smooth white, not marble, small grass and trees . . . dust . . . building on a hill overlooking water and land below . . . incredibly beautiful place . . . elevations near. . . .' It turned out that this was Russell's first afternoon on the island of Mykonos, a hundred miles off the Greek coast, in the Aegean Sea. I had no idea that he would be visiting such a place. When Russell returned from his travels, we compared notes. He explained that at the time of my viewing he had been extremely happy (and very hot) standing on a hilltop watching the crystal clear, turquoise water surrounding the island. Immediately afterward, he went to a jewelry shop and bought a silver ring with a turquoise blue stone as a memento of this exceptionally beautiful location. As we went back over the remote viewing transcript, Russell was able to provide feedback, by showing me the blue stone in the ring he had purchased that day and his photographs of the brilliant white buildings of Mykonos and the sparkling blue water surrounding it."

We can also use psi power to help find things. Informal experimentation has repeatedly demonstrated that it is possible to develop the skill of "psyching out" where an empty parking place is, where lost or misplaced possessions can be found, where buried power lines lie, or where pesky animals have hidden themselves, when there is no way of figuring out the problem through logical inference.

This story was told to me by a friend who was taking care of a client's beloved—and valuable—show dog: "Late one night we realized that the dog was gone; somehow it had escaped from the house. We searched all over the place—the house, the grounds, the entire neighborhood. A woman neighbor mentioned that she had once gone to a psychic in New York named Yolana, and she called her. Yolana said not to worry, the dog was alive, and it was somewhere around a gray room. This description didn't fit any room in the house, and we were about to dismiss it when we remembered the van outside—gray, fitted out like a room, with benches and gray carpeting. The dog was huddled under the van."

Psi can even assist us in tracking down people from the distant past, whose present whereabouts are completely unknown. Again, it seems to depend simply on noticing messages that usually fail to impress our conscious minds, which have been rigidly structured by learned limitations. Consider, for example, what happened to Claire Goldberger. On a business trip to Dallas, she was idly passing some time in the public library when she came to the section containing phone books from all over the country: about twenty or thirty shelves. "I paced back and forth in front of them," Goldberger recalls, "and suddenly I found myself reaching for a specific phone book. When I lifted it off the shelf, I seemed to cradle it. The book felt warm, and I experienced a sensation of love. I instinctively thought of my mother, whom I hadn't seen since the age of five."

Goldberger and her mother had been separated during the Holocaust, in 1942. Though she had presumed her dead, she had also searched for her all her life. There in the book, forty-three years later, was her mother's name—Marne Sylvia Goldberger. She was living in a small town in upstate New York.

For weeks, she lacked the courage to call her mother. Finally, she got on a plane to see her, drove directly to the house, and screwed up the nerve to knock. "Then the door opened," Goldberger said, "and a short, youthful-looking woman stared out at me. I said, 'Mom?' Her eyes opened wide and she said, 'Clara, is that you?' "

Have you ever had a sure hunch about a winning poker hand, or a number that was going to come up in the lottery? Many people have applied their psychic abilities toward improving their personal fortunes. Two Vietnam War buddies, Steven Nathan and Hubie Cranston, have apparently learned to use their psychic abilities to win at the racetrack. They honed their skills during the time they spent in the service. Cranston, always aware of his abilities, recognized that the pliable, open Nathan would respond to his subliminal suggestions. They would practice communicating for hours, in the hope that they could help each other get out alive in a battlefield situation. On patrol, they could alert each other to the enemy's position without saying a word, and taught themselves to discover the position of snipers by blanking out their minds. Here's their racetrack technique: They each have a racing form. Five minutes before a race, each man meditates for about thirty seconds; then each circles the name of the horse he feels will win. If they are not in agreement, they don't bet. But if they both pick the same horse, they bet heavily. They win 65 percent of the time! "Most bettors have their lucky and unlucky streaks," says Nathan. "We only place bets when our combined instincts blend together. It seems to be our insurance policy. And it works."

According to former casino security specialist Serge L. Derumeaux, a man known on the casino circuit as "Emerald Al" amassed a mind-boggling $15 million a year gambling on the strength of his psychic insight: "I worked in casinos from Monte Carlo to Singapore to London, and Al turned up in all of them from time to time. My job was to watch out for chiselers, and it didn't take long for me to notice a pattern—Al always won, and he always won big. He would breeze in, make several large bets, and clear out before things got sticky. I always figured he had to be cheating, but I couldn't figure out how. I saw him in a London club, and I said, 'Al, I'm retired now. Tell me how you do it.' I played on his ego. I said, 'I'm fascinated by your ability to win and never lose. You must show me.' He said, 'I have a special power. I can see the future.' I told him to prove it, and he said, 'Pick a casino.' I picked one, and we went there. He said, 'Pick any roulette table.' I walked over to one, and he followed me. He said the next six numbers would be 17-13-23-9-17-26. I wrote them down in my notebook, and they came up exactly in that order. Then we walked to the craps table and he called eighteen out of twenty rolls of the dice right on the money. We sat at a poker table and he told me what hands would be dealt him and the others before they were dealt."

PSI IN BUSINESS

In the memoirs of such people as Henry Ford and Bernard Baruch, psychic ability has been shown to play a vital role in business-world success, although the individuals who exercise that ability may use other, more socially acceptable terms for it. William W. Keeler, former board chairman of the National Association of Manufacturers and of Phillips 66 Petroleum, calls his psychic signals "gut feelings." He points to his solar plexus and says, "I get to feeling it right here, and pretty strong; sometimes so strong that I think of *it* as a fact. . . . I've had too many incidents that couldn't be explained as merely coincidences. I've had experiences in uncharted areas. My strong feelings toward things have been accurate, when I let myself go."

At a Phillips board meeting, for example, Keeler was asked to evaluate a theoretical process that might alleviate the shortages of aviation fuel and crude rubber. He was fully aware that the process was problematic and could take up to four years to implement, yet he surprised even himself by announcing that he could put it into operation right away. "Because of a strong gut feeling, I was satisfied beyond a shadow of a doubt that it would work," Keeler remembers, "though after I made the statement to Mr. Phillips, and had time to think, I began wondering why I had said it, and began worrying like hell." Despite his conscious doubts, he successfully implemented the program within the time span he had predicted.

More commonly, the ESP component in business-related decision-making is referred to as "intuition." Weston H. Agor, president of ENFP Enterprises, a management-consulting firm specializing in the use of intuition, conducted a survey program (which uses the famous Meyers-Briggs Personality Test) to investigate the intuitive skills of more than two thousand executives in a cross section of organizational settings. He found that upper-level managers used intuition significantly more often than middle- or lower-level managers to make decisions. Two years later, Agor recontacted those individuals who had scored in the top 10 percent on intuition. Most of them stated that intuition was especially useful when uncertainty was high or when concrete facts were limited.

When I discussed psi in business with Douglas Dean, coauthor of *Executive ESP*, he said, "A group of managers for Royal Dutch Shell told me that their top man admitted he made all his decisions for the Shell Oil Company on the basis of 'sixth sense.' They don't use the term 'intuition' in Holland, because that was Hitler's term for it. The significant thing was that the top man was willing to say that he used it."

Executive ESP is based on a 1974 study conducted by Dr. John Mihalasky, a professor at the Institute of Industrial Engineering in New Jersey, and Douglas Dean. They measured the ESP aspects pertaining to the study and discovered that 48 out of 64 company presidents in one group believed strongly in the existence of ESP. As one executive said, "I believe in ESP for one reason—because I use it."

When I approached Sharper Image about evaluating the Percep-tron™ psi-teaching game (see page 336), the sales manager said he had shown it to the president of the company, Richard Thalheimer.

I had recently seen Thalheimer in a television interview in which he said that he credited much of his success to intuition. The first time he tried the Perceptron™, the sales manager reported, he scored an incredible 17 out of 24: The chance score is 6.

Ambrose Worrall's psychic abilities were put to very practical use many times during his years at the Martin Marietta Corporation. One memorable situation came up when a mechanic suddenly noticed that there were a number of ball bearings left over after a group of twenty-eight planes had come off the assembly line. Five hundred specially engineered, nondistorting ball bearings were to have gone into each plane, with none left over. Would they have to go through the costly and time-consuming process of dismantling all the planes and counting out the ball bearings in each one? Worrall walked down the line of airplanes and ordered that one be dismantled. All the leftover ball bearings belonged in the dismantled aircraft.

John Larkin, personnel director for a large engineering firm in Detroit, says he has been using his psychic powers to make hiring recommendations for over fifteen years. Larkin boasts that he has been "90 percent accurate" in his assessments, and has this to say about his methodology: "Of course, I look at their resumes and examine their track records. But for the most part, I base my final decision on the impression I receive psychically. I try to get a good idea of their capacity for rational thought and logic and how their emotions may or may not interfere with their productivity. I can tell if a person is honest, trustworthy, loyal, a good worker, et cetera. I know who will enjoy their work and who will approach it as a necessary evil. I can determine the worker who has a 'punch-the-clock' mentality and the one who will really involve himself in a project and see it through to the end. I have certain key questions I ask in order to elicit an emotional response from the applicant. A person's face may not reveal what I am looking for, but the psychic reactions tell me what I need to know. It is very difficult for someone *not* to unknowingly reveal their innermost feelings to me."

An increasing phenomenon among successful business people is the enlistment of gifted psychics as consultants. On October 6, 1986, *The New York Times* carried a fascinating story about Brian Bricker, the head of a video company called Prometheus Productions, and Carolyn Clark, who is the resident psychic of the Akbar Restaurant on Park Avenue at Fifty-eighth Street. Clark predicted that a man in green shoes was about to walk into Bricker's life—a man who would be important to his career. She even volunteered a sales strategy. The next week, Bricker was bidding on a job when, all of a sudden, the prospective client planted his feet on the desk, flashing a pair of green snakeskin loafers. "I flipped," Bricker said, "and, of course, we got the project."

Pat Barnes is a Manhattan tarot-card reader. Years ago, Barnes says, most of her clients were women in fashion or the arts. Today, her following includes a lot more men, many of them lawyers, bankers, real estate agents, and stockbrokers. A manager of an E. F. Hutton branch office in New Jersey called every week for four years, asking Barnes the most auspicious times to buy real estate and racehorses. "Having made his fortune," Barnes remarked, "he's gone off to meditate in the Himalayas or someplace like that."

Doris Haber, a psychic at the Gypsy Tea Kettle, a popular East Side restaurant, gets a large professional crowd during the lunch hour. She has a theory about why young executives are coming for readings: "They grew up in the 'Age of Aquarius,' and so they have some affinity for this sort of thing. Now they are working at high-stress jobs and faced with difficult decisions." She also points to the fact that women, historically more prone to consult psychics than men, are gaining more and more top management positions these days, so that more and more of her sessions are organized around such matters as personnel and investment advice.

One of the largest fees ever paid to a psychic was paid by commodities broker Pete Dixon to psychic Beverly Jaegers in 1976. As Jaegers confided to sociologist Dr. Laile E. Bartlett, it all started on December 30, 1974, when Dixon first came to see her:

"The first thing, he handed me a sealed envelope. 'Please tell me what you see.' I had no idea what the envelope contained, but ran my fingers over it carefully, all around the edges, and tried to concentrate hard. Suddenly, I *did* start to see things, right behind my eyes. There was a tree, covered with reddish-colored berries. I didn't know what they were, but some kind of natives were picking them —dark people in big hats. Oh yes, and it was raining, not just a drizzle, but hard. They had large baskets, which it seemed to me should have been full, but there was only a sprinkling of berries in the bottom, and some of those were shriveled and wizened. 'What a crazy thing!' I thought, and I asked him, 'Does this mean anything to you?' 'I'll say it does!' he shouted, in a funny kind of voice. 'In that envelope is my personal hunch that the price of coffee will go up. Now you confirm it! What you've told me, loud and clear, is that the supply will go down.' With that, he dashed off to invest every penny he could scrape together, $24,000 in all, in coffee futures. The rest is history, as they say. Everything happened to the coffee market after that, and all of it was bad. There was a sudden freeze in Brazil; in Angola political unrest, even Cuban agents and fighting. The price of coffee started to skyrocket, and Pete Dixon is now a millionaire."

John Krysko currently offers psychic advice as well as more conventional financial-planning services to a Wall Street clientele through an organization he founded called the K.R.I. Corporation. It's interesting to note, however, that he doesn't advertise his psychic services or the astrological genesis of some of his information in his promotional literature. Long before he became a professional financial counselor, Krysko had tried to use his precognitive psychic abilities to advise friends and acquaintances, but the typical response was a disappointing kind of resignation. "I found I could give the information, but it actually stultified the person's growth," Krysko said to me. "I'd keep trying to feel I could change the pattern; but most of the time, all that would happen is that the person would say, 'Oh, my God, then this is going to happen to me!' and they'd have no sense of freedom, or heightened power, once they knew. That's why I turned to people who were in the business community."

After reportedly using his psychic healing abilities to guide Mel Glazer, a former executive at Chanel, through a difficult operation, Krysko started offering highly profitable advice to Glazer concerning his stock investments, his marketing decisions, and his career strategy. The ultimate result was the K.R.I. Corporation. "I like working with business people a lot, because they have an active approach to precognitive information," Krysko explained to me. "They aren't passive; they're very aggressive. They say, 'Okay, this is the pattern. I'm going to go out there and work with it and do something about it!'"

Psychic consultation has now become so popular in the private sector that a business meeting can sometimes lead to an amusing psychic confrontation. When Joe Sugarman was in the process of selling a piece of property in Wisconsin, he took his psychic friend Stuart along to size up the buyer and to see if he was serious and legitimate. When they got to the house, the buyer wasn't there, and they decided to go to a nearby restaurant to kill some time. As they were leaving the house, the buyer drove up with two people in the back seat. He told Joe that he wanted them to see the house, and then they would all meet at the restaurant. As Joe remembers:

"We waited in the restaurant and in comes the buyer with the other two people, a young man and woman—who is staring at me intensely—and I introduce Stuart, and the buyer asks me who he is and I say, 'Well, Stuart is a kind of psychic.' And I looked at the woman and said to her, 'Do you know what a psychic is?' and she says, 'Yes, because that's what *my* profession is.' So what happened is—it was pretty funny—he brought his psychic and I brought mine. The buyer wanted to see if the purchase would be successful and if I was bluffing about the other potential buyers I'd told him I had. That's how it is these days."

Sometimes, psi ability fuels an entire business enterprise. In 1982, Russell Targ and Keith Harary joined Anthony White, the manager of a family fortune, in founding Delphi Associates, an experimental commercial enterprise whose charter was to explore the potential applications of psi to real-world problems. Commercial success, they reasoned, was just what the psi field needed to be taken seriously. "Somebody had to get their feet wet," Harary said. "Somebody had to get out there and start doing it."

As reported in *The Wall Street Journal* on October 22, 1984, Delphi Associates was hired by one client to forecast how much silver prices would change between Thursday's closing and Monday's opening prices on the commodities market. In all the first nine attempts, and three additional pilot trials, Harary made accurate predictions. Delphi got into the market on only seven of them, but the investor still made well over $120,000.

By far the most dramatic application of psi potential in the business world involves the ancient art of "dowsing." Traditionally, a dowser is one who seeks extrasensory perception of underground water supplies by roaming over the land holding a tool, such as a forked hazel twig or a willow wand or, in more recent times, a bent coat hanger. Presumably acting on the psychic signal received by the dowser while he or she is in a state of active concentration, the tool will dip or jerk directly over the spot where water can be found. In the contemporary business world, dowsing is more often called "remote sensing"; the target is more often oil, precious minerals, or promising archaeological sites than water; and the methodology forgoes tools and even actual landscapes in favor of sheer mind power, with or without the aid of maps.

As with other attempted psi applications in business, the test of validity is financial rather than scientific; and results that translate into easily quantifiable dollars are very difficult to ignore. *Executive ESP* tells the story of oil billionaire H. L. Hunt, who in 1976 was interested in an offshore oil-drilling proposal affecting more than

5,000 acres. Several lots were open for bidding. Hunt's geologist reported that four of those lots were potentially lucrative, but Hunt turned to a dowser for final advice. "Which of these lots will be most profitable?" he asked. "Bid on lot #207," the dowser insisted, "and be sure you bid high enough to get it." Hunt followed the advice and got lot #207, making a bid that was $11 million above the nearest competitor's. "That piece turned out to be the best in the entire area," Hunt testified later. "It was fantastically profitable."

Hoffman–La Roche, the giant pharmaceutical company, employs a dowser to do a landscape analysis whenever it plans a new factory. When questioned about this practice, its spokesperson, Dr. Peter Treadwell, answered, "We use methods which are profitable, whether they are scientifically explainable or not. The dowsing method pays off."

Knowing that Keith Harary has successfully used remote-viewing techniques to locate oil reserves, I asked him to describe a particularly memorable case. Here is his immediate choice:

"A driller came to us and he said, 'I'm drilling a well.' That was the extent of the information provided. And I said to him, 'There's orange mud in this place.' I drew a map of a peninsula with water and mountains in a certain position, and an X on the map where he was drilling. He confirmed that that was in fact the place. Using remote viewing, I looked into the well and said, 'There is no oil in this well, I'm very sorry to tell you; there is, however, hot water down there, which is a surprise.' And he said, 'Oh, that's great! I'm not drilling for oil, I'm drilling for hot water!' A month or so later he called to say that he'd hit hot water in that well, just as predicted."

Debate rages on how dowsers (or remote viewers) get their information. Are they responding to abnormal electromagnetic characteristics of the sites they "visit," or is the answer more metaphysical? Thomas Gold offers this intriguing theory: "Where oil is first found, in the final analysis, is in the minds of men. When no man any longer believes more oil is left to be found, no more oil fields will be discovered, but so long as a single oil-finder remains with a mental vision of a new oil field to cherish, along with the freedom and incentive to explore, just so long new oil fields may continue to be discovered."

Remote viewing can also be of great value in archaeology. In 1982, the Möbius Society, a nonprofit research foundation chaired by Stephan Schwartz, conducted a famous field experiment in "psychic archaeology" called the Alexandria Project. The goal of the experiment was to use teams of remote viewers to locate the Soma, the long-lost tomb of Alexander the Great buried deep beneath the present ground level of Alexandria, Egypt. The team approach, according to Schwartz, was a crucial element in the experiment's protocol:

"When I began to consider how to design applied experiments, it seemed to me that the researcher had three options, or some combination of the three. You could have a stronger signal, which is pretty hard to do if you don't know what the signal is. You could develop better receivers, which is currently a marginal activity—although we are becoming better at it. Or you could have a number of receivers that picked up the same signal, and you could average it out—essentially the same kind of thing that a reporter or a detective does in investigating a story. If someone were to dash in here and throw green paint all over me and run out again, and each of us were interviewed, not all of us would have seen everything that happened. Not all of what we reported, however strong our conviction, would be accurate. But if all of us were interviewed independently and the transcripts of these interviews were then put together it is, we know from practice, possible to create or recreate fairly clear descriptions of those events and who carried them out."

Remote viewers assigned to the Alexandria Project, which was funded in part by the Egyptian Government, were asked to perform tasks of three different kinds: describing the Soma itself, describing features on the surface of the ground near the Soma site, and marking the site location on maps of the city. Initial diggings following these suggestions have begun by both Egyptian and Polish teams; and all signs—such as "sightings" already unearthed—indicate that the consensus of the remote viewers is indeed accurate. Since any excavation process is prolonged and costly (especially in a densely populated metropolis), final confirmation is probably years away.

Commenting on the experiment at a symposium held shortly after the publication of his book *The Alexandria Project*, Schwartz confessed:

"I got interested in archaeology . . . because it is such a clean, testable sort of situation. . . . It was pretty easy to find out from the ethno-historical record whether anybody thought anything was there, whether anybody had dug there. It was easy to ascertain that the soil layers had not been disturbed. It was possible to eliminate all of the possibilities of intellectual contamination. Did they read about it in a book, had they heard about it on their grandmother's knee—whatever. And if you dug and the material was there, then you confronted that issue."

DETECTION AND PROTECTION

On a blustery April evening in Bath, Maine, Bob Ater, a Baptist minister, heard on the six o'clock news that two students who had set out to climb New Hampshire's Mount Washington were missing in a blizzard. Ater was the father of two boys who were the same ages as the missing climbers, so he felt a strong personal desire to locate them. He marked the Presidential Range in a Texaco Road Guide and concentrated on the spot where the climbers' car had been found, asking himself, "Where is the trail the hikers took?" Suddenly, Ater recalls, the pen moved "as though in a track" toward Pinkham Notch, around Mount Clay, to a point between Mount Adams and Mount Jefferson—a route very different from the one indicated in the broadcast. Ater was convinced that the students were safely sheltered there. He phoned the information to Jonathan Lingell, the weather observer atop Mount Washington; and Lingell acknowledged that the area indicated by Ater was the only one the search team had not explored. Eight days later, Jane Gilotti and David Cornue, the lost students, were discovered in a sheltered spot at Edmand's Col, nestled between Mount Jefferson and Mount Adams. Because of continuing bad weather, it took another day to get them out.

Ater's story is representative of numerous accounts given by individuals who felt psychically compelled to intervene in events of public interest concerning human safety and well-being. Sometimes, as in the Ater case, these incidents involved the detection of people who were known to be in danger—kidnapping victims, mentally impaired people who wandered away from caretakers, workers trapped in collapsed mines. Other times, they involved the detection of people who posed a public threat, such as criminals at large.

During the fall of 1979, the county of Yorkshire in England began to be terrorized by a serial woman-killer who was dubbed "the Yorkshire Ripper" because of the ferocity of the assaults. In October, after twelve women had been murdered, Mrs. Nella Jones of South London contacted Shirley Davenport, a reporter for the *Yorkshire Post*, claiming she had received psychic information that might help in the identification and apprehension of the guilty party. Over the next year, Davenport collected details from Jones, but they were dismissed by her editors and the police. At the beginning of November 1980, Jones told Davenport that she had had a vision of another killing, which would occur on the seventeenth or the twenty-seventh of that month. On November 17, the thirteenth woman was murdered, and Davenport became certain that Jones was communicating vital clues, even if the people who could act on them continued to ignore them.

In January 1981, the killer, Peter Sutcliffe, was finally apprehended; and the facts that emerged about him astounded Davenport. Sutcliffe was a truckdriver employed by Clark Transport. Davenport recalled that a year and four months prior to the final arrest, Jones had said that the Yorkshire Ripper was a truckdriver named Peter, who had a word beginning with "C" painted on the side of his cab. Exactly one year before the arrest, Jones told Davenport that the killer lived in a big house in Bradford—addressed "No. 6"—that was elevated above the street behind wrought-iron gates, with a stairway leading up to the front door. Sutcliffe lived at No. 6 Garden Lane in Bradford. The house was large, elevated, and fronted by a wrought-iron gate and stairsteps up to the main entrance. "It went far beyond anything coincidence or guesswork could possibly have provided," commented Davenport. "And you have to remember that for the previous two years, all the public signs had been that the police were looking for a man who came from the northeast of England, a hundred miles away, and who worked in an engineering plant."

Police do not always turn a deaf ear to psychic input. In many difficult investigations, they actually solicit it. The trouble is that no simple method has yet been devised for distinguishing probable psychic "hits" from "misses" or for processing all possible psychic leads efficiently.

The same baffling problem plagues another category of psychic contributions in the public interest—those aimed at protecting groups of people or famous people from some future danger. London's Premonitions Bureau and New York City's Central Premonitions Registry have files bursting with predictions of plane crashes, assassinations, earthquakes, floods, and volcano eruptions—many of which later proved to be uncannily accurate. Whether to act on such predictions, however, remains an issue of individual faith. Agencies responsible for public protection can't afford to follow a policy of checking out all psychically acquired information or of passing it along to those individuals whose fates might be directly threatened. Even when predictions are made available to great numbers of people, only rare individuals will inconvenience themselves to take advantage of them. When I discussed this situation with the famed psychic Irene Hughes, she volunteered this story from her own experience:

"In August of 1966 I was on a railroad track in Chicago trying to go through a seance about a terrible train accident when all of a sudden it was like this great snowstorm happened, and it told me the dates January 28, 29, and 30 and February 1–4. Well, those dates were published in the paper, and sure enough—an unprecedented snowstorm hit Chicago during that exact time span and caused $50 million in damage. A famous writer I know, Alan Spraggett, came to town just before that storm. I met him in the Pump Room at the Ambassador West Hotel and said, 'You'd better get out of town, because the greatest snowstorm in the world is going to hit this city and you'll never get out.' He left, and wrote about the incident in his book *The Unexplained*."

The following story is excerpted from a 1986 letter sent to psychic Tony Cordero, signed by John E. Thoen, Director of Nursing, and Carmen Quiroga, Administrative Assistant, of Florida's Dade County Medical Center:

"We all were amazed at things you told us about ourselves and other co-workers, but did not expect some of your other predictions to be so accurate. That night you told us that we should have a fire drill soon, and have our fire alarm system checked. You stated that a fire would occur and the alarms would not function. We assured you that the alarms had been recently checked and were functioning properly. The next morning a fire did occur out in the hallway, in the garbage container. When the alarms were pulled, they did not function."

GOVERNMENT AND MILITARY USES

Just how extensively the U. S. Government has researched potential uses of psi during the past few decades is unknown (see Chapter 2). Occasionally an isolated story will surface regarding psi experimentation in the military branches. During the years of the Vietnam conflict, for example, U.S. Marines at Camp Lejune in North Carolina were successfully trained to "dowse" for mines and enemy tunnels. In part, their training programs were based on South Vietnamese models. Captain Vo Sum of the South Vietnamese Navy gained a widespread reputation during the late 1960s and early 1970s for psychically locating opium fields, lost ships, and enemy troops.

In 1984, C. B. "Scott" Jones, a former naval intelligence officer who is now a member of Senator Claiborne Pell's staff, performed a fascinating experiment for the navy in interspecies communication, working with a bottle-nosed Atlantic dolphin at Sea-Arama, Galveston, Texas. Three judges agreed upon the outcome of six sets of blind instructions telepathically sent to the dolphin by a human transmitter. Four of the outcomes were scored as hits: The dolphin carried out the multipart set of instructions in the designed sequence and at the time requested. One outcome was correct, but was accomplished immediately *before* the transmitter opened the envelope of instructions. The remaining outcome was not carried out as instructed, but the dolphin performed a "close substitute" maneuver that may have been the only one possible given the physical constraints of the dolphin enclosure. Among the potential applications of human/dolphin telepathic capability that Jones cited in his report of the experiment are:

- increased search rate for any man/sea mammal search-and-detection system;
- accurate reporting of new or changing underwater threat;
- improved neutralization capability of underwater threats;
- beach reconnaissance;
- mine placement;
- antisubmarine-warfare sensor placement.

Of far more interest to parapsychologists and the general public alike, however, is whether the U.S. Government has been making a concerted effort to keep up with the Soviet Union in psi studies relating to "distant influence." As defined by Larissa Vilenskaya, "distant influence" refers to the possible ability of a psychic individual or a psi-imparting force (such as low-level electromagnetic waves) to affect the thoughts or emotions of people without their knowledge or consent, regardless of how far away physically the people may be. "From my experience," Vilenskaya maintains, "I clearly see that while Western psi researchers are interested in extending human awareness and our realm of perception, official Soviet scientists are interested in using psi primarily to develop extended means for mental influence at a distance." The implications of distant influence are terrifying. Theoretically, it could be used to handicap the performance of enemy leaders and negotiators, to enforce the cooperation of key enemy personnel, or even to undermine the resistance of an entire enemy population.

To the best of our knowledge, the government of the Soviet Union is more committed than the government of the United States to the investigation of psi phenomena in general; and the main object of its commitment does appear to be further information pertaining to "distant influence." Nevertheless, few parapsychologists seriously believe that the horrific applications mentioned above are possible. Psi power doesn't seem likely to lend itself to such complex motives, and there are far more tangible modes of espionage and warfare to fear first. What parapsychologists are concerned about is the more basic issue of a potential knowledge gap existing between the United States and the Soviet Union: Will Soviet superiority in psi studies eventually give the Soviets an edge in overall scientific, economic, and social development? Is the fundamentally negative attitude toward psi in the United States retarding its growth as a nation vis-à-vis the Soviet Union?

In late 1984, the National Academy of Sciences began a two-year study of psychic phenomena under a $453,000 grant from the Army Research Institute. The group in direct charge of the study is called, innocuously, the "Committee on Techniques for the Enhancement of Human Performance," and it operates under the academy's Commission on Behavioral and Social Sciences. The committee's objectives are singularly ambitious: It hopes to establish the scientific validity of claims made by "proponents of existing technologies for the enhancement of human performance," to identify what kinds of scientific research are needed to evaluate these claims, and to recommend research needed to "advance understanding of human capabilities and their enhancement."

Regrettably, what could be a major breakthrough effort in regard to government interest in psi seems to be prejudiced from the start against psi. In the original proposal submitted by the National Academy of Sciences, this is how the seven different "human technologies" to be investigated are described:

"Growing out of the human potential movement of the 1960s, together with more recent developments in psychology and psychophysiology, these 'human technologies' include such things as sleep learning, split brain learning, meditation and biofeedback techniques to reduce stress and increase concentration, neurolinguistic programming to increase organizational effectiveness, and accelerated learning. *At one extreme are the so-called 'incredible technologies,' including parapsychology*"(italics mine).

People associated with the project have openly displayed their reservations about studying psi. When the project was formally announced, Dr. David A. Goslin, executive director of the commission, insisted, "This is not a witch-hunt. It is not a debunking exercise." At the same time, however, he said as a spoof on the parapsychologists that the Pentagon had already developed "a wholly different approach to remote viewing—it's called 'satellite.' " One of the actual committee members, Ray Hyman, a University of Oregon psychology professor and known psi debunker, admitted his concern about the claims being made in published reports of "pseudoscience" research, saying:

"The stuff that seems to get emphasized is stuff that even parapsychologists are alarmed at in the sense that it is very far-out. I'm a little hesitant to tell them [military agencies] not to look at it at all. If you put yourself in the shoes of the military people, they've got to hedge their bets, I suppose."

Hyman's supposition is reinforced by a comment Scott Jones made to me about a 1983 symposium sponsored by Kaman Tempo, a research division of Kaman Sciences Corporation, that brought together top psi researchers with forty-five representatives of different government agencies. Speaking about the government representatives, Scott said:

"The message I got from that meeting was that there's no way they're going to stick their heads out until a different set of political signals is sent. One of them told me, 'Hey, if Jack Anderson hears about this and talks about it, we're dead. I'll never be able to talk to you again, Scott, because I'll be afraid that we'll get the Golden Fleece Award; we'll get the diamond-studded, platinum-plated Golden Fleece Award for being so foolish as to spend any money on this nonscientific area."

The fear of ridicule—and of psi itself—is almost laughable sometimes. One of the participants in this symposium was Dr. Peter A. Sturrock, professor of Space Science and Astrophysics at Stanford University and president of the Society for Scientific Exploration. In his address to the other attendees, Sturrock was moved to comment, "The fact that this meeting is being held in a 'secure area' is indicative that interest in the psi area is still somewhat heretical." That's real cloak-and-dagger stuff, the "safe house" or secret meeting place. Sturrock added:

"A scientist who makes a careful investigation of a UFO case cannot present it at a normal scientific meeting or publish it in a normal scientific journal, yet these steps are essential if he is to receive the best available criticism and if he is to be able to inform other potentially interested scientists of his work. . . . I soon realized this situation is not peculiar to UFO research, but is common to almost all areas of research into anomalies, including parapsychology."

Given this official climate, the Committee on Techniques for the Enhancement of Human Performance has a rather daring mission; and its membership is suitably impressive. The group includes John

A. Swets, chairman of Bolt Beranek & Newman, Inc.; Robert A. Bjork and Gerald C. Davidson from UCLA's Department of Psychology; Paul W. Holland from the Educational Testing Service in Princeton; Lloyd G. Humphries from the University of Illinois' Department of Psychology; Daniel Landers from Arizona State University's Department of Physical Education; Sandra Ann Mobley, a training executive from the Hewlett-Packard Corporation; Lyman W. Porter from U.C. at Irvine's Graduate School of Management; Michael I. Posner from Washington University's Department of Neurology; Walter Schneider from the University of Pittsburgh; Jerome Singer from the Uniformed Services University of Health Sciences; Sally P. Springer from SUNY at Stony Brook's Department of Psychology; and Richard Thompson from Stanford University's Department of Psychology. Unfortunately, the membership mix is not well balanced in favor of psi study. Referring to the committee as a whole, Mary Maruca, editor of the National Park Service *Courier*, noted:

"The . . . scientists are certainly qualified in their fields, but none of them are parapsychologists or have any psychical research experience. If each of the seven areas of inquiry received equal treatment, a considerable amount of the approximately $65,000 allocated for parapsychology was probably consumed in bringing the committee up to speed in an area foreign to most of them. Any one of dozens of highly qualified parapsychologists could have provided resident committee expertise. It is too bad the committee was organized without this competence."

Despite criticisms, the mere existence of the committee is a major, positive step forward in U.S. Government and military investigation regarding practical applications of psi. Scott Jones said to me, "Over half a million dollars is not an inconsiderable sum to spend on this, even though parapsychology is only one of seven items. If you look at what is being spent on parapsychology by the government otherwise, there is a significant investment by the government to find out something about psi phenomena. The army will respond one way or another based upon what this committee turns out, and it will all be in the public domain."

THE PSI IMPERATIVE

Undeniably, the most important reason for exploring and developing psi power is that it promises to broaden our understanding of who we are as human beings, of our individual relationships to one another, and of our role in the natural universe. Already it bids us challenge our rigid notions of time, space, human interconnections, and human capabilities. In an age that is increasingly oriented toward technology, attention to psi phenomena can keep us mindful of our ever-mysterious humanity. The eminent British mathematician and computer pioneer A. M. Turing posited the theory that the only discernible difference between human intelligence and computer intelligence might ultimately be that the latter cannot directly experience psi!

Scott Jones gave me a more pragmatic slant on the same basic theme:

"I think psi is ubiquitous. I think that everyone is involved in what we on the average call 'psi' right now, and that it's a basic survival mechanism for humans. It's sort of a guardian. It gives you clues and hints; sometimes you'll follow and sometimes you won't. The more attuned you get to those clues and hints, the safer your life will be."

CHAPTER NINE

MODERN MIRACLES: PSYCHIC HEALING

"Healing by the laying on of hands is about as miraculous as radio."
—Bernard Grad

Over the past decade, a revolution in health care has occurred. A sharp rise in the incidence of complicated, stress-related health problems—including cancer, heart disease, immune deficiency, allergies, hypertension, and musculoskeletal pain—has made a flexible, multifaceted, "system" approach to therapy far more sensible and attractive than the conventional drugs-and-surgery approach. This fact, plus the skyrocketing cost of institutional medical care, has inspired widespread popular experimentation with all sorts of alternative healing models.

Some of these approaches—such as massage, hypnosis, and visualization—have endured successfully for centuries. Temporarily eclipsed by the rapid growth of surgical-medical technology, they are now being rediscovered and revitalized by a more informed, more motivated public. Other therapies—such as polarity, biofeedback, and reflexology—are more recent in origin. Responding to what science and human experience now suggest about the potential benefits of non-invasive, personalized healing procedures, these more recent therapies have been specially designed to assist the mind and the body in working their own, integrally connected restorative powers.

Taken as a whole, both the long-standing and recent therapies constitute a vast, newly popular universe of healing arts which already have a strong spiritual—even psychic—component. In fact, we are coming to realize that there may be no more powerful application of psi ability than in the area of healing. As more and more people take it upon themselves to examine all their health-care options, an increasing acceptance and use of psi ability in healing seems inevitable.

Even most scientifically trained doctors will tell you they cannot cure a patient who doesn't have the will to live, which means that in addition to medicine and surgery we invariably depend upon "the powers of the mind" to effect healing. This chapter investigates nonscientific therapies, therapists, and processes that have demonstrably tapped these mental powers and have resulted in apparent cures for which no traditional, scientific explanation exists.

The process of healing is as mysterious as the process of life. In fact, many scientists tell us it *is* the process of life—a tendency toward well-being characterized by a quickening force that we have yet to identify or understand. We know some procedures for assisting this tendency, but the tendency itself remains a paradox. It's magically natural, and it's naturally magical.

The same paradox applies to the ability we call "psi"; and psi power does seem to be a factor in many, if not all, cases of healing. But every case of healing also involves a complex of other factors that are physical, psychological, and environmental in nature. How can we distinguish a "psychic" healing from a "normal" healing, if healing in itself is such a mysterious and complicated process?

In truth, we can't make any clear distinction. We can only suggest that a psychic healing is one that appears singularly unusual. In some cases healing occurs when or where it isn't expected. In others, the pattern of healing is bizarre, or the rate of healing seems unaccountably rapid, or the extent of healing is atypically great. Depending on the circumstances surrounding such a healing, or the observer's point of view, that unusual quality may be attributed to psi functioning associated with one (or more) of the following events:

- the application of a systematic healing therapy that has no validity in terms of Western science;
- the ostensible intervention of a supernatural being;
- the exercise of paranormal powers by a healer;
- the exercise of paranormal powers by the healee.

We'll consider each of these possible explanations for psychic healing separately (bearing in mind that they may overlap), and then look at the experiments parapsychologists have devised for studying psychic healing.

NONSCIENTIFIC THERAPIES

For over twenty thousand years before the development of scientific medicine, organized healing, to most of the world's population, was what we would call a magic art. Diagnosis was closely related to divination; and treatment was, in essence, a mystic ritual. Nevertheless, patients were often cured; and this form of healing, now called shamanism, still survives. To the people who believed, and continue to believe, shamanism was, and is, as real as medical science is to most Westerners.

The word "shaman" derives from Siberia and has been used by anthropologists to describe the practitioner of a type of therapy found in most tribal societies throughout history all over the world. Dr. Michael Harner, who became an initiate in 1961 during his anthropological work with the Conibo tribe in the upper Amazon, says that shamanism takes the same basic form whether it's encountered in ancient Gaul, Scythia, Kush, or Peru, or modern Arizona, Australia, Finland, or Zaïre:

"A shaman is a person who changes his or her state of consciousness to enter another reality for the purpose of helping others. A shaman moves *at will* between what I call an Ordinary State of Consciousness (OSC) and a Shamanic State of Consciousness (SSC). It is in the SSC that one 'sees' shamanically. This may be called 'visualizing,' 'imaging' or according to Australian aborigines, using 'the strong eye.' "

Usually, Harner explains, the SSC is achieved through ritual chanting, drumming or dancing; and the actual therapy consists of the shaman's "seeing" and "touching" the patient while simultaneously inhabiting two levels of reality: the SSC and the OSC.

Thousands of anecdotes from the past and the present link shamanic therapy with the remission of symptoms, but there's no way to prove a direct causal connection. Harner offers a typical example from his own experience:

"In one case where I led a group, demonstrating a shamanic healing method, the woman we worked with had a terminal blood illness. She had been under close observation—with continuous monitoring and laboratory testing of her condition—for five years. Ten days after the shamanic experience she went in for her usual laboratory tests. The physicians found no evidence of illness at all. Since the illness was incurable, the only conclusion they could arrive at was that all their diagnoses and tests of the previous five years had been incorrect."

Here is an especially intriguing story concerning Native American shamanism that was told to me by Elizabeth Brandt, a professor of sociology at the University of Arizona:

"The British-born wife of one of my colleagues was too weak to have cancer surgery that she desperately needed when I first took her to see Phillip Cassadore, a medicine man I've worked with. He spoke to her and then performed ritualistic chants over pollen that he placed in the four directions. After that, he gave her some advice, telling her to follow it for four days, at which time her fever would break. Though she sometimes doubted and lost heart, she followed his advice. Four days later, her fever broke, and she gained enough strength over the next couple of months to have the surgery. Neither she nor I had any particular explanation for why she got better, or whether it in fact had anything to do with Phillip's intervention. On the day before her operation I happened to see Phillip and mentioned to him, not knowing why, that she was having surgery the next day, and I asked him to pray for her. He explained to me that what he would actually do was call upon the sixty-four medicine men who, according to Apache tradition, watch over the sick, and he'd get them to do what they could for her.

"I sent a short note to my colleague's wife, telling her that I was thinking about her, and that I'd asked Phillip to pray for her. But I said nothing else. Her husband called me after the operation to tell me that the first thing she said when she came out of the anesthesia was that a bunch of old Indian men had been standing around her while she was in the operating room."

Assuming that the shamanic exercises were responsible for the recoveries of the women in these two situations, the healings have to be considered "psychic" healings, for they cannot be explained according to the known laws of nature or medicine, as interpreted by Western science. The same holds true for mainstream Eastern medical practices, such as yogic therapy (the balancing of bodily energy among a metaphysical system of chakras) and acupuncture (the manipulation of a vital force called "ch'i" that flows through body meridians).

Today, increased contact with Asian and African cultures in particular has made Westerners more familiar with and knowledgeable about nonscientific healing traditions; and many elements from those traditions have been borrowed, adapted, and incorporated into Western-style "holistic therapy." Hence the growing use of acupuncture, Chinese qigong and t'ai ch'i, and various forms of yoga and meditation. Homeopathic medicine and herbalist remedies, common to cultures from Tibet to the Hopi reservations, are again popular. Frequently the adaptation involves giving the original healing technique a more "respectable" name and ideology: Hence, shamanism, for example, is picked apart and recast as "guided imagery" or "biofeedback"; the laying on of hands seems more acceptable as "therapeutic touch." Possession, divination with chicken bones, or potions made from toads' hearts are no longer favored, but somewhat cleaned-up ritual attends many current healing practices.

DIRECT SUPERNATURAL INTERVENTION

In the opinion of people who harbor strong religious beliefs, all that may be needed for a miraculous healing is prayer to a supernatural entity. Called God, Jahweh, Buddha, the Great Spirit, or any one of thousands of other names, depending on the particular religion, this transcendent being is perceived as a benevolent force that watches over human affairs and is capable of restoring health to stricken mortals by direct appeal.

There is a huge body of anecdotal literature attesting to positive healing results achieved through prayer. Among the best-documented examples are those centered around the Roman Catholic shrine of Lourdes in France. Since 1858, a team of medical examiners, known as the International Medical Commission at Lourdes, has applied stringent criteria to the investigation of more than 6,000 claims of miraculous cures that have been submitted since 1858. Many of these claims cite the complete and instantaneous cure of such diseases as cancer, multiple sclerosis, and Parkinson's disease, which are considered incurable by Western medical science. To date, only 64 of the cases studied by the commission have been accepted as "miraculous" by the Roman Catholic Church; but the occurrence of even one miraculous cure should be enough to challenge non-believers.

One cure that is not included in the Church's list of miracles was impressive enough to convert one of twentieth-century France's most distinguished scientists, Dr. Alexis Carrel. Despite his rigorous train-ing and his professed agnosticism, Carrel was open-minded enough not to discount the possibility of paranormal healing. In 1903, he agreed to accompany one of his patients, a young woman named Marie Bailly, on a trip to Lourdes. Everyone in Bailly's family had died of tuberculosis, and at this time she was in the final stages of tubercular peritonitis. The infection had spread to her body cavity, and death was expected within a matter of days. When she reached the front of the Grotto of Lourdes, however, Carrel observed a re-markable change in her appearance. Bailly's distended abdomen had shrunk to its proper size, and color had returned to her ashen fea-tures. He immediately checked her pulse and respiration rates, and they were normal for the first time in months. Later that evening, Carrel and three other physicians thoroughly examined Bailly and reportedly found that she was completely cured.

From that moment on, Carrel declared his belief in the miraculous healing of his patient—a stand that caused him to be expelled from his position at the University of Lyon in 1905. He subsequently joined the staff of the Rockefeller Institute in New York, and in 1912 he received the Nobel Prize for his work on organ transplantation and the suturing of blood vessels.

THE GIFTED HEALER

Cures that are attributed to nonscientific medical therapies or to the direct intervention of a supernatural being are not what are com-monly termed "psychic healings," although they may in fact result from psi functioning. When we think of psychic healings, we usually think of a psychic healer—a person who uses strange mind powers to relieve patients of their physical complaints. Psychic healing, then, may be perceived as psychokinesis applied to a biological system. Many parapsychologists accept the theory that psychic healing is a form of psychokinesis. The only problem with this interpretation is that it doesn't match the description many psychic healers give of how they believe the healing process works or how it feels to them.

The healers we'll be looking at in this category are not working within the context of a particular systematic health therapy (as, for example, shamans are), but they may be working within the context of a particular religion. Frequently, psychic healers will speak of themselves as "channels" for a supernatural power, just as seance mediums say that they are channels for discarnate spirits. This definition implies that psychic healing may be closer to telepathy—albeit a "supercharged" telepathy—than to psychokinesis.

Spiritual healers of the Christian faith are quite active among their congregations—especially in Great Britain, where there are more than five thousand licensed spiritual healers who have their own paramedical organization, the National Association of Spiritual Healers. I spoke to the head of this organization, Dr. Don Copland. He affirmed his view that "spiritual healing is just a healer acting as a channel for a divine energy which is available from God." He also relates this energy to "thought" energy:

"A group of us will get together on Wednesday night and project the love of God to patients who have been referred to us. It's really a transmission of energy of thought which starts with the request by the person in behalf of the patient. In other words, someone has taken the bother to worry about someone else, and has turned on a light switch."

In the United States, spiritual healers are not licensed, but spiritual-healing centers and programs abound. Eva Graf, for example, directs the Center of the Light, an 83-acre "retreat" complex affiliated with the Church of Christ Consciousness in Great Barrington, Massachusetts. The center holds training workshops in all sorts of nonmedical, holistic health approaches; however, as Graf makes clear, the emphasis is on "touching your own deep well of compassion, wisdom, and God connection that you can draw on for helping."

For more than thirty years, Gilbert N. Halloway has performed psychic healings during private sessions, public lectures, and hundreds of television and radio appearances across the United States. Describing himself as a "spiritual counselor" and "impressional sensitive," Halloway claims that all diseases are psychosomatic and that what he does during a healing is analogous to what the Bible calls "the casting out of devils." As he explained to me:

"Man has a physical body and a spiritual body. The spiritual body is primary, causative. The physical body is the effect. Whatever I think and believe in my inner consciousness, my body becomes. All disease is caused by error—a negative thought in some way. The theory of psychic diagnosis is this: If I am attuned to you, I feel in my own spiritual, psychic body what is in your spiritual, psychic body. I don't enter into the condition itself, but I feel its presence. Sometimes just this sharing can eliminate, either gradually or imme- diately, the error that is there. Sometimes it's a matter of following an appropriate good-health practice that fits the diagnosis."

A similar kind of "psychic" help is offered in Hispanic communi- ties by *espiritistas*—psychic healers and advisors who treat their clients for illnesses that seem to have a spiritual basis. Common complaints will be "I don't sleep well," "I have no appetite," "I'm losing weight," or "I cry a lot." When I talked with Dr. Virginia Garrison, an anthropologist who has made extensive studies of *espi- ritista* centers in the urban United States, she commented:

"As the Hispanic clients perceive it, they have spiritual forces within them. The ones that particularly relate to them are good— their guides, their guardians, their angels. But they could have bad spirits around them too. These people are just describing their inner experiences in those concepts. What they talk about are 'spirit prob- lems' that are manifesting themselves in physical ways, and they go to a medium for help. The mediums are doing something very much like what psychotherapists are doing."

Miraculous healing is easier to recognize as a psi phenomenon when we examine the work of healers who have a more secular orientation. The best-known psychic healer of the twentieth century was Edgar Cayce, a simple man with little formal education who made diagnoses and prescribed treatments for thousands of individ- uals while he was in a self-induced trancelike state. As manifested by Cayce, the paranormal healing power resembles clairvoyance more than psychokinesis. Many of his patients were people he never saw, and many of the ailments he described were extremely compli- cated, rare, or even unknown. Nevertheless, his success ratio was astounding.

Cayce's treatments themselves were way ahead of their time. Long before the theoretical foundations of psychosomatic medicine were laid, Cayce stressed that tensions and strains were responsible for stomach ulcers. Thirty years prior to the scientific revelation of a rabbit-serum treatment for cancer, Cayce had prescribed it and detailed how it should be prepared. Once he recommended "clary water" for a man suffering from rheumatism. No druggist had heard of "clary water," so the patient advertised in a trade paper. A man from Paris wrote saying that his father had developed the product nearly fifty years before but it was never publicized or put on the market. He enclosed a copy of the original prescription. Meanwhile, Cayce had gone into another trance to find out how to make it. The trance information corresponded exactly with the actual prescription, and the success of the subsequent treatment helped to popularize "clary water" for the first time.

In 1910, when Cayce's remarkable career was just beginning, Dr. Wesley Ketchum made this report to the American Society of Clinical Research in Boston:

"I have used him in about 100 cases and to date have never known of any errors in diagnosis, except in two cases where he described a child in each case by the same name and who resided in the same house as the one wanted. He simply described the wrong person.

"The cases I have used him in have, in the main, been the rounds before coming to my attention, and in six important cases which had been diagnosed as strictly surgical he stated that no such condition existed, and outlined treatment which was followed with gratifying results in every case."

Since Cayce's death in 1945, hundreds of healers have followed his suggestions and have successfully treated thousands of people who could not otherwise find help. His papers are preserved by The Association for Research and Enlightenment in Virginia Beach, an organization that continues to sponsor workshops and programs which attract people interested not only in Cayce, but also in psychic healing in general.

Unlike Cayce, most psychic healers establish some sort of physical bond with their patients—touching, stroking or manipulating the injured spot or simply holding their hands over it. This procedure can make psychic healing appear to be a form of psychokinesis. Like psychokinesis, it may be a power we all have to some degree, but one that we ignore, disavow, or fear. I was getting into the back seat of a taxi in Seattle once, and the driver noticed I was carrying some papers on psychic subjects. He said, "You're interested in psychic things? I think I'm a healer. When my friends have headaches, I put my index finger to their head and their headache is gone. I've even seen a light come out of the palm of my hand, but I'm afraid to tell it to anyone. They'll think I'm crazy. They'll lock me up."

It was during this trip that I met Bob O'Dell, who first became aware of his psychic healing abilities when he was forty years old and has been a practicing psychic healer for twelve years now. I asked him what a healing session felt like, and he replied:

"It's like a light, a warmth passing through me. It comes out in the palm of my hand and then my index finger. It can come out in several different ways. If a person has itchy or broken skin, it comes out like a heavy cream, like a salve, and spreads all over the skin. If the trouble is inside a bone, like the inside of a joint, it goes in like a laser. I can generally see a color in the affected area of the person's body. I don't see an aura on the outside. I see it inside. I see, for example, a dark spot on a person's body and then I can run my hands over it and I can feel heat. I thought everybody could feel that, but they can't. Most people can't feel that heat that I can feel."

Valerie Hunt, who taught physiology at Columbia University and has developed a sophisticated procedure for recording brain waves on an electromyograph, is convinced that a person's aura offers important clues about his or her physical condition: namely, changes of light or heat that can guide a psychic healer, consciously or unconsciously, to locate and alleviate trouble spots on the body. She shared with me a fascinating account of a psychic healing performed by a friend of hers, which was simultaneously monitored by someone claiming to be able to read the aura and by Hunt herself, using an electromyograph:

"A friend who is a psychic and a healer had been sent from the Neurological Institute a man who had had pathological brain waves since birth. She asked if I would record her healing, and I agreed. She brought an aura reader with her, so we had two simultaneous types of monitoring: As the healer performed, the aura reader described what she saw happening and I kept track of what was happening on the electromyograph. I couldn't figure out what the healer was doing. Among other things, she made noises and blew on the patient's knees. But whenever the aura reader described 'spurts of energy' in the aura, I saw 'spurts of energy' on the machine. Throughout the healing (which turned out to be successful), I scientifically recorded that there was a significant change in brain-wave activity at exactly the times when the aura reader indicated that things were happening in the aura!"

Organized medicine in the United States, unlike its counterpart in

Great Britain, continues to take a dim view of psychic healing. It wasn't until 1959 that the American Medical Association approved hypnosis as a patient treatment, and no doubt it is a long way from acknowledging the diagnostic possibilities of aura reading. Still, it's been difficult for doctors and nurses to ignore the fact that some people seem to be naturally gifted healers, capable of producing effects that can't be attributed either to orthodox medical procedures or to the patient's stimulated will to recover. Independent studies sponsored by a number of different hospitals have recently established that a modified version of "laying on of hands" called therapeutic touch, which has been used by a growing number of health practitioners over the last fifteen years, does produce distinct physiological effects, including the relief of pain, the reduction of anxiety, and the increase of oxygen-bearing hemoglobin in the blood.

According to Dr. Dolores Krieger, professor of nursing at New York University Hospital, therapeutic touch is a technique whereby the healer "centers" his or her self on an intent to heal, and then moves his or her hands over a patient's body to detect areas of excess energy. The hands do not actually have to touch the body, and the healee does not need to be aware that the process is going on. The healers themselves do not have to possess special talents or powers —they only require instruction and practice in the proper execution of the technique.

Krieger has trained more than two thousand nurses in therapeutic touch, among them Dr. Janet Quinn, an associate professor who is assistant director of nursing research at the University of South Carolina at Columbia. Quinn reports, "The working hypothesis is that there is a transfer of energy from the healer to the patient." Individual patients claim that they feel heat emanating from the healer's hands, even when those hands are held six inches away from the body's surface. Quinn cautions, "Therapeutic touch is not a panacea. People don't throw down their crutches or get cured of cancer"; but the reported results so far have been significant enough for the federal government to award Quinn the first grant for studying the subject.

On March 26, 1985, the main story in the "Science Times" section of The New York Times announced the federal grant and described a study that Quinn had conducted at St. Vincent's Medical Center in New York among sixty heart patients. Nurses were first divided randomly into two groups. One group was fully trained in therapeutic touch: that is, the nurses were taught how to concentrate on healing while passing their hands over the patients. The other group was not given the crucial part of the training; the nurses were merely told to count backward from one hundred by sevens while performing the correct motions with their hands. The two groups were videotaped as they practiced with patients, and observers were unable to tell who were the real healers and who were the mentally distracted counters. The patients also did not know the difference—or the real purpose of the experiment. They were told that the nurses were trying to determine "what could be learned about the body through the hands."

The patients' anxiety levels were monitored before and after exposure to the real and placebo healing exercises. Those patients whose "healers" were centered on healing experienced a highly significant reduction in anxiety compared with those whose "healers" were just counting. As Dr. Quinn reported in the professional journal *Advances in Nursing Science*, anxiety levels in the authentically treated patients dropped by 17 percent after only five minutes of therapy, whereas there was no change in anxiety whatsoever among patients who did not receive authentic treatment.

Far more difficult to accept than manual psychic healing—or even psychic healing at a distance—is psychic surgery, whereby the healer supposedly enters the patient's body and removes or manipulates body tissues, using no medical instruments, causing little or no pain, and leaving slight or no scars. I talked with one such healer, Sister Sarita, who practices psychic surgery in San Diego. She says her first encounter with psychic healing occurred when she developed "an ulcer in the chest" twenty years ago. Desperate to get rid of the pain, she went to a psychic healer in her native Mexico and watched as the healer removed fourteen stones from her body and laid them one by one on a tray with wads of blood-soaked cotton. "I thought it was all on the physical level," Sarita said through an interpreter, "but it wasn't. After the operation, there were no visible stitches. Twenty-two days later, all my symptoms disappeared and I was completely well."

Psychic operating procedures vary greatly among healers. From the Philippines, we get the image of rusty knives and nonsterile conditions used in surgery that has all the appearance of being physically real. The Brazilian psychic surgeon Arigo had the reputation of being able to use dull table knives to make swift, painless incisions that healed overnight without stitches or clamps. Most healers, however, perform nonvisible surgery, which means that there are no legal problems about practicing medicine without a license. Sarita falls into this latter category. She says that she visualizes surgery on a higher level. Were the observers as evolved as she is, she claims, they would be able to see the operation taking place themselves. In one case, a patient named Geneva Cody, who suffered from "fluid in the lungs," agreed to let reporters from *Holistic Living News* watch while Sarita operated on her. Here is the reporters' account of their experience:

"Stretched out on Sarita's operating table, Geneva was prepared for surgery with a psychic anesthetic injection [Sarita visualizing an injection and imitating it with her hand]. Sarita then began to press on Geneva's neck and chest, her fingertips leaving trails of red marks as she lifted her thumb and made cutting motions, as if she was penetrating the skin with an etheric pair of scissors.

" 'It felt real sharp,' Geneva recalls, 'like her fingers were cutting, but it didn't go deep, just below the skin.'

"Turning Geneva [over], Sarita located and cleaned out a black spot she had seen psychically on her lung. Following a 'blood transfusion,' Geneva's fifteen-minute operation was complete. Sarita recommended an herbal remedy and made an appointment for Geneva to return the following week to have her 'stitches' removed.

" 'When Sarita found the spot where she said all the infection was,' says Geneva, 'it hurt. I could tell when she gave me the anesthetic. It felt like she was really inserting a needle. Then I felt removed from the whole thing, just like I did when I had a sinus operation under a local anesthetic. Afterwards, I was exhausted, just as if a real operation had taken place.' "

Whether or not anything actually happened in the physical dimension, Geneva felt a definite improvement after the psychic surgery.

There seems to be a good deal of evidence to show that much of the blood and gore of psychic surgery is just for show. In a number of cases where psychic surgeons actually "pulled" tumors from bodies, the tumor material was later discovered to be putrid animal tissue that could have been palmed by the psychic surgeon. Surprisingly, such discoveries, like similar discoveries relating to seance mediums in the nineteenth century, have done little to discourage believers. The explanation offered by those who have investigated the field is that tangible results may well be initiated by the procedure, however contrived the procedure itself may be. In discussing psychic surgery, Dr. Virginia Garrison pointed out to me:

"You can say it's phony because they're not doing what we do for surgery. But on the symbolic level, it's not phony. I'm not denying the psychic healer's claim that there is some real surgery that takes place—there's a semantic problem here. But most of the things psychic surgeons do, like most of the things *espiritistas* in general do, involve manipulating the invisible powers on the person. It is strictly symbolic. That doesn't mean that it's not effective."

The mention of "invisible powers" leads us into the next category of psychic healing—the healing apparently initiated by the healee.

THE DOCTOR WITHIN

As long as human beings have practiced medicine, they have been aware of a mysterious force in patients now called the "placebo effect." Through the placebo effect, a patient's beliefs or expectations appear to trigger a healing response that can be as potent as any other therapy, including drugs, surgery, or psychotherapy, for a wide range of physical and psychological problems.

To most people, a placebo is a kind of sugar pill—a harmless, ineffectual substance given to a patient who insists on taking something that will in itself "make things better." In many cases it succeeds, apparently because the patient has decided it will succeed. This strengthens the argument that psi may be an innate and powerful dimension of human consciousness.

An especially provocative illustration of a placebo effect was reported by Dr. Bruno Klopfer in 1957. A man with advanced cancer insisted that his doctor give him an experimental drug called Krebiozen, which was then being advocated as a "miracle drug" by a small faction of the medical community. After only a single dose of Krebiozen, the man's malignant tumors "melted like snowballs on a hot stove" and he was able to return to his normal lifestyle. Sometime later, the man read about new studies showing Krebiozen to be of no value in cancer treatment, and immediately his tumors began growing again. Realizing there was little else that could be done, his doctor urged the man not to believe these studies and then treated the man with an "improved" Krebiozen that was actually only water. Once more, the patient's condition improved dramatically. He stayed in remission until he read that Krebiozen had been conclusively proved worthless. He died several days later.

The placebo effect, however, does not always involve "phony" medicine, nor does the patient need to be ignorant of the placebo effect's existence for it to work. Placebos have worked even when patients knew they were getting placebos. Somehow, willing submission to any act associated with healing may be all that's required for the patient to begin a self-generated recovery. "The placebo effect is proof that there is no real separation between mind and body," says Norman Cousins, former editor of *Saturday Review* and author of the 1979 best-seller *Anatomy of an Illness*. "Illness is always an interaction between both."

When Cousins was forty-nine, he came down with an unspecified cellular disease which caused general achiness, stiffness of the limbs, and nodules on the hands and feet. Medical specialists gave him "one chance in five hundred for recovery," and so he developed his own, unorthodox, "mind-over-matter" therapy. He checked into a hotel and treated himself to a marathon program of humorous books, Marx Brothers movies, and old *Candid Camera* television shows. Almost immediately he began to recover, and today the disease has completely disappeared.

Some parapsychologists claim that the placebo effect is evidence of personal psi ability applied to one's own physical and mental problems. Others say that incidents of healing attributable to a placebo effect need to be discounted as possible incidents of psi capability— that psi ability is a different process which manifests itself more dramatically. The majority, however, seem to be caught in the middle. One of these is Joseph Chilton Pearce, who has studied parapsychological phenomena for years and conducts child-raising seminars.

Pearce suggests that the placebo effect is only the remnant of a much greater ability—once possessed by the race as a whole and now evidenced among many children at a young age, before social and mental conditioning takes hold. He discusses an example of this greater potential in his book *The Magical Child*:

"A man came to a magical-child seminar as the result of an experience that had unnerved him and threatened his academic and rational world view. His eight-year-old son was whittling [when his] knife slipped and severed the arteries in his left wrist. Following an instant's panic at the sight of the spurting blood, the father, as if in a dream, seized his screaming son's face, looked into his eyes, and commanded, 'Son, let's stop that blood.' The screaming stopped, the boy beamed back, said 'okay,' and together they stared at the gushing blood and shouted, 'Blood, you stop that.' And the blood stopped. In a short time, the wound healed—and the father's world almost stopped as well. . . . He did not understand that the child is biologically geared to take reality cues from the parent; he did not know of the high suggestibility of the eight-year-old—or that [children of his age are] peculiarly susceptible to ideas about physical survival. But some part of him *did* know and broke through in the moment of emergency. All the son needed, of course, was the suggestion and the support."

In recent years, the rapid growth of the holistic health movement has spurred an inclination to consider what is mental and what is physical as different aspects of the same entity: the healed (or whole) human being. As I mentioned before, the holistic health movement is in many respects simply a rediscovery and reacceptance of healing techniques long employed by shamans, faith healers, and other "nonscientific" health practitioners. Nevertheless, the movement takes advantage of modern breakthroughs in technology, physiology, and psychology. Through biofeedback mechanisms, for example, any patient can now listen to his or her heart, brain, and respiratory rhythms and learn to effect positive moderations: something adept yogis have been doing on their own for centuries. Perhaps the most interesting psi-related holistic health development, however, is the refinement of an ancient practice into what is now known as "visualization."

Visualization is basically a meditative exercise, in which patients conjure up their own mental visions of the healing process in the belief that the visions themselves will assist recovery. One of the major exponents of this practice is Dr. Carl Simonton, who is convinced that psychology plays an important role in the generation of cancer and that psychology can be mobilized to treat it. Simonton describes the visualization process he recommends as "imaging": a combination of creativity and positive thinking.

In one example of "imaging," a man in the late stages of throat cancer began mentally picturing his radiation treatments as a stream of tiny bullets striking all body cells but destroying only the weaker ones (the cancer cells). Then he envisioned the body's white cells coming in and removing the dead cells by "flushing" them through the liver and kidneys. He was instructed to end each session by visualizing a much smaller tumor and a return to health. "The results of treatment were both thrilling and frightening," Simonton declared in a 1976 interview published in *Prevention* magazine. "Within two weeks, his cancer had noticeably diminished, and he was rapidly gaining weight."

Nowhere else is the link between mind and body so strangely apparent as in the case of a person who is clinically diagnosed as having multiple personalities. In one person's body, brain waves and blood chemistry can change radically from personality to personality.

One personality may have an allergy, or a heart ailment, or an astigmatism that no other personality has. The fact that different personalities in the same body can have such different physical conditions is potentially an important clue to the role of psychic ability in healing.

When I discussed multiple personalities with Dr. Allan Goldstein, professor and chairman in the department of biochemistry at the George Washington University School of Medicine, he said, "This facility of multiple personalities indicates that your mind can change some of the physiological parameters associated with disease. What this implies is that in some cases you can cure yourself within, but you also have the enemy within you that may be the seed of your own destruction."

Today, millions of research dollars are being spent to explore mind/body links—with special attention to biochemistry and neurology. Inevitably, this research touches on the field of psychic healing. According to Goldstein, we are witnessing the advent of a new science, psychoneuroimmunology, which is founded on the premise that neither the mind nor the immune system can be excluded from any theory that proposes to explain the onset of human disease.

In a 1986 article in *Science* magazine written in conjunction with his colleague Nicholas Hall, Goldstein states:

"The discovery of pathways that bind the brain and the immune system rescues the behavioral approach to disease from the shadowy practices of witch doctors and places it squarely within the rational tradition of Western medicine. Aware now of the complex physiological basis for behavioral modification of the immune response, physicians can spend less time fielding criticism and more time exploring which types of therapy are of the greatest benefit. . . . Unquestionably, much more research regarding the behavioral approach to illness such as cancer has to be done. But in the meantime, the most immediately realizable applications of behavioral medicine lie elsewhere. The first, and in the long run, the most valuable, clinical spinoffs of psychoneuroimmunology will be in disease prevention—initially, in the development of ways to manage stress. As we study further the relationship between behavior and the biochemistry of immunity, the aim should not be to replace the witch doctor with a Western equivalent so much as to reduce the need for both."

OFFICIAL REPORTS

Because psychic healing is so inextricably tied to real-life situations, it is difficult to design laboratory experiments that can verify its existence or establish how it operates. The process of healing in itself remains mysterious, and any unusual healing can be explained as a quirk of nature. It's no wonder, then, that there has been very little scientific experimentation regarding claims of psychic healing.

We've discussed the therapeutic-touch studies of Quinn and Krieger, and have considered the experiments conducted during the 1960s by Dr. Bernard Grad in which the healer Estebany appeared to have a positive effect on the recovery of injured mice and the growth of plants (see Chapter 5). In 1970, Sister Justa Smith, head of the departments of chemistry and biology at Rosary Hill College in Buffalo, New York, invited Estebany to participate in a different series of experiments. She filled test tubes with an enzyme that speeds up biochemical reactions associated with wound healing. She then sealed the tubes and had Estebany hold them while assistants checked their reactivity every fifteen minutes on an infrared spectrophotometer. The results were significant enough for Smith to say that an influence from Estebany's hands was apparently able to bring about a marked acceleration in the enzyme's activity.

About the same time, Graham and Anita Watkins conducted another group of experiments with mice at the Institute for Parapsychology in Durham, North Carolina. They inflicted mild poisoning on mice by rendering them unconscious with ether. Then they randomly divided the mice into pairs: One mouse was targeted for healing, the other wasn't. A total of thirteen subjects were directed to try to heal the targeted mouse in a given pair. Of the thirteen subjects, ten claimed healing powers; and nine of these ten produced impressive results. The experiment has been successfully replicated in other laboratories since the Watkinses' thirty-two initial runs, and in each replication, the results suggest that some paranormal healing force was at work.

Most scientific investigations into psychic healing, however, have featured personal demonstrations by gifted healers rather than tests conducted according to strict scientific protocols. Olga Worrall, probably the most famous spiritual healer of the post–World War II era, submitted to a wide variety of examinations by scientists before her recent death. At a university in California, for example, she allegedly helped bacteria to resist the effects of drugs. At the Holmes Center for Research in Los Angeles, she altered the crystalline structure of copper salts, turning them blue instead of the normal green.

Wanting to see if "energy waves" did in fact emanate from Worrall's hands, Dr. Robert Miller, a chemical engineer in Atlanta, invited her to try to leave an impression in a cloud chamber—a sensitive instrument normally used to detect subatomic particles. Basically, a cloud chamber consists of a glass cylinder which is saturated inside with an alcohol vapor kept at an extremely low temperature. High-energy particles that pass through this vapor leave an ionized path which can be seen and photographed. When Worrall put her hands 3 inches above the chamber, pulsating waves—one per second—were observed inside the chamber parallel to her hand. Since Worrall was well known for distant healing, Miller asked her to try to affect the cloud chamber in Atlanta from her home base in Baltimore at a prearranged time. The same pulsation occurred. This astonishing performance was repeated several times for different scientists.

In 1977, Dr. C. Norman Shealy, a neurosurgeon who directs the Pain and Health Rehabilitation Center in La Crosse, Wisconsin, and Dr. Elmer Green, a biophysicist at the Menninger Foundation in Topeka, Kansas, devised an experiment to test Worrall's effect—at a distance—on human physiology. Twelve of Shealy's patients, all of whom suffered from chronic pain, volunteered to be hooked one at a time to a series of physiological monitors for twenty minutes. Worrall, sitting in a room 70 feet away, was asked to concentrate on the person being monitored during the last five minutes of each twenty-minute session. The patient was not told that Worrall would be doing this.

In four of the patients, Shealy and Green detected an orienting reflex (a complex response indicated by changes in brain waves, heart and respiratory rates, and temperature and electrical conductivity of the skin) within seconds of Worrall's signal that she had begun concentrating. One patient spontaneously stated that he felt as if an aurora borealis were going off inside his head. He fell into a trance state and later said that he felt as if he were being electrocuted. "His recording pens went off the chart," noted Green.

Shealy emphasizes that the Worrall test does not prove anything about psychic healing. Nevertheless, one of the volunteer patients, who had suffered four unsuccessful operations for pain relief, felt well for a full week after the experiment. Another patient, who had endured twenty-six years of continuous pain, began to feel better the second day after the experiment and remained pain-free for at least a year, at which time Shealy lost track of him. "What we saw went far beyond just a mental contact," says Green. "It's as if Olga was manipulating a real energy."

Dean Kraft, a New Yorker, is another psychic healer who has conducted numerous demonstrations for scientists. In 1977, Dr. John Kmetz, director of the Science Unlimited Research Foundation in San Antonio, asked Kraft to hold containers of cells from a virulent pelvic cancer known as HeLa (for Helen Lane, the patient from whom the cells originally came) and to visualize the cells exploding. If the HeLa cells died, they would float to the top. The results were remarkable. So many HeLa cells floated to the top each time that the solution became cloudy. Cells even died when Kraft simply moved his hand above a container, instead of holding it.

Given the odd variety of these experiments and demonstrations, and their overall estrangement from the circumstances of psychic healing that are revealed in the anecdotal material, few researchers have been able to develop a coherent theory about how psychic healing operates. The "energy" that the healers themselves claim to feel while they are healing doesn't seem to be energy in the strict sense in which a physicist defines the term. Instead, it is "energy" that pertains to a special mental state upon which the healer draws. Most healers refer to this state, but each healer has a different way of describing how he or she accesses the state. Olga Worrall calls it "shifting into neutral." Dolores Krieger calls it "centering." Dean Kraft calls it "entering the void."

One person who made a major effort to assimilate the existing evidence and articulate a coherent theory about how psychic healing works is Lawrence LeShan, who studied the subject thoroughly and then designed and successfully tested his own psychic-healing technique. In the past ten years, he has taught this technique to hundreds of people in workshop settings. A typical training seminar consists of about ten participants—mostly psychologists and people involved in the human-potential movement—who, among other qualifications, possess a strong ego structure (to enable quick "recovery" from deep meditation) and a good ethical approach to life. Over a five-day period of three lengthy sessions per day, the attendees perform a carefully structured series of contemplation and meditation exercises. On the last day, a small group of individuals with medically described physical problems come in one at a time and workshop participants engage in "healing encounters."

LeShan's concepts regarding psychic healing, as well as his personal healing experiences and those of some of his students, are recorded in his book *The Medium, the Mystic, and the Physicist*. He divides all psychic healing into two categories, which he calls "Type 1" and "Type 2." In a Type 1 healing, the intended healer goes into an altered state of consciousness (ASC) in which he or she and the patient can be viewed as one entity. No attempt is made to "do something" to the healee; the endeavor is simply to unite with this person in a caring bond. LeShan calls this ASC the Clairvoyant Reality. After reviewing the techniques of many famous psychic healers (including Worrall, Harry Edwards, Agnes Sanford, Edgar Jackson, the Christian Scientists, Paramahansa Yogananda, and Sai Baba), LeShan concluded:

"At one moment, the healer was operating in the metaphysical system of the Clairvoyant Reality to the degree that he 'knew' it was true. This was a moment of such complete knowing that nothing else existed in consciousness. In some way, this was transmitted to the patient. I could use the word 'telepathy' or else could point out that —for a moment—the healer's assumptions about how-the-world-works were true and valid. . . . Since at this moment of intense knowing on the part of the healer it was valid and the healee was an integral and central part of the system, the healee knew it too.

"Knowing this at some deep level of personality, the healee was in a different existential position. He was back at home in the universe; he was no longer 'cut off.' . . . In a way, he was for a moment in what I would call 'an ideal organismic position.' He was completely enfolded and included in the cosmos with his 'being,' his 'uniqueness,' his 'individuality' enhanced. Under these conditions there were sometimes positive biological changes."

In Type 2 healing, which LeShan considers less common and less important, the healer tries to heal through a "healing flow," a perceptible pattern of energy emanating from his or her hands and passing across the afflicted area of the patient. LeShan is not sure what accounts for this energy, but he does make an intriguing guess:

"I know how to 'do it,' to 'turn on' my hands and teach others how to 'turn on' theirs. It seems perfectly reasonable to me that we may be dealing with some kind of 'energy.' It also seems reasonable to me that Type 2 may be a sort of 'cop out' on Type 1 in which healer and healee say, in effect: 'We are both too frightened of all this closeness and uniting that is a part of psychic healing. Let's pretend with each other that all that is happening is a flow of energy coming out of the hands and treating the problem. That way we will both be more comfortable.' "

LeShan, like other parapsychologists who have studied psychic healing, still has more questions than answers. What are the limits of psychic healing? How can psychic healing be effective in mental and emotional disturbances? How can gifted healers be identified and trained? How might psychic healing techniques best be integrated with conventional medical therapies? The field has enormous practical potential, but we have only begun to explore it.

INTERLUDE · THREE
STILL MORE TALES OF THE PARANORMAL

A close friend told me this intriguing story: "When I was studying with Rudolph Steiner, I learned how to do astral travel. There's a meditation that they teach, where you relax, meditate, and go backward through your day. You give the people in the astral world good feelings in exchange for knowledge. So I passed on the good things about my day and asked to have an out-of-body experience. Before I went to sleep, I thought about a friend, a very intuitive and sympathetic person, who had moved to San Francisco, whom I had never visited. I was in that twilight stage just as you fall asleep, and I felt my other, 'spirit' body, that started at my feet and came out my head, so that it was standing over me, and I could see myself lying in bed sleeping below. Then I had a feeling of being in space, as if flying, and I 'landed' in my friend's living room, which had big bookcases in it. He was reading and he had a glass of white wine next to him. It was around midnight where he was. I tried to get his attention, but he couldn't see me, so I looked around the room, made note of certain things, and then I went back to my bed. The next day I called him. 'François, I came to visit you last night.' 'What are you talking about?' he said, in a strange voice. 'You were reading Thomas Hardy, and you were drinking white wine.' There was a long silence. 'I did an astral trip, and came to visit you.' Then I described everything I had seen, and indeed, it was all accurate."

"As a young girl," another friend told me, "I used to fantasize about the man I would marry. Lots of girls do this, of course, but I had a sense that I really could sometimes see him—he lived in England, which I knew nothing about. Since I've been with Anthony [her English husband], I've had flashes of jumping back in time with him—quick pictures or scenes will materialize. In one 'flash,' I got his name, as Albert. I've seen several glimpses of us in different parts of a house in England during the Victorian era, in different situations. We were sister and brother, or half-sister and brother—I can't tell which, though I seem to be a couple of years older, and we are lovers; we have an incestuous relationship. As well as I can piece it together, neither of us married; we lived quietly in the house, to the shock of our family."

Hal Puthoff and Russell Targ tell the following story in *Mind Reach*. Like so many stories, it's hard to categorize: synchronicity, coincidence, telepathy? And like so many stories, it centers around Uri Geller, that catalyst for seemingly strange happenings. They and a colleague were meeting late at night in a hotel room to try to make sense of some photographs which showed Geller trying to bend a metal rod—but which also seemed to show an extra arm suspended over Geller's head. Their colleague also told them that the photographer had recently awakened at night to see an apparition of an arm floating above his bed. As the photographer described it, "the arm was totally real-looking, covered with plain gray cloth, and was rotating, with a hook at the hand end." Targ goes on, "That sounded more sinister to me, but Hal [Puthoff] said lightheartedly, 'That's the sort of thing that you could expect from a three-dimensional hologram projected by a second-class extraterrestrial civilization that wanted to scare a man in bed.'

"By that time it was midnight, and we were all feeling a little silly from the jet lag and the late hour. At that point, we heard a rattle at the door. Somebody had just put a key into the lock and was opening our hotel-room door. After a half-hour of ghost stories, we were frozen in an instant. The door continued to swing open, and a man walked into our room—a man who wore a plain gray suit and had only one arm.

"The explanation was simple, of course. He was only looking for his suitcase, which had been moved elsewhere when the hotel had shifted him to another room to make a place for us. The hotel had unfortunately neglected to tell him of the move. We assumed our colleague had set us up. He assumed we had set him up. None of us could find evidence to support our respective hypotheses. Of such coincidences are the lives of psychical researchers made."

• • •

Physician Rex Gardner of Sunderland District Hospital in Britain has investigated several inexplicable cases of apparent healing through prayer. In one, a woman asked the parishioners of her church to pray for her recovery from a severely ulcerous varicose condition in her leg. Her doctor had told her that even if she were healed, the scar would require skin grafting; but the ulcer healed completely the day after the prayer meeting, and no grafting was required. In his report, Gardner says that the story is "so bizarre that I would not have included it had I not been one of the doctors who examined the patient's leg at the next monthly prayer meeting and had all the people who had been present not been available for interrogation."

Stories involving animals, and their possible psychic abilities, pop up regularly in the psychic literature. Here is a funny personal anecdote from Russell Targ: "We have a large, attractive mixed-breed cat named Mushroom. She has luxurious long fur, which is a uniform beige in color, hence the name. We call her Mush for short.

"For some unknown reason, this affectionate cat began to piddle on the living-room rug, instead of outdoors as was her usual custom since she was a kitten. As time went on, she became more and more bold and would even urinate with the whole family in the room. Needless to say, such activity was vigorously discouraged. A whole research program was mounted to try to figure out a way to get the damn cat to quit peeing in the house. Nothing succeeded.

"Finally my wife decided that the cat had to go. Joan called the animal shelter and arranged to have the cat received, and probably 'put to sleep,' the next afternoon. On the morning of the appointed day, Joan spied the cat curled up on a chair, sleeping in the morning sun. She wished she could find a way to tell the cat that it was really important that she mend her ways. But at that point it was too late; only a miracle could save her. However, with one's life hanging in the balance, miracles are seemingly not so hard to come by.

"As the children were dressing for school, we heard a shout of excitement. Joan and I came to see what the commotion was about. The source of the wonderment was the cat, who was standing on the toilet seat, urinating into the toilet.

"One can only conclude that she got the message. Six months have gone by, and she has never gone back to her old life-threatening ways. It is interesting to note that even if she had happened to go outdoors on that fateful morning, that would not have saved her. It required something really momentous."

Another famous case from the psychical literature concerns the well-known nineteeth-century landscape painter Arthur Severn and his wife, Joan, as investigated by John Ruskin. The year is 1880. Mrs. Severn testifies: "I woke up with a start, feeling I had had a hard blow on my mouth, and with a distinct sense that I had been cut and was bleeding under my upper lip, and seized my pocket-handkerchief and held it (in a little pushed lump) to the part, as I sat up in bed, and after a few seconds, when I removed it, I was astonished not to see any blood, and only then realized it was impossible anything could have struck me there, as I lay fast asleep in bed, and so I thought it was only a dream!—but I looked at my watch, and saw it was seven, and finding Arthur (my husband) was not in the room, I concluded (rightly) that he must have gone out on the lake for an early sail, as it was so fine.

"I then fell asleep. At breakfast (half-past nine) Arthur came in rather late, and I noticed he rather purposely sat further away from me than usual, and every now and then put his pocket-handkerchief furtively up to his lip, in the very way I had done. I said, 'Arthur, why are you doing that?' and added a little anxiously, 'I know you have hurt yourself! but I'll tell you why afterwards.' He said, 'Well, when I was sailing, a sudden squall came, throwing the tiller suddenly round, and it struck me a bad blow in the mouth, under the upper lip, and it has been bleeding a good deal and won't stop.' I said then, 'Have you any idea what o'clock it was when it happened?' and he answered, 'It must have been about seven.'

"I then told what had happened to me, much to *his* surprise, and all who were with us at breakfast."

Valerie Hunt tells me that she gets information in all kinds of ways when she's "channeling," or going back through past lives with her subjects. Sometimes she will see a complete picture, like a movie, of what's going on. Sometimes information will appear like a banner blazing across the sky. Perhaps she'll feel their pain, or actually take on their symptoms. "Sometimes I will smell things, things that are in the 'field' from which they are transmitting. The first time I did this it was with Rosalind Bruyere [a well-known healer] and it blew my mind because I could smell gin. That was back when I used to drink martinis, and I knew gin very well, and I kept smelling this gin and I thought, I'm going to get drunk smelling this gin. Eventually she got to the information. She was an alchemist during the Black Plague in Europe and she was crushing juniper berries. She didn't know gin came from juniper berries. I knew it. That was the first time, but it happens consistently, that I smell information."

One of the problems with establishing credibility in reported healings is that it's difficult to get hard, documented evidence, or to establish that the healing didn't come about naturally, or through a doctor's intervention. People who have been cured by healers know it; they just can't prove it. Ruth West, director of the Koestler Foundation in London, is aware of this problem, but has her own story to tell. She had injured her back playing tennis, and nothing seemed to repair the damage, even consultation with a specialist in sports physiology. Yet she feels she was cured by Lady Raeburn, the wife of a major general in the British Army, whose specialty is skiing accidents (she is herself a skier) and who has been known to heal even broken bones. "I had three sessions with Lady Raeburn, whom I had known for years—three sessions a week apart. She laid her hands on my forehead, and I felt like I was going into a yogic-type trance, and I just manipulated myself. It was the most extraordinary experience, because I don't do yoga; I hate it. But it felt as if I was just sorting myself out. She never charges any money for what she does."

Ruth West also told me about a healer in Sussex named Phillip Edwards, who had studied with Sai Baba. She recounted how he had cured the knee problem of an airline stewardess who had been thrown during a flight, and who doctors felt would never walk properly again. "How does someone like that make a living?" I asked her. "Well, Phillip used to be an electrician," she said, "but he gave it up when he discovered he had healing ability. His wife was part of a seance circle, and they use the seances, through his wife, to play the football pools. Now he just keeps going through donations and the money from the football pools."

Some stories seem to point to the theory that powerful emotions may be a clue to psi at work. A Los Angeles salesman named Bill Anderson, on an unexplainable urge, decided at the last minute to take an Amtrak train to a convention in Chicago. "I was confused by this, but I reasoned it away, thinking that maybe I just needed a break from my routines."

As soon as he was on the train, he was overcome by powerful anxieties, and for hours couldn't sit still, couldn't work, couldn't eat or sleep. "It was as if some force had overtaken me. I was *possessed*." He began walking from car to car, feeling out of control, trying to calm down, getting off the train at each stop feeling that he couldn't go on, but then getting on the train again each time at the last minute. Exhausted, he gave in to the restless feelings; but just a few hours out of Chicago, his appetite returned and he rushed into the dining car.

"I saw a woman sitting alone, eating. For some reason, I couldn't take my eyes off her, no matter how hard I tried. And the longer I stared at her, the more my anxiety started to leave me. It was most strange.

"Finally the woman smiled at me and asked me to join her at her table. As I nodded yes, I felt a lightness overcome my entire body, and a sense of calm rushed over me. For the first time in hours and hours, I felt normal again."

During dinner, he told the woman about his strange feelings. "Suddenly a look of amazement came over her. Then she told me that she too had taken the train on a whim, altering her plans to drive across the country without being able to explain her change of mind. And she too was feeling lost and anxious—as though part of her was missing—until I walked into the dining car minutes before!"

Anderson feels that someone or something arranged that train ride so they could meet. He says that they are tremendously compatible, that they feel like "soul mates," and can often communicate without speaking. "I think fate stepped in and made it possible for me to find her."

I was stunned when a friend of many years, whom I'd always thought of as the most pragmatic of people, confessed to me that for years he had been aware of "sharing" his body with another person. "For many years, it was just a feeling, a strange sensation that someone else was part of my thoughts, somehow lived inside me. It was very uncomfortable, to say the least, but I eventually got used to it, and whatever it was felt almost comfortable, a part of me. Finally I tried to befriend this 'being.' Slowly I have gotten information about him. It seems that he is a teenage boy who was killed in a bombing in France near where I grew up during the war [World War II]. His explanation is that he 'didn't make it' to the other side, and so took up residence inside me."

• • •

Judy Silver tells me about the time she went out to dinner with a customer and his wife, who brought along a friend who claimed to be psychic, and who during dinner told her and her husband many intimate things about themselves. "I was somewhat turned off by her religious bent," Judy says, "but she certainly seemed to be accurate in what she said, and accused me of being 'of little faith.' Then she told me that in April—this was November—something very dramatic was going to happen to me, and I would turn to my husband and say, 'Oh, thank God he's all right.' We continued our conversation, but the mood had changed, and I sensed that something was going to happen to one of the children. Later on, the psychic must have picked up my mood, because she said to me that she didn't intend to be threatening, and everything would work out okay.

"As time went by, I completely forgot about the whole incident. In early April we were in Florida for a business convention and were to fly to Orlando to pick up Norman's fourteen-year-old son, Jimmy, to take him to Disney World. Friday night, getting ready to go to a black-tie dinner, we decided to call Jimmy and say, 'Hi, we'll see you tomorrow.' When we called, we found out that Jimmy had fallen down an air shaft from the fifth floor in his high school, and by some miracle hit a very small ledge on the third floor; it broke under him, but he was able to hang on there until the police lowered someone in to support him. He was there for four hours while they dug him out—they had to keep him flat because they didn't know if he'd injured his spine. Norman flew immediately to Jimmy—got there at five in the morning, spent the day there. I ran around getting things together. Then he came back to get me and we were running to get the other kids, and he told me what happened and that it was phenomenal Jimmy had survived. And I turned to him and said, 'Oh, thank God he's all right.' And it wasn't until that moment that I remembered what the psychic had said."

"Joel and I had been out hiking in the mountains," recalls Rebecca Eisenberg, "and I was carrying the sixty-pound pack to show him how macho I was—two sleeping bags, a watermelon, bottles of water, and all. I've climbed glaciers in Alaska and am a pretty experienced mountain climber. There was a lot of flooding in the mountains, and little did I know that you can't ford an icy, rushing stream in thongs. Joel was wearing good hiking boots. Anyway, I was crossing, and all of a sudden the wind grabbed me, my legs separated, and I slid down the torrential river, over the waterfalls, in the icy cold. I was at the bottom of the river looking up. I was numb; I don't know if I was in shock, carried along the bottom of the river. I think I started drowning, because I relaxed completely and felt very warm and full of love and good and happy. I remember wanting to take a deep breath, and then I heard this voice like I've never heard before, and remember trying to turn to see the voice, which said, 'Well, are you ready then? Are you ready to come?' I said to myself, 'Now, wait a minute, wake up,' and I couldn't see anyone else there, and I said, 'Well, yes; everything is fine and ready. I feel good.'

"Then all of a sudden, something inside of me said 'No, you're not ready, you have several unborn children.' With that, my pack came off—I had been trying to get it off earlier, but I don't remember—and I floated to the surface. But the weird thing is, I had this conversation, and those wonderful feelings. Was it the mind playing tricks? I can't explain it."

"I've gone several times to a psychic named Mrs. Lorenz, and I'm forever amazed at how much she knows about me, and how many different directions her 'vision' takes," says Trudy Mellon, whom I happened to talk to while standing in line at a wedding reception. "She 'knew' I was divorced and that I have two children. Once when I saw her she mentioned something wrong with my son's knee or ankle, and he broke his ankle twice after that. Another time she mentioned that I was going to need medical assistance soon; an hour later I was hemorrhaging. When I was thinking about selling some real estate and moving to California, she sorted that all out. It was like talking to someone who had read my mind; she was able to suggest places to go and has been very much involved with my finances. I had gone to her originally on a lark with a girl who was working for us, and I was paranoid because of the name Mellon, but she's very discreet and completely shuns publicity. I took Patty Burns there, whom you met, and she was leery because she figured the woman would know her from KBKA television, where she's news anchor, but it was not an issue. I have found her to be completely concerned and helpful. One day I went there and there was a woman leaving who was dressed in every signature designer thing possible, and had a limousine outside waiting for her. She looked out of place in this fold-up chair in the hall of this little house in Greensburg, Pennsylvania. And Lorenz said to me, obviously worried, 'That person who's with her only wants her father's money.' Now, I knew who the woman was; I don't think her father was famous, but he was a very successful retailer in New York. Now, I'm just capsulizing this, and I'm making it sound silly, but Mrs. Lorenz seemed genuinely concerned about the girl."

In 1968, New York publishing executive John Migliaccio had a near-death experience when he came close to drowning at the New Jersey shore. While swimming in the heavy tides, he became overtired; he felt himself leave his body and hang 500 feet above the water, "like being in two places at one time." He felt as if he were watching himself struggle to survive as he went on swimming. When he reached shore, he blacked out: "I just let go. I went straight into this blackness, traveling what seemed like a million miles a second. I went up into this great void. The only way I can describe it is that I was part of everything in the universe. Everything fit together and made sense to me." The experience changed his attitude toward death. When his grandmother had died the year before, he reports, "I went hysterical." But he felt different when his grandfather died the following year: "I felt inappropriate—everyone was upset but me."

Former Ohio Congressman Bill Feighan has been to several of the country's leading psychics, and told me he has used their knowledge in many areas of his life. "In 1960 I ran for office and I won by eight votes. I beat Carl Stokes, who later, in '62, joined me in the state legislature, and then became mayor of Cleveland; he's now a judge. I couldn't tell Carl, but I knew in advance the outcome of the election. A psychic had told me that I would win, and how it would happen, and what to do. I knew Carl and I knew his family, and his mother was very religious and didn't believe in that sort of thing, and I actually was a coward and a little embarrassed to mention to anybody that I believed in that. But it gave me a tremendous edge during the campaign. When I had to meet him during the campaign, or when I gave speeches or was at rallies, it gave me tremendous confidence to know that I would win the election."

Joe Sugarman, president of the JS&A mail-order electronics firm, says he has found the counsel of psychics useful in many areas of his life. He tells a funny story about a reading from a psychic named Linda Fallucca. "She tells me that 'a guy named Miller is going to call you, and you're going to get involved in a very exciting and successful new product.' So I say, 'Okay, fine,' and the next day a guy named Miller calls me and says, 'I've got this new product and I want to see you.' So I say, 'Absolutely, I've been waiting for you,' and I schedule an appointment. About an hour later I get a call from another guy named Miller with the same story—'I've got this concept and a product that I'd like to discuss.' 'Well, okay,' I say, 'come in.' Next day, *another* Miller calls me up. Now I have three Millers, and I don't know which one it is.

"So I call up this gal Linda, I go over, and I say, 'Look, is this some kind of a joke? This is unfair—you tell me a Miller is going to call me and three Millers call me. Which one is it?' So she says, 'Well, give me their first names,' and I reel them off. 'Oh, it's Dave Miller,' she says; 'that sounds good.' And that's how it worked out. She often gives me names—that seems to be her strong point—and she's usually right. So I believe it exists; I generally believe it. What I've been trying to find out is why it exists, how it exists, and how to tune in to it."

I met renowned veterinarian and whale specialist Dr. Jay Hyman on an airplane. He has a rather amazing story, especially given his once-skeptical stance. "I first met psychic Gladys Hanagan in 1981, when I tagged along with my wife when her friend was unable to keep the appointment. I don't remember being impressed or unimpressed with what she said, but she seemed like a lovely lady, and I took notes, which I always meant to go back to and see if anything came true. Then in July of '81 I had my accident. [Dr. Hyman was critically injured when he crash-landed his plane on the Taconic Parkway, in an incident that made the television news and the front pages of most East Coast papers.]

"Gladys saw the accident on television, and she didn't remember me at all, but she started getting a flashing vision of the initials J.B., and a feeling of having a relationship to the man in the accident, and then the next day got the message that it was me. So she called my wife, who was, as you can imagine, very distressed, and told her that she had this vision of someone with the initials J.B. and that his spirit was with me and would protect me. She also told my wife that she was a healer and would try to use her healing powers on me, and that she was very concerned about fluid that was leaking from my nose and ears. Now, this was just what was going on, though there was no way she could have known it. It was cerebrospinal fluid, leaking through a skull fracture, and as a doctor, if I'd been conscious, I'd have been concerned too. Anyway, she said not to worry, I'd come through this crisis, but that in another week or two there would be a crisis involving my chest cavity. Sure enough, I developed pneumonia.

"The next part of the story unfolds when my stepdaughter Leslie goes to see Gladys, and Gladys again mentions J.B. (whom Leslie has never heard of) and tells her that I went to college with him, and that I have something of his in my possession. Now I realize that this is Joseph Brenda, a guy I roomed with for two years at Cornell, and who died flying a jet at age twenty-five. That was the first time death touched me, and it upset me deeply. So Gladys tells Leslie that J.B. is saying that I will be all right, that he wouldn't let it happen a second time. But I couldn't for the life of me imagine what possession of Joe's I might have. It was only when I separated from my wife, Elaine, and moved to the house in Piermont and all kinds of crap came out of the basement—I had nothing much to do but sort it out during my recovery—and out comes a box, full of pictures and prom favors, and there in the box is a silly little beanie that we had to wear for our first two weeks as freshmen at Cornell, and in the headband was Joseph Brenda's name.

"There's a third part to the story. First my wife, Elaine, then my stepdaughter, Leslie. Now, while I was recovering, I had round-the-clock nursing care. Usually it was a hit-or-miss thing. Some would work two hours a week, or two shifts a week. With one exception. One nurse would come every single morning at seven o'clock, get me up and shaved and dressed, and take me to the hospital for my therapy. Sometimes we'd have lunch together; then I'd rest and she'd read the *Times* to me. She was a great source of comfort during all these troubles, and she was the only person who could make me laugh.

"A close girlfriend of hers was having marital troubles and went to see a psychic, and my nurse went along with her. The psychic told her, 'I see you working with a man who has been terribly damaged in an accident, torn apart from head to toe. But don't be concerned, I see a rod of steel down this man's back; he has the will to make it.' She said, 'I get the initial J. with this man, like blue jay.' She was actually saying my name. 'This man was traveling north when the accident occurred. If he had reached his destination first, he would not be alive today; the quick medical attention saved his life.' All this is true. I was headed to the Arctic, and if the plane had acted up later, I would have been too far from civilization to get help. Then she said that she saw this man writing a book about his experiences, not for his own gain, but to help others to go through difficulties.

"Now, I knew nothing about this at the time. It was a long time later. I had hired a full-time housekeeper to live with my daughter and me. But I kept in touch with the nurse, and one day she came over with her girlfriend for a drink. And I start telling them how I've had the inspiration to write a book because of all I've been through, and my family, to help others to cope with this kind of situation. Well, they both looked at each other with these very funny looks on their faces, and said, 'We have something to share with you,' and for the first time told me about their experiences with the psychic. And of course the psychic turned out to be Gladys."

This story comes from Linda Delgado, a counselor and instructor at New Paltz (New York) State College, who told me that she can often tell when something important is going to happen, even if she can't quite tell what it is. She feels she's always known when something was wrong with one of her children, and had been able to see financial problems, her father's losing his job, her sister's promotion. "My grandfather and I were always close. My mother's his oldest child; I was the oldest granddaughter, and the first to have a great-grandchild. At eighty-eight my grandfather had a stroke, and the doctors didn't feel he would come out of the hospital. I had gone to see him, and he was doing better, out of intensive care and all. The next day I came home from work, the kids were home from school, and I was trying to get dinner together when we heard the front door close. I looked at the time—I have a tendency to do that to coordinate things—and I asked the kids to check and see who had come in. The kids went out and said that nobody was there. But I felt that somebody had come in—you know how you get the feeling that someone's there? I went back to the kitchen and started doing dinner, but things were going wrong; water boiled over, things on the stove were burning, the kids were arguing, I broke a dish—four or five minutes of things' being very chaotic. And then we heard the door slam again —really slam. So again we went out to check and again there was nobody there. But everything got quiet. All of the disruptions in the house just stopped. And I just had a funny feeling, so I called my aunt to see how my grandfather was doing. When I called, my uncle answered the phone and he was crying, and I knew exactly what was going on. They had just hung up the phone from the hospital; my grandfather had died just at the time that all this craziness was going on. When I told my mother the story, I thought she was going to be skeptical and make fun of me, but her response was that my grandfather and I were very close, and that he had stopped to see me on his way to wherever he was going."

CHAPTER · TEN

THE ULTIMATE QUESTION: DOES CONSCIOUSNESS SURVIVE DEATH?

"We have no scientific proof concerning the annihilation of consciousness at the death of the body."
—Lawrence LeShan

"The whole purpose of life's campaign against matter is to establish continuity, to overcome 'forgetfulness'; this is the purpose behind instinct and racial memory and the DNA code. These are all forms of survival of bodily death; if other forms did not exist, it would be, to say the least, an extraordinary waste of opportunity."
—Colin Wilson

At the root of much interest in psi phenomena lies one main question: Is there a supernatural dimension of existence? In the so-called natural world, the one that we inhabit and perceive with our physical bodies, each life begins and ends in mystery. Is there no life at all until a moment of time when a particular egg is fertilized by a particular sperm? Does life cease altogether when the physical body dies? Or is life a force that transcends the physical, just as the mind seems to transcend the body during the natural course of existence?

This question has historically been a crucial one to people involved in religion or metaphysics; but now it is no longer strictly their province. More and more people—from hard-core scientists to the skeptic on the street—are opening their minds to the issue. Every indication of something that operates outside the limits of nature—whether it be a telepathic message, a clairvoyant image, or anything else that seems inexplicable by scientific knowledge—helps us to believe what we secretly most want to believe: that our birth into this life may have some "supernatural" explanation and, most important, that we may not cease to exist when our body dies.

This primal desire to overcome the ultimate natural barrier—death —accounted for the overwhelming popularity of various forms of "spiritualism," as well as the first systematic investigations of survival after death by scientific researchers. Eventually, however, these researchers reached—you might say—a dead end. In 1903, Frederick W. H. Myers summed up the official position at the time in his book *Human Personality and Its Survival of Bodily Death*: There is no valid evidence of life beyond death nor any conceivable manner of acquiring it. J. B. Rhine echoed Myers' conclusion (and frustration) three decades later, claiming that since any unusual "information" regarding life beyond death can always be attributed to ESP, science cannot go beyond understanding ESP first.

Despite these discouraging words, interest in the topic refuses to die. Recent scientific breakthroughs in the field of subatomic particles (revealing operations that defy standard concepts of time and space) have challenged parapsychologists anew to study the possibility of a life apart from life as we know it. As excited as they are about tackling the "survival question," they know that it resists any direct answer. By its very nature, the question is a metaphysical one, and any answers can be only conjectural. Researchers can never "scientifically" examine death as a transformational experience without being able to replicate firsthand experience under controlled conditions. Since the days of the Fox sisters, anyone who wants to investigate life beyond death has two alternatives:

(1) examining analogous states of being—times when consciousness is experienced as existing detached from the body, known clinically as out-of-body experiences (OBEs);

(2) examining anecdotal material that supports the notion of an

existence beyond the cycle of birth and death, such as recollections of near-death experiences (NDEs), reports of spirit communications (via mediums, trance channeling, ghosts, past-life hypnosis, or ESP), or life-stories suggesting the possibility of reincarnation.

Let's take a look at each of these possibilities separately.

THE OUT-OF-BODY EXPERIENCE (OBE)

We've already discussed an experiment involving Keith Harary and his pet cat, in which Harary, while he was having an OBE, apparently influenced his cat's behavior (see Chapter 5). Harary is one of those rare individuals who can self-induce OBEs and even signal to others when a particular OBE begins and ends. This does not mean, however, that an OBE is an uncommon experience. People in every culture and every walk of life report having spontaneous OBEs. From the testimonies of these individuals, we can formulate some basic characteristics of an OBE, characteristics which suggest that an OBE may be, indeed, a state analogous to life beyond death —that is to say, an existence independent of the body:

- The person having an OBE often feels that he or she is split into two or more aspects: one characterized as "physical" (the human body) and the others characterized as mental (the conscious state of being—one's awareness, even though the body itself may continue to perform as if it were still governed by a brain). In different accounts this "mental aspect" may be called a spirit, an astral body, an etheric body, or simply "awareness." In some accounts, the physical and mental aspects are experienced as being connected by a "thread" or "cable" (analogous to an umbilical cord). A common sensation (technically known as "autoscopy") that is associated with having an OBE is the experience of seeing one's physical body from an external vantage point. It's also a frequent sensation in dreams and in states of mental dissociation or near-death experience (NDE), where it may or may not be a harbinger of a true OBE.
- The experient often identifies his or her existence with the mental aspect of the split and, as this mental aspect, feels he is perceiving things in the environment that cannot be perceived from where his physical body is known to be located at the time. The mental aspect can experience traveling around, for example, and apparently witnessing scenes at remote distances—seemingly transcending barriers of both time and space—or it may

examine objects from a perspective that is impossible in terms of the position of the body.

- Many people report undergoing OBEs during the course of sleep or drug-induced states of consciousness. Once the OBE has begun, however, the person may feel that he possesses a "charged" wakefulness—details often seem clear and impress the observer as real, not dreamlike or fantastic. Some people report that they feel a "tingling" sensation, as if a mild wave of energy was surrounding them or passing through their body.

Sylvan Muldoon and Hereward Carrington called this mental aspect of an OBE the "astral body" in their 1929 ground-breaking book on the topic, *The Projection of the Astral Body*. According to Carrington: "The Astral Body may be defined as the Double, or ethereal counterpart of the physical body, which it resembles and with which it normally coincides. . . . The phantom body is the condenser of cosmic energy—the very energy you employ moving about. This energy is the 'breath of life'—omnipresent in every living thing. . . . Without this breath of life, man would really be nothing but the dust in the ground. . . . When the astral and physical body coincide, you are physically alive. When the astral body moves out of coincidence, you are physically dead—*unless* the astral cable, running from the energetic body to the physical body, is intact. That is the purpose of the astral 'line of force': to deliver the breath of life to the physical body, while the finer body is projected."

More modern researcher/practitioners of OBEs avoid such imaginative hypotheses, noting only a sensation of being free of bodily limitations during the OBE. One of the most interesting of these researcher/practitioners is Robert Monroe, whose 1971 book *Journeys Out of the Body* chronicles ten years of personal experimentation with OBEs, some of them under modified laboratory conditions set up by Dr. Charles Tart at the University of California at Davis.

Monroe, president of a large corporation, was at first terrified by his spontaneous OBEs, which occurred during his nightly sleep periods. Eventually, however, he decided to confront these experiences and investigate them in whatever ways he could. Through trial and error, he developed the ability to self-induce OBEs. In one of his most intriguing "experiments," he attempted to establish the sort of direct contact during an OBE that he felt would prove that he had indeed left his body. Here is an excerpt from a journal entry written immediately after the experiment:

"R.W., a businesswoman . . . and a close friend aware of my 'activities' (but somewhat skeptical still, in spite of rather unwilling participation), has been away this week on her vacation up the New Jersey coast. I do not know exactly where she is vacationing other than that. Nor did I inform her of any planned experiment, simply because I hadn't thought of it until today. . . . I lay down in the bedroom about three in the afternoon, went into a relaxation pattern, felt the warmth (high order vibrations), then thought heavily of the desire to 'go' to R.W.

"There was the familiar sensation of movement through a light blue blurred area, then I was in what seemed to be a kitchen. R.W. was seated in a chair to the right. She had a glass in her hand. She was looking to my left, where two girls (about seventeen or eighteen, one blond and one brunette) also were sitting, each with glasses in their hands, drinking something. The three of them were in conversation, but I could not hear what they were saying.

"I first approached the two girls, directly in front of them, but I could not attract their attention. I then turned to R.W., and I asked her if she knew I was there.

" 'Oh yes, I know you are here,' she replied (mentally, or with that superconscious communication, as she was still in oral conversation with the two girls). . . .

"I stated that I had to be sure that she would remember, so I was going to pinch her.

" 'Oh, you don't need to do that, I'll remember,' R.W. said hastily.

"I said I had to be sure, so I reached over and tried to pinch her, gently, I thought. I pinched her in the side, just above the hips and below the rib cage. She let out a good loud, 'Ow,' and I backed up, because I was somewhat surprised. I really hadn't expected to be able actually to pinch her. Satisfied that I had made some impression, at the least, I turned and left, thought of the physical, and was back almost immediately."

Later Monroe asked R.W. if she could recall what she had been doing that Saturday afternoon at about three o'clock. Here is his report of her response:

"On Saturday between three and four was the only time there was not a crowd of people in the beach cottage where she was staying. For the first time, she was alone with her niece (dark-haired, about eighteen) and the niece's friend (about the same age, blond). They were in the kitchen-dining area of the cottage from about three-fifteen to four, and she was having a drink, and the girls were having Cokes. . . .

"I asked R.W. if she remembered anything else, and she said no. I questioned her more closely, but she could not remember anything more. Finally, in impatience, I asked her if she remembered the pinch. A look of complete astonishment crossed her face.

" 'Was that you?' She stared at me for a moment, then went into the privacy of my office, turned, and lifted (just slightly!) the edge of her sweater where it joined her skirt on her left side. There were two brown and blue marks at exactly the spot where I had pinched her.

" 'I was sitting there, talking to the girls,' R.W. said, 'when all of a sudden I felt this terrible pinch. I must have jumped a foot. I thought my brother-in-law had come back and sneaked up behind me. I turned around, but there was no one there. I never had any idea it was you! It hurt!' "

It is interesting to note that when Monroe questioned R.W. after she returned home, she could not remember that she had experienced telepathy, yet Monroe had felt a strong telepathic connection with her during his OBE—a connection that she "verified" at the time. This may support the theory that our conscious mind normally screens out psi information.

Charles Tart has also conducted experiments designed to study the potential of OBEs. In one of the most successful, he placed a five-digit number on a high shelf in the same room where his subject lay in bed. Following a reputed OBE, the subject was able to identify the number correctly. Unfortunately, this feat can also be attributed to simple clairvoyance. Even Monroe's "pinch" might be characterized as long-distance PK, or "action-at-a-distance."

A classic story in the psychical literature about OBEs concerns a Mrs. S. R. Wilmot who "visited" her husband in 1863 while he was aboard the steamship *City of Limerick*, en route from Liverpool to New York. Mr. Wilmot reports:

"Toward morning I dreamed I saw my wife, whom I had left in the United States, come to the door of my stateroom, clad in her nightdress. At the door she seemed to discover that I was not the only occupant of the room, hesitated a little, then advanced to my side, stooped down, and kissed me, and after gently caressing me for a few minutes, quietly withdrew.

"Upon waking I was surprised to see my fellow-passenger, whose berth was above mine, but not directly over it—owing to the fact that our room was at the stern of the vessel—leaning upon his elbow, and looking fixedly at me. 'You're a pretty fellow,' said he at length, 'to have a lady come and visit you this way.' I pressed him for an explanation, which he at first declined to give, but at length related what he had seen while wide awake, lying in his berth. It exactly corresponded with my dream."

Mr. Wilmot's sister was also on board, and was shocked when Mr. Wilmot's roommate, Mr. William J. Tait, asked her if she had been in to visit her brother during the night. He described to her the woman in white who had "visited" her brother; Mr. Wilmot described his dream to his sister. When, after landing, he saw his wife, Mr. Wilmot reports, "Almost her first question when we were alone together was 'Did you receive a visit from me a week ago Tuesday?' 'A visit from you?' said I. 'We were more than a thousand miles at sea.' 'I know it,' she replied, 'but it seemed to me that I visited you.' "

Mrs. Wilmot went on to explain that because of the severe storms she had been very worried about him, and couldn't sleep, and it seemed to her that at about four in the morning she had "gone" to seek him, crossing the stormy sea to his ship, and then to his cabin. She described to him the room, with one bunk sticking farther out than the other, described Mr. Tait staring at her, and her actions in kissing and caressing her husband. For the record, Mrs. Wilmot also claims to have told her mother about her vivid dream, so strong that she felt happy, and that her anxiety had been allayed.

People who have had OBEs are usually sure that what they felt was genuine. Many have produced concrete evidence to verify that something of a psi nature definitely happened during the time span of their OBE. Nevertheless, we have no concrete evidence to verify that an OBE is what it appears to be—a literal detachment of the mind (or consciousness, or spirit, or soul) from the physical body. What is striking about the anecdotal material is the sheer number of people who report OBEs, and how similar in kind these reports are. The same pattern applies to near-death experiences (NDEs)—accounts of what happened to people when they came close to dying or were actually pronounced clinically "dead."

THE NEAR-DEATH EXPERIENCE (NDE)

The approach to death is a stressful period, particularly when there has been little or no time to prepare for it. All at once, a car strikes a pedestrian and the victim's life hangs in the balance. A patient undergoing a surgical operation takes a sudden, sharp turn for the worse. An entrepreneur with a weak heart learns that his business has failed and immediately suffers a life-threatening heart attack. In some cases, all symptoms of life cease and the person is pronounced dead; but then, moments later, with or without medical assistance, life returns. Whether or not they actually crossed over the threshold between life and death, many people who faced death under traumatic conditions later report having sensed intimations of an existence beyond that of physical life.

For a long time, such reports were largely ignored. If they reached the general public at all, they were quickly dismissed as hallucinations: the fantasies of minds temporarily deranged by shock, injury, illness, or drugs. The public attitude changed radically in 1975 with the appearance of the book *Life After Life*, by Dr. Raymond A. Moody, Jr. In his book, Moody offers more than one hundred case histories of subjects who experienced clinical death and then revived, with stories to tell of unearthly, "postlife" experiences. The cases are well presented and authoritatively discussed; but what made the book a runaway best-seller was that the experiences in themselves unanimously seem to suggest a positive, even rapturous, existence beyond life as we know it—the most cherished hope of humankind, the bedrock of religious sensibilities.

Early in the text, Moody draws a composite picture incorporating the classic elements of what he labels a "near-death experience," or "NDE." In fact, most NDEs typically involve only some combination of these elements:

"A man is dying and, as he reaches the point of greatest physical distress, he hears himself pronounced dead by his doctor. He begins to hear an uncomfortable noise, a loud ringing or buzzing, and at the same time feels himself moving very rapidly through a long dark tunnel. After this, he suddenly finds himself outside of his own physical body, but still in the immediate physical environment, and he sees his own body from a distance, as though he is a spectator. He watches the resuscitation attempts from this unusual vantage point and is in a state of emotional upheaval.

"After a while, he collects himself and becomes more accustomed to his odd condition. He notices that he still has a 'body,' but one of a very different nature and with very different powers from the physical one he has left behind. Soon other things begin to happen. Others come to meet and to help him. He glimpses the spirits of relatives and friends who have already died, and a loving, warm spirit of a kind he has never encountered before—a being of light—appears before him. This being asks him a question, nonverbally, to make him evaluate his life and helps him along by showing him a panoramic, instantaneous playback of the major events of his life. At some point he finds himself approaching some sort of barrier or border, apparently representing the limit between earthly life and the rest of life. Yet, he finds that he must go back to the earth, that the time for his death has not yet come. At this point, he resists, for by now he is taken up with his experiences in the afterlife and does not want to return. He is overwhelmed by intense feelings of joy, love, and peace. Despite his attitude, though, he somehow reunites with his physical body and lives."

At first glance, the NDE seems to be very similar to the OBE. In fact, though they both involve a separation between the body and consciousness that is often accompanied by feelings of joyful release, there are characteristics more typical of (though not exclusive to) the NDE.

In the NDE, the subject sees individuals who have died—or supernatural beings—and landscapes that are visionary, not real. The subject is also keenly aware that the "disembodiment" is a stage of passage into another dimension of existence. Often the subject experiences an overwhelming euphoria at making this transition, which he or she has to fight in order to return to the body. Consider, for example, this actual case history:

"I was hospitalized for a severe kidney condition, and I was in a coma for approximately a week. My doctors were extremely uncertain as to whether I would live. During this period when I was unconscious, I felt as though I were lifted right up, just as though I didn't have a physical body at all. A brilliant white light appeared to me. The light was so bright that I could not see through it, but going into its presence was so calming and wonderful. There is just no experience on earth like it. In the presence of the light, the thoughts or words came into my mind: 'Do you want to die?' And I replied that I didn't know, since I knew nothing about death. Then the white light said, 'Come over this line and you will learn.' I felt that I knew where the line was in front of me, although I could not actually see it. As I went across the line, the most wonderful feelings came over me—feelings of peace, tranquility, a vanishing of all worries."

The following story was told to me by a woman whom I've always considered one of the most pragmatic, down-to-earth people I know:

"This was one of my deep, dark secrets as a young woman. I'd returned to live with my parents after my divorce and had just gotten a good job with the Albany newspaper, when I found out I was pregnant by a man I'd been dating—but I was not in love with him. Well, I was devastated—I had no real friends since I'd moved back, my parents would have been horrified, my nice new job was in jeopardy, and this was still in the days of sordid back-room abortions. But I had grown up in England, where abortions were available at clinics, and I knew of one outside London. I contrived to take some vacation time, ostensibly to visit old friends and relatives. All alone, I went to the clinic, where the people were very warm and competent, and had my abortion. I woke up, feeling fine but very groggy, and got up to go to the bathroom.

"In the stall, I suddenly felt very faint, and felt like I was losing consciousness; in fact, I felt like the life was leaving my body. I tried to hang on and call someone, but I couldn't call out.

"I felt myself being swept down a tunnel, and there was a light at the end. There was a feeling of complete peace, of comfort and happiness—I've never felt anything like it before or since. But there was a part of me that felt I wanted to stay where I was, with my body, and I had to fight with myself not to succumb to this wonderful feeling, and to stay with my body, to try and recover, and live, though I didn't put it in so many words. I don't know how long this struggle went on, but I was aware of having to fight not to let go and follow those wonderful feelings, go to that wonderful place. Suddenly I realized that I was looking down at myself from somewhere near the ceiling. I saw myself slumped on the floor by the toilet, saw how pale I was. I could see the whole room, and hear and see people in the hall. I saw a nurse come in—she must have heard me groaning —and find me on the floor, and heard her call out. Then there were a dozen people around, and I was given a shot, and they were pumping my chest—I could see it all.

"And then I was wrenched back into my body, and remember nothing until I woke up later, with anxious faces peering down at me. They'd thought I was a goner, my blood pressure was so low. I remember coming back to London on the train, and feeling euphoric all the way; as you know, I'm not the least bit religious, but I've never since feared death."

In 1977, Dr. Karlis Osis and Dr. Erlendur Haraldsson published the results of a survey based on physicians' and nurses' observations of 877 NDEs in two countries: the United States (442 patients) and India (435 patients). Of these patients, 714 were terminally ill, but conscious during their last moments. The remaining 163 patients recovered from near-death conditions. The majority of these NDEs contain the principal elements we've already examined: apparitions, otherworldly landscapes, and a feeling of elation and serenity. The objective of the survey was to determine if NDEs could be attributed to the influence of other factors besides "ESP of or from 'another world.' " They could immediately eliminate the possible influence of medical factors: Those which often cause hallucinations did not increase the frequency of NDEs, and those which impede sensory contact with the external world also reduced the incidence of NDEs. Next, Osis and Haraldsson looked at psychological factors:

"Severe stress, especially in situations of drastically reduced social contact, can find release in hallucinations. Psychiatrists suggest that deathbed visions actually are schizoid episodes through which patients cope with very stressful situations by hallucinating pleasant fantasies of another world. A careful analysis of the data revealed no support of this counterhypothesis. Stress was not significantly related to the core phenomena of deathbed visions. In both the American and Indian examples, the trend went in the opposite direction: stress tended to reduce the survival-related aspects of these experiences. Patients' desires, wishes, and expectations also had no significant influence. In a large number of cases, patients experienced apparitions which appeared to be in opposition to their own motivations, although consistent with our hypothesis of post-mortem survival."

Finally, Osis and Haraldsson reviewed the most likely alternative theory to explain NDEs: that they are the products of cultural conditioning. Mindful of the fact that NDEs seemed to happen to people regardless of their religious beliefs or feelings about death, they analyzed their data to determine if similar NDEs occurred to people regardless of their culture:

"In childhood and youth, cultural beliefs are transmitted to us in various ways. Could they reemerge in the visions of the dying—a kind of playing back of old records? The cross-cultural survey in India was primarily done with this question in view. Our model assumes that individual and cultural factors will completely shape deathbed visions, provided they are *caused* by these factors. However, if they are based on perception of some form of external reality, of ESP glimpses of 'another world,' we hypothesized that only modest differences between cultures would emerge, with the main features remaining the same. An analogy could be found by contrasting a typically American and a typically Indian painting of a mountain: the details would be quite different while the basic characteristics of a mountain would be clearly recognizable. . . . The sex of the hallucinatory figure was largely determined by culturally conditioned preferences which, in turn, seem to influence the proportion of dead and religious figures. Religion had a comparably slight influence on the main phenomena, though it did, of course, determine the naming of the religious figures. We interpret these modest cultural differences according to our model: they seem to support the hypothesis that deathbed visions are, in part, based on extrasensory perception of some form of external reality rather than having entirely subjective origins."

If NDEs are so common, then, why aren't they more generally known? Most people who comment on this question (including Moody, Osis, and Haraldsson) have the same response: Contemporary civilization, which sets such a high value on science, technology, and progress, discourages any discussion of death, let alone the possibility of survival beyond death. Fear of ridicule keeps people who have NDEs from sharing them with others, and prevents many researchers from studying the phenomenon more closely. People who do hear about NDEs are apt to disregard them, consciously or subconsciously, since there is nothing in their world that relates to these accounts. This issue of apparent "irrelevance" may also explain why we are not more cognizant of yet another reported phenomenon: telepathic, clairvoyant, or psychokinetic communications from people who are experiencing the very moment of death or who have been dead for some time.

SPIRIT COMMUNICATIONS

No aspect of parapsychology is more provocative than anecdotal accounts of apparent communications from the spirits of dead people. As we've already seen, some of these accounts involve crisis-oriented telepathy or clairvoyance (Chapter 4), while others involve psychokinetic manifestations (Chapter 5). Mediumship and trance channeling often seem to be the means by which "departed souls" communicate with us earthlings. The most controversial form of communication, however, is the visit of an apparition—the "spirit" of a dead person made visible. Commonly called a "ghost," this apparition may be described as a "filmy" or solid image of a dead person, similar to the apparitions that turn up in NDEs.

APPARITIONS

In some cases, the apparition of a dying person presents itself at the very moment of death. Dr. Christiaan Barnard, the South African surgeon who became famous when he performed the first heart transplant, shocked an Italian television audience in 1985 with his story of a "moment-of-death" apparition that had occurred eighteen years earlier:

"I was in a private room with a door and a window. My bed was near the window and there was some light coming from outside. Around 10 P.M., a woman entered the room. She walked toward my bed, put her hand on my chest, and began pushing against it. I looked up at her and saw she was very thin and pale, with blue eyes and gray hair. She was pressing strongly on my chest. I took her wrists in my hand. They were very fragile. I pushed her back and realized she was extremely light. Then, as if she were reacting to my pressure, she levitated and disappeared through the window."

Barnard immediately rang for a nurse, but had to wait several minutes before one finally appeared.

" 'I'm so sorry,' she said, 'but I couldn't answer your first call, because a woman was dying in my ward just when you buzzed.' I asked her to describe the woman. She told me she was thin, with blue eyes and gray hair, and was wearing a white nightgown—the same woman I'd seen! And there was no question of my ever having seen the woman before. She had been in the women's ward, while I was in a private room."

Barnard's account is unusual among records of apparitions in several respects: The apparition appears very close to the moment of death itself (perhaps even before that moment!), Barnard does not recognize the apparition, and he has relatively intense physical contact with her.

Typically, an apparition appears some time considerably after the moment of death and behaves rather formally. The person who sees the apparition is tired, stressed, or perplexed. An apparition of someone the person knew in life suddenly presents itself, and the person is stunned into a wondrous passivity. The apparition offers critical input: for example, soothing, admonishing, or informing the person. In a very short time, the apparition vanishes as suddenly as it came.

Dr. Elisabeth Kübler-Ross, who has performed ground-breaking work involving the acceptance of death and the succor of the dying, tells a personal story regarding the visit of an apparition that follows this common format, but with an unusual twist: The apparition left physical evidence of her visit. Kübler-Ross was just finishing the last engagement in an extended speaking tour and was completely exhausted. She said to herself, "I've done enough of this now! I've got to phase out this work." Moments later, as she stood in front of an elevator, a former patient whom she had helped to die took shape instantly beside her. The apparition greeted her warmly, but then said in a deeply serious tone, "You can't give up this work for the dying! It's *much* too important." The apparition stayed with her as she rode down the elevator and walked along a deserted corridor. "This can't be happening," Kübler-Ross told herself. "I'm surely imagining it!" When they were finally inside Kübler-Ross' room, the apparition insisted, "Promise me you won't give up your work!" Still utterly amazed, Kübler-Ross grabbed a piece of paper and said, "Give me your autograph." The apparition complied, and then disappeared out the door. Kübler-Ross ran after her, but the corridor was empty. She stood there awestruck, holding the signed piece of paper in her hand.

A great number of anecdotes center around the visiting spirit of a former spouse, lover, or especially dear friend or relative who has died. Ingo Swann (echoing the opinion of Carl Jung) comments, "The appearance of the spirit of a departed loved one is so common it's a wonder it's controversial." Far more bizarre—and terrifying—is the sudden appearance of the spirit of a stranger. A friend reports the following encounter:

"I had been living in a house outside the city. Actually, it was more like a castle—the house had been owned by Washington Irving. In the 1960s, friends of mine had bought this big house, and unbeknownst to them, another buyer had recently bought what had been part of the same property. It had a cottage on it that had originally been part of the larger house; they had torn it down to build a new house.

"When my friends went to move into their new 'castle,' their dogs wouldn't go into the house, and their four young children couldn't sleep, complaining of chills, noises, and 'seeing things.' Not knowing what to do, but knowing that something strange indeed was going on, my friend brought a well-known psychic into the house. He was able to to reconstruct what happened, and confirm it through historical records.

"Apparently one August night during the 1850s two men had stopped at the house looking for a place to stay the night. There was a big party going on at the house, so the host offered to let them stay in a cottage down by the river. It was not until two days later that anyone remembered to wonder what had become of the travelers. Down at the cottage, they found both men hanged from the rafters, and the story of their fate was never learned. The ghosts of these two men were said to have haunted the cottage and the area down by the river for years. Now, it seemed, with the cottage gone, the restless and displaced spirits had moved up into the main house. The psychic performed some kind of ritual to calm the ghosts, and the next day the dogs came into the house, and the kids were able to sleep.

"But the ghosts were still there, though they were benevolent. They kept to the first floor of the house; their arrival would be preceded by an icy chill, and sometimes there were rattling noises, and candles or lights would go out momentarily. But the family got used to it, and even got to feel at home with their resident ghosts.

"One day we were sitting around the big living room in front of the huge fireplace, drinking wine and talking; two of the kids were there. A woman friend of theirs came to visit, and Tina, one of the daughters, started telling her about the ghosts. The woman kept making fun of Tina and laughing at the whole idea—'That's stupid and ridiculous!' Suddenly the room got icy cold, and the lights flickered. Tina and I couldn't help giggling. 'He's here,' Tina said. Suddenly, a big bronze sculpture of a hand in a heavy wood base (made by our host, who was a sculptor), jumps six feet in the air and crashes down next to the woman, tipping her wineglass onto her dress.

"Some time later, I was getting ready to move to Paris. I was in the sunroom of the house and I was feeling brave, and I decided to say good-bye to the ghosts. So I just started talking to them—it was a bit silly, but I just felt like doing it. I said I was happy to have made their acquaintance, and I was leaving for Europe and wanted to say good-bye, or some silly thing. Then I went upstairs to bed.

"I woke up in the middle of the night and got up to go to the bathroom. I went out in the hall—it was a huge, wide, long hall, very well lit because of the children, and the bathroom was down at the other end, around a corner. Behind me was a large window. As I started down the hall, all of a sudden I felt that icy chill, and I knew that the ghost was behind me. I was totally awake. I turned around and there, standing in front of the window, was a man. He was dressed in black, he looked sort of smoky, and he was about a foot off the ground—and he was staring at me. I took one look and said, 'Oh, my God,' and ran down the hall and slammed the bathroom door behind me, and couldn't bring myself to come out for half an hour. When I actually finally saw the ghost, I was a total chicken— although I probably scared him as well."

MEDIUMSHIP AND TRANCE CHANNELING

Mediums claim to be able to contact spirits of people who have died, as we've already discussed (Chapter 5). In this respect, the most remarkable medium yet investigated—by William James, among others—is Mrs. Lenore Piper, an American woman who practiced around the turn of the century. Originally she worked through a "control" spirit, a Frenchman calling himself Dr. Phinuit. (Lawrence LeShan makes the point that spirit guides or controls are sometimes unlikely characters, but you have to accept them as they are. Dr. Phinuit, for example, knew nothing of medicine, understood little French, and could not find his way around his "hometown," Carcassonne.) In any case, Dr. Phinuit acted as an intermediary between people who attended Mrs. Piper's seminars and the spirits with whom they desired to communicate.

In one seance in England, Sir Oliver Lodge, a scrupulously thorough investigator from the Society for Psychical Research, waited until Mrs. Piper had already entered her trance and then presented her with a watch. He did not tell her that it had belonged to an uncle of his named Jerry. "Uncle Jerry" promptly announced himself, spoke of his brother, and said that the watch had belonged to him. Lodge pressed for information about Jerry's early life, about which Lodge knew nothing but which he could corroborate with Jerry's surviving brother, Robert. "Uncle Jerry" was agreeable. As Lodge recorded:

" 'Uncle Jerry' recalled episodes such as swimming the creek when they were boys together, and running some risk of getting drowned; killing a cat at Smith's field; the possession of a small rifle, and of a long, peculiar skin, like a snake-skin, which he thought was not in the possession of Uncle Robert. . . . All these facts have been more or less completely verified."

Later, back in the United States, Phinuit was superseded by "G.P.," the spirit of a young man who in fact had died in an accident in 1892. At a large seance of 150 sitters, all strangers to Mrs. Piper, "G.P." correctly recognized 30 people he had known when he was alive—and *only* those 30. He also behaved differently with each individual, in accordance with the relationship he had had with that individual during his lifetime.

Lawrence LeShan tells a pertinent story about Eileen Garrett, the highly gifted psychic with whom he worked for many years. It concerns the biography of a deceased physician and philanthropist— whom LeShan calls "Dr. X"—that his widow and sister were trying to write. They were having tremendous difficulty writing the first part of the book; and it had been rejected by several publishers when they decided to consult Garrett at her publishing house, Helix Press, having once had a brief correspondence with her. Here is LeShan's firsthand report:

"I met the widow and the sister with Eileen at the Parapsychology Foundation [which Garrett founded], and we discussed the problem of getting the biography of Dr. X published. Then I had an idea. I suggested that the first section of the book should be tape-recorded and then played back to Eileen, who would go into trance and try to get the spirit of Dr. X to 'come through,' that is, speak through her voice. We would then let 'him' correct the first section. The arrangements were duly made.

"The next morning we went into the 'seance room,' in which we had two tape recorders and a shorthand secretary, and Eileen went into trance, that is, she manipulated her breathing and her consciousness, her head fell back onto the back of the couch, and she appeared to be unconscious. In a few moments (probably about thirty seconds) she raised her head and, speaking in a different tone and speech pattern, identified herself as 'Uvani' (her 'gatekeeper,' who always appeared first in any trance and decided what was possible and what was not for a particular session. He claimed to be an Arab who had been killed by a Turk in 1851 and was an amazingly consistent persona in trance transcripts over a fifty-year period).

"Uvani, speaking in his usual 'stage Persian' ('Greetings, sahib . . . ,' and so on) asked what was wanted and I asked if we could speak to Dr. X. He replied, as he usually did if we asked to speak to a specific spirit, 'One moment, I'll see if he is around!' (Where, I always wondered, was 'around'? And if he was not 'around,' where was he?)

"Eileen then appeared to become unconscious again and when, twenty or thirty seconds later, she seemed to recover consciousness she was speaking in a different voice and with a different speech pattern, which both the sister and the widow immediately identified as belonging to Dr. X.

"Dr. X called the widow by pet names she claimed only the two of them knew and recalled incidents that had the sister screaming they were known only to the two of them. At the end of half an hour each of them was holding one of Eileen's hands and talking animatedly, and very convincingly, to Dr. X.

"I said at this point it was time to go to work. I put on both tape recorders, one with a blank tape and recording, the other playing the first section of the book. Every few minutes Dr. X would interrupt with suggested changes. As soon as he started to talk I could turn off the playback machine but continued to record. In this way we had a complete running record of the session duplicated by the shorthand secretary. (The editorial changes made by Dr. X seemed to me, then and afterwards, to be excellent ones. It should be said here, however, that Eileen had been a professional editor for several years during her life.)

"From my own experience with Eileen's trance work, I had learned that during this period of her life, if she stayed in trance for up to one and a half hours she would wake up as refreshed as if she had taken a long nap. If she stayed in trance any longer she would awaken exhausted and drained. At the end of an hour and a quarter, therefore, I said, 'We will have to stop now. We can continue tomorrow.'

"Dr. X replied, 'Hell, no, we're not going to stop. I've waited five years for this.'

"I said, 'Dr. X, I am concerned about the health of the instrument.'

"He replied, 'Young man, I'm a physician and you're not. I know more about health than you do. Furthermore, I'm in here and you're not, and I know a lot more about what's going on than you do.'

"In a moment I was in the midst of an argument with a man who claimed to have been dead for five years. It was a confusing situation to say the least.

"After the argument had gone on for a while, I said, 'Dr. X, I have no way to get you out. But if you aren't gone in thirty seconds, I'm going to turn off the tape recorder and erase the tape and all the work we have done will be for nothing.'

"He replied, 'Okay, if you will agree that we finish this section and start promptly tomorrow at 10 o'clock.'

"I agreed. We finished the section in five minutes. Dr. X said, 'See you tomorrow at ten.' "

Garrett herself spent much of her life trying to understand where her abilities came from and what they were about. She could never resolve whether such experiences were really visitations from the dead, multiple-personality split-offs, or a very high-level telepathy. She told LeShan:

"Larry, I have to answer you in what seems to be a light and humorous way, but it's the best that I can do. It's as if on Monday, Wednesday and Friday I think that they are actually what they claim to be. And as if on Tuesday, Thursday and Saturday I think they are multiple-personality split-offs I have invented to make my work easier. And as if on Sunday, I try not to think about the problem."

Unlike many mediums, both Mrs. Piper and Garrett convinced every single person who investigated them that their abilities were genuine, but even this fact does not support the notion that people who have died survive in spirit form and are capable of communicating with the world of the living. Their results can invariably be attributed to extrasensory perception, or other processes, no matter what they—or their observers—may believe. Perhaps it's telepathy, by means of which they could have gleaned information from living people who possessed knowledge of the dead person. (As Garrett once reminded LeShan, "Never forget, Larry, that awake or in a trance, I am very telepathic, and that the stage lost a great actress in me!") Perhaps it's retrocognition, by means of which they could have "witnessed" events from the dead person's life. Perhaps it's a form of ESP that so far remains unarticulated—or some other process altogether.

We've already looked at a couple of examples of channeled information, in Ruth Montgomery's spirit-guided automatic writing and Luiz Gasparetto's "channeled" paintings by departed masters (Chapter 5). And by now many people have heard of the channeled books *Seth Speaks* and *A Course in Miracles*, a three-volume work which is pored over in study groups all over the country. Another intriguing case of channeled information is that of England's Rosemary Brown, to whom dozens of famous composers have dictated new works—from beyond the grave.

Mrs. Brown seems to be on rather intimate terms with the composers who visit her. Liszt was the first composer to show up; it was he who persuaded her to accept the strange role she now plays and showed her how to let the spirits guide her hands so she could play the unfamiliar and sometimes difficult music. Liszt, she says, sometimes helps her add up her bills at the supermarket. Bach is very stern, and never talks to her—just dictates his music and runs. Schubert is diffident, and apologizes for inconveniencing her. Chopin is mischievous; Mrs. Brown suspects that he often watches her in private moments: He once reminded her that she had forgotten to put on her bed socks. Gershwin, she claims, is very moody. He's been to see her a couple of dozen times, but he leaves right away if things aren't just right. He once became angry when Mrs. Brown told him that she doubted she could play the piece he wanted to dictate to her, for she knows little about jazz.

In fact, Mrs. Brown has only the most rudimentary musical training, which is one of the things that most baffle the musicians, music scholars, and psychic researchers who have investigated her. If Mrs. Brown is a fraud, she has taken on a particularly difficult hoax to pull off. As her investigators—every one of whom has come away amazed but convinced—have noted, it is one thing to try to produce one piece in imitation of one composer. But to turn out more than four hundred original compositions that are true to the known works and styles of so many composers would be beyond the scope of even the most expert musicologist.

Many of those who have come to check out Mrs. Brown start out with the attitude that some crazy joke is being played, but they are quickly disabused of that idea. Malcolm Troup, of the London Guildhall School of Music, found Mrs. Brown "utterly amazing. I have played some pieces by her, particularly the works by 'Schubert,' and they are absolutely charming. I would never guess they were not by Schubert. They are, in character and essence, the very heart of his work."

"I do not understand," said Leonard Bernstein, "how anybody with such limited training as she has could possibly write in so many different styles." Bernstein played a piece "dictated by Rachmaninoff." "It was marvelous the way he played it," remembers Mrs. Brown. "When he was finished, he looked up and said, 'Without a doubt, this is Rachmaninoff.'. . . I didn't tell Bernstein that just before my meeting with him, the composer came to me and gave me a nudge, pointing to the manuscript where I had written down the piece he had dictated. It was clear he knew where I was going and he wanted Bernstein to play his piece—which he did."

Automatic writing, paintings, and music are less common versions of what currently seems to be the most popular metaphysical diversion: trance channeling. Trance channeling is the modern mode of mediumship, and yesterday's "spirit guide" is today's "channeled entity." But today's channeled entity might take any number of forms: It might be a departed spirit from some earlier era, an extraterrestrial from some other dimension of time and space, or some being who's never had an incarnation anywhere. Channelers allow their "entities," of whatever stripe, to temporarily occupy their bodies, so that they can impart their wisdom to whoever happens to be within range. In some cases, this is an individual who has paid for a private session with the channeled spirit. More often it is a large audience—from dozens to thousands of people—and sometimes it is a nationwide television audience. Most channelers go into a trance in order to remove themselves so that the entity can take over. In the trance, the channeler is transformed into the entity, who typically speaks English, but with some form of strange accent and quirky, formalized speech pattern.

In their day, mediums attracted many well-known clients, from Arthur Conan Doyle and Henry Ford to William Butler Yeats and William Randolph Hearst. Today it's corporation executives and celebrities like Michael York, Linda Evans, Richard Chamberlain, and (no surprise!) Shirley MacLaine. It was through the televised version of MacLaine's *Out on a Limb* that millions of viewers got to see two trance channelers at work, reenacting—evidently in trance—scenes from the book. And it was MacLaine who introduced a broader public to Ramtha, the entity who speaks through J. Z. Knight. A small, blond, fortyish woman, Knight lives in a multimillion-dollar house in Yelm, Washington, with a stable of Arabian horses and a Rolls-Royce, paid for with the fees of those who have come to listen to a 35,000-year-old male spirit who claims he was a king who conquered the lost kingdom of Atlantis. Ramtha first appeared to Knight in her kitchen, while she was toying with a handful of amethyst crystals that she had bought on a whim. Ramtha's message is a variant on what many of the entities have to say for themselves: God is within us; we all have power, and we should own that power; we are loved. Ramtha also makes some dire predictions, saying that natural cataclysms—hurricanes, earthquakes and volcanoes—will devastate the earth, leaving the Pacific Northwest among the few untouched areas. Ramtha encourages his followers to prepare themselves—to move to a safe area, and stock up on food and disaster rations; many have done just that. Like many of her colleagues, Knight claims that when she awakens from her trance state, she has no memory of what Ramtha has said while she was "away." "I go through a tunnel, and there's a whistling sound and a light at the end. As soon as I hit the end, I come back [as Ramtha]."

There are several other channelers today who, like Knight, have a huge following and have become full-fledged enterprises—complete with channeled books, tapes, weekend seminars, and closed-circuit TV hookups. Thomas Jacobsen channels "Dr. Peebles," a nineteenth-century Doctor of Philosophy. Jamie Sams channels "Leah," a "sixth density entity" from a planet six hundred years in the future. Malcolm Luckin channels advice on gold and silver investments from the Star Community of Brandon. Jack Purcell reanimates as a "multidimensional energy." Penny Torres' entity, Mafu, was last incarnated as a leper in first-century Pompeii.

What makes channelers, and their followers, tick is a matter hotly debated by investigators. Some feel that channelers are in a waking dream, a self-hypnotic state which mesmerizes an audience already predisposed to accept the "wisdom" of the entity. Some compare it to religious fervor. Ray Hyman, a psychology professor at the University of Oregon and a CSICOP member, feels that there is a self-validating mechanism involved. "It's a symbiotic relationship. It's like the old way witch doctors and shamans worked. If you go to a psychic, you want to have help. You want to validate psychic powers by finding meaning in what they tell you.

Ninety-five percent are not conscious frauds. Some are split personalities. Everyone has the potential. People have enough information to act out hundreds of personalities with details. Creative artists and writers have learned to tap this. Most of us haven't. It comes out under severe conditions, when hypnotized, when sick or deprived, or in some mystical ritual."

The findings of Margo Chandley, who studied many channels for a Ph.D. in transformational psychology, seem to concur. Chandley found that many of the channels she studied were traumatized as children—by seizures, serious falls, emotional abuse. Many of them withdrew into a powerful inner life, and they were often extremely religious, reporting mystical experiences at an early age. What investigators need to address, however, is whether this kind of traumatic experience and isolation causes the opening of psychic channels or the creation of entities in response to trauma, emotional disturbance.

REINCARNATION AND PAST LIVES

Each era in history seems to favor one particular aspect of "supernatural" phenomena. Today, the possibility of reincarnation captivates the general public: A 1982 Gallup poll revealed that 23 percent of Americans believe in reincarnation. Perhaps it has something to do with the recent escalation of consciousness studies, or with the emerging union between Western scientific thought and Eastern religious thought, or with a heightened fear of death due to crime, terrorism, or nuclear holocaust. Maybe it can be attributed to the efforts of Moody and Kübler-Ross, whose recent best-selling books have made NDEs familiar to the general public and have spurred widespread speculation about all sorts of afterlife possibilities. Whatever the reason, people feel they have permission to talk about reincarnation now, which wasn't true fifty years ago.

Among those who are talking, celebrities, as usual, are getting most of the attention. In her best-selling book *Out on a Limb*, Shirley MacLaine speaks of numerous past lives uncovered while in a light trance, including one life as a court jester who was personally beheaded by Louis XV of France for telling impudent jokes: "I watched my head rolling on the floor. It landed face up, and a big tear came out of one eye." Under hypnosis, Sylvester Stallone recalled a life as a boxer who died in the ring in 1935, eleven years before Stallone was born: "I was caught with a tremendous blow that knocked me out in a title fight—and I died later without coming around." According to H. N. Bannerjee's 1980 book *Americans Who Have Been Reincarnated*, Glenn Ford found out during a series of hypnotic sessions that he had lived previous lives as a Roman Christian martyr, a seventeenth-century British sailor, a cavalryman for Louis XIV, a Scottish piano teacher in the early 1800s, and an American cowboy. Ford credits these revelations with helping him conquer his fear of death: It was "as though a great eraser had scrubbed it from my life."

A consistent element in each of these celebrity accounts is the use of hypnotic (or trance) regression to send the celebrity back to previous lives. Hypnotic regression is a highly controversial mode of acquiring information. Many experts feel that it improves recall. A subject, for example, can be led back to imagine a time when he or she was five years old; and a whole host of memories relating to that time, long forgotten, will suddenly become as vivid as if they were present realities. Whether or not this means the subject has actually "become" five years old again in his or her mind is a moot point. The veracity of further regression to previous lives is definitely a matter of faith—or credulousness. Either you believe in it or you don't. People of scrupulous honesty stake their reputations on the assertion that they did indeed realize previous existences under hypnosis; many claim to have detected correlations between their past lives and present life which they feel helped them improve the quality of their present life. Critics, however, scoff at the authenticity of *any* experience attained under hypnosis. In their book *Anomalistic Psychology*, Dr. Leonard Zusne and Dr. Warren H. Jones are exceptionally harsh:

". . . Because suggestion is part of hypnosis, suggesting that the subject go back beyond the point of his or her own birth and examine his or her previous lives achieves precisely that result—the subject all too willingly proceeds to do just that. This, however, is no proof of reincarnation. The cases that have been thoroughly investigated show beyond the shadow of a doubt that one is dealing with hypnotic hyperamnesia [improved recall] coupled with the subject's unconscious wish for exhibition, for romance to liven up a drab life, for fantasy as an ego defense mechanism, and similar psychological needs, all reinforced by the hypnotist's own beliefs in the reincarnation doctrine."

Whether or not hypnosis actually links the subject with past lives, it has reputedly been successful as a psychiatric treatment in the context of what is called "past-life therapy." Among the first to perform this type of therapy was Dr. Denys Kelsey, a British psychiatrist who was the husband of Joan Grant, a psychic and the author of many books on reincarnation. One day in the 1950s, a patient came to him who was suffering from extreme guilt. He was under the delusion that he was directly responsible for his father's arthritis. He explained that when he was seven years old, he had run a damp cloth over his parents' mattress at a time when he was deeply angry with his father. When all other stratagems failed, Kelsey tried hypnosis. The patient regressed far beyond the seven-year-old stage into a vision of a previous life as a woman in Edwardian times. The woman wanted to marry a local curate; but her aunt, who controlled the woman's wealth under the terms of her dead father's will, disapproved of the match. Desperate, the woman dampened her aunt's bed each night in the hope that her aunt would get ill and die. When the aunt discovered the plot, she flew into a rage and had a stroke. The woman was forced to tend her bedridden aunt for the rest of her life. Following this hypnotic regression, the patient was cured of his obsession. As Kelsey says in his book *Many Lifetimes*:

"When I brought the patient slowly back to the present and out of hypnosis, he had a clear memory of all he had been telling us and felt no doubt at all that it was a part of his own long history. He was completely satisfied that at last he had discovered the true source of his guilt—guilt that had become transferred to his father."

Hypnotic regression is not the only means by which one can feel an intimation of a possible past life. Meditation can also be a route. A friend tells the following story:

"One of the most profound—and scary—experiences I've ever had was during an advanced type of meditation called the mirror meditation. You sit cross-legged in front of a mirror on a pillow in a small room. I remember wearing loose white pajamas, and there was a crack in the wall behind me that was the only distraction. Anyway, you stare at yourself in the mirror, and stare at your 'third eye'—on your forehead between your eyes—and repeat your mantra over and over. My eyes were open and I became very relaxed, and after a while I realized I was levitating: I was several inches off the ground. As I stared into the mirror, images kept popping in and out real fast. I could see my face changing and saw myself in many guises, always going back in time. I was in England, in India, in what looked like Holland or Denmark, in the Middle Ages, in a very ancient culture. I was a man, a woman, a boy, a servant, a laborer, a craftsman, a mother—picture after picture, boom, boom, boom, until suddenly I was looking at a blank wall. Nobody was there, and I could see the crack in the back wall. I remember saying to myself, 'Now, don't freak, this is tricky, okay, I'm not here, but I can come back. I can see the wall behind me, I can see the crack, I just have to concentrate.' Then I just popped back in, and settled back to the ground, and it was over."

Spontaneous waking visions, dreams, and feelings of déjà vu can also provide clues to the possibility of previous existences. Take the experience reported by this woman, who was driving with a friend through New Jersey:

"We were driving down the New Jersey Turnpike, and I felt very strange, all this landscape was very familiar to me. . . . I turned to Joanne, and said, 'You know, I have never been here before, but I believe about a mile or so down the road is a house I used to live in.'

"As we went down the turnpike (heading north), everything was familiar. . . . and I began describing *what* we would see before we came to it.

"Approximately three miles or so passed, and I told my friend that around the bend we would come to a small town, it was set very close to the turnpike. I told her that the houses would be white frame, two-storey homes, rather close together . . . and that I felt that I lived there when I was six years old or so, and that I used to sit with my 'granny' on the front porch. The memories overwhelmed me, and I could remember sitting on the swing, on the front porch, and my grandmother buttoning up my high-topped shoes. I could not do it myself. When we got to the town, I recognized the house immediately, only the front porch swing was not there . . . however, at the time I lived there with my granny, there was also wicker furniture on the porch with green cloth cushions. I told my friend I *remembered* sitting there, and also that my granny used to walk two blocks down the street with me, to a drug store, and there was a high marble counter, white, and we used to get lemonade from the drug store, and I liked to go there. As we drove down the little street, I took her to the drug store, or where it *used* to be. It was still there, or rather, the building was still there, much the same as it used to look, but it was boarded up, and we could not look inside. As we stood there, I 'knew' that I had died when I was about 6 or 7 years old . . . and I tried to get Joanne to let me direct her to the cemetery where 'I' was buried, but she was so frightened that she would not take the drive. As we were leaving the town I told her, 'In about three blocks there is a small hill, rolling, and the cemetery is *there*, and that is where they buried me.' It was true . . . the cemetery *was* there and as I had described it.

"We got on the turnpike again, and went on to Paterson . . . and I still know that once, around the early 1900s, that I lived there, and died there."

Dr. Ian Stevenson's *Twenty Cases Suggestive of Reincarnation* was published in 1966 after twenty years of research. Stevenson felt that the most fruitful subjects to interview were children who had referred to previous existences, since their memories were likely to be fresher and less susceptible to contamination by things they had read or seen. The children selected for in-depth study were all from cultures that offered some support to belief in reincarnation: seven from India, three from Sri Lanka (Ceylon), two from Brazil, one from Lebanon, and seven from Alaska.

Perhaps the most interesting case Stevenson covers is that of Jagdish Chandra, who was born on March 4, 1923, in Uttar Pradesh, a district in northern India. When Jagdish was three years old, he began demanding that his father, Sahay, bring "his" car to him. Sahay couldn't figure out what he meant, but gradually he became aware that his son was talking about a previous life. Fortunately, Sahay started keeping elaborate notes of his son's memories from this point on. Jagdish said that his car was at the home of his "father," whom he called Babu or Babuji, in Benares. He described the house as having a guarded gate outside and a safe sunk into a wall in an underground chamber. He also spoke of a stairway (or "ghat") leading from the house to the Ganges River that was known as the Dash Ashwamadh. He claimed his "real" father's family name was Pandey and that the man had a wife who had died and two sons.

Sahay (who had never been to Benares) submitted a letter to the regional newspaper detailing his son's claims, and the newspaper published it. Soon he received a note from a city employee in Benares who said he knew Babuji Pandey and could verify the accuracy of

Jagdish's memories. Sahay also learned that one of Babuji's sons, Jai Gopal, had died as a child a few years before. On August 13, 1926, Sahay took his son to Benares, and Jagdish was able to direct his father to his "home" and to identify, unassisted, several of Jai Gopal's surviving relatives. Sahay says the following in his records:

"The boy was taken to the Dash Ashwamadh Ghat which he recognized from a distance. He took his bath twice with great pleasure in the arms of a panda [an aide at the ghat] whom he recognized at first sight. He was not at all upset with the sight of the swelled volume of the Ganges in August which flowed so violently, making a terrific noise. The volume of the Ganges in August did not bother him and he behaved as one who was very familiar with this site. The panda offered him a betel [a leaf commonly chewed in India] which Jagdish refused, saying that he being a bigger panda [i.e., of higher status] could not accept from one who was a small panda."

What makes this behavior remarkable is that Jagdish knew nothing about such customs from his present life and had never been near a major river. There were further indications that Jagdish had "inherited" not only memories but behaviors: He preferred food prepared according to Brahmin tradition, although he came from a lower class and knew nothing about this tradition, and he often asked for bhang —an intoxicant with which he was unfamiliar.

Several of Stevenson's cases featured a particularly astonishing phenomenon: the apparent transfer of a wound or birthmark from a past life to a present life. Victor Vincent was a Tlingit Indian living on one of the small islands off Alaska's southern coast. In 1946, when he knew he was dying, he told his beloved niece Mrs. Corliss Chotkin that he would be reborn as her next son and that she would know this by two scars the child would receive from him. Vincent had a livid, one-inch surgical scar on his back and a less distinct scar at the base of his nose. A year and a half later, Mrs. Chotkin gave birth to Corliss, Jr., who has two birthmarks that exactly match the scars on Vincent's body. Dr. Stevenson examined the one on Corliss' back and noted, "Along its margin one could still easily discern several small round marks outside the main scar. Four of these on one side lined up like stitch wounds of surgical operations."

As Corliss grew a few years older, more evidence of a reincarnation emerged. He spontaneously recognized people on the street whom he had known as Victor, he could recount incidents from Victor's life about which he had never been told, he stuttered like Victor, and he demonstrated a precocious affinity for repairing engines—a task at which Victor had been notably skilled. As he grew older, however, his memories of a past life faded. When Stevenson revisited Corliss in 1972, Corliss was in his twenties and had forgotten everything from his previous life, even though many of his personality characteristics were uncannily like those of his grand-uncle.

If we discount the possibility of reincarnation, how do we account for the massive quantity of so-called past-life visions contained in the anecdotal material? Aside from fraud, there are at least four possible explanations:

1. The subject may be hallucinating and confusing a particularly vivid scene (perhaps suggested by book, movie or excursion) with a "past-life" memory.

2. The subject may be getting information via ESP: specifically, telepathy or retrocognition, perhaps in the form of precognitive dreams.

3. The subject may be tapping a "genetic" memory system: an inherited collection of images that can be associated with his or her direct ancestors or with the race as a whole.

4. The subject may be a victim of cryptomnesia, whereby he or she taps previously absorbed information that has been forgotten by the conscious mind and mistakenly attributes this information to personal experience.

The hallucination theory is provocative, but how can one be sure that hallucinatory material is not in fact supplied by memories of a previous life? We've already discussed the ESP hypothesis. As for existence of a genetic memory, this is purely conjectural (as is the whole idea of reincarnation): We don't know, in fact, whether such a thing exists. The final possible explanation, however, holds a great deal of merit. We know that cryptomnesia is a fairly common event, and it has surfaced as a likely contributing factor in numerous incidents of alleged past-life recall (which is one reason Stevenson favored cases involving young children, who would have had far less time to acquire—and forget—information).

The human mind may be capable of remembering everything it encounters, if only subliminally. There is even good suggestive evidence that memory can be formed by an unborn baby in the womb. The smallest sense impressions may be permanently retained and recast into dreams, thoughts, and even other memories. In the 1960s, Dr. Reima Kampman, a psychiatrist at the University of Oulu in Finland, assisted a nineteen-year-old student to uncover eight supposed past lives during hypnotic regression. The most impressive was a life as a thirteenth-century English girl named Dorothy. Dorothy gave a detailed account of society at that time and even sang an old folk song in Middle English—a language the student did not know. When the student was awakened, she said that she had no idea where she could have come across such a song. In a later hynotic session, Kampman took the student back to a time when she was thirteen years old. Quite by chance, she once picked up a book in a library. She didn't read it; she merely flipped through the pages. She remembered that the authors were Benjamin Britten and Imogene Holst, and that the song was in that book. Kampman tracked down the book and there was the song—in Middle-English.

Without a doubt the most famous case involving possible reincarnation is that of Colorado housewife Virginia Tighe, the subject of Morey Bernstein's best-selling book in 1956, *The Search for Bridey Murphy* (in which Tighe is called "Ruth Simmons"). By means of hypnotic regression, Bernstein allegedly put Tighe in touch with a previous existence as Bridey (Bridget) Kathleen Murphy, a Protestant Irishwoman who lived from 1798 to 1864. "Bridey" was able to recall an amazing wealth of details about her own life as well as life in Ireland during that period, many of which were later corroborated by original historical research (that is, by "first-time" discoveries previously unavailable to Tighe or anyone else). No records mentioning Bridey herself—or her parents or husband—have ever been discovered; but this in itself is not significant. Record-keeping in Ireland during that time period was very spotty.

The Bridey Murphy case so intrigued readers that it was analyzed over and over again. Facts were proved and disproved. It still remains, in the words of D. Scott Rogo, a parapsychology researcher and consulting editor of FATE magazine, "unresolved and totally inexplicable." Cryptomnesia may, however, account for some—if not all—of Bridey's "memories." Virginia Tighe once lived with an aunt of Irish descent; and an Irishwoman, Mrs. Bridey Corkell, once lived across the street from Tighe's aunt and uncle. It's conceivable that Tighe may have subliminally retained some of her information from stories told by these women; but this doesn't wrap up all the loose ends. Rogo comments:

"The problem was that both the believers and the debunkers took an all-or-nothing approach to the mystery it [the case of Bridey Murphy] presented. To the press and to the readers of *The Search for Bridey Murphy*, the case either proved reincarnation or was the product of subconscious fantasy. Few partisans realized that perhaps the case represented a mixture of both elements."

And so we come full circle. The question of survival after death touches not only upon every aspect of psi, but also upon every aspect of human existence. It governs both the truths and the fantasies we live by. Whatever explanations we develop to solve the riddles of OBEs, NDEs, spirit communications, or reincarnations, the existence of life beyond death will always be another possible explanation. LeShan offers this "illuminating" analogy:

"A flashlight is pointed up into the sky and turned on. After a few moments we turn the flashlight off and then take a hammer and destroy it. The beam of light continues to travel through space. Even if we hold a full funeral for the flashlight and bury it in hallowed ground, the beam of light goes on. What we have done is to take some object in the sensory realm—batteries, wires, an electric bulb, a switch—put them together in a particular way, and produced an entity in a different realm, an entity that did not exist before.

"Our two entities—the flashlight and the beam of light—turn out to be in different realms, and to have different fates. The second survives the destruction of the first.

"Therefore, when we say the body has death inevitably awaiting it, and ask if this is also true of consciousness, which exists in a different realm of experience, the question is not as simple-minded as it may appear at first."

BOOK TWO

THE PSI-AWARE SELF

CHAPTER
ELEVEN
PSI-SEARCH:
GETTING STARTED

There is no reason why a man should not learn the basic tricks of telepathy, or even "astral projection," as he might train his memory to greater efficiency . . . though he would still not be able to explain it, even to his closest friend.
—Colin Wilson

A remark reportedly made by Dr. Albert Kinsey illustrates a paradox in the psychic arts: "Most people do two things that they never talk about," he said. "They masturbate, and they read their horoscope."

Masturbation may have come out of the closet since then, but we still live in an age when it is more acceptable to admit that you slept with someone on the first date than to say you've been to an astrologer. Most Americans are embarrassed to admit an interest in the psychic arts. It's not surprising, given the proliferation of all manner of questionable cults, gurus, psychic gobbledygook, and paraphernalia—and the media's propensity for giving them lots of attention while ignoring responsible psychic consultants and serious parapsychology research. Outwardly, at least, today's "thinking" man or woman is interested in what's sure and scientific, not the amorphous and imprecise.

There's no denying, however—judging from the burgeoning interest in everything from astrology to metal bending—our ongoing fascination with the psychic arts. Whether it's the irresistible urge to read our horoscope, a consciousness of a particular lucky number, the full moon, or a premonition to call your mother, we all function on the fringes of some other type of awareness without being fully aware of it. We move through life, from day to day, often knowing that we feel a particular way but not *why*. Our understanding of why we start to think of a particular person only to have that person phone or write "from out of the blue" is far from complete. What we do know is that these things happen: Even the most dogged rationalist is bound to come up against a premonition, an unexplainable coincidence, a dream that came true, a feeling of déjà vu.

AVENUES OF EXPLORATION

There are two basic ways to explore psychic functioning personally, and they can be combined. One is to try to develop your own latent psychic abilities; the other is to consult the professional practitioners themselves—astrologers, card readers, or graphologists.

In the chapters that follow, we will take a look at several disciplines that seem to offer ways of getting information not usually accessible through normal channels—namely, general ESP, astrology, numerology, tarot, I Ching, palmistry, graphology, and bio-rhythm. Though they are largely shunned by parapsychologists, it has been my experience that these disciplines provide a useful access to psychic functioning (though in some cases their practitioners disclaim their psychic component) and are a good way for the novice to investigate his own psychic potential.

The most important chapter in this how-to section is the next one, on developing basic psychic skills. It discusses ways to explore and develop your own abilities, and it provides a good foundation for the discussion and practice of the psychic arts that follow. Included are some simple, fundamental exercises that can help you limber up your ESP abilities and, in turn, expand your psychic horizons.

No one discipline is right for everyone. As you read the ensuing chapters, some will elicit sympathetic reactions, while others will sound like just so much drivel. Some will think astrology makes perfect sense, while others will be mystified by its machinations and doubtful that one's whole life might be influenced by the random minute of one's birth. Others will be impressed by palmistry but laugh at numerology. Some areas will be interesting because they offer almost instant gratification; they can be tried with very little study and without special accoutrements, while others require experience, skill, and occasionally, expensive gear. In practice, some practicioners come to use a particular branch of their specialty that they find most significant. Others may combine two systems or otherwise adjust the criteria to fit the particulars into a framework that has meaning to them.

If you are up-to-date on matters in the mantic arts, you might notice that certain of the newer, trendy divinatory arts are not included here. (Cartouche, for example, consists of a group of twenty-five ancient Egyptian symbols, printed on cards, that can be read, like the tarot, to answer questions and give advice. Another, runes —currently popularized by Ralph Blum's book *Rune Play*—uses an ancient Viking system of thumb-size stones marked with hiero-glyphic-like symbols that have individual meanings and uses in interpretation.) Indeed, other avenues of investigation—healers, spirit mediums, trance channelers, past life therapists, and the like—are out there for those who want to pursue them.

HOW DOES THIS STUFF WORK?

This is the $64,000 question. It seems preposterous, on the face of it, to think that the moment of one's birth, the shuffle of a deck of cards, or the numerological value of one's name could have any influence on our lives. Yet such tenuous information often turns up uncanny correlations to our personal experience. It seems illogical that by adding the numerical values of our name and birth date, or by shuffling a deck of picture cards to answer a question, we can come up with information that truly pertains to us. But it is hard to dismiss the detailed—and often uncannily accurate—readings that are gleaned from just such information. To Carl Jung, the responses of the I Ching and tarot were examples of classic synchronicity at work—the idea that accidents or coincidences are in some way linked to the subconscious mind. The psychic aspect comes into play in the unconscious influence exerted upon the shuffle of the cards, the throw of the coins. It is this assumption that is used to explain all prophecy and clairvoyance.

One theory that makes a great deal of sense is that these disciplines function as tools for gaining access to psychic information. A numer-ologist is likely to have a feel for the intrinsic logic of numbers—the ability to play with them, to move them around, to see how they "add up." He is attuned to the accumulated meanings that we give to numbers, the power with which we subconsciously endow them. A tarot card reader has a powerful response to the visual stimuli of the cards, to the accumulated psychological meanings of their symbolism; his deep study of the cards enables him to see the hidden story in their order and juxtaposition. A graphologist depends on his subject to expose himself in the unique idiosyncrasies of his handwriting and is able to integrate many seemingly insignificant nuances into a revealing portrait. The elaborately calculated position of the planets at the time of birth, a seemingly nonsensical starting point, is the particular entrée the astrologer has to hidden information. It is quite an experience to watch the dexterity and ease with which an adept uses his "tools"; they seem to pry open a crack through which the adept penetrates to a deeper level of meaning.

One parapsychologist, however, skeptical of the potential for garnering information in such an improbable way, conjectures that the highly evolved, elaborate methodology for some of the divinatory practices—tarot, astrology, numerology—is just a way to make it seem scientific, and to distance the practitioners from having to acknowledge their own powers of pure psychic divination.

Psychic Beatrice Rich refers to the deck of ordinary playing cards she uses as "my tools. They're catalysts; they mean nothing in the sense that the two of spades means one thing and the three of clubs another. There's no attached meaning." Other adepts depend on similar devices. Some like to touch a person; others insist on holding a hand. Still others practice what is known as psychometry: They feel they get information through holding one of the subject's cherished possessions. Some just need to look at their subject; others can work through the mail or by telephone with no apparent disadvantage. John Krysko has done many readings by telephone. He says, "I don't have to have a voice; I don't have to have a piece of their clothing or a watch or a ring. A name is almost always sufficient."

How do adepts get their information? Two things stand out: They don't really understand it fully themselves, and each has his own bands of reception. (Chapter 6 is helpful background reading on this issue.) Psychic Frank Andrews, a popular New York reader of palms and the tarot for many celebrity clients, describes what he sees when doing a reading. "I am actually seeing a flow of pictures in my mind's eye. Being clairvoyant is like a constant state of watching TV." Beatrice Rich sometimes sees images around the heads of her clients, "like a transparent film."

Irene Hughes tells of her behavior as a nine- or ten-year-old: "I used to say, 'Hey, that person is an old crab'—right to the person's face, and my mother would ask why I said that, and I'd say, 'Because I see a picture of a crab above her head.' I didn't realize they were astrological symbols until much, much later. It still happens fairly often; I'm out and all of a sudden, I can look at a person, and psychically I can see their sign dancing around their head."

Since about 1960, author Ruth Montgomery receives her messages via automatic writing from her "guides." Before she begins to meditate, she asks the questions that pertain and sits at her typewriter, ready to receive. In her meditation, she reaches what is known to physiologists as the alpha state, and the writing comes through her automatically. The content of the writing, she vows, is unknown to her: "I wouldn't be able to tell you what came through if I did not have it written. I'm vaguely aware of the subject matter but never enough that I could tell anybody what it said or remember it myself."

Clarisa Bernhardt sees auras of color around her subjects. "Ever since I was a child, I have had the ability to see lights around people —and pretty colors. I would notice that when people were very happy, the auras around them would be very beautiful, but if they were angry, it would become very, very filled with black or a darker color. Now, I use the aura as someone else would use a computer: They've got a code they type in to get at the information; I use their aura to get in tune with their energy." According to Bernhardt, auras do somewhat resemble Kirlian photography (see page 138), but only to a point. "I see them a little differently. I see colors. I see locations. I see combinations and, maybe six months from now, a person's aura could be different, but they always keep the same basic colors. If I saw lavender in one corner of an aura, it would mean one thing to me, but if it were over in the other direction, it would tell me something altogether different."

Some adepts "go by the book." They claim no particular psychic component in their readings, only that study and experience enable them to make a sophisticated interpretation based on the considerable published literature of their particular subject. In some cases, such as the interpretation of the I Ching, they are aided by their enhanced understanding and knowledge of the culture that spawned it.

Others claim to be using their psychic talents. Astrologer Julien Armistead acknowledges the psychic component of what he does: "From time to time, things I say turn out to be exactly right. I don't see blue lights. I don't have sudden hot flashes. I have no way of knowing. It is sometimes more frequent than you'd think random chance would work. When I'm looking at a chart and have some intuitive sense of what it may be about, I really make myself find it in the chart. I really try to make the distinction in my own head between what is hunch and intuition or psychic awareness and what is there in the astrology."

When I talked with him, noted graphologist Felix Lehmann recalled a story about Rafael Sherman from Vienna, who would "sit in a café and take a piece of paper and write down a word. Then he would go over to a stranger at another table in the café and ask that person to write the same word. The handwriting would be the same; he would have anticipated it exactly. This man had absolutely psychic abilities that were turned on by handwriting. He would look at a person and he would know all about him."

Rolla Nordic, a well-known New York tarot card reader, openly acknowledges the psychic aspect of her work. "I've been psychic all my life. My family had it; I had an aunt who was in her day a well-known psychic in England. I became familiar with it as a child. There's nothing strange about it; it's just a way of reading. There's a kind of rapport. Perhaps it is because I am trying to help them through the tarot and I am concentrating on just one person."

The timing of events is something that is tricky for many practitioners, time being "something else" in the clairvoyant reality; it is often hard to see a fixed past, present, or future clearly in the context of a reading. Another tarot reader, Pat Barnes, says succinctly what several of her peers have experienced: "My timing can be off. I can't always be sure. I can say it hasn't happened yet but I can't be sure if it will happen tomorrow or not. Sometimes it does happen the next day, sometimes it's six months later, and sometimes it's a year. I don't think that any psychic is a hundred percent on timing." Beatrice Rich warns her clients that she cannot always tell whether an event she sees has happened in the recent past or will soon come to pass.

ARE THE PRACTITIONERS LEGIT?

In conducting the interviews for this section of *Intangible Evidence*, I met and talked at length with dozens of adepts: the onus was on me to find the best. I wanted to locate the real pros, those who had established a reputation for outstanding abilities in their respective fields. It was easy enough to avoid the carnival Gypsies and storefront tarot readers. For all their questionable reputation in the public mind, I felt that only a small number of those beyond the fairground fringe could be considered quacks. If there was a problem, it was that there is among them a broad range of demonstrable skill. I found that most psychic advisors seem to be well-meaning people with some (often considerable) talent; what many lack is that extra "kick" that the best of them seem to possess, that spark of inspiration which makes you feel as if they have a direct line to extraordinary knowledge. Talent among practicioners varies just as it does among dentists, dancers, and drivers—each does his best, though some are clearly more gifted than others. It is that "tuned in" group I sought out. This group appeared to have rather astounding abilities.

I was amazed at the consistency among readers in various disciplines. In order to introduce them to this far-out subject, I took the publisher and editor of this book to see psychic Beatrice Rich, tarot readers Anka Junge and Pat Barnes, and astrologer Lenore Cantor. They were struck by the overlap and agreement among the readers: by their estimate, about 80 percent. In my own travels, Clarisa Bernhardt spoke of my lavender aura; Pat Barnes called it bluish-lavender; Valerie Hunt in her lab picked up lavender/blue.

To address another question often asked by people who have never consulted a psychic advisor, I found the level of integrity among these professionals to be unfailingly high, irrespective of their abilities. All of them seemed to have received their share of criticism and condescension and were very sensitive to it. It seems to go with the territory. They become accustomed to it and have found ways of coping with it. Chicago-based astrologer and psychic Irene Hughes shows visitors the commemorative plaques bestowed on her by the grateful police departments whose cases she helped solve. Others keep files of letters and newspaper clippings that are testimony to the actual occurrences of their predictions or just to their integrity and professionalism.

Numerologist Ellin Dodge emphasizes that disbelievers and detractors are forever trying to prove her wrong. She adds her personal speculation to the debate: "Astrology and most of the parasciences have a lot of fear and superstition attached to them. The reason is that in the early days, only the educated or the people who were bright enough to put two and two together had the knowledge, and they kept it to themselves; it was secret. Consequently, today people fear the occult sciences. I call it psychic whoopee because to me, anything that works, I'll take. I'll take all the help I can get. I don't understand why numerology works, it really doesn't make sense, and I will probably spend the rest of my life trying to find out why it works." And, no doubt, she'll keep trying to prove numerology's validity to skeptics as well. She continues: "I call them the make-me-laugh group. Do you remember the old days when the audience used to sit with their arms folded and say to the comedians, 'Make me laugh'? The professional people—especially psychologists—are the make-me-laugh group. It has happened several times that a person comes to see me, I sit there for an hour talking and talking, reading for them. They say almost nothing until, finally, I say, 'My throat hurts, my mouth hurts, I'm finished. And they say, 'Oh, my God! I'm so impressed. I'm a psychiatrist—I had to come because a patient brought me your tape.' They can't believe it."

Don't judge all adepts by what you read in the papers. The hocus-pocus of newspaper astrology columns or tea room fortune tellers is a far cry from what you'll find if you consult a talented professional. You are perfectly capable of judging each one's skills and ethics—just as you would judge a lawyer, doctor, or dry cleaner. For one thing unless you're a very susceptible person who would get swept away by a street-corner cult, it's unlikely any harm can be done. Most adepts are in "the business" because they sincerely want to help, and even those who aren't mightily talented are sympathetic listeners/counselors who attempt to give useful advice or support.

FINDING AND USING AN ADEPT

Depending on where you live, finding an adept may or may not be difficult. The easiest and best way I know of is through word of mouth. Find someone who shares your interest and talk to him about the practitioner he consults. Find out his likes and dislikes about the consultant he uses. Keep in mind that adepts vary widely in their own ways: Some are concerned primarily with predictions, some with the psychological aspects, some with the spiritual, and so on. Make sure that you will be seeing someone whose bent is compatible with what you seek—don't ask someone who specializes in the spiritual when you'll be getting your next raise or whom to marry. Accordingly, if relationships are what concern you, look for someone who seems to have a feeling for people and character and someone who doesn't find these earthly concerns to be beneath him or her.

If you don't know anyone who uses an adept, look in the major city telephone books. Certainly large urban areas are logical places to start, by dint of their higher population. Go to the library and ask for a file of professional organizations, or look for specialty publications and write to them for advice or help in locating a professional. Many of the psychic disciplines do not require face-to-face confrontation, so it is not necessarily vital that the adept be geographically close. Astrology, numerology, palmistry, and graphology can be done long-distance as long as the adept is in possession of the pertinent information or samples. Some readers can do tarot by telephone, especially if they know and have an ongoing relationship with the client. Many adepts travel extensively in their work and may be available near your home at specific times of the year. Contact them to find out what arrangements can be made. Also, don't fear fame. Many "famous" readers are as willing to read for you as for anyone else. Contact them and determine if they can fulfill your needs and expectations.

When you have located someone who sounds promising, it is absolutely reasonable to conduct a brief interview to determine pertinent information, such as the fee, length of reading, how he or she goes about the reading, areas of special interest, and what might be needed in the way of preparation. Don't expect the practitioner to be weird. He or she is likely to be a "normal" person who will not look or act differently from anyone else. If there are histrionics of costume or character that seem untoward—if the tarot card reader wears a satin turban and sits in a tent, for example—you might want to look elsewhere or be quite thorough in your questioning. Avoid anyone who seems like a phony in any way. Don't be afraid of the reader or the reading. Use and accept the information from the reading only if it makes sense in the context of your life—just as you would with anyone else's advice. Do not give the adept's advice extra weight—not everything you're told will manifest itself; many things can change. Accept only what is understandable at a very simple level, and apply it to your life in a reasonable way. Use the insight as a catalyst for increased self-knowledge or change. Never lose sight of the real objective; the goal is self-understanding and a wider vision of one's life and potential for the future.

When you find an adept whose talents suit your needs, cultivate the relationship and let it develop. Keep in mind that many of the psychic disciplines require infrequent consultations—about once a year for most astrologers or numerologists, more frequently for some of the question-specific disciplines. For example, a person might want to have his cards read each time a problem comes up, or to throw the I Ching every day. It may take several sessions to get comfortable with your advisor; on the other hand, many clients claim they feel as though they've known their reader for years, because he or she seems to know all about them.

There is little to fear—and a great deal to gain—from a consultation with a gifted practitioner. Almost universally, practitioners of the psychic arts have "gone public" in order to help others. Take, for example, Carroll Righter, said to be Ronald Reagan's longtime friend and personal astrologer: "The Bible says not to deny a man the hope that is in him. And we all have a hope; we all want to do something; we all have traits; we all want to express them. To find a means to do that, I think, is wonderful. Astrology is one of those ways." Julian Armistead sees astrology as a counseling tool in a helping profession.

Is it true that most readers have steady repeat clients? You bet they do. In fact, several clients go to more than one reader within a particular discipline. Dianne Frattini, astrology client of both John Maraschella and Julian Armistead, uses her two advisors for completely different approaches to her life. She explains, "With John, I have found that I get a lot of real good hands-on approaches to how to handle things like my job and relationships. Whereas with Julian, I've been targeting my work with him toward internal processes that I'm going through, rather than the external. And I have found them both to be extremely accurate and helpful."

There is no particular "typical" person who is likely to become a seeker of parascientific advice. Clients include housewives, lawyers, artists, and businessmen. By and large, clients of those who practice the psychic arts seem to get what they're looking for from their advisors. If you ask most people who have had readings whether they plan to have more, the answer is almost always affirmative. They don't necessarily plan to continue the same kind of reading, but they do plan to continue to seek information of a similar but different kind. They seek a moment of advance warning, a word of caution that could give them the edge in an important situation. They seek increased self-knowledge and a more complete understanding of the world they live in.

WHERE TO GO FROM HERE

The brief treatments of the psychic arts included here are merely a chance to get your feet wet—to establish a rudimentary understanding of these disciplines to see which ones, if any, might hold some appeal for you. Like foods or colors or sports, each person will choose his or her favorite based on an individual set of interests and affinities. The rudiments of some disciplines can be learned in a fairly brief period of time and require little technical skill. Others, like the I Ching or astrology, will produce results even for the beginner, but they are complex subjects to truly master. Years of research, experience, and practice will be needed to understand the subtleties or to have an "instant" response. All roads lead to the same place, but there is a different path for each person.

If you choose one discipline to specialize in, at some point you'll want more information, more hands-on experience than you can get on your own. Look for books, classes, teachers, and workshops or conventions in your area. *These are the tools that will help you understand.* Don't hesitate to adapt techniques and systems to your own way; experiencing meanings and spotting correlations is far more important than technique. Go slowly, test out your theories, see what works for you, and discard what doesn't. Have fun with it, but don't go overboard. Taking something this amorphous too seriously can ruin it; part of the fascination is tied up with its inaccessibility. Psychic knowledge requires understanding and responsible behavior. It is not a talent to be abused.

If you choose to pursue further study of any of the subjects covered here, you will do well to read and practice. Only by casting many natal charts will you become a competent astrologer; only by throwing the coins (or yarrow sticks) and then interpreting the findings will you truly master the I Ching. Volume upon volume has been written on all these subjects; what you find here are the briefest treatments. Check the Bibliography on page 569 to determine what other sources exist and what approach they take to the subject. Some will focus on theory, others on research, and still others on case histories. All of it is instrumental to your clearer understanding of the discipline you choose.

CHAPTER
TWELVE

EXPLORING YOUR
EXTRASENSORY
SELF

When I set out to write this book, there were two major points I wanted to make: one, that psychic phenomena are a legitimate issue worthy of serious attention, and two, that we can, with practice, "recapture" and put to valuable use our own psychic abilities. This second objective is the goal of this chapter: This is the place where you may begin to grow into and own your natural psychic abilities. It is also the place to "warm up" the intuitive skills that augment the divinatory arts discussed in the following chapters.

Diana Gazes, who conducts metal-bending workshops in New York City, refers to her sessions as "high play." That's what I hope this chapter will give you—a chance to learn something important, that also happens to be fun.

While, as we've seen, exceptional psi abilities seem to be inherited, research suggests that we all have these abilities to *some* degree and that these abilities can be enhanced with the use of certain techniques —and with practice, support, and discipline. Referring to the capability for successful remote viewing in their book *The Mind Race*, Russell Targ says: "We never found anyone who couldn't learn to do it."

Being psychic could have a definite advantage on the day you've misplaced your car keys or when you have an important meeting coming up with someone you've never met. Whether it's a matter of finding a lost wallet or meeting creative challenges, life may be easier for those who are "tuned in" to their psychic abilities. The purpose in developing psychic skills is not to be able to perform parlor tricks but to add a useful and natural skill, to develop an inherent though repressed potential. Psychic abilities can empower; they provide access to the hidden parts of our selves.

Ingo Swann feels that children have psi abilities that are far greater than those of adults. Researchers hypothesize that these psi reactions are programmed out of us through conditioning, by the rational pragmatic atmosphere in which we are reared. In his autobiography, Swann writes:

> The world of children does not match very closely the carefully guarded parameters of the respectable, social adult. No one really cares about the perceptions of the child—only that he should somehow be brought into proper conditioning and respect. Anything untoward involving a child can be attributed to vivid imagination and fantasy. Slowly, pervasively, restrained by parents, teachers, religionists, and finally the unyielding social fabric itself, the child is settled into the system. No one really knows what a human unimpeded by conditioning and learning would become. . . . As a child, I used to watch with great fascination the fluttering forms or colors sparkling from objects and people— from my mother, father, grandmothers, and ordinary people—as well as from caterpillars, leaves, rocks, and so forth. As might be expected, describing these marvelous rainbows and energetic flares to my peers left me very impressed with the fact that one was not supposed to see such things, and certainly not to talk about them if one did. . . . Eventually my response to such perceptions faded from consciousness, and many years passed before I once more began to solicit them.

Swann's understanding and grudging acceptance of his loss led him to add later in his book, "The fact is that one has to degrade one's natural psychic awareness considerably in order to participate in life and society as it is structured on this planet."

He goes on to talk about the "everydayness" of psi: "I am personally convinced that the 'problem' presented by things psychic, if it is indeed a problem, is not the strangeness of paranormality or extrasensory occurrences but the ways men permit themselves to perceive, the ideas held by society, groups, or even individuals about human potential." In other words, things psychic are not basically a scientific 'problem,' but a social one. Swann feels that the key to gaining access to our psychic functioning is to have actual firsthand experience of psi, not an episode that could be coincidental, but an experience that is the result of active seeking, that causes a "reality shift'' from the mind-set we have been carrying around, so that we can't deny the existence of psi. This way we become convinced that it exists and that we can use it. This is different from just believing in psi without any real experience, because as he says, "We can't deal philosophically with ourselves in that way; you need a reality shift rather than a philosophical shift." You have to bring yourself to the point of having an experience that *forces* the readjustment of your personal stance vis-à-vis psychic functioning. As Swann says, "This is in fact true for everything—in the absence of personal experience it all stays intellectual and analytical, and doesn't bring about a deep-seated emotional shift at the level of the deeper being." He explained to me that "the best way to understand ESP is to evoke it in yourself. . . . Once you evoke it, you have a reality shift. . . . Then you need to create an exterior universe that reflects the inner reality. If you can't do that, then you're not going to reinforce it. . . . When you see that ESP can operate as a function of your will, or your desire for it to function within you, then consciousness has to begin to change its reality. Whereas a purely spontaneous thing can happen, but unless it's powerful enough the conscious mind won't necessarily realign itself."

There are no psychic miracles and no special rarefied atmosphere that is singularly psychic. These abilities are for use in the everyday world, to help us function optimally in our regular lives, not to set ourselves apart from it. Psychic functioning is a matter of developing your inherent but neglected personal skills. The remarkable strides reported by the Chinese in psi research tell the story. Their tremendous progress, even without sophisticated machines, high budgets, computers, or well-equipped labs, is heartening. They have concentrated on making the *human* system operate better through rigorous personal discipline. In this area, they may have a jump on us Westerners—a tradition in which such skills are recognized and developed: in ta'i chi, meditation, karate, and even in such practices as the tea ceremony, flower arranging, and sumi painting. It is the kind of discipline we associate with Indian yogis, Zen masters, Hindu adepts, and Tibetan Buddhists—who find trance states, levitation, walking across beds of nails, and materializing objects out of thin air basically "old hat."

The point is: psi isn't magic. Wishing won't make it so. Don't expect major transformations in your life—at least, not without serious discipline and practice. In *From Newton to ESP*, Lawrence LeShan refers to "my own experience in learning to shift my consciousness

—a learning procedure that took me a year and a half of about thirty hours work a week." That's four to five hours a day, for eighteen months! LeShan was making a determined effort to master certain techniques as a prerequisite to learning to be a healer. Improving your own psychic functioning to a noticeable, usable level will not require that kind of commitment. But it won't happen overnight, and your success will reflect a combination of ability, willingness, time expended—and your belief in yourself. LeShan underlines the fact that part of the task is simply to learn to trust and recognize your existing psychic abilities. Another factor is learning to recognize the ways in which you personally acquire and use psychic information.

As Stephan Schwartz of the Möbius Society (see page 228) points out: "It's very clear that biases you have in your normal waking state carry over into this 'altered reality' state. Now the people I work with are not in trances. They're not channeling dead people. They're not mediums, and they're not professionals. Let's see. Right now, I'm working with a physicist, an aeronautical engineer, a psychiatrist, a fine arts photographer, a best-selling author, a motion picture director, a French rock-and-roll singer, a historian, a documentary filmmaker, and a newspaper photographer. . . . All people who are functional, successful. They do well in their careers. If you met them at a party and asked, 'What do you do,' they wouldn't say, 'I'm a psychic.' This is not their primary self-definition. But they are very good psychics."

We are entitled to our psychic selves. I hope that the following exercises will help you see the way to achieve that mind shift, so that you will believe in–and use–the psychic abilities that belong to you.

EVALUATING YOUR PSYCHIC SELF

The purpose of the following questionnaire is twofold: to help you recognize the psychic experiences you have already had, and to help you evaluate your own "style" of psychic functioning. I have found that everyone has different ways of operating on a psychic level; sometimes there are different "channels" on which they send and receive or, perhaps, different skills or tactics for which they might have an affinity. (For example, one person may not ever feel they communicate telepathically but may have precognitive dreams or repeated winning streaks at the racetrack. One gets information visually, while another is sensitive to sounds or smells.) This test will help you identify your own experiences—how they come about, through what channels, in what situations or states of mind. You can learn to see your own patterns so that you can actively bring about psychic functioning more often.

Before you look at the questionnaire, make a list of any and all personal experiences you can remember that might even possibly be called psychic—dreams, hunches, feelings of déjà vu, seeing an aura around a friend's head, the correct prediction of a roll of the dice, an "apparition," intuitive knowledge that something was wrong with a child or parent, the apparent ability to make a friend contact you or an immediate "understanding" of something that is otherwise alien to you, such as a foreign language, the workings of a machine, or tarot cards. Include everything that comes to mind. Then use the following test to jog your memory, to remind you of the many possible avenues that psychic functioning may take. For the moment, don't write off anything as coincidence (though this is sometimes the logical explanation). Coincidences can add up.

Write down everything that comes to mind. Try to remember how you felt when these things happened to you. Were you just about to fall asleep? Were you tense? Hot? Cold? Resting? Busy? Did you visualize a scene, or did a particular voice or scent come to mind? Did you feel a breeze or draft? How did you feel inside? Buoyant? Saddened? Nauseated? Happy? In what way did the psychic information feel different from other ongoing thought, or from imagination?

There's no right and wrong, no scoring at all on this test. It is just a means of getting started, a way for you to begin evaluating your present level of psychic awareness and to begin to identify your own psi patterns or tactics. Keep your list so that after you have spent some time on the exercises that follow, you'll be able to look back and see how far you've progressed.

PSYCHIC SELF-TEST

Have you ever known who was calling—friend or foe—before you picked up the telephone?

Indeed, have you ever known the telephone was going to ring just before it actually did?

Did you ever know what your mate or best friend or even a complete stranger was going to say before he or she said it?

Do your hunches—negative or positive—about people or events often prove to be true?

Have you ever found yourself humming a favorite song only to turn on the radio and hear it playing? Were you and the radio ever at the exact same place in the song?

Have you ever had a premonition or dream of bad news or misfortune that has to do with someone close to you, and then had the event come to pass?

Have you ever warned someone of impending bad news or bad luck, based on your intuition?

Have you ever had a "flash" that something particular was going to happen to you or to someone you know?

Have you ever known that the card you needed to win the poker hand was coming directly your way?

Does your lucky number work for you at the roulette wheel?

Have you ever placed a bet that was based on a hunch?

Are you ever inspired to play the lottery on the spur of the moment? Did you win?

Have you ever dreamed about an event that had nothing at all to do with you and then found out that it came true?

Do you ever feel extremely lucky?

Do you feel that you have a "sixth sense" about people?

What was the most recent "coincidence" you can remember?

Have you ever felt an inexplicable sense of impending doom and then had something awful occur?

Have you ever had a premonition of a national disaster?

Have you ever known what was in a letter or package before you opened it?

Have you ever made a business decision based on a hunch?

Have you ever felt that something other than your own everyday brain "inspired" you in your professional or creative work?

Have you ever gotten so involved in work or play that you completely lost track of time?

Has the solution to an irritating problem ever come to you in a dream or daydream? In a "flash" of inspiration?

Have you ever gone to a strange place for the first time and known your way around as though you had visited many times before?

Have you ever had a feeling or a dream about someone and then received a phone call or letter from that person?

Do you often choose the line at the bank or grocery that actually moves the fastest?

Do you often know the correct time without consulting a clock?

Have you ever had a detailed dream of something—a dress, a house, an event—only to find or experience its exact duplicate shortly thereafter?

When you were a child, did you have an imaginary friend?

Can you close your eyes and envision the face of a friend you haven't seen for a long time?

Have you ever slowed your car for no special reason, only to find that the road was obstructed in some way or that some danger lay ahead?

Have you ever been singing a particular song, only to find out that a friend has had the same tune running through his or her head as well?

Do you and your best friend, or your mate, frequently say the same thing at the same time?

Do you ever sense the onset of bad weather (and take an umbrella to work in the morning) even when predictions say it will be clear and fair?

Do your dreams ever come true—in alarmingly accurate detail?

A FEW GENERAL INSTRUCTIONS

Before we get to the exercises themselves, I want to cover a few points that pertain to all of them.

1. *It is okay to be psychic.* Don't be afraid of it; don't think that people will stare and point at you; don't think that talent for or interest in psi is something to hide or be ashamed of—we probably *all* have it, and we all could benefit from learning how to use it in many aspects of our everyday life. Many of us resist our psi abilities because we fear being labeled a kook. We lead our lives convinced that coincidence runs rampant; if we computed the frequency of such coincidences and compared them to statistical possibilities, our argument for coincidence simply wouldn't stand up. Free up your feelings

about your psychic capabilities. Go as far as to say out loud (even though it may seem foolish) before you begin each exercise: "I give myself permission to have—and to use—my inherent psychic abilities. I know that it is safe to be psychic and that no harm can come from exploring my psychic potential." Open yourself to this new experience and grow with it; expand your psi horizons. As we use our psi skills, we become comfortable with them and learn to trust them more and more. You will realize that there never was any cause for fear. If your initial successes with psi exercises astound you—you may be floored that you actually are capable of getting results—remember that psi is natural; it is a normal part of human functioning.

2. *Learn to discriminate psychic from nonpsychic functioning and to identify your own psychic style.* There are many avenues of perception—the senses, memory, fantasy and the imagination, hunches, flashes of inspiration. Each of these kinds of experience has a different feel to it, and we can usually pinpoint the origin of our perceptions. Sometimes, however, they get confused. Did we dream something, or did it really happen? How does one account for the feeling of déjà vu that comes over us suddenly in a given situation—have we really been there before?

There are many kinds of mental and psychological noise that can interfere with our ability to identify clearly psychic functioning. We may be influenced by our mood or by our state of health. We may react to someone, or something, in a way that is influenced by an unconscious memory: Without realizing it, we take a dislike to someone because he or she is wearing a color we hate, or because the person reminds us of someone who was involved in an unpleasant incident in our past. Each of us responds to different stimuli, and each of us has certain senses and modes of perception that are more highly developed than others. You may have a highly developed visual sense but not be highly sensitive to texture and touch. Smells may trigger memories. You may never tap into your psi ability through your dreams, but you may have an uncanny ability to decipher people when face-to-face. You may trust your hunches completely, or you may feel more comfortable using the tarot cards or throwing the I Ching. If we hope to increase our psi ability, we have to become aware of how we operate—our "receiving channels," our idiosyncrasies—and recognize what it feels like to access psychic information.

The difference between mental noise and psychic functioning is a difficult one to define. Russell Targ and Keith Harary say in *The Mind Race:* "Intuitive impressions are usually more *gentle* and *fleeting* than mental noise." Be skeptical of any images that come to you in great detail. Psychic functioning usually grows slowly into a full impression, but seldom arrives in full bloom. Trust your impressions but don't analyze them, or the psi atmosphere will be overpowered by everyday thinking.

3. *Keep track of your progress.* Research shows that continual feedback about one's performance contributes to successful psychic functioning. You *need* to know how you are doing. Keeping good records gives a written comparison of our hits versus our misses, and the circumstances in which they occurred.

Keep an informal notebook and record your psi learning progress. When the phone or doorbell rings and you feel you know who's calling, write it down so you can verify the accuracy of your hunches. Accumulate evidence. Keep track of all of it—from a premonition you had in a dream or the sudden thought of a friend you haven't seen for a long time, to a so-called coincidence, hunch, or sensation. Leave space in your book to follow up on any premonitions you had, recording when they occurred or how.

Take notice not only of the impression you received but what form it took. Was it a color? A scent? A dream? Did anything in particular trigger it? Write down everything you can remember about your impression. Were you lying down? Falling asleep? In the shower? On the fifth mile of your daily run? From time to time, sit down and read your notebook. The growth will be right there; let it reinforce your feelings about psi.

4. *Practice and be patient.* Unless you have unusually accessible psi proficiency, don't expect instant results. Remember that psi is a subtle, erratic signal, sensitive to many external influences. If you find it difficult to relax, spend extra time with relaxation and focusing techniques. You *must* be relaxed for your psi potential to come to the fore. If you've never relaxed in your life, start now and stick with it. Don't set a deadline for yourself—that's part of what you want to get away from. Don't concentrate on results; concentrate on what your experiences teach you. Also, shop around. Perhaps one visualization technique works better than others; use what suits you. People tend to have "strong suits" in psi—an affinity for one discipline over another. Think of your practice as a sport or a type of mental or emotional fitness, and devote a reasonable amount of time to it each day. Just as learning tennis, golf, or crocheting takes time, so, too, does psi.

5. *Integrate your psychic abilities into the rest of your life.* Don't confine psi to the hour you set aside to practice it every other day. Reinforce it as much as you can. Use it to find your way in a strange town, to locate the store that has dungarees in your size, to assure yourself that the kids are all right. Psychic talents are not meant to take you away from the here and now into another world that's far from the madding crowd. Psi can help you understand yourself better, to enhance your ability to make decisions, to be a better friend or partner. It can enrich your life in many ways, but don't go overboard. Don't suddenly devote your life to learning to read minds or travel astrally to far-off places. Psi is not something mysterious and exotic; it's an ability that can help us through life. Enjoy it, have fun with it, play with it, and take it lightly. Have a sense of humor about it—and use psi in good faith.

EXERCISES FOR DEVELOPING YOUR PSYCHIC AWARENESS

In the pages that follow are some simple exercises that, with practice, can increase your psychic functioning. Think of them as a way of limbering your psychic muscles. The first exercises are aimed at setting the stage for increased psychic awareness by developing your ability to relax and clear your mind of extraneous information—the constant jabber of the conscious mind. They will help you observe the world around and within you and learn to make your unconscious more "user-friendly." Then you'll move on to trying specific psychic feats.

Don't rush. Take one exercise at a time, and make some progress with it before moving on to the next. Build your skills on a strong foundation.

RELAXATION TECHNIQUE

Lie down on your bed (the sofa is probably too small), making sure you are unencumbered in every way. Remove your shoes; loosen your belt. If you are wearing tight clothing, loosen it. If you are weighed down with heavy or noisy jewelry, remove it; try to be as unrestricted as possible. Adjust the lighting to medium or low and make sure it is not glaring into your eyes. Choose a place that is quiet —away from street noise, the cries of children playing, or of radio, television, or conversation. If the drone of air conditioners or air traffic is unavoidable, so be it; you will soon learn to tune it out.

You are going to start at your toes and proceed to the top of your head, tensing each group of muscles as you inhale for a count of five, then completely letting go, relaxing that area for a count of five as you exhale.

Very slowly, consciously flex and then relax your toes. Moving upward, one area at a time, tightly tense and then relax the bones and muscles of your feet. Go on to your ankles, calves, knees, thighs, hips, pelvis, waist, and upper torso. Take your time and concentrate on a full contraction, or tension, of each area, followed by a complete letting go, or relaxation. Breathe deeply and evenly, inhaling on the contraction and exhaling with the relaxation. With each exhalation, say to yourself, "I'm becoming completely relaxed."

As each area feels relaxed, forget it and move on to the next area. Some areas might take longer to let go than others—work on it; the relaxed area should feel heavy and limp. Relax your fingers and then the palms of your hands. Move on to the wrists, forearms, elbows, and upper arms. Think of the individual muscles and how they stretch from arm to shoulder to neck. Trace them in your mind and let them go limp. Take time with the shoulder and neck areas—they are customary tension points. While concentrating on your neck, try to relax it fully, starting from between your shoulder blades all the way up to the base of your skull. Move all the way up your skull and relax it and the muscles that support it. Relax your jaw, your mouth, your eyes, and especially your forehead. Try to feel so heavy that moving would be a tremendous effort, an insurmountable task.

When your body is relaxed, clear your mind of all thoughts and take notice of nothing at all. Breathe easily, without being self-conscious. Think of a lush and comfortable, beautiful and peaceful place you've visited, or imagine a Camelot-like setting where everything is sheer perfection. Develop the picture of this special place in your mind's eye —the color of the sky, the fleecy clouds. Can you feel the breeze, hear a rushing stream or a birdcall? Is there a mountain, a meadow, a waterfall? Are there birds, antelope, lush flowers? Come back to this place mentally each time you do this exercise.

Some people prefer to visualize a soothing color, a long road, or a graceful stairway going up or down. Try to mentally go to and become part of that place or that color. Think of the pale green of a lush meadow, the clear blue of the sky on a cloudless day—whatever works for you and lets the world fall away into the background.

If you are just learning to relax, it is important (though somewhat contradictory) that you take note of and remember the feelings you associate with relaxation. Without doing anything to break the "spell" or atmosphere you have set up, try to remember how you feel when you are relaxed, how it feels to have a slack jaw, loose fingers and feet, or to "feel" beige or blue. Take note of these feelings so you will recognize them in the future. With practice, you can learn just what strings to pull within yourself to bring on total relaxation in just moments, but first you have to learn to induce these feelings in this slow, deliberate way. When you are thoroughly relaxed, you should feel serene and loose.

The goal of the relaxation and focusing techniques is to enable your brain to reach "alpha"—a measurably slowed-down brain-wave frequency that produces a relaxed but still-wakeful state. In alpha, the brain functions at 8 to 13 cycles per second, compared to the 13 to 30 cycles per second of our usual active, conscious, beta state. Everyone experiences alpha; think of the relaxed time just before you fully wake after a good night's sleep—that is alpha.

Variations on relaxation techniques can be tried in almost any circumstances. Try them sitting in a comfortable chair during the early evening hours, just before sunset. Try them at your desk when you're feeling particularly stressed. Speed through the muscle relaxation and spend extra time thinking of that peaceful place or that soothing color. Audio and videotapes designed to help you relax are available; you might give them a try. The object is to relax—how you manage to do it doesn't really matter. Keep track of what works for you and use it to your advantage.

FOCUSING TECHNIQUE

In her book *Develop Your Psychic Skills*, Enid Hoffman offers the effective focusing technique that follows. It is an excellent method for stilling that incessant inner dialogue.

Relax in a comfortable position and close your eyes. Silently say "one" and keep repeating it until your mind interrupts you with an unrelated thought. At the interruption, go on to the next number and repeat until the next interruption. "Two, two, two," you will repeat. Then "three, three, three." Experience this and be aware of the frequency of interruptions. Now get yourself a timer. Set it for three minutes and do this exercise. When the timer rings, jot down the number you have reached.

The first time I tried this I reached seventeen within one minute! Holding your attention to a point is difficult, but the ability to do so will really pay off when you are exercising your psychic abilities, so keep at it. Sometimes it is enlightening to make note of the ideas and thoughts that interrupt your practice. These often come up because they have not been able to reach your awareness under other conditions.

Try this focusing technique whenever you can—riding the bus to work, in a boring meeting, during the commercials on television. See if you can tune out effectively in a variety of circumstances. This exercise is especially good because it not only builds the ability to focus and concentrate, it gives you a progress report on your increasing ability to do so.

OBSERVATION TECHNIQUE

One avenue of increasing your psychic ability is to increase your powers of observation. You've probably read that agents being trained for service in the CIA are taught to absorb every detail of what they see—what we see as blue carpeting, a good observer sees as wall-to-wall teal-blue carpet with medium-high nap, indentations where a chest or hassock once stood, two burn holes, and three inch-long pieces of red lint.

In your everyday ramblings, make a determined effort to notice things in more detail. Pretend you are Sherlock Holmes. Try for short periods of time to take it all in—at the seashore, walking on the street, or watering the lawn. Spend some time feeling your way through your home or office, noticing smells and textures, colors and sounds. Use the five apparent senses as thoroughly as you possibly can—if only to give you a larger bank of knowledge to work from.

Go outside on a pleasant day and choose a comfortable place to sit down and relax. Settle into an easy position, and close your eyes. Focus on the sounds you hear—all the sounds. Listen to your breathing. Can you hear your heartbeat? Pick up on every single sound there is. If a fly buzzes past, hear it as clearly as you do piano practice at the house next door. Street noises, airplanes flying overhead, even the hushed rustle of leaves or the sound of an apple falling off a tree—hear them all; they all count. Be a sponge and soak up all the sound there is.

After ten minutes or so, open your eyes and you'll feel assaulted by visual input into the serene world you had created. Notice how sight fills in so many of the sounds but also seems to detract from them.

You're having to split your attention; do your best to take it all in.
Slowly begin to add other senses to what you have and observe the
change they make in your perception. Notice colors, textures, scents,
drafts, flavors, and rhythms. Get up and feel movement and the spon-
giness of the ground, or stay right where you are and "walk around"
in your head. Take a mental stroll to a real or an imaginary place and
try to sense everything with total realism, including all its dimensions.
If you see a flower, know how big it is, the shade of green of the stem,
the size and texture of the petals, its scent. Picture a vase of them or,
indeed, a whole bush or field. Increasing your sensory powers is a step
on the way to increasing your extrasensory powers.

GETTING TO KNOW YOUR UNCONSCIOUS MIND

One part of our mind may record *everything* that occurs in our lives
—ever. The problem lies in accessing the information. Developing a
more direct line to our unconscious can be a boon to retrieving so-
called long-lost information; people have been known to dredge up
minute details from the past when it was important or necessary.
More important, it shows us that we can tune in to information—*and*
to a way of seeing and feeling—that has apparently been closed off
to us for lack of practice. If you don't use it, you lose it, as the saying
goes.

This exercise, a variation on one from David St. Clair's *Lessons in
Instant ESP*, will help you learn how to call up information from the
unconscious mind. It is useful for reinforcing our confidence that we
can get at this information when we need to, and it gives us practice
in making our unconscious more available to us. We are often faced
with the inability to remember something that we "used" to know.
Think of the time that you were desperately trying to remember who
wrote *Ah, Wilderness!*, or when you were going half mad because you
couldn't remember the name of the actor who played Gerald O'Hara
in *Gone With the Wind*. Remember that when the answer was blocked
and you just couldn't pull it from your memory, you had no choice
but to abandon the thought. But later, when you were relaxed and
not thinking about it at all (or as you slept), there was the answer,
clear as day—Eugene O'Neill and Thomas Mitchell. Sometimes
when we least expect it, the answer comes to us.

Think back into the past and try to remember the first and last names
of someone you once knew perfectly well but who was not a close friend
—for example, your dancing teacher, the person who hired you for

your first job, the girl whose locker was next to yours in tenth grade. Be sure that you cannot remember the person's name. Visualize the person as he or she was at that time, remembering what he or she wore, the expression on her face, placing him or her in the proper location and moving around, if possible. Formulate a command to yourself to identify this person, to recall his or her name: "Tell me the name of my Little League coach at Carver School." Repeat the command two more times and forget it. Think of something else—don't give his name another thought. Generally, within a few minutes or hours, the person's name will come to you. If it doesn't, repeat the procedure and try again. Still no luck? Try again tomorrow morning, but, in between, forget about it. You'll be surprised to find that you are capable of recalling the information you want from your subconscious.

LIMBERING UP YOUR TELEPATHIC SENDING AND RECEIVING CAPABILITIES

Here are several quick and simple exercises that are easily done on an informal basis. Remember to keep track of your hits and misses.

This exercise is to be done alone, every time your telephone or doorbell rings. The object is to identify the caller before you know his identity. Therefore, every time the telephone rings, try to "know" who's calling before you answer. When the doorbell rings, quickly tell yourself who's at the door. Do not try to figure out who it is. Follow your hunch— and quickly write it down. If you have no hunch, don't force it. Helen Hammid, a photographer with considerable psychic abilities, talks about "looking at" a friend's home to see if the person is there before she calls. If the person is out, she looks in later on and phones only if the friend has returned home.

Another exercise that requires instant action is this: When thoughts of a particular friend suddenly pop into your head for no apparent reason, call right away and ask if he was thinking of you. Don't forget to jot down these hunches—correct and incorrect. The record you keep is an important part of the learning process.

When your friend is not around, try "commanding" him to get in touch with you. Try it with a friend who lives in a distant place. Send adamant mental messages and see if you don't get a letter or phone call in response to your demand.

With one friend as your partner, choose a group of common items, say, flowers. Ask your friend to look directly at you and think hard about a particular type of flower, sending you a message or picture of it. Concentrate on receiving the message. Record your message; after a minute, move on to another flower. After a minute on that one, move on to another. Do not choose categories that require much thought or that have details or associations that get in the way of focusing. Try the exercise with colors or animals or foods.

DRAWING FROM THE UNCONSCIOUS

Making a sketch or pictorial representation of something hidden is an excellent—and often successful—psychic skill that's very much worth developing. Studies show that psychic information is usually processed nonlinguistically, often visually, in simple pictographic forms that convey "meaning" rather than language—as do the crude drawings of children.

This is a simple exercise involving a partner (it can also be done with a group). One person, with his back turned or in a separate room, makes a simple drawing. It should, however, be more interesting and complicated than just a plain geometric shape. While making the drawing, and when it is complete, the sender concentrates on communicating the drawing to the partner, who tries to reproduce it. The receiver should be careful not to analyze the thing being drawn, just to try to reproduce the imagery in simple pictorial terms. Uri Geller, who often performs this feat (he did so successfully with me), observes that it is uncanny how often the receiver will reproduce the drawing almost identically— not only in content but in size as well.

AN EXERCISE IN REMOTE OBJECT VIEWING

As you've read, research in remote viewing has been highly successful and has demonstrated that most people have or can develop psychic ability. The next two exercises, based on the work of Hal Puthoff, Russell Targ, and Keith Harary, are excellent learning techniques.

Your mission in this first exercise is to describe, and then to identify, an object chosen by your partner, using remote viewing techniques. You will need at least one or, ideally, two partners to perform this exercise correctly. You will be the "viewer," and the second person will be the "interviewer."

In another room, have a third person choose a small object and place it in a bag, a box, or an envelope so that you cannot possibly know what it is. The best objects are things that have several kinds of sensory detail—a piece of sandpaper, for example, would have color, texture, and sound attached to it. A tomato would have scent, color, texture, and shape. Your friend must stay there with the object, so as not to give you (or the "interviewer") any clues about its identity. From the minute the object is placed in the bag, you, the viewer, should close your eyes and begin to write down or tape-record your impressions. If you want to draw, do so. Use whatever methods come to mind. Look into the future and see the object being placed in your hand at the end of the exercise; look into the past before it was placed in the bag, smell it, taste it. Think of touching it with your hands. Do not try to guess what it is; let your impressions, and the sensory information, accumulate.

Meanwhile, the interviewer, who does not know what the object is, should ask you questions that guide you to new ways of experiencing the object and keep you from getting off the track with overanalysis or other mental noise and distractions. Then it's just a step to "looking" at it and describing what it is. If you are describing a round red object, he might ask you its texture to help distinguish a rubber ball from a beet. If you say it is red, he might try to find out if it's shiny red or dull red. He might ask if it is smooth or if it is hard, or ask you to look at it from a different angle.

Stop when you run out of further impressions and set a time limit of ten or fifteen minutes—any longer isn't necessary for a simple object. At this point, your friend should bring you the object and you should hold it in your hands. Feel it and sense all its qualities. Make a mental note of which characteristics came through clearly and which ones were muted or missing altogether. Notice whether you got sidetracked by "facts." Don't skip this holding step—it is important feedback in the process of learning to do remote viewing.

NOTE: You can do this exercise with two people, but the person who chooses the object should not also serve as interviewer. There is a chance that he will ask leading questions or influence your impressions telepathically (though it is possible, of course, that the person choosing the object might do so anyway. In laboratory experiments, the object is chosen by computer; no one knows what it is until the session is over.)

AN EXERCISE IN GEOGRAPHIC REMOTE VIEWING

This exercise is very similar to the preceding one, except that you are going to try to describe a location during the time that your partner will be at the site. Geographic remote viewing is often especially successful because the intensity and variety of sensory input far exceeds that of a simple object—it engages the viewer's interest more.

Ask a friend to go to a geographic location of his or her choosing at a specific time. It need not—indeed, should not—be an obvious landmark location. If you live in St. Louis, he probably should not choose the Arch—a restaurant, a shopping mall, a park, or a pizzeria would do nicely. One easy way of doing this exercise is to plan ahead. Your partner can then go to the viewing site while doing a round of errands or during his break for lunch.

Plan that your friend will show up at the place at a specific time and stay there for fifteen minutes. He need not try to send you information, but he should take a good look around, observing tall things, wide things, soft, round, pointed, sharp angles. He should be aware of sounds, smells, and movement. Ask him to pay attention to the location he chooses, to experience it fully.

At the prearranged hour, you should be comfortably seated and alert. A minute or two before the appointed time, begin to relax, pushing any distractions away from you. You need not meditate or do anything more than be calm. At the proper time, you should begin to describe the impressions and images of the target place. As with the object viewing exercises, you might want to have another friend there, as interviewer, to ask questions that will "center" your description. Describe the shapes, colors, textures, scents, movement—all the qualities that you feel. Look at the site from several angles—even try to hover above it. Do not try to analyze. If you like, sketch what you see, however unskilled your drawing talents may be.

When the time is up, have your friend call you and tell you the location. Visit it as soon as is feasible. The feedback you gain from visiting the site is a valuable learning tool and will underscore your success at remote viewing.

THE MAGIC TOUCH: PSYCHOMETRY

Psychometry—picking up "vibrations" about people from one of their cherished possessions—can best be practiced in a group in which you get quick feedback about the correctness of your impressions. It can also be practiced alone; it will be more difficult, though, to gauge the correctness of your answers, unless you can later follow up on your impressions by verifying them with the owner of the object.

If you want to practice psychometry on your own, ask friends or relatives to get some items for you to practice with. Make sure that they know the history of its owner but that they don't offer you any hints as to his or her identity. If you have an eccentric Aunt Sara who adored and collected emeralds, giving you an emerald ring to practice on would be fruitless. You would be unable to know whether the information you received was colored by your conscious knowledge of Aunt Sara. Beatrice Rich (p. 178) learned her "trade" this way, practicing on anonymous items provided by friends—often with amazing results.

> In any psychometric exercise, choose key rings or bracelets, watches, pins, necklaces—anything that touched its owner and was coveted by him. Beware of anything handmade like Indian turquoise jewelry—you might be picking up on the person who made it rather than the man or woman it belongs to. Whenever possible, to avoid unnecessary confusion, choose items that were worn and loved by only one owner. The longer he or she owned the item, the better, though it should not be an heirloom that has been passed down through the generations. Who knows which one of its owners you might tap in on? Hold the item in your hand, relax quietly, and see if you feel anything about it. Do you sense something about its owner? Its history?
>
> In a group, psychometry can be fun and fascinating. Gather a small number of people and ask each of them to bring two prized objects. Either ask someone who will not be participating to collect the objects at the door, or instruct your guests to place one object on each of two tables, without peeking at the other items there or their owners. You might want to have the participants come with each item enclosed in a bag or an envelope; do whatever makes sense in your situation. Have each participant choose one object whose ownership is unknown to him, unwrap it, hold it, and write down every impression he associates with the piece. If he senses temperature, color, scent, a scenario—whatever —he should record his feelings. Pass the items around until everyone has had a couple of minutes with each object that is unknown to him. The results can be read aloud and the accuracy or inaccuracy of the comments can be established. You'll be surprised how precise some of the observations may be. Continue the exercise using the other batch of personal objects.

AURA VIEWING

The subject of auras is a controversial one, but there are many who claim they see a corona of light and color around people, animals, and even objects. The interpretation of the aura—its size, hue, intensity—is also highly debated. Try the following exercise just for fun.

In an otherwise dark or darkened room, arrange a strong light so that it reflects against a smooth, light-colored, unmarred wall. Stand with your back to the light source and make sure you are casting a shadow on the clear surface of the wall. If dimmer shadows are dancing on the wall, adjust the lighting or do whatever is required to achieve as stark a shadow as possible. Hold your hands about 18" in front of your eyes, palms facing toward you with the fingers slightly spread apart and just touching fingertip to fingertip, like a policeman's sobriety test. Stare at the place where the fingertips meet, looking at the reflected shadow, not at the fingers themselves. *Very, very slowly, move your hands just slightly apart, keeping a sharp eye out for any lines or waves that seem to emanate from the fingertips or between the two hands. Concentrate on what you are seeing and look very closely and carefully. Give yourself time. Keep trying, if necessary, until you have evidence of your own aura.*

TAPPING YOUR UNCONSCIOUS WITH A SWINGING PENDULUM

Technically called radiesthesia, this use of the pendulum is a form of dowsing (p. 227). Many people consider the pendulum an excellent way to tap unconscious information. They find that it offers a good way to get true inner answers to questions without the noise, interference, and just-the-facts-ma'am attitude of rational consciousness. Some healers use a pendulum to locate illness in the body.

First it will be necessary to construct a pendulum—any small, weighted object hanging from a foot-long length of thread or string. A needle will do nicely, as will an ordinary sink washer or necklace pendant. If you like, draw a small circle—three inches or so in diameter —that can serve as the target range by which to judge the pendulum's direction and motion. It need not be perfect or fancy.

A swinging pendulum can respond only to questions that have yes or no answers, so you will have to be careful in your phrasing. Holding the end of the thread so that the weight hangs a few inches above the target circle, let the weight steady itself and become perfectly still. Start by asking a simple question that will have a definite yes answer—check the validity of your address or telephone number, or the spelling of your name. Say to it, "Is my name Kate?" Watch carefully to see if the pendulum moves in a clockwise or counterclockwise direction, and remember it. Next, ask a "ringer" question that most certainly should receive a no answer, and check the direction the pendulum moves in response to it. "Do I live in Bangkok?" The pendulum should swing in the opposite direction from the yes response and will mark the no direction. If you like, ask more questions to which you know the answers to double-check the reliability of the swinging pendulum. (The yes/no directions may be the opposite for someone else.) You can now use the pendulum to tune in to your real feelings or to get information you don't think you have. Am I ready to go on a serious diet? Will my sister give birth to a girl? Will I get a raise? Is Abigail a true friend? Will the governor be reelected? Is today a good day to play the lottery?

What your subconscious feels will often be revealed in the answer, even if it seems counter to what your conscious reaction would be and seemingly contradictory of the "facts." Even though you think you have found the house of your dreams, ask questions about it before you close the deal. Perhaps you'll want to know if the location will become a nuisance once the "romance" of its out-of-the-way site wears off. Or go the mundane route and ask if the roof will really last through three more winters as you hoped. The pendulum will often indicate what you feel in your unconscious mind.

AN EXERCISE IN PSYCHOKINETICS

If you don't believe you have the ability to affect the movement of another object by mental energy alone, read on. A simple experiment will show that it may be possible to influence other objects that share space with us in our lives.

Light an everyday candle and place it several feet away from you, where the action of your breathing or movement will not cause the flame to flicker. Look at the flame to make sure that any movement by you is not affecting the flame. Make sure that the room you choose is as draft-free as it possibly can be. Check for even the slightest air currents; ideally, there should be none.

Concentrate on the flame and send it a message to move to the right or left side—your choice. Will the flame to obey your command by moving in the direction you indicate. Be patient, give it a bit of time, and you'll find that the candle does indeed do as you commanded it.

When it obeys, let go of the thought and let the flame return to normal —perfectly upright. Don't get discouraged; if it doesn't work, try again another day.

GROUP EXERCISES IN PSYCHIC FUNCTIONING

If you know others who are interested in increasing their psychic abilities, create a group exercise class or just an evening of light-hearted experimentation. The feedback you gain can be very valuable and the group energy often seems to improve individual psi abilities.

Card guessing, using cards patterned on the Zener deck of ESP cards, works as well at a party or workshop as it does in laboratory studies. The Zener deck consists of twenty-five cards, each marked with one of five simple symbols—a circle, a square, a plus sign (+) or cross, a star, and three parallel wavy lines. If you have several decks (they're easily made), several people can participate simultaneously.

Divide the group into pairs and send one member of each pair into another room. They will be the receivers. Each of the remaining participants should be given a deck of the Zener cards. At an audible-to-all signal, the sending parties should turn over the deck and concentrate on sending the symbol on the top card. Their partners in the other room should attempt to receive the message and draw the symbol they receive on a piece of paper. After thirty seconds, an audible signal sounds to alert the senders to move on to the next card. At the end of the twenty-five-card series, the card sequences are compared to the answers to determine how well the receivers fared in the experiment. Five out of twenty-five would be a chance level of performance. Results frequently are statistically significant, that is, higher than chance expectations.

(NOTE: The Zener deck is sometimes criticized because the simple images are too boring to elicit psychic interest. You may want to make your own deck of cards. One way is to buy five to ten cards each of five different postcards, chosen for their interesting but visually clear subject matter—flowers, buildings, food. You can also cut pictures from magazines and paste them on 4 x 6–inch file cards.)

An effective group exercise in clairvoyance involves wrapping a number of objects in many layers of paper or cloth to conceal their identity completely, and then sealing them in plain envelopes or bags. The objects chosen should be similar in size and familiar—a key, pen, small key ring, tweezers, money clip, pin, or coin. Choose everyday items and keep the test simple so that positive results are not impossible to get. Have someone who is not participating number the envelopes and write down their contents.

Each person gets one envelope to contemplate. You may touch it, hold it, or whatever else—short of unwrapping it—you feel is necessary to try to determine what's inside. Don't be overly deductive. Don't try to name the object until the end—concentrate on shape, texture, color. Open your mind to its feelings and hunches. Write down— and sketch—the impressions you receive and spend only two or three minutes.

Another exercise is to try as a group to influence the roll of a single die. Decide on a number from one to six that you want to come up. Have one group member throw the die sixty times, while everyone concentrates on that number. If you do better than ten hits, you've beaten chance. Pass the die to another group member and try another series of sixty rolls.

Children often enjoy games like this—and are often exceptionally good at them. Children who excel at games such as Button, Button, Who Has the Button? or Hide the Eraser may be exhibiting psychic functioning. If a particular child is particularly adept at quickly going right to the place where he is "hot!," chances are he is having some psychic help in getting there so quickly.

WHERE TO GO FROM HERE
We've barely exposed the tip of the psi-ability iceberg in this brief chapter. There are other types and styles of psychic functioning that also merit exploration. One exciting development is the availability of a new, inexpensive ESP-teaching machine, marketed under the name Perceptron™. It is more than a game. Perceptron™ is based on a machine that was originally developed by SRI for a NASA study. The machine uses a built-in random-number generator, which makes thousands of decisions per second, to choose which of four colored lights will be triggered *next* by the machine. The player tries to intuit the machine's choice and correctly predict the correct color by pressing one of four buttons. The great advantage is that Perceptron lets you know *right away* whether your intuition was correct or incorrect —that all-important immediate feedback factor.

The game is played in sequences of twenty-four trials. A pleasant beep lets you know if your choice was correct, and a light indicates the correct color button, whether you pressed it or not. A series of lights and sounds indicates your success and scoring in each trial. As you use the machine over time, you learn to recognize the feelings—physical, mental, emotional—that accompany your correct guesses, and you learn to tune in to that feeling. Perceptron™ is available from JS&A Products, Northbrook, Ill. and Fairfield Marketing Corp., New York, N.Y.

For those who would rather read than play, several authors, including Enid Hoffman in *Develop Your Psychic Skills* and David St. Clair in *Lessons in Instant ESP*, delve into some of the far deeper psychic subjects—astral travel, out-of-body experiences, dowsing, séances, trance channeling, past life regression, automatic writing, etc.—that are too specialized to be covered here. These techniques are better attempted in a class or workshop situation with the guidance of an experienced teacher or guide. High-quality, responsible workshops do exist, though they may be difficult to locate outside major cities.

For the adventurous, and for those who seek vivid, concrete proof of abilities, there are several psychic disciplines that seem to work better or even to *require* the atmosphere that only a group can summon, at least during the learning stage. Metal bending is one. This usually takes place at PK (psychokinesis) parties (see p. 151), at which groups of fifteen or more people gather and, after a couple of hours of instruction and meditation, learn to bend metal—spoons, forks, rods—as though they were working with modeling clay. Firewalking is even more amazing and seems to work best with large groups, usually several hundred people. Again, after just a few hours of "indoctrination," participants walk barefoot over beds of red-hot coals without feeling pain or suffering burns. Séances and table tipping are other activities in which the group dynamic seems to enhance the paranormal action, as though they require a larger amount of energy, a greater concentration of power.

Many readers are already aware of their psychic abilities and able to put them to use. For most people, however, psychic functioning is new territory and requires new thinking, new discipline, the awakening of unused potential. Do not be discouraged if you don't get immediate results; your patience will more than likely pay off. And don't have unrealistic expectations. Remember that most of us have modest psychic skills; many can play the piano, but few are Vladimir Horowitz. But even the development of modest abilities can give us pleasure and enhance our day-to-day lives.

CHAPTER
THIRTEEN
ASTROLOGY

Astrology, which *The Shorter Oxford English Dictionary* defines as "the art of judging the occult influences of the stars upon human affairs," is probably the most popular and familiar of the psychic arts. Kinsey is right: People *do* read their horoscope. They may not remember it or plan their month or day based on it, but they do read it. Think of all the magazines and newspapers you read that include horoscopes—there are dozens. I once calculated that the circulation of newspapers and magazines carrying horoscope columns (in the United States, Europe, Japan, and South America) was over 700 million! There's a good reason for that: They're tremendously popular —publishers don't spend money or column inches on topics that don't have a readership. A newspaper editor once told me that he got *thousands* of calls from irate readers when the paper inadvertently left out the horoscopes one day.

Who, in this Age of Aquarius, doesn't know his sun sign and isn't familiar, at least on a rudimentary level, with the dates and basic character traits of his sign? The days when asking "What's your sign?" was the classic cocktail party conversation opener may have passed, but many people would nevertheless like to know it, if only to feel that they could get some "free" insight into your character and personality.

Ironically, few people understand the derivation of the meanings of their sun signs and the vast body of knowledge and complicated astronomical calculations that astrologers use as the basis of their interpretations. In fact, most people have never bothered to think about the premise behind astrology: that everything on earth is affected by time and tides, by the push and pull of the heavenly bodies, and that the moment you personally join into their "flow" influences every aspect of your life.

The idea that our lives can be influenced by the position of distant cosmic forces seems illogical and is the main reason for skepticism about astrology. Yet the idea that the movement of heavenly bodies affects our weather and tides and other creatures of the earth (see p. 346) is well established. Do you remember when, early in 1987, the term *syzygy* briefly became a household word? Syzygy refers to a rare cosmic alignment of the earth, sun, and moon: perigee, the point in its monthly orbit when the moon is closest to earth; perihelion, when the earth is closest to the sun; and a tidal bulge that occurs when the moon is at the southernmost point of its orbit. Syzygy wreaked meteorological havoc all over the world with tides and flooding. In the United States, there were surging, destructive tides along the East coast from New England to the Carolinas; the West Coast recorded the highest tides in twenty years. Now, our bodies are more than 70 percent water; does it not follow that we, too, are subject to tidal, lunar influences, albeit internal and unconscious? It is not as though the sun or moon "does" something to us: It is that our unique position in the cosmic scheme of things has an influence —one among many influences in our lives—that we can better understand and make use of.

You will not learn to cast your own horoscope in this brief chapter —that takes long work and intense study. But it will explain and clarify the terms you've heard and the factors that interact to make up the horoscope. Why are sun signs important, and why are they assigned particular characteristics? What does it mean to have Libra rising or your moon in Capricorn? Why are Libra and Aquarius considered to be compatible but not Libra and Cancer? What are the "houses," and what do they mean? What is the difference between a fixed and a mutable sign? An earth and a fire sign? What is a "conjunction"? An "opposition"? How do the pieces fit together to tell your astrological story? In this section, you will find enough information to test the validity of astrology for yourself and to try your hand at some basic interpretations. And, finally, a short section addresses the growing interest in Chinese astrology. These Oriental animal signs, which are based on the year of birth, are briefly explained so that this new information can be "layered" onto the traditional Western horoscope and enrich those interpretations.

But first, how it all began.

A BRIEF HISTORY OF ASTROLOGY

It is safe to say that the earliest humans were interested in astrology. Sumerian records show their observation of the sky dating back to 6000 B.C., though fragments of specifically astrological data don't show up until around 2900 B.C. in the form of the astrological predictions of Sargon the Old and the Babylonian tables of the royal astrologers. The Chaldeans (a group that consisted of early Babylonians and Assyrians) practiced the dual science of astrology/astronomy and wrote the first ephemerides (books that list astronomical tables charting the movement of the planets), using the twelve primary constellations (i.e., the zodiac) that the sun and moon pass through. Astrology is a deductive process: The movements of the heavenly bodies were tracked and compared over years of observation, and patterns were noted. Eventually, using information implied by those patterns, people found they were able to predict events that threatened their world—wars, famine, flood, or drought. Abraham, patriarch of the Jews, was a Chaldean; Old Testament records confirm his astrological knowledge.

Every cradle of civilization had its own set of beliefs based on the movement of the sun, moon, and stars. The primitive Beaker people of the early Bronze Age, who are credited with the construction of Stonehenge in England, most probably had the study of the stars and the desire to make a calendar in mind when that amazing circle of stones was planned. It is possible to calculate the eclipses and solstices by using various stones, built from massive ten-thousand-pound stones (quarried, by the way, several hundred miles away), as markers and points against the sun, horizon, and so on. The absolute precision of these huge, rough-hewn stones is remarkable and not fully understood to this day. Certainly Stonehenge is not merely an ancient temple of worship. No accident of nature or the innocence of primitive people could produce such a finely tuned astronomical tool.

It was the descendants of Abraham who brought Chaldean astrology to Egypt, where astrology was already being studied. The Egyptian pyramids are remarkably precise astronomical instruments. Though study, and controversy, undoubtedly will never end, it is clear that the pyramids (2686–2160 B.C.) were not simply ostentatious tombs for maniacal pharaohs but precisely constructed edifices that allowed for sophisticated stargazing from within. Special holes or tubes allowed pinpoint observation of specific segments of the sky. When the Israelites fled Egypt in the Exodus, they took with them their sophisticated astrological knowledge. The ancient Jews amassed the greatest fund of astrological and esoteric knowledge in the Western world.

The Mayans, whose monuments reveal similar astrological orientation, cast charts for five-day-old boys and decided the child's future occupation on it. As early as 250 B.C., Beroses, a Babylonian astrologer, set up a school for astrologers.

It was Ptolemy in the second century A.D. who wrote the first astrology textbook, *Tetrabiblos*, a formalized version of the work of the Chaldeans, which rationalized the planets, houses, and signs of the zodiac and their functions. By 70 B.C., Greek horoscopes were based on the exact time of birth.

In Rome, astrology was varyingly popular, depending on whether it interested the reigning emperor. The Julian calendar, introduced in 46 B.C. by Julius Caesar with the help of Egyptian astronomers, set the length of a year at 365¼ days and decreed that every fourth year would be 366 days long. The calendar as we know it was made possible by astrological texts.

After the fall of Rome, astrology—like many aspects of the various cultures—became more fragmented, often preserved in secret by clandestine groups. It was not until the beginning of the Middle Ages that a new interest in astrology surfaced in Europe.

Arabic texts were translated and sparked the interest of learned men. St. Thomas Aquinas, Chaucer, Dante, Milton, Spenser, and Shakespeare referred to astrology in their work. In their time, scientists used astrology, astronomy, and mathematics to increase current understanding of the physical universe. Tycho Brahe, a Dane, studied the motion of the planets. Johannes Kepler proved three laws that later were incorporated in Newton's study of dynamics. Galileo Galilei wrote books about astrology and built early telescopes. In the early seventeenth century, William Lilly, an English astrologer, correctly predicted the beheading of Charles I, and in the nineteenth century, Goethe believed that heavenly bodies could influence our lives.

The twentieth century has brought a renewed interest in this occult science. No less than Albert Einstein, Sigmund Freud, and Carl Jung showed interest in the viability of astrology and its inclusion in valid scientific thought.

ASTROLOGY IN THE TWENTIETH CENTURY

Astrology has not necessarily had an easy time of it in the twentieth century. Though it is phenomenally popular in newspapers and magazines, it has often had to defend itself against twentieth-century rationalism. Noted scientists have kicked sand in its face, and many prominent astrologers have had to fend off rigorous attacks from rabid rationalists—in the press, on the air, and at times, in a court of law.

The first to have to defend her beliefs and practice was a woman named Evangeline Adams, one of the most famous astrologers to date. She moved to New York City at the turn of the century at the precise time her horoscope said the move would be providential. After staying for one night in a particular hotel, the next day she warned the owner of the hotel that his astrological aspects were extremely negative. He should be careful; the conditions surrounding him were not at all friendly. That night the hotel burned to the ground, killing the hotelier's wife and several other family members. Adams, of course, immediately was hailed by the press and became someone to be reckoned with virtually overnight. Among her famous clients were J. P. Morgan, Charles Schwab, Mary Pickford, Enrico Caruso, and King Edward VII. In 1914, she was taken to court on the grounds that astrology was fortune telling and, therefore, illegal. Given the birth data for an anonymous party, she was called upon to interpret the chart before a judge. She proved her mettle by doing just that, giving an uncannily accurate reading for a Mr. X—who turned out to be the judge's son. The judge was so impressed by the accuracy of the reading that he immediately ruled that Adams "had raised astrology to the dignity of an exact science."

The Catholic Church, long a foe of astrology, was the adversary in a different kind of court case involving a prominent Manhattan-based astrologer—funny, spunky, and knowledgeable—who was born into a wealthy, aristocratic—and devout—Spanish Catholic family. Throughout her life, she had been a "good" Catholic, adhering to the tenets of her church and attending Mass regularly. For her, there was no conflict between her religion and her practice of astrology, but she was mortified when she was called to defend herself before her church. "One of my clients was mad at me because I continued to consult for her husband after their messy divorce, and she reported me to the Church, knowing how terrible it would be for me." Challenged by a council of bishops to defend her astrological practice before a closed session at St. Patrick's Cathedral in New York City, she was in dread of what would happen. Treated at the session like a criminal by the bishops who sat in judgment against her, she was given four birth times and told to cast the horoscopes. In the imposing chambers, trembling, this tiny woman stood up to the bishops in their robes of office and said: "I don't know whose horoscopes these are [she suspected she had the charts of the bishops themselves], but I can tell you this: One of them is an illegitimate child. Shall I go on?" The inquiry ended with no action being taken.

Serious media interest in the astrology research of the French scientist Michel Gauquelin (p. 344) and the unabated public interest in astrology incited the most intense contemporary attack on astrology. In the autumn of 1975, *The Humanist*, a magazine that "attempts to serve as a bridge between theoretical philosophical discussions and the practical applications of humanism to ethical and social problems," published "Objections to Astrology: A Statement by 186 Leading Scientists." In it, Bart J. Bok, professor emeritus of astronomy, University of Arizona; Lawrence E. Jerome, science writer from Santa Clara, California; and Paul Kurtz, professor of philosophy at the State University of New York at Buffalo, authored a one-page condemnation of astrology. They railed against "the increased acceptance of astrology in many parts of the world," against "the unquestioning acceptance of the predictions and advice given privately and publicly by astrologers," and were "especially disturbed by the continued uncritical dissemination of astrological charts, forecasts, and horoscopes by the media and by otherwise reputable newspapers, magazines, and book publishers." They continued, "This can only contribute to the growth of irrationalism and obscurantism. We believe that the time has come to challenge directly, and forcefully, the pretentious claims of astrological charlatans." Following this discourse were the names and titles of 186 scientists, including 18 Nobel prize winners: an impressive group. In a public relations maneuver that was just short of brilliant, *The Humanist*, under editor Paul Kurtz, sent copies of the manifesto to thousands of newspaper editors throughout the United States and abroad, urging them to print it, "particularly if they carry a daily or weekly horoscope column," in the "interest of responsible journalism." And print those publishers did, raising a ruckus that noted astrologer Sydney Omarr argued with relish in his newspaper column on October 12, 1975. In it he relates a call he made to Nobel prizewinning scientist Linus Pauling: " 'Dr. Pauling; this is Sydney Omarr with the L.A. Times Syndicate.

I didn't know you had made a study of astrology . . . ' 'I don't know anything about astrology, but it is a lot of nonsense.' " When Omarr asked why he had signed such a statement when he had never studied astrology, Pauling responded that he had read about it in the encyclopedia once.

The prominent scientist Carl Sagan declined to sign the manifesto, explaining that it was "not because I feel that astrology has any validity whatsoever, but because . . . the tone of the statement is authoritarian. The fundamental point is not that the origins of astrology are shrouded in superstition. This is true as well for chemistry, medicine, and astronomy, to mention only three. To discuss the psychological motivations of those who believe in astrology seems to be quite peripheral to the issue of its validity. That we can think of no mechanism for astrology is relevant but unconvincing."

It would appear that several of the scientists who signed the manifesto did not really think about what they were signing, so eager were they to discredit the rampant spread of softheaded nonsense. But they did themselves and their cause a great disservice. Indeed, to make such a statement without thorough scientific investigation is singularly unscientific—exactly Omarr's point. Interestingly enough, a Gallup poll conducted at the time of the controversy established that the manifesto had little effect on the 32 million Americans who believed in astrology and/or consulted their daily or weekly horoscopes.

Because astrology is indeed a highly charged and controversial issue—especially in an age when science exerts an ever stronger, ever more dogmatic influence over our lives—few scientists have condescended to study astrology. This skepticism is part of what makes certain findings so interesting.

It is the research of just a few serious scientists that has bolstered the case of the astrologer, seemingly confirming the universal influence of heavenly bodies on our earthly ones. In 1950, confirmed nonbeliever Michel Gauquelin (later joined in his studies by wife Françoise), a psychologist and statistician, was gathering statistical research about planetary rhythms. Gauquelin was amazed when his data showed that a statistically significant number of doctors were born at a time of day or night when Mars or Saturn had just risen or was at its highest point. The results of a random sample of people from a mixture of other occupations showed no such planetary position correlations.

Because Gauquelin didn't believe his findings, he decided to go further and to come at the problem from another direction. His second study started with the birth data for five hundred French physicians—with comparable statistical results. In the ensuing years, Gauquelin's sophisticated statistical studies have continued, with findings that have isolated additional groups of occupational/astrological correlations. For example, his data show that soldiers, politicians, and actors—outgoing types who crave public attention—seem to have a special influence from the planet Jupiter. Similarly, he found that writers are influenced by the moon and that babies who were to grow into strong or even professional athletes were born with Mars rising or culminating on the day of their births, a phenomenon referred to as the "Mars Effect." For those who are not familiar with statistical research, many of Gauquelin's findings have odds of millions to one against chance occurrence.

In his studies, Gauquelin was able to isolate different personality types, specifically the "lunar temperament," showing the influence of the moon in the chart, as with writers. He even showed some success at linking the birth of a child with the birth of his or her parents, showing that there might be an inherited tendency for a child to be born under a particular planet.

It's not hard to imagine that many scientists just wouldn't believe the accuracy of Gauquelin's studies. The very skeptical Professor Hans Eysenck, a prominent English psychologist, set out to use Gauquelin's testing methods to determine whether there is a statistical astrological difference between introverts and extroverts. He expected no correlation; indeed, he expected to disprove the Gauquelins altogether. But much to his surprise, Eysenck found that introverts were likely to be influenced by Saturn and extroverts by Mars or Jupiter—precisely what Gauquelin had determined.

In 1978, the Committee for the Scientific Investigation of Claims of the Paranormal (CSICOP, see page 83) conducted a research project, apparently with hopes of disproving Gauquelin's findings. Imagine their horror when the study supported rather than debunked Gauquelin's. Seemingly out of fear that his added research would advance the cause of astrology and promote further studies, the Committee failed to give a clear presentation of the results. Instead they presented the data couched in a dubious statistical analysis that served to produce a negative conclusion. Since this looked to many like a cover-up—an attempt to rationalize the results—the ploy did not go over well with some CSICOP members, who felt that the findings—however damaging to CSICOP's case—should be fairly presented in the interest of open-minded scientific inquiry. Several years of internal infighting, and of trying to justify their course of action, ensued. In the end, it was unhappy and disgusted members of CSICOP who made public the information about the study and its findings; several members resigned over this issue. It was not until six years after the study, in the Spring 1983 of CSICOP's journal, *The Skeptical Inquirer*, that they admitted, in rather lukewarm fashion, that "the procedure used by Gauquelin appears to have been validated." Marcello Truzzi, a CSICOP member who earlier had resigned, says, "Dogmatic denial and skepticism are not the same." This controversy is recounted in "sTARBABY," by Dennis Rawlins, in the October 1981 issue of *Fate* magazine.

Within the scientific community, it is standard practice for findings —positive and negative—to be made public to advance the general body of knowledge.

In addition to the thought-provoking research from the Gauquelins numerous studies about the electromagnetic forces of the earth, the action of the tides, and the importance and effects of solar and lunar cycles have added some interesting fuel to arguments for the validity of astrology. Dr. Frank A. Brown, a professor of biology at Northwestern University, has done what I don't hesitate to call amazing research about electromagnetic forces at work. Many years ago, Brown took oysters from Long Island Sound off Connecticut to his laboratory in Illinois, near Lake Michigan. For two weeks, the oysters responded in their accustomed way, opening their shells to feed at the time of Long Island Sound's high tide and closing them for protection when the tide would have been at its low. Then a shift in timing occurred. Without an actual tide to respond to, the oysters— all of them, not just an individual or two—adjusted their schedule: They adjusted it to coincide with the time the tide *would have come in and gone out* if that particular geographic location in Illinois had been on the East Coast. The oysters adjusted their timetable to their location, a thousand miles west of their home. Brown went further in his tests, making sure that the oysters were not responding to sunlight and darkness; he kept them in total darkness. The same adjustment took place: the oysters were opening their shells when the moon was directly above their geographical location—proof that in a totally baffling way, the influences of the moon and its rhythms can affect the most basic workings of life on earth.

It is a sign of the recent growth of interest in serious astrological research that in 1986, two major astrology conferences were held for the first time. One, the First Eysenck Research Seminar, held over a four-day period at California State University, Long Beach, featured the Gauquelins, Marcello Truzzi, Professor Martin Fiebert, and Eysenck himself actively participating in serious roundtable discussions and presentations. The other, the five-day United Astrology Congress, drew five thousand amateur and professional astrologers to hear dozens of lectures and seminars on every imaginable aspect of astrology.

Some of the world's most influential leaders have used astrology, and others have "used it back" in an attempt to figure out what the opponent was thinking. Scientists may give astrology a hard time, but governments have used it when they felt that doing so would put them on a more equal standing with the opposition. Indeed, Sydney Omarr claims that he was "the only soldier in the U.S. Army ever given full-time duty as an astrologer." During World War II, it was known that Hitler regularly consulted an astrologer. The renowned Carroll Righter claims that he knew the astrologer Churchill hired in reaction to Hitler's astrologer. "I knew him; I had lunch with him and he told me all about it." He continues, "Nicholas Murray Butler, who used to be president of Columbia University, said that he met five astrologers of Hitler's. . . . They [the astrologers] advised him not to go into Russia." In her book about Sydney Omarr, *Omarr: Astrology and the Man*, Norma Lee Browning reports that Butler was told by Hitler's advisors that "the month of September [1939] would be the high point of his career." She goes on to relate that Hitler's private Swiss astrologer, Karl Ernst Krafft, "according to Professor Hans Bender at the University of Freiburg, drew up Hitler's horoscope, in which it specifically stated that the Führer's climax would come in 1941–42 and that he would have to win the war by 1942 at the latest or else catastrophe would occur in 1945." She goes on to include Goebbels and Rudolf Hess among the believers in astrology who surrounded Hitler and cites a passage from Goebbels' diary that includes a mention of recruiting "specialists in prophecy of every type."

Louis de Wohl, a famous Hungarian astrologer, was employed by the British to try to outguess the Nazi astrologers. He advised Churchill not on what the Allies should do but as to what advice the astrologers were giving Hitler. It's interesting that de Wohl and Krafft had studied at the same astrological institute.

Carroll Righter told me that he was about to work with the U.S. government to figure out what the Vietnamese astrologers were forecasting when the war ended. In May of 1965, just above its "Letters to the Editor of The Times," *The New York Times* published a facetious piece by C. L. Sulzberger suggesting that perhaps the time had come for the United States to find a "good White House astrologer." He went on to report on executive decisions made by several foreign heads of state who had taken the advice of or been affected by the predictions of their psychic advisors.

Other political figures have been rumored to believe in astrology. Though Carroll Righter is singularly closemouthed on the subject, other astrologers claim that Ronald Reagan has long been Righter's client. Sydney Omarr told me, "I would say one of the world's worst-kept secrets is Ronald Reagan's interest in astrology." Rumor has it that Reagan's inauguration as governor of California was advanced to 12:23 A.M., rather than being held later in the day as was customary, so that it would occur under more auspicious aspects. Omarr goes on to mention that Henry Wallace's diaries "show that when he was vice president, he was worried about Roosevelt because of Roosevelt's deep interest in astrology."

HOW ASTROLOGY SERVES

Since millions of people continue to have an honest, ongoing interest in astrology, perhaps it's a good idea to ask, "What can astrology do for me?" For the answers, I talked to dozens of astrologers and their clients.

When Colette Michaan, an astrologer in New York City, was asked, "What is the most valuable thing one can get from astrology?" her response was,

> *An affirmation of the Divine order in the universe. Everything has purpose and meaning. Everything happens for a reason, nothing is random, there is no chaos. There is a wisdom in the order of events in life. The astrological lens affirms this by offering insight into the timing of the unfolding of life. Just as the planet is evolving, so are we, and astrology gives insight into the evolutionary cycles of the individual and collective.*
>
> *Astrology is a language of symbolism based on Nature. To align*

oneself with the energies of Nature facilitates growth, change, and trust in evolution as an ongoing rhythmical process. To be aware of the "natural" order is a way of consciously connecting with the universe. Whether one acknowledges the celestial influences or not, they do indeed filter through our lives. The recognition that we live in translation of the great cosmic dance of the planets is an empowering one, offering an invaluable sense of connectedness.

The horoscope is a mandala, a symbol of the personal imprint of the quality of energy operable in the universe at the time of birth. The natal chart (birth chart) is indicative of one's unconscious predisposition, it is one's terrain. The greater the familiarity with the terrain, the greater the possibility for integration and consciousness. The greater the consciousness, the more choice one has vis-à-vis how one wishes to respond to one's predisposition. Transits [the positions of the planets at any given point in time, and their relationship to the natal chart] are like weather conditions. If we know where we are in a cycle, and what the cycle is, we can know how to counteract the cycle to aim for balance. The awareness of transits affords the individual the opportunity to position her/himself accordingly, with perspective and a greater understanding of the manner in which a particular period may serve overall growth.

Many people contend that a belief in astrology precludes free will. Michaan, however, like most of her colleagues, disagrees; she believes we have free will, and that what is predestined is just the framework within which we must work. For example, if you are an American Indian born in Taos, New Mexico, in 1936, or an Irish farmer born at the turn of the century, or an aborigine in Australia's outback, you will live your chart within the framework of the culture that nurtures you. Or consider the case of two people born the same day, month, and year: actor Dana Andrews and Senator Barry Goldwater share their birth dates, as do Carol Channing and Norman Mailer, Charles Darwin and Abraham Lincoln, and Marlon Brando and Doris Day. Certainly their lives are different—perhaps because of their birth times. Similarly, a baby born in Watts will live a vastly different life from one born at the same time in nearby Beverly Hills.

What Michaan stresses is that

planets are our sources of energy and each planet represents different principles of energy. In becoming familiar with the qualities of each

*planet, when under an influence, by transit, one has a very good idea
of what one is specifically being asked to develop. Whatever comes to
us is part of us, and the chart shows what, when, where, and how we
may attract that. As planetary energy sifts down in planes, the quality
of the energy, the duration of the influence, and the areas of life affected
can be easily predicted. However, the manner in which one translates
a particular energy is where I believe free will enters. The weather may
be predetermined; making the weather conditions work for you is a
choice. Regarding transits, clients often ask: "Is this good or bad?"
The chart simply shows what is; whether it is good or bad depends
entirely upon one's personal consciousness.*

Michaan closed her remarks with a favorite quote, from an anonymous source: "Astrology is magical only in the sense that insight is
magical. When you make an observation, draw knowledge and
strength from that observation, and the knowledge changes your life,
that is *magic!*"

Mark Vito, an astrologer in Los Angeles, states simply, "Astrology
is just another way of looking at what's going on around us." Zoltan
Mason, a well-established American astrologer, says, "What is astrology? Just interpreting one language into English. . . . I am not a
politician; I am not anything but an astrologer, that's all. If somebody
is sick, go to a doctor. If somebody has a legal problem, go to a
lawyer." Carroll Righter speaks along the same lines: "Some people
seek legal, medical, or whatever other type of advice appeals to them.
There are all these mediums through which man expresses himself.
He selects the one that he likes."

ASTROLOGY—THE HELPING PROFESSION

In interviews with dozens of professional astrologers—Sydney
Omarr, Carroll Righter, Frederick Davies, Maria Crummere, Zoltan
Mason, Julien Armistead, John Maraschella, Lenore Cantor, and
Maria Napoli among them—one theme is recurrent. All of them
state, in one way or another, that they view astrology as a helping
profession. They do not pretend to be psychologists, though there
are a few astrologer/psychologists, and several psychologists do use
astrology to gain quick insight into their patients. They are, however,
confident that they can help clarify aspects of modern life in a helping, advisory way. They can instill confidence in those who are unsure; they can warn the impatient to wait, the cowardly to be brave.

They can, as playwright Ed Dunn, a client of New York City astrologer John Maraschella, says, "give general boundaries, guidelines, and I have found him [Maraschella] to be extremely intuitive for the information he has given me. . . . I think the motivation in going to an astrologer or a psychiatrist or a psychologist is totally different. I don't go for a reading or consultation with John to get better or to change a condition I'm dissatisfied with. I go to John for his interpretation of my astrological chart, and I have found it to be always, always a beneficial experience."

Astrologer Lenore Cantor says, "I believe that the purpose of all kinds of psychological counseling or astrology is to help people gain control over their lives." The act of counseling is and must be a careful one. Julien Armistead elaborates: "I believe that we're looking at astrology from a counseling point of view. Astrology is a subset of reality: you really need to know how the person has dealt with their life, where they're at, what they're aware of, what they've solved, what they haven't solved. To read for somebody at the age of twenty-two is quite a different thing from reading for someone at the age of fifty-two. You need to know the bases in order to help, but it is the client who's doing the work. It is he who is, to put it in a rather funny way . . . it is he who is saving his own soul. To the extent that I can be of some help along the path, I'm delighted, and that's why I'm here."

On a lighter note, Frederick Davies thinks astrologers have a common personality trait that influences their choice of profession: "If they weren't doing astrology, they'd probably join in the Boy Scouts or the Red Cross or they would be helping the neighbors."

Psychologists—and not just the Jungians—have begun to use astrology as a quick way to round out their knowledge of their clients. Jung explained the astrology/psychology connection this way: "Everything born or done at this moment of time has the qualities of this moment of time. . . . As a psychologist, I am chiefly interested in the particular light the horoscope sheds on certain complications in character. In cases of difficult psychological diagnosis I usually get a horoscope. I must say that I very often found that the astrological data elucidated certain points that I would otherwise have been unable to understand."

Getting a patient's horoscope can save lots of time-consuming work in the early stages of therapy, according to several psychiatrists and psychologists I spoke to. John Maraschella, himself a psychologist, is a member of the Association of Astrology and Psychology, a coalition of professionals from each discipline who use astrology to help them in their therapy and counseling sessions with clients. Maraschella is quick to point out, however, that astrology works "as a tool to clarify the client's problems, his obstacles, his nature, his personality, and the things in his psychic makeup. . . . I think that it speeds up the counseling process because it gets to the root of the problem. . . . I am a psychotherapist as well as an astrologer. From my end of the work, the chart can very quickly let me see what the client is about. But that's not necessarily going to speed up the client's growth. We can only grow when we are ready to grow."

An attorney friend telephoned me minutes after leaving his session with Colette Michaan. "That was an amazing experience. I feel like I had four years of therapy in two hours. How can she describe my relationship with my father and be so on target knowing nothing about me except when and where I was born?"

Astrologers help in other ways as well. Several experts predict Wall Street successes and touchy financial timings with better-than-average statistical results. There's Arch Crawford, former analyst at Merrill Lynch & Co., author of the newsletter *Crawford's Perspectives*, and there's Bill Foster of Rocky Mountain Financial Forecasting— he's right a whopping 62 percent of the time. He charts horoscopes based on the founding dates of companies, the date they begin trading stocks, the date of reorganization or merger. The possibilities are endless—he can even do charts for company CEOs and the like.

Who goes to astrologers? Besides judges, bishops, and presidents, astrology apparently has appeal for many people in the entertainment industry (or perhaps it's just that we recognize their names). Sydney Omarr is or has been astrologer to several—Susan Strasberg, Angie Dickinson, Doc Severinsen, Arlene Dahl, and Anne Bancroft, among others. Frederick Davies has done readings for no less than Lauren Bacall, Goldie Hawn, Olivia Hussey, Rona Barrett, Olivia Newton-John, Joan Hackett, Debbie Reynolds, Carrie Fisher, Joan Collins, Michael York, producer Robert Stigwood, and Michael Crawford. Very early in his career, when he was hard put for an "instant prediction," Davies blurted out that Liza Minnelli and Peter Sellers (a hot item at the time) would *not* get married, and gained a new client—Liza Minnelli. It was instant astrologer-to-the-stars–dom for him. But, he will tell you, the rich and famous have the same problems and questions as you and I. Maria Crummere has many celebrity clients (she was cast astrologer on *Hair* during its entire run on Broadway), including Jane Fonda, Peter Fonda, Arlene Francis, and many others.

And why do people go to astrologers? Like so many astrologers, Maria Crummere has a specialty. What she really likes is to get involved in the fun aspects of her clients' lives. "I love to make a marriage." She continues: "Oh, I have an awful time with my clients sometimes. I carry on like a—I scream and yell. Oh, I am terrible. They're afraid of me, some of them. I say, 'Now, listen, if you want me to help you, you've got to listen. I won't tell you what to do; I won't tell you to make choices, but I'm going to tell you what your choices are. Now, if you go right, you'll win; if you go wrong, don't come back here and tell me it didn't work.' " One of her clients told me that he'd reconciled with his wife, at a time when he was sure he would lose her, by following some very specific advice from Crummere. I confirmed this story with her, and she told me in detail exactly how she'd known—from the charts of her client, his wife, and his wife's lover at that time—what would happen if he played his cards right.

If you take a look at an astrologer's clientele, sometimes his or her focus becomes clear. Some specialize in the spiritual aspects of life, others, the physical or psychological. We've already seen that some do financial analyses only, offer advice about real estate conditions, or otherwise limit their practice to one particular facet of astrology.

With years of experience, many adepts reach the point where intuition combines with their years of knowledge to give them an immediate and "whole" response to a chart—before they even break it down into its many influences and aspects. They can gain some almost instant basic understanding in the same way that a mother can recognize her child's cry in a busy nursery. And this intuitive response is as valid for the astrologer as is the "hunch" of the doctor, researcher, police officer, or mother who knew that something required further investigation. Indeed, Sydney Omarr, the well-known and widely published astrologer, calls his talent "intuitive intellect"; he won't go so far as to call it psychic. In interviews with prominent astrologers, the question of this intuition always makes for an interesting discussion. Though many adepts feel psychic to some degree, most spoke of their intuitive senses without necessarily calling themselves psychic.

Professional astrologer Julien Armistead talks about dealing with astrology in a whole-world sense. "If you practice astrology, you know it's more than 'rational' consciousness. What you're looking at is patterns, and you're looking at echos to patterns and you're looking at a way of having a kind of sense of what people are like, based on where the planets are at the time of their birth. . . . I don't think you can read an astrological chart if you're not intuitive." Armistead goes on, though, to confirm the mathematical and scientific foundations of astrology, seconding the claims of colleague Charles Jaynes: "Jaynes really makes a very good point, which is that even on the days when your intuition is off, you can still do a hell of a good job with astrology, and I think that is so. I think that astrology implies a perceptible pattern underlying various periods of time. I think there are certain patterns that astrology does pick up, regardless of whether you're intuitive or not, but I would not think that a nonintuitive astrology works very well at all, because it can't. Then you get into computer stuff, and as bright as computers are, they can't do as many different evaluations in their heads as a human being can."

THE BASICS OF ASTROLOGY

On a very simplified level, astrology can be divided into four basic parts: the signs of the zodiac; the planets; the houses; and the spatial relationships, or aspects, of the planets to one another. An understanding of these basic elements, the terms that explain them, and how they interact will lead to a clearer idea of what astrology is all about. Learning the subtle ways in which one factor affects another makes the study of astrology a lifelong learning experience, but becoming familiar with even the broadest meanings can make astrology more accessible and much more fun for the novice.

What follows is a simplified look at these important elements of astrology, with short interpretations that will guide you in making your own conclusions. First we'll go through the signs of the zodiac and learn what the sun sign, rising sign, and moon signs actually are. Then an explanation of the "qualities" and "elements" of the signs will add some further meaning. A discussion of the planets will follow, describing how a planet "rules" a particular sign—what that means and how it affects a chart. Finally the aspects—what they are, what they mean, how they are calculated.

After that background information is in place, I'll explain the two-part how-to process: casting the horoscope and interpreting the horoscope. You'll find out how to look at and cast an astrological chart. A brief discussion of Chinese astrology and the new trend of combining it with Western astrology follows. And after that, you'll get an idea of what more there is to astrology—and some advice on consulting a professional astrologer and where to go from here. First, though, here is the groundwork you'll need to know.

THE SIGNS OF THE ZODIAC

The *zodiac* consists of the twelve constellations that span the sky and make up the astrological *signs:* Aries (the Ram), Taurus (the Bull), Gemini (the Twins), Cancer (the Crab), Leo (the Lion), Virgo (the Virgin), Libra (the Balance), Scorpio (the Scorpion), Sagittarius (the Archer), Capricorn (the Goat), Aquarius (the Water Bearer), and Pisces (the Fishes). Depending on his date of birth, everyone falls into one of the signs of the zodiac.

However, the signs do not begin on January 1, at the beginning of the calendar year. The zodiac begins with the spring solstice in mid-March and moves through the year in roughly thirty-day divisions until it passes through all twelve signs.

A person's *sun sign* is the sign of the zodiac that the sun was passing through at the moment of his birth. For example, if you were born on April 30, your sun sign is Taurus because Taurus is the sign of all births that occur between April 21 and May 21. This is the sign you read about in newspaper and magazine columns; the sun sign is said to have the greatest importance in determining a person's character, what you really are. Many astrologers, however, would say that the sun sign is overstressed and oversimplified because of the popular astrology columns. Necessarily brief and simplified to suit their mass audience, they give short shrift to the many other factors that are equally important in astrological interpretation. In addition to the sun sign, two other signs are key elements in astrology: the rising (ascendant) sign and the moon sign.

The *rising sign,* or *ascendant,* is the sign that was rising on the eastern horizon at the minute of your birth. If you were born at sunrise, your ascendant would be the same as your sun sign. In astrological parlance, if your sun sign is Pisces and your rising sign as well, you are a "double Pisces." The rising sign is said to represent your outer self: your personality, how you behave in the world, and how you express yourself.

The *moon sign* is the sign of the zodiac that the moon was in at the time of your birth. The moon moves through the sky on its own 28½-day schedule, spending two to three days in each sign. The moon sign is said to represent the inner self: the way we feel about things, the emotional side of our being.

As you read the sign descriptions that follow, keep in mind that the influences of the rising sign and moon sign will powerfully affect the behavior of the sun sign. However, generally speaking, the traits listed for each sign should ring true. The "compatibility factor," though few astrologers take it seriously, is included because it seems to be of considerable interest to novice astrologers.

ARIES (March 21 through April 19)
KEY WORDS: I am
PURPOSE: to pioneer, to initiate
POSITIVE: forceful, energetic, ambitious, enthusiastic, pioneering, free, courageous, and enterprising
NEGATIVE: impatient and selfish
COMPATIBILITY: Sagittarius and Leo
The Arian will do just about any amount of work before he collapses. He can compete with the best of them, work under almost impossibly chaotic conditions, and still do a thorough, intelligent job. Though the Aries lacks diplomacy and tact, he has the ability to get to the crux of a situation, decide on a plan of action, and carry it out before going on to something else that requires his attention. He is forever questing the new—some would say it is so that he can get as much attention as possible. This sign wants to be first.
FAMOUS ARIANS:

Marlon Brando	April 3, 1924
Julie Christie	April 14, 1941
Harry Houdini	April 6, 1874
Thomas Jefferson	April 13, 1743
Claire Booth Luce	April 10, 1903
J. P. Morgan	April 17, 1837

TAURUS (April 20 through May 20)
KEY WORDS: I have
PURPOSE: to possess, to own
POSITIVE: stable and persistent, patient and solid, practical and warmhearted, builder
NEGATIVE: possessive and inflexible
COMPATIBILITY: Capricorn and Virgo
If ever you have to be rescued from some potentially awful situation, pray for a Taurus to come to your aid—he will not quit until you are safe. This sign will not rest until the goal is reached, though the way

might be a bit tough going and the course plodding and slow rather than lightning fast (like an Aries). For the shoulder to rest your weary head on, search for a Taurus, because that soft, strong, wide shoulder will protect and nurture in an affectionate way. But beware the bitter Taurean—if too many years have been spent dwelling on misfortunes, you couldn't find a more rigid or unyielding person if you tried.

FAMOUS TAUREANS:

Oliver Cromwell	April 25, 1599
Bing Crosby	May 2, 1904
Queen Elizabeth II	April 21, 1926
Sigmund Freud	May 6, 1856
Barbra Streisand	April 24, 1942

GEMINI (May 21 through June 21)

KEY WORDS: I think

PURPOSE: to communicate, to inform

POSITIVE: lively and clever, intelligent and versatile, communicative and spontaneous

NEGATIVE: inconsistent, gossipy, and superficial

COMPATIBILITY: Aquarius and Libra

Ah, Gemini—which one of you will it be? The kindly, smart, ever-so-articulate gentleman or the bossy, catty little brat who, though amusing, gets really tiresome in mere minutes. The Gemini is easily bored—he likes to concoct solutions to problems and leave the details to someone else while he runs off to put out more fires. He can't do without too much to do. The members of this sign spend a good deal of their time talking—opining vociferously and to anyone who'll listen about whatever has caught their fancy most recently. Geminis are seemingly well versed on a variety of topics, which makes them good company in any social situation.

FAMOUS GEMINIS:

John F. Kennedy	May 29, 1917
Marilyn Monroe	June 1, 1926
Laurence Olivier	May 22, 1907
Cole Porter	June 9, 1893
Queen Victoria	May 24, 1819

CANCER (June 22 through July 22)

KEY WORDS: I feel

PURPOSE: to nurture, to care for

POSITIVE: sympathetic, imaginative, nurturing, shrewd, protective, kind, parental

NEGATIVE: messy, overemotional, self-pitying

COMPATIBILITY: Pisces and Scorpio

There's nothing like a Cancerian to be your mommy, cook you food, take care of you when you're sick, read to you, help you choose new dishes or flatware, help you choose new curtains or wallpaper, or just be a friend. That's a Cancerian in a good mood. On the other hand, the mood can change quickly so that this formerly sweet soul becomes a harridan, and a tough one at that. Generally, though, the Cancer will dutifully tend her stamp collection after working in the garden, and while the stew is simmering on the stove, she'll probably write a cheery letter to a friend she hasn't seen for years. She's organized and kind—as long as she's in a good mood. Beware the bad.

FAMOUS CANCERIANS:

Ingmar Bergman	July 14, 1918
Pearl Buck	June 26, 1892
Marc Chagall	July 7, 1887
Ernest Hemingway	June 21, 1899
Helen Keller	June 27, 1880
Ringo Starr	July 7, 1940
Andrew Wyeth	July 12, 1917

LEO (July 23 through August 22)

KEY WORDS: I will

PURPOSE: to create, to be

POSITIVE: generous, expansive, dramatic, spirited, creative, organized, and optimistic

NEGATIVE: pompous, snobbish, and power-hungry

COMPATIBILITY: Sagittarius and Aries

If you like to be in charge, you might well be a Leo. This is the sign of the natural executive—quick-thinking, charming, and someone who makes opportunities where none existed before. Leo will take center stage whether it's his turn or not, but the act he performs will be showy and thrilling—quite worth the price of admission. The Leo is a hard worker, well organized, and may become a mentor to promising underlings. The Leo at his worst can be intolerant of any way but his own and is sometimes bossy.

FAMOUS LEOS:

Julia Child	August 15, 1912
Henry Ford	July 30, 1863
Alfred Hitchcock	August 13, 1899
Napoleon Bonaparte	August 15, 1769
Jacqueline Onassis	July 28, 1929
Dorothy Parker	August 22, 1893

VIRGO (August 23 through September 22)

KEY WORDS: I appraise

PURPOSE: to judge, to serve

POSITIVE: organized, meticulous, tidy, modest, efficient, service-oriented

NEGATIVE: overly practical, fussy, finicky

COMPATIBILITY: Capricorn and Taurus

Virgos are personally perfect—their socks never have holes in them, their suits are perfectly pressed and without a hint of lint, their nails show recent signs of a manicure, and nary a hair is out of place. They can be too perfect—who needs four showers a day? Or too organized —indexing and cross-indexing their files to death. This is the sign most adept at jerry-rigging something when it's necessary to make do or at analyzing the real reason the VCR won't record. The Virgoan ability to work hard for sustained periods of time makes him a valued employee who will follow through until every last detail is exactly right.

FAMOUS VIRGOANS:

Ingrid Bergman	August 29, 1917
Queen Elizabeth I	September 7, 1533
Greta Garbo	September 18, 1905
Lyndon Baines Johnson	August 27, 1908
Peter Sellers	September 8, 1925

LIBRA (September 23 through October 23)

KEY WORDS: I balance

PURPOSE: to harmonize, to equalize

POSITIVE: cooperative, just, fair, romantic, idealistic, diplomatic, easygoing

NEGATIVE: indecisive, frivolous, gullible

COMPATIBILITY: Aquarius and Gemini

Typically, a Libra child is the teacher's pet who grows up to be liked by most of the people he meets. He will be charming, a master of diplomacy—always able to see the good in something as well as the bad. And there's the rub. Libras *always* can see both sides of any situation and, therefore, they frequently try to solve problems that are bigger than they are. It's not a matter of boastfulness or conceit; Libras are blessed and bothered by the need for fairness and equality, always taking the side of the underdog, even if doing so goes against their first, more "natural" choice. Libras may have a difficult time with decision making—again, they're looking at both sides—but will take positive action the minute a decision finally is made.

FAMOUS LIBRANS:

Sarah Bernhardt	October 22, 1845
Truman Capote	September 30, 1924
George Gershwin	September 26, 1898
John Lennon	October 9, 1940
Eleanor Roosevelt	October 11, 1884
Bruce Springsteen	September 23, 1949

SCORPIO (October 24 through November 21)

KEY WORDS: I want

PURPOSE: to change, to alter

POSITIVE: emotional, passionate, imaginative, disciplined, discerning

NEGATIVE: secretive, jealous, ruthless, obstinate

COMPATIBILITY: Cancer and Pisces

The Scorpion can be vicious. He can sting with a whiplike motion of his tail, and you can never be sure if he will attack or not. Be careful —chances are he will strike or, at least, he'll want to very much. Scorpios are secretive; so secretive that it's hard to believe. They'll go for a walk leaving you no idea of what they are doing or if they'll return in ten minutes or ten years. We're talking about secrecy about inane things—what's for dinner, what came in the mail today, a friend's telephone number (it's listed in the book). All spies should be Scorpios; if caught, they'd be predisposed never to give up their secrets. This sign likes to win, and chances are they will—at just about any cost, if winning is important enough to them. Hope that a Scorpio friend's chart has some softening influences that take away some of the toughness—he'll need them.

FAMOUS SCORPIONS:

Richard Burton	November 11, 1925
Indira Gandhi	November 19, 1917
Charles de Gaulle	November 22, 1890
Katharine Hepburn	November 9, 1909
Pablo Picasso	October 25, 1881

SAGITTARIUS (November 22 through December 21)

KEY WORDS: I search

PURPOSE: to define, to clarify

POSITIVE: open, optimistic, dependable, curious, sincere, aspiring

NEGATIVE: careless, irresponsible, tactless, immature

COMPATIBILITY: Aries and Leo

Natural-born explorers, the original hobos, Sagittarians have a severe case of wanderlust and, what's more, they indulge it. This is the sign of the traveling salesman, the sailor, the astronaut, the deep-sea diver. It's not so much that this is a boisterous or macho sign; it's curious first, and then careless enough not even to think, much less worry, about the consequences of his actions. The Sagittarian's interest in travel and delving into the unknown need not necessarily be physical. He is interested in original research into topics he knows nothing about, and he delights in what he finds. His mind is keen and capable, like his attitude toward life.

FAMOUS SAGITTARIANS:

Beethoven	December 17, 1770
Winston Churchill	November 30, 1874
Noël Coward	December 16, 1899
Mary Martin	December 1, 1914
Frank Sinatra	December 12, 1923

CAPRICORN (December 22 through January 19)

KEY WORDS: I use

PURPOSE: to attain, to achieve

POSITIVE: organized, disciplined, reliable, ambitious, able, instinctive

NEGATIVE: miserly, conventional, rigid

COMPATIBILITY: Virgo and Taurus

The Capricorn competes and, most often, he wins. He will go to war in full battle regalia (three-piece pinstripe suit, baseball jersey, or military uniform) and fight hard to win. As a businessman, the Capricorn is excellent—thorough, imaginative, ambitious, talented, and lucky. He invariably does excellent work and is well respected among his contemporaries. Though his sense of humor is marvelously dry, not that many people are aware that he has a sense of humor. Capricorns don't take time out to play too often—they have to look to other signs for that impulse.

FAMOUS CAPRICORNS:

Humphrey Bogart	December 25, 1899
Marlene Dietrich	December 27, 1904
Cary Grant	January 18, 1904
Richard Nixon	January 9, 1913
Albert Schweitzer	January 14, 1875

AQUARIUS (January 20 through February 18)

KEY WORDS: I know

PURPOSE: to cooperate, to enhance

POSITIVE: original, independent, inventive, friendly, human, faithful

NEGATIVE: rebellious, tactless, perverse

COMPATIBILITY: Libra and Gemini

The Aquarian is one of the most well-rounded signs in the zodiac. They are understanding of human frailties, they can sympathize with weaknesses, they are helpful and friendly, and they are smart. What more can a person ask? Aquarians are something like sages; they seem to be wise beyond their years, to possess knowledge of the universe. They are incredibly calm. This very independent person is good alone or in company and is sometimes thought to be a bit eccentric—usually in terms of his personal style. They seem not to care what others think and, indeed, they don't—they don't have to.

FAMOUS AQUARIANS:

Charles Darwin	February 12, 1809
Mia Farrow	February 9, 1945
Clark Gable	February 1, 1901
Charles Lindbergh	February 4, 1902
Vanessa Redgrave	January 30, 1937

PISCES (February 19 through March 20)

KEY WORDS: I believe

PURPOSE: to accept, to succor

POSITIVE: sensitive, compassionate, kind, humble, emotional

NEGATIVE: confused, impractical, weak

COMPATIBILITY: Cancer and Scorpio

The Piscean is an impressionable person who is somewhat chameleonlike. It's sometimes difficult to comprehend his ideas unless they are acted out in some way—through some artistic mode of expression. The Piscean is usually better on paper than in words. When he writes, it's all perfectly, beautifully clear. The Piscean is emotional, almost to a fault, and frequently spends a good deal of his time trying to discover just what's the best way for him to spend his time. The people of this sign should take care to stay away from drugs or other addictive substances that can obscure the personality and talents of this truly creative individual.

FAMOUS PISCEANS:

Albert Einstein	March 14, 1879
Vaslav Nijinsky	February 28, 1890
Rudolf Nureyev	March 17, 1938
Elizabeth Taylor	February 27, 1932

THE QUALITIES IN ASTROLOGY

These qualities, or modes, also called quadruplicities, divide the zodiac into three groups: cardinal signs, fixed signs and mutable signs.

They are divided as follows:

CARDINAL	FIXED	MUTABLE
Aries	Taurus	Gemini
Cancer	Leo	Virgo
Libra	Scorpio	Sagittarius
Capricorn	Aquarius	Pisces

These groups are referred to as modes of expression, since the signs within each division tend to share certain qualities, though they express them differently.

THE CARDINAL SIGNS are said to be the initiators, the doers, the originators. These people get things started, they create, they solve problems as they happen, and usually are successful within their ambitions. They may have to rely on a person who is a fixed or mutable quality to complete the projects they have begun, since the urge to get on to initiating new things is very strong. Negatively, cardinal signs are hasty, domineering, and imprudent.

THE FIXED SIGNS are fixed in their habits and attitudes and tend to resist change—at almost any cost. This is not a group known to be too flexible about life; they are great managers who will carry out the work that was begun by a cardinal sign and fulfill it perfectly. The fixed signs are firm, businesslike, generally conservative, and quite determined. Negatively, fixed signs are lazy, stubborn, and vain.

THE MUTABLE SIGNS are adaptable, social, able to cope, and get along in the world. They tend to be the harmonious links between the energy of the cardinal signs and the conservatism of the fixed signs. They are the peacemakers, the diplomats. Negatively, mutable signs can be indecisive, scattered, and critical.

The completed astrological chart includes the distribution of the sun, moon, and planets throughout the zodiac, and each of them is positioned in one of the twelve signs. Ideally, the signs in the chart will be divided rather evenly among the three qualities so that the subject has the benefits and the balance of all three different types of attributes.

THE ELEMENTS IN ASTROLOGY

The elements, also called triplicities, divide the twelve signs into four groups. The planets within each group tend to work together in a harmonious way. The elements are divided as follows:

FIRE	EARTH	AIR	WATER
Aries	Taurus	Gemini	Cancer
Leo	Virgo	Libra	Scorpio
Sagittarius	Capricorn	Aquarius	Pisces

THE FIRE SIGNS are dynamic. They are the movers and shakers of any particular group, the ones with the inspirations about what to do and how to do it. Creative and spontaneous, fire signs are the life of the party, since they are ebullient and outgoing, always inventive and fun.

THE EARTH SIGNS are practical, grounded, interested in the physical, temporal, concrete world. They are serious and they take care of details. They build cities and companies and their reputations as well. These are upstanding citizens who like to live comfortably, peacefully, and safely.

THE AIR SIGNS, generally speaking, are the thinkers of the zodiac. They concern themselves with the mental, the intellectual, the sphere of ideas. Because these signs are multifaceted and can adjust to almost any situation, they tend to bring balance and harmony to situations that lack them.

THE WATER SIGNS are sensory, sensual, sensitive, and emotional. They are the antennae of the zodiac, picking up all the vibrations and attempting to bring them together in a harmonious way. The water signs represent psychic abilities and an element of mystery. This group of signs is sympathetic and sharing.

As with the qualities, it's good when the elements in a chart are balanced in number, producing a personality that is well rounded. A predominance of a particular element indicates facility in that realm; a misalignment can mean problems. Combine the characteristics of the qualities with the elements and it becomes clear that, for example:

Aries = Cardinal/Fire = forthright and assertive, energetic

Taurus = Fixed/Earth = organized and persistent, kind

Gemini = Mutable/Air = clever and inventive, versatile

Cancer = Cardinal/Water = patient and compassionate, changeable

Leo = Fixed/Fire = proud and in charge, bossy

Virgo = Mutable/Earth = organized and choosy, exacting

Libra = Cardinal/Air = affectionate and fair, sociable

Scorpio = Fixed/Water = passionate and willful, changeable

Sagittarius = Mutable/Fire = restless and curious, energetic

Capricorn = Cardinal/Earth = solid and steady, ambitious

Aquarius = Fixed/Air = human and humane, seeking

Pisces = Mutable/Water = susceptible and impressionable, kind

THE PLANETS IN ASTROLOGY

The *planets* in astrology rule the signs; that is, each sign is linked to a specific planet and is said to possess the qualities of that planet. For example, Libra is ruled by Venus; therefore, Libra is associated with Venusian characteristics—femininity, beauty, symmetry, and the like. The planets symbolize aspects of each person's personality and how they express themselves, as well as offering a hint about what motivates a person's actions. It can be said that the planets and signs are two faces of the same person, one in profile and one full-front.

Astrology includes the sun and the moon with the planets, since their attributes and powers are so clearly tied to the signs and aspects of the personality.

SUN ☉ rules Leo.

The sun is the conscious mind of man, the expression of one's major purpose in life. It is the ego, the positive side of a person, and it forecasts the way in which a person will go after his goals.

MOON ☽ rules Cancer.

The moon is the unconscious side of the personality. The maternal urges are associated with the moon, as well as the instinct, the emotions, and the heights of the imagination. The moon is the source of growth, memories of our youth, and our moods.

MERCURY ☿ rules Gemini and Virgo.

Mercury represents our ability to apply knowledge to a situation, to express ourselves, to communicate. It is the intellect—the way in which we utilize logic and information to make decisions or create ideas.

VENUS ♀ rules Taurus and Libra.

Venus is attraction—to the arts, the beautiful, to anything aesthetic, or to the aesthetic in anything. It is the planet that most thoroughly concerns itself with harmony and cooperation. It has a feminine connotation and sense of refinement.

MARS ♂ rules Aries.

Mars is energy. The planet, like the god of war for which it was named, represents the external in our personalities, whether we are talking about the daily battles in business or on a personal level. Mars is assertiveness and the impulse to action, our drive in the public world.

JUPITER ♃ rules Sagittarius.
Jupiter is expansion; it is growth, and it symbolizes a sense of public learning and development. Jupiter is the art of garnering sophistication and worldliness, of coming to understand philosophical, spiritual, and religious ideas; it is "higher" education.

SATURN ♄ rules Capricorn.
Saturn denotes limitation and restriction in the astrological chart. It can restrict one's ability to be comfortable with oneself, to develop a behavior that is natural. Saturn is discipline and caution, the sign of the isolationist.

URANUS ♅ rules Aquarius.
Uranus is dynamic and quick. When thinking of Uranus, always stress the quickness and speed, the unexpectedness of events. It represents individuality, unconventionality, eccentricity, pioneering energy, freedom of expression, and intuition. It is the sign of the ugly duckling who finally emerges a swan.

NEPTUNE ♆ rules Pisces.
Neptune is the planet that best represents illusion and receptivity. This ability to reach out and accept usually applies more to feelings or to ideas than to tangible, straightforward actions. It often has to do with spiritualism or mysticism; it can imply confusion, deception.

PLUTO ♇ rules Scorpio.
Pluto is the planet of regeneration, of death and rebirth. It points to areas in which we may be obsessive/compulsive and leads to the realization that some aspects of our lives must change, must be torn down and rebuilt from nothing.

THE BASIC COMPONENTS OF ASTROLOGY

The chart below provides a simple way of seeing the information that has just been discussed. It will help familiarize you with the glyphs for the signs and planets and should give a better understanding of the relationships of the different elements to one another.

NAME	DATE	GLYPH/SYMBOL	QUALITY	ELEMENT	RULER	GLYPH	CHARACTERISTICS
ARIES	3/21–4/19	♈ RAM	CARDINAL	FIRE	MARS	♂	ENTERPRISING, INITIATING
TAURUS	4/20–5/20	♉ BULL	FIXED	EARTH	VENUS	♀	IMPULSIVE, CURIOUS
GEMINI	5/21–6/21	♊ TWINS	MUTABLE	AIR	MERCURY	☿	AMBITIOUS, CALCULATING
CANCER	6/22–7/22	♋ CRAB	CARDINAL	WATER	MOON	☽	HUMANE, COOPERATIVE
LEO	7/23–8/22	♌ LION	FIXED	FIRE	SUN	☉	IMPRESSIONABLE, ARTISTIC
VIRGO	8/23–9/22	♍ VIRGIN	MUTABLE	EARTH	MERCURY		POSSESSIVE, SOLID
LIBRA	9/23–10/23	♎ BALANCE	CARDINAL	AIR	VENUS		CLEVER, VERSATILE
SCORPIO	10/24–11/21	♏ SCORPION	FIXED	WATER	PLUTO	♇	SENSITIVE, NURTURING
SAGITTARIUS	11/22–12/21	♐ ARCHER	MUTABLE	FIRE	JUPITER	♃	POWERFUL, GENEROUS
CAPRICORN	12/22–1/19	♑ GOAT	CARDINAL	EARTH	SATURN	♄	ANALYTICAL, EXACT
AQUARIUS	1/20–2/18	♒ WATER BEARER	FIXED	AIR	URANUS	♅	JUST, SYMNPATHETIC
PISCES	2/19–3/20	♓ FISHES	MUTABLE	WATER	NEPTUNE	♆	INTENSE, PASSIONATE

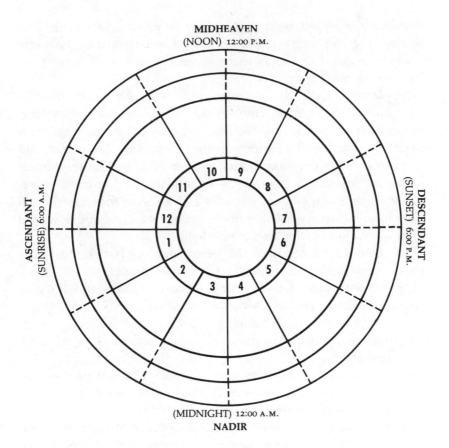

MIDHEAVEN
(NOON) 12:00 P.M.

ASCENDANT
(SUNRISE) 6:00 A.M.

DESCENDANT
(SUNSET) 6:00 P.M.

(MIDNIGHT) 12:00 A.M.
NADIR

THE HOUSES OF THE HOROSCOPE

The wheel used to plot horoscopes is separated into twelve equal wedges, each traversing 30 degrees of the circle. Each of these wedges is called a *house*, and each has a specific meaning in relationship to the whole of the chart. Each house delineates, or defines, the arena of a specific part of the life experience, whether it be childhood, health, business, or philosophy.

As you will see, when the chart is plotted, the planets will be distributed around the wheel, locating themselves in the various houses according to their positions at birth. Sometimes there will be several planets ganged together in a single house or two, while in other charts, they will be spaced fairly evenly around the circle. The meaning of each planet is further enhanced and defined by the house in which it "lands": Venus in the fourth house is different from Venus in the tenth house.

The planets are distributed through the houses based on their location at the time of birth. Think of the horoscope as a twenty-four-hour clock (see illustration). The first house, at the 6 A.M. position of the circle, coincides with sunrise. As the sun moves clockwise around the earth every twenty-four hours, the sun is in each of the houses in turn for about two hours. The twelfth house, therefore, corresponds in time to the hours just after sunrise. As I mentioned, each house has its own special significance in one's life; what follows is a brief explanation of what each house tell us.

The FIRST HOUSE describes the personality, disposition, and appearance and has a major effect on your environment.

The SECOND HOUSE defines your financial prospects and attitudes about possessions, personal security, and ways to make money.

The THIRD HOUSE rules travel, studies, communication, writing, and publishing. It also governs brothers and sisters, close relatives, and neighbors.

The FOURTH HOUSE explains your attitudes about your domestic life, your early life with your family, your home and property decisions, as well as investments in land and buildings.

The FIFTH HOUSE rules love affairs, romance, children, resorts, entertainment, show business, theater, television, movies, speculation, gambling, sports, and all the pleasures of life.

The SIXTH HOUSE has a strong effect on your work, your co-workers, employees, and the type of work you will be attracted to. Food and clothing are strongly affected by this house, as well as commodities for the general public. Work connected to the medical fields and your own health traits are highlighted.

The SEVENTH HOUSE is the house of partnerships, both marriage and business relationships, contracts, papers, and important documents and how you handle them. It indicates great attractions as well as open enemies or rivals.

The EIGHTH HOUSE rules your income, inheritance, legacy, gifts, antiques, heirlooms, and other people's money, especially a partner's money.

The NINTH HOUSE rules travel, long journeys, places far from the birthplace, foreign affairs, international business, education, higher mind studies, religion, philosophy, and your visions of the future.

The TENTH HOUSE rules your career, ambitions, honors, awards, prizes, and other achievements. It indicates fame, the government, your reputation, and worldly standing.

The ELEVENTH HOUSE is associated with your friends and social life, your own personal desires, dreams, hopes, and wishes in life.

The TWELFTH HOUSE defines your enemies, limitations, the way you may do things against yourself, attitudes toward seclusion and solitude, and what goes on in your subconscious mind. It is the house of self-undoing.

The illustration that follows numbers each house and gives a key word or two to help you remember its meaning.

THE ASPECTS

It's worth repeating that the birth chart is a graphic representation of the planetary positions at the moment of birth. An *aspect* is the specific geometric angle formed between two points on a chart, whether between two planets or between a planet and one of the divisions between the houses (called cusps) or with some other important point in the chart. The angle—whether it is just a few degrees, 90 degrees, or 180 degrees—determines the *aspect* between the points. Not all planets will be positioned so that they can be aspected, and that's nothing to worry about. Each individual chart will have different alignments between and among the features in it.

Aspects may be powerful, moderate, or weak, and positive or negative. Like the other elements in the chart, they point out factors that may need attention in everyday life. Five of the most important aspects are explained here.

A CONJUNCTION, indicated by the symbol ☌ , between two planets means that they are basically 0 degrees apart or within just a few degrees of each other. Conjunctions symbolize a joining of forces between the conjunct planets' influences.

An OPPOSITION, indicated by the symbol ☍ , means that the two planets are opposite each other—180 degrees—and manifests a separation of forces, a negative aspect.

A SQUARE, indicated by the symbol □ , is another negative aspect in which one planet is 90 degrees apart from another. The square represents an obstacle.

A TRINE, indicated by the symbol △ , is a positive aspect that occurs when a planet is positioned 120 degrees from another. The trine is an omen of good fortune.

A SEXTILE, symbolized by a ✳ , is created when two planets are 60 degrees apart. It is a sign of opportunity and is a positive influence when it appears in the chart.

LOOKING AT AN ASTROLOGICAL CHART

At one time or another, nearly everyone has seen an astrological chart or a horoscope. But to the uninitiated eye, it is filled with unfamiliar symbols and odd-looking marks that signify nothing that has any customary meaning. The *glyphs,* or picturelike symbols, make up the shorthand that astrologers use to save space and make their work more concise in a visual way.

We have seen the houses distributed around the circle of the chart. In a completed chart, some of the houses will have symbols written in them and others will not. Even without knowing a thing about the meaning of these symbols, we can learn something about the individual.

Take a look again at the illustration on page 371. It shows an "empty" chart—before the planets have been written in their proper places.

The first division of the horoscope that we should take a look at is the horizontal line through the circle; the line that separates houses 1 through 6 from houses 7 through 12. We know that the point on the left where this horizontal line touches the circle (the 6 A.M. position) is called the ascendant, the position of the rising sun at the time of birth. The opposite point (the 6 P.M. position) is called the *descendant* and is the position of the setting sun.

When looking at a chart, if we see that the majority of planets are *above* the horizontal line, we can assume that the person is principally concerned with objectivity or externalizing that which he knows. He will be very outgoing, an extrovert. If the majority of the planets are *below* the line, the person is concerned with subjectivity, introspection, or relating all experience and knowledge to himself in a very personal way. This person will be rather quiet and may seem shy, an introvert.

The next major division to look at is the line dividing the circle vertically. The top point (at the noon position) is called the midheaven and is the place of the sun at noon on the day you were born. The bottom point is called the nadir and is the midnight position of the sun.

In the second division, we learn that when the majority of the planets are to the *left* of the vertical line, the person has greater free will and independence and has a great deal of control over his own destiny. If the reverse is true and the majority of planets are to the *right*, the person is somewhat limited or dependent upon circumstances or the actions of others.

When we take a look at an actual chart, keep these simple facts in mind. It's surprising how much we can know just by looking at the overall picture of a chart.

CALCULATING THE ASTROLOGICAL CHART

Though it is possible for an amateur to cast his own chart, frankly I do not recommend the self-cast horoscope—especially if the person calculating it is a novice. So many factors must be considered that even experienced professionals double-check themselves to be sure their calculations are accurate. My best advice is to have a professional do your chart, or go to one of the computer services that can cast the chart. A professional astrologer uses the ephemeris, a book of astronomical tables that lists the position of the planets on a day-to-day basis as they move through the heavens, but it takes practice to familiarize yourself with the information and how to use it. Avoid any temptation to save time, trouble, or money by buying a so-called quick method for casting your chart. There are too many pitfalls for the amateur: the exact longitude and latitude of the birthplace must be established; but, even more tricky, the birth time must be converted to sidereal (star) time, taking into consideration such factors as Greenwich Mean Time, Daylight Savings Time, and even War Time (if you go back that far). Leave the calculation to the experts and their computers. The challenge of astrology is not in casting the horoscope but in its interpretation.

The precision of the few facts you must provide to the astrologer or computer service is crucial: the geographical location of birth, and the year, month, day, and *exact time* of birth—to the minute, if possible. If the precise birth time does not appear on your birth certificate, it is worth the effort to try to track it down by consulting hospital records or calling upon the memories of those who were present at the birth—the mother, doctor, or other relatives. If determining the exact time is impossible, a professional astrologer may be able to "rectify" the time of birth—a painstaking, time-consuming process through which the astrologer must "discover," using the specifics of your past, the actual time of birth.

GLYPHS

SIGNS   PLANETS

♈	Aries	♎	Libra	⊙	Sun	♃	Jupiter
♉	Taurus	♏	Scorpio	☽	Moon	♄	Saturn
♊	Gemini	♐	Sagittarius	☿	Mercury	♅	Uranus
♋	Cancer	♑	Capricorn	♀	Venus	♆	Neptune
♌	Leo	♒	Aquarius	♂	Mars	♇	Pluto
♍	Virgo	♓	Pisces				

INTERPRETING THE HOROSCOPE

When, finally, your very own completed astrological chart is in front of you, it will look something akin to the one below, which was calculated for March 24, 1947, at 10:46 P.M., in New York City.

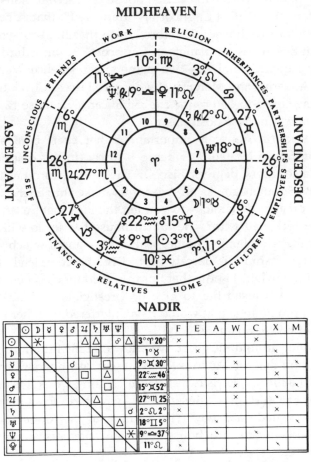

F·FIRE   E·EARTH   A·AIR   W·WATER   C·CARDINAL   X·FIXED   M·MUTABLE

Now you may be completely confused. Look at the chart. What we *do* know about the chart is based on the signs, planets, houses, and aspects. We know that this person—Susan—is an Aries, a cardinal fire sign. We can be sure that the ascendant (sitting on the cusp of the first house) is 26 degrees Scorpio, and we can check the charts on pages 366 and 369 to see what that means. We know that the mid-heaven (the point at the very top of the chart, in the position of noon) is Virgo and that the second, sixth, eleventh, and twelfth houses are empty.

We can see that the first house is ruled by Scorpio (the rising sign) and that Jupiter, the largest planet of them all, is in this house. Check the list of planets on pages 365–67 and the list of the meanings of the houses on pages 369–71 to determine what significance there is to having Jupiter in Scorpio in the first house. The second house is ruled by Sagittarius, and all of Capricorn is "transitted," that is, completely contained, in that house; therefore, since that house is empty, we learn that Susan has no planets in Capricorn. Susan's third house is ruled by Aquarius and has two planets in residence: Venus at 22 degrees Aquarius and Mercury at 9 degrees Pisces. Check the planet and house charts to determine the significance of these two planets being situated in these positions.

Susan's fourth house is important in her chart because this is where her Sun is located, at 3 degrees Aries. (In this case, her Mars is there also, at 15 degrees Pisces). The Sun, a cardinal fire sign, represents Susan's ego. As an Aries, that makes her energetic, forceful, enterprising, dynamic—do you get the idea that Susan is someone to be reckoned with? The fourth house has to do with Susan's domestic life—her family, home, real estate—about which Susan, in typical Aries fashion, is fiercely protective and completely devoted. Because I know her, I know that Susan's need for closeness to family and home has caused her to give up prestigious and lucrative job offers and promotions that would have interfered with her nonworking time at home. So far, so good.

Continuing around the chart, we know that the fifth house is ruled by Aries, and that the Moon is located there, at 1 degree Taurus. The Moon in the fifth house is especially interesting when it is applied to Susan. At age thirty-nine, Susan finally gave birth to a long-awaited, much anticipated baby boy. The location of the Moon (nurturing, motherhood) in the fifth house (children and pets and pleasures) makes sense.

Both the sixth and seventh houses in this chart are ruled by Taurus, though the seventh is home to Uranus at 18 degrees Gemini as well. The eighth house, ruled by Gemini, wholly contains the transitted sign of Cancer. And in the eighth house, we discover what is a new element to us. In this house, the planet Saturn is retrograde at 2 degrees Leo. *Retrograde* denotes the *apparent* backward motion of a planet; the planet does not actually move backward; it merely appears to do so as seen by the human eye because of a decrease in longitude when viewed from Earth. Interpreting the meaning of a retrograde planet in your chart is difficult; some astrologers think that retrograde turns positive influences into negatives, others think it has no real effect at all, and still others think it has some effect only when the planet again goes *direct* (when the apparent motion would reverse and move in the expected direction).

The ninth house in Susan's chart is ruled by Leo and contains Pluto at 11 degrees Leo. See if you can decide what significance that has for the chart. The cusp of the tenth house, the location of the mid-heaven, is ruled by Virgo. This house features Neptune retrograde at 9 degrees Libra. I would have to consult a professional to get an idea of just what that means. The eleventh house is ruled by Libra and the twelfth by Scorpio.

Look now at the boxed information beneath the chart. This is a guide to the aspects in Susan's chart. It shows us that she has two conjunctions: between Mars and Mercury and between Saturn and Pluto; six trines: between the Sun and Jupiter, Saturn and Pluto, between Venus and Uranus, between Jupiter and Saturn, and between Uranus and Neptune; four squares: between the Moon and Saturn, Mercury and Uranus, Venus and Jupiter, and Mars and Uranus; two sextiles: between the Sun and the Moon and Neptune and Pluto; and one opposition: between the Sun and Neptune. What does this all mean? Take them one at a time: Mars conjunct Mercury would combine Susan's intellectual and communicative skills (Mercury) with her considerable drive (Mars). This bodes well for her if she wants to go into politics, work as an anchorperson, or become a lecturer. There's no question about it, though; only the most astute student of astrology could possibly synthesize all this information or have the slightest idea of what is going on among all these aspects and planets and signs. No one said astrology would be easy; there are so many factors to consider. Clearly it's time to call in an expert —a professional astrologer. But first let's have a quick look at the newcomer on the astrological horizon: Chinese astrology.

THE CHINESE ZODIAC

One of the newest trends is combining Eastern and Western astrology. In this manner, a person may be a Virgo/Rat who differs greatly from a Virgo/Monkey and certainly from a Capricorn/Rat. It is the combination of the two types of astrology and of the descriptive qualities of each that enhances the reading of an individual's chart. It's easy to see how the possibilities increase. Effectively, each Western astrological sign can be interpreted in twelve more ways—one for each of the twelve animals of the Chinese horoscope.

A fairly recent book on the combining of Western and Eastern astrology, *The New Astrology,* by Suzanne White, is a wonderful, instructive introduction to combining the two astrological systems. In it, White offers 144 complete personalized character readings—one for each Western/Eastern sign combination. If the idea of combining appeals to you, be sure to take a look at White's book; she has done an excellent job of synthesizing the two disciplines. Also, the entire inside of the book jacket is a huge chart that shows your compatibility with other dual sign combinations

To call the Chinese system astrology is in a way a misnomer. Unlike Western astrology, it is based on animals of the earth rather than on the planets and stars of the sky. In fact, instead of dealing with the sky at all, the animals in Chinese astrology are said to make a ring around the equator rather than across the heavens. The animals are known as the Earth Branches, and, like Western signs, each animal has been assigned an element (the Chinese use five elements—wood, fire, earth, metal or gold, and water) and a magnetic pole, that is, a positive or negative force. In addition, the Chinese use their own lunar calendar, which dates from before 2500 B.C., and it differs greatly from ours in that each cycle is sixty years long, divided into five twelve-year segments. An animal is assigned to each of the twelve years in each segment and, therefore, each animal sign occurs only once every twelve years.

Regardless of what status they might hold in the modern American way of thinking, all the animals of the Chinese zodiac are revered in that culture. All of them are honorable animals, so don't be put off if you find that you are a pig or a snake; the connotations aren't comparable from culture to culture.

In comparison to the Western zodiac, determining your sign by the Chinese method is extremely easy. Your sign is based on the year of your birth—no complex calculations here. Only those born between mid-January and mid-February need to be careful in determining their sign (this is the time of Chinese New Year and the beginning date of the New Year differs from year to year). If you were born during this changeover period, look in a book about Chinese astrology to get the specific beginning date for each year.

The signs of the Chinese zodiac change in sequence over a twelve-year period, moving through the year of the rat, ox, tiger, cat or rabbit, dragon, snake, horse, goat or sheep, monkey, rooster or chicken, dog, and pig or boar. Look at the chart that follows to determine your sign.

RAT	1900	1912	1924	1936	1948	1960	1972	1984	1996
OX	1901	1913	1925	1937	1949	1961	1973	1985	1997
TIGER	1902	1914	1926	1938	1950	1962	1974	1986	1998
CAT (or Rabbit)	1903	1915	1927	1939	1951	1963	1975	1987	1999
DRAGON	1904	1916	1928	1940	1952	1964	1976	1988	2000
SNAKE	1905	1917	1929	1941	1953	1965	1977	1989	
HORSE	1906	1918	1930	1942	1954	1966	1978	1990	
GOAT (or Sheep)	1907	1919	1931	1943	1955	1967	1979	1991	
MONKEY	1908	1920	1932	1944	1956	1968	1980	1992	
ROOSTER (or Chicken)	1909	1921	1933	1945	1957	1969	1981	1993	
DOG	1910	1922	1934	1946	1958	1970	1982	1994	
PIG (or Boar)	1911	1923	1935	1947	1959	1971	1983	1995	

A brief description of each animal sign's personality and traits can give you an idea of what Chinese astrology is all about.

RAT—The rat is a social animal who is charming and outgoing. He usually knows the "right" people and is intellectually stimulating.

On the downside, however, he can be an uptight, power-hungry pest who should be avoided at any cost.

OX—The ox, like the animal this sign is named for, is a solid citizen who works hard to get ahead. And usually he succeeds. In public, the ox is strong, reserved but friendly, and perhaps somewhat imposing. Negatively, just try to get the ox to move if he doesn't want to. Good luck; this animal is determined to get what he wants, and he will succeed.

TIGER—The tiger likes to move around at will, openly, freely, unfettered by the demands of anyone else. He thinks that only his opinions count, no matter how bizarre or conventional they may be, and he is not very tolerant of what others think about anything. At his worst, the tiger is the typical rebel; he may be drunk and disorderly, obstinate, or just plain ornery, but this is the side of the tiger that isn't too pretty or pleasant.

CAT OR RABBIT—Cats are the ever-so-elegant sign of the Chinese zodiac, unerringly sensing what is the best of any bunch. The cat is knowledgeable about the arts, music, literature, design—whatever has aesthetic qualities that are pleasing to the senses. When the cat is naughty, it can be picky, childish, unnecessarily mysterious, and precocious.

DRAGON—The dragon is the king of Chinese beasts, always self-assured, always successful, good-looking, charming, and bright. It's hard to keep this good man down. This is the born winner—best of class, best of show. When he's bad, he's boringly intolerable—who wants to hear how wonderful he thinks he is anyway?

SNAKE—Snakes are wonderful people—honestly helpful and considerate. They are best when they can be of help to friends. Their advice is well thought out and personalized, if you will, not rehashed pop wisdom they read in a magazine somewhere. The negative side of the snake is not so bad, with one exception: You've never met a lazier person in your life, and if you're a true friend, you'll have to help your snake pal fight that do-nothing streak.

HORSE—The horse is the original rebel who grows up to become an inventor. Chances are the invention will not be another handy take-off on something that already exists; nope, the horse creates an industry where one never existed before. He is quick and clever, handy and interested in many subjects. He can be nervous, selfish, and downright mean when things aren't going his way.

GOAT OR SHEEP—The goat is a born loner. He works hard and is perfectly content to work nonstop when there's nothing that he needs to bother with. The goat would make the best computer "hacker"—totally involved, very good at what he does, and oblivious of anything else in the world. In bad times, the goat can worry himself to death or become a child who must be coddled and cajoled into a quick return to adulthood.

MONKEY—The monkey is like a monkey—cute, funny, agile, quick, and charming. Everybody likes them, and why not? They make great friends, great guests, great bosses, and great children. The problem is, sometimes they *are* children. When they're bad, they can be exasperating—mischievous, naughty, and silly—to a fault.

ROOSTER OR CHICKEN—Roosters like to crow about themselves. Sometimes you'll find one who's a tad too boisterous, but generally, they just like to tell the world what they like, what they've done, and what the world should do. The rooster is on top of everything that's current. He knows the best restaurants, stores, vacations, barbers, and tailors. And usually he's right. Negatively, the rooster's boasting will drive you crazy.

DOG—The dog is a warm, caring person who really likes to help others. He will work hard and be there for the crises; just be sure to thank him or pet his head from time to time to make him know he's needed. The dog follows up on things that bother him and might sometimes complain a bit too much, but his instincts are right and good; he means well. Don't let him get too critical about himself or others; say something to raise his self-confidence.

PIG OR BOAR—The pig is kind and straightforward, always looking for a way to better himself and increase his knowledge. He is especially hungry for the new experience. In addition, the pig is, well, always hungry. He loves to eat—especially *good* food—and he likes to eat with other people. The pig is happy around others and he'll stay that way until something makes him angry. And when a pig is angry, watch out! His temper is ferocious, and there will be nothing you can do about it. Only time will help.

THE PROFESSIONAL ASTROLOGER

A professional astrologer can cast your chart for you, making sure that all the calculations are correct and that any of the odd details about time changes and the like have been taken into consideration. Having prepared the birth chart, he or she can interpret it for you and can tell you about your life now and forecast upcoming events by comparing your birth chart with the placement of the planets today and in the near future. The astrologer will be able to see the placements at your birth and compare them to the experiences of everyday life. It is this interpretive work that takes time and study, practice and experience. There is no single book or text or teacher that can be read or studied or followed exclusively. Indeed, hundreds of good books have been written on the subject, but there is nothing like a personal interpretation to start you off and make you more familiar with the language of astrology. It is the synthesis of the many factors of the horoscope that makes astrological interpretation so difficult and also so fascinating. (Keep in mind that this brief chapter has only scratched the surface: There are many more considerations, from quincunxes to the moon's nodes, that haven't even been mentioned here.)

Generally, after making an appointment with an astrologer, you, the client, should have ample opportunity to decide what it is you would like to pursue in the reading. Write down all your questions and take them with you—the astrologer will welcome your preparedness. If you intend to ask multitudes of questions about your chart in relation to someone else's, be sure to have the data you will need so that the astrologer can intelligently compare your chart with the other person's. If you are skeptical about astrology, tell the astrologer so that he can present the material to you in a way that helps you understand. By all means, ask questions. This is your session; do not expect the astrologer to read your mind. If you are concerned about money, ask about money. If your career is cause for concern, ask for advice. If you think you'd like to move to Nova Scotia, check it out.

Before you arrive for your appointment, your astrologer will have prepared your chart and studied it (most astrologers prefer to cast the chart for themselves—some have their own computers—rather than take a chance that someone may have erred in calculating any existing chart you might have). The professional astrologer will begin his or her interpretation, usually first telling you things about your life in general and then moving into more specific territory. One friend of mine was amazed that on the first visit, her astrologer was able to pinpoint major life events that the astrologer could never have known about to specific two-week periods that occurred twenty years before they met. In other words, don't be surprised by what your astrologer knows about you.

Let your first session flow naturally through your list of questions, dwelling first on priorities and moving into less important territory if there is time. Most sessions last from ninety minutes to two hours, and you'll be quite surprised at how quickly the time goes by. Expect to pay anywhere from about $50 to $125 for a reading, though famous astrologers may charge as much as $500. Some astrologers charge by the hour and others by the reading or consultation. After your first session, generally you can expect to be given a copy of your chart to take home with you; not all astrologers do that, however. Virtually all astrologers do tape-record their sessions with you so that you have an audio record of what transpired. If, by chance, your astrologer does not provide this service, ask if you may bring a recorder; having a record of the conversation is extremely valuable weeks or months after the fact, when memory fades considerably.

WHERE TO GO FROM HERE

If your curiosity has been piqued by astrology, there's no time like the present to delve into it. Books are an excellent, if passive, way to study astrology; indeed, you'll have to do some reading. There are a multitude of books on the subject; several for the novice and many, many excellent ones that deal only with specific aspects of astrology. A good way to get a more active start might be to have your chart done by a professional. Or you might even want to go to *several* astrologers to see which ones you prefer to others and why. You might inquire about whether they teach classes or if they can guide you to someone who does. I think you'll find that most astrologers truly are help-oriented. They want to lead you, if possible, to the information you seek.

Depending on where you live, finding a professional astrologer may or may not be difficult. The American Federation of Astrologers offers a list of certified astrologers and will send it upon request. But by far the most common way to find an astrologer is through word of mouth. You need to talk with people who have found an astrologer they like and then ask them for a referral, just as you would with a new dentist, lawyer, or baby-sitter. Nearly every astrologer I interviewed said that the bulk of his or her clients came via other clients. Remember, many astrologers "specialize"—some lean toward psychological interpretations; others like to advise on money matters.

If you are reading an astrological publication and find an author you particularly admire, write to the astrologer in care of the publication. Astrologers sometimes travel outside their home base and could see you if they are in your area; others will be perfectly content to talk to you via tape or telephone. Only a few astrologers think it is vital to see their subjects in person, though many do prefer it that way, on a strictly human level.

What's vital to the pursuit of astrology is that you do it—as often as you can, with or without a professional astrologer. Learn to cast charts and do lots of them, for all your friends and family. Choose a specific part of astrology and become an expert on it before you move on to your next specialty. In time, you'll see all the pieces begin to fall in place and you'll wonder what you ever found confusing about it. So many other specific areas are of interest: You'll want to find out about transits (where the planets are today as compared to where they were at the time of your birth), to compare your chart to someone else's, to do a chart for a business or house you're building, about the Age of Aquarius and what that means, about the moon's nodes, returns, malefics, harmonics, and scores of other individual aspects of astrology.

For more information about astrology, you might want to contact one of the following groups: The American Federation of Astrologers, Inc., P.O. Box 22040, Tempe, AZ 85282; The Astrological Association of Great Britain, BM Astrology, London WC1 N3X, England; The Faculty of Astrological Studies, Hook Cottage, Vines Cross, Heathfield, Sussex TN21 9EN, England; and The International Society for Astrological Research, P.O. Box 6874, Los Angeles, CA 90504. Also see page 570 for a list of astrology texts.

CHAPTER
FOURTEEN
NUMEROLOGY

It's clear that we all have some unconscious understanding or feeling for numbers and that we assign them significance throughout our life experiences. Think about what made your "lucky number" become so special to you, or about the way certain numbers seem to recur constantly in your life. How do they influence you? A number that you "live with" for years—a telephone number, an address, your Social Security number—may come to have some relevance for you. Some people won't live on the thirteenth floor of a building; indeed, some building and hotel owners know better than to assign a number to what is, in reality, the thirteenth floor of their building —the elevators stop at twelve and at the floor above: fourteen. In our culture, the number thirteen is considered bad luck: we even have a word for it, triskaidekaphobia. (In the study of tarot, the number thirteen relates to the Death card.)

Whole cultures have feelings about certain numbers. In Malaysia, the number seven is especially meaningful: The day is divided into seven parts, each marked by one of the Seven Ominous Moments (a system used in divination). An argument can be made for the significance of the number five in Java and Bali and the number seven in China. Ask any gambler in Las Vegas, Atlantic City, or Monte Carlo if he has a number; the answer will be a resounding yes—and he will have his own very logical reason for his choice.

Numbers are the tool of choice for the numerologist. Much as an astrologer uses the position of the planets at the time of your birth as the basis for analysis of character and to forecast your future, numerologists use calculations based on the numerological values of your name and birth date. How can numbers have any predictive value? How can they reveal character? Numbers, say the adepts, have accumulated meanings in the collective unconscious to which we unknowingly respond. Our name, our birth date, is an intrinsic part of our makeup; we are under its influence. We also build personal associations to numbers throughout our lives, which add to the universal associations another layer of significance.

Many adepts claim that numerology is not actually the study of numbers so much as it is the study of the *symbols* for the numbers and their cultural and psychological significance, both conscious and unconscious, symbolic and literal. Thus, to understand the meaning of a number—say, three—it is necessary to understand the triangle, the trinity, the concept of threeness. Stephen Calia, a New York City numerology professional, advises his clients to "use what's implied behind the meaning of the number or the symbol for the number. For example, the number five relates to the five senses. The number four implies a box, a square, and that will have different meanings for different people. The number two connotes duplicity, two-faced people, liars; alternatively, it can imply coupling or cooperation, or the alternate faces of actors' masks. It is necessary to take a symbol and use it in your own language. When I look at numbers, they are pictures to me."

In 1986, a front-page article in *The New York Times* reported on the powerful influence of numerology in Japan, where a lunar-year cycle consists of periods of six lucky days, followed by six unlucky days, and six in-between days. It is often pointed out that the attack on Pearl Harbor took place on the unluckiest day of all, *butsu metsu*. The twenty-fifth and forty-second years are felt to be unlucky for men; the nineteenth and thirty-third for women. When naming children, parents count the brush strokes required to write the characters to be sure they don't add up to an unlucky number.

If you ask professional numerologists what got them interested in the subject, you frequently find that they were doubtful initially but, as Stephen Calia says, "experiencing the numbers and learning what they mean was an inspiration." Ellin Dodge, a leading American numerologist, has been practicing her craft for seventeen years. When she started, she was "ex-director of Silva Mind Control in New York City. I'm a New Yorker. I never believed that just having faith in something could make it come true. To me, if it wasn't tangible— if I couldn't taste it or feel it or smell it or spend it, it wasn't real. . . . I chose numerology because it's the nearest thing to bookkeeping I can find—it balances, it makes sense, it's very direct." She continues, "I think that astrology is absolutely fabulous, and it's numerology's sister science, but I prefer to be able to predict each hour in a day, and I can do that in numerology."

She explains how she went about learning numerology. "There aren't too many teachers around. I started with books—in particular, a book written by Florence Campbell called *Your Days Are Numbered*, which, by the way, I think is the Bible of numerology. I just read it and reread it and reread it again, and then I started to work. I started to read for people and started to get—my goodness, I got reinforcement—the things I would say—they were happening, they were coming true. . . . I don't understand why numerology works; it really doesn't make sense, and I will probably spend the rest of my life trying to find out why it works."

Several people have spent their lives trying to figure out more about numerology and how it works. In the late nineteenth century, Wilhelm Fliess, a surgeon in Berlin and for almost ten years one of Freud's best and closest friends, spent much of his time and energy informing medical and scientific experts of his theories about the numbers 23 and 28. Through extraordinary machinations that employed these two numbers, Fliess found it possible to explain almost any aspect of the physical world: these twenty-three- and twenty-eight-day cycles explained it all. And for a while, at least, Freud, apparently, was one of his biggest fans. In time, though, even Freud's belief wavered in light of Fliess's increasing fanaticism and of other, opposing evidence.

It would seem that every numerologist has his or her own system. Some use only the first name or the name that the client prefers, completely discarding the widely accepted Pythagorean theory that you are the name (and, therefore, number) you were born with. Prince Hirindra Singh, a numerologist for twenty-five years, has developed his own unique system. He maintains that "the only numerology system that can predict the past, present, and future is the date, month, and year of birth. . . . Name numerology is brilliant in its analysis of character of an individual, but when it comes to predicting the future, name numerology cannot do that." Don't think he merely uses the date of birth; Singh proceeds to break the day into nine sectors and assign times to them. But, for his own purposes, he doesn't take the name into consideration at all.

Singh is very much interested in predictive numerology. His sister is one of the top Supreme Court lawyers in India and he consults with her from time to time. In 1981, Singh predicted that Prime Minister Indira Gandhi "would not survive 1984 and that she would be shot. But the numerology could not say whether it was a heart attack, which is considered to be a shot in numerology, or was it a bullet?" He narrowed down his answers to his sister's queries to predict that Indira Gandhi would "be shot within nine months from June, 1984, and she will be shot dead." When pressed, he narrowed that time down to "October, November, or December, but definitely before March, 1985. It appears psychically that it will be before 1984 ends." If you remember, Indira Gandhi was shot and killed on October 31, 1984.

Ellin Dodge says she is able "to pinpoint—just simply by doing a chart—the excessiveness and compulsiveness in a person's nature." However, she adds that her job is something altogether different: "I'm not out to tell my clients what's going to happen tomorrow. I'm out to tell them how to get the most out of the experience; it's up to them what they do with the experience—I can't be a button on their coat that tells them exactly how to handle it." She can, however, help guide the way. Dodge's clients include TV entertainment reporter Rona Barrett, architectural designer Sam Botero, Rita Hayworth's daughter Yasmin Khan, as well as actress Lindsay Crouse and her husband, David Mamet. She continues, "I picked the day that David Mamet's play, *Glengarry Glen Ross* would open, and before David won the Pulitzer Prize for it, I said, 'You're going to win a big prize, David.' And he did. I also named their baby, Willa. I told the man who was West Coast distributor for Häagen-Dazs ice cream that he was going to sell out at a good profit. He sold for $11 million at a time when he didn't think anything like that was going to happen at all."

A number can be calculated for almost everything in the world. In fact, one person can have many numbers—one for his or her given name (Elizabeth Smith), one for the shortened name (Liza Smith), one for the nickname (Sissy Smith), one that uses a woman's maiden name as her middle name after marriage (Elizabeth Smith Jones), one for her former middle name and new last name, and so on and on. Each of the numbers calculated for each of the different names emphasizes a different aspect of the person, a different layer or mask. The numerical value of each name is interesting when considered in the context in which it is used. Does the number for a nickname describe the way a person acts around old friends and family? Does the meaning for the number of one's formal legal name vary wildly from the way the person behaves when relaxing at the beach but fit quite well when he or she is talking to the IRS man? Does "Junior" act differently with his family than when he is Osgood during the work week, and does that behavior correspond to the respective number? All this discussion does not even include considerations of aliases, *noms de plume,* or stage names.

Many people choose to change their names or adjust the spelling of their names in order to attain a different, more advantageous set of personal numbers. They might choose a number that will help emphasize a specific talent they wish to develop. For example, someone who wants to become a successful actor might want to adjust his name or create a new name that emphasizes the number 2 or 9. Both include leanings toward dramatic abilities. If a designer didn't like his name, he might choose a name that calculates into a number 6 or even a number 1. Think of your friends' real given names. It would seem that we live in a society that takes great freedom with our labels —perhaps because we are named by others, not by ourselves. One friend claims that she feels weak when she has to be Marcia (her given name) but full of energy when she goes by her nickname, Marty.

Sometimes important numbers are missing from our names. Numerologist Stephen Calia says that his actual given name is Steven, spelled with a *v*, not the *ph* he now uses. He changed the spelling of his name to "fill in a number gap," that is, to add the qualities of a number that was previously missing from his "chart." These *karmic numbers*, those that are missing in your name, are important in rounding out and balancing a person. When the lack of a particular number's influence is actually felt, it's worth taking steps to remedy the problem. The late television personality Guy Lombardo is reported to have won many speedboat races *after* he changed the name of his boat—on his numerologist's advice.

Indeed, many numerologists advise clients on potential personal name changes, company names, and the like. There really is no end to what can be studied through numerology. Your street address, telephone number, zip code, even the city you live in has a number assigned to it. You can glean knowledge from looking at the numbers that surround your life and comparing them to your own name and birth numbers, remembering always to consider their meanings in the proper context.

A BRIEF HISTORY OF NUMEROLOGY

Numerology has been around for a long time. Some experts date its beginnings to the creation of the first alphabet, others to the ancient Hindu culture. Certainly every civilization that constructed an alphabet or a written language might well have contributed to the evolution of numerology, but it is the history of written numbers that is most important. Ellin Dodge claims that Jean M. Auel, best-selling author of *The Clan of the Cave Bear*, *The Valley of Horses*, and *The Mammoth Hunters*, a trio of books about early man's coming to terms with the elements, "has given me documentation for the fact that the cave people had symbols for the cumulative values. In other words, let's say a caveman built a fire with four sticks, and it was a good fire —it was a solid fire that burned for a long time. So the caveman then identified the number 4 with something solid and foundational that one could depend upon. The number 4, or the symbol for number 4, had another value now. Now it became 4, meaning also a constructive foundation, a solid, practical thing."

Unquestionably, numerology's hero is the ancient Greek philosopher and mathematician Pythagoras, who established his school in about 632 B.C. Here he proclaimed his mathematical theories while training his students in astronomy, music, mathematics, philosophy, and numerology. Pythagoras originated the Science of Numbers, his belief that numbers offer the key to understanding everything in the universe; and he established the system of tying the symbolism of each of the numbers 1 through 9 to a particular phase of the life experience. Thus the number 1 became linked to the idea of origin or God, 2 to marriage or companions, 3 to trinity or wisdom, 4 to solidity, and so forth. Pythagorean doctrine was based on the idea that the entire universe vibrates at a specific rate and that each individual has a personal vibration rate as well. How the personal rate relates to the universal rate accounts for the differences among people.

LEARNING NUMEROLOGY

Of all the predictive arts, numerology probably is the most accessible to the layperson and the easiest to try on a rudimentary level. All you need is pen and paper, an elementary knowledge of arithmetic, and your date of birth and given name.

Stephen Calia has given me permission to share his methods in this book. This brief course, part of what Calia teaches to his beginning students, will make it easy to calculate and understand your four personal numbers; your personal day, week, and month numbers; and your peak point and action points. Keep in mind that each number and its interpretation should be considered in context, and its interpretation will be colored by its importance in your life. For example, your birth force number should have more impact on you than the number you determine for, say, the address you lived at for the first twenty years of your life. The birth force number would affect life decisions—who or when to marry, where to live, what job to take—whereas your address number might denote a favorable or lucky location (if your childhood was a happy one) or a number that represents strife, confusion, and hurt (if your childhood was unhappy). A 3 as your birth force number might mean that you are the happy optimist who seeks to enjoy life to the fullest. A 3 as your soul number, however, means that you seek a joyful life, though you may not have it at the moment. Take care that you don't assign more importance to a number than it deserves; don't apply too much significance to relatively minor numbers in your life.

THE MEANING OF THE NUMBERS

For the beginning student of numerology, only thirteen numbers are of primary significance. All other numbers are reduced to one of these simple numbers. The numbers that matter are 1 through 9 and what are called the master numbers: 11, 22, 33, and 44.

The interpretations that follow indicate the descriptions and qualities of the individual numbers. Depending on which of your personal numbers it fits, the meaning should be applied to suit that category of considerations. For example, the way someone *acts* (his personality number) does not necessarily bespeak the way he *feels* (the soul number). Always apply the interpretation of the number within the correct context.

Also, pay attention to the shapes and design of the numbers themselves. Try to understand how they came to look the way they do and see if you can get an impression of their spiritual and psychological significance. Look at the representational drawings Calia uses in his readings to determine what they mean to you. Try your best to "get inside the numbers"—let them talk to you.

1. *The key word here is* WILL. A number 1 person will be an innovator who is unique and forceful, with strong focus. He will be a pioneer who is willing to set out alone for uncharted territory, looking for new beginnings and new ways of being independent and individualistic. He is a good leader who can inspire trust and loyalty while making rapid decisions that are well based on logic. At his worst, the number 1 can be pushy, narrow-minded, and self-absorbed. He may behave with an air of superiority and have a tendency to isolate himself.

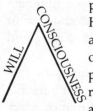

2. *The key word here is* COOPERATION. A number 2 person will be the reasoning force in any situation. He is the one who will see both sides of an argument and will be able to explain the situation calmly to overheated parties. He will be group-oriented, a person who looks for and enjoys partnerships, who relishes working out things with people. He may be a counselor of some type, or he might display some amount of acting ability. At his worst, the number 2 can be duplicitous, shy, self-conscious, and reclusive. He might avoid groups or relationships of all kinds or be tense when forced to deal with them.

UNIVERSAL LOVE
COMPASSION
WISDOM

3. *The key word here is* JOY. The number 3 person has fun and wants others to have fun, too. He enjoys life and lets all the bad roll off his back. This person is dynamic, imaginative, and lucky—perhaps the most well-rounded personality of them all. At his worst, the number 3 can be all talk and no action. Or the balance of this fun sign can be off kilter so as to make the individual overly introverted or overly extroverted.

4. The key word here is FOUNDATION. The number 4 person is hardworking, dedicated, sometimes overly serious. He needs stability so desperately that nothing else matters as much. His goal is solidity at any cost. The powers of concentration here are enhanced, and the number 4 will be efficient, organized, and creative in a very down-to-earth way. This person is goal-oriented in that he prefers a job that has a beginning, a middle, and an end, rather than work that is more or less ongoing. At his worst, this person is dour, fixed, inflexible, and very slow to change. There is a tendency to box oneself in by setting too many limits, or by having too many limits imposed.

SELF-
CONSCIOUSNESS

4

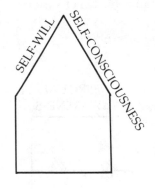

5

5. The key words here are EMOTIONAL PROGRESS. The number 5 person is an independent traveler who loves his freedom. The number 5 will likely be sexually attractive, loving, and able to express anger in a healthy way. This person has self-doubts and fears but is successfully striving to conquer them —and he will. He is a good decision-maker who is interested in growth and almost constantly on the move. This person learns through hands-on experience rather than through study or logic. At his worst, the number 5 can be indecisive, overly self-indulgent, hot-tempered, dissatisfied, and generally, no fun at all to be around.

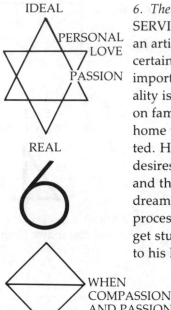

IDEAL

PERSONAL LOVE

PASSION

REAL

WHEN COMPASSION AND PASSION ARE ONE

6. *The key words here are* HUMANITARIAN SERVICE. The number 6 person may be an artist or may perform his work with a certain type of artistry. The home is important to a number 6, since this personality is a nurturing one that likes to focus on family and career. He is unselfish, at home with himself, and relationship-oriented. He finds it easy to empathize and desires to balance the problems of people and the world. He strives to make his dreams real and to learn about the creative process. At his worst, the number 6 can get stuck in a home or career that is not to his liking, or he may spend all of his energy on others, to the exclusion of his own needs. Behavior can be obstinate because his belief systems are fixed.

7. *The key word here is* STUDY. The number 7 person is very cerebral, both intellectually and intuitively. He is very interested in introspection, meditation, and the search for perfection. This is the soul who needs to get away from society, to get back to nature, to think in the forest or on a mountaintop. Number 7s need to specialize in something in order to succeed financially. They need to know everything there is about a subject, and they will drive themselves unmercifully to attain that goal and be "the best." At his worst, the number 7 can be secretive, gossipy, overly analytical, or cynical. Their desire to be the best can get the best of them, causing low energy and sometimes even illness, the function of which is to slow them down so that they can listen to their wisdom. This is the person who thinks he can accomplish superhuman tasks in a single day. Seven is the number of safety and of occult intelligence in the Kabala. The

SPIRITUAL AWARENESS

person whose number is 7 *must* regularly get "in touch" with his needs and listen to the inner self.

8. *The key words here are* ETHICAL LEADER-
SHIP. The number 8 person will be responsible, powerful, and an excellent leader and/or
teacher. He might preside over a company or
corporation, where his strength and leadership
can be noticed and rewarded. Finances are important to the number 8, as is authority. The
number 8 needs close personal ties in his family life and strong professional bonds at work.
At his worst, the number 8 can be overly demanding and boisterous—a person who loves
to toot his own horn.

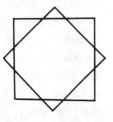

SELF-AWARENESS

He may be irresponsible, may steal or cheat or
in some way repress others. He will want the
job done his way or not at all.

HIGHER SELF

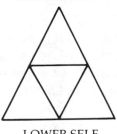

LOWER SELF

9. *The key word here is* IDEALISM. The
number 9 person is a born teacher,
guru, or leader of some kind. He is
concerned with humanitarian causes, is
compassionate and loving. Many leaders
in the arts and sciences are number 9s
and frequently dramatic ability is considerable. These people seem to have the
qualities of a sage; they understand the
oneness of all, the larger perspective. In
fact, they need to understand the big
picture in order to do their small part:
They cannot perform an isolated task on
an assembly line unless they understand
every step in the process. At his worst, the number 9 is too sentim-
ental, never knowing when to let go. He may be moody or depressed, may live too much in the past, and may be careless with
his finances. This is the person who changes direction at the very
brink of success—almost as though he needs to fail, or at least, fail
to succeed. He may, in fact, love himself too much.

THE MASTER NUMBERS

En route to calculating their single-digit personal numbers, some people will first arrive at a total of 11, 22, 33, or 44. If you do, *you may reduce these numbers to a single digit, but you should retain the double-digit number as well.* These numbers are the "master numbers" I referred to earlier, and they are important and providential in one's numerological "chart." The master numbers have an additional strength and meaning: They heighten the effect of their base number—that is, 11 heightens the qualities of a number 2; 22 heightens the qualities of a number 4. This heightening is not necessarily positive or negative; it is simply enhancement. *Both* numbers are significant; don't get overly involved in the master number to the exclusion of the base number to which it reduces. Many numerologists assign special meanings to these master numbers; if your name or birth date adds up to a master number, you might want to pursue it; take a look at whole chapters of discussion and interpretation in books such as *Numerology for the New Age* by Lynn M. Buess. If you continue your study of numerology, you should try to determine their meaning for yourself.

HOW TO DETERMINE YOUR FOUR PERSONAL NUMBERS

YOUR BIRTH FORCE NUMBER

The birth force number, also known as the life lesson number, is the most important personal number of them all. It is the one that explains your *reason for being*. This number represents the positive talents and also challenges you have brought into this lifetime. You can change your name but you can't change your birthday. Therefore, the positive and negative influences of this number will *always* be felt. The birth force number can be compared to the sun sign in astrology; it describes the strongest single manifestation of the person who bears it.

To figure out your birth force number, first print your birth date on a sheet of paper, using numbers to represent the month rather than words. We will use the example of Violet Armstrong, born February 24, 1942. Her birthdate would be written:

2–24–1942

To find the birth force number, just add the digits: 2 + 2 + 4 + 1 + 9 + 4 + 2 = 24. Add the parts of this two-digit number and you get

2 + 4 = 6. The birth force number is 24/6. This person is a 6; the number is always written this way, separated by a slash so that the double-digit (compound) number can also be considered. (This calculation may *seem* complicated but it isn't at all; you're doing the most elementary arithmetic.)

Compute your birth force number and read the description of the positive and negative traits that corresponds to your number. In the case of Violet Armstrong, she would look up the number 6; she could further interpret that 6 by looking up the digits of her compound number 24 (2+4) to see the path by which she arrived at that 6. (More about compound numbers on p. 405.) Keep in mind that the descriptions of the qualities of the numbers given here are merely brief overall interpretations. But these basic interpretations, combined with your own feelings and associations, are all you need. The only difference between what you and a trained numerologist come up with is the experience the latter has in making sense of all your personal numbers, integrating them into a pattern to see how they work together to tell your story.

THE NUMBERS IN YOUR NAME

Now we move on to calculating your soul number, personality number, and the integrated self number. These numbers are determined by using different combinations of the letters of your name.

Print your given name on the paper, leaving space above and below the letters. Use the name that is printed on your birth certificate, even if it is incorrectly spelled or otherwise wrong. (Here's when I feel sorry for my friend Don Smith, the fourth of seven children. Since Don's parents were convinced that he would be a girl, no boy's name was chosen. By the time his parents finally did agree on a name, it was too late; the birth certificate had been filed, listing his name as Baby Boy Smith. He had to go to court to have his name "changed" to Donald. For numerological purposes, though, Don would figure his numbers based on his given name, Baby Boy Smith.)

NUMERICAL EQUIVALENTS OF THE ALPHABET

1	2	3	4	5	6	7	8	9
A	B	C	D	E	F	G	H	I
J	K	L	M	N	O	P	Q	R
S	T	U	V	W	X	Y	Z	

Numerology assigns a numerical value to each letter of the alphabet. Use the chart of equivalents to determine the value of each letter in your name. Following the sample here, write the vowel value *above* each vowel in your name and the consonant value *below* each consonant in your name. (*Y* is a vowel for these purposes.) Here is an example of what your paper should look like:

```
   9   6      5              1                      6
   V   I   O   L   E   T      A   R   M   S   T   R   O   N   G
   4       3       2          9   4   1   2   9       5   7
```

Now you are ready to calculate your remaining personal numbers.

YOUR SOUL NUMBER

The soul number signifies what you really are *inside*. It is the spiritual body; it represents the inner soul urge or desire. Make sure this number vibrates well with any partners (romantic or business). The soul is interested in growth and wisdom, and it is expressed through the personality. Others might not even be aware of this "hidden" side of your self.

To discover your soul number, add the value of the *vowels* in your name. Thus, this soul number would be:

$$9 + 6 + 5 + 1 + 6 = 27: 2 + 7 = 9$$

The soul number for Violet Armstrong is 27/9. To interpret the soul number, read the description for number 9 (as well as for 2 and 7), and apply it to understanding your internal self.

YOUR PERSONALITY NUMBER

The personality number indicates the way you appear to others—your outer public image and appearance. It is the physical body. It represents how you see yourself in relationship to your environment and how people see you. Your personality number represents the way you express your personality publicly, though in rare cases, that behavior can be false, an "act" to hide the true personality from the public's eye.

Find your personality number by totaling all the *consonants* in your name, in this case:

$$4 + 3 + 2 + 9 + 4 + 1 + 2 + 9 + 5 + 7 = 46: 4 + 6 = 10 = 1$$

The personality number for Violet Armstrong is 46/1.

YOUR INTEGRATED SELF NUMBER

The fourth personal number, the integrated self number, is the mental/emotional body. It represents the highest ideal you wish to express on the physical plane in this lifetime. The full name is the map of how you are going to accomplish your life lesson or birth force. You may change your name to emphasize a certain talent you wish to develop. Martin Luther King, Jr.'s, 1964 Nobel Peace Prize was the work of his integrated self, the culmination of his work as clergyman, orator, and civil rights advocate.

Calculating the integrated self number is easiest of them all; the work is already done for you. Simply add the double-digit soul and personality numbers together to get one total, or add the single-digit soul and personality numbers together. Reduce the numbers as necessary, for example:

27 (soul) + 46 (personality) = 73 = 10 = 1 (integrated self); or,
9 (soul) + 1 (personality) = 10 = 1 (integrated self)
Violet Armstrong's integrated self number is 73/1.
To sum up, the four personal numbers at work here are:

> *Birth force number: 24/6*
> *Soul number: 27/9*
> *Personality number: 46/1*
> *Integrated self number: 73/1*

NUMEROLOGICAL INTERPRETATION AND UNDERSTANDING

Now is when the art of numerology comes into play: the interpretation of the numbers. It is important that the beginning numerologist approach the subject reasonably. Look at the shapes of the numbers and remember your reactions and thoughts and associations. Calculate the personal numbers for many of the people you know well so you can apply their traits to the numbers to help you remember and understand them. (Jim is the quintessential 6 because all children and small animals absolutely adore him, and he'd rather paint the den or rake leaves than have box seats at a World Series game; Susie is a 5, in fact, she even *looks* like the number 5, and she behaves like one, too.)

Don't get discouraged if you get confused; learning and remembering the meanings of the numbers is not necessarily easy. It is only with time and practice that the meanings will become more "automatic" to you.

DETERMINING YOUR PERSONAL CYCLES

Cycles—daily, weekly, monthly, yearly—have a big influence on our lives physically, emotionally, even economically. Cyclical patterns are an important aspect of astrology and biorhythm, and they have a place in numerology, too. Since your personal numbers—the birth force, soul, personality, and integrated self numbers—apply to your entire lifetime, they must always be kept in mind. But it is also useful to know the numbers that govern cyclical periods of our lives —the month of June, next year. Such calculations can help us foresee upcoming problems and opportunities, help us to understand the general tenor of times to come. We find our place in a cycle and can see its progression day to day, month to month, year to year. Certainly all of us have wondered from time to time if a particular meeting would be more auspicious scheduled for today or delayed until Friday. Anyone who has ever proposed marriage has done some thinking about the proper time. Timing is all, and numerology can help you determine your own "best" times. The following section shows you how to determine your annual, monthly, and daily cycles.

THE DIVISIONS OF THE CYCLES

Each cycle—whether it is a daily, monthly, or annual cycle—is divided into four parts: Halfway between the beginning and the end of the cycle is a "peak point"; and there are two "action points"— one halfway between the beginning and the peak point, the other halfway between the peak point and the end of the cycle. If you place points on a line, they would divide the line into four sections, each representing one quarter of the cycle.

For numerological purposes, your personal cycles are calculated from your birth date and time. For example, Violet Armstrong's personal year starts on her birthday, February 14 (not January 1), and ends on February 13 of the following year. Her monthly cycle begins on the fourteenth of each month and ends on the thirteenth of the following month. Her personal day begins at her time of birth, 7:17 A.M. (not at midnight) and ends the following morning at the same time. Only people born at midnight on January 1 can synchronize their cycles to the calendar year. The peak point in a year is always six months from the date of birth, the action points at three and nine months respectively. The peak point of a given month is approximately two weeks from the birthday, and the action points one and three weeks respectively. The daily peak point is always twelve hours from your birth time, the action points respectively six and eighteen hours from the beginning of the daily cycle. (A method for calculating the peak and action points of cycles is given on p. 404.)

DIVISIONS OF THE CYCLES

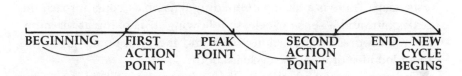

| BEGINNING | FIRST ACTION POINT | PEAK POINT | SECOND ACTION POINT | END—NEW CYCLE BEGINS |

A SAMPLE YEARLY CYCLE BEGINNING ON 2/14/1986:

FEB 14, 1986		AUG 14, 1986		FEB 13, 1987
	MAY 14, 1986		NOV 14, 1986	

A SAMPLE MONTHLY CYCLE BEGINNING 9/1:

| 9/1 | 9/7–8 | 9/15 | 9/22–23 | 9/30 |

A SAMPLE DAILY CYCLE BEGINNING AT 3:00 a.m.
(THE BIRTH TIME)

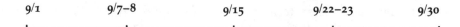

| 3 A.M. | 9 A.M. | 3 P.M. | 9 P.M. | 3 A.M. |

Within a full cycle, the *first action point* is situated 25 percent of the way along the line. It denotes a time that creates motion, internally or externally, toward the peak point. The *second action point*, three quarters of the way between the beginning and ending points, creates motion toward the new cycle by first putting the events of the earlier part of the cycle into perspective and then preparing for the start of the new cycle. The *peak point* is midway in any cycle. It represents the culmination of the cycle. It is the time when what you have been doing or working on over the first half of the cycle manifests itself. There is a feeling of building tension as you approach the peak point and a sense of release following it. Looking at the numbers that represent the action points and the peak points gives you an added idea of what the cycle is about.

The numbers you calculate for the various cycles will give you clues as to what to expect during those periods. A number 1 year or month is a time for beginnings; a 9 is a time for culmination, fulfillment, wrapping up. It is good practice to write in the numbers you calculate for each cycle or section of a cycle to help you forecast what's coming up during that period. It is also useful to note those times when the cycle number corresponds to one of your four personal numbers. It is at these times that the influences of the cycle are accentuated and the cycle becomes more meaningful in correlation with the personal number. For example, if your integrated self number is 5 and if June 8 is a 5 day, decision-making should be careful and deliberate. Perhaps this represents a time when you can draw on all your resources. Look at the qualities of a number 5 person on page 393—if you have to make a decision, do so, but focus on major issues only so that the negative traits don't get a chance to go to work. If there's a chance that you will make an unwise investment on a certain day, why not postpone the decision to a more fortuitous day? If you know that your peak day this month is the twenty-eighth, try to arrange it so that's when you present your proposal to a new client. All the hard work you've put into the project will culminate for you at that time.

Here is a good experiment for testing numerology's usefulness to you on an individual basis. Calculate your month number and your numbers for each day of the month, making note especially of the peak points and action points. Next, look up your number for each day and read the corresponding interpretation. Choose one word that characterizes that number and write it on a calendar to be your "word of the day." Check the calendar on a daily basis, beginning your numerological day at the time of day you were born, and see if you can find any correlations. In fact, you might want to check each day starting at the traditional new day of midnight as well as at the hour of your birth. It's important to stay with it for a month, since numerology, like many of the parasciences, is based on the cyclical repetition of predictable factors.

DETERMINING YOUR PERSONAL YEAR NUMBER

The calculations for personal year are not unlike those for the personal numbers. To determine the personal year number, here's a quick fill-in-the-blank formula:

Birth date + Month   =
Present year   = _____
Personal Year Number =

Therefore, for Violet Armstrong, the equation is:

2 + 4 + 2   = 8
1 + 9 + 8 + 6   = 24
Personal Year Number = 32 and 3 + 2 = 5

Her personal year number for 1986 is 5—that is, the year beginning on 2/24/86 and ending on 2/23/87. Very broadly looking at 1986, Violet can look forward to an eventful year highlighted by great activity and personal growth and stimulation, a year in which she must make a decision. By logical progression, beginning on 2/24/1987, Violet's personal year number will be a 6.

DETERMINING YOUR PERSONAL MONTH NUMBER

To determine Ms. Armstrong's personal month number, we'll use another formula and assume that today's date is 2/25/86:

Personal Year Number =   5   (from above)
This Month's Number = +   2   (for February)
Personal Month Number =   7

Her personal month number is 7—that is, the month of February 24 (24 being her birthday) to March 23. If the current month were a 7, she could anticipate an introspective month of learning about herself and her own needs. She should try to avoid being too hard on herself. Next month, March 24 to April 23, will be an 8 month.

DETERMINING YOUR PERSONAL DAY NUMBER

To determine the personal day number, we'll use Calia's formula combined with today's date, 2/25/86:

Personal Month Number $\quad = \; 7$
Today's month + day $(2 + 2 + 5 = \underline{+\;7}\,)$
Personal Day Number $\qquad = \quad 14 = 1 + 4 = 5$

A number 5 personal day could mean that Violet will be happiest if she is kept very busy, very active—perhaps she should be traveling. She is apt to feel angry or frustrated if she doesn't in some way experience movement or expansion.

DETERMINING YOUR PEAK POINTS AND ACTION POINTS

Your peak points and action points are calculated using your personal year, personal month, or personal day number (depending on the period for which you want to make the calculations).

For example, to determine your critical points over the next year, use the following formula and plug in the numbers that apply to you in place of those I'll use for Violet Armstrong, whose birthday is 2/24.

The First Action Point:
Personal Year Number $\qquad = 5$
Month number that is 3 months
after your birthday $\qquad = 5$ (3 months from 2/February)
First Action Point $\qquad = 10: 1 + 0 = 1$

The Peak Point:
Personal Year Number $\qquad = 5$
Month number that is 6 months
after your birthday $\qquad = 8$
Peak Point $\qquad = 13: 1 + 3 = 4$

The Second Action Point:
Personal Year Number $\qquad = 5$
Month number that is 3 months
before your next birthday $\qquad = 11$
Second Action Point $\qquad = 16: 1 + 6 = 7$

If you wanted to plot that on a line, it would look like this:

DETERMINING YOUR PEAK AND ACTION POINTS

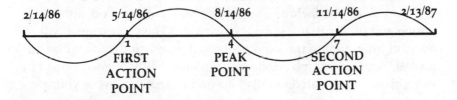

WHERE TO GO FROM HERE

Much earlier in this brief lesson on numerology, I admonished you to keep track of the double-digit numbers that were your totals for the birth force, soul, personality, and integrated self numbers. In case you don't remember, Violet Armstrong's were as follows:

birth force number: 24/6
soul number: 27/9
personality number: 46/1
integrated self number: 73/1

These double-digit, or *compound*, numbers have a meaning all their own in the advanced study and practice of numerology; however, knowing how to interpret their significance is something that comes with time and study. A professional numerologist finds the compound number as interesting as the number it reduces to. For instance, though the compound numbers 62 and 53 both reduce to 8, the professional numerologist will have two completely different readings from them, since the compound numbers are different, indicating that very different paths led to the same end. For example, if someone is a 24/6 (Violet Armstrong), the progression is "cooperation" (2) in "work" (4), leading to "commitment" (6). Thus in Violet's case, the number 6 is indicative of creating committed, stable relationships. Stephen Calia sees these compound number progressions as "processes." These compound numbers will take on significance to you as well as your knowledge of numerology increases.

If you go to a professional numerologist, you can expect an interpretation that includes your current cycles along with dates to watch in the future. Like any professional, the numerologist's experience and study makes him particularly adept at seeing the overall picture and interpreting the dovetailing influences of your various numbers. And, naturally, the professional has the advantage of being a stranger to you—all he or she knows about you is what the numbers tell. Forecasts can include some days that nothing you do can be wrong and others that will be the opposite. The professional will be adept at intertwining the aspects of spirit, mind, and body with your mental, emotional, physical, and intellectual tendencies—again, using more complicated calculations and interpretations of your personal numbers. If you need to be careful for some reason or for some period of time, the numbers will be clear about exactly when that time will occur in your life. Expect the fee for a reading to range from about $25 to $75.

Like any of the psychic disciplines, numerology is useful only to those who give it a chance. Give it a try to see what it can do for you, whether you're choosing a date for a party or trying to decide on a name for your baby. If you're torn between which of two houses to buy, work out the numbers in their addresses; maybe one will be fortuitous and the other a clear second choice. Let the numbers guide you as your future unfolds.

CHAPTER
FIFTEEN
TAROT

The word *tarot* is familiar to almost everybody, though most might be hard-pressed to define it. The image that immediately comes to mind is that of a wild-looking Gypsy fortune teller holding a large deck of strange-looking cards. We've seen her (to be sure, the tarot card reader in literature is almost always depicted as a woman) in the play *The Killing of Sister George*, in the James Bond film *Live and Let Die*, and, no doubt about it, there was Vanessa Redgrave "throwing the cards" in the title role of the film *Isadora*. Though the tarot reader is invariably portrayed as a kook of some type, to students of the psychic arts, the tarot offers a valid and serious method for seeking answers to questions that concern all phases of life.

The tarot deck is a set of seventy-eight cards that can be separated into two parts: the Major Arcana, a group of twenty-two key, or "trump," cards, and the Minor Arcana, the remaining fifty-six cards, traditionally divided by "suit" into four groups of fourteen cards each. Tarot cards are highly pictorial, with each colorful card crammed full of symbols and elaborate graphic detail that have mystical meaning.

Tarot card reading—interpreting the meanings and relationships of the tarot cards and applying them to various aspects of a person's life—can be practiced by anyone who has the time and interest to involve himself with the cards. There are dozens of tarot decks available, from different eras, different cultures, each with its own graphic interpretations and refinements. Tarot card readers use the deck to which they feel the most attraction or empathy. As with the symbols for the numbers in numerology, the meaning of the cards is influenced as much by what you, the reader, bring to them, as by the traditional interpretations that can be found in books. It is pretty much the same with all the parasciences: A powerful reading results from the combination of classic connotations and personal "English" that one brings to the interpretation.

Again, we are dealing with tools, in this case, cards, with which someone with an aptitude or an affinity can seemingly gain access to hidden information. The gift of the talented tarot reader seems to be the ability to use the visual and psychological information inherent in the cards to trigger psychic and intuitive insights. We are again reminded of the conjecture of Jung and others that there is a psychic, synchronistic factor that occurs when the cards are shuffled, so that they mysteriously seem to answer the question asked, to bring to the surface unconscious knowledge that had resisted awareness.

Though tarot cards can be used to give a life reading that is similar to having the natal chart read by an astrologer, it is tarot's ability to zero in on specific, more mundane questions that makes it so applicable in everyday life. If a student wants to know which college to attend, the tarot will help guide him. If an executive wants to know whether to accept a competitor's job offer, the tarot will elucidate the choices. If there are queries about love or money or health, the tarot can offer guidance. For people who are interested in dealing more efficiently with the day-to-day machinations of life, the tarot can be a positive influence on their decision-making.

John Green, author of *Dakota Days* and for more than five years tarot card reader for John Lennon and Yoko Ono, writes of his involvement in their busy lives. Using tarot, he conferred with Yoko Ono on an almost daily basis, generally acting as business advisor. Frequently he was called upon to help with more personal questions, such as choosing a numerologically correct name for their soon-to-be-born son, Sean. In the introduction to his book, Green says, "Tarot cards are a wonderful device for seeing into people and the situations in which they find themselves. Clients tell their card readers things they wouldn't tell anyone else—their lovers, their spouses, their families, or their friends. As a student of mine put it wonderingly, 'People unzip themselves!' So a reader has an excellent opportunity to see into his fellow man in a way that is denied to others."

A card reader's clients may come from many walks of life. Pat Barnes, a professional tarot card reader for more than seventeen years, has clients from many professions, among them doctors, lawyers, and teachers. She finds that "the educated people want to find out more about their inner self . . . everyone is looking within." Rolla Nordic, a reader since 1947, reads for many businessmen. They consult her regarding "mergers and very important meetings. They ask questions, and usually the tarot will give them a clue as to the temperament of the men they have to meet and how to handle the situation." Anka Junge, a full-time professional tarot card reader, estimates that "most of my clients are college-educated professionals." Clients' two main topics of concern are career and love. Like many adepts, she frequently travels to see clients in other places, away from her home base. "I go to Washington, D.C., about every six weeks. . . . I have seen people from different branches of government. Naturally they don't tell me exactly what they do, but if they, for example, work for the CIA or the FBI, that's very easy to see."

The cards seem to be consistent. Pat Barnes says she doesn't know how it works. "It's eerie. Sometimes, after you've picked a card, the same card comes back over and over again. If you do twenty drawings, it will come back fifteen out of twenty times, and when it doesn't come back, there's usually a card that's similar in meaning. I can't figure it out, but the cards *are* consistent. Perhaps it's this consistency that makes prediction possible."

Anka Junge tells a story that seems unbelievable, since there are so many factors that nobody could have foreseen. She says:

> I have a client, a young woman who was living with someone, and I told her that soon she would meet someone from the past—a man she had known or met before, who was married and had children—and this man would get a divorce and marry her and she would move far away from New York. Three months later, she met him and rushed back for another reading. . . . He got divorced and I went to their wedding. I predicted they would have difficulty. Don't buy a house in Denver, I told her, because I don't think you are going to stay; I think you are going to move to Texas. Neither of them believed it because he was in a very good, secure position in Denver. . . . When they returned from their honeymoon, his job, for some reason, was coming to an end, and one of the last things he did on the job was go on a business trip to Washington, D.C. An old friend there, not knowing any of the circumstances, said, "If I didn't know you had such a fantastic job, I would have just the job for you in Texas." So, of course, they moved, found the right house, and they live happily in Texas. Just this past summer they visited and I told her she would be pregnant within a few weeks, if she wasn't pregnant already. She called back soon after and said she had gotten pregnant within ten days after seeing me. It seems to be an unreal story, but it's true. It happens so quickly.

Irene Krawitz, a psychic researcher and inventor of Tarot Wheels of Destiny, claims that her own research and experience has shown her that "a 'sensitive' can tune in to another's subconscious and reveal information that the subject may be unaware of, because the subconscious records all information a person is exposed to in a subliminal manner. It is a depository for all emotions, reactions, and hostilities." Apparently, several psychologists agree. Mary Ann Maniacek, a psychotherapist for Dorothy May, Ph.D., & Associates, in Glenview, Illinois, uses tarot to release memories that may be hidden in her patients' subconscious memory. She asks her patients to make up a story, using the design of one of the twenty-two cards of the tarot's Major Arcana as the basis of the tale. Patients almost invariably create stories that are about themselves and about how they feel regarding some person or thing in their life. Often Maniacek is able to isolate subconscious memories that help patients become aware of problems and issues they have been hiding. The use of parapsychology within the framework of her usual psychotherapeutic methods is valuable to Maniacek. "We can't see it; it's not concrete, but this does not mean it does not exist. *Para* means 'alongside of, beyond or closely related to.' "

Psychologist Carl Jung would agree. He claimed that the tarot is a compilation of archetypes—universal images that are "hardwired" into man's mind, irrespective of time, culture, and country. These images, or "keys," as he called them, are links to the subconscious mind. If you let them, he maintained, these images will "speak" to you; they will prod a train of thought relevant to the matter at hand; they will prod your subconscious. When you look at the pictures on the cards and compare them to the traditional meanings for the cards, you will understand what he means.

The practice of tarot card reading first came to the attention of educated Europeans near the end of the eighteenth century. In the ensuing two hundred years, the tarot has accrued as many interpretations and derivations as it has followers. It has been traced variously to Egypt, China, India, and Morocco and has been linked to astrology, numerology, and the Jewish Kabbalah. If, as some people believe, the tarot is the key that tied together all the ancient esoteric traditions, its history and its relationship to the other psychic disciplines make it worthy of a closer look.

A BRIEF HISTORY OF THE TAROT

The origins of the tarot are lost in time, though theorists have come up with myriad possibilities over the years. In 1781, Antoine Court de Gebelin, a French theologian, linguist, and archaeologist, published the eighth volume of his vast work *Monde Primitif*, which included an article on the tarot. He believed the tarot deck to be thousands of years old, based on an ancient Egyptian initiation rite associated with the worship of Thoth, the god of magic and wisdom. The Book of Thoth, he surmised, was the record book of all Egyptian wisdom and knowledge of the occult. The first prophet of this Egyptian-based divination of the tarot was in the person of Alliette, a Parisian barber and friend to Court de Gebelin. Under the pen name of Etteilla (yes, all he did was reverse the order of the letters of his name), he published numerous tracts and pamphlets explaining the Egyptian mysteries behind the cards. In addition, Etteilla designed a tarot deck of his own, incorporating many aspects that would make the tarot's Egyptian ancestry seem even more pronounced. Tarot's newfound popularity on the Parisian social scene and Court de Gebelin's theory that the tarot originated in Egypt combined to convince people that the tarot was, indeed, Egyptian in nature, and this thinking was for a long time accepted as truth and fact.

Other historians and researchers thought the origins of the tarot could be found in India, in the Hindu religion. Some suggested that the tarot deck evolved in the marketplaces of Morocco as a graphic "language" that could convey similar meanings to people who spoke different languages. Perhaps the tarot was invented, as some claim, by Jacquemin Gringonneur, an artist who is said to have designed the cards solely for the pleasure and entertainment of King Charles VI.

Another popular belief is that the tarot is the cultural property of the Gypsies. The first writer to expound on this view was a Frenchman named Boiteau d'Ambly, who further supposed the Gypsies to be of Indian origin. However, timing would seem to disprove this, since the first definite appearance of Gypsies in western Europe was in 1417, a time when both card games in general and the tarot specifically seem already to have been known. It is much more likely that upon their arrival in Europe, the Gypsies adopted the deck and perhaps originated the custom of using it for divination.

In the middle of the nineteenth century, the tarot acquired the bulk of its occult traditions in the work of Alphonse Louis Constant, who, using the name Eliphas Levi, was the most celebrated magician of his time. Levi's primary contribution was to associate the tarot with the Kabbalah (a body of wisdom that is represented by a series of letters and numbers), the esoteric side of Judaism. He assigned each of the twenty-two trump cards to a letter of the Hebrew alphabet, with corresponding numerological significance. It is the wisdom that is illuminated by the Infinite Light *(Ain Soph Aur)* through the various paths of the Tree of Life. The twenty-two keys of the Major Arcana correspond directly with the twenty-two paths of the Tree of Life.

Around the turn of the century, in London, several learned men, among them Samuel MacGregor Mathers, Dr. Wynn Westcott, and Dr. William Woodman, founded a magical order that revolved around the tarot, the Hermetic Order of the Golden Dawn. The members thought themselves compelled to study and record existing information on magic and ritual to shape a complete chronicle of the occult. This club followed the ten levels of the Kabbalah and divided the levels into various ritualistic grades, seven of which were attainable by mere mortals, with three levels left to the Secret Chiefs, spiritual superiors who would steer the order and contribute magical inspiration. The movement attracted many new members, opening societies in four cities within eight years. Many of the intellectual elite became involved with the Hermetic Order of the Golden Dawn, including poet William Butler Yeats and occultist Aleister Crowley. A. E. Waite, a tarot scholar and creator of one of the most widely used tarot decks, was one of the early members of the order. These men studied the existing information and expanded the written body of knowledge on the occult. Most current interpretations are based largely on the writings of the order's members, such as Westcott's *An Introduction to the Qabalah* (1910), Waite's *The Holy Kabbalah, The Holy Grail, The Real History of the Rosicrucians,* and *Azoth.* The members were aware of two levels of meaning in the use of the deck: a lesser divinatory system and a greater allegorical reading, which they hinted at or purposely obscured. On the deeper level, they believed the images of the Major Arcana to represent stages of knowledge leading to mystical enlightenment—the secret doctrine of a hermetic religion. And for all their mumbo jumbo, infighting, and dissimulation, their views on the Major Arcana appear to be correct.

THE HISTORY OF THE TAROT DECK

There has been much speculation as to whether the Major and Minor Arcana were not once separate; this seems quite likely. The Major Arcana can be considered a full deck in itself, while references to cards that resemble the Minor Arcana exist throughout the latter part of the fourteenth century without any mention whatsoever of the distinctive and far more puzzling cards of the Major Arcana. These citations were usually in the context of gambling. The first definitive reference to the Major Arcana records the purchase of three decks of cards by Charles VI of France in 1392, without mention of the Minor Arcana.

The most probable place of origin for the Minor Arcana is Italy of the late thirteenth or early fourteenth century. Cards had existed in the East before they were used in Europe, and Italy, particularly the city-states such as Venice, had more contact with the Chinese, Indian, and Muslim cultures than other parts of the Western world, having taken over the bulk of that trade after the fall of the Byzantine Empire. There is also evidence that most of the early decks assigned the cards Italian names, despite their country of manufacture. Further, the Taro River of northern Italy might be the source of the name.

THE IMAGERY OF THE TAROT DECK

Though the idea of using cards for games is an Eastern one, the imagery of the tarot deck probably is Western. Historians have pointed to earlier instances of Indian and Chinese use of symbols similar to those of the four suits, but this is probably more an indication of the archetypal nature of these images than of any direct cultural borrowing.

The images of the Major Arcana come from more obscure sources than the rest of the deck. They are most probably gnostic in origin, that is, based on the early Christian beliefs that matter is evil and that salvation is available to man only through the revelation of the spiritual truths. Since the beginning of the Christian era, the Church had long sought to suppress the various gnostic heresies that were to make appearances well into the thirteenth century. Gnostic sects, including the Manichaeans, the Albigensians, and the Essenes (the Jewish community that was the source of the teachings of John the Baptist, and probably Jesus as well), believed in a strict dualism. At its simplest, gnosticism stated that the material world was evil and the spiritual, good. The Demiurge, the God of the Old Testament, was an imperfect god who had created the world and its inhabitants, who were, it follows, imperfect. The God of the New Testament, the greater of the two, had entered history to bring man to a state of perfection. Man's story was the battle between the two.

It should be remembered that for most of history, well into the early modern era, literacy was a function of the Church. Until printing was invented and books became relatively easy to come by, an essential part of learning was "the art of memory." The mind's ability to link simple images with elaborate ideas allowed the illiterate population of Europe to possess a great deal of information in an ordered fashion, to a degree that we would find astounding. Though considered heretical, such "books" as the Major Arcana were an important means of conveying doctrine forbidden by the Church.

Since the gnostic connection to the tarot was first pointed out about a hundred years ago, it has received a good deal of attention. Tarot scholars such as Alfred Douglas have since demonstrated a one-to-one correspondence between the Major Arcana and gnostic teachings. Though there will probably never be definite proof, this seems its likely provenance.

The pictures on the cards have evolved constantly over the centuries. In some early decks, many of the cards depicted specific members of the nobility (the Medicis and the Sforzas, in one case), while some modern decks are almost abstract. But running through all of them is a thread of continuity, some integral key to the image that is always there.

The subject of the design of the various decks is an interesting one. In reality, anyone could design a tarot deck; the challenge is to design one that is mystically correct, that is, that suggests enough to give rise to interpretation while still staying within the traditional feeling and meaning of the card. The Rider-Waite deck, designed by artist Pamela Coleman-Smith under the guidance of A. E. Waite, is probably the most popular tarot deck in the world. Some 160 different decks are available in the United States, among them the Tarot of Marseilles, the Visconti-Sforza Tarot, the Tarot of the Witches, the Aleister Crowley Tarot, the Golden Dawn Tarot, and the Tavaglione Tarot. Decks of nontraditional design should be studied by the reader to see if the cards communicate and give rise to the imagination. If they "speak" to you, by all means, use them; if the cards confuse you, try a simpler, more conventional deck.

Fans of artist Salvador Dali should look for the tarot deck he designed in 1983—a blend of the traditional and nontraditional with signature Daliesque motifs as well as Key cards marked with astrological symbols and Hebrew letters of the alphabet. The deck is interesting in that Dali has included all the historical possibilities for the tarot, offering the reader several layers of interpretation at a single glance.

I highly recommend a new and quite elegant "package"—a deck of cards, a silky black cloth with the Celtic spread diagrammed on one side (which you can wrap the cards in when not in use), and a book detailing the use and interpretation of the cards, titled *The Mythic Tarot*. Written by Juliet Sharman-Burke and Liz Greene, the cards are especially appealing because they have been redesigned in accord with images of the Greek gods, so that they feel more familiar to us Westerners.

THE TAROT DECK

The Major Arcana consists of twenty-one numbered cards and an additional card, the Fool, which may be unnumbered or designated as either 0 or 22. The Minor Arcana includes four suits, each having ten numbered cards—ace through 10—and four Court cards—King, Queen, Knight, and Page. Traditionally, the ten numbered cards were illustrated with simple designs of the suit emblem, as is a deck of modern playing cards—which comes from the tarot. (Note, however, that whereas the playing cards we're accustomed to have only three Court cards—the King, Queen, and Jack—the tarot deck has added a fourth—the Knight.) Since 1910, when A. E. Waite supervised the design of the Rider-Waite deck, most decks have followed his lead and assigned allegorical illustrations based on the traditional divinatory values to the numbered cards. (We will be using the Rider-Waite deck for illustration purposes, as it is probably the best known and is very suggestive in its imagery.) The interpretations offered in this chapter were culled from a large number of sources. They are not meant to be definitive, but merely suggestions. Your reading of the cards will depend on who and where *you* are. If an image suggests a train of thought at odds with orthodox interpretation, accept it; that will be a "truer" reading—if it comes from within you.

THE MAJOR ARCANA

In the following paragraphs, interpretations are provided for cards in both upright and reversed (upside-down) positions. However, a reversed card is open to several different interpretations: It can connote the exact opposite meaning of an upright card; its meaning might merely be tempered from the positive or upright meaning; its meaning can be tempered by the cards that surround it in the spread. Determining which interpretation is the applicable one is another knack altogether. You will want to consider the question being asked and the range of possible answers to see which one is most likely to apply. When reading the explanations of each card, think, too, of the symbolism of the number that correlates with it; try to apply the number to the message the card conveys (for more on numerology, see p. 385).

<u>0</u>   THE FOOL

THE FOOL.

An innocent-appearing youth is walking toward the edge of a cliff on a bright sunny day; his eyes are focused upward, and on his face is a look of contemplation or wonderment. He is unaware of the chasm in front of him. Over his shoulder he carries a bundle tied to a stick, sometimes said to contain his past experience and sometimes said to contain the suit symbols. In his left hand is a white rose, and at his feet, his dog, happily romping along with him. In some decks, the dog, or alternatively a cat, is attacking his leg, though the young man seems oblivious of it.

Interpretation: Innocence and possibilities, the beginning of a journey, the contemplation of unlimited choices. Divine wisdom and divine folly. Both the benefits and drawbacks of innocence and naïveté.

Reversed: Extravagance, lack of discipline, the desire to achieve the impossible.

THE MAGICIAN.

<u>I</u>   THE MAGICIAN

A man—young, strong, and handsome —stands behind a table, wearing a white monk's-type robe with a scarlet surplice over it. On the table are the four suit symbols—a sword, a wand, a cup, and a pentacle. His right hand, clasping a wand, reaches upward toward the sky; his left hand points down toward the earth. He wears as a belt the snake biting its own tail —symbol of the infinite universe. Above his head is a lemniscate, the sideways number eight that is our mathematical symbol for infinity. In some decks, his appearance is closer to a carnival magician, a mountebank, or a juggler.

Interpretation: Will, originality, creativity, intellect. The ability to focus divine powers to earthly ends. Skill, dexterity, organizational ability. Diplomacy and self-confidence.

Reversed: Cunning, deceit, and trickery.

II THE HIGH PRIESTESS

A dark-haired young woman, seated, wears the blue-and-white robes of a priestess. To either side of her are pillars, one black and one white. They are marked with the letters B and J—B for Boaz (negation) and J for Jachin (beginning). At her feet is the waxing crescent moon, and she wears on her breast a cross with arms of equal length—the solar cross, not the Christian. On her lap, she holds a scroll— the Torah—or a Bible, partially hidden by her robe. She wears a crown representing the waxing, waning, and the full moon. Behind her is a tapestry of palm leaves and  pomegranates. This card has also been designated the Papess, and Juno.

Interpretation: Serenity, intuition, common sense. Learning and education. The occult, hidden influences, mystery, undeveloped talent. Nature and inspiration; the subconscious.

Reversed: Conceit, sensuality, decadence, and cynicism.

III THE EMPRESS

A blond woman, older than the priestess, is seated outdoors. In the background are trees and flowing water; in the foreground, ripening wheat. Her robe is decorated with halved pomegranates, and she holds a small staff with an orb in her raised right hand. Her crown is made of stars, and nearby is a shield bearing the symbol for Venus, the female.

Interpretation: Abundance, material gain, and fertility. Stability, wealth, comfort, and contentment. The Earth Mother. Pregnancy, physical love, positive sensuality. The fruition of projects.

Reversed: Overindulgence, idleness, sterility, poverty, dissipation, debauchery.

IV THE EMPEROR

An Emperor, a solid, stern-faced, older-looking bearded man, is seated on a throne ornamented with rams' heads. In one hand he holds an orb, in the other a staff that is topped by the *crux ansata*, or ankh, signifying life and immortality. In the background, mountain peaks.

Interpretation: Leadership, authority, power, stability. Endurance and dominance. A reasoning intellect. Temporal power, as opposed to spiritual. Paternity, potency, and virility. A builder.

Reversed: Tyranny, war, and ambition.

V THE HIEROPHANT

THE HIEROPHANT

A pope, dressed in scarlet robes, is seated on a throne, between two pillars. He wears a triple-tiered crown, surmounted by a W. His right hand is raised in the gesture of a two-fingered blessing. In his left hand is a staff ending in the papal cross. Kneeling before him are two monks in supplication, and at his feet are the crossed keys of St. Peter. The Hierophant was the high priest of the Eleusinian Mystery religion. This card has also been designated the Pope, and Jupiter.

Interpretation: Humility, mercy, kindness, servitude.

Reversed: Orthodoxy and dogma. The observer of the outward aspects of religion; thus, conventionality.

VI THE LOVERS

THE LOVERS.

Adam and Eve stand in the Garden, being blessed by an archangel, a radiant sun behind him. Behind Adam is the Tree of Life, sprouting fruits of flame; behind Eve, the Tree of Knowledge, around which the Serpent is coiled. Adam looks toward Eve, while Eve looks upward. Other versions have depicted a youth choosing between two women, interpreted as Vice and Virtue, Wisdom and Beauty, Mother and Lover. Many included a figure of Cupid.

Interpretation: Physical, passionate love, attraction, perfection, harmony. Matters dealing with marriage and affairs. Sacred as opposed to profane love. Love unsullied by material desire or ulterior motives. A choice between powerful attractions.

Reversed: Jealousy, infidelity, general bad tidings in love.

VII THE CHARIOT

A young and powerful-looking blond man in light armor stands upright in a chariot drawn by two sphinxes, one black and one white. In the background is a walled city. The blue curtain that adorns the chariot is decorated with white stars, and the man's gold crown is topped by an eight-pointed star. Upon his shoulders are *Urim* and *Thummim*, representations of the crescent moon used by the ancient Hebrews for the purpose of divination. He wears a radiant square medallion on his chest. The front of the chariot bears a winged sun and a stylized yoni and lingam.

THE CHARIOT.

Interpretation: Conquest, triumph, victory. The triumph could be over anything—money, health, enemies—but is most likely to be on the material plane. Winning through long hard work. Loyalty and obedience; authority under authority.

Reversed: Quarrels, trouble, and vengeance. Struggles and obstacles.

STRENGTH.

VIII STRENGTH

A woman, clothed in a loose white dress, wears both a crown and a belt of flowers. She might be gently holding shut the mouth of a lion, or she may be petting him. Above her head is a lemniscate; in the background, a mountain. Some versions show her opening the lion's mouth.

Interpretation: Strength and courage tempered by judgment. Spiritual strength overcoming weakness. Mind over matter. Fortitude and the joy of life.

Reversed: Obstinacy, abuse of power. Weakness. Danger.

IX THE HERMIT

A tall, hooded monk stands in profile atop a mountain peak, looking downward. In his left hand, he holds a staff; in his right, a lantern. Within the lantern shines a star.

Interpretation: Prudence, wisdom, and caution. Illumination from within. Solitude and withdrawal from things of this world. Wisdom offered, a teacher or an advisor, openness to advice.

Reversed: Fear, timidity, refusing sage advice.

THE HERMIT.

X THE WHEEL OF FORTUNE

WHEEL of FORTUNE.

Suspended in the blue sky is a wheel bearing the letters T-A-R-O, alternating with the Hebrew letters for Y-H-V-H, spelling Yahweh, the forbidden name of God. The center of the wheel bears the symbols for mercury, sulfur, salt, and water. Sitting atop the wheel is a sphinx with a sword resting over its left shoulder. Rising to the right of the wheel is Anubis, the Egyptian deity that carried the dead to final judgment. Descending to the left is a snake. In the four corners of the card, resting on clouds, are the Four Beasts of the Apocalypse, all reading books. Earlier decks depict Blind Fate turning a wheel, at the top of which sits a joyous couple, often a King and Queen. The female figure looks over her shoulder at a man who has just fallen off the wheel.

Interpretation: Destiny, fate, luck, fortune. The law of karma: past actions come back to you. That which is out of our hands. An unexpected turn for the better.

Reversed: An unexpected turn for the worse.

XI   JUSTICE

The traditional image of Justice: Justice is seated, with a sword in the upraised right hand, a scale in the left. This blond figure is not blindfolded; she has her large, clear eyes wide open, enabling her to see all that takes place before her.

Interpretation: Fair judgment, balance, fairness. Often associated with legal matters, lawsuits. Clearness of vision.

Reversed: Bigotry, prejudice, bad judgment. An incorrect choice.

XII   THE HANGED MAN

A blue-smocked blond man hangs upside down, tied at one ankle, from a cross of living wood. The free leg is crossed behind the other to form an inverted 4. Hands behind his back—perhaps tied, perhaps not—his head is encircled by a golden aura. The look on his face clearly is *not* one of suffering; his expression is one of joy or contemplation. He looks relaxed. Some decks show coins falling from his pockets.

Interpretation: A turning from the outer, material world to the inner, spiritual world. Surrender and transition. Intuition and prophecy. Sacrifice, or self-sacrifice. A complete reversal in one's way of life.

Reversed: An overattachment to the material. An obsession with one's own delusions.

XIII   DEATH

Riding a huge white horse, a skeleton in black armor looks down at a bishop wearing a miter. The bishop is praying—either pleading with death or preparing for it. A king lies dead beneath the horse's feet, his crown fallen from his head. On their knees are a child and a young woman. Death carries a black banner bearing a white rose. In the background, a ship sails, and on the horizon, either rising or setting, the sun is shining between two towers. Most decks show Death with a scythe.

DEATH.

Interpretation: Death, destruction, loss, failure. Vast changes, sudden changes. Renewal and rebirth. A clearing of old things to make way for new. Violence, political unrest. Liberation through change: sought-after or avoided.

Reversed: Lack of change, stagnation, loss of hope. Forced change.

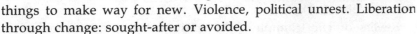

TEMPERANCE.

XIV   TEMPERANCE

An androgynous white-robed winged angel stands with one foot on land, the other in water. The angel pours water from a cup in the left hand to a cup in the right. On its chest is a triangle within a square, and on its forehead a golden disk. An aura surrounds its head. Yellow irises grow nearby, and fertile countryside with distant mountains is in the background.

Interpretation: Moderation, harmony, discipline, and balance. Management, diplomacy, and accommodation. Temperance literally, thus a mixture of the proper proportions.

Reversed: The opposite of all the foregoing.

XV THE DEVIL

THE DEVIL.

A huge horned devil with batlike wings crouches on a pedestal. Between its horns is an inverted pentagram. Its right hand is raised in a sign that can be attributed to black magic; its left hand grasps a torch, held downward. Loosely chained to the pedestal are a pair of figures, the female on the left, the male on the right. Both have horns and tails. The male's tail ends in flames; the female's sprouts a bunch of fruit. This image clearly parallels both card V, The Hierophant, and card VI, The Lovers.

Interpretation: Bondage to the material; the triumph of material desire over spiritual inclinations. Impulse, ambition, and temptation —all in their most negative senses. Perversity, sexual or otherwise. Physical illness. Danger.

Reversed: The triumph of the spiritual over the material, or the other meanings tempered.

XVI THE TOWER

THE TOWER.

A tower aflame, seen at night, has been struck by a jagged and pointed bolt of lightning. A large gold crown has been dislodged from the top and is about to topple. Falling from the tower are two figures, one wearing a crown. This card has also been called the Lightning Struck Tower and The House of God.

Interpretation: Disruption, calamity, unforeseen catastrophe. Revelation piercing an established set of beliefs. Deception. Bankruptcy: financial or spiritual. Traditional associations with the Tower of Babel, thus punishment for the crime of hubris.

Reversed: Illumination, inspiration, freedom bought at a great cost. A lesser manifestation of the negative meanings of the card.

XVII   THE STAR

A young and beautiful naked blond woman kneels at a shoreline, her left knee on land, her right foot in the water. With a pitcher in either hand, she pours water both onto the earth and onto the water. Directly above her is a large yellow eight-pointed star; around it are seven smaller white stars. In the background is a tree with a bird standing in its foliage.

Interpretation: Hope-expanded horizons, the promise of satisfaction. Unselfish help, unexpected help. Faith. Insight and inspiration.

Reversed: Doubt, self-doubt. A closed and rigid mind. Pessimism and disappointment.

THE STAR.

THE MOON.

XVIII   THE MOON

A dog and a wolf or jackal are howling at the moon. The moon shows its face both full and crescent. In the foreground is a pool of water, from which crawls a lobster or crayfish. A path starting at the pool winds its way between the two canines and in the distance passes through the square towers to vanish on the horizon in a darkened and mountainous landscape. Tears or dewdrops fall from the sky.

Interpretation: The specific symbolism explains itself here. The dog and wolf are aspects of the human mind—the domesticated and the wild. The creature crawling from the water represents impulses arising unbidden from the depths of the subconscious—thus, instinct, intuition, and superstition. The mysterious, the hidden, and the occult. Dreams. The female aspect of things.

Reversed: Fear of the irrational and the unknown. Hidden dangers, deceit, savagery.

<u>XIX</u> THE SUN

In front of a walled garden with sun-flowers growing inside, a smiling naked child sits astride a white horse. A red plume is in his blond hair, and in his left hand, he holds a long orange banner on a pole. A stern-faced sun shines above all.

Interpretation: Success and accomplishment, health and pleasure. Attainment: material, emotional, or creative. Thought and intelligence. Imaginative and daring ideas justified; winning over great odds. The outward and manifest, and thus the masculine (in contrast to card XVIII, The Moon).

Reversed: Uncertain future, troubled relationship. Danger of loss or failure.

<u>XX</u> JUDGEMENT

An angel emerging from clouds blows the Last Trump. Attached to his trumpet is a banner of a red cross on a white field. In the foreground three naked figures—man, woman, and child—arise from three coffins floating in the sea. Their arms and faces are raised in welcome and praise. In the distance, similar figures arise from coffins.

Interpretation: Transformation and changes. Confrontations and determinations. The union of opposing forces; the spiritual and the material combine in perfect harmony.

Reversed: Loss and guilt, deserved punishment. Weakness and overdeliberation; delay.

XXI   THE WORLD

Within an oval wreath of leaves, the figure of a young woman dances, holding a white rod in each hand. Her naked body is draped in a long, flowing purple scarf. In the four corners of the card are the heads of the Four Beasts of the Apocalypse: angel, eagle, lion, and bull.

Interpretation: The union of the individual with the universe; man as, and united with, god. Fulfillment of all desires, success in all undertakings. An awaited reward. Freedom and liberation.

Reversed: Stagnation and inertia. Blindness: moral, spiritual, or physical.

THE MINOR ARCANA

Like the Major Arcana, a wide variety of opinion exists as to the meanings of the Minor Arcana. Although the fifty-six cards are too many to describe individually in this beginner's look at tarot, some general interpretations can be offered for use in divination. Once you've purchased a deck, look for a book that explains that deck, or read up on the tarot in general by consulting several of the books listed in the bibliography.

THE SUITS

Very generally speaking, Pentacles and Cups are considered the "good" suits and have a female identification. Wands and Swords are cards of force, the male suits, and are negative.

PENTACLES: Deal with matters of business, finance, and money. When each suit is assigned to one of the four Elements, Pentacles is associated with Earth. (Here's an astrology connection; see p. 338.)

WANDS: Have to do with matters of work, force, energy, and agriculture. Element: Fire.

CUPS: Refer to creativity, emotion, and intuition. Element: Water.
SWORDS: Indicate authority, intellect, and strength. Element: Air.

A related set of values that can be of some use in readings associates each of the suits with an aspect of medieval society. Thus, Swords represent nobility; Cups, the clergy; Pentacles, business people or merchants; and Wands, peasants or laborers.

Within the suit divisions, the Court cards (King, Queen, Knight, and Page) generally are taken to represent specific people: Kings, older men; Queens, older women; Knights, young men; and Pages, young women or children. Further, the following definitions are often used:

WANDS represent people of fair coloring—blonds and redheads.
CUPS represent people slightly darker—dark-complected blonds and those with light brown hair.
SWORDS represent those with dark brown hair and complexions.
PENTACLES represent those with black hair.

When doing a reading, meanings of function or character should be considered more important than those of coloring. Therefore, a Knight of Pentacles is more likely to be a young male executive than a dark young man.

As the Court cards generally refer to people, the numbered cards generally refer to events or circumstances. The meanings now in common use are rooted in the readings derived by Waite and Mathers from numerology and the Kabbalah. The meanings of the numbers remain the same, but they are interpreted within the context of the suit. Therefore, the number 5, classically a number of bad luck, could signify trouble in a love affair if it were the 5 of Cups, or it could signify financial problems if it were the 5 of Pentacles.

The following list of key words was presented by Alfred Douglas in his book The Tarot. Based on the work of members of the Golden Dawn circle, these words were selected as useful guides in reading the Minor Arcana. They are not, however, definitive—merely suggestions of meanings that can be assigned. The numbered cards are not as "strong" as the Major Arcana and are more subject to the influences of the circumstances surrounding them and the other cards in the spread. Your reading should come primarily from the images of the cards in the context of the situation and the question at hand.

WANDS	CUPS	SWORDS	PENTACLES
1—Fire	1—Water	1—Air	1—Earth
2—Dominion	2—Love	2—Peace	2—Harmonious
3—Established	3—Abundance	Restored	Change
Strength	4—Blended	3—Sorrow	3—Material
4—Perfected	Pleasure	4—Rest from	Works
Work	5—Loss in	Strife	4—Earthly
5—Strife	Pleasure	5—Defeat	Power
6—Victory	6—Pleasure	6—Earned	5—Material
7—Valor	7—Illusionary	Success	Trouble
8—Swiftness	Success	7—Unstable	6—Material
9—Great	8—Abandoned	Effort	Success
Strength	Success	8—Shortened	7—Success
10—Oppression	9—Material	Force	Unfulfilled
	Happiness	9—Despair and	8—Prudence
	10—Perpetual	Cruelty	9—Material
	Success	10—Ruin	Gain
			10—Wealth

Remember also, that like the Major Arcana, a numbered suit card is at its full strength when upright, and either tempered, weakened, or its opposite when reversed.

SPREADING THE CARDS FOR A READING

There are dozens of ways of arranging the tarot cards so that they can be read. One elaborate method for determining a life reading involves using all seventy-eight cards and takes most of a day to do. Another type of spread, the Destiny Spread, is taught by Rolla Nordic in her classes. "It goes into some of the past life. I have found that, often, aspects of a person's past life relate to fears they have today, and that some of their fears don't relate to this life at all. They have to be finished with it, get rid of it, otherwise they'll carry it throughout their lifetime. I often find that someone who died from fire in a past life, however long ago, has an inclination to be an alcoholic today. It seems as if they are trying to put that fire out all the time. One of my students said he was so afraid of fire that he would run back home to make sure he had completely put out his cigarette butts, and he was an alcoholic. When he understood what was behind this fear, he got over it. But it was very helpful to explain his 'certain feeling.' They don't understand why they've got it; there's no visible cause." Nordic thinks she has been associated with the tarot for a long time. She identifies strongly with the Oracle at Delphi, a place she has visited. "The astrologers were the wise men in the Bible whom the tarot readers would call the oracles. The priestesses in the temple used to give their answers to the tarot. Strangely enough, the oracles were very often women—mostly women—the astrologers were mostly men. The tarot card readers were the oracles; they go way back in history."

Many professional readers find the Celtic spread useful and informative, and it is not too complicated for the novice. It is explained on page 431. First, here are two shorter, less complex techniques to try your hand at:

- To obtain a quick yes or no answer to a question, the cards are shuffled and cut. Then all the cards are laid out, face down, on a table. Three of the cards are chosen and placed, face up, in front of the reader. If all the cards are right side up, the answer to the question is yes. If only two cards are right side up and the other reversed, the answer is yes, but with some qualifiers. If two cards are reversed, the answer is a qualified no, and if all are reversed, the answer couldn't be a more definite no.

- Another method is called the Three Aces Spread. The cards are shuffled and cut. Then up to thirteen of the cards are dealt, face up, into a single pile until one of the four Aces appears. If an Ace doesn't appear within the first thirteen cards, up to thirteen more cards are dealt into a second pile, until an Ace is revealed. Once an Ace has been dealt or after the second stack of thirteen cards has been revealed, a final group of up to thirteen cards is turned over, until an Ace is uncovered. If no Aces are turned up, the tarot is not yet ready to address the question. If one or two of the stacks is Aceless, a period of time will have to pass before the solution to the problem or question will be possible. If just one Ace is revealed among the three piles, it will represent the answer to the question; if more than one Ace is revealed, the solution will be begun as regards the Ace on the far right and will be completed by the action of the Ace or Aces to its left.

Literally dozens of other arrangements exist, some in circles, crosses, parallel lines, and so on. What works for you is what is best.

THE CELTIC SPREAD

One of the most popular techniques—and the one we'll use here —is the Celtic Spread. It is relatively simple to learn; its yield of information is considerable, and it generally is considered to be the most suitable for looking at a situation or finding the answer to a specific question, whether stated aloud or not.

Before anything else is done with the cards, it is necessary to choose the *significator*, the card that will represent the subject of the reading, called the *seeker* or the *querent*. The significator can be chosen from among the Court cards according to their meanings (i.e., the Queen of Cups to represent an older woman involved in the arts; the Page of Wands to represent a teenage boy with blond hair and blue eyes), but a good general card to use as the significator is the Fool, because of its implications of beginnings and possibilities. Some adepts prefer to look at the pictures on the Court cards and make their choice based on intuitive feelings about which card best represents the seeker.

When the significator is chosen, remove it from the deck and set it aside. Shuffle the remaining tarot cards as you would regular playing cards, making sure that some of the cards are reversed in handling them. For example, if the reader divides the deck into two parts and turns one group of the cards upside down, one group will be reversed in comparison to the other. It is important that some cards be reversed in the shuffling process. Remember, the meaning of reversed cards is not always negative; therefore, there is no virtue in trying to keep all the cards right side up.

When the cards are shuffled, they are passed to the seeker, who, speaking aloud or simply thinking about it, concentrates on the matter or question he hopes to illuminate. The seeker uses his left hand to cut the deck twice to the left, creating three stacks of cards. The reader then picks up the cards, going first to the first stack, then the middle stack, and finally to the last stack, placing the pile that had been on the bottom on the top of the deck.

The significator is placed, face up, in the center of a clear flat surface at least two feet square. The reader, taking cards from the top of the deck, arranges them, face up, as follows:

at least two feet square. The reader, taking cards from the top of the deck, arranges them, faceup, as follows:

THE CELTIC SPREAD

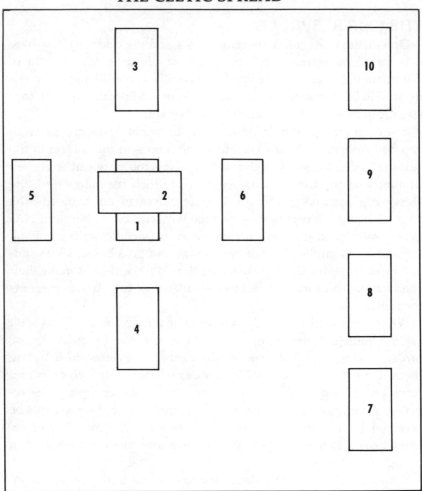

1. The first card is placed on top of the significator, covering it. This card indicates the dominating influence in the situation, what is currently influencing the seeker most.

2. The second card is placed sideways over the first. This indicates what stands in the way of the seeker, what opposes him. (This card is *always* read as upright; reverse interpretations do not apply.)

3. The third card is placed above the significator. This card indicates the most that can be attained in the present circumstances.

4. The fourth card is placed below the significator. It indicates the background of the situation and hidden influences.

5. The fifth card is placed to the left of the significator. It indicates the past, the immediate past, or a recent development or situation.

6. The sixth card is placed to the right of the significator. This card indicates the future, or developments likely to come about, given the current situation.

NOTE: The last four cards are placed to the right of the first six cards, in a column, one above the other.

7. The seventh card is placed at the bottom of the column. This indicates the seeker—the next step in his progress, a new development, or a strengthening influence.

8. The eighth card is placed above the seventh. It refers to the seeker's environment, often a person—a friend or member of the family.

9. The ninth card is placed above the eighth. It indicates the seeker's fears or hopes, his feelings about the situation.

10. The tenth card is placed above the ninth. It indicates the outcome of the situation or the answer to the question.

INTERPRETING THE CELTIC SPREAD

Having laid out the cards, it is important to look at them as a whole. Considering that only eleven cards of the seventy-eight have been used, check to see if the spread includes an inordinate number of Key cards from the Major Arcana. If so, there are powerful influences bearing on the situation that are out of the seeker's control. Is any one suit—perhaps Cups—disproportionately represented? If there are more than three or four Cups cards, then perhaps the situation, whether one of business or romance, is largely subject to the influence of emotion. Are Court cards heavily represented in the spread? Are there a surprising number of threes or sixes or any particular number? These observations and their meanings are general impressions that should be kept in mind as the specific cards are interpreted. Different adepts read a preponderance of types within a spread in different ways.

Rolla Nordic adds that there are nuances to the cards, little twists and turns that must be considered. "A card might mean one thing in a certain group of cards, and it might refer to something else among others. Now, someone might ask you a money question and a love card will come up. You think, 'Why would a love card come up with money?' But it's that they love money. You see, you have to relate the cards to the subject."

If you are just beginning your study of tarot, let your feelings guide you or check the book of an author you find interesting. Many strongly tie the tarot to numerology, since each card has an assigned number, and those numbers can have different meanings for different people or situations. If the tie between the tarot and numerology appeals to you, take a look at the chapter on numerology.

If the question or problem was asked aloud, the reader can begin to talk his way through the cards, reading them in order, beginning with the one in the first position (see the illustration) and moving through to the tenth. Each card will not only be relevant in itself and its position in the spread, but it will further explain the implications of previous cards. In this way, the spread will yield as much information as possible. (The seeker can be of help here to the novice reader, guiding the reader as much as possible. Adepts, however, often do not even need to know the question beforehand. They can look at the arrangement and progression of the cards and uncover the answer to the unspoken question.)

The process of reading the spread should produce a "story," dictated by the guidelines of the cards, fleshed out by the reader's interpretations and the specifics that the seeker can provide. The final card in the tenth position will resolve the question. If the last card has ambiguous meaning, it indicates that there is uncertainty, and the entire process should be repeated, using that final card from the original spread as the significator. If, after a second reading, the answer is still not clear, it is best to stop and try again another time; an answer cannot be forced.

A word should be added about handling the tarot cards. If the cards do not belong to you, do not grab them or touch them in any way without first ascertaining whether their owner objects. Some readers are very sensitive about their cards. Storage of the cards is important to some people—many prefer to wrap them in a dark-colored piece of silk or otherwise treat them specially. The protocol is not necessarily vital, but it's best not to offend a reader or his cards.

ASTROLOGY AND THE TAROT

Tarot's ties to astrology make all manner of different readings possible. Each sign of the zodiac is tied to one of the keys of the Major Arcana; therefore, an astrological "chart" can be cast, using tarot cards to explain the influences of the houses and planets in the chart. The tarot card reader needs to be well aware of astrology before attempting such a divination, but with patience, the correlations can be drawn. The Horoscope Method or spread requires that the shuffled cards be placed, one at a time, faceup, in a circle similar to that of a natal chart. The first card will be placed in a corresponding position to the first house, and eleven more cards will be turned up to correspond to the remaining eleven houses. The reader then interprets each tarot card as it relates to the classic meaning of the particular astrological house.

The Solar Chart Method uses only the Key cards that correspond to the signs of the zodiac. Therefore, the reader will remove the following cards:

Aries—The Sun, Key 19
Taurus—The Hierophant, Key 5
Gemini—The Lovers, Key 6
Cancer—Temperance, Key 14
Leo—Strength, Key 8
Virgo—The Hermit, Key 9
Libra—Justice, Key 11
Scorpio—Judgment, Key 20
Sagittarius—The Chariot, Key 7
Capricorn—The Devil, Key 15
Aquarius—The Star, Key 17
Pisces—The Moon, Key 18

If the sun sign of the seeker is Virgo, the Hermit card will be placed next to the first house on the chart and the remaining Key cards will be distributed, in order—Justice, for Libra, through Strength, for Leo —around the remaining houses in the chart. The chart then is read, correlating the meaning of the house with the meaning of the Key card that "rules" it.

WHERE TO GO FROM HERE

Learning the tarot is a complicated process that is well worth the time and effort to the truly interested. The dabbler, however, might do better at another discipline that has fewer variables or a smaller range of interpretation. The interesting and difficult part of the tarot is that each card signifies many things in and of itself as well as being extremely affected by its location, its proximity to other cards, and also to the question being asked.

A person who is interested in learning the tarot would do well to choose a different card from the Major Arcana every day and to concentrate on that card all day long. He or she should study the colors used on the card, the facial expressions of the people, the elements that make up the background, the frills, the relative size and importance of different aspects in the design. Some people will learn much by comparing the designs of the cards from one deck to the designs of another, noting which elements are shared, which ones change, what colors predominate, and so on. What is important is that the interested reader begin to "feel" the meaning of the card and to gain a clearer, more personal understanding of its intent and relationship to a situation.

A good practice session involves randomly selecting any two cards and trying to interpret them individually and then in relationship to each other. When those parallels become rather easy to do, start combining three cards and using different bases of comparison.

Naturally, reading what the experts have to say on the subject of the tarot will enlighten you about its history and its historical implications. Since tarot is so definitely based on past interpretations and mythology, a clearer and more detailed understanding of those subjects will add to your ability to read the cards. Expect a person-to-person reading with a professional to cost between $30 and $100, and be sure to go to your appointment well armed with questions about matters that concern you. Remember, the tarot is especially useful as a tool for guidance; we should use it to clarify specific situations and to point the way toward besting our shortcomings.

CHAPTER
SIXTEEN
I CHING

Despite the opening of China's closed doors in recent years, most Americans have little familiarity with I Ching. Perhaps they know that it has to do with throwing sticks or coins, or that the concept of yin and yang is somehow involved, but beyond these basic facts, most people just aren't conversant with the I Ching. I wasn't, either, but I made it my business to study the I Ching and to talk to people who have had some experience with it; now I can confidently say that the I Ching, or Book of Changes, is worth looking into for anyone, Eastern or Western.

At first glance, the I Ching seems obscure and inaccessible, filled with sayings about pigs and fishes, dragons and mares, and the hides of yellow cows. Colin Wilson remarks: "I can only say that a close acquaintance with the I Ching and its symbols soon begins to reveal a remarkable inner consistency. At first, the landscape is strange and disconcerting; soon it becomes familiar and everything is seen to be logical." Hellmut Wilhelm, whose book *Eight Lectures on the I Ching* is the standard introduction to the material, suggests that "we must accept this at first, as we accept a musical composition in which it is not always immediately evident why this or that modulation or harmony stands in this or that place, yet the whole composition carries conviction." This is fine advice, but it must be admitted that Wilhelm's father, Richard, was one of the most important scholars and translators of the I Ching, and Hellmut certainly started out with a good bit of understanding. Most of us need first to realize the importance that the book holds in Chinese culture in order to approach it with the appropriate attitude.

Suppose you were to take the King James Bible and the complete works of William Shakespeare, with all their poetry, moral lessons, and insights into humanity, and combine them in one book. Add to that the commentaries of every major Western thinker, from Plato to

Einstein, from Marx to Machiavelli, from St. Augustine to Thomas Jefferson, all written after a lifetime of studying the result. For a final measure, destroy every other book our culture has produced. If you can imagine the significance that book would have to us, you will understand the importance the I Ching holds in Chinese culture.

Hellmut Wilhelm puts it this way: "The essential thing to keep in mind is all the strata that go to make up the book. Archaic wisdom from the dawn of time, detached and systematic reflections of the Confucian school of the Chou era, pithy sayings from the heart of the people, subtle thoughts of the leading minds: All of these disparate elements have harmonized to create the structure of the book as we know it." Remembering this, we can begin to examine the material that makes up the I Ching.

THE TEXT OF THE I CHING INTERWOVEN WITH A BRIEF HISTORY

The core of the I Ching consists of sixty-four hexagrams. Each hexagram is a complex of six horizontal lines, one atop the other. Each of the six lines is either broken in half or solid. These lines, called yin and yang respectively, represent the dualities that make up the world. Some of these qualities can be summarized as follows:

YIN	YANG
DARK	LIGHT
FEMALE	MALE
YIELDING	STRONG
RECEPTIVE	CREATIVE

Note that nowhere in these attributes is the idea of good as opposed to evil. Both the yin and the yang are necessary to make up the world; one could not exist without the other.

The basic unit of the hexagram is the trigram, or three horizontal lines; each hexagram is made up of two trigrams. There are eight trigrams, each being one of the eight possible combinations of the broken and unbroken lines when grouped in threes. Like the lines, the trigrams have certain attributes. The concepts that the trigrams represent parallel somewhat the Western idea of Platonic ideals; that is, they are basic qualities underlying reality, on which our world is modeled. Further, each trigram is assigned a familial position. The names and various qualities of the trigrams are shown in the chart that follows.

THE TRIGRAMS

	Name		Quality	Image	Position
☰	Ch'ien	creative	strong	heaven	father
☷	K'un	receptive	devoted, yielding	earth	mother
☳	Chen	arousing	inciting movement	thunder	first son
☵	K'an	abysmal	dangerous	water	second son
☶	Ken	keeping still	resting	mountain	third son
☴	Sun	gentle	penetrating	wind, wood	first daughter
☲	Li	clinging	light-giving	fire	second daughter
☱	Tui	joyous	joyful	lake	third daughter

Tradition credits the creation of the eight trigrams to the mythical character Fu Hsi, in a period about five thousand years ago. They are most likely derived, whether by Fu Hsi or not, from the markings on tortoiseshells; reading the tortoiseshell for oracles, known as scapulomancy, was a tradition precedent to and superseded by the I Ching.

The present arrangement of the sixty-four hexagrams—all the possible combinations of the eight trigrams in pairs—is attributed to King Wen, a historical figure whose son founded the Chou dynasty around 1100 B.C. The first of the ten commentaries, or Wings, attached to the hexagrams is also said to be the work of King Wen. These are called the Judgments—short statements or poems describing the character of each hexagram. A second commentary, called the Great Images, is derived from the combinations of qualities of the trigrams represented in each hexagram, such as Fire on the Mountain or Wind over Lake. The Small Images are commentaries attached to each line in the hexagram. Both the Great and Small Images have been attributed to Tan, the Duke of Chou, who was the son of King Wen and for some time regent of the dynasty.

The remaining commentaries have been traditionally attributed to Confucius, but historically, only some of the teachings could have been his. Some of these most probably are, and a great deal may be the work of a group of his students, carrying on his teachings.

Another legend concerning Confucius and the I Ching tells that when, in 213 B.C., Ch'in Shih Huang Ti, the ruler of the newly founded Ch'in dynasty, ordered all books of the previous dynasty destroyed, the I Ching survived only because Confucius hid a copy in the walls of his home. Probably closer to the truth is that with the general destruction of books—which did, in fact, take place that year and is one of the major events of Chinese history—a select group of scientific works were allowed to survive. The I Ching, as one of the few remaining repositories of the teachings of previous thinkers, received even greater attention.

THE I CHING AND THE WEST

The I Ching has always fascinated the Western mind. The first to come in contact with it were the Jesuit missionaries who traveled to China bearing the teachings of Christianity. The Jesuits were the most finely trained thinkers of their time and were, in addition, fanatically dogmatic about Christianity. To demonstrate that fanaticism, it need only be pointed out that those who took up the study of the I Ching were pronounced either heretic or insane.

Leibniz, one of our great mathematicians and philosophers, believed that in the I Ching he had discovered a universal binary calculus—a mathematical system within which all the truths of science could be expressed. He took the yin and yang to represent 0 and 1. (A binary system such as this that uses only two digits, as opposed to our ten-digit decimal system, underlies all the operations of modern computers.)

Finally, Carl Jung, one of the great minds of our time, took up the study of the I Ching toward the end of his life and, like Confucius, is said to have expressed the wish for another lifetime to devote to its study.

The I Ching has been shown to be compatible with our way of thought; we need only a key. Fortunately, within the translation of the book itself, we are provided with it. The classic commentaries serve as a wise and patient guide, explaining the obscure imagery and obtuse references. Understanding them, however, requires patience, experience, and time for serious contemplation.

Howard Goodman, a Chinese historian currently doing research at Princeton, studied the I Ching over a fifteen-year period while he was preparing his dissertation on the subject. His pursuit of the meaning of the I Ching was based on his personal desire to understand it in order to better comprehend Chinese history. When he speaks of the Book of Changes, he is very much the cautious scholar.

Goodman's reaction to the Wilhelm translation is very positive. "I think a lot of it. Richard Wilhelm knew the language—it's still, to my mind, one of the best translations there is. He based himself on the received Chinese understanding of the text as it came down especially with thirteenth- through nineteenth-century commentaries, which were also based indirectly on earlier ones. . . . The James Legge translation is good, too." Goodman goes on to relate that Legge himself didn't make much of the I Ching, and said so in his introduction to his translation. He translated it because he thought it important that it be done. According to Goodman, Richard Wilhelm, on the other hand, "welded a philosophical system to his understanding of the text. And the system could rightly be called Jungian, with qualifications. . . . He read Jungian writings and saw bigger movements in the lives of human beings in the text of the hexagrams. . . ."

When asked if a person needs a special psychic talent to be able to use the I Ching, Goodman answers with a definite no. Apparently one needs no particular metaphysical knowledge whatsoever, though "a knowledge of the different systems of rules the Book of Changes draws on is helpful. They're not all in the Book of Changes, they're in Chinese culture. You have to draw them out, and if one set of rules doesn't seem to be working, you plug in another. . . ." According to Goodman, the question "Why was the I Ching written?" is an interesting one. He responds with his own theory: "As a tool for understanding the universe, for understanding one's place in the universe; and the function of the tool was probably very much in the everyday lives and in the symbols of power of socially prominent people, people of political power."

But the insights available from the I Ching are not the quick and easy aphorisms the West prefers. Goodman is clear about the expertise required for its use. He thinks that both the expert on classical Chinese studies and the layman can use the I Ching equally well. "You'll get something—a different approach—if you take it to somebody who truly understands classical Chinese, understands the text of the book itself and the history of the commentators who wrote on it for fifteen hundred or two thousand years. Questions asked of the I Ching can be as specific as you want them to be. . . . Belief is the key word."

The I Ching demands wisdom as well as yields it. Confucius put it this way:

> First take up the words
> Ponder their meanings
> Then the fixed rules reveal themselves.
> But if you are not the right man,
> The meaning will not manifest itself to you.

The teachings are derived from a complex system of relationships among the trigrams, the hexagrams, and the lines themselves. The fifth line of a hexagram, for example, is said to be the ruler; the fourth, the minister; and the sixth, a sage. Therefore, a hexagram with a broken yin line in the fourth place and a solid yang line in the fifth is said to contain a minister who yields to a strong ruler. A yang in the sixth place and a yin in the fifth would be a ruler who follows the teachings of his sage.

Another set of relationships derives from the positions of the trigrams. Chi'en, the father, over Chen, the first son, shows a proper familial relationship, the father having authority over the son.

The positions of the trigrams as images is another source of the teachings. Chi'en, as heaven, naturally moves upward; K'un, as earth, has downward movement. In hexagram 12, Ch'ien over K'un, heaven and earth pull in opposite directions, creating a negative situation. With the trigrams reversed, in hexagram 11, K'un over Ch'ien, they pull toward each other, creating a positive situation.

Let's look at a specific hexagram from Wilhelm's *The I Ching* and see how this works. In hexagram 10, *Lu*, Treading (or Conduct), Ch'ien, heaven, the father, is over Tui, lake, the daughter. The Judgment reads:

> Treading upon the tail of the tiger.
> It does not bite the man. Success.

This seems initially meaningless. The commentary, however, explains: Tui, as the daughter, is the weaker. Tui follows under, or behind Ch'ien, the father, the powerful. Thus a man walks behind a powerful tiger and chances stepping upon its tail. But Tui, whose quality is joy, does so without presumption, with a nonchallenging attitude—the proper conduct for a daughter. Thus the powerful father, the tiger, does not take offense, and does not bite.

The image for this hexagram—again, from Wilhelm—reads:

Heaven above, Lake below.
Thus the superior man discriminates between high and low,
And thereby fortifies the thinking of the people.

From the image, Wilhelm derives this lesson: "Heaven and lake show a difference of elevation that inheres in the natures of the two, hence no envy arises. Among mankind also there are necessarily differences of elevations. But it is important that differences in social rank should not be arbitrary and unjust, for if this occurs, envy and class struggle are the inevitable consequences. If, on the other hand, external differences in rank correspond with differences in inner worth, and if inner worth forms the criterion of external rank, people acquiesce and order reigns in society."

This example goes a long way toward showing how lessons for living can be derived from the hexagrams. But it brings up another question. Throughout the text, there are references to "the superior man." Who is the superior man? This is a simple and easily translated concept. The superior man is the person who conducts himself properly given the situation. It can be expressed in the Western saying "God grant me the serenity to accept the things I cannot change, the courage to change the things I can, and the wisdom to know the difference." Proper behavior in any given circumstance is the ultimate lesson of the I Ching.

THE USE OF THE I CHING

In both the East and the West, the I Ching has had two distinct uses. The first, as a book of wisdom, treats the I Ching as simply that: a repository of wisdom to be read and savored, studied and learned from. As such, it should be approached as any great book is approached, with respect and patience. There is enough insight here to keep anyone occupied in contemplation for a lifetime, just as a Christian might study passages from the Bible for the lessons it offers.

The second use of the I Ching—and the one that has earned it its mystical reputation—is as a book of oracles. In this case, one asks a question and is pointed to an answer in one of the hexagrams. There are two methods used to ask the answer to a question. The first is the complicated traditional method involving yarrow stalks—the stalks of a wild herb. Starting with fifty stalks, one proceeds to divide them at random, repeatedly counting them out until they indicate the six lines of a hexagram. The simpler and more common method is one you can try for yourself. It requires just three coins.

How does the "psychic" factor enter into the throwing of the I Ching? Brian Inglis writes, "The act of throwing yarrow stalks or coins is psychokinetically linked to the results obtained. The arrangement of the tarot cards after they are dealt, or the passages in the I Ching indicated by the way in which the stalks or the coins have fallen, are believed in themselves to provide paranormal divination through synchronicity." Howard Goodman adds that throwing the sticks is the more desirable method. "You'll get certain numbers more—you'll get a broader range with the sticks. With the coins there tends to be a statistical sink in which you'll get two of the four numbers more often."

D. Scott Rogo refers to an experiment that yielded interesting conclusions:

> There was an experiment done—I believe by Rex Stanford—with the I Ching where people would consult the I Ching and then they would be given two responses. One was the response they got through the throwing of the sticks or whatever procedure they used, and one that was randomly chosen. These people were able to pick out to a statistically significant degree the one that did match the question. The point was that it only worked for people who believed in the I Ching. It did not work for people who did not. That seemed to indicate that there may have been some sort of psychokinetic activity when they actually threw the sticks. There are loopholes in the techniques that can allow psychic functioning to take place.

How a random process such as throwing sticks or coins could answer a question is certainly open to debate. The Chinese tradition cites *Shen*, "spiritlike things," as causing the stalks or coins to result in a particular configuration. Carl Jung referred to the phenomenon of synchronicity and was convinced that it provided a rationale for divination through the I Ching. He found the I Ching infallible. In his explanation, it is believed that the subconscious mind knows the answer to the question and thus influences the result of the throws. Does it work? Howard Goodman says that I Ching works if you believe.

Rogo continues the discussion, citing a phenomenon in parapsychology known as the psychic shuffle. Tarot cards are shuffled and laid out. Then a person shuffles another deck of the cards and stops when he thinks there is a decent match between what he is shuffling and the preorder of the other deck of cards. Rogo says, "Statistically, it worked very well in the lab. Obviously, somehow psychically, the shuffler is keeping track of what's going on in the deck as he's shuffling it. Couldn't tarot be a very similar situation, where the person shuffling the deck uses some sort of psychic ability to stop shuffling or manipulate the shuffling in such a way that it does seem to reflect what is going on in the life of the client?"

Colin Wilson describes his first experience with I Ching:

As to my own personal experience with the I Ching, it has certainly disposed me to treat it as perhaps the foremost of all such works. I first came across it in the period I have already spoken of, when I was living in Wimbledon. Obviously, the first thing that any would-be writer consults an "oracle" about is his future as a writer; he wants a "long-range forecast." I took three pennies, and threw them down six times. Each time, there was a preponderance of heads, giving a hexagram made up of six yang lines: the first one in the book, with a judgment that reads:

The creative works supreme success
Furthering through perseverance.

In the hundreds of times I have consulted it since then, the coins have never given six unbroken lines. Obviously, I was disposed to be convinced.

A SAMPLE THROW

Probably the best way to try I Ching is to jump in with both feet. Since the yarrow-stalks method is time-consuming, and since yarrow isn't so easy to find in most places, I opt for the coin method. First, find three coins (here the Chinese would choose three of their round coins that have a square hole in the center; you might use three quarters or three dimes).

If you follow the instructions given by Da Liu in his book *I Ching Coin Prediction*, after choosing your coins, your next step would be to burn incense. During this time, the querist should pray, introducing himself, giving his address, the question, and the reason for asking the question. Talk to the I Ching directly, just as though it were a person right there in the room with you. Then, according to Da Liu, "he shakes the three coins in the smoke of the incense—these should be held in clasped hands or in a special container—and throws them on a table or some other flat surface. This ritual is no mere superstition; it has a specific purpose: to concentrate our thoughts and quiet the mind. Only when a person has clearly and definitely in his mind what he wants to know can the I Ching give a clear and definite answer." In other words, a calm and meditative attitude—if not prayer and incense—is the best way to approach the I Ching.

For the actual tossing of the coins, heads (yang) are assigned a value of 2, and tails (yin) are assigned a value of 3. Throwing the coins a total of six times, each throw will yield a total of 6, 7, 8, or 9. You can thus build a hexagram—*always building from the bottom to the top*—using 6s and 8s as yin, or broken, lines, and 7s and 9s as yang, or solid, lines. Further, 6s are read as "old yin" lines, that is, yins that are in the process of changing into yangs; 9s are read as "old yang" lines, those in the process of changing into yins.

Using this three-coin method for a sample throw, I arrived at the following values and lines:

Throw 1: three heads, value 6 = old yin
Throw 2: two heads, one tail, value 7 = yang
Throw 3: two tails, one head, value 8 = yin
Throw 4: three tails, value 9 = old yang
Throw 5: two heads, one tail, value 7 = yang
Throw 6: two tails, one head, value 8 = yin

The graphic representation would be this:

The two trigrams are thus Tui (⚌) over K'an (⚍). Consulting the chart on page 447, we find that this hexagram is number 47, K'un.

Here is where I have done my best to simplify your initial understanding of the I Ching. In the pages that follow, I offer Frederick Davies' Westernized interpretation of each trigram of the I Ching. These readings are much condensed to make them more accessible to the novice. Turn to number 47 and read the paragraph of explanation. This approach has deleted the poetry of the I Ching in favor of clearer, more immediate understanding. It has been written to apply directly to everyday life, avoiding nonspecific allusions. If your interest is deeper and you want to pursue further study of the I Ching, it will be necessary to work with one of the classic translations of the text—either the Wilhelm or the Legge or both.

DETERMINING THE HEXAGRAMS

Trigrams Upper→ Lower ↓	Ch'ien	Chen	K'an	Ken	K'un	Sun	Li	Tui
Ch'ien	1	34	5	26	11	9	14	43
Chen	25	51	3	27	24	42	21	17
K'an	6	40	29	4	7	59	64	47
Ken	33	62	39	52	15	53	56	31
K'un	12	16	8	23	2	20	35	45
Sun	44	32	48	18	46	57	50	28
Li	13	55	63	22	36	37	30	49
Tui	10	54	60	41	19	61	38	58

If you were to use the Wilhelm book, first you would read the Judgment and its commentary, and then the Image and its commentary. Next you would consult the commentaries for the individual lines of the hexagram. You would read the commentaries only for changing lines, that is, those with values of 6 or 9, such as lines 1 and 4 in the sample throw. These readings provide specific advice for the situation.

The final step would be to change those lines with values of 6 and 9: The first line is changed from a yin to a yang, and the fourth line is changed from a yang to a yin, thus:

The new combination yields K'an over Tui, hexagram number 60, Chieh. The Judgment and Image of the new hexagram are consulted to determine what will be the final outcome or result of the question being asked. Commentaries on the individual lines are ignored in interpreting the second hexagram.

Another facet of the reading involves the nuclear trigrams, the "inner" trigrams formed by lines 2, 3, and 4, and lines 3, 4, and 5 (in this case the trigrams Sun and Li). When used, these are read after the interpretations and before the individual lines of the first hexagram. They are used to determine the internal tensions of the first situation. But this method requires a great familiarity with the I Ching and is not advised for the beginner.

THE HEXAGRAMS

1.   CH'IEN, The Creative

ABOVE   Ch'ien   **The Creative, Heaven**

BELOW   Ch'ien   **The Creative, Heaven**

You have control over your destiny, for you are creative and practical in all that you do. Everything you get involved with will be a success and go according to your well-organized plans. Not only will you achieve the recognition you seek but also fame, honors, and public acclaim in your community. Beware of being too arrogant and demanding on others, as that will slow your progress and lessen the loyalty of your supporters.

2.   K'UN, The Receptive

☷   ABOVE   K'un   The Receptive, Earth

☷   BELOW   K'un   The Receptive, Earth

You will be led into the right path by following your intuitive feelings and by being led by others who come into your life at different times. Never act impulsively, as you are apt to make mistakes that cannot be reversed. Your personality and attitudes attract the right people, and if you always listen to your heart, you won't go far wrong. Listen to the wise words of teachers and advisors and of your spiritual leader. Once you have found your guru, you will have sublime happiness.

3.   CHUN, Difficulty at the Beginning

☵   ABOVE   K'an   The Abysmal, Water

☳   BELOW   Chen   The Arousing, Thunder

Success finally comes from great struggle and much hard work. There will always seem to be obstacles put in your way, and you must think of new and original ways to get around them each time. Keep your principles and never give in to others whom you do not believe in totally. Happiness and material rewards are there if you are willing to go after them in all weather, good and bad. New ventures need patience and careful encouragement.

4.   MENG, Youthful Folly

☶   ABOVE   Ken   Keeping Still, Mountain

☵   BELOW   K'an   The Abysmal, Water

Listen to those who are older and wiser, for you are apt to jump into situations and relationships without thinking about the consequences. Things may appear to be slow, and you must not allow this to hold back your enthusiasm for life and adventure. Ask advice; don't jump into an unknown pit without finding out ahead of time what is in it. You will have great success once you behave with maturity.

5. HSU, Waiting

☵ **ABOVE** K'an — The Abysmal, Water

☰ **BELOW** Chi'en — The Creative, Heaven

You must always wait for the appropriate time to act. There is much to be gained by just doing nothing. Inaction physically gives you time to think. You can attain all your goals and aspirations, for you have the strength and character to persevere. Never rush or behave impulsively, for you must weigh every act before carrying it out. Your long-term planning finally pays off with many big rewards and happy results.

6. SUNG, Conflict

☰ **ABOVE** Ch'ien — The Creative, Heaven

☵ **BELOW** K'an — The Abysmal, Water

Now you are aware of the many conflicts that you attract in every area of your life. But you can gain more by being aggressive and taking advantage of these conflicts than by being tactful and passive and ignoring them. Obstacles bring out the best in you in your strategic planning. The bruises you suffer to your spirit will soon heal. Whatever happens, people will remember you and admire your stamina and your determination.

7. SHIH, The Army

☷ **ABOVE** K'un — The Receptive, Earth

☵ **BELOW** K'an — The Abysmal, Water

Working with the masses will bring you the greatest success in life, for you like to lead and direct others into the most practical and useful paths. But you are also willing to take orders from other people, and you respect their position in society or the rank and office they hold in business or in other organizations. Always uphold your faith and your beliefs. Don't be led by lesser men or women to be motivated by greed.

8.   **PI, Holding Together, Union**

☵   **ABOVE   K'an**   **The Abysmal, Water**

☷   **BELOW   K'un**   **The Receptive Earth**

Unity in love and business brings much happiness and much success. Think of others before you take any action that could embarrass them or put their position and reputation in jeopardy. Joint ventures will be rewarded, for you help show others how to improve their lives. The public will approve of any ideas you may have and will be regular customers or clients. They will give you the same loyalty you have shown them.

9.   **HSIAO CH'U, The Taming Power of the Small**

☴   **ABOVE   Sun**   **The Gentle, Wind**

☰   **BELOW   Ch'ien**   **The Creative, Heaven**

Keep to your beliefs and never relax. You have the ability to do great things. Patience is necessary, but without the support of large organizations of the government, you can still accomplish what you strive for. Once the obstacles and restrictions disappear, your luck will suddenly change and much happiness will be bestowed on you. Never be pessimistic. Always keep up your courage. You have the strength of the lion when it comes to a crisis.

10. **LU, Treading, Conduct**

☰ ABOVE Ch'ien **The Creative, Heaven**

☱ BELOW Tui **The Joyous, Lake**

Taking your time, you can surmount all the dangers that may be around you. Walk steadfastly but slowly, for you could suddenly encounter a situation that may be unusual and foreign to you. Never take the offensive, as others will interpret that as a bad and critical attitude. Maintain a cool stance. Stand firm and you will receive blessings and rewards for your humility.

11. **T'AI, Peace**

☷ ABOVE K'un **The Receptive, Earth**

☰ BELOW Ch'ien **The Creative, Heaven**

The future has much in store for you, and you will get what you go after. Studies, business, and romance will bring much happiness. There will always be opportunities showing themselves, and you must be willing to take chances at times. Life will have very few surprises or problems. You seek peace of mind more than wealth, but you may attract it subconsciously without making the effort. Luck comes to you early.

12. **P'I, Standstill**

☰ ABOVE Ch'ien **The Creative, Heaven**

☷ BELOW K'un **The Receptive, Earth**

You will have to work hard to overcome much of the hard luck that surrounds you. There could be much separation from your loved ones, which will give you much unhappiness. Only by waiting patiently, in quiet study and in restful repose, can you conquer any adversity. The pendulum rises and falls; the swing of the pendulum brings you as much luck and success as it has given you sadness and sorrow.

13.   **T'UNG JEN, Fellowship with Men**

≡   ABOVE   Ch'ien   The Creative, Heaven

☲   BELOW   Li   The Clinging, Flame

Everything you do in conjunction with others will have much success. You will always be protected by your associates. When you have found the perfect partner, good fortune and wealth will be bestowed upon you. Try to avoid arguments with others, as you do not come out at your best on such occasions and will resort to selfish and uncharacteristic behavior.

14.   **TA YU, Possession in Great Measure**

☲   ABOVE   Li   The Clinging, Flame

≡   BELOW   Ch'ien   The Creative, Heaven

Great fortune and luck will be bestowed on you and your family. The masses will like your style, and you will attract rich supporters to your business, your talents, and your ideas. More caution is necessary if you are going to retain this success and status in the place where you live. Beware unnecessary expenditure, as you are apt to be extravagant and impulsive. Generosity is a good trait but can be excessive and foolhardy. However, luck will always be on your side.

15.   **CH'IEN, Modesty**

☷   ABOVE   K'un   The Receptive, Earth

☶   BELOW   Ken   Keeping Still, Mountain

It is very important that you behave in a modest and humble fashion. All goes well for you, and better than you dreamed, but if you show off or are unkind or unfair to those who take care of you, then you will lose your protective luck. Even in your goals in life, don't be too greedy or demand too much, or you will not be satisfied. By aiming lower than usual, you can accomplish everything you set out to do and shine.

16.   YU, Enthusiasm

☷☳ ABOVE Chen   The Arousing, Thunder

☷☷ BELOW K'un   The Receptive, Earth

Luck comes to you in many ways, but you cannot stand still and just hope for everything to fit into place. You must make things happen. Your enthusiasm and excitement about what you do will always encourage others. Because of your faith in other people, you put yourself in a position where you can be robbed or embezzled. Get all your papers, documents, and contracts into a safe place.

17.   SUI, Following

☱☱ ABOVE Tui   The Joyous, Lake

☳☳ BELOW Chen   The Arousing, Thunder

Success comes by following the example and the advice of others who have gone the same path before. If you try to impose your ideas and personality onto others, there may be a clash of wills. Fame is yours once you are willing to tie yourself to the glory of another and share the spotlight together. Your loyalty will be recognized and a position of power may be given to you in the shadow of your guru, partner, or spouse.

18.   KU, Work on what has been Spoiled, Decay

☶☶ ABOVE Ken   Keeping Still, Mountain

☴☴ BELOW Sun   The Gentle, Wind

You meet many obstacles and problems before you can have the success you strive for. Everyone you meet seems to be against what you want to do and to deliberately set out to set traps for you. By being independent and not allowing yourself to become stagnant, idle, or lazy, you can combat this negativity and shine through all the problems. Sickness in the family brings about extra pressures. You are finally rewarded for your devotion to duty and for your perseverance.

19.　　　LIN, Approach

☷　ABOVE　K'un　　　The Receptive, Earth

☱　BELOW　Tui　　　The Joyous, Lake

The way in which you treat other people will be the way in which others will think of you. You will have much success in life, but the amount depends on your behavior and how well you deserve such rewards and honors. Be humble but not subservient. Be generous but not extravagant, and never be unkind, arrogant, or superior. Happiness comes to you naturally if you follow your instincts.

20.　　　KUAN, Contemplation, View

☴　ABOVE　Sun　　　The Gentle, Wind

☷　BELOW　K'un　　　The Receptive, Earth

Great advancement in life comes from winning the support of wiser and older people. Meditate and think about the future, for you have the ability to see what is about to happen and to use this knowledge for the betterment of mankind. By treating others with sincerity, you create an atmosphere of tranquillity, and peace of mind is your reward. Think and analyze your moves before you make them.

21.　　　SHIH HO, Biting Through

☲　ABOVE　Li　　　The Clinging, Flame

☳　BELOW　Chen　　　The Arousing, Thunder

Aggressive action will get you through life, and you must allow yourself to speak out, to say exactly what is on your mind. Being passive brings unhappiness, for you will not be in control of your life. You will achieve your many ambitions and make a mark in history if you are willing to go forward with strength and purpose. Don't ever rely on others to negotiate on your behalf, as you could be the loser. You do best when you take life into your own hands.

22.   **PI, Grace**

☷☷   **ABOVE   Ken**   **Keeping Still, Mountain**

☲   **BELOW   Li**   **The Clinging, Flame**

Much success comes to you through following your natural creative talents. The arts attract you and will give you happiness and honor. Be satisfied with small achievements at first, for it will take time for you to build the reputation and publicity that you deserve. If you are conceited, or expect too much in the beginning, you will meet with many obstacles, and supporters will be only halfhearted instead of behind you totally.

23.   **PO, Splitting Apart**

☶   **ABOVE   Ken**   **Keeping Still, Mountain**

☷   **BELOW   K'un**   **The Receptive, Earth**

Caution is necessary in all that you do, as luck is not often on your side. Precautions are to be taken to ensure that others don't take advantage of you. Make sure you don't give them ammunition for gossip or to do you harm. Take a good look at all the options before you move ahead, and always retreat and reevaluate your strategy before making any reckless or risky moves.

24.   **FU, Return, The Turning Point**

☷   **ABOVE   K'un**   **The Receptive, Earth**

☳   **BELOW   Chen**   **The Arousing, Thunder**

Having overcome many difficulties and much bad luck, you now enter a beneficial and happy period. Good fortune is in your future. Take your time, for there may still be a few minor obstacles in your way. Impulsive actions will prove costly, and you must forever watch a tendency to be lavish and extravagant. Success is yours if you are willing to make the necessary sacrifices and work hard. This is a new beginning, a real turning point.

25.   **WU WANG, Innocence, The Unexpected**

☰   ABOVE Ch'ien   The Creative, Heaven

☳   BELOW Chen   The Arousing, Thunder

Be sincere in all your dealings, and allow others to go after greedy ambitions. You must seek a well-balanced life by accepting little and going after only ambitions that will help others. Pleasure will come from the delight of other people whom you would have helped up the ladder of success. Your selflessness will bring you the joy and happiness you seek and take away many pressures.

26.   **TA CH'U, The Taming Power of the Great**

☶   ABOVE Ken   Keeping Still, Mountain

☰   BELOW Ch'ien   The Creative, Heaven

Things may not go as well as you dreamed, but you must persevere. Success and happiness come from hard work and the ability to take adversity in your stride. You cannot be held back, and you are never completely disappointed. You will save much money and be given important work to do. Promotions and rewards come from others watching your diligence and sophisticated approach to life. You have magnetic power over others, and they are under your spell and will do your bidding.

27.   **I, The Corners of the Mouth, Providing Nourishment**

☶   ABOVE Ken   Keeping Still, Mountain

☳   BELOW Chen   The Arousing, Thunder

Actions must be carefully thought out before or you will have bad luck. Study and develop your abilities, talents, and skills so you will ensure your success in life. Only by sincere and devoted hard work will you achieve your goals. Success is there if you go after it. Be careful not to neglect your health, diet, and nutrition if you are working or studying excessively.

28.   **TA KUO, Preponderance of the Great**

☱   **ABOVE   Tui**   **The Joyous, Lake**

☴   **BELOW   Sun**   **The Gentle, Wind**

Be willing to throw off the burdens that are resting very heavily on your shoulders. These things can hold you back. Let others share these responsibilities. Decide what your strong points are and concentrate on developing them. Overcome any weakness or characteristics that you find restrictive to your career and ambitions. Your luck changes when you are willing to make personal changes.

29.   **K'AN, The Abysmal**

☵   **ABOVE   K'an**   **The Abysmal, Water**

☵   **BELOW   K'an**   **The Abysmal, Water**

Life will bring you many hardships, and you will learn many lessons from other people's behavior. By being patient, your luck changes for the better, but you cannot force it. Give yourself some well-defined goals and go after them. Ignore obstacles; get around them the best you can. Others may want to cheat you or take something away from you. Make sure your valuable possessions are protected.

30.   **LI, The Clinging, Fire**

☲   **ABOVE   Li**   **The Clinging, Flame**

☲   **BELOW   Li**   **The Clinging, Flame**

Much good luck comes to you because your motives are pure and you are on the right path. By remaining friends with associates from the past, you give security to relations you have with others, both in business and in romance. You must always listen to the wise advice of older people, for they will steer you in a safe direction and save you years of suffering. Impulsive actions bring you defeat, so think first before any major contracts are made.

31.   **HSIEN, Influence**

☱   **ABOVE**   Tui   **The Joyous, Lake**

☶   **BELOW**   Ken   **Keeping Still, Mountain**

Much happiness and good fortune are in store for you. All your goals are easy to reach, and any joint venture with others will have success. Romance and love cause you much distress, but finally you come out a winner and can expect a long and happy relationship. If someone is taken out of your life, that person was not meant to be there. Another will replace him or her with much more joy.

32.   **HENG, Duration**

☳   **ABOVE**   Chen   **The Arousing, Thunder**

☲   **BELOW**   Li   **The Clinging, Flame**

Wealth and prosperity are possible for you, as you work hard and, being sincere, people trust you. Be conservative in your approach to life, for the rich will stay away if your presentation is radical and complicated. You will be able to endure long hours of work and accomplish many tasks during your life and receive honors and rewards fitting your person. Make your ambitions material ones as well as spiritual ones for the best success.

33.   **TUN, Retreat**

☰   **ABOVE**   Ch'ien   **The Creative, Heaven**

☶   **BELOW**   Ken   **Keeping Still, Mountain**

Take great care in whatever you do financially, for you will instinctively get warnings of danger yet you will ignore them. Save your money and don't allow yourself to speculate recklessly. Being cautious, you will save your home, property, business, and wealth. Carelessness will take away everything you worked for and that means much to you. Good fortune comes after much struggle.

34.   TA CHUANG, The Power of the Great

▚   ABOVE   Chen   The Arousing, Thunder

☰   BELOW   Ch'ien   The Creative, Heaven

Whatever you do will be successful, and you will become great in
your community and in your profession. Keep a warm and friendly
disposition when dealing with others, for you could become so busy
with your work that your personal life will suffer. You could end up
alone, in solitude and without close friends, if you don't make an
effort. A change of attitude brings happiness.

35.   CHIN, Progress

☲   ABOVE   Li   The Clinging, Flame

☷   BELOW   K'un   The Receptive, Earth

Good fortune shines on you and on all your ventures and ambitions.
Let others who have much more experience and who are wiser give
you a hand, for that will save you a lot of worry and anxiety plus
make them feel very important to your success. You will naturally
meet many people who are envious, jealous, and harmful, so be
aware of their motivations and don't trust everyone who attempts to
be helpful. Ask yourself why.

36.   MING I, Darkening of the Light

☷   ABOVE   K'un   The Receptive, Earth

☲   BELOW   Li   The Clinging, Flame

Element of danger. By being more self-confident and by sticking to
routines that you are familiar with, patience and loyalty pay off, and
you will achieve much success by allowing life to take you along
quietly until the time comes for your luck to change, at which time
everything you are striving for becomes possible.

37. **CHIA JEN, The Family**

☴ **ABOVE** Sun The Gentle, Wind

☲ **BELOW** Li The Clinging, Flame

Much happiness, success, and good fortune in all that you do. Always stick to your goals and remember the reputation of the family and you will always have good luck. Beware of rash changes, for others will be bewildered and unhappy. Trust those around you who love you, but beware the jealous and envious relatives who resent your achievements in life and try to sabotage them.

38. **K'UEI, Opposition**

☲ **ABOVE** Li The Clinging, Flame

☱ **BELOW** Tui The Joyous, Lake

Life will be difficult, but you must keep going for you will finally achieve your goals and be deliriously happy. There will be one obstacle after another put in your way, but you have the fortitude to ignore them. Once you have found a firm footing in life, in your profession, or in your personal relationships, take a strong stance and don't try to advance too quickly, as you will then suffer loss.

39. **CHIEN, Obstruction**

☵ **ABOVE** K'an The Abysmal, Water

☶ **BELOW** Ken Keeping Still, Mountain

A change of location may be favorable, especially as you meet with so many obstacles in your present location. Be courageous and go after goals that you have always dreamed about, and ignore the hardships, restrictions, and the rivalries that you are about to encounter. Natural disasters as well as human failings seem to plot against your rise in life. You are able to overcome all and have much success and good fortune.

40.   HSIEH, Deliverance

☳ ABOVE   Chen   The Arousing, Thunder

☵ BELOW   K'an   The Abysmal, Water

For years you may have to struggle to overcome difficulties, but you are finally successful, and good luck and fortune shine on your life. Whenever chances appear for you to improve your life or your income, take them, even though it may mean drastic changes in life-style and in relationships. Addition to your family means much to you, and happiness comes from those close to you.

41.   SUN, Decrease

☶ ABOVE   Ken   Keeping Still, Mountain

☱ BELOW   Tui   The Joyous, Lake

Joint ventures help you to protect any money and success you have achieved so far. Any problems or difficulties you have had to face gradually change, and you overcome them. You will see many opportunities but may not be in a position to take advantage of them. You must try to grab them when they appear, even at the risk of creating other problems in the home or in your profession.

42.   I, Increase

☴ ABOVE   Sun   The Gentle, Wind

☳ BELOW   Chen   The Arousing, Thunder

Stop thinking and procrastinating, for you must put your ideas into action. Benefits come to you and to those around you, for your charisma will have a positive effect on everyone you meet. Good fortune comes to you in many ways. Finding a colleague or loved one to help you reach your goals brings you double happiness and luck. Family joy is imminent, and much love surrounds you.

43. KUAI, Breakthrough, Resoluteness

☱ ABOVE Tui   The Joyous, Lake

☰ BELOW Ch'ien   The Creative, Heaven

Hang on to your wealth and possessions, for there will be times when you will have to go through difficult and poor periods. Stop putting your trust in people who do not have your welfare at heart, as they may betray you when they feel that it will benefit them to do so. Your careless attitude and ideas about contracts and other valuable documents can cause you lots of unhappiness. Success comes by making a resolution and keeping to it.

44. KUO, Coming to Meet

☰ ABOVE Ch'ien   The Creative, Heaven

☴ BELOW Sun   The Gentle, Wind

Much of the good luck you have been having may change if you are not cautious. Don't trust others with your life or your wealth, for they will be careless and extravagant with it. You must take it upon yourself to prevent loss and to budget carefully. The gradual losses can soon pile up, and you may lose much. A prominent woman could encourage you to spend recklessly. You must hold on to the purse strings.

45. TS'UI, Gathering Together, Massing

☱ ABOVE Tui   The Joyous, Lake

☷ BELOW K'un   The Receptive, Earth

You can achieve a great deal, and the more ideas you sow and put into action, the more success you will have. You are a winner and must allow yourself to keep up the good luck and good fortune by going after all your goals and aspirations. There is nothing that you cannot do if you set your heart to it. Large corporations and organizations will have an effect on you and will help you to attain your dreams and give you honors and rewards.

46. SHENG, Pushing Upward

☷ **ABOVE K'un** The Receptive, Earth

☴ **BELOW Sun** The Gentle, Wind

Timing is very important. You must work quietly and methodically, as you will have more success by being patient than by rushing. Things will go according to plan and you will have much success and good fortune in life. There is much more success in your career, promotion, raise, and honors. Children will bring you much happiness, and there could be an addition to the family. You are very lucky and well protected.

47. K'UN, Oppression, Exhaustion

☱ **ABOVE Tui** The Joyous, Lake

☵ **BELOW K'an** The Abysmal, Water

Financial difficulties have to be overcome, and you must be willing to cut down on your overhead and your extravagant habits. Working hard and long hours is the only way that you can keep your bank balance in a positive manner. You are able to rise above any problems and attain much success once you have gotten everyone in your family and in your place of work conscious of the need to save money. Lady Luck shines on you always.

48. CHING, The Well

☵ **ABOVE K'an** The Abysmal, Water

☴ **BELOW Sun** The Gentle, Wind

Success and good fortune come from a peaceful life and not from putting unnecessary pressure on yourself. A calm, serene, and quiet disposition brings rewards and peace of mind. Aggressiveness in others will upset you, and you must not be tempted to follow their behavior, as this would be your downfall. Once you have reached a successful plateau, be satisfied and live a life of tranquillity.

49.   **KO, Revolution, Molting**

☱   **ABOVE**   Tui   **The Joyous, Lake**

☲   **BELOW**   Li   **The Clinging, Flame**

There will be many changes; be prepared for the new adventures life has in store for you. Once you have your own life in order, then you can include others. But don't allow them to affect any important professional decision or one about the location where you live and work. Domestic change brings happiness, and you should be on the lookout for ways to eliminate problems and people who hold up your good fortune and luck.

50.   **TING, The Caldron**

☲   **ABOVE**   Li   **The Clinging, Flame**

☴   **BELOW**   Sun   **The Gentle, Wind**

Your talents will be recognized at a very early age. A teacher or guru will guide you into the correct path. Your fortune will be waiting for you if you have the drive and the discipline to go after it. Whether in a team or in partnership, you will do well as others blossom in your company, and you do your best because of their faith and love. Much happiness is there for the asking, and the more ambitious and enthusiastic you are, the more good fortune for you.

51.   **CHEN, The Arousing, Shock, Thunder**

☳   **ABOVE**   Chen   **The Arousing, Thunder**

☳   **BELOW**   Chen   **The Arousing, Thunder**

Fame and fortune lie ahead, and you will win the respect and admiration of the public and your peers. There will be many difficulties and obstacles to overcome, but you grow with the challenge. Be logical in your work and not overambitious openly, for others will then be very jealous and envious of your success and enthusiasm. Care is needed, and too much self-confidence will take away much of that which is charming in your personality.

52.   **KEN, Keeping Still, Mountain**

☶☶   **ABOVE**   Ken   **Keeping Still, Mountain**

☶☶   **BELOW**   Ken   **Keeping Still, Mountain**

Be firm in your beliefs and in your convictions, and good luck will eventually come your way. There will be many obstacles that you have to overcome, and at times, your life may feel like it is standing still, but underneath there is much activity and progress in your heart and mind and soul. Worldly gains do not attract you so much as position in your profession and in your community. Good fortune comes to you; just wait; be patient.

53.   **CHIEN, DEVELOPMENT, Gradual Progress**

☴   **ABOVE**   Sun   **The Gentle, Wind**

☶☶   **BELOW**   Ken   **Keeping Still, Mountain**

Good fortune comes to you, and everything develops slowly without pressure and without anxiety. The future awaits you with many surprises, honors, and rewards, for you deserve them for being patient and strong in your faith. Each stepping-stone brings you nearer to your goal, and gradual progress ensures wealth and security. Travel brings great joy, happiness, and prosperity.

54.   **KUEI MEI, The Marrying Maiden**

☳   **ABOVE**   Chen   **The Arousing, Thunder**

☱   **BELOW**   Tui   **The Joyous, Lake**

You may surprise other people with your nonconforming attitudes and behavior, and some will take offense at your fresh approach to life and to love. Happiness comes from work connected with giving others pleasure and through the entertainment and artistic pursuits you enjoy so much. Tact, diplomacy, and discretion are your protective traits, and you must beware in whom you confide your most intimate secrets. You will find a wealthy sponsor to help your career, and this person may be infatuated with you.

55.   FENG, Abundance, Fullness

☳   ABOVE   Chen   The Arousing, Thunder

☱   BELOW   Tui   The Joyous, Lake

Good fortune shines on whatever you do, and you will get more out
of life than most people. Without too much trouble and effort, you
will reach your goals and attain honor and fame in your community.
If you are attracted to the arts, you will have amazing success and
may become rich through your talents. You will make much money
but must beware of the natural tendency to waste it through extravagant purchases and impulsive investments.

56.   LU, The Wanderer

☲   ABOVE   Li   The Clinging, Flame

☶   BELOW   Ken   Keeping Still, Mountain

Until you know what you want in life, you will drift from one thing
to another, one person to another, and one place to another. Settle
down as quickly as possible and set up your business and family.
Once a secure footing is made, then you can take trips, travel to
foreign places, and get involved in as many adventures as you like.
But having the security of a home and family to come back to gives
you the confidence and the luck to be the daredevil you seem to want
to be. Restlessness brings unhappiness for you and others. Discipline
brings wealth, success, and joy.

57.   SUN, The Gentle, The Penetrating, Wind

☴   ABOVE   Sun   The Gentle, Wind

☴   BELOW   Sun   The Gentle, Wind

There will be many ups and downs in your fortune, and you will be
blown from one success to another like the weeds in the desert. Yet
you would do well to allow the fates to take you in their palms and
place you in the position and location in which you would do well.
Since you are of gentle personality and disposition, others will want

to impose their will on you. You cannot hang on to the wind or on to your fortune, yet you are able to amass one fortune after another. Be humble in dealing with your associates. You will need one another on many occasions.

58.　　　TUI, The Joyous, Lake

☱　ABOVE　Tui　　　　　The Joyous, Lake

☱　BELOW　Tui　　　　　The Joyous, Lake

There will be much happiness and joy in your life and you will attain fame and fortune whether you purposefully go after it or not. Your joyous personality attracts others and they will shower money, gifts, and love onto you. Be sincere in the handling of other people and their problems, for you will reap what you sow in this life. A careless word or remark could hurt your reputation and credibility, so be cautious what you pass on to other family members or work colleagues.

59.　　　HUAN, Dispersion, Dissolution

☴　ABOVE　Sun　　　　　The Gentle, Wind

☵　BELOW　K'an　　　　The Abysmal, Water

Good fortune and happiness come from international work and business. Your love of travel combined with your own particular talents bring you much recognition and success. There is a major change of fortune, which will bring joy to your heart, for you are leaving a period of delay and disappointment. Relaxation is good for you, but you must not slow down your efforts to attain your goals, as you will lose a lot of the natural enthusiasm that keeps you and your professional work attractive to others.

60. **CHIEH, Limitation**

☵ ABOVE K'an   The Abysmal, Water

☱ BELOW Tui   The Joyous, Lake

Take your time, for there are some obvious obstacles and problems that you must overcome as quickly as possible. Beware of being too greedy in your pursuit of fame and good fortune, as that motivation will be your undoing. Better to be more philanthropic in your outlook and do things for the good of mankind and your community. Be more discriminating in whom you put your trust. By being aware of the limitations around you, you will be able to see the bright roads that will lead you to success and prosperity.

61. **CHUNG FU, Inner Truth**

☴ ABOVE Sun   The Gentle, Wind

☱ BELOW Tui   The Joyous, Lake

Truth is your goal in all things, and it is this honesty in your personality that shines through and makes others come to you for guidance and advice and in return leads to your fame, fortune, and general happiness. You will be aware of any evildoings of others, and you must make sure you expose them to others to protect their health. Much travel to other parts of the world will be more of a pilgrimage than a need for relaxation and pleasure.

62. **HSIAO KUO, Preponderance of the Small**

☳ ABOVE Chen   The Arousing, Thunder

☶ BELOW Ken   Keeping Still, Mountain

Know what you want in life and stick to it, as there will be people who will want to take you off your path and destiny to help them with theirs. Keep to what you know best and you will have great success, and money will flow toward you. Separation at an early age from your home will give you the self-confidence and character that you need to fight for yourself the battles you will encounter. Great fortunes await you as long as you are willing to do your own thing instead of worrying about others.

63.   CHI CHI, After Completion

☵   ABOVE   K'an   The Abysmal, Water

☲   BELOW   Li   The Clinging, Flame

Your happy and carefree attitude wins you much admiration and love from others. You will achieve much and you will be able to list many of your accomplishments at an early age. But study and practice remain important and you will never be able to give up and just relax. You must always be willing to go on to your next ambitious goal once you have attained the current one. A winner at heart, you will win the hearts of many people and the public en masse.

64.   WEI CHI, Before Completion

☲   ABOVE   Li   The Clinging, Flame

☵   BELOW   K'an   The Abysmal, Water

You must make an effort to get along with your family, your colleagues at work and at school, and with those you love. There is a tendency to be reckless with the emotions of other people. You should always take others' advice and opinions seriously, as they have your welfare at heart. Success comes through steady hard work and optimistic enthusiasm. Joint ventures have the best results.

CHAPTER
SEVENTEEN
PALMISTRY

When I went to interview graphologist Felix Lehmann (see p. 503), I took along a friend, a man in his mid-fifties. Somehow, before the interview began, Lehmann looked at my friend's hand and said, "You're married; you've had two serious long-term affairs; there may be a third. They were serious; you didn't just pick someone up in a bar." When we left, the man was very shaken. He admitted he'd had two affairs in his twenty-five years of marriage.

Many people who read palms take exception to the words "palmist" and "palmistry," because they fear association with Gypsy fortune tellers and similar shady denizens of the occult fringe. They prefer, instead, to call themselves hand readers, practitioners of the science of hand reading, or chiromancy. Their claim is that they can read a person's character from the marks on the palm of the hand. Here, again, the claim is that experience proves that certain lines, characteristics, and patterns have particular meanings, which turn up again and again and can be read like a book. Certain lines we are born with; they are the key to our nature, both internal and external. Other, smaller lines change slowly yet observably and are a mirror of changes in our life and character. As farfetched as this might seem, modern science is turning up a good deal of evidence linking the markings of the hand with various physical characteristics and with certain diseases (p. 476). If the palm can reveal hidden illness, is it not possible that it can reveal what is hidden in the mind?

The first time I encountered a professional hand-reader, Marion Coe Palmer, I was not at all prepared for the woman who received me. Miss Palmer, well into her eighties, is a mother, grandmother, and great-grandmother. When she was six years old, her family's Irish cook read Marion's mother's palm and predicted two things: She was going to have another baby and, as a result, the family would move to another, larger house. She continues, "My mother said we weren't going to have another baby, and that we certainly were not going to move. When I was seven, we had a baby and we moved. It all made a great impression on me."

Marion was fascinated by a deck of cards the cook owned, explaining the lines of the hand. She went on to read extensively. One book in particular fascinated her: *The Laws of Scientific Hand Reading: A Practical Treatise on the Art Commonly Called Palmistry*, by William G. Benham, published in 1900 by The Knickerbocker Press. (A new revised edition of the Benham book is published by Hawthorne Books, New York, copyright 1974.) "I read Benham's," she recalls. "It's the best book. That was my Bible really." In college, her ability to read a person's character from his palm frequently made her the most popular person at the party, thereby getting the shy young woman through some otherwise unamusing social situations.

"Your hand is your map," Miss Palmer will tell you, and she continues, "The left hand [if you are right-handed] is what you're born with, the right hand is what you do with it. I have never seen anything bad in any hand in my life. Ever. You always have free will." She goes on with great animation to explain her thrill when a new grandchild is born: "Whenever anybody has a baby, I go to the hospital to see his or her hands. I just can hardly wait. They come into this world with these little maps and it's just so exciting. Here's their whole life in front of them."

Her enthusiasm is genuine. In her opinion, palmistry is really a tool. She explains, "I can guarantee you that with a reading, I can really help you to understand yourself better, and you can zero in on why you are the way you are. I don't believe in telling the future. I think only God knows the future. In five minutes, I could teach you enough that you could understand someone better. You can tell whether a person is stingy, whether they are extravagant, whether they give in or want peace and harmony too much, whether they want to control people. I can tell a lot about the hands I see for only a minute on television—whether they're stubborn or passionate or have difficult lives from just glancing. You know, it's a tool."

When asked if she can see the future in a palm, Miss Palmer is adamant. "I always see the past. I see a *tendency* toward the future, but I don't believe in influencing people without being very, very careful. I take this very seriously. I could predict, but I have to be sure I'm right. I think everybody is psychic. Everybody has it—to some degree. There are lines in your hand that show if you have it.

The more intuition you have, the more aware you are. I'm more intuitive than I am psychic. I'm very intuitive. I feel people; I care."

Miss Palmer, at one time secretary to the eminent astrologer Carroll Righter, is well known in the Los Angeles area, where she has been reading palms, frequently at parties, for years. Besides her private clients, she admits to having read many famous hands, including those of President and Mrs. Reagan, Betsy Bloomingdale, Jimmy Carter, Frank Sinatra, Katharine Hepburn, Sophia Loren, Jaclyn Smith, Angie Dickinson, and John Wayne. The rich and famous, it would seem, are just as curious about having their palms read as anyone else.

A BRIEF HISTORY OF PALMISTRY

Though the true origins of palmistry will probably always be debated, it is believed that it began in India more than two thousand years before Christ's birth. Written records, if there were any, have not survived, but it is clear that consistent, solid information about palmistry was passed along verbally, and reference is made to it in ancient Indian texts. Additionally, art of the time contains clearly delineated lines on the palms of the hands.

Chinese texts about palmistry date from before the fourth century B.C. and clearly describe a study that was well established—not new —by the time it was recorded.

The Bible is said to contain several references to the marks of the palm. Proverbs 3:16 says, "Length of days is in her right hand; and in her left hand riches and honor." Job 37:7 reads, "He sealeth up the hand of every man; that all men may know His work."

Though its route to the West is unclear, there is no question that palmistry was practiced by the ancient Greeks. Aristotle refers to it; Plato, Hippocrates, and Galen are known to have used it. Whether it was brought by Indians, Chinese, or Arabs is not known for sure.

References to palmistry can be traced to Arab texts from the eleventh century, and other references proliferate in the twelfth and thirteenth, but it is not until the fourteenth century that manuscripts solely about palmistry can be found. The first text on the subject was Die Kunst Chiromantia, published in 1475. The popularity of palmistry was well established and began to grow throughout Europe, leading to its inclusion in the curriculum at the University of Leipzig during the late seventeenth and early eighteenth centuries. However, the 1700s were a dark period in the history of palmistry. The rise of rationalism caused all such subjects to fall by the wayside until 1800, when Adrien-Adolphe Desbarolles and Count Casimir D'Arpentigny revived it by publishing their theories and classifications of palms. The credence they accorded the subject was quickly embraced by a society that was willing and ready to understand human behavior.

Napoleon, before he reached his height as emperor of France, when he was still the ambitious and capable General Bonaparte, had his palm read by a woman named Marie-Anne le Normand. A friend of Napoleon's later confirmed that he was an eyewitness to her predictions that Napoleon would marry Josephine—"a beautiful woman who already had two sons"—that he would realize his dream of becoming commander of the Republican army in Italy, and that he would attain "sufficient glory to make him the most illustrious of all Frenchmen."

Don't think that Mlle. le Normand or Marion Coe Palmer are alone. Throughout history, hand-readers have made their reputations by reading the palms of the famous. In the late nineteenth century, one of the most famous among them was a man who came to be known as Cheiro (born Count Louis Hamon). He told England's King Edward VII, "You will not die, sir, until you are in your sixty-ninth year. . . . But a namesake will give up his crown for love." In May 1910, at age sixty-nine, Edward VII died. It was not until 1936, though, that Edward VIII gave up the throne to marry the woman he loved, Mrs. Wallis Simpson.

In another now-famous consultation, Cheiro informed the much celebrated Lord Kitchener that he would die by drowning. Horrified because he did not know how to swim, Kitchener quickly learned, though ultimately to no avail. He drowned in 1916, when the ship he traveled on was sunk by a German mine en route to Russia. Similarly, Cheiro predicted another's drowning, this time to well-known newspaper editor W. T. Stead, who was aboard the ill-fated *Titanic*.

But perhaps Cheiro made his greatest prediction in foretelling his own death. At age seventy, he asked his publisher to rush galley proofs of his most recent manuscript to him because he thought he would die soon, specifically, on October 8, 1936. Unfortunately, he was again correct.

In America around this same period of time, a tiny woman named Nellie Meier was impressing celebrities of her day with her hand-reading talents. She charged her clients $5 for each reading and became quite popular for donating her earnings to charitable causes. While she was crisscrossing the country on a lecture tour during the

1930s, newspaper and magazine stories popularized her work and she collected the handprints of around twenty thousand personalities. She used some of the most illustrious in her book *Lion's Paws, A Story of Famous Hands*, which was published to great acclaim in 1937, and continued doing readings for the famous until her death in 1944. Her clients included Franklin Delano Roosevelt, who once summoned her to Washington for a reading; Eleanor Roosevelt; Amelia Earhart; Joan Crawford; James Whitcomb Riley; George Gershwin; and Walt Disney. Tuckaway, Nellie Meier's home in Indianapolis, Indiana, now in the National Registry of Historic Places, is testament to her interesting life. The house is preserved much as she left it, filled with autographed photos of her clients as well as thousands of signed palm prints, photographs, and signed first editions. Meier's readings for the famous are marked by her sharp observations; she found a highly developed, original imagination at work in Walt Disney's hand and said, "The mark of intuition leading to genius is there, and coupled with the development of the mount [of the moon], it makes a bottomless well of joy upon which he can draw." She found Amelia Earhart to be courageous, meticulous, and cautious. Joan Crawford's love of power and material things was clearly present. Highly impressed by George Gershwin's handshake, Meier found his palm to reveal a just and honest man who possessed great willpower and supersensitivity; he had the ability to persevere. In 1938, Meier read the palm of journalist Benjamin Meiman, the skeptical correspondent for the *New York Forward*. Though he had come to scoff and debunk Meier's talents, he was amazed when, on looking at his hand, Meier described him as "a mental explorer, so obstinate that the other fellow will want to kill him, that he would fall for a sob story although he would try to act hard-boiled, that he would go the limit for those who are cold and hungry, and that he was a winner at a poker game." Meiman left the meeting impressed, later admitting that Meier knew him better than he knew himself.

PALMISTRY AND SCIENCE

Though it had captured the interest of scientists for hundreds of years, it was not until this century that the revelations of the palm's markings began to gather credentials that were enough to impress the members of the serious scientific community. With increased interest and study, it has been shown that signs of certain physical characteristics appear in the hand. If this is so, it reinforces the hand-readers' claim that character and personality are also revealed.

Dermatoglyphics, the scientific study of the skin patterns on the insides of the hands and feet, is a comparatively new science that dates from around 1926. Criminologists have been interested in the ridges and furrows of the skin ever since it was discovered that fingerprints are unique to each person and that they do not change. When genetic science was in its infancy, dermatoglyphics looked like a possible avenue of inquiry. According to an article in the February 11, 1985, edition of *Medical World News*, "The most successful application has been the identification of dermatoglyphic parameters that reliably correlate with Down's syndrome. One analysis for Down's that relies on four dermatoglyphic traits has a diagnostic accuracy of 87 percent." The article goes on to say that *perhaps* there is a dermatoglyphic indicator for Alzheimer's disease and that studies are underway that seek correlations for diabetes, various cancers, and seizure disorders. Who knows what will turn up?

In *Supernature*, Lyall Watson synopsizes a study that found "about thirty different congenital disorders [that] have been connected with particular patterns in the palm, some of which are apparent even before the disease appears. In 1966, abnormal palm prints were linked for the first time with a virus infection. Three New York pediatricians palm-printed babies born to mothers who had caught German measles during early pregnancy and found that, even if the babies were not affected in any other way, all had a characteristic and unusual crease in their hands."

In talking about the awesomely intricate physiology of the hand, Watson points out that we have an uncommonly huge number of nerve sensors in the palm of the hand. If, he postulates, our proportions were determined only by the nerve supply to any particular area, "we would have hands the size of beach umbrellas."

Watson is fascinating on the subject. He goes on to surmise that since it is known that the ridges on the skin are formed by the twentieth week of fetal development—at the same time and from the same ectoderm of the embryo as goes into the makeup of the brain, nervous system, and sense organs—then it is possible that their common origins could indicate "that they maintain very close connections throughout life, and it is not at all unreasonable to assume that many internal events will show up externally through the skin." He adds that jaundice and rheumatoid arthritis do, and that there is "a very close connection between many skin diseases and mental states."

The skin is a strange thing. Watson points out that "the distribution of the ridges [on the surface of the skin] is determined by the arrangement of sweat glands and nerve endings and is so firmly established that it is impossible to destroy or change the pattern permanently. They reappear as healing brings the natural skin to the surface again after severe burns and even after skin grafting." Keep in mind, though, that while the fingerprints seem to be immutable, the minor markings on the palm subtly change and evolve all the time. Presumably that is why the palm should be read from time to time rather than just once in a lifetime; it is in a constant state of flux, changing, somehow, as we do, from day to day.

The seeming consistency of the palm's revelations was demonstrated in a fascinating study conducted over a three-year period in the early 1950s. It tested the ability of one woman—palmist Maria Gardini of Bologna, Italy—to predict past, present, and future facts about the lives of twenty subjects. The subjects were complete strangers, and she could use only what information she could gather during a ten-minute session with a dowser's pendulum and a twenty- to forty-five-minute hand-reading session. The subjects could answer only "yes" or "no" to statements she made and then only when absolutely necessary. At the end of the sessions, Gardini's affirmative statements were read and the subject stated whether her findings were correct or incorrect. When her predictions were evaluated, using medical tests and psychological observations for backup when necessary, Gardini's results were 72.52 percent correct, 4.74 percent incorrect, 18.4 percent had to do with the future and were unanswerable at the time, and 4.34 percent were unanswerable because of lack of complete information. These findings were astounding given the total of 506 statements—about 25 per subject. With other research continuing at a fast pace, perhaps it will finally be shown that the whorls and lines of the skin on the hands have more meaning than we ever guessed.

But now it's time to put science aside and take a look at the hand itself—to see what the practice of palmistry involves.

LOOKING AT THE HANDS

The principal lines of the hands are formed before birth and change only slightly throughout life. It is the minor lines that tell the true story. Why they change is still open to conjecture. It has been observed that the thousands of nerve endings located in the palm are linked to the frontal lobe of the brain, where the impulses of conscious thought, memory, and imagination are found. Therefore, it is possible that, when aroused, this area of the brain may send messages via the nerve endings to the palm, affecting the formation of these tiny capillary lines. Because they change, these lines are indicative of the status of the health and of life events, as well as the psychological state.

There is always some difference between the lines on the left and right hands. Some hand-readers refer to the writing hand as the active hand, the hand that changes most as your life changes, while the other hand is the passive hand, the hand that reveals your inherent characteristics. But many modern hand-readers have dismissed this old idea in favor of new theories. One is that the left hand reveals the unconscious ideas we were born with, while the right reveals our experiences in life. Put a different way, it is said that the left hand reflects brain impulses stimulated by the subconscious and thus reflects our internal and private world, while the right hand reflects impulses triggered by our external world and thus shows our reactions and adaptation to the world.

Because of the differences, it is advisable to look at both hands. Most hand-readers recommend working from the more general observations to the more specific. With that in mind, the first thing to look at is the shape of the hands, then the size of and shape of the fingers, then the size and shape of the thumbs—considered to be more important than any individual finger—and, finally, the lines and mounts (mounds) of the hands.

There are seven specific areas that these signs can illuminate: the physical body, the emotional nature, the will and individuality, worldly and material success, talent, imagination and creativity, and overall self-fulfillment.

One final note before we go on to the specifics of hand-reading. All descriptions are relative. When we speak of long fingers, we mean long in relation to the individual's palm—a person with tiny hands may have "long" fingers, while those of a very large person may be rather stubby. The degree to which an individual possesses a particular quality can be determined by the degree from which he or she deviates from the average or norm—you will learn to distinguish between "slightly" long fingers, for example, and "very" long fingers. Remember, too, that the hands you will be looking at will not match the drawings here and will not fit perfectly into the categories: Most hands are actually a combination of characteristics. You will learn from experience how to make judgments.

GENERAL CHARACTERISTICS OF HANDS

Before going into details of hand shapes, finger characteristics, and particular lines, there are some preliminary observations to be made. The first, hand strength, can be determined by shaking hands with the subject. Palmistry offers two insights into the handshake: An overly strong grip, rather than pointing to a strong and self-confident personality, points to the likelihood that this person is doing his best to impress. With this in mind, you can make some guesses as to the possibility that this person has feelings of inadequacy and attempts to compensate by being overly assertive.

The other side of this coin is the limp, weak handshake. This can be interpreted as the grip of a person who wants to be protected by others—someone who is ready to leave the responsibilities and decisions in the hands of another.

Another qualification that can be made on the basis of a handshake is that of skin quality. A soft and delicate skin indicates a highly sensitive and emotional type, unlikely to be found engaged in physical labor. Rough, hard skin shows the opposite—a lack of sensitivity and a tendency toward practicality. There is also a skin type that falls somewhere between the two: an elastic, springy skin. This is prevalent among professionals: doctors, lawyers, executives, and independent types. This person usually is able to conceive his or her own ideas and apply them practically.

The color of the palm is another primary factor. We are used to responding to the color of another's face—how often have you said, "You look pale; why don't you sit down and rest?" But the sensitive palm reflects the body's state just as well. Here are four gradations, based on color, that palmists often use:

- pale—a lack of vitality and initiative
- yellow—an inhibited, sardonic nature
- pink—a normal constitution and a healthy degree of aggressiveness
- red—a hyperactive personality and a forceful nature

HAND SHAPES

Since the nineteenth century, when Casimir D'Arpentigny, called the father of modern palmistry, delineated seven basic types of hands by shape, these same categories have been acknowledged by most palmists. Two of these, the elementary and the knotty hand, have been dropped by many readers, due to the infrequency of their appearance.

The five hand types into which almost all people neatly fit are the square hand, the pointed, or psychic, hand, the conic, or artistic, hand, the spatulate hand, and the mixed hand, which shows assorted characteristics of the other four types.

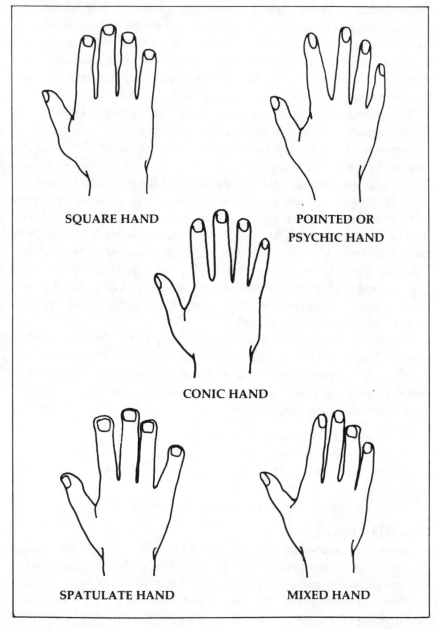

SQUARE HAND

POINTED OR PSYCHIC HAND

CONIC HAND

SPATULATE HAND

MIXED HAND

The **square hand** is a practical hand. It can be easily recognized: It actually appears square, the width of the palm equal to the length. Although finger length will vary, the tips of the fingers will be flattened, squared off. The lines of the palms will be few but deep and clear, and often rather straight.

The possessor of the square hand is practical and realistic. Though he may be lacking in imagination, this is not a drawback in this type of character. People with this hand shape are competent and steady, pursuing things from beginning to end. They tend to be materialistic and "earthy." They are most likely to be found in occupational niches that require skill and knowledge but not necessarily originality, such as medicine or engineering.

The **pointed, or psychic, hand** is slim and delicate, found more often, though not exclusively, in women. It is slightly wider at the base of the palm than at the top and tapers gracefully. The fingers are long and pointed; the lines of the palm are pronounced, though not deep.

These are the hands of dreamers and dilettantes. The possessor is marked by an inability to deal with practical matters of the world and will often be taken care of by another. On the positive side, though these aren't the hands of the great creators of the world, they are the hands of those who most appreciate the achievements of others. A highly developed sense of art and music is often found. And, given a positive and nurturing environment, protected from the world, these are the hands of those most likely to develop psychic ability.

When left to fend for themselves, these people are often left behind in the crowd.

The **conic, or artistic, hand** is wider at the base than the top, like the pointed hand; however, it is more substantial. It is also greater in depth—thicker—at the bottom than at the top. The fingers are generally long and cylindrical rather than pointed.

This person is a cross in characteristics between the square hand and the pointed hand. He is imaginative and creative, but also able to apply original ideas practically. If the hand is soft and fleshy rather than firm, the person might well be given to self-indulgence.

If this person can avoid the pitfall of self-indulgence, he might be a successful artist or painter, or if in a profession, someone who originates ideas that others bring to fruition.

The **spatulate hand** appears odd at first but has a certain grace of its own. It is usually wider at the top of the palm than the bottom and squarish-looking. It might have unusual-looking bumps or angles to it, and the fingers are often knotty and slightly crooked. Further, the fingers will usually be broadest at the tips.

This is the hand of the inventive problem-solver. Highly energetic and demonstrative, this person is always working on various projects, to which he brings ingenious solutions. An inveterate do-it-yourselfer, this person will always find a place for himself in the world.

The **mixed hand** is, as one would guess, a hand that shows mixed qualities of all the others. These people are versatile, jack-of-all-trades types. They usually know a little bit about everything, being curious about everything around them. They are fascinating to talk to and usually successful. They can be found in those professions that call for generalists: teaching, journalism, entrepreneurial businesses.

THE FINGERS

The fingers of the hand have come to be known by the names borrowed from astrology. The first, or index, finger is called the Jupiter finger. The second, or middle, finger is called the Saturn finger. The third, or ring, finger is called the Sun or Apollo finger. The fourth, the little finger, or pinkie, is called the Mercury finger.

There are two ways to look at these astrological names. One view is that the names of the fingers were assigned in accordance with the astrologically defined characteristics of the planets they represent. The skeptic's view would be that the characteristics were assigned according to the name. Either way, the following list shows the qualities generally associated with the size and shape of each finger.

- First—This is the finger of ego. When it is long (in relation to the palm), it indicates self-confidence, diplomacy, and pride in achievement. When short, it indicates impatience. If it is excessively long, it indicates vanity, conceit, and overconfidence. If it is crooked, it indicates a person who has original ideas but finds it difficult to carry them out.
- Second—This is the finger of the material world: business, finance, and wealth. If it is long, it suggests success through hard and steady work, caution, and careful planning. If short, it indicates constant struggle and failure. If excessively long, it indicates the overly cautious, and through that, missed opportunities. If crooked, it shows poor judgment in material situations.

- Third—This is the finger of the arts, love, and beauty. If it is long, it shows an appreciation for the arts and sensitivity toward others. If short, it shows a lack of appreciation for the arts and an unfriendly individual. If excessively long, it shows an inclination toward gambling and fame—"life in the fast lane." It also indicates an overly passionate type who is guided almost entirely by emotion. If crooked, it indicates a quiet and aloof personality.
- Fourth—This is the finger of intellect. If it is long, it denotes intelligence and an ability to express ideas well. If short, it indicates a quick and perceptive mind but one that is fragile and unstable. If excessively long, it indicates excessive cleverness, without substance: all form and no content. If crooked, it indicates an individual who often jumps to conclusions, usually on the basis of instinct or hunches.

Another important aspect of the fingers is flexibility. Do the subject's fingers bend back easily? Or do they not bend back at all and stay tightly grouped together?

The fingers normally bend back at a 45- to 90- degree angle. This indicates a mind that, though firm in its convictions, is willing to hear and consider others' ideas. Fingers that bend less show a stubborn and dogmatic individual who is convinced of his being right. Fingers that bend too far—all the way back—indicate a person too easygoing for his own good, easily swayed, and never quite sure of himself.

THE THUMB

Perhaps it's because the thumb has become a symbol for man's rise from the apes, as well as being the means for the handling of tools. Perhaps it's because it sticks out, if you will, like a sore thumb. Whatever the reason, the thumb has become the single most important factor making up the totality of palmistry. It must be taken into consideration whenever a reading is done.

Although at first glance the thumb appears to be made up of two segments, it is, like the fingers, composed of three. The lowest segment forms what palmistry calls the Mount of Venus, which appears as a large swelling in the palm below the thumb.

Each of the three segments has been assigned specific significance. The uppermost portion, that which sprouts the thumbnail, represents the individual will. The middle segment is related to logic. The bottom section, with its connection to the Mount of Venus, is related to love and sexual vitality. The way the three segments are related to one another can be read in conjunction with the overall length of the thumb. The standard applied to determine overall thumb length is that it should be equal to the length of the fourth finger.

- A long tip segment and short lower segment indicates a strong-willed individual. A slightly longer tip segment indicates a reasonable degree of stubbornness. If the tip segment is untowardly long, the individual is overly willful and lacking in discretion.
- A long middle segment and short tip segment indicate an individual whose advice and actions are considered and deliberate; often, though, this person will delay too long through deliberation and miss opportunities.
- A thumb in which the top two segments are of equal length shows a good balance between thinking out a situation and putting conclusions into action.
- A thumb in which the lowest (palm) segment predominates is one that points to a person who is ruled by his crudest impulses, his animal nature.

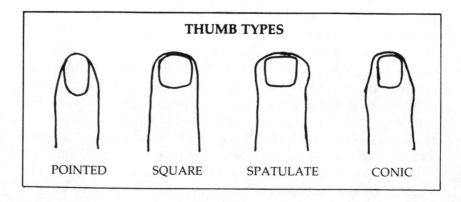

THUMB TYPES

POINTED   SQUARE   SPATULATE   CONIC

Another important index of character is the shape of the thumb. The illustrations show the possible shapes the tip might take.

- A slender thumb tip shows opportunism and an ability to manipulate others.
- A pointed thumb tip shows an individual who can take advantage of opportunities without being exploitive of others. Also, diplomacy is indicated, and a quick and impulsive nature.
- A conic thumb tip indicates a lack of willpower.
- A square thumb tip indicates a mixture of common sense and stubbornness.
- A spatulate thumb tip shows impatience, excess energy, and tactile sensitivity.

The final characteristic revealed by the thumb is determined by the angle made between the thumb and the first finger when the thumb is held comfortably away from the palm. This angle is called the angle of generosity.

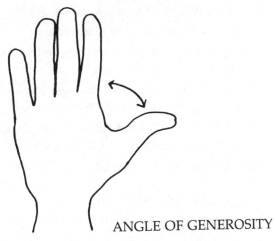

ANGLE OF GENEROSITY

The average hand will form an angle of about 90 degrees. A noticeably greater angle indicates a noticeably generous person. A lesser angle would suggest one who is "tightfisted." This quality becomes even more pronounced in the case of the double-jointed thumb, which might bend completely back. In this case, it shows extravagance, material or emotional. A double-jointed thumb that bends back only to a normal degree points to adaptability in addition to whatever amount of generosity is indicated.

LINES AND CREASES OF THE PALM

The lines and creases of the palm, known in anatomy as lines of flexure, are not formed by the actual use of the hand, as is commonly thought. These patterns, as unique to each person as the loops and whorls of the fingerprint, are developed in the fetus by the twentieth week of pregnancy. They are part of the genetic endowment, like height and the color of hair and eyes.

These lines are the indices we all identify with palmistry—even someone who knows nothing of the subject knows what his life line is. Before we analyze the meanings of the individual lines and their formation, there is information to be garnered from the overall impression. A quick look at the palm will reveal which of the following categories a given hand fits into.

- Fine lines indicates subtle perceptions.
- Sparse lines in conjunction with coarse skin indicates physical energy.
- Few clearly marked lines and fine, delicate skin indicates well-directed intellectual energy.
- Many lines indicates nervous energy.
- Many lines with the main lines well marked and the minor lines light shows constructively channeled nervous energy.
- Main lines no deeper or strongly marked than minor lines indicates a high-strung and impressionable type.
- The characteristics described in the paragraphs above, combined with fine skin, shows extreme sensitivity.
- Most lines deeply marked indicates deep feelings and inner conflict.
- Main lines marred with breaks and other markings shows nervous or physical strain and a tendency toward hysteria under pressure.
- Minor lines wavering and tangled indicates overstimulation or a depleted physical condition.
- Lines broad and deeply marked in coarse skin shows undeveloped intelligence.
- Pale lines shows a lack of energy.
- Yellow lines indicates nervousness and inhibitions.
- Red lines indicates feelings deeply felt.
- Well-marked pink lines shows general health and well-being.

Before we look at the four major lines of the hand, I think it's important to point out the special marks that are to be found in many, but not all, hands.

SPECIAL MARKINGS

No matter whose hand you study, you will notice very quickly that the palm and fingers will be covered with odd little scratchlike marks. These special markings point to events in life. Some or all these markings are to be found on most palms; if you're lacking any of them in your own palm, there is no need to worry. They act as aspects to the meaning of the line or area they affect, and their meaning is determined by their particular placement in the hand.

Since the marks are determined by their location, there is no easy way of saying what each one means except in the most general terms. Their interpretations vary with frequency and placement. Keep an eye out for the following marks:

CROSSES	+ ✗ + ✗ ✗	signify sudden or drastic change that may be positive or negative.
STARS	✳ ✳ ✳ ✳	also signify sudden or drastic change that may be positive or negative.
ISLANDS	⌁ ⌁	denote difficulties or obstacles.
CHAINS	∽∞∞ ∞∞	denote minor obstacles, usually physical or psychological.
SQUARES	▢ ◊ ▭ ▢	have a positive effect.
GRILLES	▦ ▦ ▦	denote a temporary obstacle that is difficult but not insurmountable.
TRIANGLES	▷ △ ▽	denote good luck and positive energy.

In the pages that follow, we will be looking at the four dominant lines: the life line, the head line, the heart line, and the fate line. We will also look at the mounts of the hand as well as the lines of travel and marriage and some special areas created by the lines of the palm.

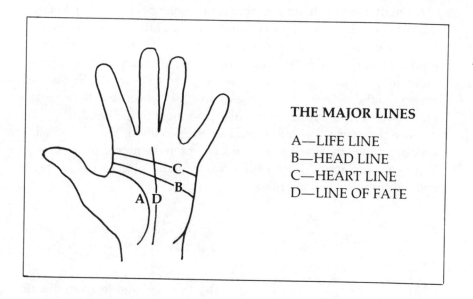

THE MAJOR LINES

A—LIFE LINE
B—HEAD LINE
C—HEART LINE
D—LINE OF FATE

THE MAJOR LINES

In the preceding diagram, the major lines are clearly marked. They may not be so obvious in the palm you are examining. One of the frustrations for the novice palmist is that the human hand is so unique that the hand you are examining rarely conforms to the drawings in palmistry texts. It is best to learn the positions of the lines in relation to one another as well as the general shape of the hand. This will make it easier to discern the pattern when one or more of the lines are indistinct or absent or uniquely placed, as is often the case.

The **life line** is the most important source of information in the marking of the palm. It begins between the thumb and the index finger, descends in a curve around or through the Mount of Venus, and ends somewhere near the base of the palm.

The life line indicates not only the length of life but the energy one brings to it. To judge when events occur in the course of a life, divide the line into thirds, each segment starting from the top of the line indicating a twenty-five-year portion of the life span.

- A broken life line does not always indicate sickness or death; it can instead indicate a major change in the course of one's life. It could be indicative of career, location, or marriage.
- The closer the life line stays to the base of the thumb, the more that person will tend to stay in his or her original surroundings. The farther it winds away from the thumb, the greater the scope—not the length—of a person's life.
- When the life line and head line begin together, it indicates caution and judgment. The farther they travel along the same line, the more deeply ingrained are these traits. When these lines begin separately, they indicate independence and self-confidence. When the life line ends abruptly, it suggests a quick and unexpected death; when it slowly fades out, the reverse is true.
- A cross touching the life line at some point indicates the death of someone close at that point of life. A life line that branches out widely at the bottom indicates a life that broadens in scope or activities late in life.

Following is a list of other observations that can be made from the life line:

- When the life line is well defined, deep and unbroken, it suggests good health and vitality.
- When the life line is broken in places, it suggests abrupt changes.
- When the life line has many fine lines all about it, it suggests nervousness and uncertain health.
- When the life line is straight with little curve, it suggests controlled emotions.
- When the life line is deeply curved under the base of the thumb, it suggest deep emotion and long life.
- When the life line is very long but thin, it suggests an even disposition and less vitality.
- When the life line is short, with few other lines, it suggests a placid and uneventful life.
- When the life line is short and shallow, it suggests a life influenced by another.
- When the life line is accompanied by parallel lines, it suggests constant protective forces at work.
- When the life line is long and runs into the wrist, it suggests an unusually long life.

- When the life line is found to begin above the head line, it suggests energy and a dynamic personality.
- When the life line is branched upward in the beginning, toward the index finger, it suggests perseverance and determination.
- When the life line is touched by a cross at the beginning, it suggests an accident or illness early in life.
- When the life line is touched by a square, it suggests protection from someone at that point in life.
- When the life line is opened into an island, it suggests hospitalization or some other enclosure due to breakdown or failing of some sort.
- When the life line is broken by deep and distinct lines, it suggests a serious illness, accident, or upset.
- When the life line gets darker and stronger, it suggests better health and confidence as life progresses.
- When the life line is crossed by small light lines, it suggests minor worries.

The **head line** is the second most important line in the palm. If there is only one horizontal line, it is the head line. It starts between the thumb and index finger and continues across the palm. The head line yields information about the strength and application of the mind, the attitudes toward life and its problems, and can be considered a guide to the general mental outlook.

As with the life line, it should be divided into thirds to indicate youth, prime, and age.

- When the head line starts under the index finger and is clear and straight, it suggests logical thinking, determination, self-control, and good judgment.
- When the head line starts at more than a quarter-inch above the life line, it indicates a rash and impatient sort.
- When the head line starts within the life line and crosses it on the palm, it suggests a nervous, worrying type who imagines problems that aren't really there.
- When the head line is short and starts in the middle of the hand, it suggests a lack of clear thinking.
- When the head line starts high and close to, or connected with, the heart line, it suggests pettiness and jealousy.
- When the head line starts low on the hand, in line with the

thumb joint, and runs upward toward the little finger, it suggests an imaginative mind.

- When the head line branches off the heart line under the second or third finger, it suggests a person who is completely controlled by emotion.
- When the head line becomes a chain, it suggests mental agitation.
- When the head line is long and dips downward, it suggests a dreamer who has creative powers.
- When the head line is deep and straight, with few or no markings, it suggests a stable mind.
- When the head line wavers, twists, and turns, it suggests indecision and a lack of concentration.
- When the head line forks toward the end, it suggests immense mental capacity.
- When the head line is straight, clear, and unbroken, it suggests leaning toward the material rather than the theoretical.
- When the head line is perfectly straight, all the way across the palm, it suggests the foregoing, coupled with an argumentative nature.
- When the head line begins straight and then slopes downward, it suggests a mixture of practicality and imagination.
- When the head line has branches reaching upward, it indicates optimism.
- When the head line is wavy throughout, it indicates a mercurial, erratic personality.
- When the head line is broken, it suggests severe mental strain or breakdown.
- When the head line is darker than the other lines and is erratic, it suggests a hot temper.
- When the head line is chained at the beginning, it suggests nervousness and sensitivity in early life.
- When the head line is very curved, it suggests impulsiveness.
- When the head line is very pale and indistinct, it suggests mental feebleness and lack of vision.
- When the head line is broken by a short line, it suggests an undeveloped mind or a lack of education.
- When the head line is broken by a long line, it suggests extreme shocks to the mind.
- When the head line is connected to the heart line by one or more lines, it suggests a good balance between mind and emotion.

- When the head line has an island or a cross, it suggests a mental crisis.
- When the head line has a star, it suggests a mental achievement.
- When the head line has a square, it suggests advice or guidance.

The **heart line** is read in the opposite direction of the other lines. That is, it is considered to *start* under the fourth finger and to run across the palm toward the first finger. The heart line is read to reveal the emotional nature, the depth of feelings, and the sorts of relationships a person might have.

- A long, deep heart line is a basic indication of loyalty, trust, and sincerity. A short line indicates fickleness, distrust, and jealousy.
- The higher in the hand, that is, the closer to the fingers, the heart line is found, the stronger and more acted out the emotions. The lower and closer to the head line, the more reserved the emotions. When there is only one horizontal line across the palm, it is considered to be the head line and the individual is likely to rule his emotions with reason.
- If the head and heart lines run separately for the most part and then join, the individual is undemonstrative but is capable of strong, lasting, and sincere relationships.
- When the heart line swings upward and ends under the first finger, it suggests strong loyalty to the point of mindlessness.
- When the heart line swings upward and ends between the first and second fingers, it indicates possessiveness and affections that are more passionate than idealistic.
- When the heart line is doubled, it strengthens what is revealed in the main line.
- When the heart line has breaks in it, it suggests emotional disturbances.
- When the heart line is very red, it suggests violent emotions and temper.
- When the heart line is marked by a cross, it indicates the death of a loved one.
- When the heart line is marked by a square, it suggests the nurturing of a loved one.
- When the heart line is well defined and long, it suggests strong and lasting affections and a capacity for self-sacrifice.

- When the heart line is broken in many places, it indicates disappointments, disillusionments, and inconstancy in love.
- When the heart line is chained or wavering, it suggests capriciousness and lightly given love.
- When the heart line is very thin and pale, it suggests that the major love object is oneself.
- When the heart line has small lines moving upward, it indicates a successful love life.
- When the heart line has small lines moving downward, it suggests disappointments in love.
- When the heart line creates a star, it indicates marriage at that point in time.
- When the heart line is short, it shows a lack of interest in the emotional realm.

The **line of fate,** also called the line of destiny or the line of Saturn, is a vertical line that starts near the wrist at the center of the palm and runs up through the center of the palm toward the head and heart lines. This line indicates the effect of fate upon one's life. The stronger and deeper this line is, the more strongly the life is shaped by fate.

- When this line dominates the hand—is stronger and deeper than the major lines—it indicates a life totally dictated by fate. When the fate line is weak or absent in contrast to the three major lines, it shows a self-made individual. This is also indicated when the fate line is joined to the life line at its beginning.
- When the line of fate begins low in the middle of the palm and runs straight up to a point below the middle finger, it suggests security in life.
- When the line of fate starts clear of any other lines at the wrist, and farther up joins with the life line, it suggests sacrificing one's self-interest to another. If it separates again later on, it means one's life once again is one's own.
- When the line of fate starts within the curve of the life line and branches outward, it suggests others—family or close friends —being extremely helpful in the course of life.
- When the line of fate is joined by a second line from the base of the palm, it suggests a life greatly influenced by a romantic interest.

- When the line of fate breaks at the head line but then continues at another point, it suggests a successful change of career.
- When the line of fate runs up to the third finger, rather than the second, it shows the arts having a large part in life. If it ends there in a star, it suggests a very successful career in the arts.
- When the line of fate ends in a star under the index finger, it suggests success in whatever career is indicated elsewhere.
- When the line of fate ends in a star under the middle finger, it suggests success after much hard work.
- When the line of fate has breaks or islands, it suggests periods of hard luck.
- When the line of fate has a square, it indicates protection and help from an unlikely source.
- When the line of fate is broken by strong, dark lines, it suggests that others' lives will interfere in one's own destiny.
- When the line of fate has many lines branching upward and downward from it, it suggests a life with many ups and downs.
- When the line of fate is made up of many short lines, it suggests indecision and fear of taking chances.
- When the line of fate is broken at the heart line, it suggests unhappy friendships and affairs.
- When the line of fate is very deep, long, and straight, it suggests unusually good luck.
- When the line of fate is faint, but long and straight, it suggests luck but accompanied by many worries.

THE MOUNTS OF THE PALM

The mounts of the palm are the fleshy mounds of skin that can be found at the base of the fingers or on either side of the heel of the hand. Depending on your profession or hobby, these areas of the palm may become calloused if used for strong movements like digging with a shovel or handling rough-textured things such as bricks or stone. The mounts may not be very high in the hand or may be a mixture of high and low or even nonexistent. Indeed, some hands have almost no mounts at all. Generally speaking, the rule to remember is that prominence heightens meaning and lack of prominence subtracts from the interpretation of the mounts. The direction in which a mount points or leans, as well as its size and location, also affect a mount's meaning in the hand.

There are eight major mounts in each hand. The illustration indicates their general location.

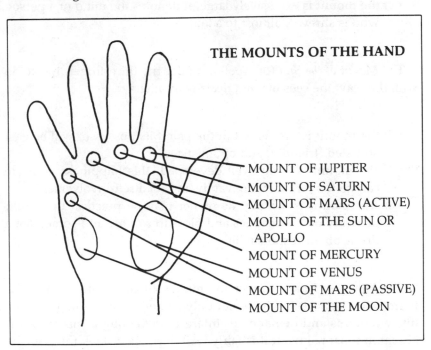

THE MOUNTS OF THE HAND

MOUNT OF JUPITER
MOUNT OF SATURN
MOUNT OF MARS (ACTIVE)
MOUNT OF THE SUN OR
  APOLLO
MOUNT OF MERCURY
MOUNT OF VENUS
MOUNT OF MARS (PASSIVE)
MOUNT OF THE MOON

The *Mount of Mercury*, under the fourth finger, addresses the practicalities of everyday life as well as business concerns.

- If the mount is well developed and firm, it indicates a practical person who is in control of his life and his business interests. There may be interest in the sciences. If the mount is undeveloped, the person may be scatterbrained, always a step or two out of kilter or off balance.
- If this mount is highest on the side near the ring finger, the possessor will have an acute interest in the arts, possibly even being involved with the arts as a business.
- If this mount is lacking altogether, it indicates a person who is a born follower, probably unable to initiate any type of activity on his own behalf.
- If the mount is excessively large, it denotes the mind of a person who is shrewd, almost to a fault.

The *Mount of the Sun* (or Apollo), under the third finger, has to do with the way one sees life and deals with others.

- If the mount is prominent in the palm, its possessor will be well adjusted, friendly, and optimistic.
- If the mount is really well developed, this happiness with life can go too far, showing vanity and total self-involvement.
- If this mount is lacking, its owner may be practical to a fault, unaware of the beauties and pleasures of life and somewhat a drone about responsibilities.

The *Mount of Saturn*, under the middle finger, is the sign of the hermit, the iconoclast who is not only content to be alone but absolutely requires and demands it. Interestingly enough, this mount is absent in most palms. If it is fairly well developed, look for one who is taken by philosophy and/or mysticism.

The *Mount of Jupiter*, under the index finger, is tied to one's position in life—as a person, as a professional, or as a spiritual being. A well-developed mount here signals one who is an upstanding citizen, proud, loyal, and honorable. If the mount is lacking altogether, its possessor doesn't hold himself in much esteem and probably will lack ambition. An excessive mount here warns of the selfish person who cares of no one except himself.

The *Mounts of Mars* are located in two different areas of the palm. One—the active mount—can be found under the Mount of Jupiter and above the Mount of Venus. This mount, when it is well developed, indicates poise and grace, the sign of a person who is in control of himself and most situations. He may be an adventurer of sorts. If it is unusually large in this position, it denotes an argumentative person who is unpleasant and rude. The passive Mount of Mars— on the opposite side of the hand, between the Mount of Mercury and the Mount of the Moon—denotes a person who is affable and friendly, with the best intentions. He may, however, be overly talk- ative or boisterous. If this area is truly flat and not developed at all, it indicates emotional extremes—passions and sometimes violence that may not be completely under control at all times.

The *Mount of Venus*, usually the largest of the mounts, is the heel of the hand, just below the thumb. When it is well developed, it signals the sociable person who is thoughtful, warm, and helpful. If this mount is lacking or very small, its possessor no doubt will be unfriendly, suspicious even, and not at all given to social interaction —a real curmudgeon. If the mount is excessively large—enough to make the hand look somewhat misshapen—look out for extreme behavior. This person is so passionate that his feelings can get frighteningly out of control.

The *Mount of the Moon*, located just across from the Mount of Venus at the base of the palm under the fourth finger, addresses itself to intuition and imagination. If the mount is lacking, these qualities will be lacking as well. The subject will be all logic and no hunches—very cut and dried. If the mount is well developed, its possessor will have good imaginative powers and intuition. He will trust his urges and follow them. If this mount is overdeveloped—really outstanding in the palm—the possessor may be mentally aberrant, prone to hallu- cinations, or other signs of psychosis.

SPECIAL AREAS

The life, head, and heart lines create two special areas in the palm: the angle of luck and the quadrangle.

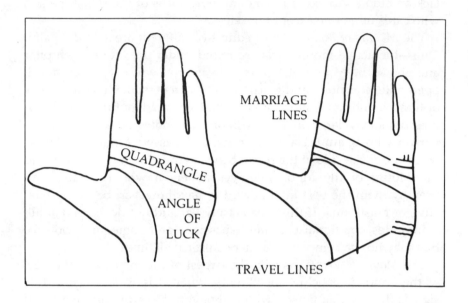

The *angle of luck* is formed by the head line and the life line. The greater the angle is, the more luck is indicated in the person's life. The *quadrangle* is formed by the head line and the heart line. The broader this space is, the wider the interests and the broader the outlook on life.

MARRIAGE, CHILDREN, AND TRAVEL

In the diagram here, the minor lines that indicate travel and marriage are illustrated. The number of small horizontal lines below the fourth finger suggest the number of marriages or major love affairs. Small, clearly marked lines running perpendicular to a marriage line indicate the number of children one will have, either from that marriage, or, if all such lines come from the top line, the total number.

Below this, horizontal lines on the base of the palm opposite the thumb indicate the number of major journeys one will take. The length of both travel and marriage lines indicate the relative length of such events.

READING A PALM

GETTING STARTED

For those interested in learning more about hand-reading, it will be necessary to gain experience with many, many different hands. Using only your own palm can be frustrating, since it is individual unto itself and no hand can include well-defined examples of all the possible factors. You'll be shocked to see how much palms vary from person to person. Different lines look different on each hand; some will be absent. Also, it is important to remember that reading a hand is not simply a step-by-step investigation of the various aspects of the hand. Probably more information can be gleaned from the overall impression of the whole hand—its color, shape, size, and so on— and from the comparison of left and right hands than from the interpretation of individual lines and mounts. The features of the palm are interdependent; their meanings offset other factors in the hand. The ability to take in the whole palm and to get a feeling from it before you investigate the details is a goal worth working toward.

Reading a palm for someone else involves responsibility. The person who asks for the reading is seeking information about himself; he is, to some degree at least, vulnerable. As a reader and an advisor, you must keep the subject's mental state in mind. Be careful about which words you use; your job is to help and to guide, not scare, your subject. If you are not sure of how to interpret specific aspects of the hand, don't irresponsibly take a stab at it. What you say will be remembered.

HOW TO MAKE A PALM PRINT

If you are interested in pursuing palmistry, you will want to start a collection of handprints. To this end, it will be necessary to convince friends and family to help. To make a print, you will need about ten sheets of unlined plain white paper, a large cloth-covered red ink pad (not the foam rubber variety), and a soft-leaded pencil.

Working with one small area of your clean, dry hand at a time, press your hand and fingers on the ink pad to coat it thoroughly. Continue pressing, covering more and more territory until the entire hand is coated with red ink. Using several sheets of paper underneath for padding, press your palm on a sheet of the paper, taking care to push down so the center of the palm print will register on the paper, and hold the hand in place while you trace around your palm, fingers, and thumb with the pencil. When you lift your hand, check the print. Is it smudged? Did you use too much ink? Not enough? Continue inking your hand and making prints of *both* hands until you have two good prints of *each* palm. Take care that the fingers are in a natural position when you make the print—not too close together but not widely spread apart, either.

Collect prints from whomever of your friends is willing to submit to your ministrations. Not until you have a good cross section of lines, mounts, hand shapes, finger shapes, and special markings will you truly be able to understand and enjoy the infinite variety of each palm.

WHERE TO GO FROM HERE

There is much more to palmistry: bracelets, plains, rings, wrinkles, arcs, curves, and other elements. If your interest in palmistry goes beyond the basic information discussed here, look for books on the subject and compare the interpretations of several authors. Keep charts of your own observations and practice reading palms—there is nothing better than experience. Seek out hand-readers in your area. One of the nice things about palmistry is that though it's good to be able to see the color of the skin and to feel the hand, a good palm print is enough to work from. If you locate a hand-reader in another city, perhaps you can arrange a reading by mail. Expect to pay from $25 to $75 for a reading of about one hour. See the Bibliography on page 572 for books on palmistry.

CHAPTER
EIGHTEEN
GRAPHOLOGY

Graphology, from the Greek *graph*, or writing, and *ology*, the science of, is the study of handwriting, usually for purposes of character analysis. Though we do it without thinking, writing is a highly complicated feat of hand–eye coordination. Each stroke of a writing implement is a very small, finely controlled movement, governed by the brain and produced through the impulses of the nerves to the muscles. When you think about it, our ability to perform such intricate movements in infinite and constantly changing variations over prolonged periods of time is really quite amazing. No wonder we get writer's cramp; we're lucky that our brains don't cramp from the effort as well.

Handwriting is the face man presents to the world. Yet for every word we write, we subconsciously respond to the idea that the word represents. The combination of these influences makes for a unique map to the personality. Graphologist Nadya Olyanova, author of four books on graphology, says, "Handwriting is really mindwriting. It's a photograph of how your mind works. If you're mentally disturbed, that will show in your handwriting." Likewise, if you are an optimistic type with great nurturing instincts and a dry sense of humor, that will show, too. Edward B. O'Neill, author, lecturer, and noted graphologist, says it this way in his *Graphological Journal:* "If we see handwriting as not merely a series of static forms but as a human being symbolically moving through space and time, we must then realize that we are seeing that human being move in his own personal way (smoothly, rhythmically, jerkily, spastically, hesitantly, timidly, inhibitedly, impulsively, compulsively, quickly, slowly, etc.)." Handwriting is one of man's ways of showing his individualism. Like fingerprints, a person's writing is almost totally individual, with the odds of exact duplication being calculated at trillions to one.

The graphologist's work often is twofold in nature. Many professionals interpret handwriting for character and personality analysis for private individuals or corporations. Others, sometimes called handwriting analysts, work with police, art dealers, museums, or lawyers to help determine authenticity, forgeries, and clues to the identity of the authors of threatening letters. Some graphologists do both. In her book *Handwriting Tells . . .* , Nadya Olyanova clarifies the differences: "The handwriting expert deals primarily with the physical structure of handwriting, examining it almost as an intern might a cadaver, with no thought that this might once have been a human being. The graphologist is concerned with the human equation, which includes the feelings, hopes, goals, and talents of the individual, the sum of his character. Often he has to read between the lines to arrive at a conclusion, whereas the handwriting expert is concerned only with the lines. However, the expert graphologist also examines the lines and structure of a handwriting to reach his conclusion, and he can therefore do everything the handwriting expert can do." Handwriting experts (or analysts) can be licensed so that their testimony is admissible in court in matters involving the validity of documents, the authorship of documents, and sometimes how, when, and where documents may have been drafted.

Many graphologists are quick to distance themselves from any association with the paranormal or the occult, yet few deny that intuition plays an important part in their interpretations. Again, it may be just a matter of the language. It is accepted that graphology is a way to read the unconscious, though the exact connection between the letter forms and the hidden thought is hard to prove. And, of course, permeating the unconscious is our psychic component; the handwriting becomes yet another device for extracting that buried treasure.

It is interesting to find that most graphologists know very little of the parasciences; here is how Nadya Olyanova compares her work to astrology: "Astrology is dealing with the unknown; whereas, in graphology, you have it all right in front of you. You have the writing, which is the person. To me, the handwriting *is* the person." Doubters of graphology would of course debate whether a graphologist has it all "right in front" of him, either.

No doubt about it, a heightened intuitive sense is useful in the study of handwriting. After learning the meanings of the individual variable factors in the handwriting and after becoming aware of every aspect that comes to bear on a reading, often it is intuition that assures the professional which elements have meaning in a given sample and which are mere flukes. Felix F. Lehmann, a leading American graphologist, stresses that "graphology is a science. Even if it's not a complete science, it is a science. Intuition certainly helps. Sometimes friends of mine will borrow my book [Casewit's *Graphology Handbook* (see Bibliography), in which Lehmann is extensively quoted] and come back three weeks later, saying, 'You can have your book back. I don't think I'll ever be able to manage it.' There are some people, like my children, who look at a handwriting and have an immediate idea of what a person is like."

Nadya Olyanova, on the other hand, thinks of graphology as "more of an art than a science." She explains, "I'm not psychic. I go according to the handwriting and that's it. It's true, you can't be a good graphologist without intuition—it plays a big part."

GRAPHOLOGY AND BUSINESS

In addition to having private clients, graphologists are frequently consulted by large corporations to help with personnel decision-making—to determine a potential employee's honesty, emotional stability, competence, initiative, self-confidence, sales ability, executive ability, or creativity. Sometimes the handwriting is used to flush out an existing employee who may be suspected of dishonesty or to pinpoint someone who might be worthy of a promotion or transfer to a different department, based on qualities not necessarily apparent in his current position.

In a front-page story in the September 3, 1985, issue of *The Wall Street Journal*, staff reporter Roger U. Ricklep reported that "These days, some French job-seekers actually are finding that weak-willed capital letters can stop their careers quicker than ordering red wine with the *truite aux amandes* at a job-interview lunch. And a good many executives have decided that studying penmanship can help them find people with the right stuff. 'Even if I think a person will be good, I won't take him if our graphologist advises against it,' says Geoffroy de Vogue, the chairman of Credit Français International, a private bank here [in Paris]. 'At least eighty of France's one hundred biggest companies use graphology in hiring, especially for executives and professionals,' says Jean Bousser, an executive recruiter.

"He continues, 'Nicole Borie, a Paris graphologist, says company demand for handwriting analysis has also doubled. Besides French companies, numerous subsidiaries of American concerns like Coca-

Cola Co., General Foods Corp., and Chase Manhattan Corp. now make use of handwriting analysis in hiring. 'We find it quite reliable,' says Jacqueline Dulestre, the personnel chief at Coca-Cola France."

In my days as a public relations executive, I had the opportunity to experience firsthand the European penchant for applying graphology to big business. I discovered quite by accident that before I was hired as a consultant to a major German corporation, my handwriting was very carefully scrutinized by the staff graphologist. Luckily I passed.

Though the United States still lags behind Europe, the trend toward using graphology in personnel selection is growing in this country. As this book was going to press, I noticed a large employment ad in the business section of *The New York Times* requesting that applicants send in their résumé "along with a short *handwritten* essay . . ." The following week an article in *Direct Mail News* discussed the use of graphology in evaluation of prospective employees, pointing out that the New School for Social Research offers several semesters of graphology in their psychology curriculum.

Barbara Harding, of Concord, Massachusetts, has been a graphologist for almost twenty years. She can document how rapidly her business-consulting services have grown: "I've been working with companies in personnel selection since 1980. And I have to say that I probably had ten clients in 1980 and in 1985 I had one hundred fifty. . . . I don't tell them whether or not to hire the person; that isn't my function. My function is to describe the personality and character, and particularly as it pertains to the job description that they have outlined for me." In addition, Harding sometimes compares her findings about the potential employee with those of the person he or she would report to, in order to determine compatibility. Typically, corporations seek to know about specific qualities that have to do with specific jobs. Is the potential sales manager aggressive under pressure? Is the comptroller candidate honest; does he have personal and professional integrity? Can the public relations director really get along with just about everyone?

Stan Sherman, a management consultant in Waltham, Massachusetts, has found Harding's services to be of value to his clients. He relates the following anecdote: "A company down south used my services to survey its employees' attitudes about the work environment. In working with the client, I became somewhat familiar with the president of the company. One day, he said, 'It's too bad that you're so far away because I don't feel like sending candidates up to Massachusetts to see you, but I've got a problem that's really bugging me. The productivity of one of my managers is really falling down tremendously and I don't know what's bothering him.' At that point, I thought about Barbara Harding. Since the president wasn't going to send the man up to see me, this would be a good opportunity to experiment with graphology. I told the president to send me some handwriting samples from several years ago and current ones as well. I turned them over to Barbara Harding. She studied them and said that the man was under tremendous emotional stress and that she had some questions in her mind about his honesty. I passed her comments along to the company president. He called in his accountants and had them do an audit of the books. The man in question was the firm's comptroller, who had, indeed, been stealing from the company. That's the most dramatic of the stories that I know personally."

A bit closer to home, several years ago Sherman was prescribed Valium for a bad back. After he wrote a letter to Harding, she telephoned to ask what was wrong with him. She knew that he was not well and said she suspected that he was on drugs of some sort. He continues, "Having had many occasions to see the normal handwriting, she identified the change in it immediately. I certainly have enough evidence to believe that there is merit to graphology."

DIAGNOSING ILLNESS THROUGH GRAPHOLOGY

Every professional graphologist I talked with believes it is possible to diagnose certain ailments through the study of graphology. Felix Lehmann adds, "Many times, I do see various handicaps in the handwriting. Let us say that somebody has great trouble with his legs. I would see that in the writing, in the lower zone. We have legs, the lower zone; the torso, the middle zone; and a head, the upper zone. And each of these zones is portrayed in the handwriting. The upper zone, the ascenders such as the b, d, h, k, l, and t, would be the head, but also let's say the conscience, aspirations, spirit, authority, the superego. The middle zone, the torso, from the neck down to the lower part of the body, would be the letters a, c, e, m, n, o, r, s, u, w, and x. If the top was the intellect, this would be the will, the daily life, the experiences. The lower zone, the legs, shown in the letters f, g, j, p, q, y, and z, would be what is below the regular ego, what is hidden—the subconscious, sex drive, family roots, and certain kinds of emotions." It is the interplay of these zones that is different from person to person. To Lehmann, variances in a particular zone make him suspicious of the health in the body parts that are in that zone.

When asked if she can tell illness in the handwriting, Nadya Olyanova says, "Yes, definitely. Certain types of illness are very apparent—especially heart disease, but also pulmonary—anything that has to do with the chest. I can't account for it; it's just an empirical rule. There are breaks in the upper loops of the handwriting that definitely show heart disease. In one of my books, I give an example of a salesman who had a heart condition. He was in a hotel when he had an attack and he wrote something. You couldn't make out what he was writing, but the sign of the heart condition was so prevalent that there was no mistaking why he died."

Olyanova claims also to be aware of other physical maladies— neuroses, alcoholism, drug addiction, potential suicides, brain damage, hysteria, and tuberculosis. Though she claims she cannot tell if someone has a predilection to drugs, she "can see if some people are on drugs. Very often I can tell if someone is under the influence of something, and very often I can see suicidal tendencies."

Indeed, many of the examples she cites are convincing. In light of the renewed interest in the events surrounding Marilyn Monroe's death, Olyanova stands by what she wrote about Monroe in the 1969 edition of *Handwriting Tells . . .* :

From her handwriting, which shows none of the signs of the suicide, we can only conclude that her death was an accident. For here we see a love of life, a heightening of the energies on the least provocation, and certain visionary ideals that she realized in her position in show business.

It is true that there were mild paranoid trends in her makeup, but no more than would be found in anyone in her position at the top—after starting at the bottom. The rightward flow tells us that she had an absolute need for human companionship, and could be generous with those who showed her love. There are signs of talent, of a dramatic instinct, of a desire to be outstanding—in the form of the capital M, as well as in the underscore. Though large, the writing does not show much expansiveness, and despite her desire to give, this was attended by fears of being hurt if she did. She could be rigid and unyielding in some instances, as shown in the angular formation of the s in "soon" and in the short finals. Neverthe-less, she could make a generous gesture, as the long final in "Friend" shows; but essentially Marilyn was a child with a longing for something she never had, and she sometimes despaired of ever finding it. Her last gesture would appear to be one lacking in judgment rather than a delib-erate taking of her life, for she was compulsive, and in following a comp-ulsion she overdid what might have been a tem-porary escape from reality.

(It is interesting to compare Olyanova's remarks to Bob Slatzer's story of Monroe, page 172.)

Huntington Hartford, philanthropist, heir to the A & P fortune and founder of the Handwriting Institute, spent a considerable amount of money supporting research in graphology. On his staff were medical doctors, Ph.D.'s, graphologists, and others—all looking for evidence that would advance the acceptance of graphology as a science. One man, Alfred Kanfer, received a grant from Hartford to study the use of handwriting in detecting cancer. For years, Kanfer examined the handwriting of cancer patients, isolating specific characteristics that he found to be worthy of note. He worked in a small lab in New York's Strang Clinic and, according to Felix F. Lehmann, "he believed in it and he was a very serious man. He was an excellent graphologist and a very fine humanitarian and he felt he had something. When he got sick, he analyzed his own handwriting and said that he had cancer, and he died from it. . . . As far as I can remember, his method was to enlarge the stroke two hundred times. A little hair-thin stroke would look huge, magnified two hundred times, and then he saw in the flow—in the width, breadth, and the irregularities —he saw cancer." It is to be hoped that in the future, dedicated graphologists will have more opportunities to work with doctors and scientists to test the efficacy of graphology.

GRAPHOLOGY AND THE LAW

Graphology or handwriting analysis frequently are used for legal or law enforcement matters. The need for expert testimony in matters of forgeries and the like is vital. Nadya Olyanova says, "I can usually tell when a handwriting is faked. You know, it's very strange about forgers. They have a very common, ordinary handwriting of their own, because their character seems to be affected by the person whom they're imitating. There was a man called Scratch McCarthy, a very well-known forger—I love that name—and I saw his handwriting. It was just simple, ordinary—like a Palmer hand. He was a great forger, but that was because he took on the characteristics of the person whose handwriting he was forging." Felix Lehmann agrees: "A phony is a phony, and I always say, the more we disguise, the more we show. But you have to have experience. If you're really in doubt, ask for another sample. If something doesn't click, it doesn't; you just feel that something is wrong."

Forgeries, however, have different scopes. They can range from the ten-year-old's attempt to duplicate his mother's signature on a not-too-wonderful report card to the large-scale, multimillion-dollar hoax of the modern-day publishing world.

The Clifford Irving trial over his so-called authorized Howard Hughes autobiography is a good example of the use of graphologists for legal purposes. In writing the book, Irving produced more than twenty pages of contracts and letters he claimed were from Hughes's private files. In reality, the pages were forged by Irving, who had never seen an original specimen of Hughes' handwriting. The documents were submitted to five top-notch handwriting experts, all of whom examined the work and unanimously declared the papers to be genuine—written by Hughes himself. In a piece called "Clifford Irving's 10 Best Forgers of All Time" that he wrote for *The Book of Lists*, Irving lists himself among his choices for the top ten. He quotes one expert, Paul Osborn, as having said that the forgery of such a mass of material "would be beyond human ability."

Just a few years ago, the Hitler diary hoax embarrassed the German magazine *Stern* in much the same way. The so-called diaries—all sixty volumes—were written in a virtually illegible hand and were judged to be authentic by several notable experts. Later, after simple forensic testing, the diaries were shown to be forgeries, but for a few intense days just prior to that evidence being released, experts vacillated wildly, one day declaring the diaries to be real and reversing their opinions the following day. It was a circus atmosphere, and an expensive one at that. Gruner & Jahr, the publisher/owner of *Stern*, lost $8.6 million in the debacle.

THE LIMITS OF GRAPHOLOGY

Having looked at the major ways that graphology is used, it's a good idea to consider just what it can and can't do. As we've discussed, graphology *can* reveal character and personality as well as instinct, creativity, kindness, anger, physical or mental illness, fear, energy, and many other qualities of feeling or behavior. What graphology *cannot* reveal includes the sex of the writer, his or her age, race, marital status, or occupation. (I should add, though, that Felix Lehmann claims to be able to ascertain information about the subject's life that is reflected in the handwriting. He says, "I can probably tell, in 90 percent of the cases, whether a woman is divorced for some time. You can tell that from a certain reflection on the past. There's a certain kind of sadness or taking it into consideration, a happening in the past. It shows.")

Graphology cannot reveal whether two parties are related. Within a single family, each member may write completely differently from the others, since handwriting is the expression of the individual, not his genes. On the other hand, the daughter who is very close to her mother might consciously or subconsciously try to emulate her mother's penmanship because she desires to be like her mother. By the same token, schoolchildren or even groups of adults who work together often pick up particular flourishes within a limited-size group of people. Think of all the people who at some time in their lives dotted their i's with a small circle. Think of the teenagers who, if only for two weeks, deliberately slanted their writing to the left. Indeed, don't forget whole offices full of people who cross their number 7's and z's with bars—in the European manner—because the boss does so.

Most people are surprised—and thrilled—to find out that the prettiness or legibility of their handwriting has no bearing whatsoever in graphology. It is not a beauty contest or an art exhibit. We write the way we write, and the artfully scripted hand has no particular advantages or disadvantages.

A BRIEF HISTORY OF GRAPHOLOGY

In one sense, the analysis of handwriting reaches back into antiquity. Confucius cautioned, "Beware the man whose writing sways as the reed in the wind." Aesop, Aristotle, Julius Caesar, and Cicero were believers, as was Nero. Graphologists are fond of quoting one of Nero's letters, in which he says, "I fear this man at court because his writing shows him treacherous." The Roman historian Suetonius Tranquillus, in his book *The Lives of the Caesars*, written in the second century A.D., repeatedly comments on the idiosyncrasies of his subjects' handwriting. A medieval Chinese philosopher, Jo-Hau, wrote that he could tell if a man was noble or vulgar by his handwriting.

Yet although the connection between handwriting and personality is one that scholars seem always to have been aware of, the true inception of graphology didn't start until the seventeenth century. The reason for this is self-evident: From the fall of Rome until the rise of modern Europe, almost everyone was illiterate. What writing was done during this hiatus was largely the province of scribes, whose specific job was to copy exactly what the original document showed. Their writing was highly stylized, as seen by the surviving manuscripts and records.

It wasn't until about 1630 that modern graphology had its start. Camillo Baldo, a professor at the University of Bologna and a scholar, wrote the first book on the subject, *Tratto come da una lettera missiva so cognoscano la natura e qualita del scittore*, or *How to Know the Nature and Qualities of a Person by His Letters*. In the early 1870s, two French abbots, Abbé Flandrin and Abbé Jean-Hippolyte Michon, discovered Baldo's book and developed an enthusiasm for the subject. Flandrin wrote a textbook of sorts that catalogued his findings about handwriting, and Michon, who coined the word *graphology*, produced the first popular work on the subject. M. Crepieux-Jamin joined Michon in his studies and revised the first book to publish a second edition that is a classic in the field.

Since that time, graphology has gained much popularity and respect in Europe. In the late 1800s, interest was piqued among the Germans, who began cataloguing data and showed themselves to be willing and able scholars of graphology. Criminology began to embrace graphology in Germany, Italy, and England, where it was used to classify different types of criminals and criminal behavior. The intelligentsia of Great Britain became quite interested, including several noted physicians, scientists, and even writers Elizabeth Barrett and Robert Browning, who were enthusiasts. The painter Gainsborough kept a handwriting sample of his subject next to his easel to study when the model was absent

Throughout France and Germany, many universities maintain courses of study in graphology, usually within their departments of medicine or psychology. As a method of personality analysis, graphology is being accepted more and more in the United States, and though hundreds of books have been written on the subject, learning the basics of graphology is not all that difficult.

ANALYZING THE HANDWRITING

In some ways, the analysis of handwriting in the United States is easier than elsewhere. Europeans are taught much more complex and variable letter forms—somewhat similar to what is called the Spencerian hand—whereas virtually all Americans are taught to write according to the Palmer Method.

No doubt this script is more than familiar; after all, it was tidily tacked above the blackboard in every classroom in America. Remember penmanship class—the slanted upstrokes and the slanted continuous ovals that looked, if you did them correctly, like a Slinky?

Remember the alternate forms for the letters *t* and *r* that were strictly verboten? But we must keep in mind that we are not sheep. By the time we become adults, most of us have developed our own letter forms that vary from the Palmer models to some degree. The amount and direction of that variance is the barometer of graphology.

What follows is a guide to the basics of graphology. It will explain how to "take" a writing sample and what it should contain, as well as what information the graphologist needs to know about the subject. Then we look at the primary factors of graphology to see what they are, how they vary, and what they mean. After that, there is a checklist of the factors to consider in interpretation, and finally, we look at where to go for further study.

Throughout the next sections, Nadya Olyanova has generously given me permission to cull illustrative examples from her vast published writings, handwriting samples, and interpretations. You'll see how these illustrations enhance the quick comprehension of this material.

OBTAINING A WRITING SAMPLE

Because so many factors are important to the analysis of handwriting, it is important, whenever possible, to secure a proper sample of the writing.

- The subject should sit comfortably at a table or desk.
- Provide a choice of writing instruments—a fine ballpoint pen, a medium ballpoint pen, a fountain pen, or two with different-size nibs. Avoid pencils, which lose their points too quickly, and felt-tip pens, which require almost no pressure from the hand.
- Give the subject several sheets of standard-size unlined smooth white paper. Avoid very thin paper, highly textured paper, odd sizes of paper, tinted paper, and, above all, do not use

lined paper. (I suggest you supply several sheets, because some people dislike writing on a single thickness; they like the "padding" provided by several backup sheets.)

- Have the subject write at least one-half to a full page about whatever he or she chooses—it might be about what he or she ate for breakfast, favorite hobbies, or a television show watched the night before. (Ideally, the person will use the word "I" in his or her writing, and, if you are very lucky, some other potentially "emotional" words will be included. Try to have the subject write about a personal experience to increase the chances that such terms will be used.) At the bottom of the page, ask the person to give a signature. (I feel that asking the subject to write the alphabet in capital and lowercase letters can be helpful, but it is not a standard graphological practice.) If the subject has more than one style of handwriting—for example, my friend whose most commonly used "public" handwriting style is almost printed, but who when hurriedly taking notes or jotting down ideas for her eyes only, lapses into script—try to get a sample of both styles. Urge the subject to relax and write as he or she would normally write; attempts to prettify the writing style can influence the analysis. Remember, legibility does not matter.
- Determine the sex and approximate age of the subject for your own use, since these factors will color your interpretation. Also, determine whether the writer was educated in the United States or elsewhere. If schooled in a foreign country, certain letter forms will vary and should not necessarily be considered different from the norm. (This is difficult to read if the graphologist is not familiar with other handwriting styles.)

Some cautionary remarks about the writing sample: Some graphologists prefer a sample that was written in the normal course of everyday business—a friendly letter or business letter, the notes for a résumé, class notes, a complaint to a company, or instructions to the housekeeper. If the sample is several pages long, analyze the writing toward the end of the document, because the writer would have been "warmed up" by then. If you are present while the sample is being written, note the speed of the writing—is it quick or slow? Some graphologists like to have a handwritten sample from several years before—just for comparison. This would be especially helpful for certain types of determinations.

THE PRIMARY FACTORS IN HANDWRITING

SLANT

The first thing to look at in analyzing someone's handwriting is its slant. Do the letters lean forward or backward, or are they straight up and down? If they lean in one direction or another, to what degree? The slant represents the writer's approach to others, his introversion or extroversion. Nadya Olyanova uses the "Emotional Barometer" to measure the amount of slant in a subject's handwriting.

EMOTIONAL BAROMETER

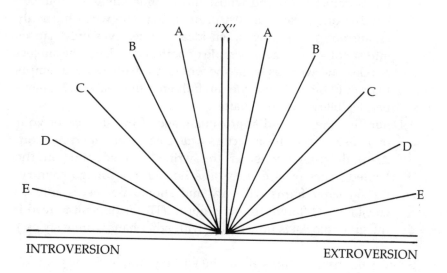

INTROVERSION   EXTROVERSION

A *pronounced leftward slant* (introversion C, D, and E) shows an extremely introverted character, given to overriding emotional impulse with intellectual considerations. There is a fear of the future here and a tendency toward dwelling in the past.

A *slight leftward slant* (introversion A or B) shows a slight wariness of the future, someone who holds back from expressing emotion openly, and a tendency to evaluate things logically rather than emotionally. (Many left-handed writers will write this way naturally; in that case, it is not a valid basis of interpretation.)

Straight up and down writing ("X") shows a rigid and controlled attitude, not introverted but still overly intellectual, with a firm control of the emotions. This person generally is savvy about practical considerations and can take care of his or her own needs.

A *slight forward slant* (extroversion A or B) is the way most Americans are taught to write. It indicates both a healthy attitude toward the future, without ignoring the lessons of the past, as well as a good balance of emotion with pragmatism.

A *pronounced forward slant* (extroversion C, D, and E) indicates a headlong approach to the future, diving into it and ignoring practical considerations. It shows an extroverted character, one whose impulses are acted out rather than evaluated, as well as a highly emotional personality. At the extreme, it indicates emotional instability.

BASELINE

Baseline is the incline present in a *line* of writing: uphill, downhill, or straight across—as though on a printed line. In order to get a good sample of the natural baseline, it is important that the writing be on unlined paper.

Handwriting that climbs *uphill* like that above shows an optimistic attitude toward life and a character whose actions are often shaped by enthusiasm.

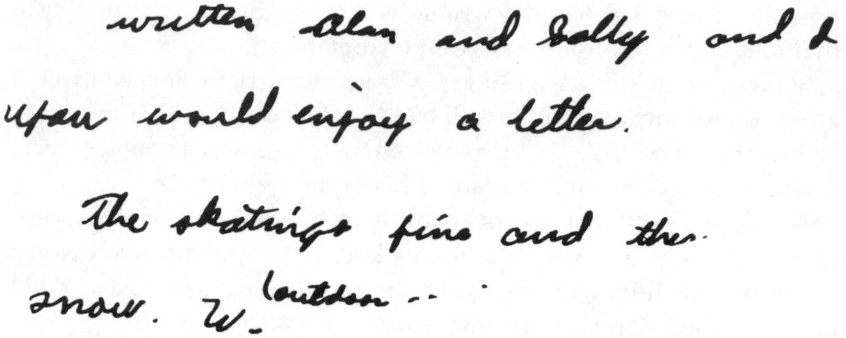

[handwritten sample]

The *downhill* writing shows a depressed personality that treats life with a caution that will often edge into pessimism.

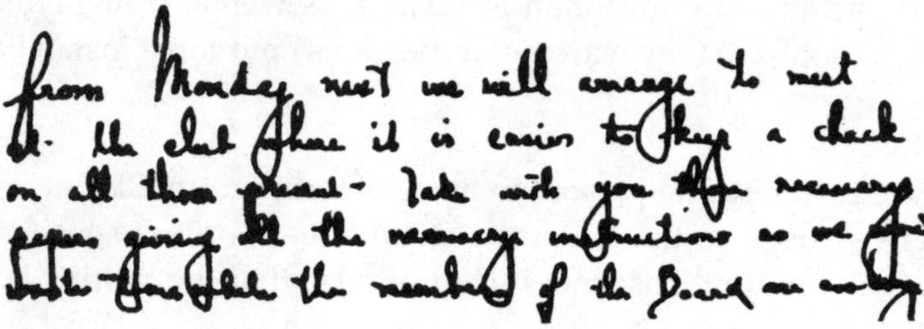

[handwritten sample]

An *even baseline* shows a coolheaded approach to life, neither pessimistic nor optimistic, but realistic—someone who reacts to the world as circumstances dictate, not approaching things with a predetermined attitude.

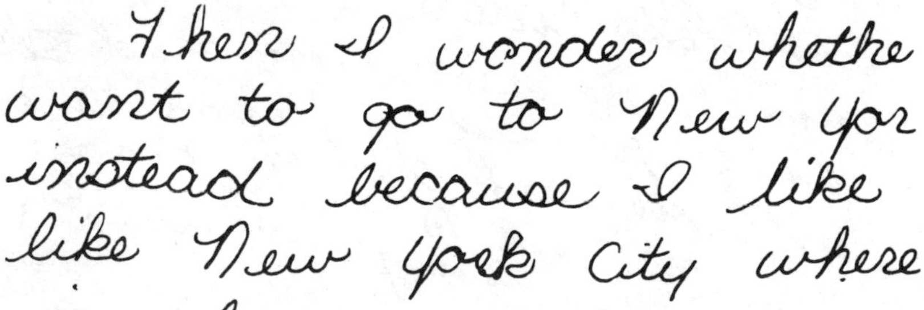

[handwritten sample]

A handwriting with a baseline that *changes from uphill to downhill or vice versa* indicates fits of moodiness and temperament. They can be overenthusiastic or overly negative, but generally will be at some extreme of the spectrum.

The more extreme the baseline runs in any direction, the more pronounced the attitude. An extreme uphill writer is not merely optimistic but realistic, reacting to the world as circumstances dictate, not approaching things with a predetermined attitude.

MARGINS

1 WIDE MARGINS

2 CROWDED MARGINS

3 WIDE LEFT MARGIN NARROW RIGHT MARGIN

4 WIDE RIGHT MARGIN NARROW LEFT MARGIN

5 MIXED MARGINS

6 REGULAR MARGINS

A writer's margins are used to evaluate, specifically, his attitude toward money, and generally, his expansiveness of character. This is guided by a very logical correlation—the larger the margins, the more paper is required to write out a given amount of words.

1. Wide margins left and right: Someone with a basically generous nature, not given to worry about cost or other types of expense. Someone who would offer help when needed without thinking about time or effort for himself.

2. Very small or nonexistent margins: Someone who is aware of the expense of everything; he avoids waste in every situation, though he is not necessarily cheap or greedy. He simply is aware of the value of his own time and considers that before making a decision.

3. Wide left and narrow right margin: A person with a naturally extravagant nature who does his best to overcome it. The wide left margin shows an immediate impulse to be generous, and the narrow right margin shows the attempt to budget time, money, or effort.

4. Narrow left and wide right margins: The naturally thrifty person who makes a conscious effort toward generosity.

5. Mixed margins—inconsistent: The person who starts out with the best intentions of staying within a budget, but who can't overcome an overly generous nature.

6. Regular margins: Not specific enough to work with—ask for a longer document. This could indicate good balance but only if other factors corroborate that finding.

The margin between the top edge of the paper and where the writing begins is thought to indicate the writer's attitude toward the addressee. A large top margin shows a great deal of respect, even awe, on the part of the writer. It shows someone who is careful not to encroach on the addressee's "territory." On the other hand, a small or nonexistent top margin indicates familiarity or a certain lack of respect.

SPACING

The spacing between words and between lines generally indicates two separate sets of characteristics. One school of thought holds that spacing is another indicator of generosity, as it is with margins. That is, a relatively large amount of space between words and lines shows generosity and extravagance, while little space between them shows a person with a tendency toward thriftiness. A second way of interpreting spacing is to view it as an indicator toward "personal space."

1. A person with a strong sense of privacy. He likes to stand back from people and doesn't join in or get involved too quickly.

2. A gregarious person who desires the company of other people. There is an indication toward sharing thoughts and feelings with others.

3. This extreme example shows just what it seems to: confusion, illogic, and difficulty in expressing oneself. It is the sign of a convoluted mind, with thoughts interfering with one another and extreme difficulty in making decisions.

1. *I would be very interested to have the analysis of my own.*

2. *I am quite interested in drama and was thinking seriously of transfering to the Northwestern School of Speech*

3. *(illegible handwriting sample)*

PRESSURE

Because of the diversity of writing instruments available, it often is hard to judge what degree of pressure was used in writing a given sample. A fine-line ballpoint pen will only produce a thin line, no matter what. Some felt-tip pens do both; indeed, some writers deliberately mash the tips to make them wide, while to others, a wide line means it's time to discard the pen. The best way to judge for pressure is to actually *feel* the back of the paper. It will take some time to get used to, but after some experience, you will be able to judge the amount of pressure involved.

A sample written lightly, with the point of the pen just touching the page, indicates a sensitive and responsible individual. This person is aware of the people around him and responds to their needs and emotions. The values of this person are more spiritual and aesthetic than material.

Someone who presses down heavily on the page will parallel the writer who makes overly large letters. In fact, the two qualities often are found in pairs. This is the loud and domineering sort, given to material values, and while not necessarily inconsiderate, he is clearly more concerned with himself than with others.

SIZE OF LETTER FORMS

The size of the handwriting can be seen as how "loudly" we are speaking. Like the forms of letters, we are taught a standard of size —about ⅛-inch for lowercase letters. Deviation in either direction— smaller or larger—shows our personal inclinations and "speaking volume."

1. Small: Unusually small writing such as this indicates modesty and humility as well as a natural ability for self-criticism and a talent for concentration. This person can be single-minded and unstoppable when he or she decides to pursue a task to its completion.
2. Medium: Neither small nor large, the medium-size letter form indicates a fairly normal person. Look at other factors for idiosyncrasies.
3. Large: This person likes to do things right, and usually that means big. This person is good under pressure and may be not so good until the pressure is applied. Generally, though, he likes himself and you might, too.
4. Extralarge: The exhibitionist, the extravagant, the flawed. Something is out of kilter here—the flamboyance is too extreme. Poor powers of concentration.

1 ⟶ Coaches come from everywhere and from Toronto
to the distant reaches of the province where the
fun and the feeling can banish care for a

2 marrying. Will you please
tell me whether or not you
think that we have an

3 what is the future

4 the check, for you
Life _is_ quite a

finest cinema

CONNECTEDNESS

This quality usually is thought to be indicative of the subject's thought processes.

1. Completely connected: Shows logical thinking, a person who proceeds from premise to conclusion and relies on facts for decisions.
2. Somewhat connected, showing some breaks: A good combination of logic and intuition; good powers of concentration and reasoning.
3. Disconnected writing: Decides things on intuition, an instinctive thinker who often operates on hunches. While this could show a flighty personality, it might also indicate creativity.

1   *[handwritten sample]*

2   *[handwritten sample]*

3   *[handwritten sample]*

INITIALS, OR LEAD-IN STROKES, AND TERMINALS, OR ENDINGS

What a writer chooses to keep in his writing and what he finds superfluous is always interesting. So it goes with initials and terminals. They are details that can be deleted or altered without any loss of meaning to the words.

In the Palmer hand, the lowercase letters b, e, f, h, i, j, k, l, m, n, p, r, s, t, u, v, w, x, y, and z all start with lead-in strokes before forming the body of the letter itself. The retention or deletion of these strokes, or the addition of strokes or endings to other letters, are good indicators of personality.

1   *Christmas greetings*

2   *when you come*

3   *There will be plenty of time to talk*

4   *the other + young son are she working*

5   *bank's personnel Analyst my Vaults*

    Sincerely yours

1.   Lead-ins to all words: Conventional. Believes in tradition and maintaining proper standards. There may be an element of dependence on others. Finally, it shows a reluctance to dive into things; the lead-ins are a delaying tactic against getting to the matter at hand.

2. No lead-ins: Has dispensed with the unnecessary. Traditions that don't serve a purpose are eliminated in life as they are in this script. This person is comfortable going against conventions if he or she doesn't agree with them. Also, a readiness to deal with problems without delay.

3. Up-sloping finals: An affable person who likes to be surrounded by others. Not a loner in any way. This person probably is very likable and socially stimulating.

4. Flattened or drawn-out finals: Denotes a generous and curious nature. Has good powers of concentration and will stick with something to the end.

5. Down-turned finals: A very serious nature, possibly cruel or extremely moralistic. This is the sign of the judgmental personality who has written his own set of unpublished rules.

CAPITALS

There are so many variations on capital letters that it would take dozens of pages to try even to mention the possibilities. Generally speaking, look at capitals for consistency. Are three of them printed and all the others written in script? What does the capital *I* look like? It's an interesting combination of a letter, a capital, and a word that bespeaks the self.

1. rounded A: maternal instinct that wins out over reason.

2. old-fashioned A: traditional, conservative

3. printed A: creative and loving

4. large-bottomed B: generous, expansive, sometimes gullible

5. small-bottomed B: cautious and skeptical

6. lead-in stroke on capitals: impatient with small matters, concerned with appearances and possessions

7. simple, printed letter forms: clear thinking, manual dexterity

8. single-stroke I: clarity of thought, an acute aesthetic sense, and real sophistication

9. blocked-off I: constructive thinking

10. open-top D: openness, frankness, talkativeness

11. closed-top D: cautious, reserved, secretive

12. loop-top D: flirtatiousness, sometimes with reserve

13. ornamental capitals: vulgarity, lack of aesthetic sense

14. big-loop L: generosity, sensitivity

15. M with angular-top, round bottom: keen mind, gentle nature

16. M with first mound higher: dignity, family pride

17. M with second mound higher: if mound is rounded, gentle self-assertion, desire for authority; if mound is angular, misplaced authority, self-righteousness, disagreeableness
18. G-clef S: musical ability, rhythm
19. open-bottom S: expansiveness, good temperament

t-BARS

The way we cross our t's is said to be an indication of willpower and an idea of how well adjusted or neurotic we are. Again, there are dozens of possibilities; here are just a few.

INDECISIVENESS	WELL-BALANCED	ENERGETIC
OBSTINATE	TENACIOUSNESS	INTROVERSION
PROCRASTINATION	AMBITION	PERSISTENCE
ADVENTUROUS	FUN-LOVING	MYSTICISM

i-DOTS

A few i-dots have special significance, which is enhanced if other factors, such as t-bars, correlate with them. Nadya Olyanova adds another interesting point: "Since we are all taught to dot our i's, a good memory is revealed when dots appear consistently."

METICULOUS	IMAGINATIVE	CRITICAL	HUMOROUS
ENTHUSIASTIC	CAUTIOUS	ECCENTRIC	AGRESSIVENESS

LOOPS

Loops denote emotion and how it comes to the surface. They represent the path of our feelings and fantasies.

ASCENDING LOOPS

Normal loop:
Idealism

High loop:
Imaginative

Wide loop:
Sensitive

Compressed loop:
Repression

Back-formed loop:
Maladjusted

Ragged or broken loop:
Unhealthy (heart)

Short loop:
Practical

No loop:
Precise

Squared loop:
Aggressiveness

DESCENDING LOOPS

Normal loop:
Realistic

Swooping loop:
Physical

Short fat loop:
Vain

Short loop:
Physical weakness

Backward stroke:
Clannishness

Broken stroke:
Fearfulness

Fancy loop:
Compulsiveness

Angular loop:
Aggressiveness

Single downstroke:
Determination

Upstroke to right:
Altruistic

Backward loop:
Cautious

Tiny loop:
Shyness

SIGNATURES

Because signatures are so often repeated, they seem to have a life and a style of their own. Often, they do not resemble a person's normal handwriting. Signatures are, of course, one of the most telling facets of handwriting—but in an odd way. If there is a marked difference between a person's handwriting and his signature, what you are looking at is the difference between the writer's true nature and what he would like to project about himself. Some people develop a distinctive signature naturally. Think of the executive who signs dozens of business letters and checks every day, in his quick threaded scrawl. But, generally, a signature is consciously developed and reveals the writer's self-image. (It's hard to deny that some names almost "beg" for a special signature, whereas others take some real consideration as to what can be done with them. On the other hand, John Hancock did a great job with a fairly ordinary name, and, though his name is rather special, Leopold Stokowski did a really amazing job with his; see below.)

Interpretation of the signature should include consideration of the size, shape, position, slant, and any additional fillips that might be added by the writer. In addition, it's important to check the relative size and predominance of the given name versus the family name. The smaller given name and larger family name often shows a person who is cowed by his family, one who feels that he is not measuring up to their expectations. If the given name is larger, the subject may be ashamed of his family in some way; he might dislike his father or the entire family, though he may or may not think he is a good person relative to them.

Surprisingly, if the signature veers in a different direction from the other writing, the subject is adaptable in many ways. Otherwise, the slant can be interpreted using the standard guidelines for slant.

Lyndon B. Johnson

James Cagney

John Lindsay

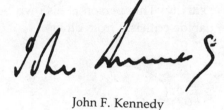

John F. Kennedy

Frank Lloyd Wright

Henry Fonda

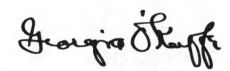

Georgia O'Keeffe

Tallulah Bankhead

Ernest Hemingway

Albert Schweitzer

Some people, it would seem, can't leave well enough alone. They sign their name and then they add to it. These embellishments mean something. For example:

Gamel Abdul Nasser

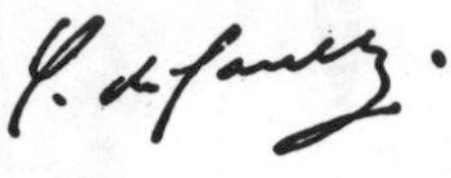

Charles DeGaulle

A period after the name shows sensitivity, especially personal sensitivity. This person is his own best and biggest critic, so he cannot abide criticism from others.

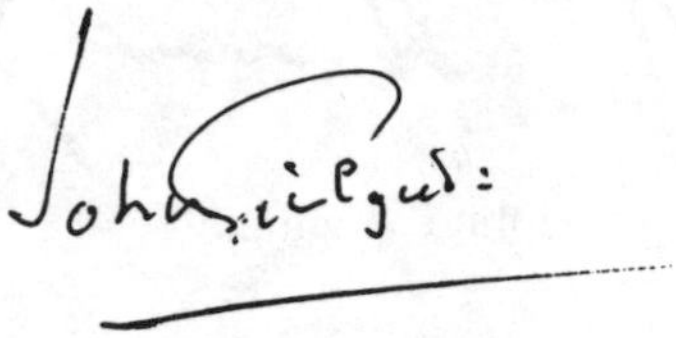

John Gielgud

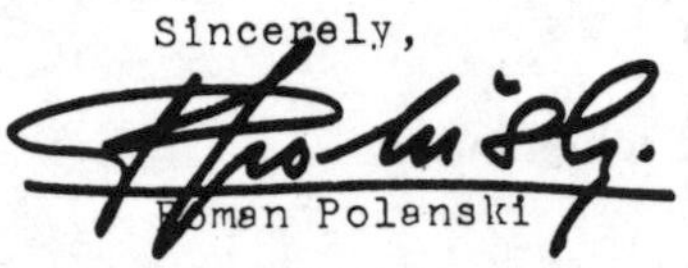

Roman Polanski

Underlining the signature once, as in Gielgud's and Polanski's signatures, indicates a healthy ego and self-confidence. An elaborate underscoring denotes an increased sense of pride.

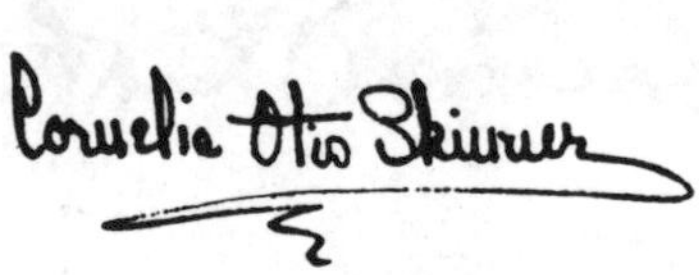

Cornelia Otis Skinner

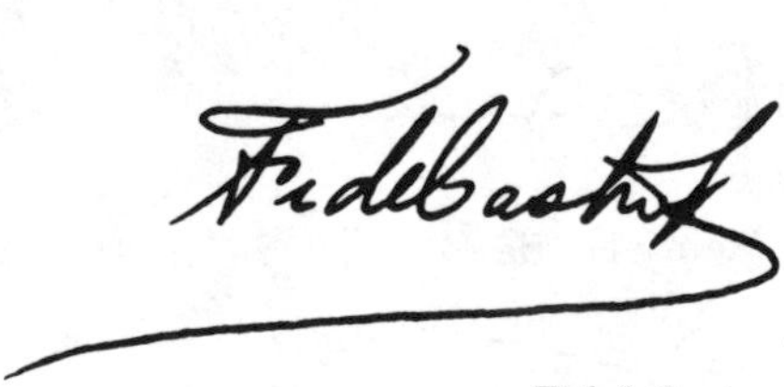

Fidel Castro

Olivia De Havilland

A simple squiggle, whether connected to the name or not and whether curving or straight, is the sign of a creative person who can assert himself and who, basically, likes himself.

George Bernard Shaw

An encircled signature is the sign of someone who wants to have a secret and who may be reclusive or otherwise stingy of himself.

Ravi Shankar

Marilyn Monroe

Joan Crawford

Elaborate squiggling, either within the signature or underneath it, can be the sign of the show-off. This is the person who loves to be the center of attention. Take into consideration that Europeans and others born prior to about 1940 will have fancier penmanship since they were taught the Spencerian method of writing.

 "Bluebeard," the pirate. (Count Gilles de Rais (Retz) de Laval)

Robert F. Kennedy

The illegible signature usually belongs to a person who would like to be secretive. Often, these people feel that if they can read their signature, others can read their inner thoughts. If it is truly an eccentric collection of shapes and forms, the signature can be a sign of creativity.

LEFT-HANDEDNESS

Those who write with the left hand are just as open to graphological interpretation as are right-handed people. Indeed, left-handed writers may even possess some special ability as well. Granted, they do hold a writing implement differently—frequently they are poorly instructed in writing—and sometimes they actually pull or push the pen or pencil in a way that is foreign to right-handed writers, but their penmanship is as much an indication of their character and personality as it is for right-handed people. If the left-handed writer didn't feel comfortable with the way he wrote, presumably he would change it or modify it until it was, at least, comfortable.

One very interesting study of left-handedness is the case of Admiral Horatio Nelson, who lost his right hand in battle. Nadya Olyanova compares his former handwriting with his acquired left-handed script, written ten years after his injury:

Horatio Nelson

Written With The Right Hand

Written With The Left Hand

In the right-handed sample, we see an ardent, outgoing, impulsive person, strongly sexed but controlled. His involved capital H shows a tendency to get into tight situations, from which, by logic and strategy, he could emerge. The embellished ending on the signature is larger than the rest of the writing, gives us his sense of the dramatic, and shows a dominant personality.

In the sample written with his left hand, ten years after he lost the right one, the angle is notably changed and vertical, showing a prevalence of reason over emotion. Intuition has developed in these intervening years, as shown in breaks in words, which do not appear as often in the earlier sample. His capital N now takes on an old-fashioned form, revealing a paternalism which became more distinct after his adventurous life. Both specimens show some similarities, as in the capital B. He had become more realistic and less romantic in his approach to life; his emotions were tempered by reason, and he derived pleasure from reading and reflecting, where formerly he was a man of action.

CHECKLIST OF IMPORTANT GRAPHOLOGICAL TRAITS

Start with a sample of your own handwriting. Using the following checklist, first fill in the second column to correspond with what you observe about your own writing. I've included some words or questions that will remind you of important factors, but you might want to refer to each individual section in the foregoing text to refresh your memory and see some samples. After the second column is completed, refer to the text again for ideas about interpretation. Remember, go with what you see; if there's nothing there, look elsewhere. Fill in the entire third column. If you come to a factor that completely mystifies you, skip it—at least for now. Maybe it will be clarified with further study.

GRAPHOLOGICAL CHECKLIST

FACTOR	CHARACTERISTIC	INTERPRETATION
SLANT	RIGHT? LEFT? VERTICAL?	
BASELINE	UP? DOWN? STRAIGHT? BOTH?	
MARGINS:	LEFT: RIGHT:	
SPACING	BETWEEN WORDS? LINES?	
PRESSURE	LIGHT? MEDIUM? HEAVY?	
SIZE	LARGE? SMALL? HUGE?	
CONNECTIONS	ALL? SOME? NONE?	
INITIALS	WITH LEAD-IN? WITHOUT?	
FINALS	UP? FLAT? DOWN?	
CAPITALS	PALMER? PRINTED? ODD?	
t-BARS	COMPLETE? PLACEMENT?	
i-DOTS	SHAPE? PLACEMENT?	
LOOPS	ASCENDING? DESCENDING?	
SIGNATURE	STYLE? SHAPE? POSITION? SLANT? FLOURISHES?	
OTHER	SPEED? LEGIBILITY? ZONES? OVERALL SHAPE? PUNCTUATION MARKS? ODD FORMATIONS THAT ARE CONSISTENT BUT UNIQUE?	

INTERPRETING THE SAMPLE

First take a good long look at the writing sample before you. Take note of everything you see or feel about it; you'd be surprised at the accuracy of first impressions—even if you're just a beginner. Whatever you do, don't be cowed. Handwriting is a solid thing that is there on the paper in front of you and won't run away. There's no race, so take your time and consider the factors fully. I suggest you keep paper handy so you can jot down random impressions or words that occur to you. And I can think of no better advice than Nadya Olyanova's most basic rule: "A sign occasionally shown indicates an occasional trait. When plentiful, it shows a habit. When scarce yet evident, it reveals a tendency." Keep these words in mind and you can't go too far off track.

Use your checklist. If you think of additional factors that matter to you, add them at the end of the list. But I always find it useful to have it all there, written down, in front of me. If there is some aspect that confuses you, discard it. Felix Lehmann admits to not putting too much trust in t-bar theory. He says, "More important are the syndromes. Various clusters of features go together. One t-bar and one i-dot don't make the world, and I would consider it sensationalism to say it does. It might be what the public wants to hear, but I wouldn't go for it." This concept of clusters, or recurring traits, is one that really does occur. It's finding the ones that go together in each specimen and determining their meaning as a group that makes graphology so interesting.

WHERE TO GO FROM HERE

If your curiosity has been piqued by what you have seen and read here, I urge you to pursue this interest. Many good books on graphology have been written (see Bibliography, p. 577, for a suggested reading list), most of them chock-full of samples and interpretations. But before that, by all means, start collecting samples of handwriting on your own. Ask your friends and relatives for samples and cajole them into digging out things from their past—letters or notes written several years ago. Read several authors to make sure that you get a rounded idea of the meanings, and test yourself by writing down what you see in a sample before you compare your findings to a text. Choose one aspect that really interests you and become an expert on it; once you've increased your knowledge in one area, you'll be surprised how quickly other matters fall into place.

If you want to have a reading with a professional graphologist, consult the Yellow Pages of the telephone directory. Expect to pay $25 to $100 for a session with a professional.

CHAPTER NINETEEN

BIORHYTHM

THE RHYTHMS OF LIFE

You don't need to be a genius to know about or observe patterns in life. After all, the sun rises and sets daily, and it does so at *predictable* times. The tides go in and out, the moon waxes and wanes— *predictably*. To everything there is a season: Springtime in the eastern United States will no doubt be wet and warm, and the swallows will return yet again to Capistrano.

Cycles are normal in our lives, so much so that we don't think of them as special. The early-rising "lark" doesn't wonder why he is more efficient in the morning and really rather "out of it" after sunset; he's used to it. The "owl"—a person who doesn't really seem to wake up fully until nighttime—frequently has a very difficult time adjusting to a typical nine-to-five business day that was built, one would think, by larks, for larks. Shift work in factories, mines, and hospitals offers one of the best opportunities to study man's behavior under different schedules, and the findings are telling. People seem to function naturally on a twenty-four-hour-per-day schedule. They can do shift work—especially when the shift in times is gradual rather than sudden—and, as Jane Brody writes in *The New York*

Times, "Studies have shown that it is easier for people to adjust their bodies to a day that starts later than one that begins sooner than they are accustomed to." She goes on to liken the situation to the kind of jet lag one experiences when flying east to west—a somewhat easier adjustment for most people than the more disruptive west to east, which requires a forward adjustment in time.

All of mankind is affected by the cycles produced by planetary movements, though we take them mostly for granted. There is the effect of the earth rotating on its polar axis, creating a circadian (meaning "about a day") rhythm. There is the rotation of the earth around the sun, which accounts for our seasons and fluctuations in the amount of light we receive. There is also the influence of the moon on the earth, creating month-long lunar cycles that affect the tides.

Within our own bodies, literally hundreds of patterns or cycles are at work. The heart of an average adult beats sixty to eighty times per minute; we take about twelve breaths per minute under normal unstressed conditions; we sleep about eight hours a night; and insurance statistics tell us that men live to an average age of sixty-eight and women to seventy-four. Because of the internal rhythms of our bodies, researchers have found that certain drugs for the treatment of cancer are more effective and have fewer adverse side effects if administered at one particular time of day than at another. An asthma drug has been found to be virtually ineffective if administered late in the afternoon, yet the same drug is very effective when taken earlier in the day. Most people are aware that their performance is generally lackluster after a large lunchtime meal. They require a few hours—a siesta, perhaps—to get past the lull brought on by the food. Human blood pressure rises as much as 20 percent over the course of a day, being at its highest in the afternoon and its lowest in the morning. When the body temperature begins to rise, we are energized; we wake up. When it falls, we become tired; we seek rest and sleep.

The sum of all these rhythms means something. There is an orderliness to the universe and to everything in it, including you and me. There would seem to be a master clock by which all aspects of life are timed. And since so many factors occur regularly *and* predictably, there is reason to assume that all these individual rhythms create a larger pattern, just as the combination of the woodwind, string, and other sections of an orchestra create a whole that is the sum of its parts. That is the underlying premise of biorhythm. Biorhythm's champions feel that by understanding our place in the pattern of the universe, the cosmic flow in which we inexorably join at the moment of our birth, we gain insight into a hidden mechanism that influences our lives, but of which we normally remain unaware. But before we discuss the mechanics of biorhythm, let's take a look at how it got started.

A BRIEF HISTORY OF BIORHYTHM

Just prior to 1900, biorhythm was discovered almost simultaneously in two European cities—Berlin and Vienna. Also at that same time, Dr. Sigmund Freud was in the midst of tying together the clinical knowledge he had gathered while treating the emotionally ill to create his theory of psychoanalysis. Both these new discoveries had one major factor in common: They offered ways to explain the hidden roots of our actions and our lives.

The study of biorhythms has two fathers and one very important "great-uncle." The fathers were Dr. Hermann Swoboda, a professor of psychology at the University of Vienna, and Dr. Wilhelm Fliess, a physician specializing in otolaryngology (ailments of the nose and throat) in Berlin. As frequently happens with discoveries, they were working independently of each other but along amazingly similar lines. What's most significant is that without mutual consultation, their findings were virtually identical.

Swoboda was fascinated by reports of seemingly rhythmic mental changes in patients. His own patients reported their feelings to Swoboda, who noticed that certain states seemed to recur on a regular, cyclical basis. Their dreams, ideas, and creative impulses seemed to have a pattern behind them; and his patients who were new mothers became anxious about their child's safety at the time of their own biorhythmically critical days or the days just before and after them. He became a fanatic and meticulous researcher, accumulating all manner of data based on observation of both physical and mental states. In time, patterns began to emerge, indicating two cycles—one a physical cycle that was twenty-three days in length, and another, an emotional cycle twenty-eight days long. In 1904, his first book was published, *The Periods of Human Life (in their psychological and biological significance)*, soon followed by *Studies on the Basis of Psychology*. Four years later, he invented and produced a slide rule of sorts that made it easy and quick to calculate one's critical days. To explain its use and something about biorhythm, he included a booklet, *The Critical Days of Man*.

Swoboda is best known—and rightly so—for one of his last books, *The Year of Seven*. Within its six hundred pages, he takes steps to prove biorhythm by using mathematical documentation from his study of the life events in thousands of families. The book is a discussion of his observations of periodicity within a family—births, deaths, illnesses—starting from the first day of life. Before he died in 1963, Swoboda actively wrote and lectured about biorhythm all over the world. He was honored by universities and lauded by followers who saw and respected his findings about the recurrence of events in everyday life. Unfortunately, he never received the popularity worldwide that he rightly deserves for his landmark work.

The man who got most of the credit was Dr. Wilhelm Fliess, who was doing work with biorhythm in Berlin at the same time as Swoboda was working in Vienna. As co-discoverer of biorhythm, Fliess deserves attention and respect; however, his methods and his particular "madness" were vastly different from Swoboda's and displayed a more "crackpot" type of approach to his studies. You see, Fliess was obsessively enamored with the numbers 23 and 28. In his thinking, the number 23 was masculine and 28, feminine. He became convinced that these two numbers or their multiples ruled every aspect of life. He constructed elaborate tables and charts filled with virtually every possible combination of his two numbers, adding them together, multiplying—multiples of 23, multiples of 28, the sum of 23×28, 23×23, 28×28, $23 + 28 \times 23$, and so on and on, forever. To say he was obsessed is putting it far too mildly. He wrote volumes about his mathematical studies, proving in his eyes that these two numbers governed organic and, perhaps, inorganic phenomena. His writings, however, were filled with confusing and irrelevant wanderings of his mind and lacked the clarity and relative simplicity of actual scientific proof. Clear communication was a problem for him.

What gave Fliess the edge was his friendship with Freud. Apparently Freud held certain of Fliess' theories in great regard. They were mutually fascinated with Fliess' theory of the bisexuality of everything larger than a single cell, which he considered to be hermaphroditic. He thought that in growing beyond the one-cell size, cells differentiated into male and female, with each retaining some vestige of the opposite sex within its makeup. It was this bisexuality that was the basis of his assigning masculine qualities to the twenty-three-day physical rhythm and female qualities to the twenty-eight-day emotional cycle.

In his research, Fliess became convinced that the two cycles were heavily influenced by certain "genital" spots on the interior of the nose—remember, he was a nose and throat specialist—and actually performed two operations on Freud's nose. After a time, his friendship with Freud waned, largely because Freud began to disagree with some of Fliess' precepts, and Fliess turned more and more to publishing his findings. At the time of his death in 1928, Fliess had not had the pleasure of seeing his work widely accepted in his native Germany.

An engineer, Alfred Teltscher, who lived and worked in Innsbruck, Austria, was biorhythm's "great-uncle," responsible for discovering the third biorhythm cycle. Using data gathered from his students' performance on examinations, he found that humans' ability to absorb and synthesize data was stronger at some times than at others, and that the ability for self-expression varied as well. His data, based on the birth dates, test results, and test dates of scores of high school and college students, clearly pointed to a thirty-three-day intellectual cycle. Unfortunately for Teltscher, he was unable to explain the reasons for the cycle, though interestingly enough, some of his medical colleagues suggested that this cycle could be influenced by glandular secretions that had specific actions on the brain. What scientists have since found confirms this guess: Hormonal secretions from the pineal and thyroid glands do, indeed, affect brain function.

Since the time of these three pioneers in biorhythm, enormous quantities of data have been gathered and studied, much of it underlining the existence of these three great cycles. Biorhythms have been the basis for many studies that have to do with people who do shift work—miners, automobile plant workers, steelworkers, and the like. And the findings from the studies have caused manufacturers worldwide to adjust schedules to avoid times of inefficiency resulting from the inability of the workers' inner clock to adjust to the time change. The same types of studies have helped doctors come up with a way to fight jet lag. As anyone who has ever flown through several time zones knows, several days are needed for the body and mind to adjust to the new schedule. Meanwhile, efficiency and time are wasted. Now, however, several formulas have been created—based mostly on a change of sleep patterns, dietary restrictions, and limits on caffeine—that prepare the body for the trip and cut down on time lost on account of jet lag. New scientific studies are regularly being released that support the existence and the effect of the different and unsuspected rhythms that influence us every day. A tremendous amount of attention is being paid to the fledgling field of chronobiology, the study of man's internal biological rhythms. According to chronobiology, we respond not only to the predictable stimuli but to more subtle influences of space, time, and well-being. We are different people biochemically at 6 A.M. than we are at midnight, different in Timbuktu than we are in Chicago, different under the influence of various chemicals. The master clock in our brain and the billions of satellite clocks that regulate our biological processes take their cues from external sensory factors. Changes in the preordained circadian rhythm can put us in a transient state of "dysynchronism." I am confident that the future holds ever more revealing and convincing information about the viability of biorhythm and that this relatively infant science will grow with great speed.

THE USES OF BIORHYTHM

If you feel that all this makes sense, you might benefit from being aware of your daily biorhythms to see how they affect your everyday life. We can't stay in bed every time we're near a critical or low time and still live a normal life in the twentieth century. But we can take action to accommodate our biorhythms on critical days. Take the Japanese, for example, the most avid practitioners of biorhythm today. Their belief in biorhythm verges on astonishing. In factories, biorhythms are closely plotted and followed. On and around critical days, workers wear armbands that declare their susceptibility to harm and they are shifted away from dangerous or precarious jobs to safer positions until the critical period is over.

Paying attention to biorhythms can have health benefits. I find that testing biorhythms by using famous people and events yields interesting results. For example, on November 11, 1960, George Thommen was the guest of Long John Nebel on radio station WOR. Thommen discussed the biorhythm chart he had done for Clark Gable following Gable's first heart attack on November 5. He warned that Gable would have another physically critical day on November 16 and that his doctors should take special care to monitor his condition that day. On the sixteenth, a second heart attack killed Gable. Biorhythm statistics show that others might have been able to avert disaster or unfortunate circumstances had they paid attention to their critical days. Judy Garland's death of a drug overdose was at a difficult time in her chart. She was emotionally critical, with both her physical and intellectual rhythms in low. Daniel White, the man who killed San Francisco Mayor George Moscone and Supervisor Harvey Milk, was experiencing an emotionally critical day as well as extreme lows in his intellectual and physical cycles. Jack Ruby shot and killed Lee Harvey Oswald on an emotionally critical day. Marilyn Monroe's death on August 5, 1962, followed a physically critical time and an emotionally low period on August 4, the night of the actual overdose. Much the same is true of singer Janis Joplin, who died of a drug overdose on October 4, 1970, a physically critical day. Elvis Presley died with his intellectual and emotional cycles in a low and just after a physically critical day.

Using biorhythm to predict the outcome of sports events is a popular and interesting pastime because so much of physical competition relies on the individual athlete. I have watched the biorhythms of scores of sportsmen, from Mark Spitz's performance in the Olympics to football and boxing matches. Boxing offers an especially interesting case because it pits a single athlete against another, producing rather dramatic results. In a rematch between Ingemar Johansson and Floyd Patterson, Johansson was the favorite. However, Johansson's negative physical and emotional rhythms made Patterson's job much easier. No doubt it helped that Patterson was at the top of his cycles at the time. The Ali–Norton upset in March of 1973 was no surprise to fans who were aware of biorhythm; Ali was physically and emotionally critical and Norton took advantage—he smashed Ali's jaw.

Many people who have read my biorhythm book have reported to me on their own experiences with biorhythm. Dr. Phillip Costin of Ottawa, who was information officer of Canada's equivalent of the National Institute of Health, found that most acts of heroism in combat occurred on critical days—presumably when the hero was not clearly thinking about his own safety. His research also showed that accidents due to a soldier's personal negligence often occurred on critical days.

A Chicago-based plastic surgeon called to tell me that after reading my book, she had gone back through her surgical records and found that most cases involving postoperative bleeding occurred on *her* critical days. For a year thereafter, she did not operate on her critical days and had no instances of postoperative bleeding complications. Other doctors and nurses have noticed correlations to heart attacks and deaths but are reluctant to share their findings with the skeptical medical community.

An inquisitive Eastern Airlines pilot has taken to checking the personal biorhythms of pilots involved in near-misses in the air. He found a high correlation with emotional and intellectual critical or low days.

On a more personal level, the actors Jackie Gleason and Ed Begley, Jr., both call my office periodically for updates on their biorhythm charts and claim this has been of great value in their work and lives.

It should be pointed out that proponents of biorhythms eschew any connection with the occult. Biorhythm is not a predictive art; it is solidly based on scientifically collected data. Its interpretation, however, requires experience with each individual subject, since we all have some rhythms that are stronger than others. There is no "sensitivity" involved; anyone can calculate and understand his or her biorhythm.

Several recent studies done in the United States, Canada, and England seem to disprove biorhythm. Some seem to be valid; some use information selectively or disregard important data. (For example, one study on athletes' performance disregards the prior biorhythm history of the subjects: Some athletes perform better under pressure and *consistently* perform better on low or critical days.) Although it is discredited by many, biorhythm still enjoys great popularity with people all over the world, with people who have kept long, detailed personal records and found that it works for them; I have a great deal of correspondence to attest to this. As I have said many times in lectures, in print, and on the air: I don't know if biorhythm works or not; the real test is whether it works for you. That is why I call my book *Biorhythm: A Personal Science*.

But, enough *about* biorhythm; by now, you must be chomping at the bit to know how to calculate yours.

HOW TO CHART YOUR BIORHYTHM

Charting your own biorhythm is mostly a matter of elaborate calculations. Though relatively simple, they are time-consuming and should *not* be done with a calculator. Quite honestly, I suggest that you invest in a book that includes all the instant biorhythm charts you may need or, better yet, a computer-charted biorhythm analysis that includes a day-by-day or weekly interpretation for the forthcoming year. I would suggest this even if I weren't in the business, not only because it eliminates the drudgery, but simply because it cuts out the possibility of human error, takes all the exceptions into consideration, *and* it includes a broad-based interpretation that gives the novice a good starting point. If you are looking for a book, I naturally

recommend mine—*Biorhythm: A Personal Science*, published by Warner Books, and updated with new charts every two years. It contains
my own quick calculating method, interpretations, compatibility
charts, and three years worth of monthly charts so that you can plot
your biorhythm ahead and have a good reference point for the days
in the recent past. If you are interested in a computer-generated
forecast of a year's biorhythms, try one from the Institute of Biorhythm Analysis, Box R, Summit, N.Y. 07901.

In the interim, however, for you impatient souls who can't wait to
see for yourself how it works, what follows is a do-it-yourself
method. It shows you how to calculate your current place within
each cycle—physical, emotional, and intellectual—and also how to
place each number on the proper sine curve so you can determine
your critical, positive, and negative days.

CALCULATING YOUR POSITION WITHIN EACH CYCLE

First, we are going to go through the necessary steps to determine
your *base number* for today, the starting point from which all other
numbers are calculated. The steps use simple arithmetic; have a
good-size piece of paper handy.

1.   Multiply your present age by 365.
2.   Check the Leap Year Chart that follows and count the number of
leap years that have passed since the year you were born and now.
Count the number of years and add it to the total of step 1.

LEAP YEAR CHART (since 1860)

1860	1888	1916	1944	1972	2000
1864	1892	1920	1948	1976	2004
1868	1896	1924	1952	1980	2008
1872	1900	1928	1956	1984	2012
1876	1904	1932	1960	1988	2016
1880	1908	1936	1964	1992	2020
1884	1912	1940	1968	1996	2024

Example: For Martha, born on September 30, 1929, there would be
14 leap years between the year she was born and 1987. She would
add 14 to her previous total.

3. *Including* your birthday, count the number of days that have passed between then and today, *including* today. Therefore, for example, Martha, born on September 30 and calculating for today's date, February 16, would add together:

1 for 9/30 of last year
31 for October
30 for November
31 for December
31 for January
16 for February to date, including today.

Figure the total number of days since your last birthday and add the sum to the total you got in step 2. This is your base number.

You now have your base number. Using long division—*not* a calculator—divide your base number by 23 to get your *physical biorhythm number*. The **remainder** represents the day you are on in your physical cycle; it will be the number you will plot on a graph. Keep track of it for the moment.

Again, using long division, divide the base number by 28 to get your *emotional biorhythm number*. Keep track of the remainder as before.

BASE NUMBER CALCULATION

Finally, using long division again, divide your base number by 33 to calculate your *intellectual biorhythm number*. Make a note of the remainder. Check your division to be sure that you haven't made any errors in your calculations.

The example that follows shows the actual calculations Martha would use to determine her biorhythm. She was born on September 30, 1929, and wants her biorhythm computed for February 16, 1987.

57	(age)
× 365	
20805	
+ 14	(leap years)
20819	
+ 1	(9/30/86)
31	(10/86)
30	(11/86)
31	(12/86)
31	(1/87)
16	(to date)
20959	BASE NUMBER

PHYSICAL NUMBER: (divide by 23)	EMOTIONAL NUMBER: (divide by 28)	INTELLECTUAL NUMBER: (divide by 33)
911	748	635
23)20959	28)20959	33)20959
207	196	198
25	135	115
23	112	99
29	239	169
23	224	165
REMAINDER: 6	REMAINDER: 15	REMAINDER: 4

Martha is on day 6 of her physical cycle, day 15 of her emotional cycle, and day 4 of her intellectual cycle. The remainder is the number that counts; it represents the exact number of days—your position—in each cycle.

PLOTTING YOUR BIORHYTHM CYCLES

Following are three graphs, representing the three biorhythm cycles.

23 DAY PHYSICAL RHYTHM

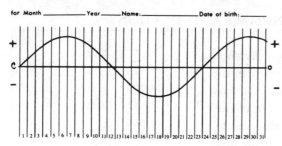

for Month _____ Year_____ Name:_____ Date of birth:_____

28 DAY EMOTIONAL RHYTHM

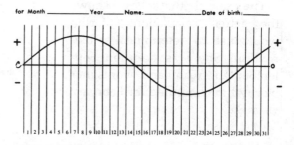

for Month _____ Year_____ Name:_____ Date of birth:_____

33 DAY INTELLECTUAL

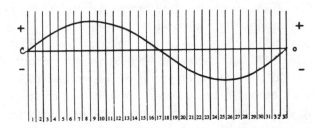

Note that each is divided vertically to mark off the days of the cycle, and each is divided horizontally into three parts: a large upper zone marked with a plus (+) sign, a narrow middle zone marked with a C, and a lower zone equal in size to the upper zone and marked with a minus (−) sign. The first graph is labeled PHYSICAL, the second EMOTIONAL, and the third INTELLECTUAL. Each graph shows the sine curve of that cycle, starting on the left at a critical point (C) and traveling across the graph in a wave that first goes up through the + area and then curves down through the C line and farther down into the − area and then up again to the C line. Notice that on the physical graph, it takes twenty-three days for a complete cycle, and that the curve crosses the critical line at the beginning, midway through, and at the end of the cycle. The same is true on the emotional graph, but the cycle is twenty-eight days long; the intellectual cycle is thirty-three days long.

Using the numbers we calculated for Martha, we see that the remainder for the physical chart is 6. This means that Martha is on day 6 of her physical cycle. Look at day 6 on the physical chart and it will show Martha's physical biorhythm for February 16, 1987—in the positive phase. (On February 17, it will be in position 7, etc.)

Look at the remainder we calculated for Martha's emotional cycle. It is 15. Using the emotional graph, check the location of the curve on day 15. It is in the beginning of the negative phase. (The cycle will change day by day as indicated by the wavy line.)

Look at the remainder for Martha's intellectual cycle—4. Just as you did before, look at the curve at day 4 and you'll see that intellectually, Martha is in a just-past-critical positive phase.

Once you have calculated your numbers for today, you can progress your numbers by just adding one day at a time, proceeding through each cycle and beginning again at the next. For example, Martha is on day 6 of her physical cycle today. Tomorrow she will be on day 7 (yesterday was day 5). Tomorrow her emotional day will be 16; intellectual, 5.

If you feel the need for some practice, calculate the positions for friends or family. This method will work perfectly every time; its only drawback is that you will have to count forward laboriously for each cycle to see what's coming up next week, or count backward to see what was going on when you had that fender-bender last month. The ideal method, as I said before, is to have a computer-generated forecast, or a book that gives you an instant-calculation chart that covers a few years. It's much clearer and less confusing, and it keeps your records together in one place, so you can see your biorhythms over a longer period of time.

THE PHASES OF THE CYCLES

Your next question, no doubt, is, "So how do I know what these silly graphs mean?" And it's a good one. Interpretation is the key to learning how to use biorhythm for your personal benefit. But before I give you that, let's talk about the phases of each cycle.

It is important to review some basic facts about biorhythm. All three of your biorhythmic cycles begin in the positive phase on the first day of your life and continue regularly thereafter until death. We can draw a continually undulating sine curve to represent the movement within each cycle. Since each cycle is based on a different number of days, they rarely coincide.

As I've shown you, the first cycle is the physical. It is the shortest and the least ambiguous, lasting over a period of twenty-three days. The first half of the cycle—the positive phase—is 11.5 days long. During this positive time—especially for the first six days—we are incredibly energetic. We are strong, very able and capable of hard work, hearty, coordinated, more immune to disease, and at our physical best. During the negative phase of the cycle, we are in the act of recharging our batteries and accumulating energy. We will be more easily tired, sometimes weak, depleted, less resistant to disease —we're in a slump. But the negative phase is not necessarily a bad phase; it is passive, a gathering of strength. It is only during the critical phase—days 1 and 11.5, during the change from the positive to the negative or vice versa—that extra caution is advisable; at this time, the physical rhythm is unstable and erratic.

The emotional cycle is twenty-eight days long, with fourteen days in the positive phase and fourteen in the negative. This is the easiest of the cycles to keep track of because it recurs on a biweekly basis from the date of birth. If you were born on a Thursday, every alternate Thursday for the rest of your life will be an emotionally critical day (since the other cycles have different lengths, they won't stay in step with the emotional cycle). Keep track of this two-week cycle— do you see any evidence of recurring mood swings? Are you highly excitable, depressed, angry, elated? See if there seems to be an emotional pattern that makes sense in your life.

The fourteen-day positive phase of each emotional cycle is marked by a positive outlook, a cooperative attitude, openness, sociability, and creativity. During the negative phase of the emotional cycle, caution may be in order: While we recharge emotionally we may be prone to being short-tempered and hotheaded. It is a bad idea to perform any dangerous tasks or attempt herculean feats at this time. Chances are your timing will not be what it should be. Our reactions and judgment just aren't at their best on these negatively influenced days. Moreover, on the critical days (1 and 14), we are even worse off—these are the most dangerous days of all. These times leave us open to seemingly irrational disagreeableness, argumentativeness, and the possibility of self-inflicted harm. If you have an emotionally critical day combined with a critical day either intellectually or physically, take all the precautions you can—why take unnecessary risks? The majority of industrial and transportation accidents occur during your negative emotional phase.

On the other hand, the strength and power of the emotional cycle can modify both the physical and intellectual cycles. The athlete who is in a negative physical phase but whose emotional cycle is high might be able to overcome the physical lull with his extremely positive emotional outlook and attitude. Or if you are in an intellectual down phase but need to come up with a brilliant idea, a strong emotional phase can add the needed spark of creativity or insight.

For some very good reasons, the intellectual cycle has been studied the least—perhaps because it has the least impact on survival. Little is understood about the intellectual rhythm. The cycle is thirty-three days long, with a 16.5-day positive phase and a 16.5-day negative phase. In the positive direction, we have retentive memories, heightened perceptions and deductive powers, quick comprehension of new information, and we are adaptable. Diets, exercise regimens, and any self-improvement plans have a better chance for success if begun when the intellectual phase is at its height. Negatively, there is a distinct lack of inquisitiveness. The person seems just a bit too weary of it all; the extra expenditure of energy is just beyond his or her limits. The critical times of the intellectual cycle, days 1 and 16.5, bode badly if extremely important decisions must be made. If what you have to deal with is vitally important to you, your work, or the community, it's a good idea to try to postpone or delay for a short time in order to avoid making a potentially serious mistake.

Keep in mind that the relative strength of each cycle varies with the individual. The professional athlete's physical cycle may be enhanced while the astrophysicist's intellectual cycle may be strongest of the three. Inheritance plays a major role. If you inherit highly coordinated genes from your choreographer father and dancer mother, chances are good that you will have a heightened physical sense; your genes will strengthen your biorhythmic physical cycle.

PAYING ATTENTION TO CRITICAL DAYS

Day 1 and day 11.5 are the critical days of your physical (P) cycle.

Day 1 and day 14 are the critical days of your emotional (E) cycle.

Day 1 and day 16.5 are the critical days of your intellectual (I) cycle.

Using the foregoing formulas and knowing what day of each cycle you are on *now* makes it possible for you to count ahead to find out what days will be your critical days, as well as the low days just before and after your critical days. These are the days when you should consider what you do. If you are in a physically critical period, you might think twice about going mountain climbing for the first time. If you are in an emotionally critical time, maybe it's not the optimum time to decide to divorce your spouse or fly off into the Brazilian jungle with a novice pilot—you might be overreacting. Similarly, when you are in an intellectually critical zone, don't think that the first draft of anything will be your last—chances are much of the work you do will be discarded and redone after the critical period is over.

INTERPRETING YOUR COMBINED BIORHYTHMIC CYCLES

The first step in interpreting your biorhythm is to take a look at how your different cycles mesh. Every day of the year you have all three cycles working at once. Sometimes, though it is very infrequent, two or three of your cycles will be in critical periods at the same time. Alternatively, at other times two or three of your cycles will be in favorable positions. It's a good idea to evaluate the combined positions of your three cycles on a day-to-day basis. This is done very simply. Write down what zone each of your cycles is in (in correct order: physical, emotional, intellectual) and look up the interpretation that follows for your particular cluster of cycle phases. If the point on the graph is in the upper (+) area—no matter where in that area—it is interpreted as a +. The same is true of any point that is in the lower (−) area. Example: Today Martha's reading would be + C +.

Keep in mind the meaning of the + and − symbols. The + signifies a high or strong influence; the − represents a low or weak influence. C, of course, means critical.

POSSIBLE COMBINATIONS

C C C   All systems are at zero today and you might do well to rest and let your batteries recharge. Don't stick your head in the sand and hide—it's not *that* bad—just consider carefully anything and everything you do. Don't get into details, and stay away from high pressure or stressful situations.

C C +   Deal with your head, not your heart or your hand. Physically and emotionally today won't be wonderful, but intellectually it's just fine. Why not catch up on work or read something that's not emotionally threatening—say, the *Encyclopaedia Britannica*.

C C −   Be careful today—you don't have a lot going for you—better take notice and keep cool and calm. Don't get caught up in anything too complex. Sitting under a tree might do, or watching game shows on TV shouldn't cause you any trouble. Hold off on things that really matter to you—you won't do them justice with so many factors working against you today.

C + C   Today is a good day to do something social but safe. In other words, go to a film with friends, but don't even consider playing touch football all afternoon on the lawn. It's best to delay making heavy-duty work-type decisions until a more propitious intellectual day.

C + +   A good day for those who sit in one place—at home—to do their work. Physically you will be accident-prone today, but otherwise, things look pretty good. It's another think day—a good time not to take risks physically but to go for it in emotional and intellectual matters.

C + − Another accident-prone day, but at least you shouldn't be depressed about it. Your thoughts may be somewhat muddled today—it's that intellectual low that does it—but it won't upset you unnecessarily; you know it will pass in a day or two. If you feel exceptionally clumsy, it's a phase, and this, too, shall pass.

C − C Today won't look like much fun at all. Physically and intellectually you are stressed, and to go with it, there's that emotional low that is downright depressing. Watch old movies, read a good book, and hope that tomorrow will be better—it couldn't be much worse.

C − + Today you might feel tired in body and spirit, but the mind will be racing with good ideas and plans. Let your brain take over and put your physical transition and emotional low in abeyance for the interim. Stay away from physical challenge or stress and don't even try to be social; catch up with your work, pay bills, or plan a vacation.

C − − Go easy on yourself today. Physically you are at zero, and you are experiencing lows both intellectually and emotionally to boot. You might well feel like an old dishrag—tired, down, and dull—so go slowly, and surely this unpleasant period will pass.

+ C C It's workout day. Today is the day that you are at your physical best but not your emotional and intellectual best. It's a good day to go to the gym or jog or sail, but only if you've done those things before and are used to them—don't let your emotions or mind make any foolish daredevil decisions for you. Play it safe and you can go the distance.

+ C + Today you are hot. Physically and intellectually you couldn't be in better form. Go out and slay that dragon. Emotionally, however, you are in transition. You'll be better at your desk than at a barbecue, so use the day to be enormously productive. You're a star, so go ahead and shine.

+ C − Plan your day today and follow the plan. Don't be tempted to reach beyond the logically doable, because you just won't be able to come through. Physically you're terrific—be sure to indulge yourself with a good run or walk and maybe a massage or sauna afterward. But follow your list of things to do and baby yourself a bit in the other phases of your life.

+ + C   Cross your fingers that today is a Saturday, because if it is, you will be in the pink. Today, you're *on*—be with friends and have a good time. Have a picnic in the park, play a bit of softball, go dancing, be as social as you want to be. Just beware of making any decisions, and don't sign anything except a credit card slip at dinner.

+ + +   Don't waste a minute of this perfect day. You are in the best of all three cycles and you should take advantage of it —to the hilt. You will be energetic, emotionally confident, and very stable, and if you have to make a presentation or ask for a promotion, chances are you've got it. Trust yourself—it's a red-letter day.

+ + −   Two out of three ain't bad. Today is a good one, so be sure to enjoy it. The only caution: don't make any vital decisions until your intellectual cycle has taken an upswing; other than that, you're absolutely okay.

+ − C   Today is an odd one—physically you're at your peak, but emotionally you're down, and intellectually you're not your best. It's a good day to avoid stressful work or sensitive situations and to have a good time with mindless physical activities. Play games—tennis, golf, croquet, or whatever—but make sure that it's not chess; you'll be in check before you know it.

+ − +   Today is the day you can figure out which play will stymie the opponents and you can execute the play flawlessly, but it's a no-joy sort of win. It's a winning day without the thrill of success. Emotionally you are at a low, and there's not a whole lot that will pull you out of it. Best to concentrate on the mental and physical and set the emotional aspects aside for another day.

+ − −   Today is a good day to be physical and mindless. With two lows at a time, you're better off doing something that requires physical rather than mental work. Clean out the garage or wash and wax the car; be productive in a passive way and let the hours pass quickly.

− C C   With a physical low and emotions and intellect in transition, today may not be the best day of your life, but it's certainly not the worst. Take it slowly and move deliberately; you won't accomplish anything earthshaking today, but it won't be a total waste, either.

− C +   It's idea day—think. Physically you're low; emotionally you're blah, but when it comes to thinking, you're terrific. Take advantage of this intellectual high and come up with a brainstorm so brilliant it surprises you. Let the physical and emotional aspects of life pass you by as you actively pursue your ideas.

− C −   It's pamper-yourself day. Go ahead, take a long hot bath, have a manicure, or read a trashy book. Eat some of your favorite foods, listen to your favorite music, and do what you feel like doing. You're at a low intellectually and physically and in transition emotionally, so it's a great day to treat yourself well in time-tested ways.

− + C   It's an emotionally high day, so it will be good. Let this strength work for you to place the physical low and intellectual zero in the background. Be social, be warm; today's your day to gather a loving audience around you, because you are thoroughly entertaining.

− + +   If you need to convince someone of something, today is the day to give it a try. Physically you're dull, but both emotionally and intellectually you're on a high. You can be a super salesman today—whether it be an idea, a product, or even convincing someone you care for that you're the best thing that ever happened to her or him.

− + −   Be inquisitive today. You have positive thoughts and feelings, even though you're in a physical and mental lull. Keep your mind and eyes open for new thoughts and ideas. There's a good chance that today will be a highly creative one for you; take advantage of it.

− − C   Avoid hassles today. In fact, avoid a lot of things; it probably won't be a terrific day at all. With two lows and a transition of your mental powers, what can a person expect? Take it easy—avoid stress, put off what you can, and deal carefully and slowly with what must be accomplished today.

− − +   Look at it this way: Intellectually you're on a roll. Go sit at your desk and think and work and be busy, but be careful getting to your desk and don't be offended by a casual comment on the way. Use this time to accomplish work-related things; when your emotional and physical cycles change for the better, you'll want to have your work out of the way.

— — — Don't think this is an all-time low day and you must stay in bed. On the contrary, this is the day that you get to be a spectator. You need not feel any pressure to do much of anything. Float around in the pool, sit in the stands at a ball game, watch a movie, or listen to music—all these pleasant, calming activities are just what the biorhythm ordered. Enjoy yourself; you don't even have to think of being a hero today.

WHERE TO GO FROM HERE

I have found that besides the constant influx of more scientific data that supports biorhythm, one of the most interesting aspects of biorhythm is my constant testing of its accuracy. I have tried every combination—paying no attention to what it tells me and seeing what happens, paying strict attention to what my day should be like according to my chart and working within those guidelines, paying attention only to the positive aspects and ignoring the negatives and vice versa.

For those who are interested in the biorhythm phenomenon, I suggest keeping a diary of your own internal states—physical, emotional, and intellectual—over a month or more. *Do not* look at your biorhythm charts for that time but do it on your own, writing down what you feel. Record the occurrences of the day so that when you look back you get a real, personalized idea of what happened. It's important that you keep a wholly honest assessment of your feelings and experiences and that they not be biased in any way. After a month or so, compare the results with what would have been predicted from biorhythm for the same period of time. Biorhythms' accuracy will be immediately apparent. This test is the best way I know to get a feeling—personally—about biorhythm.

Other times, I keep a biorhythm diary in which I start every day's entry with the sum of my phases that day—for example, $+ - C$ or $- - +$. Then I describe the events of the day and my feelings about them. If I was thwarted in business, I say so. If I felt that I needed to be alone and wasn't fit company for man or beast, I write it down. When the same combination of factors comes up again, I check the previous times I experienced one of those days to try to learn from it. Sometimes I have had to learn—the hard way—that a low physical day just isn't the right day to traipse through the Louvre, or that a high emotional day but a low intellectual day is a bad day to do business—I negotiate with my head, not with my heart.

Many biorhythm enthusiasts like to keep in practice by figuring out the biorhythms for their friends and family or even for strangers or people in the news. I recently received a letter from a Tennessee woman who has been charting her biorhythms for ten years. She wrote to tell me that after twenty-four years in an unhappy marriage, she had divorced her husband. She claimed that they shared next to no interests in common and that their biorhythms were wildly incompatible. She writes: "As I began to work out the compatibility factor, it became clear as crystal. It wasn't anybody's fault—we were just functioning on different levels. Prior to your book I had used astrology as a guide of sorts—thinking that it would be of some help, and it was. But I feel that this [biorhythms] is even more important than astrology. . . . This is by way of thanking you for the insight, and to tell you that since reading the book, and being convinced of the soundness of the concept, I have been very aware of things I read about people, and the experiences of people close to me."

People such as this woman become what I call mundane biorhythmists, and they specialize in figuring out the biorhythm of worldly things. They can tell you what went wrong with certain public events —fires, murders, accidents—but, unfortunately, they often have to work after the fact, when they have the details necessary to compute the biorhythm of the people involved. Their findings, however, often are food for thought. It seems that so many things might be different today if certain key people had paid more attention to their changing cycles.

However you choose to use biorhythm in your life, I hope that you find it as enlightening as I have. As scientists continue searching for explanations of physical phenomena, perhaps the factors behind biorhythm will become clearer. For my part, I find them a highly interesting and instructional way of leading my life.

EPILOGUE

A human being is part of the whole called by us the "universe," a part limited in time and space. He experiences himself, his thoughts and feelings, as something separate from the rest . . . a kind of optical delusion of his consciousness. This delusion is a kind of prison for us, restricting to our personal desires and to affections for a few persons nearest to us. Our task must be to free ourselves from this prison by widening our circle of understanding and compassion to embrace all living creatures and the whole of nature and its beauty.
—Albert Einstein

With every passing day, it becomes more crucial that we change our lopsided vision of man. All the ways in which we perceive ourselves as separate—individually, religiously, racially, nationally—have left our planet riddled by war, inequality, corruption, and dwindling resources. We are victims of the blinders with which we view the human condition, and our world cannot survive much longer unless we begin to remove those blinders.

The study of psi offers us no less than a new model of man, one whose connection to all others and to all else in the universe is as real, as concrete, as his individuality. If psi is consciousness, if it is interwoven in the very fabric of nature, we will not be fully ourselves until we admit the reality of psi into our everyday lives. What we think about ourselves determines what we will become. It is our responsibility to learn more about the workings of consciousness so that we can collectively create a vision of ourselves that will survive —and thrive.

GENERAL
BIBLIOGRAPHY

Abell, George O., and Barry Singer, editors, *Science and the Paranormal: Probing the Existence of the Supernatural*. New York: Charles Scribner's Sons, 1981.

Achterberg, Jeannie, *Imagery in Healing*. Boston and London: New Science Library, 1985.

Alcock, James E., *Parapsychology: Science or Magic: A Psychological Perspective*. New York: Pergamon Press, 1981.

Bartlett, Laile E., *PSI Trek*. New York: McGraw-Hill, 1981.

Beloff, John, "On Trying to Make Sense of the Paranormal." *Proceedings of the Society for Psychical Research*, Vol. 41, 1961, pp. 41–46.

Betty, Stafford L., "The Kearn City Poltergeist: A Case Severely Straining the Living Agent Hypotheses." London: *The Society for Psychical Research*, Vol. 52, No. 798, October 1984, p. 345ff.

Bohm, David J., "A New Theory of the Relationship of Mind and Matter." New York: Journal of the American Society for Psychical Research, Vol 80, No. 2, April 1986, p. 113ff.

Castaneda, Carlos, *The Fire from Within*. New York: Simon and Schuster, 1984.

Cerf, Christopher, and Victor Navasky, *The Experts Speak: The Definitive Compendium of Authoritative Misinformation*. New York: Pantheon Books, 1984.

Chang, Kwang-Chih, *Shang Civilization*. New Haven and London: Yale University Press, 1980.

Child, Irvin L., "Psychology and Anomalous Observations: The Question of ESP in Dreams." *American Psychologist*, November 1985, pp. 1219–30.

Christopher, Milbourne, *Mediums, Mystics, and the Occult*. New York: T. Y. Crowell, 1975.

Claire, Thomas C., *Occult/Paranormal Bibliography: An Annotated List of Books Published in English, 1976 through 1981*. Metuchen, New Jersey: Scarecrow Press, 1984.

Cohen, Daniel, *The Far Side of Consciousness*. New York: Dodd, Mead, 1974.

Cole, K. C., "Is There Such a Thing as Scientific Objectivity?" *Discover*, September 1985.

Cousins, Norman, *Anatomy of an Illness*. New York: W. W. Norton, 1979.

Crapanzano, Vincent, and Vivian Garrison, editors, *Case Studies in Spirit Possession*. New York: John Wiley and Sons, 1977.

Crichton, Michael, *Electronic Life: How to Think About Computers.* New York: Alfred A. Knopf, 1983.

Davis, Wade, *The Serpent and the Rainbow: A Harvard Scientist's Astonishing Journey into the Secret Society of Haitian Voodoo, Zombis and Magic.* New York: Simon and Schuster, 1985.

Day, Harvey, *Occult Illustrated Dictionary.* London: Kaye and Ward, Ltd., 1975, and New York: Oxford University Press, 1976.

Dean, Douglas, et al., *Executive ESP.* Englewood Cliffs, New Jersey: Prentice-Hall, 1974.

Ebon, Martin, *The Satan Trap: Dangers of the Occult.* Garden City, New York: Doubleday, 1976.

——, *The Signet Handbook of Parapsychology.* New York: A Signet Book, Published by the New American Library, 1978.

——, *Psychic Warfare: Threat or Illusion?* New York: McGraw-Hill, 1983.

——, editor, *True Experiences in Prophecy.* New York: A Signet Book, published by the New American Library, 1952.

Edge, Hoyt L., et al., *Foundations of Parapsychology: Exploring the Boundaries of Human Capability.* Boston and London: Routledge and Kegan Paul, 1986.

Eisenbud, Jule, *Parapsychology and the Unconscious.* Berkeley, California: North Atlantic Books, 1983.

Ellison, A. J., and C. Eng, "Mind, Belief and Psychical Research." London: *Society for Psychical Research,* Vol. 56, May 1978, p. 236ff.

Erikson, Erik H., *Gandhi's Truth.* New York: W. W. Norton, 1969.

Eysenck, Hans J., and Carl Sargent, *Explaining the Unexplained.* London: Weidenfeld and Nicolson, 1982.

——, *Know Your Own Psi-Q.* New York: World Almanac Publications, 1983.

——, and Kamin, Leon, *Intelligence: The Battle for the Mind.* London and Sydney: Pan Books, 1981.

Fairley, John, and Simon Welfare, *Arthur C. Clarke's World of Strange Powers.* London: William Collins Sons, 1984.

Ferguson, Marilyn, *The Aquarian Conspiracy: Personal and Social Transformation in the 1980s.* Los Angeles: J. P. Tarcher, 1980.

Frazier, Kendrick, editor, *Science Confronts the Paranormal.* Buffalo, New York: Prometheus Books, 1986.

Free Inquiry, Spring 1986, Special Issue: *Faith Healing: Miracle or Fraud?*

Gardner, Martin, *Fads and Fallacies in the Name of Science.* New York: Dover Publications, 1957.

——, *Science: Good, Bad and Bogus.* Buffalo, New York: Prometheus Books, 1981.

Garrett, Eileen J., *Many Voices: The Autobiography of a Medium.* New York: G. P. Putnam's Sons, 1968.

Gauld, Alan. *The Founders of*

Psychical Research, New York: Schocken Books, 1968.

Gawain, Shakti, *Creative Visualization*. USA and Canada: A Bantam New Age Book, published by arrangement with Whatever Publishing, 1979.

Geller, Uri, *My Story*. New York: Praeger, 1975.

——, and Guy Leon Playfair, *The Geller Effect*, New York: Henry Holt and Co., 1987.

Gittelson, Bernard, *How to Make Your Own Luck*. New York: Warner Books, 1981.

Goodspeed, Bennett W., *The Tao Jones Averages*. New York and London: Penguin Books, Viking Penguin, 1983.

Goodwin, John, *Occult America*. Garden City, New York: Doubleday, 1972.

Grad, Bernard, "The Biological Effects of the 'Laying On of hands' on Animals and Plants: Its Relation to Physics, Biology, Psychology, and Psychiatry," edited by G. Schmeidler. Metuchen, New Jersey: Scarecrow Press, 1976.

Gregory, Anita, editor, "London Experiments with Matthew Manning." *Society for Psychical Research*, Vol. 56, October 1982, p. 283.

Hall, Nicholas R., and Allan L. Goldstein, "Thinking Well: The Emotional Links Between Emotions and Health." *Science*, February 1986, pp. 34–40.

Hansel, C.E.M., *ESP: A Scientific Evaluation*. New York: Charles Scribner's Sons, 1966.

——, *ESP and Parapsychology: A Critical Re-Evaluation*. Buffalo, New York: Prometheus Books, 1980.

Harary, Keith, "Psi as Nature." *European Journal of Parapsychology*, Vol. 4, No. 3, November 1982.

Harman, Willis W., "Consciousness and Survival: A Perennial Issue Revisited." *Institute of Noetic Sciences Newsletter*, Vol. 13:2, Summer 1985, Sausalito, California.

Harrison, Edward, *Masks of the Universe*. New York: Macmillan, 1986.

——, "J'Accuse: An Examination of the Hodgson Report of 1885." *Journal of the Society for Psychical Research*, Vol. 53, 1986, pp. 286–310.

Harvey, Andrew, *A Journey In Ladakh*. Boston: Houghton Mifflin, 1983.

Herbert, Nick, *Quantum Reality*. Garden City, New York: Anchor Press, Doubleday, 1985.

Hirsig, Werner, *Destin de L'Homme*. Quebec: Les Éditions de Mortagne, 1983.

Hofstedter, Douglas R., *Metamagical Themas: Questing for the Essence of Mind and Pattern*. New York: Basic Books, 1985.

Honorton, Charles, "Meta-Analysis of Psi Ganzfeld Research: A Response to Hyman." *Journal of Parapsychology*, Vol. 49, No. 1, March 1985, pp. 51–86.

Honorton, Charles, Margaret Ramsey; and Carol Cabibbo, "Experimenter Effects in Extrasensory Perception." *Journal of the American Society for Psychical*

Research, Vol. 69, No. 2, April 1975, pp. 135–49.

Hooper, Judith, and Dick Teresi, *The 3-Pound Universe*. New York: Macmillan, 1986.

Hövelmann, Gerd H.; with Marcello Truzzi and Piet Hobens Hein, "Skeptical Literature in the Parapsychology: An Annotated Bibliography," from *A Skeptic's Handbook of Parapsychology*, Dave Kurtz, ed., pp. 449–494.

Hubbard, G. Scott, and E. C. May, "Aspects of Measurement and Applications of Geomagnetic Indices and Extremely Low Frequency Electromagnetic Radiation for Use in Parapsychology." SRI International, Menlo Park, California, 1986.

Hyman, Ray, "Parapsychological Research: A Tutorial Review and Critical Review and Critical Appraisal." *Proceedings of the IEEE*, Vol. 74, No. 6, June 1986, pp. 823–49.

———, "The Ganzfeld Psi Experiment: A Critical Appraisal." *Journal of Parapsychology*, Vol. 49, No. 1, March 1985, pp. 3–49.

Hynek, J. Allen, *The UFO Experience: A Scientific Inquiry*. New York: Ballantine Books, 1972.

Inglis, Brian, *The Hidden Power*. London: Jonathan Cape, 1986.

———, *The Paranormal: An Encyclopedia of Psychic Phenomena*. London: Paladin, Gratton Books, 1986.

———, *Science and Parascience: A History of the Paranormal 1914–1939*. London: Hodder & Stoughton, 1984.

———, and West, Ruth, *The Alternative Health Guide*. New York: Knopf, 1983.

Institute of Noetic Sciences Newsletter. Sausalito, California; all issues.

Jahn, Robert G., "The Persistent Paradox of Psychic Phenomena: An Engineering Perspective." *Proceedings of the IEEE*, Vol. 70, No. 2, February 1982.

Jones, C. B. Scott, editor, *Proceedings of a Symposium on Applications of Anomalous Phenomena*, Santa Barbara, California: Kaman Tempo, 1984.

The Journal of the American Society for Psychical Research, all issues.

Journal of the Society for Psychical Research, all issues.

Jung, C. G., *Memories, Dreams, Reflections*. New York: Vintage Books, 1965.

———, *Psychology and the Occult*. Princeton, New Jersey: Bollingen Series, Princeton University Press, 1977.

Kelsey, Denys, and Joan Grant, *Many Lifetimes*. Garden City, New York: Doubleday, 1967.

Krippner, Stanley, editor, *Advances in Parapsychological Research, Volume 1: Psychokinesis*. New York and London: Plenum Press, 1978.

———, editor, *Advances in Parapsychological Research, Volume 2: Extrasensory Perception*. New York and London: Plenum Press, 1978.

———, editor, *Advances in Parapsychological Research, Volume 3*.

New York and London: Plenum Press, 1982.

——, editor, *Advances in Parapsychological Research, Volume 4*. Jefferson, North Carolina, and London: McFarland and Company, 1984.

——, *Human Possibilities*. Garden City, New York: Anchor Press, Doubleday, 1980.

——, and Solfvin, Gerald, *Parapsychologie: Science ou Illusion?*, Paris: Éditions Sand, 1987.

—— and Villoldo, Alberto, *The Realms of Healing*. Millbrae, California: Celestial Arts, 1976.

Kübler-Ross, Elisabeth, *To Live Until We Say Good-Bye*. Englewood Cliffs, New Jersey: Prentice-Hall, 1978.

Kurtz, Paul, *A Skeptic's Handbook of Parapsychology*. Buffalo, New York: Prometheus Books, 1985.

——, *The Transcendental Temptation: A Critique of Religion and the Paranormal*. Buffalo, New York: Prometheus Books, 1986.

Leahey, Thomas Hardy, and Grace Evans Leahey. *Psychology's Occult Doubles: Psychology and the Problem of Pseudoscience*. Chicago: Nelson Hall, 1983.

Leek, Sybil, *The Complete Art of Witchcraft*. New York: A Signet Book, New American Library, 1971.

LeShan, Lawrence, *From Newton to ESP*. Wellingborough, Northamptonshire: Turnstone Press, 1984.

——, *The Medium, the Mystic, and the Physicist*. New York: Ballantine Books, 1966.

Lindsey, Hal. with Carlson, C. C., *The Late Great Planet Earth*. USA and Canada: Bantam Books, published by arrangement with The Zondervan Corporation, 1970.

Mackenzie, Alexander, *The Prophecies of the Brahmin Seer*. Highlands of Scotland: Sutherland Press, Golspie, 1970 (First Publ. Eneas Mackay, Stirling, Revised Edition 1899).

McRae, Ron, *Mind Wars: The True Story of Secret Government Research into the Military Potential of Psychic Weapons*. New York: St. Martin's Press, 1984.

Marks, David F., "Investigating the Paranormal," *Nature*, Vol. 320, March 13, 1986, pp. 119–24.

——, and Richard Kammann, *The Psychology of the Psychic*. New York: Prometheus Books, 1980.

Merton, Thomas, *The New Man*. New York: Farrar, Straus and Giroux, 1961.

——, *Zen and the Birds of Appetite*. New York: New Directions, 1968.

——, Stone, Naomi Burten, and Brother Patrick Hart, editors, *Love and Living*. New York: Harvest, Harcourt Brace Jovanovich, 1985.

Mishlove, Jeffrey, *Psi Development Systems*. Jefferson, North Carolina: McFarland and Company, 1983.

——, *The Roots of Consciousness: Psychic Liberation Through History, Science and Experience*. New York: Random House, 1975.

Monroe, Robert, *Journeys Out of the Body*. Garden City, New York: Doubleday, 1971.

Montgomery, Ruth, *Strangers Among Us: Enlightened Beings from a World to Come*. New York: Coward, 1979.

———, with Garland, Joanne, *Ruth Montgomery: Herald of the New Age*. Garden City, New York: Doubleday, 1986.

Moody, Raymond A., Jr., *Life After Life*. New York: Bantam Books, 1975.

Morgan, Chris, and David Langford, *Facts and Fallacies*. Exeter, England: Webb and Bower, 1981.

Moss, Thelma, *The Probability of the Impossible*. Los Angeles: J. P. Tarcher, 1974.

Muldoon, Sylvan, and Hereward Carrington, *The Projection of the Astral Body*. London: Rider & Co., 1929.

———, *The Phenomenon of Astral Projections*. New York: Samuel Weiser, 1951.

Neher, Andrew, *The Psychology of Transcendence*. Englewood Cliffs, New Jersey: Prentice-Hall, 1980.

Nelson, R. D., R. G. Jahn, and B. J. Dunne, "Operator Related Anomalies in Physical Systems and Information Processes," *Journal of the Society for Psychical Research*, Vol. 3, No. 803, April 1986, p. 261ff.

Netherton, Morris, *Past Lives Therapy*. New York: William Morrow, 1978.

Nichols, Beverly. *The Powers That Be*. New York: St. Martin's Press, 1966.

O'Regan, Brendan, "Inner Mechanisms of the Healing Response." *Institute of Noetic Sciences Newsletter*, Vol. 12, No. 2, Summer 1984, pp. 13–15.

———, et al., "Multiple Personality—Mirrors of a New Model of Mind?" *Institute of Noetic Sciences Newsletter*, Vol. 1, No. 34, pp. 1–2.

Osis, Karlis, and Erlendur Haraldsson, "Deathbed Observations by Physicians and Nurses: A Cross Cultural Survey." *Journal of the American Society for Psychical Research*, Vol. 71, No. 3, July 1977, pp. 237–59.

———, "Parapsychological Phenomena Associated with Sri Sathya Sai Baba." *The Christian Parapsychologist*, Vol. 3, No. 5, December 1979, pp. 159–63.

Ostrander, Sheila, and Lynn Schroeder, *Psychic Discoveries Behind the Iron Curtain*. Englewood Cliffs, New Jersey: Prentice-Hall, 1970.

Pearce, Joseph Chilton, *The Magical Child*. New York: Dutton, 1977.

Peck, M. Scott, M.D., *The Road Less Traveled: A New Psychology of Love, Traditional Values and Spiritual Growth*. New York: A Touchstone Book, Simon and Schuster, 1978.

Playfair, Guy Lyon, and Scott Hill, *The Cycles of Heaven: Cosmic Forces and What They Are Doing to You*. London: Souvenir Press, 1978.

Prigogine, Ilya, and Isabelle Stengers, *Order out of Chaos: Man's New Dialogue with Nature*. New York: Bantam Books, 1984.
Touch as Energy Exchange: Testing the Theory." *Advances in Nursing Science*, January 1984.

Randi, James, *Flim-Flam! Psychics, ESP, Unicorns and Other Delusions*. Buffalo, New York: Prometheus Books, 1982.

———, *The Truth About Uri Geller*. Buffalo, New York: Prometheus Books, 1982.

Randles, Jenny, *UFO Reality: A Critical Look at the Physical Evidence*. London: Robert Hale, 1983.

Rauscher, Elizabeth, "The Physics of Psi Phenomena in Space and Time." *Parapsychology Review*, September 1983, p. 93ff.

Rawcliffe, D. H., *Illusions and Delusions of the Supernatural and the Occult* (originally *The Psychology of the Occult*). New York: Dover Publications, 1959.

Reynolds, David K., *Playing Ball on Running Water: A Japanese Way to Building a Better Life*. New York: Quill, William Morrow, 1984.

Rhine, J. B., *New World of the Mind*. New York: William Sloane Associates, 1953.

———, et al., *Extra-Sensory Perception After Sixty Years: A Critical Appraisal of the Research in Extra-Sensory Perception*. Boston: Branden (1940), 1966.

Rhine, Louisa E., *ESP in Life and Lab*. New York: Macmillan, 1969.

Roberts, Henry C., translator, editor, interpreter, *The Complete Book of Nostradamus*. Oyster Bay, New York: Nostradamus Company, 1982.

Roberts, Jane, *The Further Education of Oversoul Seven*. New York: Pocket Books, Simon and Schuster, 1979.

Rogo, D. Scott, *Leaving the Body: A Practical Guide to Astral Projection*. Englewood Cliffs, New Jersey: Prentice-Hall, 1983.

———, *Life After Death: The Case for Survival of Bodily Death*. Wellingborough, Northamptonshire: The Aquarian Press, 1986.

———, *Mind over Matter: The Case for Psychokinesis*. Wellingborough, Northamptonshire: The Aquarian Press, 1986.

———, *The Search for Yesterday: A Critical Examination of the Evidence for Reincarnation*. Englewood Cliffs, New Jersey: Prentice-Hall, 1985.

Roll, W. G., *The Poltergeist*. New York: New American Library, 1974.

Rossi, Ernest Lawrence, *The Psychobiology of Mind-Body Healing: New Concepts of Therapeutic Hypnosis*. New York: W. W. Norton, 1986.

Rueveri, Uri, Ross V. Speck, and Joan L. Speck, editors, *Therapeutic Intervention: Healing Strategies for Human Systems*. New York: Human Sciences Press, 1982.

Scarf, Maggie, "Images That

Heal." *Psychology Today*, September 1980, pp. 33–46.

Schwartz, Stephan, *The Alexandria Project*. New York: A Delta/Eleanor Friede Book, Dell Publishing, 1983.

———, "Deep Quest." *Omni*, March 1979.

———, "Psychic Search." *Omni*, April 1981.

Schmeidler, Gertrude, "PK Effects upon Continuously Recorded Temperatures." *Journal of the American Society for Psychical Research*, Vol. 67, 1973, pp. 325–340.

Schmidt, Helmut, "Mental Influences on Random Events," *New Scientist*, June 24, 1971, pp. 757–58.

Shealy, C. Norman, *Occult Medicine Can Save Your Life: A Modern Doctor Looks at Unconventional Healing*. New York: The Dial Press, 1975.

Shepard, Leslie, editor, *Encyclopedia of Occultism and Parapsychology*, 2nd edition. Detroit: Gale Research, 1984.

———, *Skeptical Inquirer*. Journal of the Committee for the Scientific Investigation of Claims of the Paranormal, all issues.

Stearn, Jess, *Edgar Cayce, the Sleeping Prophet*. USA and Canada: A Bantam Book, published by arrangement with Doubleday, 1967.

Stevenson, Ian, *Twenty Cases Suggestive of Reincarnation*. Charlottesville, Virginia: University Press of Virginia, 1974.

Swann, Ingo, *To Kiss Earth Goodbye*. New York: Hawthorne, 1975.

Targ, Russell, and Keith Harary, *The Mind Race: Understanding and Using Psychic Abilities*. New York: Ballantine Books, 1984.

———, and Harold Puthoff, *Mind Reach*. New York: Dell Publishing, 1977.

Tart, Charles T., "Who's Afraid of Psychic Powers? Me?" *ASPR Newsletter*, I, xxi, January 1986, pp. 3–5.

———, *Altered States of Consciousness*. Garden City, New York: Doubleday, 1969.

———, *Waking Up: Overcoming the Obstacles to Human Potential*. Boston: Shambhala Publications, New Science Library, 1986.

Thalbourne, Michael, *A Glossary of Terms Used in Parapsychology*. London: Heinemann, 1982.

Tornatore, Rosemarie, "Psychic Phenomena in Psychotherapy." *The Humanistic Psychology Institute Review*, Vol. 3, No. 1, Spring 1981, pp. 57ff.

Tromp, S. W., *Psychical Physics: A Scientific Analysis of Dowsing, Radiesthesia and Kindred Divining Phenomena*. New York: Elsevier Publishing Company, 1949.

Ullman, M., S. Krippner, and A. Vaughan, *Dream Telepathy*. Baltimore: Penguin, 1974.

Vaughan, Alan, *Incredible Coincidence: The Baffling World of Synchronicity*. Philadelphia: Lippincott, 1979.

Vilenskaya, Larissa, *Parapsychology in the U.S.S.R.* San Francisco: H. S. Daikin Company, 1986.

Psi Research, 1982–present; all issues.

Villoldo, Alberto, and Stanley Krippner, "Quantum Theory and Psychic Healing." *The Humanistic Psychology Institute Review*, Vol 3, No. 1, Spring 1981, p. 41.

———, *Healing States*. New York: Fireside Books/Simon & Schuster, 1987.

Von Daniken, Erich, *Pathways to the Gods*. New York: Berkley Books, 1981.

Von Franz, Marie Louise, *On Dreams and Death*. Boston: Shambhala Publications, New Science Library, 1986.

Wallach, Charles, "The Science of Psychic Warfare." *Journal of Defense and Diplomacy*, September 1985, pp. 38–44.

Watson, Lyall, *Super Nature*. New York: Bantam Books, 1973.

———, *The Romeo Error*. New York: Dell Publishing, 1974.

White, Rhea A., *Parapsychology Abstracts International, Volume 1, Number 1*. Dix Hills, New York: The Parapsychology Sources of Information Center, 1983.

Wilson, Colin, *Mysteries: An Investigation into the Occult, the Paranormal and the Supernatural*. London: Panther Books, 1978.

———, *The Psychic Detectives*. London and Sydney: Pan Original, Pan Books, 1984.

Wolman, Benjamin B., editor, *Handbook of Parapsychology*. Jefferson, North Carolina, and London: McFarland and Company, 1977.

Woods, Richard, *Understanding Mysticism*. Garden City, New York: Image Books, 1980.

Worrall, Ambrose, and Olga Worrall, *Explore Your Psychic World*. New York: Harper and Row, 1970.

Wuthnow, Robert, *Experimentation in American Religion: The New Mysticisms and Their Implications for the Churches*. Berkeley, California: University of California Press, 1978.

Yogananda, Paramahansa, *Autobiography of a Yogi*. Los Angeles: Self-Realization Fellowship, 1946, renewed 1974.

Young, Louise B., *The Unfinished Universe*. New York: Simon and Schuster, 1986.

Zetetic Scholar. Journal of the Center for Scientific Anomalies Research, all issues.

Zolar, *Zolar's Encyclopedia of Ancient and Forbidden Knowledge*. New York: Arco Publishing, 1984.

Zukav, Gary, *The Dancing Wu Li Masters*. New York: Bantam Books, 1979.

Zusne, Leonard, and Jones, Warren H., *Anomalistic Psychology: A Study of Extraordinary Phenomena of Behavior and Experience*. Hillsdale, New Jersey: Lawrence Erlbaum Associates, 1982.

BOOK TWO
BIBLIOGRAPHY

CHAPTER 11: GETTING STARTED

Blum, Ralph. *Rune Play.* New York: Oracle Books, St. Martins Press, 1985.

Hope, Murry. *The Way of Cartouche.* New York: St. Martins Press, 1985.

Hunt, Stoker. *Ouija, The Most Dangerous Game.* New York, Cambridge, Philadelphia et al: Barnes and Noble Books, a Division of Harper and Row Publishers, 1985.

MacLaine, Shirley. *Out on a Limb.* USA and Canada: Bantam Books, 1983.

Omarr, Sydney. *The Thought Dial.* Los Angeles, California: Wilshire Book Company, 1962.

Smith, Alson, J. *The Psychic Source Book.* New York: Creative Age Press, 1951.

CHAPTER 12: EXPLORING YOUR EXTRA-SENSORY SELF

Arkin, Alan. *Halfway Through the Door.* New York, Hagerstown, San Francisco, London: Harper and Row Publishers, 1979.

Edwards, Betty. *Drawing on the Right Side of the Brain.* Los Angeles, California: J. P. Tarcher, Inc., 1979.

Edwards, Betty. *Drawing on the Artist Within.* New York: Simon and Schuster, 1986.

Hoffman, Enid. *Develop Your Psychic Skills.* Gloucester, Massachusetts: Para Research, Inc., 1981.

Karagulla, Shafica, M.D. *Breakthrough to Creativity, Your Higher Sense Perception.* Marina del Rey, California: DeVorss and Company, 1967.

Kreskin. *Kreskin's Fun Way to Mind Expansion.* Garden City, New York: Doubleday and Company, Inc., 1984.

Le Shan, Lawrence. *How to Meditate.* USA and Canada: Bantam Books, published in arrangement with Little, Brown and Company, 1974.

Sherman, Harold. *How to Make ESP Work for You.* Greenwich, Connecticut: Fawcett Publications Inc., 1964.

St. Clair, David. *David St. Clair's Lessons in Instant ESP.* Englewood Cliffs, New Jersey: Prentice-Hall Inc., 1978.

Swann, Ingo. *Natural ESP.* New York: Bantam Books, 1987.

CHAPTER 13: ASTROLOGY

Arroyo, Stephen. *The Practice and Profession of Astrology*. Reno, Nevada: CRCS Publications, 1984.

Browning, Norma Lee. *Omarr: Astrology and the Man*. Garden City, New York: Doubleday and Company Inc., 1977.

Crummere, Maria Elise. *Sun-Sign Rising*. New York: Ballantine Books, 1977.

Dean, Geoffrey, Arthur Mather et al. *Recent Advances in Natal Astrology: A Critical Review 1900–1976*. Bromley Kent, England: The Astrological Association, 1977.

DelSol, Paula. *Chinese Astrology*. English translation: Pictorial Presentations Ltd, 1972.

Doane, Doris Chase. *Astrology, 30 Years Research*. Los Angeles, California: The Church of the Light, 1956.

Fleming-Mitchell, Leslie. *Running Press Glossary of Astrology Terms*. Philadelphia, Pennsylvania: Running Press, 1977.

Gale, Mort. *Instant Astrology*. New York: Warner Books Inc., 1980.

Hirsig, Werner. *Destin de l'Homme*. Boucherville, Quebec: Les Presses Metropolitaines Inc., 1983.

———. *Manuel d'Astrologie*. Montreal, Quebec: Presses Select Ltee, 1978.

Innis, Pauline. *Astronumerology*. New York: David McKay Company, 1971.

Lau, Theodora. *The Handbook of Chinese Horoscopes*. New York et al: Harper and Row Publishers Inc., 1979.

Leo, Alan. *Casting the Horoscope*. New York: Astrologer's Library, 1983.

Lynch, John (ed.). *The Coffee Table Book of Astrology*. New York: The Viking Press, 1967.

McCaffery, Ellen, M.A. *Graphic Astrology: The Astrological Home Study Course*. Richmond, Virginia: Macoy Publishing Company, 1952.

Parker, Derek and Julia. *The New Compleat Astrologer*. New York: Harmony Books, division of Crown Publishers Inc., 1984.

Pelletier, Robert, and Cataldo, Lenard. *Be Your Own Astrologer*. London and Sydney: Pan Books, 1984.

Rosenblum, Bernard M.D. *The Astrologer's Guide to Counseling*. Reno, Nevada: CRCS Publications, 1983.

Rudhyar, Dane. *The Astrology of America's Destiny*. New York: Vintage Books, a division of Random House Inc., 1974.

White, Suzanne. *Suzanne White's Book of Chinese Chance*. New York: M. Evans and Company, Inc., 1976.

———. *The New Astrology*. New York: St. Martin's Press, 1986.

CHAPTER 14: NUMEROLOGY

Buess, Lynn M. *Numerology for the New Age*. Marina del Rey, California: Devorss and Company, 1978.

Bunker, Dusty. *Numerology and Your Future*. Gloucester, Massachusetts: Para Research, Inc., 1980.

Cheiro. *Cheiro's Book of Numbers*. New York: Arco Publishing Company, Inc., 1964.

———. *When Were You Born?* New York: Arc Books, Inc., 1969.

Dodge, Ellin. *You Are Your First Name*. New York: Simon and Schuster Inc., 1984.

Javane, Faith and Dusty Bunker, *Numerology and the Divine Triangle*. Gloucester, Massachusetts: Para Research Inc., 1980.

Jordon, Dr. Juno. *Numerology: The Romance in Your Name*. Marina del Rey, California: DeVorss and Company, 1965.

Konraad, Sandor. *Numerology: Key to the Tarot*. Rockport, Massachusetts: Para Research Inc., 1983.

Seton, Julia, M.D. *Symbols of Numerology*. North Hollywood, California: New Castle Publishing Company, Inc., 1984.

CHAPTER 15: TAROT

Connolly, Eileen. *Tarot: A New Handbook for the Apprentice*. North Hollywood, California: New Castle Publishing Company Inc., 1979.

Douglas, Alfred. *The Tarot: The Origins, Meaning And Uses of the Cards*. New York, England, Canada: Penguin Books, 1972.

Gerulskis-Estes, Susan. *The Book of Tarot*. Dobbs Ferry, New York: Morgan and Morgan, 1981.

Gray, Eden. *The Complete Guide to the Tarot*. Toronto, New York, London, Sydney, Auckland: Bantam Books, published by agreement with Crown Publishers, 1970.

———. *Mastering the Tarot*. New York: A Signet Book, New American Library Inc., 1971.

Nordic, Rolla. *The Tarot Shows the Path*. New York: Samuel Weiser, 1960.

Sharman-Burke, Juliet and Liz Greene. *The Mythic Tarot*. New York: Simon and Schuster, 1986.

Waite, Arthur Edward. *The Pictorial Key to the Tarot*. York Beach, Maine: Samuel Weiser, Inc., 1982.

Wolker, Barbara G. *The Secrets of the Tarot*. San Francisco, Cambridge, New York et al: Harper and Row Publishers, 1984.

CHAPTER 16: I-CHING

Blofed, John (trans., ed.). *I Ching: The Book of Change*. New York: E. P. Dutton, 1965.

Da Liu. *I Ching Coin Prediction*. New York, Evanston, San Francisco, London: Harper and Row Publishers, 1975.

Legee, James (trans.). *I Ching Book of Changes*. New Hyde Park, New York: University Books, 1964.

Sherrill, W. A. and Chuy W. K. *An Anthology of I Ching*. London, Melbourne, Boston, Henley: Routledge and Kegan Paul, 1977.

Wilhelm, Richard and Gary F. Bayres. *The I Ching or Book of Changes*. Princeton, New Jersey: Princeton University Press, 1977.

Wilhelm, Hellmut. *Eight Lectures on the I Ching*. Princeton, New Jersey: Princeton University Press, 1960.

CHAPTER 17: PALMISTRY

Benham, William G. *The Laws of Scientific Hand Reading*. New York and London: G. P. Putnam's Sons, 1900.

Cheiro. *Palmistry for All*. New York: Arco Publishing Inc., 1982.

Gardini, Maria. *The Secrets of the Hand*. New York: Collier Books, Macmillan Publishing Company, 1985.

Lawrence, Myrah. *Hand Analysis: A Technique for Knowledge of Self and Others*. West Nyack, New York: Parker Publishing Company Inc., 1967.

Meier, Nellie Simmons. *Lion's Paws*. New York: Barrows Mussey Publisher, 1937.

Squire, Elizabeth Daniels. *The New Fortune in Your Hand*. New York: Fleet Press Corporation, 1960.

Wilson, Joyce. *The Complete Book of Palmistry*. Toronto, New York, London, Sydney: Bantam Books, published by arrangement with Workman Publishing Company Inc., 1971.

CHAPTER 18: GRAPHOLOGY

Amend, Karen and Ruiz, Mary S. *Handwriting Analysis: The Complete Basic Book.* North Hollywood, California: Newcastle Publishing Company, Inc., 1980.

Casewit, Curtis W. *Graphology Handbook.* Gloucester, Massachusetts: Power Research, Inc., 1980.

Lester, David. *The Psychological Basis of Handwriting.* Chicago, Illinois: Nelson-Hall, 1981.

Mann, Peggy. *The Telltale Line: The Secrets of Handwriting Analysis.* New York: Macmillan Publishing Company, Inc. 1976.

Olyanova, Nadya. *Handwriting Tells. . . .* North Hollywood, California: Wilshire Book Company, 1969.

————. *The Psychology of Handwriting: Secrets of Handwriting Analysis.* North Hollywood, California: Wilshire Book Company, 1960.

O'Neill, Edward B. "Graphological Journal," 1984.

Rice, Louise. *Character Reading from Handwriting.* New York: Frederick A. Stokes Company, 1927.

Sara, Dorothy. *Reading Handwriting for Fun and Popularity.* New York: Permabooks, 1949.

CHAPTER 19: BIORHYTHM

Ayensu, Edward S., and Dr. Philip Whitfield. *The Rhythms of Life.* New York: Crown Publishers, 1981.

Center for International Business Cycle Research. "International Economic Indicators." September 1985. New York: Columbia University Press, 1985.

Cohen, Daniel. *Biorhythms in Your Life.* Greenwich, Connecticut: Fawcett Publications Inc., 1976.

Dewey, Edward R. *Cycles: The Mysterious Forces That Trigger Events.* New York: Hawthorn Books Inc., 1971.

Fleiss, William. *Of Life and Death.* Biological lectures, translated and edited from the German text. Printed in 1916 by Eugen Diederichs, Vienna, under the supervision of Bernard Gittelson, for IBRA, Atlanta, Georgia.

————. *The Year in Living Things.* Translated and edited from the German text (Pub. 1924) by Eugen Diederichs, Vienna, under the supervision of Bernard Gittelson, for IBRA, Atlanta, Georgia.

Foundation for the Study of Cycles. "Cycles." Vol. 36 No. 6, August 1985. Pittsburgh, Pennsylvania: The Foundation for the Study of Cycles, 1985.

Gittelson, Bernard. *Biorhythm: A Personal Science.* New York: Warner Books, 1986.

Krauze-Poray, B. J. *Primordial Biorhythms: Nature's Biological Master Clock.* Australia: Biorhythm Research and Information Centre, 1976.

Luce, Gay Gaer. *Biological Rhythms in Human and Animal Physiology.* New York: Dover Publications, 1971.

———. *Body Time.* New York, Toronto, London: Bantam Books, by arrangement with Pantheon Books, Inc., 1971.

Shap, Marle, and Alan Kahn. *The Biorhythm Decision Maker.* New York: Grosset and Dunlap, a Filmsways Company, 1979.

Swoboda, Dr. Hermann. *The Basis of Psychology.* Translated from German text printed 1905 by Franz Deuticke, under the supervision of Bernard Gittelson, for IBRA, Atlanta, Georgia.

———. *The Critical Days in Humans and Their Calculation with a Period Scale.* Translated and edited from the German text (Printed 1909) under the supervision of Bernard Gittelson, for IBRA, Atlanta, Georgia.

Tatai, Kichinosuke M.D., M.P.H. *Biorhythm for Health Design.* Tokyo, Japan: Japan Publications Inc., 1977.

Thuman, Albert P.E. *Biorhythms and Industrial Safety.* Atlanta, Georgia: The Fairmont Press, 1977.

Wernli, Hans J. *Biorhythm.* New York: Cornerstone Library, 1960.

APPENDIX A

ORGANIZATIONS AND INSTITUTIONS

PROFESSIONAL ORGANIZATIONS

Academy of Parapsychology and Medicine
P.O. Box 36121, Denver, CO 80277

American Parapsychological Research Foundation
Box 8447, Calabasas, CA 91302

American Society for Psychical Research
5 West 73rd Street, New York, NY 10023

Association for Research and Enlightenment
215 67th Street, Virginia Beach, VA 23451

Central Premonitions Registry
P.O. Box 482, Times Square Station, New York, NY 10036

Committee for the Scientific Investigation of Claims of the Paranormal
P.O. Box 229, Central Park Station, Buffalo, NY 14215

ESP Research Associates Foundation
Suite 1660, Union National Plaza, Little Rock, AR 72201

Foundation for Research on the Nature of Man
Box 6847, College Station, Durham, NC 27708

Institute of Noetic Sciences
475 Gate Five Road, Sausalito, CA 94965

International Association for Near Death Studies
Box U-20, 406 Cross Campus Road, University of Connecticut, Storrs, CT 06268

International Kirlian Research Association
2202 Quentin Road, Brooklyn, NY 11229

Metascience Foundation
Box 32, Kingston, RI 02881

Mind Science Foundation
Suite 100, 8301 Broadway, San Antonio, TX 78209

Möbius Society
2525 Hyperion Avenue, Los Angeles, CA 90027

Parapsychological Association
Box 7503, Alexandria, VA 22307

Parapsychology Foundation
228 East 71st Street, New York, NY 10021

Parapsychology Institute of America
P.O. Box 252, Elmhurst, NY 11373

Professional Psychics United
1839 South Elmwood, Berwyn, IL 60402

Psi Research
3101 Washington Street, San Francisco, CA 94115

Psychical Research Foundation
West Georgia College, Carrollton, GA 30118

Psychic Science International
Special Interest Group
7514 Belleplain Drive, Dayton, OH 45424

Saybrook Institute
1772 Vallejo Street, San Francisco, CA 94123

SRI International
333 Raven's Wood Avenue, Menlo Park, CA 94025

ASTROLOGY
American Federation of Astrologers
P.O. Box 22040, Tempe, AZ 85282

Astrologers' Guild of America
Mount Pocono Office Park, Mount Pocono, PA 18344

Centre for Psychological Astrology
26 Estelle Road, London, NW3, England

Federation of Australian Astrologers
P.O. Box 179, Coburg, Victoria 3058, Australia

International Society for Astrological Research
P.O. Box 38613, Los Angeles, CA 90038

National Astrological Society
205 Third Avenue, New York, NY 10003

GRAPHOLOGY
American Association of Handwriting Analysts
820 West Maple, Hinsdale, IL 60521

American Handwriting Analysis Foundation
1211 El Solya Avenue, Campbell, CA 95008

Council of Graphological Sciences
Box 331, Naples, ID 83847

Handwriting Analysts International
1504 West 29th Street, Davenport, IA 52804

International Graphoanalysis Society
111 North Canal Street, Chicago, IL 60606

TAROT
Associated Readers of Tarot International
Box 803, Dept. EA, Du Bois, PA 15801

JOURNALS, NEWSLETTERS, TRADE PUBLICATIONS

PARAPSYCHOLOGY AND RELATED TOPICS
American Society for Psychical Research Newsletter
5 West 73rd Street, New York, NY 10023

Association for the Study of Perception Journal
Box 744, De Kalb, IL 60115

ESP Research Associates Foundation Newsletter
1660 Union National Plaza, Little Rock, AR 72201

Institute of Noetic Sciences Newsletter
475 Gate Five Road, Sausalito, CA 94965

Journal of the American Society for Psychical Research
5 West 73rd Street, New York, NY 10023

Journal of Parapsychology
402 Buchanan Boulevard, Durham, NC 22708

Meta Science Annual
Box 32, Kingston, RI 02881

New England Journal of Parapsychology
Franklin Pierce College, Rindge, NH 03461

Parapsychology Abstracts International
2 Plane Tree Lane, Dix Hills, NY 11746

Parapsychology—Psychic Science Reports
Box 600927, North Miami Beach, FL 33160

Parapsychology Review
228 East 71st Street, New York, NY 10021

PSI Research
3101 Washington Street, San Francisco, CA 94115

Skeptical Inquirer
1203 Kensington Avenue, Buffalo, NY 14215

Zetetic Scholar
1323 Culver Road, Ann Arbor, MI 48103

FOREIGN PUBLICATIONS

Australian Institute of Psychic Research Bulletin
P.O. Box 445, Lane Cove, NSW 2066, AUSTRALIA

Autre Monde
10 Rue de Crussol, 75011 Paris, FRANCE

European Journal of Parapsychology
University of Utrecht, Sorbonnelaan 16, 3584 CA Utrecht,
NETHERLANDS

Fortean Times
96 Mansfield Road, London NW3 2HX, ENGLAND

Informazioni di Parapsicologia
Centro Italiano di Parapsicologia, Via Belvedere 87, 80127 Naples,
ITALY

Journal of the Society for Psychical Research
1 Adam and Eve Mews, London W8 6UG, ENGLAND

Light
College of Psychic Studies, 16 Queensberry Place, London SW7 2EB
ENGLAND

Psychic Researcher
37 Lilyville Road, London SW6, ENGLAND

Question de Racines, Pensées, Sciences Éclaires
10 Rue de la Vacquerie, 75011 Paris, FRANCE

Skeptic
P.O. Box 1555P, Melbourne, Vic. 3001, AUSTRALIA

Supermente
43 Colonia El Sifón 09400, Mexico, D.F., MEXICO

Zeitschrift Für Parapsychologie und Grenzgebiete der Psychologie
Franziskanerstrasse 9, Postfach 5204, D-7800, Freiburg,
WEST GERMANY

ASTROLOGY AND GENERAL INTEREST
American Astrology
475 Park Avenue South, New York, NY 10016

American Federation of Astrologers Bulletin
6 Library Court, Box 22040, Tempe, AZ 85282

Astrology and Psychic News
Box 810, North Hollywood, CA 91603

Astrology Guide
355 Lexington Avenue, New York, NY 10017

ESP News
1413 North Cabrillo, San Pedro, CA 90731

Fate Magazine
500 Hyacinth Place, Highland Park, IL 60035

The Llewellyn New Times
Box 43383, St. Paul, MN 55164

O.P.R.A. Newsletter
2801 Rubin Road, Midwest City, OK 73110

Psychic Guide
Box 701, Providence, RI 02901

Today's Astrologer
6535 South Rural Road, Box 22040, Tempe, AZ 85282

Yoga Journal
2054 University Avenue, #302, Berkeley, CA 94704

FOREIGN PUBLICATIONS
Astro-Psychological Problems, The Schneider-Gauquelin Research Journal
B.P. 317, 75229 Paris, CEDEX 05, FRANCE

Conocimiento de la Nueva Era
Viamonte 1716, 1055 Buenos Aires, ARGENTINA

Dimensione
Via Puggia 47, 16131 Genoa, ITALY

Esotera
Staudingerstrasse 7, Postfach 167, 7800 Freiburg, WEST GERMANY

Kosmos Tis Psichis/World of Soul
32 Tsiller Street, Athens 905, GREECE

Laboratoire d'Étude des Relations entre Rhythmes Cosmiques et Psychophy-
siologiques
8 Rue Amyot, 75005 Paris, FRANCE

Psychic News
20 Earlham Street, London WC2H 9LW, ENGLAND

Soekaren
S652 20 Karistad, SWEDEN

COMPUTER SOFTWARE ON PSYCHIC ARTS
Write to the companies listed below for information on their computer software programs.

ASTROLOGY
AGS Software
94 Cranberry Highway, P.O. Box 28, Orleans, MA 02653
(Apple Star Track, Astro Mapping, Astroscope)

Andrea Group
P.O. Box 24223, Washington, D.C. 20024
(Astrology Library)

Astro Computing Services
P.O. Box 16430, San Diego, CA 92116

Astrolabe
Box 28, Orleans, MA 02653

Astrology Instant Software
Rte. 101, Peterborough, NH 03458

Atari Home Computer
P.O. Box 61657, Sunnyville, CA 94088
(Software: Astrology)

Matrix Software
315 Marion Avenue, Big Rapids, MI 49307
(Astrologers Natal Package, Astrotalk)

BIORHYTHM
Alladin Software
1001 Colfax Street, Danville, IL 61832

Bluebirds Computer Software
P.O. Box 339, Wyandotte, MI 48192

Color Corp.
208 North Berkshire, Bloomfield Hills, MI 48013

K-Tel Software
11311 K-Tel Drive, Minneapolis, MN 55343

Ponder Data Quest Services
P.O. Box 95, Hatfield, PA 19440

Zephyr Services
306 South Homewood Avenue, Pittsburgh, PA 15208

I CHING
Simon & Schuster
1230 Avenue of the Americas, New York, NY 10020
(Software: ISBN 0671 30877-7)

NUMEROLOGY
Matrix Software
315 Marion Avenue, Big Rapids, MI 49307

Numerology World
P.O. Box 108, Wantagh, NY 11793

Widening Horizons
9582 Hamilton Avenue, Huntington Beach, CA 92646

PALMISTRY
BPC
P.O. Box 74157, Los Angeles, CA 91004

TAROT
Matrix Software
315 Marion Avenue, Big Rapids, MI 49307

For personal computerized reports on Astrology, Biorhythm, I Ching, Numerology, Tarot:
Stonehenge, Box R, Summit, NJ 07901

APPENDIX B

COURSES AND OTHER STUDY OPPORTUNITIES IN PARAPSYCHOLOGY

10th EDITION, JUNE 1987
DONNA L. McCORMICK, EDITOR

A NOTE

This directory contains information about undergraduate, graduate, and non-credit courses, independent study opportunities and degree programs in parapsychology inside and outside of the United States. Listings are arranged geographically.

The 10th edition of this directory contains the most recent information. However, since the educational picture is constantly changing, we suggest that you check with the college or instructor for the most up-to-date information.

The study opportunities contained in this directory were primarily obtained from a survey of those listed in the 9th edition (©1983). The sample is, therefore, not all inclusive: There may very well be courses offered in your area that are not listed in this publication. We suggest that you contact academic institutions in your area about other possible study opportunities in parapsychology.

ALABAMA

ATHENS STATE COLLEGE, Department of Psychology, Division of Behavioral Sciences, Athens, AL 35611. Phone: 205-232-1802.

INSTRUCTOR: Joseph H. Slate, Ph.D., Chairperson, Division of Behavioral Sciences.

EXPERIMENTAL PARAPSYCHOLOGY (PS 401). Undergraduate. A study of the experimental methods and procedures applicable to parapsychology. Explores the sources of parapsychological data, evaluates the problems and limitations of parapsychological research, and examines the applications of parapsychological research to psychodiagnosis, psychotherapy, medicine, forensics, education, and personal development. Laboratory included. Credit: 5 quarter hours.

SEMINAR IN PARAPSYCHOLOGY (PS 403). Undergraduate. A study of the phenomena associated with ESP, psychokinesis, unexplained events, and related topics. Credit.

Opportunities also exist for directed studies and supervised research within the Psychology Department for 1–5 quarter hours credit.

Special interest group on campus: Parapsychology Foundation.

CALIFORNIA

SOUTHWESTERN COLLEGE, Department of Math & Sciences, 900 Otay Lakes Road, Chula Vista, CA 92010. Phone: 619-421-6700.

INSTRUCTOR: Barbara K. Maze, Ph.D.

PARAPSYCHOLOGY (PSY 103). Undergraduate. A survey of parapsychology, including the areas of telepathy, precognition, clairvoyance, psychokinesis, out-of-the-body experiences, etc. The experimental and spontaneous aspects of parapsychology, as measured in the laboratory and reported in the field. Credit: 3 (option available to take the course for no credit).

INDEPENDENT STUDY (PSY 299). Undergraduate. Arrangements may be made with the above-mentioned instructor to do independent study/research on student's topic of choice in parapsychology. Credit: 1–3 units.

INSTITUTE FOR TRANSPERSONAL PSYCHOLOGY, 250 Oak Grove, Menlo Park, CA 94025. Phone: 415-326-1960.

DIRECTOR: Arthur Hastings, Ph.D.

Contact Dr. Hastings about courses and other study opportunities at the Institute.

JFK University, 12 Altarinda Road, Orinda, CA 94563. Phone: 415-228-6770.

Director: Susan Galvin

Masters Degree Program in interdisciplinary consciousness studies with concentration in parapsychology through course-work and thesis. Call or write for more information.

Saybrook Institute, 1772 Vallejo Street, San Francisco, CA 94123. Phone: 415-441-5034.

Instructor: Stanley Krippner, Ph.D. (Member: PA)

Ph.D. Program in psychology and humanistic sciences with opportunity for concentration in parapsychology. Accredited correspondence course requiring only several weeks residency/year. Call or write for more information.

Antioch University, Los Angeles, Department of Psychology, 300 Rose Avenue, Venice, CA 90291. Phone: 213-342-8513.

Instructor: Carolyn Miller, Ph.D.

Transpersonal Psychology. Graduate. Places transpersonal and parapsychological concerns within the context of Western personality theories. Credit: 2.

Masters Degree Program in (clinical) psychology with specialization in parapsychology and/or transpersonal psychology.

Also opportunity for meditation, intuitive work with Prof. Carolyn Miller.

CONNECTICUT

Western Connecticut State University, Department of Psychology, White Street, Danbury, CT 06801. Phone: 203-797-4334.

Instructor: David Sheskin, Ph.D.

Parapsychology (PS 236). Undergraduate. In addition to lectures, sessions will be devoted to in-class experiments and exercises. Credit: 3.

FLORIDA

University of Miami, Department of Psychology, Coral Gables, FL 33129. Phone: 305-284-2814.

Instructor: Jack A. Kapchan, Ph.D.

PARAPSYCHOLOGY (PSY 307). Undergraduate and Continuing Education. History, methodology and scope of parapsychology: science or pseudoscience. Implications regarding physics, religion, medicine, psychology, anthropology, transpersonal aspects. Credit: 3.

Opportunity also exists for independent study under the supervision of Dr. Kapchan.

UNIVERSITY OF WEST FLORIDA, Department of Psychology, Pensacola, FL 32514-5751.

INSTRUCTOR: William L. Mikulas, Ph.D.

UNDERGRADUATE AND GRADUATE: Students may specialize in parapsychology as part of a regular BA or MA in psychology.

ROLLINS COLLEGE, Department of Philosophy, Winter Park, FL 32789. Phone: 305-646-2178.

INSTRUCTOR: Hoyt Edge, Ph.D. (Member: PA)

INTRODUCTION TO PARAPSYCHOLOGY. Undergraduate. A basic introduction to experimental parapsychology and some philosophical implications. Credit: 3.

Opportunities for independent study also exist.

GEORGIA

WEST GEORGIA COLLEGE, Department of Psychology, William James Laboratory for Psychical Research, Carrollton, GA 30118. Phone: 404-834-1423.

INSTRUCTOR: William Roll, M. Litt. (Member: PA)

Undergraduate, Graduate coursework for credit and opportunities for independent study.

DEVELOPMENTAL AND CLINICAL PARAPSYCHOLOGY. The class will discuss the requirements needed for both developmental and clinical parapsychology and explore relevant procedures, learn about and practice techniques conducive to psi development and awareness, and ways to deal with and counsel people about disturbing psychical experiences.

LIFE AFTER DEATH. An examination of the findings suggestive of the continuation of human personality and consciousness after death. The class will also examine evidence for recurrent spontaneous psychokinesis, localized psi effects, and similar occurrences related to the survival issue.

NEUROPSYCHOLOGY, SYSTEM THEORY AND PSI. The class will discuss psi in relation to other parapsychological, psychological, biological and physical theories.

Special interest group on campus: Parapsychological Services Institute, Inc.

HAWAII

WINWARD COMMUNITY COLLEGE, Continuing Education, 45-720 Keaahala Road, Kaneohe, Hawaii 96744. Phone: 808-235-0077.

INSTRUCTOR: Gharith A. Pendragon

INTRODUCTION INTO PARAPSYCHOLOGY. Non-credit. A general survey of parapsychology, its history and prominent research, past and present. Class workshops will provide the student with the opportunity to take part in ESP experiments.

Other continuing education courses may be available in the University of Hawaii's school system. For further information about other courses and lectures, contact: Mr. Gharith Pendragon, Director, Hawaiian Society for Psychical Research, P.O. Box 4620, Honolulu, Hawaii 96813-4620; 808-247-6799.

IDAHO

UNIVERSITY OF IDAHO, Department of Psychology, Moscow, ID 83843. Phone: 208-885-7508.

INSTRUCTOR: James E. Crandall, Ph.D. (Member: PA)

PARAPSYCHOLOGY (PSY 340). Undergraduate. The course attempts to cover the whole range of topics, methods, alternative explanations, and several theoretical orientations to the subject. Credit: 3.

Opportunity exists for independent study under the supervision of Prof. Crandall for 1–3 credits.

ILLINOIS

FOREST INSTITUTE OF PROFESSIONAL PSYCHOLOGY, Department of Psychology, 1717 Rand Road, Des Plaines, IL 60016. Phone: 312-626-9250.

INSTRUCTOR: Joseph E. Troiani, MA, CAC

PARAPSYCHOLOGY (PSY 813). Graduate. This course is designed to give the future parapsychologist an understanding of psychic phenomena and the parapsychological community which is active in studying these phenomena both in the laboratory and in the field. Credit.

KANSAS

THE WICHITA STATE UNIVERSITY, Department of Religion, Box 76, Wichita, KS 67208. Phone: 316-689-3108.

INSTRUCTOR: Howard A. Mickel, Ph.D. (Associate: PA)

PSYCHIC PHENOMENA (RELIGION 2600). Undergraduate. An introduction to the great variety of psychic phenomena that have appeared in human history and, in modern times, have been investigated with scientific methods. Credit: 3.

Opportunities also exist within the Department of Religion for independent study under the supervision of Prof. Mickel.

MAINE

UNIVERSITY OF SOUTHERN MAINE, Continuing Education, 68 High Street, Portland, ME 04101. Phone: 207-780-4045.

INSTRUCTOR: Alex Tanous

INTRODUCTION TO PARAPSYCHOLOGY (CPA 101A). Non-Credit. Introductory exploration of the world of energy and the realm of consciousness. Included will be events in space, time, and mass; ESP; life after death; Kirlian photography; astral projection; reincarnation.

MARYLAND

UNIVERSITY OF MARYLAND, Department of Philosophy, 5401 Wilkens Avenue, Baltimore, MD 21228. Phone: 301-455-2103.

INSTRUCTOR: Stephen Braude, Ph.D. (Member: PA)

PHILOSOPHY AND PARAPSYCHOLOGY. Undergraduate and Graduate. Credit: 3.

MASSACHUSETTS

BRIDGEWATER STATE COLLEGE, Department of Psychology, Rm. 330, Burrill Academic Bldg., Bridgewater, MA 02324. Phone: 617-697-1200.

INSTRUCTOR: Richard T. Colgan, Ph.D.

PARAPSYCHOLOGY. Undergraduate and Continuing Education. The seminar shall be a balanced presentation of parapsychology, designed neither to persuade nor dissuade the senior scholar and scientist. It will allow the opportunity to explore an area of psychical interest, to exercise research abilities and potentialities, to make individual presentation, and to critique through discussion. Credit: 3.

Opportunity also exists for independent study under the supervision of Dr. Colgan.

MICHIGAN

WESTERN MICHIGAN UNIVERSITY, Department of General Studies Science, 338 Moore Hall, Kalamazoo, MI 49008. Phone: 616-383-0460.

INSTRUCTOR: Michael D. Swords, Ph.D.

SCIENCE OF PARASCIENCE (GSCI 432). Undergraduate. A general education science course in which each student picks a single research topic on the fringes of science, identifies the extraordinary claims, evaluates the evidence, and weighs alternative hypotheses. Credit: 4.

Possible opportunities for independent study.

EASTERN MICHIGAN UNIVERSITY, Department of Sociology, 712 Pray-Harrold Bldg., Ypsilanti, MI 48197. Phone: 616-487-4246.

INSTRUCTOR: Marcello Truzzi, Ph.D. (Associates: PA)

SOCIOLOGY OF PARAPSYCHOLOGY. Undergraduate. Critical review of psi claims plus consideration of deviance in science. Credit: 3.

Opportunity exists for independent study under the supervision of Dr. Truzzi.

MISSOURI

UNIVERSITY OF MISSOURI, Department of Psychology, 5319 Holmes Street, Kansas City, MO 64110. Phone: 276-1321.

INSTRUCTOR: Lawrence Simkins

PARAPSYCHOLOGY. Undergraduate. Introductory survey of parapsychology and the research in ESP, PK, and Theta phenomena. Critical evaluation of existing data and methodological limitations. Credit: 3.

Opportunity may also exist for independent study.

NEW JERSEY

FAIR LAWN COMMUNITY SCHOOL, Continuing Education, P.O. Box 8, Fair Lawn, NJ 07410. Phone: 201-791-7947.

INSTRUCTOR: Douglas Dean, Ph.D. (Member: PA)

ESP: NEW FRONTIER OF THE MIND. Non-Credit. Overview of the history and research findings.

PRINCETON UNIVERSITY, Human Information Processing Group, 2-S-2 Green Hall, Princeton, NJ 08544.

DIRECTOR: Dean Radin, Ph.D. (Member: PA)

HUMAN INFORMATION PROCESSING GROUP. A new interdisciplinary program integrating an unusually broad spectrum of research in cognitive science, psychology, linguistics, philosophy, and engineering. Contact Dr. Radin for further information.

NEW YORK CITY

FORDHAM UNIVERSITY, Department of Theology, Bronx, NY 10458.

INSTRUCTOR: John J. Heaney, STD. (Associate: PA)

THEOLOGY AND PARAPSYCHOLOGY. Undergraduate. A general survey of parapsychology's religious implications. Credit: 4.

KINGSBOROUGH COMMUNITY COLLEGE, Department of Behavioral Sciences, 2001 Oriental Boulevard, Brooklyn, NY 11235. Phone: 718-934-5630.

INSTRUCTOR: Philip Stander, Ed.D.

PRINCIPLES OF PARAPSYCHOLOGY (PSY12). Undergraduate. Introduces students to the interdisciplinary nature of parapsychology, its fields and subdivisions, such as telepathy, precognition, psychokinesis and clairvoyance. Current theoretical and experimental research will be reviewed. Credit: 3.

AMERICAN SOCIETY FOR PSYCHICAL RESEARCH, 5 West 73 Street, New York, NY 10023. Phone: 212-799-5050.

INSTRUCTOR: Patrice Keane (Associate: PA)

HISTORICAL AND MODERN TRENDS IN PARAPSYCHOLOGICAL RESEARCH. Non-Credit. Evaluates the state-of-the-art in psi research and presents a historical overview. Examines belief systems, experimentation on altered states of consciousness, new developments in psychokinesis research, traditional and nontraditional forms of healing. Psi induction techniques are illustrated through in-class experiments.

Note: Other seminars, lectures and classes are occasionally offered by the ASPR. Contact the ASPR for further information.

CONSCIOUSNESS RESEARCH AND TRAINING PROJECT, 315 East 68 Street, New York, NY 10021.

INSTRUCTOR: Joyce Goodrich, Ph.D.

SEMINAR IN LESHAN APPROACH TO HEALING. Non-Credit. These seminars, developed by Dr. Lawrence LeShan, are taught by a small group of people trained at length by him. Offered in central locations throughout the country, they are five days in length and residential. Optional advanced seminars are offered from time to time. The purpose is to train in depth a core group of serious people, as the project is experimental and research oriented. No person trained in this method may charge or take donations of money or valuable gifts from the healees, their friends or relatives. Also, every healee must be under an appropriate professional's care.

THE NEW SCHOOL FOR SOCIAL RESEARCH,   Division of Social Science, 66 West 12 Street, New York, NY 10011. Phone: 212-741-5600.

INSTRUCTOR: Bob Brier, Ph.D. (Member: PA)

PARAPSYCHOLOGY.   Undergraduate. An experimental approach where each student designs and conducts an experiment. Credit: 3.

INSTRUCTOR: Michaeleen Maher, Ph.D. (Member: PA)

PARAPSYCHOLOGY: 100 YEARS OF RESEARCH. Undergraduate. Within a historical context, discussions focus on a wide array of topics within parapsychology. Credit: 3.

WEST SIDE YMCA,   Adult Education, 5 West 63 Street, New York, NY 10023. Phone: 212-787-5302.

INSTRUCTOR: Nicole Lieberman

PARAPSYCHOLOGY   Non-Credit. This workshop will stress personal acceptance, evaluation and development of psi. There will be experimentation on ESP and PK. Discussions will include psi-inductive states, healing, out-of-body experiences, cosmic consciousness, etc.

ST. JOHN'S UNIVERSITY,   Department of Psychology, Grand Central and Utopia Parkways, Jamaica, NY 11439. Phone: 718-990-6161, Ext. 6368.

INSTRUCTOR: Rex G. Stanford, Ph.D. (Member: PA)

ALTERED STATES OF CONSCIOUSNESS AND PARAPSYCHOLOGICAL EVENTS. Undergraduate. Research findings and related theoretical developments in areas such as sleep and dreams, hypnosis and suggestibility, and unexplained communication with the environment (ESP and PK). Discusses progress, difficulties and controversies in these areas. Credit: 3.

Opportunity also exists for independent study under the supervision of Dr. Stanford.

COLLEGE OF STATEN ISLAND,   Department of Psychology, 715 Ocean Terrace, Staten Island, NY 10301. Phone: 718-390-7744.

INSTRUCTOR: Steven M. Rosen, Ph.D. (Associate: PA)

PARAPSYCHOLOGY. Undergraduate. Basic definitions, conventional methodology and the history of research are covered. The question of

meaning is raised and explored. Theories and difficulties are discussed. Credit: 4.

A parapsychology club is also on campus.

SUSAN WAGNER HIGH SCHOOL, Department of Continuing Education,
1200 Manor Road, Staten Island, NY 10314. Phone: 718-761-0344.

INSTRUCTOR: Rosemarie Pilkington, Ph.D. (Associate: PA)

PSYCHIC PHENOMENA: MYTH AND REALITY. Non-Credit. Covers all
major aspects of psychical phenomena and research.

NEW YORK STATE

ST. BONAVENTURE UNIVERSITY, Department of Theology, St. Bonaventure, NY 14778. Phone: 716-375-2000.

INSTRUCTOR: Rev. Alphonsus Trabold, O.F.M., M.A.

PSYCHICAL RESEARCH AND THE NATURE OF MAN. Undergraduate. The
course is concerned with the implications of parapsychology for theology and religion. It is not an experimental course in psi, but it does
evaluate quite thoroughly what parapsychology has discovered.
Credit: 3.

NEW YORK INSTITUTE OF TECHNOLOGY, Continuing Education, Carleton
Avenue, Bldg. 66, Rm. 212, Central Islip, NY 11722. Phone: 516-348-
3325.

INSTRUCTOR: Shirley Wiedmer

PARAPSYCHOLOGY. Non-Credit. Presents an overview of parapsychology and attempts to integrate relevant aspects of the field with
biology, psychology, psychiatry, philosophy and literture.

NASSAU COMMUNITY COLLEGE, Continuing Education, Garden City,
NY 11530. Phone: 516-222-7472.

INSTRUCTOR: Shirley Wiedmer

PARAPSYCHOLOGY 1. Non-Credit. Presents an overview of parapsychology and attempts to integrate relevant aspects of the field with
biology, psychology, psychiatry, philosophy and literature.

STATE UNIVERSITY OF NEW YORK-GENESEO, Department of Psychology,
Geneseo, NY 14454.

INSTRUCTOR: Lawrence Casler, Ph.D. (Member: PA)

PARAPSYCHOLOGY AND HYPNOSIS (PSY 305). Undergraduate. A critical
inquiry into the nature of the two fields with particular emphasis on
current research and practical implications. Credit: 3.

Opportunity exists for doing a Masters thesis on parapsychology under the supervision of Dr. Casler.

STATE UNIVERSITY OF NEW YORK-OSWEGO,   Department of Psychology, Oswego, NY 13126.

INSTRUCTOR: Mahlon Wagner, Ph.D. (Associate: PA)

CURRENT TOPICS: PARAPSYCHOLOGY (PSY 310). Undergraduate. This course will critically examine research and methodology associated with the study of phenomena not usually considered in conventional studies of sensory and perceptual processes. Credit: 3.

EXPERIMENTAL PSYCHOLOGY: PARAPSYCHOLOGY. Undergraduate. This course is designed to be an advanced experimental analysis of parapsychology. Students study the basic methods of data collection, experimental design, data analyses and report writing in this field. Credit: 4 with Lab.

NORTH CAROLINA

FOUNDATION FOR RESEARCH ON THE NATURE OF MAN,   Box 6847 College Station, Durham, NC 27708. Phone: 919-688-8241.

INSTRUCTOR: John Palmer, Ph.D. (Member: PA) and others

SUMMER STUDY PROGRAM.   Annually: June–July. Consists of lectures, discussions, workshops and experimental practica addressing parapsychological history, theories, controversies, experimental methods, and analytical techniques.

ADVANCED PROGRAM. Year-round residential training program affords students the opportunity to acquire thorough familiarity with the professional parapsychological literature; obtain intensive training in experimental methodology, statistical analysis, and logical interpretation of results; and to develop, implement and report original research projects.

Credit for these programs may be arranged with the institution at which the student is taking his/her degree.

UNIVERSITY OF NORTH CAROLINA,   Department of Psychology, Chapel Hill, NC 27514. Phone: 919-962-5034.

INSTRUCTOR: David Price Rogers, Ph.D. (Member: PA)

While no courses are offered, undergraduate and graduate students may arrange independent study under the supervision of Dr. Rogers.

PENNSYLVANIA

SLIPPERY ROCK UNIVERSITY,   Department of Philosophy, Slippery Rock, PA 16057. Phone: 412-794-7370.

INSTRUCTOR: Theodore L. Kneupper, Ph.D.

MYSTICISM AND PSYCHICAL RESEARCH. Undergraduate. As a philosophical exploration, this course will focus primarily on gaining knowledge of the psi dimension. It will include an introduction and an overview of the field of psychical research. Credit: 3.

A Psychic Awareness Club also exists at this school.

TEXAS

EAST TEXAS STATE UNIVERSITY, Continuing Education, East Texas Station, Commerce, TX 75428. Phone: 214-886-3067.

INSTRUCTOR: Betty Corbiere-Binder

BEGINNING PARAPSYCHOLOGY. Non-Credit.

PARAPSYCHOLOGY AND REALITY. Non-Credit.

OUR LADY OF THE LAKE UNIVERSITY, Continuing Education, Providence Building, Room 2A, 411 SW 24 Street, San Antonio, TX 78285. Phone: 512-434-6711, Ext. 392.

INSTRUCTOR: Marilyn Schlitz, M.A. (Member: PA)

PARAPSYCHOLOGY TODAY. Non-Credit. General overview of the field and experimental exercises aimed at providing insights into psi experimentation.

VERMONT

LYNDON STATE COLLEGE, Department of Philosophy and Religion, Lyndonville, VT 05851.

INSTRUCTOR: Kenneth D. Vos, Ph.D.

PARAPSYCHOLOGY AND PHILOSOPHY. Undergraduate. Examines the evidence from both spontaneous cases and data obtained from laboratory research. Explores philosophical implications of psi phenomena for our beliefs about the nature of the world and of human consciousness. Inquires how parapsychology can be put to practical use in the service of personal and social values. Credit: 3.

VIRGINIA

UNIVERSITY OF VIRGINIA, Department of Behavioral Medicine and Psychiatry, Box 152, Medical Center, Charlottesville, VA 22908.

DIRECTOR: Ian Stevenson, M.D. (Member: PA)

POST-GRADUATE FELLOWSHIPS. While no courses or degrees are offered, The Division of Parapsychology offers fellowships for the study of spontaneous cases. However, applicants must have a doctoral degree and must be on the faculty of a university where they have recognized freedom to engage in research.

VIRGINIA COMMONWEALTH UNIVERSITY, Department of Psychology, Richmond, VA 23284.

INSTRUCTOR: Glenn R. Hawkes, Ph.D.

PARAPSYCHOLOGY (PSY 307). Undergraduate. Reviews evidence on ESP and PK, plus events such as apparitions, mediums, death experiences, poltergeists, healing, dreams, mystical experiences, and concludes with theory summary. Credit: 3.

Opportunity exists for independent study under the supervision of Dr. Hawkes.

WISCONSIN

UNIVERSITY OF WISCONSIN, Department of Psychology, Stevens Point, WI 54481. Phone: 715-346-3953.

INSTRUCTOR: Daniel Kortenkamp, Ph.D.

PARAPSYCHOLOGY (PSY 285). Undergraduate. An introductory course covering ESP, PK, and Survival Research. Credit: 3.

WYOMING

UNIVERSITY OF WYOMING, Department of Psychology, Box 3708, University Station, Laramie, WY 82071. Phone: 307-766-2187.

INSTRUCTOR: R. Leo Sprinkle, Ph.D. (Associate: PA)

LITERATURE OF PARAPSYCHOLOGY. Graduate. An overview of the field and its literature, with emphasis on the psychological aspects of paranormal phenomena. Credit: 3.

Opportunity exists for independent study under the supervision of Dr. Sprinkle.

OUTSIDE THE UNITED STATES

ARGENTINA

UNIVERSIDAD DEL SALVADOR, Department of Psychology, Sarandi 65-1081 Buenos Aires, Argentina.

Instructor: Enrique Novillo Pauli, M.A. (Member: PA)

Curso de Parapsicologia—Dinamica del Inconsciente

Opportunities for independent study also exist at this institution. Contact Mr. Pauli for further information.

AUSTRALIA

University of New England, Department of Psychology, Armidale, New South Wales 2351, Australia.

Instructor: Harvey Irwin, Ph.D. (Member: PA)

Parapsychology (PSY 220-1/320-1). Undergraduate. An exploration of the bases of apparently paranormal phenomena; critical examination of authenticity of paranormal phenomena; origins of parapsychological research; problems of fraud, self-deception; review of research, theories; parapsychology as a scientific enterprise.

Opportunity exists on the undergraduate and graduate levels for independent study and/or thesis work under the supervision of Dr. Irwin.

ENGLAND

The University of Loughborough, Extension Studies, Loughborough, Leicestershire LE11 3TV, England.

Instructor: Arthur J. Ellison, D.Sc. (Member: PA)

The Paranormal. 5-week Course. Nature of science and its application to all aspects of the paranormal.

ICELAND

University of Iceland, Department of Psychology, 101 Reykjavik, Iceland.

Instructor: Erlendur Haraldsson, Ph.D. (Member: PA)

Parapsychology. Undergraduate and Graduate. Credit: 3.

PANAMA

Instituto de Estudios Parapsicologicos, Apartado 8000, Panama 7, Panama.

Instructor: Roberto Mainieri (Associate: PA)

Introduction to Experimental Parapsychology. Non-Credit. A 5-day intensive course providing an overview of the field.

SCOTLAND

UNIVERSITY OF EDINBURGH, Department of Psychology, 7 George Square, Edinburgh EH8 9JZ, Scotland.

INSTRUCTOR: Robert L. Morris, Ph.D. (Member: PA)

DOCTORAL PROGRAM: Opportunity for graduate research leading to a Ph.D. in psychology with a concentration in parapsychology, under the supervision of Dr. Morris.

THE NETHERLANDS

UNIVERSITY OF AMSTERDAM, Department of Psychology, Weesperplein 8, 1018 XA Amsterdam, The Netherlands.

INSTRUCTOR: Dick J. Bierman, Ph.D. (Associate: PA)

PARAPSYCHOLOGY. Undergraduate. General introduction, covering methodological and social issues. Credit: 6.

STATE UNIVERSITY OF UTRECHT, Parapsychology Laboratory, Sorobnnelaan 16, 3584 CA Utrecht, The Netherlands.

INSTRUCTOR: Dr. Martin Johnson (Member: PA)

For students of psychology, there are weekly seminars on selected topics of parapsychology.

DOCTORAL DEGREE: Guidance for work leading to a Ph.D.

INDEX